THE OXFORD HANDBOOK OF
SOUTH KOREAN POLITICS

THE OXFORD HANDBOOK OF

SOUTH KOREAN POLITICS

Edited by
JEONGHUN HAN,
RAMON PACHECO PARDO,
and
YOUNGHO CHO

Great Clarendon Street, Oxford, OX2 6DP,
United Kingdom

Oxford University Press is a department of the University of Oxford.
It furthers the University's objective of excellence in research, scholarship,
and education by publishing worldwide. Oxford is a registered trade mark of
Oxford University Press in the UK and in certain other countries

© Oxford University Press 2023

The moral rights of the authors have been asserted

First Edition published in 2023

Impression: 1

All rights reserved. No part of this publication may be reproduced, stored in
a retrieval system, or transmitted, in any form or by any means, without the
prior permission in writing of Oxford University Press, or as expressly permitted
by law, by licence or under terms agreed with the appropriate reprographics
rights organization. Enquiries concerning reproduction outside the scope of the
above should be sent to the Rights Department, Oxford University Press, at the
address above

You must not circulate this work in any other form
and you must impose this same condition on any acquirer

Published in the United States of America by Oxford University Press
198 Madison Avenue, New York, NY 10016, United States of America

British Library Cataloguing in Publication Data

Data available

Library of Congress Control Number: 2022940778

ISBN 978–0–19–289404–5

DOI: 10.1093/oxfordhb/9780192894045.001.0001

Printed and bound in the UK by
TJ Books Limited

Links to third party websites are provided by Oxford in good faith and
for information only. Oxford disclaims any responsibility for the materials
contained in any third party website referenced in this work.

Table of Contents

List of Contributors ix

Part 1 Introduction

1. Introduction: South Korean Politics after Transitions 3
   JeongHun Han, Ramon Pacheco Pardo, and Youngho Cho

2. The History of Korea, 1905–1945 17
   Hyung-Gu Lynn

3. The History of South Korea, 1945–1987 34
   Tae Gyun Park

Part 2 Core Concepts

4. Presidentialism with Parliamentary Characteristics 49
   JeongHun Han

5. Regionalism 68
   Kwang-Il Yoon

6. Conservative Democratisation 87
   WooJin Kang

7. The Developmental State 104
   Meredith Woo

8. Chaebol 120
   Sang-young Rhyu

9. Nationalism 136
   Jungmin Seo

PART 3 POLITICAL INSTITUTIONS

10. Constitutional Politics 153
    WON-TAEK KANG

11. Legislative Politics 167
    BYOUNG KWON SOHN

12. Executive Politics 183
    JONGKON LEE

13. Judicial Politics 198
    DONGWOOK CHA

PART 4 PARTIES AND ELECTIONS

14. Parties and Party Systems 217
    SUNGHACK LIM

15. Minority Representation 233
    KYUNGMEE PARK

16. Elections and Electoral Systems 252
    WOOJIN MOON

17. Political Communication 270
    HAN SOO LEE

18. New Issue Politics 285
    SEUNG-JIN JANG

PART 5 CIVIL SOCIETY

19. Social Movements: Developments and Structural Changes after Democratisation 305
    JIN-WOOK SHIN

20. Interest Group Politics 326
    YOOJIN LIM AND YEONHO LEE

21. Labour Union Activism 342
    SOONMEE KWON

22. Citizens' Support for Democracy 358
    YOUNGHO CHO

PART 6   CULTURE AND MEDIA

23. Cinema and Television 377
    HYANGJIN LEE

24. The Internet and Social Media 394
    DAL YONG JIN

25. The Press 408
    KI-SUNG KWAK

26. Public Intellectuals 423
    NAMHEE LEE

27. Politics and Popular Music 439
    JOHN LIE

PART 7   PUBLIC POLICY AND POLICY-MAKING

28. Political Control and Bureaucratic Autonomy 455
    HUCK-JU KWON

29. The Development of Welfare Programmes 471
    JOOHA LEE

30. Decentralisation and Local Government 491
    YOOIL BAE

31. Corruption 508
    KYOUNG-SUN MIN

PART 8   THE INTERNATIONAL ARENA

32. Foreign Policy 529
    RAMON PACHECO PARDO

33. Security and Defence Policy 546
    SUNG-HAN KIM AND ALEX SOOHOON LEE

34. Foreign Economic Policy 562
    SOHYUN ZOE LEE

35. The South Korean Development Model   578
Eun Mee Kim and Nancy Y. Kim

36. Korean Reunification   595
Young-Kwan Yoon

37. The ROK–US Alliance: Drivers of Resilience   613
Victor D. Cha and Katrin Katz

38. Evolving Relations with China   629
Heung-Kyu Kim

Index   647

List of Contributors

Yooil Bae, Assistant Professor, Department of Public Administration, Dong-A University

Dongwook Cha, Associate Professor, Department of Public Administration and Policy, Dong-eui University

Victor D. Cha, Vice Dean and D.S. Song-KF Professor of Government and International Affairs, School of Foreign Service and Department of Government, Georgetown University

Youngho Cho, Associate Professor, Department of Political Science, Sogang University

JeongHun Han, Associate Professor, Graduate School of International Studies and Chair of the EU Center, Seoul National University

Seung-Jin Jang, Associate Professor, Department of Political Science and International Relations, Kookmin University

Dal Yong Jin, Distinguished SFU Professor, Simon Fraser University

Won-Taek Kang is professor, Department of Political Science and International Relations, Seoul National University

WooJin Kang, Professor, Department of Political Science and Diplomacy, KyungPook National University

Katrin Katz, Non-Resident Senior Fellow, The Korea Society and Adjunct Fellow (Non-Resident), Office of the Korea Chair, Center for Strategic and International Studies (CSIS)

Eun Mee Kim, President, Ewha Womans University

Heung-Kyu Kim, Director, US–China Policy Institute, Ajou University

Nancy Y. Kim, PhD Candidate and Researcher, Institute for Development and Human Security, Ewha Womans University

Sung-han Kim, Professor, College of International Studies, Korea University

Ki-Sung Kwak, Chair of Department, Department of Korean Studies, University of Sydney

Huck-ju Kwon, Professor, Graduate School of Public Administration, Seoul National University

Soonmee Kwon, Professor, Korea Employment and Labor Educational Institute

Alex Soohoon Lee, Associate Research Fellow, Korea Institute for Defense Analyses (KIDA)

Han Soo Lee, Associate Professor, Department of Political Science and Diplomacy, Ajou University

Hyangjin Lee, Professor of Film Studies, Rikkyo University

Jongkon Lee, Associate Professor, Department of Political Science and International Relations, Ewha Womans University

Jooha Lee, Professor, Department of Public Administration, Dongguk University

Namhee Lee, Professor of Modern Korean History, Department of Asian Languages and Cultures and Director, Center for Korean Studies, UCLA

Sohyun Zoe Lee, Lecturer in International Political Economy, School of History, Anthropology, Philosophy and Politics, Queen's University Belfast

Yeonho Lee, Professor, Department of Political Science and International Studies, Yonsei University

John Lie, Distinguished Professor of Sociology, University of California, Berkeley

Sunghack Lim, Professor, Department of International Relations, University of Seoul

Yoojin Lim, Assistant Professor, Department of Political Science, Kangwon National University

Hyung-Gu Lynn, AECL/KEPCO Chair in Korean Research, University of British Columbia and Editor, *Pacific Affairs*

Kyoung-sun Min, Assistant Professor, Korean National Police University

Woojin Moon, Professor, Department of Political Science and Diplomacy, Ajou University

Ramon Pacheco Pardo, Professor of International Relations, King's College London and KF–VUB Korea Chair, Brussels School of Governance, Vrije Universiteit Brussel

Kyungmee Park, Associate Professor, Department of Political Science and International Relations, Jeonbuk National University

Tae Gyun Park, Professor, Graduate School of International Studies, Seoul National University

Sang-young Rhyu, Professor, Graduate School of International Studies, Yonsei University

Jungmin Seo, Professor, Department of Political Science and International Studies, Yonsei University

Jin-Wook Shin, Professor, Department of Sociology, Chung-Ang University

Byoung Kwon Sohn, Professor, Department of Political Science and International Relations, Chung-Ang University

Meredith Woo, President, Sweet Briar College

Kwang-Il Yoon, Professor, Department of Political Science and International Relations, Sookmyung Women's University

Young-Kwan Yoon, Professor Emeritus, College of Social Sciences, Seoul National University and Former Minister of Foreign Affairs and Trade, Republic of Korea

PART 1
INTRODUCTION

CHAPTER 1

INTRODUCTION

South Korean Politics after Transitions

JEONGHUN HAN, RAMON PACHECO PARDO, AND YOUNGHO CHO

1. South Korean Politics: Old and New

South Korea is best known for its economic development, democratic consolidation, proactive civil society, and, more recently, for its emergence as a cultural powerhouse. South Korea transitioned from one of the poorest countries in the world in the 1950s into a developed economy by the 1990s. Its economic development model is now being exported throughout the developing world. Meanwhile, South Korea went from dictatorship to democracy in the 1980s, thanks to the re-establishment of free and fair elections in 1987. Over three decades later, it is a consolidated democracy with peaceful transitions of power between parties. In addition, South Korean civil society has been key in the democratic transition as well as its consolidation. Today, it keeps leaders accountable, as the 2016–2017 Candlelight Uprising showed. Furthermore, South Korean culture has been gaining in popularity across the world. Both its traditional and, especially, contemporary cultural expressions are being consumed well beyond East Asia.

The starting point of this handbook is that South Korea has experienced various transitions, including political, democratic, economic, societal, and demographic, and, thus, its contemporary politics are considerably different from its traditional patterns through the process of responding to these transitions. During the 1950s and 1960s, the South Korean state was not functionally differentiated. The country was ruled by personal dictatorship, its economy was based on subsistence agriculture, and most South Koreans lived in rural areas and followed Confucian norms and rituals. Accordingly, few foreign scholars paid attention to this small, recently war-torn country for which there was little hope.

In recent decades and moving away from this old image, South Korea has created and developed specialised state organisations and the country has institutionalised core elements of liberal democracy such as free elections, multiparty competition, and civil liberties. Moreover, high-tech and service companies have been leading its economy, South Korean cultural industries have been gaining global popularity, and its society now looks hyper-modern. Owing to these dramatic transitions, international society now regards South Korea as a middle power and the country has expanded its interests, as well as its responsibilities, abroad. Overall, South Korea and its politics are far distant from the old image and the grand perspectives that tended to underappreciate the complex and diversified nature of South Korean politics.

Traditional understandings of South Korea indeed do not account for this historical evolution and the complex nature of its politics. Many scholars and political pundits specialising in South Korea describe its politics through two grand perspectives: dynamic and static. On the dynamic side, Gregory Henderson published his seminal book, *Korea: The Politics of the Vortex*, in 1968. Henderson characterised South Korean political dynamics using a physics analogy: as a strong vortex sweeping all active elements of society upwards and towards centralised power. Henderson applied the popular thesis of the politics of mass society by William Kornhauser (1959) to link South Korean politics to an agrarian and traditional society. In his analysis, the strong unity and homogeneity of South Korea were the main reasons hindering the formation of strong institutions or voluntary associations, preventing change, and, therefore, failing to construct a stable liberal democracy (Henderson 1968: 5).

On the static side, scholars emphasise the cultural legacies of Confucianism. According to this perspective, the Joseon dynasty adopted Confucianism as the state ideology and it eventually became embedded into social and private norms and values (Deuchler 1995). Since then, Confucianism has continued to play an important role in shaping the modernisation trajectories of South Korea and continues to have an enduring impact on its politics and democracy (Kim 2014; Shin 2012). While acknowledging that some aspects of these grand perspectives may still remain relevant, we need to present an updated understanding of South Korean politics, which, by and large, has been overlooked by these perspectives.

We aim to shed fresh light on contemporary South Korean politics and put together this handbook with two underpinning related principles in mind. First, most of the chapters examine South Korean politics since the 1987 democratic transition. The reason is that state development, economic growth, and social and demographic changes began to be reflected in South Korean politics after this transition, which removed the intervention of authoritarian leaders. Second, the authors take a bottom-up perspective to advance our understanding about South Korean politics. Relying on Robert Merton's (1968) mid-range theory, the different contributors integrate both theoretical and empirical research about specific aspects of South Korean politics. As South Korea has experienced various transitions over the past decades, its politics have changed in a multidimensional way. And since holistic and grand approaches are limited in detailing specific aspects of South Korean politics, we have divided the handbook into six sections: core concepts, institutions, civil society, culture and media, public policy, and foreign policy.

What changes have been taking place in South Korea's core political elements such as the developmental state, nationalism, presidentialism, and regionalism? How have democratic institutions, such as elections, the party system, and the judicial body, processed citizens' interest and values and transformed them into government policies and laws? Has the civil society of South Korea, including interest groups and labour unions, grown in size and attained democratic civility? What are the main characteristics of South Korean culture as it has modernised and globalised? What impacts and implications have decentralisation, new public management (NPM), and growing welfare programmes had on the politics and society of South Korea? And what is the current state of South Korean foreign policy towards North Korea and the superpowers surrounding the Korean Peninsula?

This handbook answers these and related questions by providing state-of-the-art analyses of all significant aspects of South Korean politics. The authors in this handbook share a desire to explain South Korean politics using both theoretical and empirical approaches and to provide a general account of the main characteristics observed in specific domains of its politics after transition. Through this project, the contributors hope that an international audience will gain new knowledge about South Korean politics either in their own right or in comparison to the experience of other countries.

2. Modern History and Core Concepts

Our handbook focuses on the contemporary politics of South Korea after the 1987 democratic transition. However, contemporary politics reflect social, economic, and political changes that the country experienced during the twentieth century. After the Joseon dynasty failed to reform and survive, the modernisation process of the Korean Peninsula was postponed until it gathered new strength following its liberation from Japanese colonialism and later occupation by the United States and the Soviet Union in 1945. With modernisation in the first half of the twentieth century proving impossible, domestic efforts to develop a liberal democracy, an industrial economy, and a modern society took place during its second half, framed by South Korea's alliance with the United States.

Because these two periods in modern Korean history are crucial to understanding contemporary South Korea, we include two chapters that take stock of what we would lose should we jump straight into present South Korean politics. Hyung-Gu Lynn (Chapter 2) examines major transformations in the period from 1905 to the 1940s such as the emergence of Korean nationalism, the polarisation of left and right independence groups, and incipient economic development under the period of Japanese occupation. While acknowledging the dominant scholarly narrative about the interplay between Japanese colonial oppression and the Korean struggle against it to achieve national independence, Lynn shows that these transformations are less self-evident than those described in school textbooks. Tae Gyun Park's (Chapter 3), meanwhile, focuses on the history of South Korean politics from 1948 to 1987. Throughout this period, South Korea underwent several political changes in terms of regime type and president. For the most part, however, South Korea spent these years under de facto or de jure authoritarian rule. Thus, there were decades-long tensions between authoritarianism and progressive forces demanding democratisation. Ultimately, the experience of South Korea during these decades and the political tensions affecting the country helped to shape South Korea's democratisation and democratic years post 1987.

After these two chapters on the modern political history of South Korea, we provide core concepts whose understanding is the basic foundation to delve into various aspects of South Korean politics. JeongHun Han (Chapter 4) posits that South Korea has been commonly known as a presidential system. However, he also points out that its performance is often questionable from the perspective of the normal dynamics of a presidential system. This is due to the existence and effectiveness of institutions observed in parliamentary systems. In particular, the institutional characteristics of institutions abnormal to presidential systems—thus providing stronger power to the executive—may help us to understand why the power of South Korean presidents is not controlled or checked by other governing institutions, including the National Assembly or the courts, but is often controlled by civil society movements.

Regionalism, covered in Chapter 5, is one of South Korea's most distinct sociological characteristics. Its importance is reinforced because of its influence on South Korean politics. Defining it as a voting behaviour tendency based on voters' birth places, Kwang-Il Yoon (Chapter 5) contends that regionalism emerged due to processes of uneven industrialisation and state repression between regions. As the leading politicians—the 'three Kims'—conducted campaign strategies to mobilise voters according to their birth places, incentives for voters to find alternative channels of representation were weakened. Even though its influence has declined, Yoon posits that regionalism is the only clear political cleavage in South Korea.

Conservative democratisation is a concept separating South Korean democratisation from some other countries. According to WooJin Kang (Chapter 6), South Korean democratisation was the result of a political pact established through a bargaining process between old political elites that remained in power. Instead of reshuffling the entire system, the democratisation process to a large extent preserved the power of the political elites of the old authoritarian regime. This clashes with the role and beliefs of new democratic elites that have emerged post democratisation and which sometimes seek to transform the regime itself. Similarly, the continuation of the policymaking patterns of the developmental state is also present in contemporary South Korea. Meredith Woo (Chapter 7), meanwhile, shows that the country was part of a group of East Asian peers including Hong Kong, Japan, Singapore, and Taiwan in which governmental, bureaucratic, and economic elites worked together to promote economic development. With the advent of democracy and the graduation of South Korea into a developed economy, these links have frayed but have not completely dissipated. Indeed, a developmental mindset characterised by state–private sector cooperation and long-term thinking continues to inform policymaking in South Korea. Sang-young Rhyu (Chapter 8) examines the chaebol using one of the three metaphors in the political economy of South Korea: angels, demons, and necessary evils. According to Rhyu, chaebol are active players in the South Korean developmental state, helping to make South Korea one of the major industrial powers. Nonetheless, the long-standing collaboration between chaebol and political elites also deteriorates the development of social organisations. Political competition has failed to escape from the pattern of conflicts between elite coalitions and the mass public. Therefore, the developmental state and the chaebol face the prospect of having to go their own ways.

Finally, this section discusses how South Korean culture's strong unity based on nationalism has evolved. Modern nationalism originated from the anti-Japanese independence movement, yet Jungmin Seo (Chapter 9) points out that political leaders have utilised and altered its forms and contents since 1948. Taking the constructivist approach to nationalism and using Benedict Anderson's definition of a nation as an 'imagined community' (1991), Seo contends that South Korean nationalism has evolved throughout major political events such as the Korean War, authoritarian state-building, democratisation, and recent globalisation. Seo concludes that nationalism conditions how politicians and ordinary citizens deal with domestic and foreign issues.

Seen from the perspective of these core concepts characterising contemporary South Korean politics, the profound changes occurring since the 1987 democratisation process might have had mixed effects on the emergence of new dynamics in South Korean politics. On the one hand, political and social divisions have changed as the interests between governing institutions as well as regions and other social sectors have become more heterogeneous. On the other hand, such divisions may not have found channels for their representation. The legacies of the previous authoritarian regime were not completely eliminated, suggesting that political dynamics are still dominated by the same centres of power. Nevertheless, recent changes seem to have weakened the negative influences of authoritarian legacies. The remaining sections of the handbook illustrate in more detail the changes taking place in South Korea.

3. Political Process

Sections 2 and 3 in this handbook examine various aspects of the political process to link peoples' preferences and public policy. During the democratic movements of the 1980s, the political interests of the whole of South Korean society were concentrated in making the authoritarian leaders step down from the centre of power. This would open the door to choosing new leaders in a democratic way. This homogeneous orientation to political and societal reform is now no longer valid. More than thirty years after democratisation, the political interests of the South Korean people have become diversified, leading to the emergence of a complex web of groups of people divided by different preferences on various social issues. The extent to which contemporary South Korea's political process succeeds in responding to this change is the main concern of these two sections.

Section 2, in this regard, explores the political accommodation of the current South Korean Constitution and identifies key defining characteristics of performance among three main constitutional institutions, namely the National Assembly, the executive, and the judiciary. In Chapter 10, Won-Taek Kang argues that the current South Korean Constitution shows clear limitations by producing 'imperial' presidents as well as failing to represent the diversity of the contemporary South Korean society. He explains that the focus of the 1988 Constitution lay in re-establishing a fair, free, and direct presidential election system. Consequently, by following the 1962 version of the Constitution, the 1988 version left other issues untouched including human rights, economic liberalism, and institutional consistency. Based on this understanding, he claims that the current Constitution is inadequate to reflect the diversity of contemporary South Korean society.

Under the Constitution, the relationship between governing institutions has sometimes failed to produce the expected checks and balances in a presidential system. Byoung Kwon Sohn (Chapter 11) argues that the role of the National Assembly is still fairly limited, preventing the development of the so-called inter-party consultative system. Instead, the dominant role of the president and the executive branch in the legislative process often results in the atrophy of standing committees and quick, majoritarian decisions without proper deliberation. In contrast, Jongkon Lee (Chapter 12) finds that the strong bureaucratic power tradition has been weakened as the ability of the National Assembly to keep the executive in check has been strengthened. The slightly different evaluation on the relationship between the National Assembly and the executive in these two chapters may lead us to reach the understanding that South Korean society is still waiting for the development of an adequate representative role for the National Assembly, independent of the seemingly weakened power of legislative initiative for the executive. As for the judiciary, Dongwook Cha (Chapter 13) points out how recent relations between the executive and the National Assembly have been mediated by the Constitutional Court. South Korean society did not pay much attention to the role of this court in the early stages of democratisation. But, as the era of dominance by the president and the government has passed, the Constitutional Court is now facing unprecedented political and social pressures to resolve the conflicts between highly polarised political forces.

Section 3 examines the process of political representation and its substantial outcomes in South Korea. Sunghack Lim (Chapter 14) confirms the stable inter-party competition over the years leading to democratic consolidation in South Korea. While blaming regional factionalism, personality-based party organisation and organisational instability for the weak party system institutionalisation of South Korea, his evaluation of South Korean parties is overall fairly positive. Lim characterises them as a fairly successful actors for democratic governance. Indeed, South Korean parties have frequently changed their labels and organisational structures. But if we make use of a one-dimensional ideological spectrum, the main liberal and conservative parties have remained as representatives of voters in their respective ideological positions. Nevertheless, ideological representation by each party does not imply a substantively successful representation. Kyungmee Park (Chapter 15) covers, in this regard, the level of political representation for different groups of people. In particular, she argues that women's representation in South Korean society is still lower than the standard for other developed countries. Park also explains that representation for migrants, as well as the younger generation, still remains at a symbolic level. Thus, the stable existence of two main parties on each side of the ideological spectrum does not guarantee the avoidance of marginalisation of some social issues in South Korean society. Woojin Moon (Chapter 16), focusing on electoral competitions in South Korea, highlights how voters' issue preferences can be weakly represented. He argues that the current mixed-member majoritarian electoral system in South Korea produces a weak proportionality between the vote and seat shares of political parties. In addition, the South–North confrontation tends to distort the programmatic mobilisation strategies of political parties in South Korea. Because of these characteristics, he argues that candidates' campaigning strategies are more likely to concentrate on mobilising personal votes form their regional base.

Meanwhile, Han Soo Lee (Chapter 17) discusses the potential development of different types of campaign strategies. He argues that the recent advancement of online communication technologies is associated with significant changes in the campaign strategies of political parties in South Korea. Even though Lee cautions against concluding that there is a direct correlation between the use of new media and offline political participation, he analyses the possibility that online communication tools will play a significant role in the process of representing the diversity of South Korean society. While Lee shows the effect of communication technology developments, Seung-Jin Jang (Chapter 18) leads us to pay attention to the effect of diverse issues in the process of representation. He finds that issues such as gender and immigration have only recently begun to become politically significant and attract public attention. Likewise, only in recent years have welfare and redistribution become a prominent area of party competition. As he shows, there are emerging political coalitions among South Korean voters focusing on those issues. Thus, he expects that political competition in South Korea will be affected by the diversification in the type of issues receiving attention.

Overall, all authors studying the representation process in South Korean politics seem to agree that the country's society no longer has a homogenous purpose as observed in the early period of democratisation. In response to heterogenous preferences, the development of political dynamics different from the early democratising period is required. And indeed, some of them are already taking hold in contemporary South Korean politics and society.

4. Civil Society, Culture, and Media

Sections 4 and 5 examine various aspects of South Korea's civil society, culture, and media as they relate to the country's politics. Section 4 focuses on the interplay between civil society and politics. Even though Henderson (1968) attributed the unstable politics of South Korea to a lack of intermediary civic organisations, the authors in this section show that economic development and democratisation have led to the tremendous growth of civil society. The authors concur that South Korean civil society initially grew out of the democratic movement against the authoritarian state before the 1987 transition. But they also show that the democratic consolidation of the 1990s dramatically facilitated its expansion and activism compared to the pre-democratic era. The two main reasons are that socio-economic modernisation equipped South Korean citizens with resources and opportunities to form civic organisations and interest groups, while political democratisation removed barriers to citizens' associationism and activism in the political process.

The authors highlight that the unity of the democratic movement during the 1980s did not hold and gave a way to diversity and differentiation within civil society. In this context, economic interest groups, labour unions, civic reform organisations, and even new issue groups focusing on issues such as gender or minorities have formed and engaged in politics since the 1990s. In Chapter 19, Jin-Wook Shin demonstrates that civic associations and activism have blossomed not only due to the democratisation movement but also because of their own success. Along with the growth of civil society and activism, three notable changes have been observed in the macrostructure of South Korean social movement: the differentiation of social movements across independent issue areas, the decentralisation of communication and mobilisation structures as well as the ecosystem of social movements, and the ideological division of civil society intensifying competition between groups pursuing conflicting values and reform agendas. Moreover, citizens actively participate in non-profit organisations and politics in comparison with other democratic countries, which confirms that South Korean civil society is vibrant at both the individual and societal levels.

Along the same lines, Yoojin Lim and Yeonho Lee explain in Chapter 20 that the growth of interest groups is evident in four areas: labour unions, economic organisations, professional associations, and public interest groups. If these interest groups were controlled by government during the authoritarian past, they have departed from state influence and demanded their sectoral interests. And if interest groups showed the features of competitive pluralism before the 2010s, they have then headed towards a conflictual pluralism in which they directly clash, and representative organisations such as political parties remain weak.

Soonmee Kwon (Chapter 21) details the internal characteristics of South Korean labour unionism. Growing out of the Great Workers' Struggle of 1987, labour unions in South Korea have faced a dilemma: they have been under pressure from globalisation and market-friendly politics, while maintaining militant activism without official channels to communicate with political parties. Indeed, labour unions are internally divided at the ideological level and have failed to shift from enterprise unionism to industrial unionism. They have also failed to establish a working class differentiated from the classes represented by the liberal and conservative parties. Accordingly, the recent dualisation of the labour market has intensified the political marginalisation of labour unions, making militant unionism, including 'sky protests', an attractive strategy among union leaders.

Youngho Cho (Chapter 22) examines recent trends and the state of civic culture in South Korea, since the health of a democracy depends on what people think about it. Since the 1990s, public support for democracy has steadily eroded and openness to strongmen and military rule has increased in South Korea. It is notable that this downward trend continued even after the 2016–2017 Candlelight Uprising. The sluggish development of representative institutions has contributed to the steady decline in public support for democracy, causing worrisome signals for the future of South Korean democracy.

The authors in this section identify three general features of South Korean civil society. First of all, large-scale mass protests have continued as evidenced in the 2016–2017 Candlelight Uprising. Second, political polarisation within civil society has been intensifying in that labour organisations have maintained militaristic activism and various interest groups conflict outside of formal politics. Finally, representative institutions have been limited in terms of incorporating and integrating differentiated interests of civil society.

Section 5 examines the links between South Korea's culture and media and the country's politics, focusing on how traditional and new communication spaces and tools shape socio-political and politico-economic dynamics. The contributors to this section show that media indeed influences politics. But as media consumption patterns have changed, online media has become more central to politics compared to other types that played a bigger rule during the authoritarian era. Also, politicisation can affect media narratives as well. Thus, media sometimes plays the role of political actor rather than being a medium for objective information to allow informed citizens to form their own views. In any case, and broadly speaking, media and cultural expressions have also served their purpose of allowing for debate among different views.

In Chapter 23, Hyangjin Lee explains the role that cinema and television have played in critiquing South Korean politics, therefore shaping the views of voters and public opinion at large. In particular, cinema and television have been critical of government interventionism, a remnant of the authoritarian years. In the case of cinema, in addition, its popularity continues to make it an influential medium. As for television, its apt use of online communication has preserved its enduring relevance. Likewise, Dal Yong Jin explains in Chapter 24, that the internet and social media have shaped voting behaviour and, more broadly, the political conversation since the early 2000s. They have democratised this conversation by influencing political messaging and giving voice to new groups which found it difficult to be represented in traditional media. At the same time, the dominance of a small number of internet portals and messaging apps give them a gatekeeper function in that they determine which ideas circulate.

In contrast, the role of the press in shaping public discourse has weakened as Ki-Sung Kwak suggests in Chapter 25. The main reason is its partisanship and identification with either conservative or liberal ideas, which has sowed divisions in South Korea and means that those with a particular ideology will only read the press that conforms to their views. In the case of the press, Kwak explains how the legacy of decades of authoritarianism still affects political reporting and the relationship between the press and political parties. But as Namhee Lee (Chapter 26) explains, the situation is different for public intellectuals that used to rely on the press to influence the circulation of political ideas. Their role has not been diminished but rather transformed. Making use of new means of communication, public intellectuals continue to shape and participate—if not necessarily to lead—public debate. Furthermore, both socially conscious celebrities and experts in a particular field have emerged as new public intellectuals since the 2000s. Meanwhile, popular music plays a different role in politics. As John Lie (Chapter 27) shows, popular music was more political during the years of authoritarianism when it channelled the thirst for democracy. Since democratisation, however, it has become a paradigm of South Korean political economy and globalisation rather than a driver of domestic political conversation. Therefore, the political role of popular music has changed. Today, popular music in general and K-pop in particular supports the political goal of economic growth and globalisation that is central to the contemporary South Korean state.

Culture and media have a big impact on the politics of post-democratisation South Korea. They shape the political agenda, represent different points of view, and provide a communication channel for political parties, civil society, and other groups. Some culture and media organisations have become stronger as the years have gone by, while others have become weaker. But all of them play an important role, as is the case in comparable democracies across Asia and elsewhere.

5. Public Policy and the International Arena

Sections 6 and 7 examine the politics of South Korea's public policy and international relations. Section 6 shows how bureaucratic government and public policy have changed in the post-developmental and democratic era. Before the 1987 transition, South Korea could be best described as an authoritarian developmental state with centralised government and minimal welfare programmes. When Park Chung-hee launched the developmental state including specific government structures in the 1960s, North Korea was more advanced and belligerent than South Korea (Greitens 2016). Thus, Park sought to avoid a reunification-first policy and direct conflict with North Korea, focusing instead on boosting security and the developmental state via economic growth. The ultimate purpose was regime survival as well as winning the 'competition' against North Korea. This approach provided the necessary impetus for the development of both the state and the economy. The South Korean government was optimised for economic development and security. However, this developmental model became unsustainable and has had to change to respond to new demands emerging from the 1990s.

In Chapter 28, Huck-ju Kwon evaluates the democratic accountability of the South Korean government. Kwon argues that the political control of elected leaders from the national to the local levels has increased, politicising and overwhelming bureaucratic autonomy. Following democratisation, South Korean presidents have undertaken reforms to dismantle the policy regime of the developmental state and to reduce the number of initiatives coming out of the bureaucracy, eventually making performance management less autonomous and effective than before. Government reforms in South Korea need to create a balanced and accountable relationship between elected leaders and professional bureaucrats.

Jooha Lee (Chapter 29) identifies the 1997 Asian Financial Crisis as the critical juncture when South Korea departed from the legacy of developmental welfarism characterised by low government spending and strong emphasis on human capital investment. While the current welfarism of South Korea has become more inclusive by increasing its spending and focusing on vulnerable groups compared to the previous developmental welfarism, its social investment strategies still mix both protective and productive purposes. It is apparent that the dualisation between regular and non-regular work and addressing the aftermath of COVID-19 are two urgent tasks for South Korean welfarism.

When analysing the decentralisation of South Korea's central government, Yooil Bae (Chapter 30) shows that institutional decentralisation has been enormous. However, the weak administrative and fiscal capabilities of local governments have led to frequent confrontation with the central government and a growing gap among them. Furthermore, dependency on fiscal transfers from the central government and shrinking local populations are expected to increase the burden of local governments and widen regional economic disparities, which may pose a threat to local as well as national democracy.

Meanwhile, Kyoung-sun Min (Chapter 31) divides corruption into two types: petty and grand. Min demonstrates that the democratisation and economic development of South Korea have dramatically reduced the petty corruption experienced by ordinary citizens and lower-class officials, but more efforts are needed to control grand corruption, especially linked to presidents. While democratisation and the use of internet technology explains a low level of petty corruption, the legacies of crony capitalism and prosecution power explain the persistence of grand corruption.

Overall, the old centralised, developmental, and authoritarian government of South Korea has been adapting to the pressures of democratisation, globalisation, decentralisation, and need for social protection. Recent governmental and political efforts have focused on institutional domains, but they are yet to create a balanced and reciprocal relationship between elected politicians and professional bureaucrats.

Section 7 examines South Korea's foreign and defence policy since the transition to democracy. South Korea has become more ambitious, dynamic, and self-confident. It has emerged as a middle power, one whose history of democratic and economic development plus military upgrading has equipped it with a strong political narrative to underpin its foreign policy. But even though politics may not have a huge impact on the ultimate goals that South Korean policymakers would like to achieve (e.g. reunification with North Korea, a strong alliance with the United States, or promoting economic growth), liberals and conservatives do not always agree on the instruments to achieve them. Thus, domestic politics influence foreign policy insofar as changes in government can lead to the prioritisation of some specific tools of foreign policymaking over others.

In Chapter 32, Ramon Pacheco Pardo shows that foreign policy has remained relatively stable in terms of structures, goals, and available tools in spite of the level of political polarisation in South Korea. To a large extent, this reflects that South Korea is a middle power, which has both advantages and constraints. One of the key advantages is that South Korean politicians and policymakers agree on the range of issues that their country should be focusing on, thus providing continuity. When analysing South Korea's security and defence policy, Sung-han Kim and Alex Soohoon Lee (Chapter 33) find that South Korea faces two key security dilemmas that underscore this stability in terms of structures and goals: the North Korean nuclear threat and US–China strategic competition. These dilemmas are decades old, which underscores the extent to which South Korean foreign policy is determined by developments outside its control. However, Kim and Lee caution, competing beliefs mean that South Korean policy choices have fluctuated between liberal and conservative administrations. This is the result of each camp having different beliefs about the best ways to promote South Korean national interests.

With regards to the economic dimension of foreign policy, Sohyun Zoe Lee explains in Chapter 34 that the overarching goal of promoting growth through foreign economic policy remains unchanged. This has been a cornerstone of South Korean foreign economic policy dating back decades, given the extent to which the country has benefited from global trade openness. But governments differ in terms of how to achieve this goal. And they also have different ideas about the role of the chaebol and other civil society groups in economic policymaking. If there is one area in which liberals and conservatives agree when it comes to foreign policy, it is in positing South Korea as a development model and an aid donor. Eun Mee Kim and Nancy Y. Kim (Chapter 35) explain that this is a cornerstone of South Korean foreign policy, given the extent to which South Korea benefited from external support when it was a developing country. And they argue that South Korea's success story ultimately is the result of policy flexibility, a lesson that the country is trying to export.

When it comes to South Korean relations with third countries, three stand out: North Korea, the United States, and China. In Chapter 36, Young-kwan Yoon finds that South Korea's policy towards North Korea has also been in flux because liberals and conservatives identify differently vis-à-vis Korea's other half. The ultimate goal of reunification remains unchanged, regardless of South Korean domestic politics, and has been a staple of the country's foreign policy since its foundation. But the means to achieve this goal do not. This is the result of opposing views about North Korea's nuclear programme and the regime's stability. Similarly, Victor Cha and Katrin Katz (Chapter 37) show that South Korea's liberals and conservatives agree on the need for a strong alliance with the United States. This has been a staple of South Korean foreign policy since the Korean War. However, liberals and conservatives differ in terms of how much autonomy South Korea should exercise within the alliance. In general, liberals believe that autonomy should take precedence over the alliance. For conservatives, in contrast, the alliance is an enabler of South Korean autonomy. In Chapter 38, Heung-kyu Kim assesses the relationship between South Korea and China. The two countries only normalised diplomatic relations in 1992, but, of course, Sino-Korean historical relations date back centuries. Kim explains that this proximity means that the gravitational pull of China inevitably affects South Korean foreign policy, particularly in an area marked by strategic competition between South Korea's neighbour and its ally, the United States. In this context, South Korea has had to learn to carefully navigate relations between the two powers to avoid being affected by their bilateral competition.

All told, the politics of South Korea in relation to its presence in the international arena have evolved substantially since the country's democratisation. As South Korea has become more developed and democratic, debates about how to pursue the country's core foreign policy interests have grown. The goals may not change much regardless of who is in power, but the means to achieve them are affected by domestic politics.

6. South Korea's Democracy

By critically evaluating the contemporary politics of South Korea in their areas of expertise, most of the contributors to this handbook point out that South Korean politics have been moving in the direction of introducing the principle of checks and balances over the South Korean presidential system. Different groups, including political parties and civil society, have developed diverse channels to make their voices heard. Strong state-led developmentalism has been replaced by a thriving market-driven economy with heterogenous demands. Instances and practices of international cooperation and mutual learning have eroded the unity of political elites, now divided into competing groups with different reference points behind their policy orientations.

Accordingly, both the vortex-like instability of Henderson (1968) and the static culture of Confucianism have limits in explaining the contemporary dynamic of South Korean politics. This is the case because South Korea has experienced social, economic, and demographic transitions over the past half-century and its democratic politics has accompanied—as well as enabled—those changes. The dynamics of contemporary South Korean politics have often followed from developments on civil society. The number of interest groups has expanded as a result of economic development, on the one hand, and the interplay between representative politics and a modernised society on the other.

In the literature analysing political development and democracy, there are two contrasting views. According to the modernisation paradigm of Seymour Lipset (1959), a stable democracy emerges as a consequence of socio-economic modernisation. Socio-economic modernisation empowers the middle class, breeds civil society with interest groups and civil organisations, and supports the accumulation of cultural capital supportive of democratic legitimacy. On the other hand, Huntington (1968) posited that socio-economic modernisation does not necessarily lead to democracy but tends to cause political instability because of the changes it brings. The reason behind Huntington's claim is that the speed of socio-economic modernisation is normally faster than that of political development, and therefore (political) democracy is not likely to attain institutional stability in changing societies. Despite the academic debate between these two views, both approaches agree that South Korea is as an exemplary case of a country which has successfully achieved socio-economic modernisation and political democracy following a sequential path (Fukuyama 2014).

Taking mid-range perspectives rather than grand theories, this edited volume aims to provide an in-depth and accurate evaluation of South Korean contemporary politics as well as the evolution of its democracy as a system and as a practice. The volume explains and discusses their strengths and weaknesses, the areas in which there has been more change since the 1980s and the areas in which shifts have proceeded more slowly, and the reasons why South Korean politics and democracy have evolved in a particular way. It is our hope that readers of this volume gain a deeper understanding of how South Korea got to the point it is at today, appreciate the country's remarkable evolution from the late 1980s onwards, and come up with their own analysis to debate the ways in which South Korean democracy might evolve in the future.

BIBLIOGRAPHY

Anderson, B. (1991), *Imagined Communities* (New York: Verso).
Deuchler, M. (1995), *The Confucian Transformation of Korea* (Cambridge, MA: Harvard University Press).
Fukuyama, F. (2014), *Political Order and Political Decay* (New York: Farrar, Straus and Giroux).
Greitens, S. (2016), *Dictators and Their Secret Police* (New York: Cambridge University Press).
Henderson, G. (1968), *Korea: The Politics of the Vortex* (Cambridge, MA: Harvard University Press).
Huntington, S. P. (1968), *Political Order in Changing Societies* (New Haven, CT: Yale University Press).
Kim, S. (2014), *Confucian Democracy in East Asia* (New York: Cambridge University Press).
Kornhauser, W. (1959), *The Politics of Mass Society* (Glencoe, IL: The Free Press).
Lipset, S. (1959), 'Some Social Requisites of Democracy', *American Political Science Review* 53, 69–105.
Merton, R. K. (1968), *Social Theory and Social Structure* (New York: The Free Press).
Shin, D. C. (2012), *Confucianism and Democratization in East Asia* (New York: Cambridge University Press).

CHAPTER 2

THE HISTORY OF KOREA, 1905–1945

HYUNG-GU LYNN

1. INTRODUCTION

THE period of 1905–1945 in modern Korean history has had a long-lasting and outsized impact on the public memory in Korea. Post-1945 political leaders such as Rhee Syngman, the first president of South Korea, and Kim Il-sung, the first leader of North Korea, mined the period as a source of political legitimacy and public appeal by invoking their anti-Japanese, pro-independence activities overseas during these years. School textbooks in both Koreas continually reinforce a binary narrative pitting Japanese colonial oppression against Korean resistance and independence movements, while legal and political issues stemming from the period have plangent resonance in bilateral relations between South Korea and Japan in the 2020s, despite the decades that have passed since liberation in 1945, and the fact that normalised diplomatic relations between the two countries were established in 1965 (Lynn 2000).

The dominant narrative in the scholarship, especially from 1945 to the mid-1980s, also focused on Japanese colonial oppression and the Korean struggle for national independence. While further documentation of independence movements and colonial atrocities remain essential areas of research, these have been supplemented by other approaches that have helped to generate additional depth, precision, and nuance. More specifically, historians have analysed the processes and the causes driving the formation or the expansion of modern Korean nationalism under the crucible of colonial rule; the intensification of fractures along the entire political spectrum; the socio-economic transformations and the emergence of a middle class during the 1930s; the implications of industrialisation, mobilisation, and militarisation that occurred from 1936 as lodestars for the array of economic planning and mobilisation, policies implemented in South Korea in the 1960s, the so-called developmental state; and the dissipation of monarchy as a sustainable form of government.

This chapter provides an analytical overview of the essential questions, issues, and debates about Korean politics from 1905 to 1945, a period during which Japan ruled over Korea as a protectorate (1905–1910) and as a colony (1910–1945). It is not intended to be an encyclopaedic or descriptive summary; rather, the aim is to highlight and examine major transformations that occurred during these years and their implications for the study of post-1945 politics.

Organised into five sections and a Conclusion after this Introduction, the chapter first outlines the implications of the Protectorate period (1905–1910) for the study of Korean politics, flagging in particular the interplay of domestic Korean modernisation efforts, imperialist jockeying for influence and control among international powers, and the impacts—or lack thereof—of major, unpredicted events and agency on Korean politics. Second, it covers the development of modern nationalism or the emergence of a collective Korean ethnic identity that encompassed, rather than superseded, other units of identity based on locale, region, class, clan, gender, and age. Third, it outlines the polarisation of politics between left and right and diversification within these categories. Fourth, it briefly assesses the attempts to trace the origins of the so-called development state of 1960s South Korea to economic planning of the colonial bureaucracy during the 1930s. Finally, the chapter addresses the emergence of republicanism and the waning of monarchy as desirable forms of government, before presenting a conclusion.

2. The Protectorate Period, 1905–1910

Japanese colonial rule of Korea officially started on 29 August 1910 with the public announcement of the Treaty of Annexation. Contemporary observers and later historians underscored the inevitability of imperialist expansion and the ineffectiveness of Korean efforts to modernise prior to 1910, but the pre-history of colonialism was in fact a complex interplay of international power politics, truncated domestic reforms, and major assassinations that raise questions about the relative importance of individual political actors relative to structural dynamics.

To be sure, imperialist ambitions and international politics did loom large over the period. From the mid-nineteenth century, Korea had been forced to wend its way between foreign powers, namely China, Japan, the United States, Britain, France, and Russia, competing for influence over it. Japan forced Korea to sign its first port-opening treaty in 1876 through gunboat diplomacy, while China held sway over the Korean Peninsula from 1885 until 1904 through its representative in Seoul, the Imperial Resident, Yuan Shikai (Larsen 2008). The First Sino–Japanese War of 1894–1895 was fought largely over indirect control of Korea, paving the way for a period of Russo–Japanese competition. Increasing tensions over Korea and Manchuria prompted Japan to shore up its alliance with Britain (Anglo–Japanese Alliance Treaty of 1902) prior to the outbreak of the Russo–Japanese War of 1904–1905. Japan's victory over Russia secured its control over Korea and recognised via the signing of the Treaty of Portsmouth in September

1905, a process brokered by the United States. The importance of international politics can be gleaned from the fact that despite lobbying from Korean leaders, US President Theodore Roosevelt's position on the Japanese protectorate in Korea was that there was really nothing to be done (Duus 1998). The *Eulsa* Treaty of November 1905, with Japanese troops from the war still occupying Korea, officially rendered the country a protectorate of Japan, a dependent state granted a degree of internal administrative autonomy, but whose major foreign policy decisions were to be controlled by its 'protector' or suzerain state. The first Japanese Resident General was former Prime Minister Itō Hirobumi, apparently sealing Korea's slide towards colonisation.

But a second major issue infusing the study of pre-1910 history is the extent and impact of domestic reforms launched by the Korean government prior to 1905. Historical accounts that focus on the machinations and jockeying of foreign powers can render Korea a marginal agent in its own history. Admittedly, numerous contemporary Western diplomats and missionaries were dismissive of the capacities of the Korean government in the early 1900s, but recent scholarship has shown that the modernisation efforts undertaken by the Korean King (Emperor after 1897), Gojong, were more comprehensive than previously depicted and that the Korean government made numerous attempts to invoke international law to prevent being colonised (Yi 2000).

Korea became the Great Korean Empire in 1897, allowing Gojong to elevate himself from King to Emperor, not for reasons of ego, but in order to gain equal footing, at least technically, with the emperors of Japan and China under international law. More substantively, Gojong undertook a programme of modernisation, called the *Gwangmu* Reforms (1897–1905), that introduced new weapons for the Korean military and new regulations governing clothing and haircuts, and initiated the construction of infrastructural services, such as the expansion of the postal system, telephone and telegraph, electricity, water pipes, streetcars, trains, and public parks. In addition, grassroots organisations, such as An Chang-Ho's *Sinminhoe* (New People Association) established in 1907, emerged in this period, propelled by the goal of increasing public access to education, medical facilities, and other social services (Yu 1997).

Korea also attempted to use international law to counter the trajectory towards colonisation in the years prior to 1910. Gojong sent a trusted advisor, Hyeon Sanggeon, as early as 1903 to convince officials in France, the Netherlands, and Russia to recognise Korea's perpetual neutrality, and declared his country's neutrality under international law at the outbreak of the Russo–Japanese War in 1904. However, European governments and the two combatants in the war ignored Korea's entreaties and filing. The Emperor also sent a letter to the Hague Conference of 1906 to again request support for Korea's neutrality and sovereignty, and in 1907 sent three envoys to the Hague Peace Conference for that year to protest Japan's violation of Korea's sovereignty (Jeon 2014). The Korean delegates were denied entry into the conference and Itō Hirobumi and his Korean Prime Minister, Yi Wanyong (whose name, much like that of Norwegian Nazi collaborator Vidkun Quisling, became synonymous with 'traitor' as he was the signatory to the Treaty of Annexation in 1910, which sealed Korea's colonisation), forced Gojong to abdicate his throne in July of the same year (Im 1993). Only five days after Gojong's son Sunjong ascended to the Emperorship, Itō pushed through the Japan–Korea Treaty (also known as the *Jeongmi* Treaty), which transferred remaining governing powers to the Japanese Resident General, and thereby allowed him to dissolve the Korean army.

The attempt to use international law was not limited to the Korean government. From 1905 through to 1907, guerrilla forces known as the Righteous Armies (*Uibyeong*), joined after 1907 by former members of the Korean army, battled the Japanese army, despite being vastly outnumbered and outgunned. In 1908, one of the guerrilla leaders, Yi In-Yeong, applied to foreign embassies in Seoul for recognition as an army at war under international law, but this effort ended in vain. While armed resistance continued, peaking in 1908 with around 70,000 Koreans participating in 1,450 clashes, there was a dramatic decline after a sustained offensive by the Japanese in 1909 to stamp out insurgents (Kang 2004).

A third area involves untying the Gordian knot of causality, motivations, and agency in the years 1905–1910. One challenge has been to recognise and study the full range of responses to colonisation among Koreans at a depth beyond the compilation of a catalogue of 'good' and 'bad' historical figures. If some of the guerrillas from the Righteous Armies made their way to Manchuria and the borderlands in the north to continue armed resistance, a minority of Korean organisations, such as the *Iljinhoe*, welcomed colonisation as a platform for equality and integration of Korea and Japan as a propellant for modernisation and as a bulwark against Western imperialism (Moon 2013). Such Pan-Asianists and other prominent 'pro-Japanese' figures, such as Yi Wanyong, have been dismissed as rapacious and corrupt traitors that do not merit research, other than as objects of condemnation and vituperation, leaving their motivations relatively under-analysed. Another challenge has been the need to sift through the seemingly contradictory beliefs within each individual. For instance, while An Junggeun is widely celebrated as a national hero in contemporary South Korea for his assassination of Itō Hirobumi at the train station in Harbin, China in October 1909, the narrative requires some finessing to integrate the facts that while An was indeed angered by Japan's exploitation of Korea, as outlined in his Fifteen-Point explanation for killing Itō, he was also a Pan-Asianist, who believed that China, Korea, and Japan had to unite to defeat Western imperialism. Further complicating matters is that some scholars underline the fact that Itō was not in favour of colonisation and sought to maintain a protectorate status against the wishes of rival politicians such as Yamagata Aritomo and the Japanese army, resulting in Itō resigning from the Residency General in April 1909 (Moriyama 1987), while others argue that Itō acceded to colonisation plans in 1909 prior to stepping down from his post in Korea (Ogawara 2010). Korean activists also assassinated a US advisor to the Japanese Residency General, Durham Stevens, in San Francisco in 1908, but the historical reality remains that the two assassinations did not prevent Korea's colonisation. Considering the causes of Korea's colonisation requires care and precision in order to avoid *post hoc ergo propter hoc* fallacy; render assessments of the relative importance of individual political actors, agency, and single events against more cumulative structural dynamics in general; and analyse the more specific possibility that individuals such as Itō and

Stevens may not have been such major players on the Korean political stage, at least by 1909, as depicted in textbook accounts.

3. Modern Nationalism

The question of when modern nationalism in Korea emerged is inextricably tied to the relative weight placed on the March First Movement of 1919. On 8 February 1919, Korean students in Tokyo, inspired in part by Woodrow Wilson's Fourteen Points speech in 1918 supporting the principle of national self-sovereignty and the sudden death of the former Emperor, Gojong, in January of the same year, read out loud a declaration of independence. On 1 March 1919, thirty-three leaders from various religions and denominations signed a declaration of independence in a restaurant, which in turn was read out loud by a student in Pagoda Park in Seoul, attracting large crowds. Gojong's funeral, which was scheduled for 3 March, also drew large crowds that chanted for independence. Peaceful demonstrations rapidly spread throughout Korea, so that by May, nearly all corners of the Peninsula had demonstrations. Most experts agree that between one and two million people, young and old, students and workers, men and women, participated in the Movement, which lasted from March to the end of the year. The Government General responded with violence, leading to several massacres of unarmed civilians, mass arrests, torture, and subsequent international attention. One of the atrocities was the Jeamni massacre on 15 April 1919, in which villagers were herded into the local church, locked in, and burnt to death by Japanese military police. Despite the Government General's attempts to cover up the massacre, the Canadian missionary Dr Frank W. Schofield was able to relay the information concerning the events to the international media (Clark 1989).

There are three notable points of debate in research on the March First Movement. First, timing of the emergence of modern nationalism is a point of some dispute. While universally acknowledged as the largest mass demonstration for national independence in modern Korean history, some scholars view the March First Movement as a culmination of a grassroots nationalism that first emerged during the late nineteenth century, while others view it as evidence of a new, modern national identity that emerged after colonisation. Regardless of whether the spotlight is directed towards latent class consciousness evident from the nineteenth century, or a new twentieth-century anti-colonial collective identity, there is agreement among academics that the oppression under the initial years under Governors Terauchi Masatake (1910–1916) and Hasegawa Yoshimichi (1916–1919), a period labelled 'Military Rule', was a major causal factor in fuelling the development of modern Korean nationalism. The colonial state, renamed the Government General of Korea, used strict controls over economic activity, censorship of the press, heavy presence of military police, violence, and systematic imprisonment of any dissidents to establish colonial rule. In the notorious '105 Persons

Incident', the Government General arrested over 700 Korean Christians who were largely members of the aforementioned *Sinminhoe* for allegedly plotting to assassinate Terauchi. Despite public protests from Western Christian missionaries that the case had been entirely fabricated by the Government General, 105 people were sentenced during the trials held in 1912 (they were eventually given amnesty in 1915 due to international pressure; Kim 2016).

A second point of dispute has concerned the core causes of March First and, by proxy, modern nationalism. The mainstream historiography has stressed the combination of the oppressive nature of the Japanese colonial period from 1910 to 1919, widely circulating rumours to the effect that the former Emperor Gojong had been poisoned by the Japanese, and the catalytic effect of an external stimulus, in the form of Wilson's Fourteen Points speech of 1918 in which the US president expressed support for the principle of self-sovereignty for the South (Manzela 2007). In contrast, scholars hewing to a grassroots or people's (*minjung* in Korean) history perspective argue that the font of nationalism should be traced to peasant rebellions of the 1800s, in particular the Donghak Peasant Rebellion of 1894–1895. In the North Korean historiography, the external stimulus takes an alternative form, namely the 1917 October Revolution in Russia, which in this account inspired farmers and workers to rise up against the Japanese colonial overloads. Others, while keeping an eye on international contexts, trace the emergence of modern ethnic nationalism to the late nineteenth century, at least among intellectuals and political elites, as they grappled with the Social Darwinist conception of competition among races and states, in contrast to research which argues that the transition from regionalised forms of identity (e.g. provincial, city, village, etc.) to national ones occurred during the Military Rule period (Kim 2010).

Third, even with the widespread acknowledgement of the significance of the March First Movement, there have been calls to diversify research on it beyond the tracing of the development of modern Korean nationalism and its impact on politics. There are at least three burgeoning areas of research in South Korean academia, fuelled in part by its hundredth anniversary of the March First Movement in 2019—local history, socio-economic contexts, and international connections. There has been an exponential growth in the number of local histories that map the ways in which the Movement spread to and manifested in towns and villages, as well as descriptions of the range of Japanese police response in these locales (e.g. Heo 2018). Studies of socio-economic factors as background conditions for the Movement have increased since the 2010s, pointing to the surge in production from the First World War boom, combined with stagnant wages and inflation as supplements to colonial oppression as the sources of resentment and alienation among the general Korean populace (Pak 2014). On the international dimensions, researchers have investigated reactions and activities of individual Western missionaries, as well as the variances in views of foreign powers among the thirty-three original signatories who anticipated some form of support from Wilson (e.g. Choe Rin, Choe Namseon), as well as others who declined to participate (e.g. Yun Chi-ho) because they anticipated no actual support from any of the Western powers. Other studies have focused on concrete efforts to recruit foreign aid, such as the case of

Yeo Un-hyeong, who met with Charles Crane, a close advisor to Wilson, in Shanghai during 1918 to push for US support of the Korean independence movement (Jeong 2017). Historians have also scrutinised the tactical indifference of the United States during the Paris Peace Conference of 1919, where the Korean delegates' efforts to gain the support of Western governments for Korean independence ended in vain, despite spending January to August in Paris (Kim, S. 2009).

March First did not result in Korean independence, but it did prompt a major shift in Japanese colonial policy. The new Governor, Saitō Makoto (1921–1927; 1929–1931), appointed after an overhaul of the top positions within the Government General in the aftermath of the March First Movement, oversaw under the banner of 'Cultural Rule' the implementation of an array of policies that combined clearer incentives and indirect oppressions, for example allowing the publications of privately run Korean newspapers and periodicals, while at the same time strengthening censorship protocols (Kang 1979). But the independence movement continued within Korea through the 1920s and 1930s, covering the spectrum from non-violent demonstrations to assassination attempts, everyday forms of resistance to advocacy via emerging mass media (Sin 2005). In fact, Saitō was the target of a bombing attempt upon his arrival in Seoul in September 1919 and evaded several other attempts on his life through the 1920s.

At the same time, many Korean organisations refocused their activities to overseas advocacy or fighting guerrilla wars along the northern border, and there would not be a repeat of the scale of the March First Movement until liberation in 1945. This is not to say that there were no independence movements within Korea, but that mass demonstrations of similar scales did not occur. For instance, when Sunjong, Gojong's successor, died in April 1926 and the funeral was scheduled for June of the same year, the Government General braced for a repeat of the March First Movement, mobilising some 7,000 troops into the Seoul area. Student activists did in fact coordinate with socialists to organise demonstrations for independence in what came be called the June 10th Movement, which resulted in around 1,000 people being imprisoned. In another case, from November 1929 to March 1930, student-organised demonstrations spread from the city of Gwangju throughout Korea, with an estimated 54,000 Koreans in 320 schools participating in what later became known as the Gwangju Student Independence Movement (Yun 2010).

4. Political Polarisation and Diversification

Another major thread of research has scrutinised the political divisions that crystallised during the 1920s and 1930s as explanatory factors for the loss in momentum of the independence movement within Korea by the late 1930s and as the fountainhead for the post-1945 division of the Peninsula. Even if Cold War calculations and the physical presence of US troops in the South and Soviets in the North were the ostensible reasons, domestic divisions had laid the foundations for the post-liberation period. While acknowledging the impact of international forces and Cold War structures on the politics of the Peninsula, in-depth research that details the extent to which communism and socialism gained traction during the colonial period has helped to generate an understanding of the origins of the Korean War beyond simply a proxy war between the United States and China/Soviet Union (Cumings 1981). Within the broad rubric of political polarisation and diversification, there are three intertwined scales and areas of research: the right–left relationship; fractures within each grouping; and the role of technology in politics.

The first area, right–left separation, has been the most densely researched, due in part to the convenient linkages to the division of the Peninsula. The inability to generate support from foreign governments despite the massive scale and scope of the March First Movement presented several choices among activists: an exodus from Korea to focus on independence activities from overseas locales; working within the incentive structures of Cultural Rule and weighing the possibility of advocating for self-rule, rather than independence, as a first step; enduring institutionalised discrimination; or exploring alternative ideologies such as socialism, communism, and anarchism. The 1920s witnessed the rapid growth of socialism, communism, and anarchism among intellectuals and students through underground publications and organisations, as well as through classrooms for Korean students in Japan and Comintern (Communist International) meetings for those in the Soviet Union and China. Moreover, the Comintern also initially encouraged communists in East Asia to embrace anti-colonial nationalism and social projects in order to generate support and momentum, allowing for cooperation with 'revolutionary' religious organisations (Tikhonov 2017). Thus, within Korea, when the industrialist Kim Seongsu, who founded the Korean daily newspaper *Donga Ilbo* in 1920, helped launch the Korean Goods Promotion Movement in 1923, communists and socialists were highly critical, labelling it a co-option of the independence movement by profiteering bourgeoise. Yet at the same time, leftists continued to cooperate with a minority of Christians and Buddhists who were sympathetic to their social action agendas. The period of relative pragmatism ended when, after multiple attempts at establishing a party that were extinguished by the colonial police, the Korean Communist Party was officially launched in 1925. This widened political rifts as the Comintern, which had begun taking a more radical turn, urged the newly established party to view the March First Movement as a 'failed bourgeoise revolution' and to take an explicitly anti-religious stance, particularly against Christianity (Sin 2019).

The second field of internal disputes has been studied on a more fine-grained scale. Despite the polarisations noted above, an organisation that presented a unified front of left and right, the *Singanhoe* (New Root/Trunk Society) operated within Korea from 1927 to 1931, alongside a sister organisation for women, the *Geunuhoe*. Some of its left-leaning members supported the Wonsan General Strike of 1929 that brought the city to a halt, and also triggered subsequent work stoppages in other cities throughout Korea. This in turn triggered intensified police crackdowns and arrests of leftist *Singanhoe* members, while those who had kept themselves at a distance from the Strike were not subject to overt harassment (Yi 1993).

In addition to police repression, internal disputes over ideology and tactics also diluted the group's cohesion. The Comintern retracted its recognition of the Korean Communist Party in 1928, citing its 'reformist' tendencies to compromise ideals, which in turn amplified divisions among factions within the socialist and communist camps based on their willingness to continue in the united front or not. The *Geunuhoe* split from the *Singanhoe* and ultimately dissolved due to a fallout between the Christian and socialist factions, and the constant marginalisation by male colleagues (Jang 2019). Division in the anarcho–communist camp and subsequent conflicts between these two groups accelerated the evaporation of cohesion in the left. Within the nationalist or bourgeoise groups, left and right divisions emerged, centred on the issue of whether or not to pursue colonial self-rule (based in large part on the Home Rule debates in Britain regarding Ireland) as an intermediary step towards long-term independence (Pak 1992).

Third, the print and communications technologies, the medium by which the 'imagined community' of the nation state was formed (Anderson 1983), had a double function in colonial Korea. On the one hand, the diffusion of print, and to a lesser extent, radio and film, helped to diffuse a standardised version of Korean identity and language. Two Korean-language daily newspapers were established in 1920, while numerous other magazines and periodicals were also published during the decade. Radio was introduced to Korea in 1927, with the broadcasts of one station using both Japanese and Korean languages. A dedicated Korean-language station was added in 1933. While all media were under strict censorship, which was particularly stringent on references to Marxism and communism, and on radio, their diffusion has been central to the notion of 'colonial modernity', the emergence of various forms of modernity under colonial conditions (Shin and Robinson 1999). On the other hand, print forums became increasingly focused or segregated, resulting in magazines that were affiliated with commercial print, socialism, socialism, or labour associations. For example, communist publications persisted largely underground and discrete from the mainstream due to the legal restrictions.

Governor Minami Jirō (1936–1942) implemented an array of wartime mobilisation policies, resulting in coerced assimilation policies and increased oppression that sharpened the divide not only between left and right, but also between those who remained in Korea and those who moved overseas. Bans on the use of Korean in public places such as schools and government offices, enforced name change policy, discouragement of the wearing of traditional white clothing, the drafting of Korean youths into the Japanese Imperial army, the mobilisation of women and men into labour corps for munitions factories and mines, the closure of privately run Korean-language daily newspapers in 1940, and the implementations of the notorious 'comfort women' system were just some of the policies that had lasting and traumatic impacts on collective memory (Higuchi 2001). In addition, state-controlled Korean-language publications featured writings exhorting Koreans to contribute to the war effort by public figures who had previously been leaders of the centrist or bourgeoise independence and women's movements (e.g. Yi Gwangsu, Yun Chi-ho, and Kim Hwallan/Helen). At the same time, the police engaged in divide-and-conquer tactics, simply imprisoning and torturing some communists and socialists, while 'converting' others to issue public apostasies of left-wing ideologies.

The complex imbrications of ideologies, tactics, gender, class, and apostasy were bundled under a narrative emphasising unified Korean opposition to Japanese colonial rule in post-1945 South Korea, obscuring the issue of who exactly was a collaborator or not. The South Korean government did hold a series of trials in 1948–1949 to judge those who had collaborated with the Japanese colonial rulers. However, due to Syngman Rhee prioritising anti-communism and bureaucratic utility over truth and reconciliation, none of those charged served their sentences; and yet, communism remains illegal in twenty-first-century South Korea. In North Korea, the government undertook a more extensive liquidation of 'collaborator' assets to expedite the process of entirely abolishing private ownership of land (Kim 2013).

5. Developmental State

When the South Korean economy was struggling in the 1950s, seemingly perpetually dependent on US aid, many observers pointed to period of 1905–1945 as having truncated economic development and growth. When the frame switched in the 1980s to explaining the sources of South Korea's 'Miracle on the Han', revisionist scholars pointed to the state-directed colonial period economy as the wellspring for capitalist development via the effectiveness of the colonial state's industrial policies; the provision of opportunities for entrepreneurial experience in a market economy; and the consequent growth in human capital (Woo-Cumings 1999). The concept of 'colonial modernisation' as an alternative to 'colonial exploitation' has been debated intensively in South Korea, in part due to the largely overlooked fact that the arguments for colonial modernisation or the Government General as genesis of the developmental state echo reports published in 1946 by Suzuki Takeo, a Japanese economist who had been a professor at Keijo [Seoul] Imperial University from 1928, who had been commissioned by the Japanese Foreign Ministry. The debates have centred on whether increases in production occurred and in what specific industries, who profited from the secular increases in output, whether Koreans who were not collaborators benefitted, and the causal mechanisms behind this development and growth. As a result, a steady stream of empirical, conceptual, and didactic research and commentary has been produced on the political economy of the period in Korean and Japanese, in contrast to the sporadic scale and scope of output on the subject in English.

The colonial state was undoubtedly interventionist in social, economic, and political arenas. Governor Ugaki Kazushige (1927; 1931–1936) explicitly prioritised industrial and agricultural growth in the 1930s; the statistics indicate significant growth in manufacturing and heavy industries during this decade. Campaigns to promote primary industries, such as the 1931 slogan promising 'sheep in the north and cotton in the south' accompanied increased investment into manufacturing and heavy industries from Japanese conglomerates. Large-scale, capital-intensive industry conglomerated in the northern regions of Korea in the form of mining operations, hydroelectric dams, and chemical industries, with the city of Hamhung becoming home to one of the largest fertiliser factories in the world during the 1930s (Kang 1985). However, whether the economic development and growth can be attributed to effective planning by a group of uber-bureaucrats appears less clear than much of the developmental state literature seems to assume.

The first issue is that economic development had multiple actors, not just the colonial state. Even in the 1920s, Korean, Chinese, and Japanese labourers, Japanese conglomerates based in Tokyo, Korean entrepreneurs, and Japanese settlers who operated small-to-medium firms held a diverse range of rights and interests. This resulted in cases where Japanese entrepreneurs wanted more Government General promotion of specific industries, yet also demanded protection of their rights against Korean competition (Uchida 2011). Moreover, some Korean-operated textile firms, such as the Kyeongseong Spinning, using cotton and wool produced in the southern parts of the colony, grew in the 1920s and 1930s during a time when the Government General was more focused on agricultural projects, such as the Rice Production Increase Plan in Korea that ran from 1925 to 1934.

Second, publications in English have been sparse on specifics in terms of institutions and individuals responsible for the economic planning in the Government General. The overwhelming majority of substantive studies on colonial decision-making and policy implementation processes have been published in Japanese and Korean (Jang 2007; Yi 2013). Therefore, there is a keen need for more precise, in-depth research published in English on the workings of the Government General in terms of personnel continuity and decision-making processes to assess whether origins of the developmental state can be traced to the colonial period.

Third, logically, the years between 1945 (the end of Japanese colonial rule) and 1962, when the South Korean President Park Chung-hee launched his First Five-Year Plan, need to be analysed to mount a persuasive case that the colonial state was the prototype of the developmental state. Indeed, Korean-language scholarship has seen an increase in the number of studies on capital accumulation, the impact of aid, economic plans and planning, and multiple other dimensions of state and private-sector economic activity in the 1950s (Yi 2012). In addition, there are promising avenues that focus on the lasting legacies of the colonial period transmitted through individual experiences imprinted into key individuals such as Park Chung-hee (Eckert 2016) that might allow for less emphasis on direct bureaucratic continuity and more focus on human capital.

A similar chronological jump also allows for assertions of continuities between the colonial period and North Korea's economic plans of the 1950s and 1960s without any examination of the specific institutions, economic theories, or individuals (e.g. Choe Yonggeon, allegedly the architect of the country's economic plans) who were essential to its operations during the 1950s and the 1960s. Details on internal debates, primary policy challenges, and changes over time over this period (e.g. gradual constriction of private enterprises that occurred in the 1950s; disputes between agriculture first and heavy industry first factions) have been elucidated in numerous publications in Korean (Yi 2004). A loose parallel to the human capital or imprinting approach for North Korea is the view of the country as a 'guerrilla state', in which organisational structures, strategies, and tactics of the country mirror through direct memory and experience those of the Korean guerrilla units that fought against the Japanese army during the colonial period (Wada 1998). The fact that North Korea's economy plateaued in the mid-1970s also remains largely unaddressed in the attempts to apply the colonial developmental state model to North Korea's economic planning during the 1960s, triggering interesting questions about the half-life of the colonial developmental state and the limited utility of using continuity or path dependence as an analytical tool.

6. Monarchy to Republic

One area of emerging research is the question of when and how the monarchy ended and republicanism began in Korea. If the transition from monarchy to republic in a recent case such as Nepal occurred only after a brutal ten-year civil war (1996–2006), the process for Korea was less clear and more protracted. When South Korea was ruled by a string of strongmen, such as Syngman Rhee during the 1950s, and Park Chung-hee in the 1960s and 1970s, several social scientists asserted that the colonial period was an interregnum that restricted access to meaningful political participation for Koreans, and thereby disabled the growth of democracy. The empirical evidence paints a more complex picture: there were Koreans appointed as provincial governors, one served a term as Education Bureau Director in the Government General (roughly the equivalent of a Cabinet minister), others were employed in large numbers in the Government General (albeit generally around half the total of the Japanese officials and concentrated in the lower ranks, with lower wages), and one former gangster employed by the colonial police to break up labour union meetings, Pak Chungeum, who made his way to Japan and was eventually elected to the Imperial Diet in 1932 and 1937 (Matsuda 1995).

The genealogical pursuit of the origins of republicanism has gravitated around the activities and limits of the Provisional Government of the Republic Korea, which was established in Shanghai on 11 April 1919 as a conglomeration of several Korean political organisations in exile. Detailed studies of its activities and internal tensions, such as the reasons why the first president of the Provisional Government, Syngman Rhee, was impeached in 1925 and why prominent figures such as Sin Chaeho left it to pursue writing and anarchism after repeated disagreements with Rhee about ideology and political tactics have been increasing in number (Seo 2012). Other works have focused on the Provisional Government's efforts to organise armed battles against Japan in China, the carrying out of assassination plans against Japanese officials, and the activities of

Kim Gu, who was the President from 1927 on, lobbying efforts in the international political arena, among other subjects.

More conceptually, there has been a continuing debate as to whether March First signalled the beginning of republicanism rather than 1926, 1945, or 1948, given that the demonstrators chanted for independence rather than mourned Gojong's death, and the fact that the Provisional Government was inspirited in large part by the scale and the scope of the movement in Korea (Yi 2019). Close readings of the Provisional Government's Constitution, the explicit reference in its name to 'republic' and its other texts have been parsed by scholars as origins for the Republic of Korea (South Korea). This argument is complicated by the relative paucity of research on the so-called Yi Gang incident, when Gojong's fifth son, Yi Gang, attempted to join the Provisional Government in Shanghai but was caught in Dandong in 1919 and returned to Korea by the colonial police. Nonetheless, available records indicate that debates between republicans and monarchists lasted intermittently into the late 1920s (Pak 2007).

The end of monarchy in de jure terms occurred when Japan colonised Korea in 1910 (although there is as yet unresolved debate among historians and law specialists concerning the legality of the 1910 Treaty), but a subject that has been relatively understudied is the process of how monarchy as a form of governance and the Korean Imperial family as possible leaders within it faded from elite and public perception. In de jure terms, the Korean royal family was incorporated into the Japanese Imperial Household system in 1910, with Sunjong demoted from emperor to a king and confined to one of the royal palaces in Seoul until his death in 1926 (Shinjō 2015). In de facto terms, Gojong's forced abdication in 1907 and death in 1919 very likely marked the end of monarchy as a viable form of government, even after liberation.

Since Sunjong did not have any offspring, the next in line within the Korean Imperial family was Yi Eun, one of Sunjong's younger half-brothers. Yi Eun had been taken to Japan at the age of seven in 1907 by Itō Hirobumi (Kim, C. 2009). In 1920, he was married to Princess Nashimoto Masako (later known as Yi Bangja/Pangja, a Korean reading of her name), a first cousin of the wife of the Show Emperor, Empress Kōjun, as a part of a series of orchestrated marriages between Korean and Japanese royals designed to symbolise the integration of the colony. The couple visited Korea with their newborn son, Yi Jin, in April 1922, to considerable media coverage. But the baby suddenly died in May, sparking rumours that Jin had been poisoned by Korean activists. The couple did not visit Korea when their second son, Yi Gu, was born in 1931. Other members of the Korean Imperial family, such as Princess Deokhye and Yi Gang also faded from public view during the 1930s. After liberation, South Korean newspapers contained only sporadic mentions of Yi Eun and his family's woes (he lost his royal status and nationality under the new Japanese Constitution in 1947 and was forced to sell the family's home in 1952).

Syngman Rhee, according to several accounts, feared the return of the monarchy, and thus refused repeated requests from Yi Eun and his family to return to the country. Rhee did meet with Yi Eun in Tokyo in 1950 during an official visit to meet Douglas MacArthur, Supreme Commander for the Allied Powers in East Asia, but declined to allow Yi to enter Korea in 1960. It was only in 1963 under Park Chung-hee that Yi Eun and Bangja were allowed to return to South Korea (Yi 1973).

7. Conclusion

Intense debates continue to roil around the extent, nature, impact, and legacy of the various changes that occurred during 1905–1945. Even in areas of apparent agreement, there are noticeable differences. March First is a major national holiday in twenty-first-century South Korea, while in North Korea, it is commemorated, in large part as Kim Il-sung in the official history is said to have participated in the event as an eight-year-old, but is not a national holiday. The difference in degrees of celebration is rooted in the fact that the North Korean state narrative places far greater weight on the role of Kim Il-sung and his guerrilla resistance during the 1930s and 1940s against the Japanese army, and highlights that the lessons learnt from March First were not just the abiding power of modern ethnic nationalism and collective demonstrations *pace* South Korea, but the futility of peaceful resistance and the need for a strong individual leader to serve as a vanguard for liberation and revolution.

Manichean contrasts between idealised independence movements and relentlessly menacing Japanese colonial state had a clear instrumentalist role to play in post-1945 South and North Korea. Consolidating the national identities in the two new countries was an urgent task, one that required sweeping narratives that accented the ineluctable rise of independence movements, whether infused by communism or liberalism, and shunting aside more complex and vexing nuances of the colonial period. Older historiography generally hewed closely to the anti-communist nationalism of the South, and the anti-imperialist communism of the North. Starting in the mid-1980s, concordant with South Korea's democratisation in 1987, a wider range of approaches on Korea's colonial period appeared in the South, including those that re-examined the roots of Korea's modern ethnic nationalism, centred around interpretations of the March First Movement of 1919; the dynamics and implications of political polarisation between the left and right and further fragmentation with each camp that materialised during the 1920s; the short-term and long-term implications of economic development and growth in the 1930s that, according to some writers, served as the template for the developmental state that emerged in South Korea during the 1960s; and the dissolution of absolute monarchy and the rise or republicanism as a desirable system of governance for a liberated Korea.

Even then, there remain several areas of elision and lacuna, some of which have been identified in this chapter. More importantly, the years 1905–1945, despite the dominating presence of colonialism, contain complex processes that cannot be merely celebrated or demonised, or wholly captured by analyses that rely on monocausal explanations, ex post facto vituperations, and essentialised categories of nation or race. Further research that delves into archival sources to develop robust foundations of empirical sources, displays a firm command of the salient scholarship in at least three languages (Korean, Japanese, and English), and engages with and applies theoretical frames with depth and precision will be essential for strengthening our understanding of, and ability to navigate, this period in Korea's political history.

Bibliography

*All Korean-language titles and author names have been rendered in Revised Romanization system, rather than the authors' preferred versions, with the exception of common variants for personal names (e.g. Kim, Pak) and places (e.g. Seoul). All Japanese names and titles have Romanized using the Revised Hepburn system, with the exception of commonly used place names (e.g. Tokyo).

Anderson, B. (1983), *Imagined Communities: Reflections on the Origin and Spread of Nationalism* (London: Verso).

Clark, D. (1989), ' "Surely God Will Work Out Their Salvation": Protestant Missionaries in the March First Movement', *Korean Studies* 13, 42–75.

Cumings, B. (1981), *The Origins of the Korean War: Liberation and the Emergence of Separate Regimes, 1945–1947* (Princeton, NJ: Princeton University Press).

Duus, P. (1998), *The Abacus and the Sword: The Japanese Penetration of Korea, 1895–1910* (Berkeley, CA: University of California Press).

Eckert, C. (2016), *Park Chung Hee and Modern Korea: The Roots of Militarism 1866–1945* (Cambridge: Harvard University Press).

Heo, Y. (2018), 'Samil undong ui network wa jojik, dawonjeok yeondae' [Networks, Organizations, and Plural Solidarities of the March First Movement], *Sahak yeongu* 132, 523–562.

Higuchi, Y. (2001), *Senjika Chōsen no minshū to chōhei* [Koreans and Conscription during World War II] (Tokyo: Sōwasha).

Im, D. (1993), 'Yi Wanyong ui byeonsin gwajeong gwa jaesan chukjeok' [The Transformation of Yi Wanyong and His Wealth Accumulation], *Yeoksa bipyeong* 22, 138–185.

Jang, S. (2007), 'Iljeha Joseonin godeung gwallyo ui hyeongseong gwa jeongcheseong' [Emergence and Identities of High-Ranking Korea Officials in the Government General], *Yeoksa wa hyeonsil* 63, 39–68.

Jang, W. (2019), 'Geunuhoe wa Joseon yeoseong haebang tongil jeonseon' [Geunuhoe and the United Front for Women's Liberation], *Yeoksa munje yeongu* 42, 391–431.

Jeon, I. (2014), 'Dae-Hanjegug ui Heigeu mangukpyeonghwa hoeuie ui teuksa pagyeon gwa sisajeom' [Implication of the Dispatch of the Great Han Envoy to the Hague International Peace Conference], *Hanguk haengjeong sahakji* 34, 29–48.

Jeong, B. (2017), 'Samil undong ui gipokje: Yeo Unhyeong i Crane ege bonaen pyeonji mit cheongwonseo' [Letter and Petition of Lyuh Woon-hyung to Charles Crane, November 1918], *Yeoksa bipyeong* 119, 223–267.

Kang, C. (2004), *Joseon tonggambu yeongu* [Japanese Residency General of Korea], Vol. 2 (Seoul: Gukhak jaryowon).

Kang, J. (1985), *Chōsen ni okeru Nitchitsu kontserun* [Nichitsu Conglomerate in Colonial Korea] (Tokyo: Fuji shuppan).

Kang, T. (1979), *Nihon no Chōsen shihai seisaku-shi kenkyū* [Japanese Colonial Policies in Korea] (Tokyo: Tokyo daigaku shuppankai).

Kim, C. (2009), 'Politics and Pageantry in Protectorate Korea (1905–10): The Imperial Progresses of Sunjong', *Journal of Asian Studies* 68, 835–859.
Kim, J. (2013), 'Haebang hu Buk-Han ui chin-Ilpa wa Ilje yusan cheokgyeol' [Liquidation of Pro-Japanese Assets in Post-Liberation North Korea], *Hanguk gunhyeondaesa yeongu* 66, 182–222.
Kim, M. (2016), 'The Politics of Officially Recognizing Religions and the Expansion of Urban "Social Work" in Colonial Korea', *Journal of Korean Religions* 7, 69–98.
Kim, S. (2009), *American Diplomacy and Strategy toward Korea and Northeast Asia, 1882–1950 and After* (New York: Palgrave).
Kim, S. ed. (2010), *The Northern Region of Korea: History, Identity, and Culture* (Seattle, WA: University of Washington Press).
Larsen, K. (2008), *Tradition, Treaties, and Trade: Qing Imperialism and Chosŏn Korea 1850–1910* (Cambridge: Harvard University Press).
Lynn, H. (2000), 'Systemic Lock: The Institutionalization of History in Post-1965 South Korea–Japan Relations', *Journal of American East Asian Relations* 9, 55–84.
Manzela, E. (2007), *The Wilsonian Moment: Self-Determination and the International Origins of Anticolonial Nationalism* (Oxford: Oxford University Press).
Matsuda, T. (1995), *Senzenki no zainichi Chōsenjin to sanseiken* [Koreans in Japan and Suffrage, Pre-1945] (Tokyo: Akashi shoten).
Moriyama, S. (1987), *Kindai Nikkan kankeishi kenkyū* [Modern Japan–Korea Relations] (Tokyo: Tokyo daigaku shuppankai).
Moon, Y. (2013), *Populist Collaborators: The Ilchinhoe and the Japanese Colonization of Korea, 1896–1910* (Ithaca NY: Cornell University Press).
Ogawara, H. (2010), *Itō Hirobumi no Kankoku heigō kōsō to Chōsen shakai* [Itō Hirobumi's Annexation Plans and Korean Society] (Tokyo: Iwanami shoten).
Pak, C. (1992), *Hanguk geundae jeongchi sasangsa yeongu* [History of Modern Korean Political Thought] (Seoul: Yeoksa bipyeongsa).
Pak, H. (2007), 'Iljesidae gonghwajuui wa bokbyeokjuui ui daerip' [Republicanism versus Restoration Theory], *Jeongsin munhwa yeongu* 30, 57–76.
Pak, S. (2014), 'Je-1cha Segyedaejeon jeonhu ui Hanguk gyeongje' [The Korean Economy after World War I], *Hyeondaesa gwangjang* 3, 72–91.
Seo, I. (2012), '1919–1923 nyeon Sin Chaeho ui ban-Imsi jeongbu roseon gwa minjok jagyeoljuui insik' [Shin Chaeho's Anti-Provisional Government Line in 1919–1923 and His Understanding of the Principle of Self-Determination of Peoples], *Hangung dongnim undongsa yeongu* 43, 43–73.
Shin, G., and Robinson, R. eds (1999), *Colonial Modernity in Korea* (Cambridge: Harvard University Press).
Shinjō, M. (2015), *Chōsen ōkōzoku* [The Korean Royal Family] (Tokyo: Chūō kōronsha).
Sin, J. (2005), *1930 nyeondae minjok undongsa* [Korean Independence Movements of the 1930s] (Seoul: Seonin).
Sin, U. (2019), 'Gukgwonhoebok(1945) ijeon "3.1 hyeongmyeong" ae daehan pyeongga, insik, mit geu uimi' [Evaluations of the March First Movement before 1945], *Seondo munhwa* 27, 293–324.
Tikhonov, V. (2017), '"Korean Nationalism" Seen through the Comintern Prism, 1920s–30s', *Region* 6, 2013–224.
Uchida, J. (2011), *Brokers of Empire: Japanese Settler Colonialism in Korea, 1876–1945* (Cambridge, MA: Harvard University Press).

Wada, H. (1998), *Kita Chōsen: yūgekitai kokka no genzai* [*North Korea: The Guerilla State*] (Tokyo: Iwanami shoten).
Woo-Cumings, M., ed. (1999), *The Developmental State* (Ithaca, NY: Cornell University Press).
Yi, B. (1973), *The World is One: Princess Yi Pangja's Autobiography* (Seoul: Taewon).
Yi, G. (1993), *Singanhoe yeongu* [*Singanhoe*] (Seoul: Yeoksa bipyeongsa).
Yi, H. (2013), *Chōsen sōtokufu kanryō no tōchi kōsō* [*The Structure of the Government General of Korea*] (Tokyo: Yoshikawa kōbunkan).
Yi, N. (2019), '3.1undong gwa gonghwajuui' [The March First Movement and Republicanism], *Simin sahoe wa NGO* 17, 79–109.
Yi, S. (2004), 'Jeonhu Bukhan eseoui sahoejuui gyeongje geonseol noseon e daehan nonjaeng' [The Debate in Post-1953 North Korea on Socialist Economic Development], *Asea yeongu* 116, 213–242.
Yi, S. (2012), 'Hanguk gyeongje gwallyo ui Ilje sigminji giwonseol geomto (1950 nyeondae-1960 nyeondae jeonban)' [Colonial Origins of Korean Economic Bureaucrats, 1950s and Early 1960s], *Minju sahoe wa jeochaek yeongu* 21, 202–247.
Yi, T. (2000), *Gojong sidae ui jaejomyeong* [*Re-Examining the Gojong Period*] (Seoul: Taehaksa).
Yu, Y. (1997), *Daehan jegukgiui minjok undong* [*Nationalism during the Great Han Empire*] (Seoul: Iljogak).
Yun, S. (2010), 'Gwangju haksaeng undong ihu haksaeng undong ui byeonhwa' [Changes in Student Movements after the Gwangju Student Movement of 1929], *Hanguk dongnip undongsa yeongu* 35, 71–115.

CHAPTER 3

THE HISTORY OF SOUTH KOREA, 1945–1987

TAE GYUN PARK

1. Introduction

MODERN Korean politics involving political parties began with the liberation from Japan in 1945. Although a parliamentary system was established in the late nineteenth century and a communist party was first organised in 1925, these were not lawfully based (Cumings 1997). The US Military Government in Korea (USAMGIK, 1945–1948) established a party system, and a general election was first carried out in 1948 under the supervision of the United Nations (UN) (Eckert et al. 1990).

This chapter examines the changes in political parties, leaders, and systems between 1948 and the 1987 democratisation. This period was characterised by an authoritarian system with a popular opposition party during the Cold War era. Though there were two people's uprisings that caused regime changes in 1960 and 1979, the military leaders held onto power, as was the case in other developing countries in Asia, Africa, and Latin America in the twentieth century.

The turning points in modern South Korean politics before democratisation in 1987 have been conventionally viewed in terms of elections, constitutional revisions, people's uprisings, and military coups. In this chapter, the political vortex resulting from the conflicts between authoritarian leaders and popular opposition parties serves as the main story for understanding the characteristic of modern politics in South Korea. This conflict reveals how the presidents and opposition leaders frequently understood and practiced a leader-orientated politics rather than policy-orientated party politics.

2. The First Republic (1948–1960)

Modern politics in South Korea began with the general election in 1948 under the supervision of the UN. Although USAMGIK planned to implement a trusteeship system on the Korean Peninsula under the United States, Great Britain, the Republic of China, and Soviet Russia, the failure of the US military and Soviet army to reach an agreement led to the handling of the Korean issue by the UN. As a result, the general election in 1948 was carried out only in the region below the thirty-eighth parallel (Cumings 1997).

The 1948 election and the first constitution were significant in several respects for setting the original conditions of modern South Korean politics. First of all, only one major party, the Korean Democratic Party (KDP), which was the founding organisation of conservative groups in South Korea and played a role as a ruling party under the USAMGIK, participated in the general election in 1948 (Park 1994). The other three major parties, the Korean People's Party (KPP), the Korean Communist Party (KCP), and the Korean Independence Party (KIP), did not participate. The absence of the KPP and KCP in the general election was more or less a predictable outcome, most of the members of which opposed a separate government in South Korea and participated in North Korea's legislative convention instead of South Korea's elections due to their political suppression under USAMGIK's strong anti-communist policy.

At the same time, USAMGIK's reluctance to clear away the vestige of the colonialism and policy for the establishment of a separate government resulted in the nonparticipation of a major conservative rightist party in South Korea, the KIP led by Kim Gu. Instead, Kim Gu, who was a leader of the Korean Provisional Government[KPG] in China during the colonial period and has been considered the most famous patriotic leader due to his life long career in the independence movement, had a meeting with the North Korean leader, Kim Ilsung, to organise unified institution. The absence of the KPG and the KIP leaders in the 1948 election has been considered as a serious defect in the South Korean government at the beginning by South Korean people, because the ROK government defined herself as a successor of the KPG in the preamble of the constitution (Seo 2007).

The second point deserving attention is that the National Assembly had relatively strong power in South Korean politics from its inception. Although the government system was characterised by a strong presidency, the president and vice-president were elected by the National Assemblymen as stipulated in the first Constitution, which was originally drafted by USAMGIK in 1947 for the Joint US–Soviet Commission. Although the first Constitution was revised four years later, when the election system for president was changed to a direct popular election in 1952, people have considered the strong power of the legislative assembly as a symbol of democracy in South Korea since 1948. And even though the opposition party was always a minor power in the National

Assembly before democratisation in 1987, the majority of highly educated people in urban areas supported opposition members to check the strong power of the president and his administration, while the rural area served as a backyard for the ruling party (Park 2018).

Third, the first Constitution included several paragraphs on the socialist economic system. The economic sections in the Constitution defined that major industries related to natural resources, infrastructure, and mining industry should be controlled by the ROK government, which was strongly influenced by social discourse at the time (Park 2005). In spite of the revision in 1954, most companies in social overhead industry, such as water, electricity, railroads, the mining industry, and so on, were controlled by the South Korean government until the liberalisation reform until the early 1990s.

Although the South Korean government was established in August 1948 and was approved by the UN General Assembly as lawful in December 1948, its jurisdiction was limited to the area in which the general election was held on 10 May 1948. This meant the southern part of the Peninsula under the thirty-eighth parallel, although the election was not implemented on Jeju Island due to the guerrilla movement that strongly opposed holding an election only in South Korea. Furthermore, the areas the UN forces and the ROK army recovered during the Korean War did not immediately return to South Korea's governance. The jurisdiction of those area transferred to the South Korean government after the UN organisation in South Korea joined the agreement with the South Korean Government in 1954. In the South Korea–Japan Normalization Treaty in 1965, the Japanese government also officially approved the ROK government as the only lawful government on the Korean Peninsula in accordance with the resolution passed by the UN General Assembly in 1948 (Seo 2007).

In spite of the initial weakness of the South Korean government, the first President Rhee Syngman dominated South Korean politics and society as a result of the war, which triggered strong anti-communism in South Korean society. The anti-communist in South Korea and the anti-American sentiment in North Korea was widely spread through massacres committed by both sides during the war. Furthermore, there were few politicians who demonstrated strong leadership and could replace President Rhee, since many of the popular politicians had been kidnaped or killed by North Korea. The Liberal Party (LP) founded in 1951 served as the ruling party under the Rhee government in a strongly anti-communist atmosphere. Although the UN Forces Command designed plans to remove President Rhee in 1952 and 1953, they were not carried out due to the lack of alternative leaders to President Rhee (Seo 2007).

The LP revised the constitution in 1952 and 1954 to strengthen President Rhee's power and prolong his presidency. The 1952 revision was passed under a martial law in Busan, the temporary capital city during the Korean War, shortly after several National Assemblymen were arrested under suspicion of being international communist spies, while the second revision in 1954 was passed in the National Assembly by rounding off the number of votes needed (Park 2018). As a result of the revisions in 1952 and 1954, President Rhee could continue to maintain presidency unless he were to be forcefully dismissed by people's uprising.

Ironically, President Rhee's unilateralism encouraged the opposition politicians to establish a new powerful party, the Democratic Party (DP), in 1955. The party members were a successor to the KDP that had strongly opposed Rhee's constitutional revisions to prolong his rule in 1952 and 1954. The Rhee government manipulated South Korean politics in order to strengthen its power both in terms of the National Assembly and executive administration without any political rival until 1960. Cho Bong-am, a strong opposition leader who was the head of the Progressive Party (PP) and received around 30 per cent of the vote in the 1956 presidential election, was executed in 1959 on a charge of North Korean espionage, while two other opposition presidential candidates died shortly before the election day in the 1956 and 1960 elections (Henderson 1968). In order to suppress the opposition party and the critical voice from intellectuals, the LP passed the security law on 24 December 1958 and a famous newspaper, the *Kyunghyang Daily*, which was published by the Catholic church and supported opposition leaders, was suspended in 1959.

The people's hope to change the regime was realised not through elections, but by the people's uprising in 1960, also known as the April Revolution, one year after the Cuban Revolution (Park 1995). The revolution was a result of the people's anger about the corrupt links between ruling party politicians and big business, as well as the rigged election in 1960. Big business engaged in rent-seeking through corrupt connections with the ruling party in the process of distributing American assistance and provided bribes to the politicians for political funds (Woo 1991). Following the week-long uprising by students and civilians in 1960, President Rhee was expelled and the ruling party's vice-presidential candidate committed suicide with his family.

3. The Second Republic, the May Coup, and the Park Government

The DP recorded an overwhelming victory in the 1960 general election under the new Constitution, which changed the political structure from a presidential to a parliamentary system. Chang Myun, who had been the vice-president since 1956, was elected as the prime minister in the National Assembly. The Chang government established a bicameral system; although it had first been introduced in the 1952 constitutional revision, it had not been implemented until 1960. The ruling party tried to carry out political and social reform based on popular demand during and after the April Revolution (Lee and Kim 2016).

First of all, the Second Republic guaranteed freedom of speech, assembly, and association. The people who were suppressed under the Rhee government began to carry out active campaigns and rallies to change the social structure. Labour movement groups, student activists, and families of victims of anti-communist killings during the Korean War were the driving force behind the rallies. Progressive politicians rebuilt political parties that had been forcefully removed shortly after the execution of Cho Bong-am in 1959. Student activist groups organised youth associations that became the axis of the 1960s and 1970s revolutionary organisations (Jeong and Lee 2010). Their activities were stimulated by the non-alignment alliance that had existed since the mid-1950s and most were critical of anti-communism. The families of victims of anti-communist killings during the war desired to restore the victims' honour and the right to commemorate them, since they were regarded as communist criminals under Rhee. Finally, some student groups loudly advocated for reunification with North Korea (Hong 2002).

Along with political reform, the Chang administration sought to achieve economic reconstruction, one of the people's strong hopes since the 1950s, by designing Economic Development Plans (Park 2005). The regime changed the name of the Ministry of Rehabilitation to the Ministry of Construction and formed several strategies: (a) to develop infrastructure through a mass campaign; (b) to adjust the exchange rate as the American government had asked for since the early 1950s; (c) to investigate illegal and corrupt connections between big business and politicians; (d) to raise fees for public services, including those for electricity and public transportation; and (e) to raise salaries for civil servants. For this plan, the government hoped to procure a development fund from the United States in early 1961 (Park 2007).

However, the reforms were not so successful for several reasons, such as the ruling party's loss of integrity after splitting in two in early 1961, social instability because of street rallies, the failure to address corruption, and so on (Lee 1987). All this amounted to the growing irritation and frustration of the people. In particular, the people believed that the Chang administration was indistinguishable from the former Rhee government and incapable of dealing with these issues, which needed to be solved through revolution. Even social discourse that the parliamentary system was unfit for South Korea's conditions emerged under the Chang government in 1960 and 1961.

The military coup succeeded in these unstable conditions. Even though people did not want to revive another dictatorship, they also wanted strong leadership. A junta was established shortly after the coup, which dissolved the National Assembly, and an Emergency Cabinet composed of military generals seized administrative, legislative, and judicial power for about two-and-a-half years until late 1963, when general and presidential elections were carried out. The junta expressed the will to succeed the people's hope expressed during the April Revolution, calling the military coup a revolution. In fact, the junta implemented social reforms as soon as it took power, by (a) writing off poor peasants' debt; (b) promoting small and medium-sized businesses; (c) arresting gangsters who supported corrupt politicians throughout the 1950s; (d) establishing a new pilot institute named the Economic Planning Board (EPB), which designed the economic development plans and coordinated positions among the different ministries; and (e) banning political activities for those involved in corruption during the Rhee and Chang administration (Han 2011).

However, most of the reforms were not successful. In particular, economic reform failed in terms of acquiring funds from the United States and in terms of currency reform to mobilise domestic capital (Park 2007). In spite of the failure, the leader of the junta, Park Chung-hee, was elected as a president in the 1963 presidential election and the Democratic Republican Party (DRP) became the ruling party between 1963 and 1979. People seemed to consider Park as relatively progressive in the election at the beginning of the Park administration, since the rival candidate, Yun Bo-seon, a member of the KDP during the USAMGIK, a Seoul city mayor in the early Rhee government, and the former weak president during the Chang administration, was regarded as outdated. Park's commitment to economic development looked more innovative than Yun, who rather focused on exposing Park's past record as a member of the South Korean Worker's Party and expressed strong anti-communism. In fact, Park and the junta had an advantage because they were able to intervene in the election using government power. In addition, strife in civilian politics provided another cause of the victory of Park, Chonghee, and the DRP in 1963 (Sim 2017).

The Park government faced a very serious political crisis shortly after the inauguration because of massive resistance to the South Korea–Japan Normalization Treaty. People were very angry about the secret negotiation between the junta and the Japanese government on the reparation during the colonial period. In fact, Korean people believed that the Japanese government should pay compensation in order to recover Korea from the exploitation during the colonial period, while the Japanese did not feel the necessity of reparation because the annexation of Korea in 1910 was lawful under the accord between the Japanese and the Korean monarch. The demonstration against the treaty was spread all over the country in 1964, like the April Revolution in 1960.

The US Embassy in Seoul thought that the Park administration would collapse due to the demonstrations and allowed the mobilisation of military forces to suppress the protests under martial law. According to the Minute Agreement made between the United States and South Korea in 1954, the ROK government could not mobilise the military forces without approval of the US forces command in South Korea (Macdonald 1992). The United States had wanted normalisation between South Korea and Japan since the 1951 San Francisco Pact, which could build strong deterrence power against the north triangle alliance between the Soviet, China, and North Korea.

Furthermore, the crisis was forgotten by South Korean people through the dispatch of South Korean combat troops to Vietnam in 1965 and the successful results of the first and second economic development plans in 1962 and 1967, the funding for which mostly came through the reparation from Japan after the 1965 treaty and the special procurement from the Vietnam War between 1965 and 1973 (Hong et al. 2018). And South Korean people received a very positive impression from the fact that the Johnson administration strongly supported President Park, who hailed to the US government request to send combat troops to Vietnam.

The DRP revised the Constitution in 1969 to allow President Park to run for a third term, one year after his re-election and the dominant victory of the ruling party in the general election in 1968 as a result of rigged elections. While the opposition party and students strongly protested against the revision, it was passed through a referendum. There were two important conditions in the late 1960s strengthening the Park government. One was the security crisis in 1968 and 1969. North Korean provocations during this time included a guerrilla attack on the presidential residence in 1968, the capture of a US intelligence vessel, the *USS Pueblo*, and the shooting down of US intelligence flight EC 121 (Park 2009). In fact, North Korea wanted to assist the North Vietnamese through the security crisis on the Korean Peninsula, which could deter more South Korean combat troops in Vietnam. The Park administration was able to strengthen its control over the whole society during the security crisis in 1968 and 1969; the resident registration system and the reserve army system were established in 1968.

The second important condition to strengthen the Park government was the economic boom owing to the special funds acquired from Japan through the Normalization Treaty and the special procurement from the Vietnam War. In particular, the special procurement from the Vietnam War played a great role in the dramatic increase in exports and the high economic growth rate as Thailand and the Philippines who joined the Vietnam War on the side of the United States in the late 1960s showed. The successful economic growth throughout the 1960s led to Park's election as president for a third term in 1971, in spite of the rise of the young opposition leaders Kim Dae-jung and Kim Young-sam (Hong et al. 2018).

4. The Yushin Regime

Although President Park and the DRP won the elections in 1971, the Park government began to try to change the South Korean political structure later that year. The decisive moment of the transition came when President Park declared the Emergency Measure in December 1971. The Emergence Measure had critical articles and paragraphs limiting basic freedoms and a contingency mobilisation programme under the jurisdiction of the president, without consultation with a legislative body. The ruling party passed the measure in the National Assembly when the opposition party was not present. According to Park, the declaration was needed because of the security crisis not only on the Korean Peninsula, but throughout the world. In fact, his plan to consolidate the regime was not all that understandable as the international order had been gradually moving towards détente (the relaxing of strained relations) since 1971, when US President Nixon announced his visit to Beijing. The Nixon administration tried to reconcile with mainland China in order to reduce tension in Northeast Asia in an effort to decrease the budget deficit caused by expenses incurred through the deployment of American troops in the hot war in Vietnam and the cold war in East Asia. Reconciliation was a precondition for downsizing and withdrawing US forces from Asia, and President Nixon expressed this idea in Guam in 1969. As a result, the US forces in Vietnam started to withdraw and those in South Korea, Thailand, and the Philippines were reduced in number, beginning in 1969. Détente and the reduction of US forces in South Korea was a signal for reconciliation from the US perspective, whereas the new policy could be seen as a security crisis from the viewpoint of the South Korean government because the downsize in troop numbers could appear as the weakening security commitment of the United States (Im 2011; Oberdorfer and Carlin 2013).

President Park declared another emergency measure, known as the Yushin regime, in October 1972, which surprised the South Korean people, as well as the United States, at the time. As the ROK government announced a joint communiqué with North Korean leader Kim Il-sung on 4 July 1972, the South Korean people began to believe that reconciliation on the Korean Peninsula, as well as in Northeast Asia, could be achieved in the near future. Meanwhile, the 3 August emergency measure, which froze private debt in order to save insolvent companies, ameliorated an emerging economic crisis. The Yushin regime was prepared without any consultation with politicians or the US Embassy in Seoul. In fact, the Park government carefully observed conditions in the Philippines, which had already declared martial law, and in Thailand, where there was a military coup in 1971. In these two countries, there were few people's uprisings and the US government was unable to intervene in domestic political affairs. This seemed to offer useful lessons to President Park (Park 2018). Being different from the situation in 1952 and 1963 when the United States deeply intervened in the internal politics of South Korea in order to prevent consolidation of the authoritarian system, the United States was not able to do this in the early 1970s because the US engagement policy towards East Asia was weakened due to the downsizing of US forces and protectionism in trade under the Nixon administration.

At the moment of the Yushin Declaration, the National Assembly was dissolved and its function taken over by the Emergency Cabinet, as had been the case with the junta between 1961 and 1963. A new constitution, called the Yushin Constitution, was announced publicly a month after the declaration and, without any discussion in the National Assembly, was passed in the Emergency Cabinet and through a referendum. Any criticism or denunciation of the Constitution or the Yushin system was strictly prohibited by law.

The Yushin Constitution concentrated political power under the president, who could do whatever he wanted. In particular, he now had the power to appoint one-third of the National Assemblymen, while the other two-thirds were elected through a multimember district system favouring the ruling party. As a result, in every general election, the ruling party automatically gained two-thirds of the seats in the National Assembly. This meant that President Park was unchecked by any opposition in the National Assembly. The president was also indirectly elected by an institution called the National Council for Unification (NCU), the members of which were elected by the people. However, the members of the NCU could not identify themselves as members of a specific political party, so people had to elect the members of the NCU without any information on for whom they were voting. President Park was elected as a president twice between 1972 and 1979, and he received 99 per cent of the vote from the NCU (Im 2011).

The most symbolic means to control society and to consolidate power were the emergency decrees passed during the Yushin regime. President Park issued nine emergency decrees during the Yushin era, which seriously limited basic freedoms and banned any critique of the president and the Yushin Constitution. Even though economic growth continued throughout the 1970s in spite of two oil crises, triggering the formation of the middle class in South Korean society, anti-Yushin sentiment grew more and more prevalent in civil society. The Park government arrested many student activists and intellectuals and executed nine people on suspicion of North Korean espionage and agitation of the student movement, but the tide of anti-government sentiment could not be stemmed during the Yushin era. In particular, politicians whose political activities were prohibited and Christian priests, both Catholic and Protestant, greatly influenced students' and intellectuals' anti-government gatherings and declarations. Despite suppression and censorship by the Korean Central Intelligence Agency (KCIA) and the Military Security Unit, the great demand for changing the political structure continued during the Yushin era (Lee and Kim 2016).

In the end, the Yushin regime collapsed with the death of President Park in October 1979. The collapse began with the general election in December 1978, in which the opposition party received more votes than the ruling party. The opposition party elected Kim Young-sam, who had strongly protested against President Park since the beginning of the Yushin regime, as party leader. The ruling party, the DRP, expelled him from the national assembly by reason of his interview with the *New York Times*, in which he asked the US government not to support President Park because he destroyed the democratic system and violated human rights. Even he blamed President Carter, who met President Park in June 1979 and did not criticise his authoritarian system publicly during his visit to Seoul. Then, shortly before the murder of President Park, students began an uprising that was widely supported by civil society in Busan, the second largest city in South Korea, and in Masan, a special export area. In spite of the fact that the Park government declared martial law in the Busan and Masan areas, disputes arose over how to stabilise the situation. Kim Jae-gyu, the director of the KCIA, argued for persuading students and civilians rather than mobilising the military to suppress them and opposed the imposition of martial law. At a dinner party in October 1979, he killed President Park, who did not agree with his position. As a result, the Yushin regime collapsed and Prime Minister Choi Kyu-hah succeeded to the presidency (Hong et al. 2018).

Coincidentally, the Park Chung-hee's economic policy had produced negative effects since the middle of the 1970s. Although the Park government successfully overcome an economic crisis caused by the first oil shock in 1973, serious inflation continued throughout the 1970s. As a result, the deputy prime minister, who was in charge of the EPB, declared the failure of economic policies during the Yushin system in April 1979. The ultra-inflation since the mid-1970s was triggered not only by the second oil shock in 1978, but also by the increase of liquidity to boost heavy chemical industry since 1973. A stabilisation policy was designed by the central bank of South Korea and the Korean Development Institute in 1978 even before the second oil shock and the sudden increase of foreign debt appeared since 1977. People started to feel fatigue from extorted market system caused by inflation in the late 1970s, while the Park government advertised what they achieved, such as 10 billion dollar export and 1,000 dollar gross national product per capita in 1977. The unemployment rate was increased in 1978 and 1979, which was one of the backgrounds in the Busan–Masan Uprising. In 1980, South Korea recorded the first minus economic growth rate since 1948.

5. The Gwangju Uprising, New Military Leaders, and the Democratisation Uprising in 1987

The collapse of the Yushin regime and the death of President Park inspired a bright vision of recovering a democratic system as had occurred with the April Revolution in 1960. People referred to the period of early 1980 as the Seoul Spring. Politicians including former presidential candidate Kim Dae-jung, whose activity had been strictly banned during the 1970s, were released from house arrest. Opposition party members, students, and intellectuals anticipated a regime change under a democratic constitution. There was a lot of discussion and gatherings regarding what would be the future political system and what should be included in a new Constitution. In terms of potential leaders, the mass media paid much attention not only to the two opposition party leaders Kim Young-sam and Kim Dae-jung, but also to Kim Jong-pil, Park's former right-hand man who had organised the DRP. However, mass media as well as political leaders at the time failed to recognise another strong group in the military cultivated throughout the Park era (Shin and Hwang 2003).

The new military group, led by General Chun Doo-hwan, carried out a military coup shortly after Park's death, arresting the martial law commander who was also the ROK army General Chief of Staff. The group seized power gradually and quietly, ceding nominal power to President Choi until May 1980. Despite rumours over this group's power and influence, major politicians and the mass media ignored the possibility that it would seize power. In fact, the group secretly contacted the US Embassy and US forces Commander in South Korea, as well as domestic politicians during the Seoul Spring, unbeknownst to the student and civil groups who wanted democratisation at the time.

Under these conditions, the group, led by General Chun, declared martial law on 17 May 1980, when more than 100,000 students gathered in the square in front of Seoul Central Station. However, the conflict between the students and the military emerged not in Seoul but Gwangju, the largest city in the Southwest region of South Korea, the most underdeveloped area during the Park era. The Gwangju people were angry about the arrest of Kim Dae-jung, who had been the representative political leader of the Southwest region since the 1970s. The new military group mobilised paratroopers who received special trains to Gwangju, and their bloody suppression of the college students angered civilians. The military soldiers' killing of more than 200 civilians marked the beginning of the Gwangju Uprising (Massacre). The civilians took control of the whole municipal area for a week without law enforcement. During this time, no crimes were reported and the people's autonomy continued. However, the people's uprising failed when soldiers were mobilised again. Most of the people involved in the uprising were prosecuted and killed, with Kim Dae-jung sentenced to death on the charge of scheming to overthrow the government (Shin and Hwang 2003).

With the failure of the people's uprising in Gwangju and the emergence of the new military government, the Seoul Spring came to an end. General Chun was elected as president by the NCU and the Chun government revised the constitution. The policies of the new government were premised on the lessons of Yushin, focusing on several points: (a) a special institution to indirectly elect the president, replacing the NCU; (b) a presidency limited to one term of seven years; (c) the reorganisation of opposition parties as 'satellite parties' without strong opposition leaders; (d) strengthening of media censorship and mergers of the mass media institutions; and (e) some liberalisation policies in order to pacify the people's protests against the authoritarian system and control civil society. The curfew restricting movement between the hours of midnight and 4 a.m. was removed for the first time since the Korean War and the strict regulation of high-school students and the university entrance exam was eased.

However, people's passion for democratisation could not be suppressed. The general election in 1985 was the first signal, when politicians who supported the strong opposition leaders Kim Young-sam and Kim Dae-jung were elected, instead of those from the satellite opposition parties. After the election, the opposition party made revision of the constitution the main political issue, above all emphasising direct election of the president. The campaign for the revision continued in 1986, while severe demonstrations continued in Seoul, as well as in smaller cities. Meanwhile, anti-Americanism had been escalating since the early 1980s because people believed that the United States supported the military dictatorship over civilians, who had sought out democracy through the Gwangju Uprising. In particular, the students condemned the US government for supporting the authoritarian regime while professing support for democracy and human rights.

In 1987, the Democratization Uprising erupted over the death of a Seoul National University student under torture in January. Civilian groups, Catholic priests, and mass media correspondents were the main agents who exposed the death, which had been concealed and misrepresented by the government and police. The June Uprising began with the indignation of the people at the time, which had been escalating since the late 1960s. In the end, the actions of the students and civilians concluded with the 29 June Declaration made by Roh Tae-woo, Chun Doo-hwan's anointed successor, which lifted the ban on political activities and promised constitutional revision introducing direct election of the president (Im 1997).

As a result, the first direct election of the president since 1971 was held in December 1987. Although opposition party leaders received more than 60 per cent of the vote, the split between Kim Young-sam and Kim Dae-jung ensured Roh Tae-woo's victory. In spite of the fact that the following two presidents, elected in 1992 and 1997, were opposition leaders, infighting ensured the delay of democratic reforms. On the other hand, democratisation signified a new political framework, with the traditional 'democratization group versus authoritarian regime' structure replaced by the new progressive versus conservative structure. The decisive event in this regard was Kim Young-sam's joining of the ruling party controlled by the new military group in 1990. This structure has shaped Korean politics into the present. A key aspect of this structure is that democracy itself has gone unchallenged. Even the new constitution, completed in 1987, has continued unrevised until now (Kang 2012).

Bibliography

Cumings, B. (1997), *Korea's Place in the Sun* (New York: W. W. Norton).
Eckert, C., Lee, K., Lew, Y. I., Robinson, M., and Wagner, E. W. (1990), *Korea, Old and New* (Cambridge: Harvard University Press).
Han, Y. (2011), 'The May Sixteenth Military Coup', in E. Vogel and B. Kim, eds, *The Park Chung Hee Era: The Transformation of South Korea* (Cambridge, MA: Harvard University Press), 35–57.
Henderson, G. (1968), *Korea: The Politics of the Vortex* (Cambridge, MA: Harvard University Press).
Hong, S. (2002), 'Reunification Issues and Civil Society in South Korea: The Debates and Social Movement for Reunification during the April Revolution Period, 1960–1961', *Journal of Asian Studies* 61(4), 1237–1257.
Hong, S., Park, T., and Jeong, C. (2018), *Hanguk hyeondaesa 2* [*Modern Korean History*, Vol. 2] (Seoul: Pureun yeoksa).
Im, H. (1997), 'Politics of Democratic Transition from Authoritarian Rule in South Korea', in S. Choi, ed., *Democracy in Korea: Its Ideals and Realities* (Republic of Korea: The Korean Political Science Association), 71–92.
Im, H. (2011), 'The Origins of the Yusin Regime: Machiavelli Unveiled', in E. Vogel and B. Kim, eds, *The Park Chung Hee Era: The Transformation of South Korea* (Cambridge, MA: Harvard University Press), 233–261.
Jeong, K., and Lee, H. (2010), *4-wol hyeongmyeong gwa Hangukminjujuui* [*The April Revolution and Korean Democracy*] (Seoul: Seoninsa).
Kang, W. (2012), 'Samdang hapdang gwa jeongdang jeongchi ui gujojeok byeonhwa' [The Three-Party Merger and Structural Changes in Party Politics]', in I. Park, ed., *Talnaengjeonsa ui insik* [*Perceptions of Post-Cold War History*] (Seoul: Hangilsa).
Lee, K. (1987). *Hanguk yadangsa* [*History of Opposition Parties in Korea*] (Seoul: Baeksan seodang).
Lee, N., and Kim, W. (2016), *The South Korean Democratization Movement: A Sourcebook* (Seongnam: The Academy of Korean Studies Press).
Macdonald, D. (1992), *U.S.–Korean Relations from Liberation to Self-Reliance: The Twenty-Year Record* (Boulder, CO: Westview Press).
Oberdorfer, D., and Carlin, R. (2013), *The Two Koreas: A Contemporary History*, Rev. edn (New York: Basic Books).
Park, T. (1994), 'Haebang jikhu Hanguk minjudang kusongwon ui seonggyeok gwa jojik gaepyeon' [Characteristics and Reorganization of Korean Democratic Party Personnel Immediately after Liberation], *Guksagwan nonchong* 58, 87–120.

Park, T. (1995), *Jo Bong-am yeongu* [*A Study of Cho Bong-am*] (Seoul: Changjak gwa bipyeongsa).

Park T. (2005), 'Different Roads, Common Destination: Economic Discourses in South Korea during the 1950s', *Modern Asian Studies* 39(3), 661–682.

Park T. (2007), *Wonhyeong gwa byeonyong: Hanguk gyeongje gaebal gyehoek ui giwon* [*Archetype and Metamorphosis: The Origin of Korea's Economic Development Plans*] (Seoul: Seoul daehakgyo chulpanbu).

Park, T. (2009), 'Beyond the Myth: Reassessing the Security Crisis on the Korean Peninsula during the Mid-1960s', *Pacific Affairs* 82(1), 93–110.

Park, T. (2018), *Gungmu hoeuirok ui jaebalgyeon* [*Rediscovering the State Council Meeting Records*], https://theme.archives.go.kr/next/rediscovery/help.do., accessed 2 March 2021.

Seo, J. (2007), *Yi Seung-man gwa che-1 gonghwaguk* [*Rhee Syngman and the First Republic*] (Seoul: Yeoksa bipyeongsa).

Shin, K., and Hwang, K. (2003), *Contentious Kwangju: The May 18th Uprising in Korea's Past and Present* (Lanham, MD: Rowman & Littlefield).

Sim, J. (2017), *Hanguk jeongdang jeongchisa* [*History of Korean Party Politics*] (Seoul: Baeksan seodang).

Woo, J. (1991), *Race to the Swift: State and Finance in Korean Industrialization* (New York: Columbia University Press).

PART 2
CORE CONCEPTS

CHAPTER 4

PRESIDENTIALISM WITH PARLIAMENTARY CHARACTERISTICS

JEONGHUN HAN

1. Introduction

On 29 June 1987, the authoritarian regime finally responded to the demands of the democratic movement in South Korea, proclaiming that the next president would be directly elected by universal suffrage. The whole of South Korean society was full of unprecedented fervour over the upcoming presidential democracy. Since a directly elected president was the only unsatisfied institutional requirement among the defining characteristics of presidentialism by Shugart and Carey (1992), such a reform was expected to be an institutional solution for emancipating the South Korean people from social oppression and the absurdities experienced under the authoritarian regimes.

However, the blueprint was not exactly realised. On the one hand, South Korean society after democratisation has often lamented the existence of an 'imperial presidency' or 'hyper-presidentialism'. Defined as a political system in which the electorate only weakly controls the president and other political actors (Rose-Ackerman et al. 2011: 247), hyper-presidentialism has been criticised for its negative influence on South Korean democratisation by reinforcing the intrinsic institutional perils of the presidential system (e.g. Linz 1990). Many studies of South Korean presidentialism in this regard highlight the concentration of power in the hands of individual presidents, and count corruption or abuses of power among its political consequences (Yang 1999; Lee 2000; Croissant 2002, 2003; Kim 2003; Kim 2004; Jeong 2009; Park 2009; Kang 2017). On the other hand, South Korean presidents have been sometimes criticised as impotent as they fail to effectively run a democratising society. Scholars have demonstrated that there have been a large number of weak and unsuccessful efforts in taking timely measures in redressing social problems or enacting their electoral promises (Kim 2017; Lee 2019).

Scholars indeed have sought theoretical as well as methodological answers to redress the problems with South Korea's poorly performing presidential system. From the methodological perspective, studies frequently point out the invalid and ephemeral evaluation of South Korean presidentialism produced from limited focus on specific time periods and contexts (Park 2004; Jang 2010; Kang 2017; Kim 2017). From the theoretical perspective, other studies particularly highlight the historical origin of ill-performing South Korean presidents (Suh 2006; Jeong 2009; Jin and Choi 2009; Kim 2012). Scholars in this area have identified some distinct institutional elements of South Korean presidentialism and traced their historical origins and impacts on the performance of South Korean presidents. Thanks to their efforts, it is now well known that the South Korean Constitution from its origin stipulated a few institutions distinct from other presidential systems, which allows us to characterise South Korean presidentialism as 'presidentialism with parliamentary characteristics' (Suh 2006; Jeong 2009; Kim 2012).

From this simple illustration of academic research on South Korea's political system, it is quite clear that the current South Korean political regime may be classified as democratic presidentialism. But what has not been thoroughly explored yet is how much its performance, equipped with some institutions observed in parliamentary systems, differs from other presidential systems. This lack of a proper examination indeed has led some scholars to mistakenly identify South Korean presidentialism as a semi-presidential system (Elgie 2007; Tasi 2009). The aim of this chapter is thus to more systematically examine the impacts of the mixture of parliamentary institutions in South Korean presidentialism.

The main task of this chapter is to show how the parliamentary elements affect executive–legislature relations in South Korea and to argue whether or not it is meaningful to identify the South Korean presidential system as presidentialism with parliamentary characteristics. In so doing, the chapter first introduces the parliamentary elements in the South Korean Constitutions and examines their chronological development. Since the institutional design of parliamentary systems has been relatively understudied compared to presidentialism (Carey 2008: 97), it might not be a simple task to identify the institutional elements specific to parliamentary systems. This chapter resolves this problem by drawing on existing literature on government typology and focusing on two distinct dimensions separating presidentialism and parliamentarism: selection of government branches and the process of policy formation.

Specifically, the chapter analyses the long-term practices concerning the most actively studied elements from each dimension. For the dimension of the selection of government branches, the chapter covers National Assembly (hereafter Assembly) involvement in the appointment or removal of the prime minister and members of the State Council by the president.[1] For the dimension of the policy formation process, focus is on the constitutional permission for the executive to introduce legislative bills in the Assembly. These two elements are chosen since they are, among others, major elements of parliamentary systems on which many constitutional studies have focused

(Croissant 2003; Kim 2003; Jeong 2009; Yoo 2010). By analysing the long-term practices of these parliamentary institutions, covering the period from 1948 to 2018, the chapter tries to answer the question of whether they have functioned in a manner which makes South Korean presidentialism a system of mutual dependence between the executive and the legislature, which would distinguish the South Korean system from other presidential systems. Findings from the analysis may help us to improve our typological understanding of South Korean presidentialism and have substantial implications for the on-going debates over constitutional revision in South Korea, as well as on the weak performance of presidentialism in the process of democratisation (e.g. Dipalma 1990; Linz 1990; Stepan and Skach 1993; Przeworski and Limongi 1997).

The chapter is organised as follows. First, it conceptualises the distinction of South Korean presidentialism by introducing the historical development of parliamentary elements. Second, focusing on a few major parliamentary institutions, it evaluates whether South Korean presidentialism is functionally different from other presidential systems. Finally, it draws out implications for the ongoing debates on constitutional revision in South Korea.

2. South Korean Presidentialism: Conceptualisation and Parliamentary Elements

2.1 Conceptualisation

The fundamental principles of presidentialism are known to be the separation of powers between the executive and the legislature, or checks and balances between them. Although the two concepts are understood equivalently, their empirical denotations rely on different historical backdrops. The argument for the separation of powers dates back to Montesquieu's seminal work published in 1748 (Montesquieu 2002). According to Cohler et al. (1989), the separation of powers underpins the control of a king's ministers by assigning executive and judicial powers to different institutional agents. However, the modern development of presidentialism does not entirely satisfy the principle of separation of powers, not even in the United States. Instead, checks and balances became a more useful concept in describing modern presidentialism, through which we understand presidentialism as a regime in which each governing branch could impose checks on the other without fear of jeopardising its own existence (Shugart and Carey 1992: 18–19). In implementing this principle, contemporary presidential governments are defined as having three basic institutional features (Shugart and Carey 1992; Shugart 2008): a popularly elected president as the chief executive, fixed terms of the chief executive and the legislative assembly without being subject to mutual confidence, and the government formation by the president with some constitutionally granted law-making authority.

Drawing on the defining institutional features of presidentialism, it can be said that South Korea's regime type has been predominantly presidentialism. For over seventy years since the promulgation of the first Constitution, South Korean society has had a presidential system, except for a short period of less than two years.[2] Specifically, the historical records presented in Table 4.1 show that most South Korean presidents have been directly elected by popular votes. Among the nineteen South Korean presidents so far, seven presidential elections were exceptional in this regard. One of them occurred under the parliamentary system during the period from 1960 to 1962. The other six cases occurred in a constitutionally presidential system. Under the first Constitution, the Assembly had the authority to elect the president. Four other cases occurred during President Park Chung-hee's Yushin era, during which the Constitution stipulated that the president was to be selected by the National Council for Unification (NCU). For the other case under the ninth Constitution, the role of the NCU was replaced by the Electoral College for the President.

When it comes to the requirement of a 'popularly elected president', this practice of indirect elections, except for the case under the first Constitution, are problematic. To be elected 'popularly', both the NCU and the Electoral College should follow the national consensus on the election of a president. But, for all five cases under the eighth and the ninth Constitutions, it was only after the two institutions formed that the candidates for the presidency were registered. Thus, the public did not know who the candidates for president would be before the institutions were formed. In addition, these indirect elections were not conducted with multiple candidates. Only a sole candidate registered after both the NCU and the Electoral College had been composed, which forces the members of the two institutions cast a take-it-or-leave-it decision for the presidency. It is thus very clear that this procedure of indirectly electing the president is significantly different from the practice of the Electoral College in the United States, whose members' votes normally follow the public preference in each state. This cautions us from labelling these regimes under the eighth and ninth Constitutions as 'democratic'.

Leaving aside those non-democratic political systems under the eighth and the ninth Constitutions, the popularly elected presidents in South Korea serve fixed terms, though the length of the terms has varied. When the South Korean Constitution has stipulated a four-year presidential term, it has commonly allowed for the re-election of the president. Meanwhile, under the current tenth Constitution, the South Korean president is elected for a single, five-year term with no possibility of being re-elected. Recently, this has become a major issue concerning constitutional revision. Jang (2010) points out that due to this constitutional design, South Korean presidents are often tempted to act as imperialistic presidents and, at the same time, suffer from the lame-duck problem in the early stage of their term.

Finally, the South Korean Constitutions also provide the president with both the powers of appointing the members of the State Council and legislative powers, including the veto, the authority to legislate by decree, and the power to propose referenda.

Table 4.1: Constitutional history and regime change in South Korea, 1948–2020

Const.[a]	Year	Regime type	Presidential election	Terms	Election year	President
1st	07/1948	Presidentialism	Indirect[b]	4	07/1948	Rhee Syngman
2nd	07/1952	Presidentialism	Plurality	4	08/1952	Rhee Syngman
3rd	11/1954	Presidentialism	Plurality	4	05/1956	Rhee Syngman
4th	06/1960	Parliamentarism	Indirect[b]	5	03/1960	Yun Bo-seon
5th	11/1960	Parliamentarism	Indirect[b]	5		
6th	12/1962	Presidentialism	Plurality	4	10/1963	Park Chung-hee
					05/1967	Park Chung-hee
7th	10/1969	Presidentialism	Plurality	4	04/1971	Park Chung-hee
8th	12/1972	Presidentialism	Indirect[c]	6	12/1972	Park Chung-hee
					07/1978	Park Chung-hee
					12/1979	Choi Kyu-hah
					08/1980	Chun Doo-hwan
9th	10/1980	Presidentialism	Indirect[d]	7	02/1981	Chun Doo-hwan
10th	10/1987	Presidentialism	Plurality	5	12/1987	Roh Tae-woo
					12/1992	Kim Yeong-sam
					12/1997	Kim Dae-jung
					12/2002	Roh Moo-hyun
					12/2007	Lee Myung-bak
					12/2012	Park Geun-hye
					05/2017[e]	Moon Jae-in

Notes:
(a) Constitution;
(b) indirect election by National Assemblymen;
(c) indirect election by directly elected National Council for Unification;
(d) indirect election by directly elected Electoral College;
(e) the election was held earlier than scheduled due to the presidential resignation through impeachment.

Although the president should often seek the Assembly's consent or approval when they appoint Cabinet members, the constitutional power of the president meets the requirement of the defining characteristic of a presidential system.

All these constitutional features thus allow us to validly identify the South Korean system as presidentialism. However, it should also be noted that South Korean Constitution includes some fuzzy elements that make it difficult for scholars to identify the South Korean system as presidential (Elgie 2007; Tasi 2009). For example, Elgie

(2007: 8) argues that the constitutional requirement of the Assembly's consent to the presidential appointment of the prime minister in South Korea cannot be regarded as a nominal, but rather as a substantial procedure, which causes him to judge the South Korean political system to be semi-presidential. While this judgement is corrected in a later work (Elgie et al. 2011), the South Korean literature indeed has identified parliamentary institutional elements in South Korean presidentialism concerning the rules of forming government and legislation (Kim 2003; Jeong 2009; Kim 2012). Five parliamentary institutional elements exist in the process of government formation, including the consent of the National Assembly for the appointment of the prime minister by the president (Article 86.1), the National Assembly's ability to recommend removal of the prime minister or a State Council member (Article 63.1), the attendance of the prime minister or members of the State Council at meetings of the National Assembly or its committees and the delivery of opinions to or answering questions of the National Assembly (Article 62.1), the obligation of countersigning all official acts of the president by a minister of the Cabinet (Article 82), and the allowance of concurrent office-holding by the prime minister or members of the State Council in the National Assembly.[3] Two parliamentary institutional elements are included in rules governing legislation, including the ability of the executive to introduce legislative bills (Article 52) and the executive submission of the budget bill for each fiscal year to the National Assembly (Article 54.2).

There are at least two reasons why we cannot view these elements as minor or small variants from common presidentialism. First, unlike Latin American presidential systems, in which certain parliamentary elements were included only after democratisation in the 1990s (Carey 2008: 95), the origins of the parliamentary elements in South Korean presidentialism date back to the first Constitution. The long history of these parliamentary elements thus makes it necessary to examine how they have been adjusted in South Korean presidentialism or have distinguished it from other presidential systems. Second, there has been no systematic analysis of the impact of these parliamentary elements on South Korean presidentialism. Scholars seem united in their waning optimism that these institutional elements constrain presidential power (Back 1995; Park 2000). However, we are not sure whether these institutions have just lost their proper roles or have rather reinforced presidential power. Bearing this in mind, this chapter examines the long-term performance of parliamentary institutions in more detail. Before that, I briefly describe their historical development.

2.2 Historical Development

Concerning the development of a modern democratic political system in South Korea, the issue of when South Korean society began to modernise is not yet resolved.[4] However, many scholars seem to agree that a democratic political system was established after liberation from Japan in 1945 (Suh 2006; Jin and Choi 2009). Interestingly, the drafters of the first Constitution in 1948 did not consider it an option to go back to the old monarchy. Due to the lack of data, we are not sure why such an option did not emerge in liberated South Korea, but what we do know so far is that there was no organised force asking for a return to monarchy (Ko 2000). Also, it is well known that, among others, the parliamentary system became an option widely supported among the drafters of the first Constitution (Kim 2000). In particular, one drafter, Yoo Jin-oh, was known to push the idea of building a parliamentary system (Yoo 1980).

Many factors, including the experience with several types of political systems in the provisional government of South Korea (1919–1945), the US military rule of post-liberation South Korea from 1945 to 1948, and reference to the constitutional developments of other countries, were said to be relevant in the choices made in drafting the Constitution at that time (Suh 2006; Jin and Choi 2009). In particular, scholars have emphasised the fact that the first Constitution is an outcome of the political competitions between groups of people who preferred a parliamentary system and those who argued for presidentialism (Yoo 1980; Kim 1997; Kim 2000; Suh 2006). In this regard, they often consider the adoption of a presidential constitution with parliamentary institutional elements to be an outcome of the negotiations between the two groups of political elites.

Table 4.2 presents how the widely reviewed seven parliamentary elements of South Korean Constitution have been historically revised. The first thing we should note is that all seven elements, despite slight revisions, have been fairly consistently maintained since the first Constitution. This is what Jin and Choi (2009: 45) emphasise by arguing that the parliamentary elements in the South Korean Constitution are not just an unstable institutional mixture, but common characteristics. In particular, except for the Assembly involvement in the appointment of the prime minister and the removal of Cabinet members, the other five parliamentary elements have rarely been changed. Although the seemingly largest variation is observed in the allowance of the concurrent executive office-holding by members of the Assembly, most Constitutions, except for the sixth, are very similar in having continued to allow concurrently holding the offices of prime minister or State Council member while serving in the Assembly, as well as prohibiting the members of the Assembly from the concurrent holdings of positions of different levels of legislature. Also, the continuation of the two elements concerning the executive power in legislation displayed in the last two columns of Table 4.2 seems remarkable. For example, after the introduction of executive legislation in the first Constitution, no revision has been made thereafter. In addition, although the executive budget power was stipulated in the sixth Constitution, it was practically exercised before the revision.

The second thing to notice is that Assembly control over the appointment of the prime minister and the removal of members of the State Council are close to being a norm. The early strong power of the Assembly to approve the appointment of the prime minister in the first and second Constitutions was weakened and abolished for a while. However, the Assembly's power to approve the appointment of prime ministers reappeared, beginning in the eighth Constitution. A similar variation in the Assembly power over the removal of members of the State Council is also observed. The early strong authority

Table 4.2: Parliamentary elements in the South Korean Constitution, 1948–2020

Const.[a]	Appointment of prime minister	Removal of Cabinet members	Cabinet Assembly attendance	Counter-signing	Concurrent office-holding[d]	Executive legislation	Executive budget
1st	Assembly approval	No Assembly involvement	Assembly request	Required	Allowed 1	Allowed	Not specified
2nd	Assembly approval	Vote of no confidence[b]	Assembly request	Required	Allowed 1	Allowed	Not specified
3rd	No office	Vote of no confidence[c]	Assembly request	Required	Allowed 2	Allowed	Not specified
4th–5th	Periods of parliamentary system (06/1960–11/1962)						
6th	No Assembly involvement	Assembly recommend	Assembly request	Required	Allowed 3	Allowed	Specified
7th	No Assembly involvement	Assembly recommend	Assembly request	Required	Allowed 4	Allowed	Specified
8th	Assembly consent	Assembly decision	Assembly request	Required	Allowed 4	Allowed	Specified
9th	Assembly consent	Assembly decision	Assembly request	Required	Allowed 4	Allowed	Specified
10th	Assembly consent	Assembly recommend	Assembly request	Required	Allowed 4	Allowed	Specified

Notes:
(a) Constitution;
(b) collective;
(c) individual;
(d) allowed 1 (allowed except the local assembly); allowed 2 (allowed except the local assembly and simultaneous positions at bicameral assembly); allowed 3 (allowed except the president, prime minister, Council members, local assembly, and legally banned offices); allowed 4 (allowed except the legally banned offices).

through the vote of no confidence has been alleviated into the recommendation of removal. But the Assembly has been continuously equipped with the power to either enforce or recommend the removal of members of the State Council.

The existing literature has judged the influence of these parliamentary elements from different perspectives. Some scholars have argued that they have the potential to reinforce strong presidential power in South Korea (Yang 1999; Croissant 2002; Kim 2004; Park 2009; Jeong 2009; Kang 2017). Others, in contrast, have pointed out that they could be institutional obstacles for the president during attempts to take timely measures in redressing social problems or enacting their electoral promises (Kim 2017; Lee 2019). Still others scrutinise how these elements can interact with other political contexts, including the emergence of divided government, the presidential election cycle, non-democratic political practices, and socio-economic contexts in South Korea (Lee 2000; Park 2004; Jang 2010; Kang 2017). This chapter cannot completely cover the existing debates over the impact of the parliamentary elements in the South Korean Constitution. Instead, by focusing on three main elements, it tries to make a more systematic examination of the long-term performance of these institutions and thus improve our understanding of the distinct conceptualisation of South Korean presidentialism.

3. Political Consequences of Parliamentary Elements

Do the parliamentary institutional elements in the South Korean Constitution make South Korean presidentialism distinct from other presidential systems? More basically, do they really have substantial influence on explicitly developing new relations between the legislature and executive in South Korea? To answer this question, this section focuses on three parliamentary elements and, if they exist, tries to identify long-term trends in the ways these elements change executive–legislature relations. Specifically, concerning the two types of Assembly control over presidential personnel appointment power, it is hypothesised that if those elements restrict the personnel appointment power of the South Korean president, they are more likely to improve the mutual dependence between the executive and the legislatures. Similarly, with respect to executive legislation, it is hypothesised that if executive legislation becomes effective under the checks and balance system, the legislative power or agenda-setting power between the executive and the legislature is more likely to be symmetrical between the two institutions. If these hypotheses are proved true, we may conclude that these parliamentary elements tend to distinguish South Korean presidentialism from other presidential systems. If not, the influence of the parliamentary elements in South Korean presidentialism may not be substantial, but more likely conditioned by other political contexts in South Korea.

3.1 Assembly Involvement in Cabinet Formation

According to Shugart and Carey (1992), assembly involvement in the appointment of Cabinet members, with the provision for censure or for dissolution to the legislature, consists of the main institution which limits the separation of origin and survival of the executive. While presidentialism is, in this regard, expected to provide the president with independent authority over personnel appointment from the legislature, it is very interesting that South Korean presidentialism allows assembly involvement in both appointment and removal of Cabinet members.

To examine the performance of Assembly involvement in Cabinet formation in South Korea, two empirical indicators are used. The first indicator is the number of nominees who fail to be approved by the Assembly. Although the South Korean president has the independent power to appoint members of the State Council, the nomination of a prime minister is commonly subject to either approval or consent by the Assembly. There have been so far a total of forty-six officially appointed prime ministers and seven nominees who failed to be appointed due to Assembly opposition. Among the seven failed nominees, five cases occurred under the Rhee Syngman government, including the nominee, Lee Yun-young, who was not approved four times by the Assembly (Lee 2006: 109). The other two nominees who did not receive Assembly consent were nominated by Kim Dae-jung in the late 1990s.

These cases, thus, might be regarded as empirical evidence that Assembly involvement in the appointment of the prime minister is a de facto process substantially weakening presidential power. However, it should be noted that setting aside the case of Lee Yun-young, the Assembly was indeed involved in the appointment in a very few cases. In addition, all seven cases occurred in divided governments, in which the conflicts between the executive and the legislature can be frequently caused by the typical dual legitimacy problem under presidentialism (Linz 1990). Moreover, the Assembly involvement did not become entangled in follow-up cooperation between the executive and the legislature. South Korean presidents indeed never tried to coordinate with the Assembly when they had to replace the nominee due to the Assembly involvement, as was the case with Lee Yun-young, where President Rhee Syngman did not easily give up trying to have his choice appointed as prime minister, despite the Assembly's opposition. In this regard, the seemingly effective control over presidential power by the Assembly through the ability to disapprove the nomination of prime ministers is not strong evidence for distinguishing South Korean presidentialism from other presidential systems.

The second indicator of the Assembly's power to intervene in Cabinet formation is the annual average number of Assembly proposals recommending the removal of the members of the State Council. Here again, the weak role of Assembly involvement in the president's personnel appointment power is also observed. Referring to Figure 4.1, only the Kim Yeong-sam government (1993–1998) shows an exceptionally high number of annual proposals. One explanation for this may be the political and economic contexts of the time, which include the failed executive response to the first

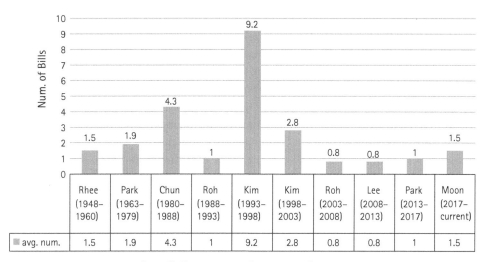

FIGURE 4.1: Average number of bills recommending removal

Source: National Assembly minutes of the bills concerning the recommendation for removal of State Council Members, 1948–2019, https://likms.assembly.go.kr/bill/main.do, accessed 5 August 2021.

North Korean nuclear crisis and the collapse of the Sungsu bridge in 1994.[5] If we ignore the stochastic occurrence during the Kim Yeong-sam government, which may be explained by random socio-economic contexts (Browne et al. 1984), the Assembly on average has recommended removal of fewer than two members of the State Council annually. Even if we add the case of the Kim Yeong-sam government, the average number of annual proposals would be fewer than three. In addition, comparing the records between governments, we find that except for three governments—Chun Doo-hwan, Kim Yeong-sam, and Kim Dae-jung—most governments in South Korea have received annually fewer than two Assembly recommendations for the removal of the members of the State Council.

The small number of proposals recommending removal of the members of the State Council, thus, implies weak Assembly involvement in the president's personnel appointment power. But what is more striking is that extremely few proposals are indeed passed by the Assembly. Specifically, there have been 167 proposals concerning the removal of State Council members. Eighteen proposals requested the vote of no confidence targeting individual State Council members prescribed in the third Constitution, and the other 149 proposals were the non-binding requests for the removal of State Council members. Among them, only six indeed passed the Assembly. The remaining 161 bills failed to be adopted by the Assembly, since they were repealed in committee, withdrawn, automatically dropped due to the end of term, or rejected during a plenary session.

The asymmetrically large number of failed proposals implies that although Assembly involvement in the removal of State Council members can be effectively used to force out ministers through criticism and pressure (Fischer et al. 2012: 511), the Assembly does not make every effort to do so, but restricts its involvement in regulating this power to a symbolic process to check the president's initiative for appointments. In addition, among the six cases in which recommendation for removal was adopted by the Assembly, only one member of the State Council was removed via a vote of no confidence during the Syngman Rhee government. The other four Cabinet members resigned voluntarily when the recommendations passed the Assembly, implying that the appointed ministers step down voluntarily before being dishonourably removed due to the Assembly's threat. In the remaining case, President Park Geun-hye rejected the Assembly's recommendation. All these records, thus, imply that the Assembly might not consider the power to recommend removal of State Council members to be an effective tool or fail to utilise it to hold the president accountable to the legislature.

In sum, the records of the Assembly's involvement in the appointment and removal of Cabinet members in South Korea show that except for the very early period of the first Constitution, the Assembly does not use this power effectively to hold the executive accountable to the legislature. In contrast, a long-term review of the practice of this power shows that regardless of its *de jure* power in Cabinet formation, the Assembly does not make it a *de facto* power, and thus leaves the privilege to the president.

3.2 Legislative Power of Presidents: Executive Bills

The South Korean Constitution provides the president with relatively strong legislative power in terms of the fact that he or she has an effective package of veto power, budgetary power, and the authority to introduce legislation (Croissant 2003: 73). This constitutional characteristic is said to be the main reason for the emergence of hyper-presidentialism in South Korea (Croissant 2002, 2003; Kim 2004). In particular, through the power to introduce legislation in the Assembly, the president can redress the passive position in which he or she responds only to take-it-or-leave-it legislative offerings from the Assembly (Huber 1996). This also allows the government to successfully and swiftly shepherd its policy agenda through the introduction of legislation (Albert 2009: 563).

However, it is not easy to identify under which conditions the executive power to introduce legislation in South Korea is considered conducive to the hyper-presidentialism. To illustrate the possible relationship between the executive-introduced legislation and the emergence of the hyper-presidentialism, let us first consider the typical system of presidentialism, where the executive may not introduce legislation. In such cases, the presidential agenda-setting power might usually depend on the president's partisan leadership, through which the president can whip his or her partisan colleagues in the Assembly (Park 2009; Kim 2017). Since the influence of partisan leadership on legislation is conditional on the partisan composition of the Assembly, we may expect that the president might wield much stronger legislative power under a unified government than under a divided government.

The executive power to introduce legislation may change the dynamic in which the president's agenda-setting power depends on the partisan composition of the legislature. The existence of the executive power to introduce legislation in a presidential system may be understood as providing the president with an alternative way of grabbing agenda-setting power without relying on partisan control over the Assembly. In addition, to the extent that the executive does not mutually depend on the Assembly, executive-introduced legislation may be likely to function as a tool for the president's legislative power.

The president's partisan leadership in this context may reinforce the function of executive-introduced legislation through the president's control of the Assembly. If this is the case, compared to legislators' proposals, which have to overcome internal conflicts within the Assembly, executive proposals may have a much higher chance of being passed, thanks to the role of the president. Meanwhile, if the executive is conditioned by mutual dependence on the Assembly, executive-introduced legislation may not be a tool for enhancing the president's legislative power, but should be coordinated with the Assembly. This is particularly plausible in South Korean presidentialism due to the possibility of the Assembly involvement in the president's personnel power. Although the president's partisan control might weaken the strength of the threat to the executive from the Assembly, there is still the possibility for executive-introduced proposals to be vulnerable to internal conflicts in the Assembly. Accordingly, the chance of executive-introduced proposals being passed in the Assembly may be lowered.

The adoption rate of executive-introduced legislation is also expected to depend on the partisan composition of the Assembly. Since partisan composition of the Assembly affects the strength of the president's partisan control of the Assembly, the President may use executive-introduced legislation more effectively under a unified government than under a divided government. Again, the degree of effectiveness of executive-introduced legislation may vary, depending on the nature of the relationship between the executive and the legislature. To the extent that the executive is concerned with mutual dependence on the Assembly, the influence of the president's partisan control of the Assembly may be weakened. If this is the case, the performance of executive-introduced legislation may not significantly differ between a unified and a divided government.

These two hypothetical expectations regarding executive-introduced legislation can be tested by measuring the success rate of bills proposed by the executive and by legislators. As long as the success rate of bills proposed by the executive is higher than that proposed by legislators, and higher under a unified government than under a divided government, the executive-introduced legislation is more likely to be a tool conducive to the emergence of the hyper-presidentialism in South Korea, and thus this institution should not be considered an effective parliamentary element.

In testing these expectations with the records of the number of proposed bills and their adoption rate from the first to nineteenth South Korean Assemblies, I omitted the records from 1960 to 1963 when South Korean society was not a presidential system. Meanwhile, I categorised the bills proposed by the committee chair as those proposed by legislators. Within the South Korean Assembly, committee chairs can amend and combine bills proposed by both the executive and legislators in the process of reviewing the proposed bills. Although some executive proposals, in this regard, may be accommodated into the bills proposed by the committee chair, this chapter follows the conventional practice in studies of South Korean legislation, which regards the committee chair's bills as the legislator's bills.

Table 4.3 shows that the long-term practice of permitting the executive to introduce legislation does not support the argument that this institution makes South Korean presidentialism different from other presidential systems. At first, it is interesting to see that, despite a valid theoretical argument to the contrary, executive bills have an overwhelmingly higher adoption rates than bills proposed by legislators. Although the

Table 4.3: Government type and legislative bills

Type	Period	No. of bills Exec.[a]	No. of bills Leg.[b]	Passed bills Exec.	Passed bills Leg.	Success rate Exec.	Success rate Leg.
Unified	4th (05/1958–07/1960)	201	123	53	39	26.37	31.71
	6th (12/1963–06/1967)	242	416	200	235	82.64	56.49
	7th (07/1967–06/1971)	291	243	255	150	87.63	61.73
	8th (07/1971–10/1972)	35	14	34	8	97.14	57.14
	9th (03/1973–03/1979)	479	154	470	102	98.12	66.23
	10th (03/1979–10/1980)	124	5	97	3	78.23	60.00
	11th (04/1981–04/1985)	287	204	279	104	97.21	50.98
	12th (04/1985–05/1988)	168	210	164	119	97.62	56.67
	13th (02/1990–05/1992)	239	257	229	93	95.82	36.19
	14th (05/1992–05/1996)	581	321	561	167	96.56	52.02
	17th (05/2004–05/2008)	1,102	6,187	880	2,886	79.85	46.65
	18th (05/2008–05/2012)	1,693	12,220	1,288	4,890	76.08	40.02
Subtotal		5,442	20,354	4,510	8,796	82.87	43.22
Divided	1st (05/1948–05/1950)	143	103	109	59	76.22	57.28
	2nd (05/1950–05/1954)	215	201	149	103	69.30	51.24
	3rd (05/1954–05/1958)	239	170	91	81	38.08	47.65
	13th (05/1988–02/1990)	129	313	126	259	97.67	82.75
	15th (05/1996–05/2000)	807	1,144	737	687	91.33	60.05
	16th (05/2000–05/2004)	595	1,911	551	1,028	92.61	53.79
	19th (05/2016–05/2020)	1,094	23,047	738	8,061	67.46	34.98
Subtotal		3,222	26,889	2,501	10,278	77.62	38.22

Notes:

(a) executive;

(b) legislator.

Source: Bill Information of the National Assembly (1948–2020), http://likms.assembly.go.kr/bill/stat/statFinishBillSearch.do, accessed 5 August 2021.

absolute number of bills proposed by legislators began to exceed that of the executive in the thirteenth Assembly, the success rates of executive bills is still higher than those of the bills proposed by legislators. Second, this characteristic is preserved irrespective of the partisan composition of the Assembly. When we compare the success rate of proposed bills between unified and divided governments, we observe that the average success rates of bills proposed by both the executive and legislators are lower during divided governments than unified governments. However, regardless of the partisan composition of the Assembly, we find that the adoption rate of the bills proposed by the executive is consistently higher than that of the bills proposed by legislators.

These results clearly imply that the impact of the executive-introduced legislation is not moderated by the potential demand for coordination with the Assembly, but indeed contributes to the emergence of hyper-presidentialism. In addition, the overall higher adoption rates of bills under unified governments implies that the degree of legislative efficacy in South Korea is strongly correlated with congruent party majorities in both the executive and the legislature (Croissant 2003; Carey 2008). However, the consistently higher adoption rate of bills proposed by the executive compared to those of legislators, irrespective of the partisan composition of the Assembly, does not confirm that the power given to the executive to introduce legislation produces checks in South Korean presidentialism by helping to build strong legislative coordination between the executive and the legislature. Based on these findings, we may fairly confidently conclude that the provision of the power to introduce legislation reinforces the power of the president in South Korea.

4. Conclusion

This chapter has examined the existing conceptualisation of South Korean presidentialism as presidentialism with parliamentary characteristics and has described the parliamentary characteristics of the South Korean Constitution. Some scholars have argued that South Korean presidentialism does not function properly due to the existence of the parliamentary institutions (Kim 2017; Lee 2019). Others often attribute the emergence of hyper-presidentialism in South Korea to these elements (Croissant 2002, 2003; Kim 2004; Kang 2017). However, existing literature has yet to provide proper guidelines of how to understand or evaluate the impacts of these parliamentary elements. This is a particularly important question, since these elements are often invoked as a major issue during discussions of constitutional revision in South Korea.

In this regard, the chapter aimed to improve our understanding of these parliamentary elements by introducing their historical development, as well as examining the extent to which they impact South Korean presidentialism. Specifically, by focusing on three parliamentary elements, this chapter has shown whether the long-term performance of these institutions has distinguished South Korean presidentialism from other presidential systems. In so doing, it first confirmed that the South Korean Constitution indeed clearly establishes a presidential system. Second, although the South Korean Constitution contains some parliamentary elements, their historical performance does not make South Korean presidentialism a political system which produces mutual dependence between the executive and the legislature.

This implies that despite the original purpose for introducing these parliamentary elements in the first Constitution, they have not substantially restrained the emergence of strong presidents in South Korea. Rather, without active efforts by the Assembly to utilise these elements, they will rarely effectively improve the asymmetric power distribution between the executive and the legislature in South Korea. In this regard, this chapter contributes to the existing debates over constitutional revision by implying that future constitutional revisions in South Korea should begin from this proper understanding of the role of parliamentary institutions, should not limit its focus to the revision of the constitutional or institutional layouts, and should extend to cover the influence of other non-institutional and socio-political contexts in South Korea.

Acknowledgement

This work was supported by the Creative-Pioneering Researcher Program through Seoul National University (SNU): [grant no. 870-20200020] and the Ministry of Education of the Republic of Korea and the National Research Foundation of Korea: [grant no. NRF-2019S1A3A2098969].

Notes

1. The State Council is a constitutional institution authorising major public policies and governing activities. It consists of the president, the prime minister, and major public officers including ministers of administrative departments, as well as heads of other governing offices. In this regard, following the existing convention which considers the State Council to be an equivalent to cabinets in other countries (Kim 2004), this chapter uses the terms 'State Council' and 'Cabinet' interchangeably.
2. From the institutional perspective, the parliamentary constitution was promulgated in June 1960 and lasted until December 1962. But, after the military coup in May 1961, the government was controlled completely by the military.
3. National Assembly Act, Article 29.1.
4. See Chang (2016) for a discussion of the modernisation of South Korea.
5. See the Assembly minutes of the 170-9 plenary session, https://likms.assembly.go.kr/bill/billDetail.do?billId=012919, accessed 6 August 2021.

Bibliography

Albert, R. (2009), 'The Fusion of Presidentialism and Parliamentarism', *American Journal of Comparative Law* 57(3), 531–577.

Back, Y. (1995), *Je 1 Gonghwagukkwa Hangukminjujuui: UihweJeongchireul Jungsimuiro* [*South Korean Democracy in the First Republic: Focusing on Legislative Politics*] (Seoul: Nanam Publisher).

Browne, E. C., Frendreis, J. P., and Gleiber, D. W. (1984), 'An 'Events' Approach to the Problem of Cabinet Stability', *Comparative Political Studies* 17(2), 167–197.

Carey, J. M. (2008), 'Presidential versus Parliamentary Government', in C. Ménard and M. M. Shriley, eds, *Handbook of New Institutional Economics* (Dordrecht, the Netherlands: Springer Science & Business Media), 91–122.

Chang, Y. (2016), 'Daehanmingukheonbeopui jeonsa: Heonbeopjejeong ijeonui heonbeopsa' [Past Records of Korean Constitution: Constitutional Records before the First Constitution in 1948], *Korea Law Review* 81, 127–160.

Cohler, A. M., Miller, B. C., and Stone, H. S. (1989), *Montesquieu: The Spirit of the Laws* (Cambridge: Cambridge University Press).

Croissant, A. (2002), 'Strong Presidents, Weak Democracy? Presidents, Parliaments and Political Parties in South Korea', *Korea Observer* 33(1), 1–45.

Croissant, A. (2003), 'Legislative Power, Veto Players, and the Emergence of Delegative Democracy: A Comparison of Presidentialism in the Philippines and South Korea', *Democratization* 10(3), 68–98.

Dipalma, G. (1990), *To Craft Democracies* (Berkeley, CA: University of California Press).

Elgie, R. (2007), 'What is Semi-Presidentialism and Where Is It Found?', in R. Elgie and S. Moestru, eds, *Semi-Presidentialism Outside Europe* (London: Routledge), 1–13.

Elgie, R., Moestrup, S., and Wu, Y. (2011), *Semi-Presidentailism and Democracy* (Palgrave: Macmillan).

Fisher, J., Dowding, K., and Dumont, P. (2012), 'The Duration and Durability of Cabinet Ministers', *International Political Science Review* 33(5), 505–519.

Huber, J. D. (1996), 'The Vote of Confidence in Parliamentary Democracies', *American Political Science Review* 90(2), 269–282.

Jang, H. (2010), *Isipjyeonui silheom: Hanguk jeongchigaehyeokui ironkwa yeoksa* [*Twenty Years Experiment: Theories and History of Political Reforms in Korea*] (Seoul: Nanam Publisher).

Jeong, M. (2009), 'Hyeonhaengheonbeopsang jeongbuhyeongtaeui uiwonnaegakjejek yosoe daehan geomto' [A Study on Parliamentary Elements in the Government Structure of the Current Constitution of Korea], *Dong-A Law Review* 44, 37–78.

Jin, Y., and Choi, S. (2009), 'Hangukjeok gwonryeokgujoui giwonjeok hyeongtae: Daehanminguk imsijeongbu (1914–1945) ui heonbeopgaejeongkwa gwonryeokgujo byeoncheonsa bunseok' [The Origins of the 'Korean Power Structure': The Changes of Power Structure through Five Revisions of the Constitutions during the Provisional Government from 1919 to 1945], *Korean Political Science Review* 43(2), 25–49.

Kang, W. (2017), 'Heonbeopgwa gwonryeokgujo: Jewangjek daetongryeongeul neomeoseo' [Constitution and Political Regime: Beyond the Imperial President], in Sam-yeol Lee, Jeong-woo Lee, and Won-Taek Kang, eds, *The Future and Challenge of Korean Democracy* (Seoul: Hanwul Academy), 69–96.

Kim, H.-Y. (2012), 'Hyeonhaengheonbeopui ulwonnaegakjejeok yosoe daehan pyeongga' [A Review on the Elements from the Parliamentary System of the Present Constitution], *Kwangwon Law Review* 32, 131–162.

Kim, H.-W. (1997), 'Jeheongukhweui jeongbuhyeongtaeron nonui' [Debates on the Type of Government in the First Constitutional Parliament], *Legislative Studies* 4, 203–250.

Kim, J. (2004), 'Comparing the Power of Korean and American Presidents: An Institutional Perspective', *Pacific Focus* 19(1), 107–136.

Kim, Y. B. (2003), 'Gwonryeokgujogaehyeokgwa gukmuchongrijedo munjewa gaeseonbangan' (The Reforms of Power Structure and Prime Minister Institution in Korea: Its Problems and Alternatives], *Journal of International Relations* 6(1), 1–24.

Kim, Y. (2017), 'Minjuhwa ihu hanguk daetongryeongjeui jinhwagwajeong bunseok' [An Evaluation of 30 Years' Democratization in South Korea: Focus on the Evolution of South Korean Presidential System and Its Future Prospects', *Journal of Legislative Studies* 23(1), 37–79.

Kim, Y.-S. (2000), *Hangukheonbeopsa* [*The History of the Korean Constitution*] (Seoul: Hakmoon Publisher).

Ko, J.-H. (2000), 'Daehanminguk imsijeongbuui seongripgwajeonge daehan geomto' [Examining the Historical Process of the Formation of Provisional Government of Korea], *Journal of Korean Modern and Contemporary History* 12, 88–127.

Lee, J.-W. (2006), *Hangukui gukmuchongriyeongu* [*A Study of the Prime Minister in South Korea*] (Seoul: Nanam Publisher).

Lee, J. (2000), 'Constitutional Choices in South Korea', *Korea Observer* 31(1), 23–40.

Lee, S. (2019), 'Daetongryeongui yaksok: Roh, Moo-hyun, Lee, Myung-bak, Park, Geun-hye daetongryeong seongeogongyak ipbeopsanchul yeongu' [The Promise of the President: Legislative Output of Presidential Election Pledges during the Roh Moo-hyun, Lee Myung-bak, and Park Geun-hye Administrations], *Korean Association for Policy Studies* 28(3), 37–61.

Linz, J. J. (1990), 'The Perils of Presidentialism', *Journal of Democracy* 1(1), 51–99.

Montesquieu, C. L. (1748/2002), *The Spirit of Laws*, rev. edn (Amherst, NY: Prometheus Books).

Park, C. W. (2000), 'Legislative-Executive Relations and Legislative Reform', in L. Diamond and D. C. Shin, eds, *Institutional Reform and Democratic Consolidation in Korea* (Stanford, CA: Hoover Institution), 73–96.

Park, C. W. (2004), 'Daetongryeongjeui jeongsangjeok jakdongeul wihan gaeheonron' [Constitutional Revision for the Normal Operation of Presidentialism], in Y. Jin, ed., *Understanding Political Regime in Korea* (Seoul: Nanam Publisher), 171–224.

Park, G.-D. (2009), 'Gwonryeokgujo nonjaengui heosilgwa daetongryeongje jeongbuui anjeonghwa mosaek: Sahwejeok biyonggwa bulhwaksilseongui chwesohwa gwanjeomese' [Searching for the Stabilization of Presidentialism through the Examination of Weakness and Strength of the Debates over the Power Structure: From the Perspective of Minimizing the Social Costs and Uncertainties], in J. Lee, ed., *Towards the Twenty-First Century of Korean Politics* (Seoul: National University Press), 173–200.

Przeworski, A., and Limongi, F. (1997), 'Modernization: Theories and Facts', *World Politics* 49(2), 155–183.

Rose-Ackerman, S., Desierto, D. A., and Volosin, N. (2011), 'Hyper-Presidentialism: Separation of Powers without Checks and Balances in Argentina and Philippines', *Berkeley Journal of International law* 29(1), 246–333.

Shugart, M. S. (2008), 'Comparative Executive–Legislative Relations', in R. A. W. Rhodes, S. A. Binder, and B. A. Rockman, eds, *The Oxford Handbook of Political Institutions* (Oxford: Oxford University Press), 344–365.

Shugart, M. S., and Carey, J. M. (1992), *Presidents and Assemblies: Constitutional Design and Electoral Dynamics* (Cambridge: Cambridge University Press).

Stephan, A., and Skach, C. (1993), 'Constitutional Frameworks and Democratic Consolidation', *World Politics* 46(1), 1–22.

Suh, H. K. (2006), 'Daehyanminguk geogukheonbeopui yeoksajeok giwon (1898–1919): Man mingongdonghwe·3.1wundong·daehanmingukimsijeongbuheonbeopui 'minjugonghwa' jeongche insikeul jungsimeuro' [The Historical Origins of the 1948 Founding Constitutional Law in the Modern Korea, 1898–1919: Focusing on the Understanding of Democratic Republic in the General People's Assembly, March 1 Independence Movement, and Korean Provisional Government', *Korean Political Science Review* 40(5), 139–163.

Tasi, J.-H. (2009), 'Political Structure, Legislative Process, and Corruption: Comparing Taiwan and South Korea', *Crime Law and Social Change* 52, 365–383.

Yang, D. (1999), 'Hangukdaetongryeongjeui gaeseongwa daeandeule daehan jaegeomto' [Reexamining the Alternatives and Reforms of Korean Presidentialism], *Korean Political Science Review* 33(3), 91–109.

Yoo, H.-J. (2010), 'Daetongryeongui ipbeopuijeroseo Jeongbubeopanui gukhwe jechulkwa tongkwaui yeonghyang yoin: Minjuhwa ihu ryeokdaejeongbureul jungsimeuro (1988–2007)' [A Study of the Factors Influencing the Introduction of Executive Legislation to the National Assembly and Its Legislative Success: A Focus on Successive Governments Since Democratization (1988–2007)', *Korean Journal of Public Administration* 48(4), 263–293.

Yoo, J.-O. (1980), *Heonbeopgichohwegorok* [*Memoirs of Drafting the First Constitution*] (Seoul: Iljogak).

CHAPTER 5

REGIONALISM

KWANG-IL YOON

1. INTRODUCTION: THE UNIQUENESS OF SOUTH KOREA'S REGIONALISM

REGIONALISM has been the determining factor in both voting behaviour and aligning the party system in South Korea, especially since democratisation in 1987. South Korean voters have been known to make voting decisions primarily based on where they were born and raised. And South Korean politics have been shaped by two regional parties which are essentially the same in terms of leadership, active members, and platform, although both parties frequently reshuffle and rebrand themselves to overcome political crises. Korea's regionalism has taken a unique, unprecedented form that is different from other democracies. For example, compared to the regionalism of Scotland in the United Kingdom, Quebec in Canada, the Basque Country in Spain, the Punjab in India, Flanders and Wallonia in Belgium, and so on, South Korea's regionalism is not based on race, ethnicity, language, or religious cleavages. Even if a party has a regional stronghold of electoral support, it competes nationally and has not pledged to commit to the exclusive interests of the regional core constituents, nor has it pursued a substantial transfer of authority to the region by seeking federalism, segregation, or autonomy (Moon 1984; Kang 2003). Moreover, South Korea's strong regional parties are not a product of either fiscal or political decentralisation, as in other democracies (Chhibber and Kollman 2004; Brancati 2007).

The regionalism of other countries, where party support is concentrated in a specific region, stems from a territorial community that is based on historical or cultural community before the establishment of the modern nation state. In contrast, South Korea's regionalism is distinct from these countries as it has a very homogeneous historical, cultural, and social composition. According to an empirical study of political cleavage structures in 117 countries around the world, South Korea constitutes a rare case where one ethnic group forms a nation (Selway 2009). In fact, South Korea, along with Portugal and Iceland, is one of the few historically mono-national states in the era of multiculturalism (Kymlicka 2007). The issue of South Korean regionalism has been characterised as unique and severe, since there are no cases of deep, extreme regional division based on political exclusion and alienation in countries without salient ethnic, linguistic, or cultural heterogeneity (Choi 1993).

South Korean regionalism brings into sharp relief more distinct characteristics than universal ones when one refers to studies of political cleavage. For example, Lipset and Rokkan (1967) explain how political parties develop to represent the constellations of historical and social rifts in Western Europe formed through the two revolutions, the national and the industrial. It is a daunting task to apply their demand-side model of party system to assess the theoretical status of the South Korean regional cleavage that has provided a monopolistic 'mobilisation market' to a small number of regional political parties, with no similar revolution and freezing process. Regional parties in South Korea, whose strongholds are all located in the periphery, have never reflected centre versus periphery nor land versus industry cleavages, although the centre, the Seoul Capital Area, has monopolised political, economic, and cultural resources in the nation-building and modernisation processes.[1] Regional or territorial cleavage in Europe appears in an overlap with decentralised elements such as language and religion or as cleavage between urban and rural areas during industrialisation (Keating et al. 1997; Kriesi 1998; Caramani 2004; Knutsen 2010) or, more recently, as a transnational cleavage (Hooghe and Marks 2018). However, it is difficult to see South Korean regional cleavage centred on the southwest Honam (Jeolla) and the southeast Yeongnam (Gyeongsang) regions as such.[2] Nevertheless, the South Korean regional cleavage appears to involve all three elements of 'full cleavage' (Bartolini and Mair 1990; Deegan-Krause 2007): structure (region), attitude (identity), and institution (party). This is because South Korea's regionalism implies territorial division between Honam and Yeongnam, politicised identity among the regional natives and residents, and the regional party system based on exclusive support by these people and the regionally biased political class recruitment.[3]

In short, compared to the major types of deep social and political divisions in other countries, South Korean regional cleavage constitutes a unique and unprecedented case. Moreover, at least in terms of regional bloc voting and exclusive party support by Honam and Yeongnam natives and residents, South Korea's regionalism remains solid enough that it is unlikely to significantly change in the near future. At the same time, there have been a few signs of change in regionalism with respect to prejudice and discrimination against Honam, as well as the regional party system. Thus, regionalism in South Korea needs a sophisticated explanation. This chapter is structured as follows: first, it discusses the origins of regionalism. Second, the chapter conceptualises regionalism according to the level of analysis and the domain of its manifestation and promotes the theoretical understanding of regionalism drawing on prejudice, social identity, and cleavage theory. Finally, it concludes with a discussion of recent developments in regionalism.

2. South Korea's Regionalism: Origins and Conceptualisation

2.1 The Origins of Regionalism

The literature includes three proposed explanations for the origins of regionalism: historical rivalry and oppression and Confucian culture, political economy of uneven development and biased elite recruitment under the authoritarian regime, and political mobilisation by regional leaders, especially since democratisation. First, historically, the intense antagonisms that exist today between Honam and Yeongnam are suggested as being rooted in the confrontation between two ancient kingdoms: Silla (BC 57–935), or what is largely Yeongnam today, and Baekje (BC 18–660), or what is largely Honam today. And the negative affect against Honam by the rest of the nation, or 'Honam phobia' which intensified following the Gwangju Uprising in 1980, is attributed to premodern Honam-discriminatory policies deliberately pursued by the Goryeo (918–1392) and Joseon (1392–1910) dynasties. Moreover, Confucianism has nurtured and reinforced premodern regional ties among natives (Shin 1996; Kwon 2004).

Second, the successive authoritarian regimes of Park Chung-hee (1961–1979), Chun Doo-hwan (1980–1988), and Roh Tae-woo (1988–1992) pursued, deliberately or not, regionally 'uneven development strategies' that heavily favoured their home region, Yeongnam, at the expense of other regions, especially the agriculture-based Honam economy. Moreover, in the economic modernisation and development processes, the talents in military, government, business, and even academia had been recruited predominantly from Yeongnam, a practice which continued under the first civilian government led by Kim Young-sam (1993–1997) (Yu 1990, 2003; Kim 1995). Facing exclusionary and alienating practices and policies seemingly imposed by the ruling Yeongnam political elites, Honam may have been obliged to act collectively rationally by exclusively supporting their own regional parties in order to defend and claim their fair share of pork-barrel benefits (Cho 1996).

These historical and cultural and political economic accounts may help us to understand the facilitating conditions for the negative stereotypes, prejudice, and discrimination towards Honam today, but they fail to account for current political regionalism that features exclusively regional voting behaviour and persistent regional party dominance in Honam and Yeongnam but not in other regions. Furthermore, both explanations are not adequate to understand maximised political mobilisation in these regions by not only the ruling Yeongnam-based parties, but also the opposition Honam-based ones after democratisation.

Thus, we have to resort to the third explanation, which emphasises politicised regional identity mobilised by political entrepreneurs who were the favourite sons of Honam and Yeongnam, with significant help from the winner-takes-all presidential elections and primarily majoritarian legislative elections. In South Korea, unlike in the

West, personal leadership or charisma, not political organisation or party, has played a decisive role in political mobilisation in certain regions; this led to people's exclusive voting and political party support for candidates from the Honam and Yeongnam regions because they were from the same hometowns. This 'birthplace-based regionalism' has been considered a key manifestation of South Korean regionalism (Kang 2016). Park Chung-hee and Chun Doo-hwan, both the authoritarian military rulers, and Roh Tae-woo, the first president after democratisation, and their civilian successor Kim Young-sam, all hailed from Yeongnam, while throughout their rule the only electorally viable opposition leader had been Kim Dae-jung, who was from Honam.[4] They all had their electoral machine-type parties, whose members were heavily recruited from the boss's home regions.

It would not take too much effort for voters in or from Honam and Yeongnam to identify who they are supposed to vote for. The voters of both regions might not understand the specific details of policies that their regional 'in-party' advocated, nor be able to attribute them correctly to their in-party, probably because Korean politics had long been dominated by the Cold War as well as anti-North Korea discourses and policies, especially after the Korean War (1950–1953) and hence the regional parties are basically similar in terms of conservative orientations.[5] Moreover, frequent reshuffling and rebranding of the regional parties has not helped voters to tell one from the other in terms of campaign pledges. Nevertheless, voters of these regions have easily been able to recognise their in-parties by the leaders at the top and their avid followers, most of whom share the same accents. Voters in Honam and Yeongnam have also been able to tell and support policies which are typically attributed to their in-parties, mainly by the media. For example, Kim Dae-jung's reconciliatory 'Sunshine Policy' towards North Korea has been identified as a flagship policy of Honam-based regional parties, while hawkish policies towards North Korea have been associated with more conservative, Yeongnam-based regional ones. Voters are able to know 'what goes with what', at least in this policy area, and support accordingly.

The winner-takes-all presidential elections and the primarily single-member-district-plurality legislative elections introduced with democratisation definitely facilitated the strategic mobilisation and politicisation of regional identity of natives of Honam and Yeongnam by their favourite sons of both ruling and opposition parties. This in turn led to regionalist voting behaviour at the individual level and regional bloc voting at the aggregate level, and consequently landslide wins by regional parties in their respective strongholds. In fact, the regional party system of Honam and Yeongnam based on regional bloc voting of natives and residents and near-monopoly of seats of regional parties in each region was first established in the 'founding' presidential and legislative elections after democratisation (Kang 2001; Jung 2015).[6] A merger of three conservative political parties in 1990, two Yeongnam-based and one Chungcheong-based regional parties with the exclusion of then opposition leader Kim Dae-jung's party, amplified political mobilisation against Honam. The stable but unique regional party system has been firmly grounded since, by any measure (Ohn 1997, 2003; Kang 2005; Jung 2015). After all, over the course of seven presidential elections and eight general elections between democratisation in 1987 and 2017, Honam and Yeongnam natives had voted almost exclusively for their regional in-parties and mostly their presidential and legislative candidates (Lee 2011; Yoon 2012, 2018).

2.2 Conceptualisations of Regionalism

Existing literature on Korea's regionalism has combined its elements or equivalent terms such as nepotism, parochialism, regional attitudes or sentiment, regional bias or prejudice, regional identity, regional conflict or cleavage, regional dominance or hegemony, under regionalism, without a clear conceptual definition of the term, much less specifying and defining its elements (J. Kim 1988; Choe and Kim 2000; Lee 2003; Kim 2004). While this highlights the distinct characteristics of South Korean regionalism, it neglects the commonality with cleavage in other democracies and fails to facilitate a theoretical and empirical understanding of the subject by drawing on social science research, let alone interdisciplinary work. In particular, conceptualisation efforts so far have subsumed not only the elements that characterise regionalism, but also its micro-level or psychological and macro-level or institutional and structural implications, preventing the parsing of causes and consequences of regionalism and convincingly tracking its changes. For instance, empirical studies on regionalism in political science have focused on the regionalist voting behaviour of Honam and Yeongnam natives and residents, regional bloc voting in these regions, and the subsequent near-monopoly of seats by regional parties in their respective bastions, without a clear definition of the term, hence blurring the causes and effects of regionalism, whatever they may be. To overcome these limitations, studies must be preceded by a clear theoretical basis and rigorous definitions of the concepts related to regionalism.

That said, I conceptualise regionalism or elements thereof in the South Korean context based on the level of analysis and the domain of its manifestation in order to facilitate an appropriate operationalisation of the concept and to foster drawing on relevant theories on regionalism in social science research. The level of analysis bifurcates into the individual and the aggregate and the former is further differentiated into three components of an individual's psychology or attitude structure: cognition (thought), affect (emotion), and behaviour. The domain of the manifestation of regionalism, where one observes its instances, dichotomises into society and politics.

Now let us classify selected terms related to regionalism. For the individual or micro-level analysis and in the domain of society, regionalism encompasses regional stereotypes and attribution bias for cognition, regional identity, regional prejudice, 'in-region' favouritism and 'out-region' animus for affect, and discrimination for behaviour. For the aggregate or macro-level analysis and in the same domain, regionalism typically refers to the regional division or conflict between Honam and Yeongnam. For the individual level analysis and in the domain of politics, regionalism subsumes stereotypes of regional parties and their politicians, policies, and ideology, along with attribution

Table 5.1: Conceptualisation of regionalism

Domain level of analysis	Society	Politics
Micro/individual: cognition	Regional stereotypes, especially of Honam; attribution bias	Stereotypes of regional parties and their politicians, policies, and sideology; attribution bias
Micro/individual: affect	Regional identity; regional prejudice, especially against Honam; in-region favouritism and out-region antagonism	Regional party identity; regional in-party favouritism and out-party animus
Micro/individual: behaviour	Discrimination, especially against Honam in the job market or in workplaces, etc.	Voting for the regional in-party and its candidates
Macro/aggregate	Conflict between Honam and Yeongnam	Regional bloc voting; regional Monopoly Party System

bias for cognition, regional party identity, in-party favouritism and out-party animus for affect, and voting for the in-party and its candidates for behaviour. Finally, for the aggregate level of analysis and in the same domain, regionalism typically refers to regional bloc voting and the regional monopoly party system. Again, it is worthy of note that all these terms apply solely to Honam and Yeongnam in the context of South Korea's regionalism. And when it comes to negative stereotypes, prejudice, and discrimination in both domains, the victim has usually been Honam, the reason for which may be attributed to the historical origin of exclusionary policies and practices, as well as persistent political mobilisation against the region discussed above. Table 5.1 summarises the conceptualisation scheme of regionalism.[7]

Each of these terms has a clear social scientific basis compared to concepts with an ambiguous theoretical basis, such as regional sentiment and regional emotion, or even regionalism per se, which have been largely circulated in the media, as well as regionalism studies in South Korea, and thus enables more systematic studies based on relevant theories and findings in academic research. For example, we can draw on social psychological approaches to study regional stereotypes of and prejudice against supporters for a Honam-based party; misattribution of policies or ideology to a regional party; sociological approaches to analyse conflict between Honam and Yeongnam as related to resource allocation; and political science approaches to understand regional party identity, exclusive voting behaviour, and persistent regional monopoly party system. Or we can utilise all these scholarly approaches in an interdisciplinary manner to study regional cleavage, which necessarily calls for combining both levels of analysis, as well as taking into account both domains of manifestation of regionalism. The following section introduces selected theories that help to understand Korea's regionalism, along with elaboration of the conceptualisation of the terms suggested here.

3. Theories on Regionalism: Prejudice, Social Identity, and Full Cleavage

3.1 Theory of Prejudice

Allport (1954/1979: 7) defines prejudice as an 'aversive or hostile attitude towards a person who belongs to a group, simply because he belongs to that group'. He claims that prejudice is based on prejudgment according to categorical thinking, and stereotypes are 'caught' during childhood, rather than formed through learning from parents, and are not easily corrected by knowledge based on a new fact or logical persuasion. In addition, prejudice often goes beyond an intrapsychic process and leads to discrimination or unequal treatment of another person because he or she belongs to a group. In other words, Allport notes cognitive, emotional, and behavioural elements of prejudice that later formed the core of studies on prejudice. We can apply this 'tripartite model of prejudice' to understanding regional prejudice, specifically negative attitudes towards Honam by people in other regions.

Thus, as a cognitive element of regional prejudice, regional stereotypes can be defined as schema or organised cognitive structures stored in memories one has about an individual because he or she resides in or is from a certain region, regardless of actual individual differences. It tends to be 'cultural knowledge' shared by many about natives and residents of a region or of Honam in particular. Once it is formed, most likely through the political socialisation process, regional stereotypes have continuity in that they do not change, despite receiving new information that contradicts the stereotype, retains and strengthens regional prejudice, and justifies regional prejudice and discriminatory behaviour. Regional stereotypes can facilitate efficient information-processing and often develops later to justify prejudice and a discriminatory behaviour (Kim 1999).

Since Lee (1959) first observed from among a sample of about forty college students that negative stereotypes against Honam natives existed, their existence and content have been confirmed and identified repeatedly in social psychology research (Kim and Cho 2015). Experimental studies have suggested that regional stereotypes, implicit or explicit, influence the formation of prejudice and prejudicial judgement, attribution bias, and discriminatory behaviour intention, mostly against Honam (H. Kim 1988, 1993, 2001; Ahn 1998).

Regional prejudice can be conceptualised as antipathy or negative affect against the people or natives of a certain region, again, particularly against Honam. It is basically an attitude and thus we can expect the same properties and functions that an attitude has been found to have. In other words, regional prejudice is formed through the classical or operant conditioning process towards the people of a certain region rather than a belief or knowledge based on facts about them. Regional prejudice with negative affect as a central ingredient does not change easily, even after the cognitive causes are forgotten, and has a lasting and lingering effect on the thought and judgement processes and behaviour.

And it is difficult to measure, since affective reactions that shape attitudes occur subliminally and the explicit expression of prejudice is susceptible to social desirability bias.

Reviews of the literature have confirmed that there exists nationwide regional prejudice against Honam in college student samples (Kim 1987; H. Kim 1988; Min 1989), as well as in nationally representative samples (Na 1990; Choe and Kim 2000; Chung 2005; Jhee 2015). Studies that used implicit measurement methods to circumvent the social desirability bias have found that prejudice against Honam is prevalent (Hong and Lee 2001; Na and Kwon 2002; Lee 2015).[8] The prejudice against Honam also has substantive effects on political behaviour. Lee (1998) found that the negative affect against Honam leads to the negative evaluation of Kim Dae-jung and his party and ultimately discouraged voting for the Honam native in the presidential election of 1997. Lee and Park (2011) observed that the positive evaluation of Honam and Yeongnam natives had a substantive independent effect on the support of regional parties of each region.

Finally, regional discrimination, a behavioural element of regional prejudice, is a behavioural response to people in or from a certain region. It involves unreasonable, inappropriate, or unfair treatment towards an individual or an entire group of a certain region or a less favourable reaction to out-region members than in-region ones, even in a similar circumstance. As in the tripartite model of prejudice, regional stereotypes and prejudice are often influenced and easily activated by automatic information-processing outside of conscious control, and significantly influences the thought and judgement processes afterwards that lead to discriminatory behaviours under favourable conditions, that is, the approval or sanction of these behaviours by in-group members. Discrimination often justifies and reinforces regional stereotypes and prejudice.

Again, the usual victims of regional discrimination have been the people of Honam. Studies using nationally representative samples have documented, since 1988, that the proportion experiencing discrimination had persistently been higher among the natives of Honam than among any other native groups (Chung 2005; K. Yoon 2017). This, along with the reports of widespread negative stereotypes and prejudice, suggests that there has existed fertile ground for the discursive and political mobilisation of Honam's regional identity by the long-persecuted favourite son, Kim Dae-jung, and his party of devoted followers. The regional party of Yeongnam constructed by the consecutive military authoritarian leaders had already been in place by the time Kim established his own regional party and acted as the natural agent of political mobilisation of the regional identity in Yeongnam.

Where, then, does the regional prejudice generating and reinforcing current regional political cleavage stem from? It is social identity theory that this chapter focuses on to answer this question.

3.2 Social Identity Theory

'Prejudice, broadly conceived', or 'ethnocentrism' behind intergroup conflict is a predisposition or readiness to reduce society into in-groups and out-groups or 'us versus them'. It entails the favouritism for the in-group, to which an individual has a sense of belonging or identity with, and the contempt, prejudice, and, in extreme cases, hatred towards out-groups are the sources and the results of intergroup conflict (Kinder and Kam 2009). Yet, the intergroup conflicts in the context of South Korea's regionalism have not necessarily resulted from interregional competition over the acquisition of limited material resources, as the realistic group conflict theory suggests. Furthermore, there is no reason that the competition should have been limited to Honam and Yeongnam, supposedly the main parties of an interregional conflict. A regional conflict in Korea tends to erupt over symbolic resources such as the in-region's reputation and pride, and the people involved in the conflict do not always perceive it as real. Thus, social identity theory is more relevant to explain the prejudice behind regionalism in South Korea.

According to the 'minimal group paradigm' of social identity theory, even if there is no history of intergroup conflict of interests or antagonism and there is no interaction among members, they tend to favour the in-group and derogate the out-group (Tajfel 1970) or to take on an 'us versus them mentality' (Kinder and Kam 2009). This is the result of the natural cognitive process of social categorisation and social comparison, which motivates one to confirm the superiority of an in-group by comparing oneself to the members of out-groups and hence to achieve positive social identity that promotes self-esteem (Tajfel and Turner 1986). Thus, a sense of belonging to a region where one was born and raised or currently resides (i.e. in-region identity) would suffice to promote in-region favouritism and out-region hostility.[9] Then, why does South Korea's regionalism feature Honam versus Yeongnam? In-region favouritism and prejudice against out-regions would not have significant political implications, nor have been limited to Honam and Yeongnam had it not been for the political mobilisation of regional identities, organised, maintained, and reinforced by the elites from Honam and Yeongnam and their regional parties. The winner-takes-all electoral system along with regional bloc voting, a key manifestation of politicised regional identities, has facilitated the regional party system since democratisation. And the media has only amplified the conflicts between these regions, real or imagined.

Studies based on social identity theory found that there is widespread in-region favouritism not only in Honam and Yeongnam (Hong and Lee 2001; Kim 2002; Bae 2009). Regional identity was also found to increase significantly the support for in-region candidates (Ahn 2000; Park and Han 2003). Kwang-Il Yoon (2012, 2017) made explicit the place where one was born and mainly grew up as a proxy for regional identity and revealed that it significantly increased the support for presidential and legislative candidates of the in-region party and for the party itself. Kim and Lee (2015) theoretically justified Yoon's identity-based regionalism and presented more evidence that hometown rather than residency matters for South Korea's regionalism. Aggregate-level approaches support the conclusion that birthplace-based regional identity had been important in presidential elections (Jung 2015: Lee and Repkine 2020).[10]

3.3 Regional Cleavage as the Only Full Cleavage

The theory of prejudice and social identity are helpful in understanding South Korean regionalism, especially at the individual level. To grasp a fuller picture of South Korean regionalism by bridging the gap between the micro- and macro-level of analysis, as well as by integrating diverse social science approaches, we need to draw on the theory of cleavage.

The historical regional division between Honam and Yeongnam qualifies as the only cleavage, the concept of which was reformulated by Bartolini and Mair (1990) in order to bring precision to the rather loose use of the term by Lipset and Rokkan (1967). Cleavage, according to Bartolini and Mair, consists of three fundamental elements:

> an *empirical* element, which identifies the empirical referent of the concept, and which we can define in social-structural terms: a *normative* element, that is the set of values and beliefs which provides a sense of identity and role to the empirical element, and which reflect the self-consciousness of the social group(s) involved; and an *organisational/behavioural* element, that is the set of individual interactions, institutions, and organisations, such as political parties, which develop as part of the cleavage.
>
> (Bartolini and Mair 1990: 215, italics in original)

So defined, the concept is invaluable in understanding the dominant conflict structure of a nation that shapes and conditions electoral behaviour and the party system. Thus, the theory of cleavage calls for integrating the levels of analysis, as well as such diverse approaches as sociological, psychological, and institutional, among others, in political science. And this 'triangular model of cleavage' of demographic-value-party is needed to help comparativists establish a common basis for something less than cleavage with all three elements or 'full cleavage' when analysing the cleavage structure of a state. Not all countries' politics are characterised by a full cleavage; some are characterised by a 'divide' with any two elements or others by a 'difference' with any one of them (Deegan-Krause 2007; Bartolini 2011; Schoultz 2017).

South Korea's regional cleavage should qualify as a full cleavage. First, Honam and Yeongnam constitute a historically, clearly demarcated, socio-structural element. Most natives and residents of each region tend to share similar political orientation and electoral behaviour with their fellow voters. Second, it has a normative element in that Honam and Yeongnam have maintained distinct regional identities that foster in-region favouritism and, arguably, antagonism towards its rival out-region in the political socialisation process. The distinct regional identity has been nurtured at home and in local milieus and has been mobilised into political identity in the form of a psychological tie to a regional in-party. Third, and more importantly, there have been political parties with regional strongholds as an organisational/behavioural element. They have successfully mobilised the natives and residents of respective regions, reinforced their political identities, and led these voters to support and almost exclusively vote for their regional in-parties. Most natives of both regions have maintained an enduring affective attachment towards their respective regional parties and have recently aligned themselves with them in terms of symbolic ideological orientation and issues which have been perceived to be closely associated with these parties, such as North Korea and reunification. For example, the people of Honam tend to identify themselves as more liberal and support the Sunshine Policy, while their Yeongnam counterparts identify as more conservative and express more hawkish policy preferences towards North Korea (Yoon 2018, 2019). In a sense, partisanship based on the regional party system in South Korea is 'a perfect distillation of all events in the individual's life history that have borne upon the way in which he relates himself to a political party' (Campbell et al. 1960/1980: 34).

Not only is the regional cleavage a full cleavage, but it is also the only one because the other alternative cleavages that have been examined both theoretically and empirically do not seem to meet the criteria of a full cleavage. For example, there is ample empirical evidence that generation divide has existed in terms of political orientation and voting behaviour; that is, the young are more liberal while the old are more conservative. Nevertheless, Koreans have not witnessed any meaningful political organisations, let alone parties, that represent or mobilise a generation. Even the politically active '86 generation' does not seem to be a homogeneous group that shares the same political identity (Han et al. 2019).[11] In other words, generation can be a divide or a difference but not a full cleavage.

Ideology is another alternative cleavage that has been studied extensively since the 'founding fathers' of regional parties retired and presidential candidates were recruited, even from rival regions. Some scholars, for example, claimed with caution that the regional cleavage would be replaced by ideological and generational cleavages (Kang 2003; Choi and Cho 2005). However, openly ideological parties have not been successful electorally, even after the electoral system changed in their favour in 2004.[12] And Western-style ideological divisions at the mass level based on economic and social liberalism-conservatism dimensions have surfaced only recently. In South Korea, ideological orientation had long been shaped by political preference towards anti-communism and North Korea and overlapped with the regional cleavage (Kang 2011). The persistent, severe underrepresentation of organised labour and 'working-class conservatism' has also blocked the formation of an ideology-driven cleavage. In any case, ideology may have found generation as an empirical element, but still lacks an organisational/behavioural element to qualify as a full cleavage.

In short, the regional cleavage has been the only full cleavage that dominates the hearts and minds of the voters of Honam and Yeongnam and shapes and maintains the regional party system. No other alternative cleavages seem to qualify as one at the moment, and probably for the long haul (Yoon 2020).

4. Conclusion

This chapter has discussed South Korea's regionalism, focusing on its origins, conceptualisation, and relevant theories that help in understanding its durability. It has argued that the regional cleavage with birthplace-based regional prejudice and identity that have determined electoral behaviour and the party system will not change significantly in the near future. Here, I examine the implications of two recent developments for South Korea's regionalism which are ripe for further research. First, although prejudice against Honam seems to have evolved to prosper in other platforms, such as social media and online communities, a recent study shows that it has almost vanished except among North Yeongnam and Gangwon natives (Yoon 2017). There have also been reports that support for the liberal, out-region party of Honam is increasing gradually among South Yeongnam natives and residents, while Northern counterparts of Yeongnam remain staunchly conservative (J. Yoon 2017; Jung and Lee 2018). Considering that personal leadership has been traditionally decisive in regional political mobilisation, this may have to do with the fact that two successful candidates of the Honam-based party in 2002 and 2017 presidential elections were from South Yeongnam, while the most prominent regional leaders in Yeongnam including Park Chung-hee and his disgraced daughter, Park Geun-hye, were from the northern part. Thus, we have to pay attention to whether the cleavage line has been redrawn between Honam and North Yeongnam. The fact that Honam has long been subject to prejudice and discrimination and the discourse mobilised by some regional leaders of the Yeongnam-based party that North Yeongnam should remain the last bastion of conservatism would help the rearrangement. Besides, the core constituents, as well as the elite members of the two major parties, both of which are similarly non-ideological in nature, still largely consist of people hailing from their respective strongholds.

Second, although there is no indication that current partisans of either party have been switching to a rival regional party, it seems that voters who have little regional loyalty and are more likely to base their party loyalties on their ideological orientation and new issues have been gradually forming a new coalition with voters with regional identity. In other words, those who are younger or live in the Seoul Capital Area are more likely to identify themselves as more liberal than those who are older or live in the country, and they have been joining Honam voters. The political class has been polarised in ideology and on multiple issues since 2004 (Park et al. 2016; Hong 2018) and voters seem to have been responding to the polarisation by sorting themselves into parties that better fit their ideology and policy preferences on North Korea and welfare, among others. Four consecutive wins by the Honam-based party that include two legislative elections in 2016 and 2020, the last presidential election in 2017, and local elections in 2018, with even stronger showings among younger voters and in capital and metropolitan areas, seem to have constituted a new, winning coalition or 'secular realignment' in the making. This whole process appears very similar to ideology-driven partisan realignment that is characterised by gradual and incremental conflict extension, not by short-term conflict displacement (Carmines and Stimson 1989; Layman et al. 2006). Whether this would fundamentally change the structure of the regional cleavage to a point where it is replaced by ideological cleavage featuring conservative North Yeongnam versus the remaining liberal regions of the nation demands close observation.

Notes

1. There has been an effort to apply Lipset and Rokkan's model to the formation of political cleavage in Korea. For example, Kang (2011) claimed that nation-state building after liberation from Japanese colonial rule and the rapid modernisation under Park Chung-hee's regime corresponded to the national revolution and industrial revolution, respectively. He also argued that the two revolutionary processes froze the current major political cleavage (i.e. nation–cold war system, economic centre–peripheral, and capital–labour cleavages), although the latter being somewhat weaker than Western experiences.
2. In this chapter, Honam and Yeongnam refer to both natives (i.e. those who were born and raised) and residents, or together the people of each region. Although current residents of each region are mostly the natives, many natives of each region live in other regions, mostly the Seoul Capital Area.
3. Regionalism in Korea typically refers to regional conflict between Honam and Yeongnam regions without explicitly specifying who harbours antagonism against whom on what. More importantly, the literature has been relatively silent on who the victims of regional prejudice are—the people of Honam. The detailed discussion on this issue will follow in the subsequent sections.
4. Except for Honam and Yeongnam, the only area that had similar regional parties is Chungcheong. Kim Jong-pil, an unsuccessful presidential candidate from the region, led conservative, strong regional parties from 1987 to 1990 and again from 1995 to 2004. Most members of these parties joined Yeongnam-based regional parties after he retired from politics.
5. The terms 'in-party' or 'out-party' and 'in-region' or 'out-region' are all attributed to in-group versus out-group distinctions familiarised by social identity theory, discussed in the section on 'Social identity theory'.
6. It has been suggested that Park Chung-hee and his electoral machine initiated political mobilisation of regional sentiment or identity of his hometown natives in the 1971 presidential election against the strong opposition candidate Kim Dae-jung, a Honam native, cultivating prejudice against the region. After his narrow win, Park abolished direct presidential elections and strengthened authoritarian rule. Kim's Honam-based regional party was first established in his failed presidential run in 1987 and 'defensive' political mobilisation of regional identity of Honam may have been launched full-scale beginning at this time, which led to the regional party system that has dominated Korean politics ever since.
7. The scheme revised and extended the one originally presented by Kim (2004: 86).
8. A study by Choi (2008) that used an unobtrusive measurement method only to find no prejudice against Honam among the rest of the nation is a notable exception.

9. Some studies have suggested that social identity has to do with in-group favouritism but not necessarily with the negativity or hatred towards out-groups (Brewer 1999, 2016).
10. There have been studies that contrasted 'birthplace-based regionalism' with 'residence-based regionalism' and presented the evidence supporting the latter (Moon 2005, 2017; Kang 2016). The result was explained in terms of regional economic voting (Kang 2016).
11. The '86 Generation' refers to those who entered college in the 1980s, when the student democratisation movement against the authoritarian regime was fierce. Most of them were born in the 1960s.
12. The best results for an ideological party in legislative elections have been 13 per cent in votes in 2004 or 4.3 per cent in seats in 2008, both won by a leftist party.

Bibliography

Ahn, S. S. (1998), 'Jiyeok-beomju Jeomhwagwajeeseo Ammugjeok Gojeong-gwannyeom Hwalseonghwawa Eogjehyogwa' [Effects of Implicit Stereotype Activation and Inhibition in Localism-Categorization], Ph.D. dissertation, The Graduate School Kyungpook National University.

Ahn, S. H. (2000), 'Tupyoeseoui Yeongojuui: Jibdanjuui Gyeonghyangseonggwaui Gwangye mich Gijeo Donggi' [Ingroup Favouritism in Voting: Its Underlying Motive and Relationships to Collectivism], *The Korean Journal of Culture and Social Issues* 6(1), 145–180.

Allport, G. (1954/1979), *The Nature of Prejudice* (Cambridge, MA: Addison-Wesley Publishing Company).

Bae, J.-C. (2009), 'Ammugjeok Yeonhabgeomsaleul Tonghan Jiyeokjeongchegam Yeongu' [The Study of Regional Identity by Implicit Association Test], M.A. dissertation, The Graduate School, Chonnam National University.

Bartolini, S. (2011), 'Cleavages, Social and Political', in Bertrand Badie, Dirk Berg-Schlosser, and Leonardo Morlino, eds, *International Encyclopedia of Political Science* (Thousand Oaks, California: Sage), 276–282.

Bartolini, S., and Mair, P. (1990), *Identity, Competition, and Electoral Availability: The Stabilisation of European Electorates 1885–1985* (New York: Cambridge University Press).

Brancati, D. (2007), 'The Origins and Strengths of Regional Parties', *British Journal of Political Science* 38(1), 135–159.

Brewer, M. B. (1999), 'The Psychology of Prejudice: Ingroup Love and Outgroup Hate?', *Journal of Social Issues* 55(3), 429–444.

Brewer, M. B. (2016), 'Intergroup Discrimination: Ingroup Love or Outgroup Hate?', in C. G. Sibley and F. K. Barlow, eds, *The Cambridge Handbook of the Psychology of Prejudice* (Cambridge: Cambridge University Press), 90–110.

Campbell, A., Converse, P. E., Miller, W. E., and Stokes, D. E. (1960/1980), *The American Voter* (New York: John Wiley & Sons).

Caramani, D. (2004), *The Nationalization of Politics: The Formation of National Electorates and Party Systems in Western Europe* (Cambridge: Cambridge University Press).

Carmines, E. G., and Stimson, J. A. (1989), *Issue Evolution: Race and the Transformation of American Politics* (Princeton, NJ: Princeton University Press).

Chhibber, P., and Kollman, K. W. (2004), *The Formation of National Party Systems: Federalism and Party Competition in Canada, Great Britain, India, and the United States* (Princeton, NJ: Princeton University Press).

Cho, K.-S. (1996), *Haplijeok Seontaek: Hankookeui Seongeowa Yukwonja* [Rational Choice: Elections and Voters in South Korea] (Seoul: Hanwool Academy).

Choe, J.-Y., and Kim, S.-H. (2000), 'Jiyeokgan Geoligameul Tonghaeseo Bon Jiyeokjueuieui Silsanggwa Munjejeom' [Understanding the Reality and Problem of Regionalism through a Sense of Regional Social Distance], *Korean Journal of Social Issues* 1(1), 65–95.

Choi, J.-J. (1993), *Hankook Minjujueuieui Iron* [The Theory of Korean Democracy] (Seoul: Hangilsa).

Choi, J.-Y. (2008), 'Jiyeokgamjeongeun Jonjaehaneunga?: Jiyeokgamjeonge Daehan Ganjeobcheugjeong Gibeobeul Jungsimeuro' [Does Regional Prejudice Exist?: A Study on Regional Prejudice through an Unobtrusive Measurement], *Journal of Contemporary Politics* 1(1), 199–222.

Choi, J.-Y., and Cho, J. (2005), 'Jiyeokkyunyeoleui Byunhwa Ganeungsunge Daehan Gyeonhumjeok Gochal' [Is Regional Cleavage in Korea Disappearing?], *Korean Political Science Review* 39(3), 375–394.

Chung, K. (2005), 'Jiyeokgamjeonggwa Jiyeokgaldeunginsikui Byeonhwa: 1988nyeon 2003nyeon Bigyo' [Changes in Regionalism and Social Cognition of Regional Conflicts between 1988 and 2003 in Korea], *Korean Journal of Sociology* 39(2), 69–99.

Deegan-Krause, K. (2007), 'New Dimensions of Political Cleavage', in R. J. Dalton and H.-D. Klingemann, eds, *The Oxford Handbook of Political Behavior* (New York: Oxford University Press), 538–556.

Han, S., Kim, J., and Choi, J. (2019), '86sedae, Gyunyeolinga? Heosanginga?: 86sedaeui Jeongchijeok Taedo Byeonhwae Daehan Gyeongheomjeok bunseok' [Is the 86 Generation Divergent or Illusive?: An Empirical Analysis of the Change of Their Political Attitudes], *Peace Studies* 27(1), 39–83.

Hong, Y.-L. (2018), 'Comparison of Representatives' Ideological Orientation', 17th–20th National Assembly, Chosunilbo, 8 January 2018, https://www.chosun.com/site/data/html_dir/2018/01/08/2018010801043.html., accessed 6 August 2021.

Hong, Y. O., and Lee, H. K. (2001), 'Ammugjeok Yeonhabgeomsae Uihan Jiyeok pyeongyeonui Cheugjeong' [Measurement of Regional Prejudice by Implicit Association Test], *The Korean Journal of social and Personality Psychology* 15(1), 185–204.

Hooghe, L., and Marks, G. (2018), 'Cleavage Theory Meets Europe's Crises: Lipset, Rokkan, and the Transnational Cleavage', *Journal of European Public Policy* 25(1), 109–135.

Jhee, B.-K. (2015), 'Minjuhwa Ihu Jiyeokgamjeongui Byeonhwawa Wonin' [Changes in Regional Antagonism and Its Causes in Korea], *Korean Party Studies Review* 14(1), 63–91.

Jung, J.-D., and Lee, J.-M. (2018), 'Yeongnam Jiyeokjueui Tupyohaengtaeui Byeonhwayeongu' [A Study on the Change of Regional Voting Behavior in Yeongnam Area], *Korean Journal of Political Science* 26(4), 59–92.

Jung, J. P. (2015), 'Daetongryeonseongeoreul Tonghae Bon Jiyeokjueuiui Sijaggwa Geu Byeonhwa Yangsang' [The Origin of Regionalism and Its Patterns of Change in Korean Presidential Elections], *Journal of Korean Politics* 24(2), 83–119.

Kang, M. (2001), 'Hankookseongeoeui Juyojaengjeom: Jiyeokjueuineun Eonje Sijakdoeeonneunga? Yeokdae Daetongryeong Seongeoreul Gibaneuro?' [When Did Regionalism in Presidential Elections in Korea Begin?], *Korea and World Politics* 17(2), 127–158.

Kang, W. T. (2003), *Hankookeui Seongeo Jeongchi: Inyeom, Jiyeok, Sedaewa Midieo* [Electoral Politics in South Korea: Ideology, Region, Generation and Media] (Seoul: Purungil).

Kang, M. (2005), 'Jiyeokjueui Jeongchiwa Hankook Jeongdangchejeui Jaepyeon' [The Changing Korean Party System?], *Korean Party Studies Review* 4(2), 249–270.

Kang, W. T. (2011), 'Hankookeseo Jeongchi Gyunyeolgujoeui Yeogsajeok Giwon: Lipset-Rokkan modeleui Jeokyong' [Formation of Political Cleavage in South Korea: Application of the Lipset–Rokkan Model], *Korea and World Politics* 27(3), 99–129.

Kang, W. C. (2016), 'Local Economic Voting and Residence-Based Regionalism in South Korea: Evidence from the 2007 Presidential Election', *Journal of East Asian Studies* 16(3), 349–369.

Keating, M., and Loughlin, J., eds (1997), *The Political Economy of Regionalism* (London: Frank Cass & Co. Ltd).

Kim, J. K. (1987), 'Younghonam Daehaksangeui Sanghogan Chaijigak Yeongu' [Youngnam and Honam Students' Perception of the Differences between Youngnam and Honam People], *Korean Journal of Social and Personality Psychology* 3(2), 113–147.

Kim, H. S. (1988), 'Jiyeokgan Gojeonggwannyeomgwa Pyeongyeonui Silsang: Sedaegan Jeoniga Jonjaehaneunga?' [Reality of Regional Stereotypes and Prejudice: Does Intergenerational Transmission Exist?', in Korean Psychological Association, ed., *Understanding Regional Sentiment from the Perspective of Psychology: Regional Stereotypes and Solution* (Seoul: Sungwonsa), 123–169.

Kim, J. K. (1988), 'Jiyeokgamjungui Silsanggwa Haesobangan' [Reality of Regional Sentiment and Its Solution], in Korean Psychological Association, ed., *Understanding Regional Sentiment from the Perspective of Psychology: Regional Stereotypes and Solution* (Seoul: Sungwonsa), 113–147.

Kim, H. S. (1993), 'Jiyeok Gojeong-gwannyeomi Gwiinpandangwa Insanghyeongseonge Michineun Yeonghyang' [The Effect of Regional Stereotypes on Attribution and Impression Judgment], *Korean Journal of Social and Personality Psychology* 7(1), 53–70.

Kim, M. H. (1995), 'Jeongchi Kyunyeol, Jeongdang Jeongchi, Guegrigo Jiyeok Jueui' [Political Cleavage, Party Politics and Regionalism], *Korean Political Science Review* 28(2), 216–237.

Kim, H. S. (1999), 'Jibdanbeomjue Daehan Gojeong-gwannyeom, Gamjeonggwa Pyeongyeon' [Stereotypes, Affect and Prejudice regarding Group Category], *Korean Journal of Social and Personality Psychology* 13(1), 1–33.

Kim, H. S. (2001), 'Jibdanbeomjue Daehan Sinnyeomgwa Hogamdoga Pyeongyeonjeok Pandane Michineun Yeonghyang: Migukeui Sungpyeongyeon, Injongpyeongyeongwa Hankookeui Sungpyeongyeon, Jiyeokpyeongyeoneui Bigyo' [The Effect of Beliefs and Affect Regarding Group Categories on Prejudiced Judgment: A Cross-Cultural Comparison between Gender and Racial Prejudice in America and Gender and the Regional Prejudice in Korea], *Korean Journal of Social and Personality Psychology* 15(1), 1–16.

Kim, S. M., and Lee, H.-W. (2015), 'Chulsinji Geojujawa Bigeojujaeui Jiyeokjueui Haengtae Bigyobunseok' [New Approach of Regionalism Based on Hometown-Residents and Non-Hometown Residents], *Korean Political Science Review* 49(5), 243–266.

Kim, B. J. (2002). 'Sahoejeog Beomjuhwaga Jiyeoggamjeong Hyeongseonge Michineun Yeonghyang', [The Influence of Social Categorization on Regional Prejudice Formation], *The Korean Journal of Social and Personality Psychology*, 16(1), 1–17.

Kim, W. (2004), 'Hankook Jiyeokjueuieui Jiyeokbyeol Teukseonggwa Byeonhwa Ganeungseong: Daejeon-Chungcheongjiyeokeul Jungsimeuro' [The Regional Characteristics and Prospect for Changes in Korean Regionalism: With Particular Focus on Daejon-Chungchung Region], *Twenty-First Century Political Science Review* 14(1), 83–105.

Kim, Y. C., and Cho, Y.-H. (2015), 'Jiyeokjueuijeok Jeongchigudoeui Sahoesimrijeok Todae: 'Sangjingjeok Jiyeokjueui'roeui Jinhwa' [Social Psychological Foundation of Regional

Political Structure: Evolution of Symbolic Regionalism?], *Korean Party Studies Review* 14(1), 93–128.
Kinder, D. R., and Kam, C. D. (2009), *Us against Them: Ethnocentric Foundations of American Opinion* (Chicago, IL: University of Chicago Press).
Knutsen, O. (2010), 'The Regional Cleavage in Western Europe: Can Social Composition, Value Orientations and Territorial Identities Explain the Impact of Region on Party Choice?', *West European Politics* 33(3), 553–585.
Kriesi, H. (1998), 'The Transformation of Cleavage Politics: The 1997 Stein Rokkan Lecture', *European Journal of Political Research* 33(2), 165–85.
Kwon, K. (2004), 'Regionalism in South Korea: Its Origins and Role in Her Democratisation', *Politics & Society* 32(4), 545–574.
Kymlicka, W. (2007), *Multicultural Odysseys: Navigating the New International Politics of Diversity* (New York: Oxford University Press).
Layman, G. C., Carsey, T. M., and Horowitz, J. M. (2006), 'Party Polarization in American Politics: Characteristics, Causes, and Consequences', *Annual Review of Political Science* 9 (1), 83–110.
Lee, J. S. (1959). 'Paldoinui Jiyeogteugseonge Daehan Seonibgwannyeom' [The Stereotypes of the Natives of Eight Provinces], *Sasanggye*, 77: 74–87.
Lee, N. Y. (1998), 'Yougwonjauei Jiyeokjueui Seonghyanggwa Tupyo' [Regionalism and Voting Behaviour in the Korean Electorates], in N. Y. Lee, ed., *The Korean Election II: The 15th Presidential Election* (Seoul: Purungil), 11–44.
Lee, H. K. (2003), *Yeongojueui (Nepotism)* (Seoul: Bupmoonsa).
Lee, K. Y. (2011), *Hankookineui Tupyo Hangtae* [Korean Voting Behaviour] (Seoul: Humanitas).
Lee, J. (2015), 'Aged Minds of Current Citizens: The Changing Nature of Regional Prejudices in the South Korean Public', M.A. dissertation, The Graduate School, Seoul National University.
Lee, K.-Y., and Park, J.-S. (2011), 'Jiyeokmin Hogamdoga Jeongdangjijie Michineun Younghyang' [Effects of Regional Feelings upon the Party Support in Korea], *Korea and World Politics* 27(3), 131–158.
Lee, H.-C., and Repkine, A. (2020), 'Changes in and Continuity of Regionalism in South Korea: A Spatial Analysis of the 2017 Presidential Election', *Asian Survey* 60(3), 417–40.
Lipset, M. S., and Rokkan, S. (1967), 'Cleavage Structure, Party Systems, and Voter Alignments: An Introduction', in M. S. Lipset and S. Rokkan, eds, *Party Systems and Voter Alignments: Cross-National Perspectives* (New York: Macmillan), 1–64.
Min, K. H. (1989), 'Gwonwijueui Seonggyeokgwa Sahoejeok Pyeongyeon: Daehaksaengjibdaneul Jungsimeuro' [Authoritarian Personality and Social Prejudice among College Students], *Korean Journal of Social and Personality Psychology* 4(2), 146–168.
Moon, S.k-N. (1984), 'Jiyeokpyeonchawa Galdeunge Gwanhan Han Yeongu: Yonghonam Dujiyeokeul Jungsimeuro' [Inter-Regional Disparities and Conflict: Focused on the Yongnam and Honam Regions], *Korean Journal of Sociology* 18(2), 51–76.
Moon, W. (2005), 'Decomposition of Regional Voting in South Korea: Ideological Conflicts and Regional Interests', *Party Politics* 11(5), 579–599.
Moon, W. (2017), 'Jiyeokjuui Tupyoui Teugseonggwa Byeonhwa: Ilonjeog Jaengjeomgwa Gyeongheombunseog' [The Nature of Regional Voting and Its Change: Theoretical Issues and Empirical Analyses], *Journal of Legislative Studies* 23(1), 81–111.
Na, E.-Y., and Kwon, J. (2002), 'Ammugjeok Yeonhab Geomsae Euihan Jiyeok Pyeongyeoneui Gangdo Cheukjeong Mich EungYong: Saturi Eumseongjageukeui Hyogwareul Jungsimeuro'

[Measurement of the Strength of Regional Prejudice by Implicit Association Test and Its Application], *Korea Journal of Social and Personal Psychology* 16(1), 51–74.

Na, K.-C. (1990), 'Jiyeok(min)ganeui Sahwejeok Georigam' [Sense of Social Distance among Natives and Residents], in Korean Sociological Association, ed., *Korea's Regionalism and Regional Conflict* (Seoul: Sungwonsa), 79–100.

Ohn, M.-G. (1997), 'Yeokdae Daetongryeong Seongeogyeolgwae Natanan Jiyeokjueuieui Chuiwa Yangsang' [Trend and Pattern of Regionalism in Presidential Elections], *Korean Journal of Sociology* 31(3), 737–757.

Ohn, M.-G. (2003), 'Hankook Jeongdangchegyeui Hyeongseonggwa Byeonhwae Gwanhan Iron (1948–2000): Jiyeokjueui, Seongeobeob, Geurigo Jeongdangchegye' [Theorizing the Formation of the Korean Party System (1948–2000): Regionalism, Electoral Rule, and Party System], *Korean Journal of Sociology* 37(3), 135–157.

Park, G. S., and Han, D. U. (2003), 'Yonghonamineui Sahoegujo Yoin Jigakgwa Sahoejeongcheseongeui Sangdaebagtalgwa Jibhabjeonlage Michineun Yeonghyang' [Effects of Perceived Social Structure Variables and Social Identity on Relative Deprivation and Collective Strategies in Youngnam and Honam Regional Areas], *Korean Journal of Social and Personality Psychology* 17(2), 59–72.

Park, Y.-H., Kim, M.-S., Park, W.-H., Kang, S.-G., and Koo, B. S. (2016), 'Je 20dae Gukhweuiwonseongeo Dangseonja Mich Hubojaeui Inyeomseonghyanggwa Jeongchaektaedo' [Ideology and Policy Positions of the Candidates and the Elects in the 20th Korean National Assembly Election], *Journal of Legislative Studies* 22(3), 117–58.

Schoultz, Å. von (2017), 'Party Systems and Voter Alignments], in K. Arzheimer, J. Evans, and M. S. Lewis-Beck, eds, *The Sage Handbook of Electoral Behaviour* (London: Sage), 30–55.

Selway, J. S. (2009), 'Constitutions, Cleavages and Coordination: A Socio-Institutional Theory of Public Goods Provision', Ph.D. dissertation, University of Michigan, Ann Arbor.

Shin, B.-R. (1996), 'Hankookeui Jiyeok Gamjeongeui Yeogsajeok Baegyeong: Honam phobiareul Jungsimeuro' [Historical Background of Korean Regional Sentiment: Focusing on Honam Phobia], in Korean Political Science Association, ed., *Reflection on Korean Politics: Premodernity, Modernity, and Postmodernity* (Seoul: Hanwool Academy), 110–139.

Tajfel, H. (1970), 'Experiments in Intergroup Discrimination', *Scientific American* 223, 96–102.

Tajfel, H., and Turner, J. C. (1986), 'The Social Identity Theory of Intergroup Behaviour', in S. Worchel and W. G. Austin, eds, *Psychology of Intergroup Relations* (Chicago, IL: Nelson Hall).

Yoon, J. (2017), 'Gyochaabryeoggwa Jiyeokjueuii Tupyoeui Byeonhwa: Je 14–18dae Daetongryeong Seongeoreul Jungsimeuro' [Cross-Pressure and the Change of Regional Voting: Evidence from the 14th to the 18th Korean Presidential Elections], *Korean Party Studies Review* 16(3), 5–45.

Yoon, Kwang-Il (2012), 'Jiyeokjueuiwa Je 19dae Chongseon' [Regionalism and the 19th General Election of South Korea], *Korean Journal of Political Science* 20(2), 113–138.

Yoon, K.-I. (2017), 'Jiyeokjueuiui Byeonhwa: 1988nyeon, 2003nyeon Mit 2016nyeon Josagyeolgwa Bigyo' [Change and Continuity in Regionalism: A Comparison of 1988, 2003, and 2016 Survey Results], *Journal of Legislative Studies* 23(1), 113–149.

Yoon, K.-I. (2018), 'Gyunyeolgujowa 19dae Daeseon: Wanjeonhan Gyunyeolroseo Jiyeokgyunyeol' [Cleavage Structure and the 19th Presidential Election: Regional Cleavage as Full Cleavage], *Journal of Korean Politics* 27(1), 241–280.

Yoon, K.-I. (2019), 'Jiyeokgyunyeoleui Yujiwa Byeonhwa: Je 19dae Daeseoneui Gyeongheomjeok Bunseok' [Persistence and Change of Regional Cleavage at the 19th Presidential Election], *Korea and World Politics* 35(2), 37–73.

Yoon, K.-I. (2020), 'Change and Continuity in the 21st General Election', *Korea Observer* 51(2), 179–204.

Yu, E.-Y. (1990), 'Regionalism in the South Korean Job Market: An Analysis of Regional-Origin Inequality among Migrants in Seoul', *Pacific Affairs* 63(1), 24–39.

Yu, E.-Y. (2003), 'Hankookeui Jiyeokjueui: Sahoe Gak Bunya Jidogeub Insa Guseonge Natanan Jiyeokpyeonjungdo' [Korea's Regionalism: An Analysis of Regional Bias in Elite Recruitment], in S.-K. Kim, ed., *What Nepotism Means in Korea: Korea's Collectivism and Network* (Seoul: Tradition & Modernity), 128–191.

CHAPTER 6

CONSERVATIVE DEMOCRATISATION

WOOJIN KANG

1. INTRODUCTION

SOUTH Korea celebrated its thirtieth anniversary of democratisation in 2017. At the same time, it experienced the unprecedented Candlelight movement, in which the power of a total of 17 million citizens finally achieved the impeachment of the corrupt President Park Geun-hye. Over the thirty years since democratisation in 1987, South Korea has successfully institutionalised democracy; during this period, the country has completed three government turnovers without suspension of the constitutional system.

South Korea's successful democratic institutionalisation has been praised by various authoritative international organisations. According to the Polity Index, South Korea's democracy is representative of a stable democracy. After democratisation in 1987, it remained at the 6-point level, just above 'democracy or a mixed system' (−5 points to 5 points) in 1989. After the peaceful regime change in 1997, the country's index rose by 2 points to achieve a relatively high and stable 8 points.[1]

Freedom House in the United States annually publishes the Liberalization Index, another representative index of levels of democracy. The index (100 points) combines political rights (40 points) and civil rights (60 points) to classify countries as free, partly free, or not free,[2] and as of 2019, South Korea was classified as a free country with an index of 83 points out of 100. According to the score converted back to a 1–7 scale, South Korea has fluctuated since 1998, but has maintained the highest level of 1–2 points for both political and civil rights.

The Economist Index Unit[3] rated South Korea a full democracy from 2008 to 2014, after the country passed a two-turnover test (Huntington 1991). Since 2014, South Korea has been ranked a flawed democracy, but as of 2019, South Korea ranked twenty-third, higher than Japan (twenty-fourth) and the United States (twenty-fifth), placing it directly in the range of full democracies.

Furthermore, in a recent analysis utilising Varieties of Democracy data, South Korea was twenty-third out of ninety-one cases that had made democratic advances since their transitions to democracy (Mainwaring and Bizzarro 2019). Furthermore, as of 2017, South Korea showed the second greatest progress following that of Portugal and was one of eight countries categorised as a liberal democracy.

However, looking at the other side of the thirty years of democratisation, we see very different results. These thirty years of successful democratisation in South Korea failed to democratise the hegemony system created in the process of industrialisation through top-down authoritarian mobilisation. Ironically, the period of successful democratisation in South Korea created another cartel system.

First, the democratic transition process established a highly centralised single-term presidential system combined with a majoritarian style electoral system. This winner-takes-all system served as a high entry barrier for new actors. Accordingly, the progressive party did not get any seats until the two-vote mixed electoral system was adopted in the 2004 legislative election.

Moreover, the party system generated during the democratic transition was based on region rather than ideology and programme. The political representation of the regional party system was ideologically homogeneous and narrow. With a frozen regional party system, the voices for minority groups, such as non-regular workers and youth, failed to get representation.

Finally, as a consequence of the nonresponsive new democratic system, South Korea's democratic support has been sluggish. Based on the Korean Barometer Survey (KDB) and the Asian Barometer Survey (ABS), despite overwhelming support for democracy as an idea and its suitability for the country, South Koreans' support for democracy as a principle and in reality has not been solid. From 1998 to 2015, South Koreans' preference for the democratic system over the alternative did not exceed 70 per cent, ranging from 44.86 per cent (KDB 2001) to 69.94 per cent (KDB 2010). Satisfaction with democracy between 2003 and 2015 was even lower, ranging from 52.1 per cent (ABS 2006) to 63.12 per cent (ABS 2015).

The question arises of how to analyse these contrasting aspects of the outcomes of South Korean democratisation. Democracy cannot be equated with elite circulation (Schumpeter 1942): Its central tenet is 'the continuing responsiveness of the government to the preferences of its citizens, considered as political equals' (Dahl 1971: 1). Over the past thirty years of democratisation, how well did South Korea's democracy realise the idea of democratisation?

The goal of this chapter is to evaluate South Korea's thirty years of experience as a democracy from the perspective of a conservative democratisation process. The main explanation for South Korea's conservative democratisation derives from two processes. First, democratisation as it derived from the dynamic process that was the June Uprising ended up maintaining the elite's political cartel, composed of both the democratic opposition and the authoritarian ruling bloc. Second, the institutionalisation of democracy that followed the democratic transition could not transform the conservative political cartel into the democratic one that reflected the preferences of the many citizens. Ironically, the historical origin of the conservative political cartel that the dynamic process of South Korean democratisation generated was the period of authoritarian rule under Park Chung-hee (1961–1979). This chapter analyses the conservative characteristics of the 1987 system created by democratisation, focusing on three dimensions (the mode of transition, setting the rules of the game, and the regional party system) and the consequences for minority representation.

2. Mode of Transition: Between Conversion and Cooperative

According to research on democratisation, there are four different modes of transition: conversion, cooperative, collapse, and foreign intervention (Guo and Stradiotto, 2014). We pay attention here to the differences and similarities between conversion and cooperative democratisation. In the case of conversion, the incumbent holds power and advantage over the opposition, and the incumbent takes the lead in democratisation. Other scholars call this process transformation (Huntington 1991), transaction (Share and Mainwaring 1986), and reform through extrication (Munck and Carol 1997).

Students of the theory of democratic transition report that the most beneficial process for the stability of democracy is the 'pacted transition (cooperative)'. Guo and Stadiotto (2014: 7–8) conducted an empirical analysis and determined that since 1900, out of 128 nations, 37 countries transitioned by cooperative pacts and only two cases (5 per cent) reverted to dictatorship. Additionally, those countries maintained ten-year polity ratings of 7.76, higher than the scores for any other transition type besides foreign intervention (8.25). In contrast, in the conversion mode of transition, out of forty-eight countries, twenty-two (46 per cent) regressed; furthermore, the ten-year polity rating for countries that transitioned by conversion was 4.60, much lower than the score for cooperative transitions.

The existing literature categorises South Korea as one of the exemplary cases of the cooperative transition between an authoritarian incumbent and the opposition (Huntington 1991; Guo and Stradiotto 2014; Im 1990). O'Donnell and Schmitter (1986) give a thorough perspective of the cooperative transition in South Korea through a strategic comparative analysis of major actors during the democratic transition, and Im (1990) advanced their theoretical framework more rigorously in the context of South Korea's democratic transition.

According to this perspective, South Korea's democratic transition was quite different from the transition in the Philippines. It did not result in the political rupture that can cause the demise of authoritarian rule. Instead, it was a compromise between the authoritarian incumbent and the opposition, and it was only possible after a protracted stand-off that convinced both camps to accept the second best as a possible solution to escape a catastrophe (Im 2020). The South Korean case is also different from Taiwan's conversion; in Taiwan, authoritarian incumbents led the democratisation process.

According to O'Donnell and Schmitter (1986), authoritarian regimes suffer from a lack of legitimacy, which leads them to liberalise their rule, and liberalisation, which allows some political and civil rights, paves the way for civil society's resurrection; this resurrection accompanies mass mobilisation. During the democratisation process, the role of civil society is critical (Fishman 2017). When an authoritarian incumbent confronts the rapidly rising cost of oppression, the regime is divided into hardliners and softliners. The former are risk-insensitive players in that they attempt to repress the democratic movement at all cost, whereas the latter are risk-averse, strategic players. The democratic opposition is also differentiated into radical maximalists and moderate reformers; the radical opposition argues for maximal mobilisation of the masses to secure fully fledged democracy, whereas reformers seek compromise to avoid high costs. The transition of democratisation hinges on the softliners' role in the authoritarian regime and that of the reformer in the opposition (Im 1990: 59–60). Even though the cooperative perspective appreciates softliners' significant roles in both authoritarian regimes and the opposition, it emphasises opposition-led negotiated pacts (Guo and Stradiotto 2014: 25).

Now there is the question of how well this perspective reflects Korea's democratisation process. Prior research focusing on the strategic choices of actors has significant limitations. First, researchers have considered the division between hardliners and softliners within authoritarian governments the most critical condition for democratic compromise, but according to those involved, there was no such division in Korea, as the authoritarian incumbent confronted the citizenry's massive resistance. According to Chun Doo-hwan (2017), Roh Tae-woo was not the person who suggested the 29 June Declaration. Chun argued that Roh refused to accept the president's direct election at first, and Chun's press secretary (Kim 1992) also confirmed that President Chun initiated the Declaration, not Roh. Roh (2011), however, gave a different story: that he had a plan and Chun had agreed to it. Details of the testimony regarding the negotiation between Chun the incumbent and Roh the successor also differ somewhat (Kim 1992; Chun 2017; Park 2005; Roh 2011). A witness on Chun's side emphasised his initiative, whereas those on Roh's side argued his central role in drawing up the declaration. Common opinion across the testimony confirmed that there was no notable split between hardliner and softliner in facing the June Uprising in 1987.

Second, this perspective underestimates the initiative of the ruling authoritarian forces in the process of democratisation. The authoritarian incumbent (Democratic Justice Party, DJP) was not a passive player forced to accept the path to democratisation after being driven to a political dead end. The authoritarian ruling forces in Korea did not pre-emptively lead the process of democratisation, unlike in other cases of conversion from authoritarian rule, but neither was the authoritarian party a group of losers who surrendered at the edge of a cliff. Prior researchers who emphasised the compromise between the authoritarian regime and the opposition parties did not properly acknowledge the first initiative.

Before democratisation in 1987, there were three important political stages: liberalisation at the end of 1983, a legislative election in 1985, and the confrontation from 1985 to 1987. Analysing the pre-democratisation process from a long-term perspective, covering all three stages, reveals that the authoritarian ruling forces actively confronted the political situation through strategic calculations, even though their efforts often went wrong. The liberation phase that began at the end of 1983 and marked the beginning of democratisation did not spring forth out of pressure from below, but came from the excessive confidence of the ruling forces.[4]

According to prior research, the 29 June Declaration was a great democratic compromise that was the political outcome of the catastrophic balance between the authoritarian regime and the democratic opposition (Im 2014: 616). It was not a pre-emptive response to the explosive increase in democratisation demand. However, it is also important to point out that the DJP played a significant role at the critical juncture of democratisation.

The 29 June Declaration was not announced after consultations with the opposition party and civil society; rather, it was a one-sided measure that the authoritarian administration carefully planned to reverse the political situation. With the declaration, the DJP was able to immediately convert the political scene. The Declaration comprised eight points: (1) amending the constitution to provide for the direct election of presidents; (2) revising the presidential election law to ensure free and competitive elections; (3) granting amnesty to political prisoners, including Kim Dae-jung; (4) protecting human dignity and extending the right of habeas corpus; (5) abolishing the country's Basic Press Law and restoring press freedoms; (6) strengthening local and educational autonomy; (7) moving the political climate towards dialogue and compromise; and (8) achieving substantial social reform. The 29 June Declaration concluded that the critical period began with the 13 April measure for maintaining the constitution (*hoheon jochi*).

With strong support for the 29 June Declaration from both the opposition party and civil society, the street's contentious politics transformed rapidly into the politics for a democratic transition. The declaration was neither a one-sided concession nor a victory for the DJP; it reflected demands raised during the liberation phase and included measures that had not been requested directly by the civil society (e.g. one for social purification). The final negotiation proposal set the limits for DJP compromise (S. Kang 2017). The DJP was neither an active player that initiated democratisation proactively nor a passive loser that had to embrace all of civil society's demands at the edge of a political cliff.

In the founding presidential election of 1987, the authoritarian regime's strategic calculation of accepting direct elections in the 29 June Declaration paid dividends. Failing to unify the candidacy, Kim Young-sam and Kim Dae-jung from the democratic opposition camp ran separately for the election, and Roh Tae-woo, Chun Doo-hwan's successor, won the election with 36.6 per cent of the votes. The authoritarian ruling power gained legitimacy by succeeding in maintaining power through direct elections by the people. In the first legislative election, the thirteenth congressional election in

1988, held the year after democratisation, the DJP failed to gain a majority of seats but maintained its status as the ruling party (125 seats out of 299). Facing political difficulties due to pressure from the opposition parties that held the majority, the DJP transformed itself into a hegemonic mega party (Democratic Liberal Party, DLP) by a three-party merger with the Reunification Democratic Party (RDP) led by Kim Young-sam and the New Democratic Republican Party (NDRP) led by Kim Jong-pil. With the creation of the DLP, with its slogan of the convergence of industrial and democratic forces, the authoritarian regime's successor was able to claim further political legitimacy.

3. Setting the Rules: The 1987 Constitution and the Majoritarian Style Electoral System

After the 29 June Declaration, the politics of the street for democratisation turned to the politics for constitutional reform. Meanwhile, a Great Workers' Struggle took place from July to September 1987.[5] The revision of the Constitution established the so-called 87 system[6] as the constitutional system.

In a representative example of the conflicts between democracy and constitutionalism during democratic transitions (Choi 2004), the 87 constitutional system had significant drawbacks in terms of its main players, processes, and contents. First, regarding the main players, the constitutional reform in 1987 was achieved by agreement between major political forces; the entire process was guided by negotiations between political elites. It is paradoxical that introducing a democratic constitutional system, which was a result of the uprising in June 1987—a civil revolution from below—was dominated by political negotiations between the major political parties outside of civil society.[7] In fact, neither did citizens play any meaningful role in the process of constitutional amendment.

Second, the basic framework for constitutional amendment focusing on restoring procedural democracy was already determined by the mode of democratic transition involving the two opposing parties (the 29 June Declaration). The 1987 constitutional reform in Korea is similar to the process in Spain in terms of the minimalist approach to the scope of the revision. The rapid constitutional amendment based on a minimalism strategy had the advantage of reducing uncertainty during the democratic transition and shortening the schedule for democratisation (Im 2014: 619).

Third, the 1987 constitutional system focused on the political interests of the opposing parties, reorganising the power structure rather than on the long-term and macroscopic goal of establishing a democratic system. Therefore, the democratic agenda raised during the June Uprising and the Great Workers' Struggle was markedly reduced (C. Park 2005: 36–39).

The ninth constitutional amendment in 1987, which was made through negotiations between the major parties, has four main characteristics (U. Kang 2017). First, Article 67, paragraph 1 introduced a direct election for a one-term president to end the military regime and prevent long-term rule.[8] To prevent military intervention in political processes, Article 5, paragraph 2 specified the military's duty of political neutrality.[9]

Second, although it was not possible to specify national resistance as an independent fundamental right, the preamble of the Constitution stipulated the succession of the 19 April revolution's democratic ideology against injustice. Additionally, the constitutional amendment introduced the right of habeas corpus (Article 12), guaranteed freedom of expression, and prohibited restrictions on the media and publications through censorship. In addition, efforts were made to guarantee labour rights. Article 32 stipulated a minimum wage system, and discrimination against women in terms of wages and working conditions was prohibited. A legal foundation was laid for guaranteeing three labour rights to public officials.[10]

Third, the ninth constitutional revision of 1987 laid the legal foundation for the practical operation of democratic checks and balances by reducing the president's power and strengthening the National Assembly's power. Article 61 revived the national audit system, which is a means of monitoring the executive branch. Article 63 eliminated the president's right to dissolve the National Assembly and maintained its function as a check on the executive branch by changing the right to dismiss the prime minister and other ministers to the right to recommend their dismissal.

Fourth, with the introduction of the Constitutional Court, the function of adjudicating unconstitutional laws became independent from the Supreme Court. The president, the National Assembly, and the Supreme Court would each recommend three constitutional judges (Article 111).[11] In many aspects, the 1987 constitution, focusing on restoring procedural democracy, was a return to the Constitution before the Yushin system (W. Kang 2017).

The 1987 constitutional amendments, which focused on changing the way of electing the president through negotiations between political elites, was weak in creating a constitutional basis for a new democracy. It was weak as well in providing an institutional mechanism to check the highly centralised administrative power (e.g. independence of the Board of Audit and Inspection). More importantly, it did not pay attention to establishing the constitutional basis for local autonomy.

Like constitutional reform, reforming the electoral system (the rules for electing representatives) was also a process of political negotiation and calculations among the four parties based on the thirteenth presidential election results in 1987. The electoral system of the authoritarian regimes before democratisation was a distorted system that brought great political benefits to the ruling party. Two representatives were elected in each district and the president in fact nominated one-third of the members of the National Assembly. After democratisation, special interest was given to reforming the electoral system in order to democratise the distorted political representation system.

The fierce negotiations among the major political parties resulted in the introduction of single-member districts based on a plurality system, while also allotting a certain number of seats in the National Assembly for proportional representation. The electoral reform assigned 224 district seats and 75 proportional seats out of the total 299 seats. Formally, the new electoral system was mixed; in practice, however, it functioned as a majoritarian system that enormously benefited the major party.[12]

The majoritarian style electoral system, combined with the centralised single-term presidency, strengthened the constitutional system's winner-takes-all character. This system performed two contrasting functions. Given the very high political prize for the winner of the single-term presidency, there was fierce internal competition among the major political parties, but the system also served as a high threshold to entry for new political forces.

4. The Frozen Regional Party System

The most important feature of Korea's democratisation is that the political party system based on regions was institutionalised through two founding elections (the first presidential election and the legislative election after the democratic opening in 1987 and 1988, respectively). The parties constituting the regional political system that emerged under the centralised presidential system have a fundamentally different character from the regionalist parties in Western Europe (Mazzoleni and Mueller 2016). The regional party's social base in Korea is not based on distinct identities such as language or ethnicity, nor does it seek secession.

In the first direct presidential election after the democratic opening in December 1987, four major leaders ran for President: Roh Tae-woo, the DJP candidate; Kim Jong-pil, NDRP candidate and successor of the Park Chung-hee government; Kim Dae-jung, Peace Democratic Party (PDP) candidate and the most influential political symbol of the democratic movement during authoritarian rule since the 1970s; and Kim Young-sam, RDP candidate and political rival cum comrade of Kim Dae-jung in the fight for democracy. The political strongholds of the four political leaders were, by accident, divergent, with Roh and Kim Young-sam taking the North and South Gyeongsang provinces (southeast region), respectively, Kim Dae-jung taking the Jeolla provinces (southwest region), and Kim Jong-pil taking South Chungcheong Province (south-central region).

In the founding (thirteenth) presidential election in 1987, the four political leaders gained overwhelming support from their political strongholds: Kim Dae-jung won 88.39 per cent of the vote, Kim Young-sam won 53.66 per cent, Roh Tae-woo won 68.13 per cent, and Kim Jong-pil won 45 per cent. After the election, the fierce negotiations among the four parties resulted in the introduction of single-member plurality districts. The first legislative election under the new system, in April 1988, set the momentum for establishing the regional party system at the legislative level that manifested in the previous year's presidential election. The PDP created by Kim Dae-jung swept all thirty-six seats in the Jeolla provinces, Kim Young-sam's RDP earned twenty-three seats out of thirty-eight in South Gyeongsang Province, the DJP controlled by Roh acquired twenty-five of twenty-nine seats in North Gyeongsang Province, and the NDRP led by Kim Jong-pil garnered thirteen out of eighteen seats in South Chungcheong Province.

A regional party system with a regional stronghold was characterised as representing the ideological homogeneity of the political party system. In the conservative bloc, the DJP and NDRP shared historical roots in the Park Chung-hee era in ideological orientation and central party personnel. In the liberal bloc, the RDP and PDP had long been part of the same democratic opposition before the split ahead of the 1987 presidential election because they could not unify behind a single candidate. The two parties were not significantly different in terms of ideology; the narrow ideological spectrum of political representation by the new political party system failed to represent new labour issues presented during the Great Workers' Struggle followed by the June 1987 uprising. In short, the new regional party system was a modern version of the previous frozen party system of 1958 (Choi 2002: 140). In this regard, it may be said that the regional political system created by democracy has its origins in the period of authoritarian rule.

With the institutionalisation of the regional party system, the democratic–authoritarian cleavage that lasted during the authoritarian period (1961–1987) was replaced by a newly emerged regional cleavage. Since then, the regional cleavage has dominated Korean politics. The political influence of the cleavage reached its culmination in the three-party merger of the DJP, RDP, and NDRP, which institutionalised the political isolation of the Jeolla region; that merger created the hegemonic DLP with more than 200 seats. The new political cleavage exercised decisive political influence when Kim Dae-jung won a narrow victory in the 1997 presidential election through a regional coalition with the United Liberal Democrats (ULD) led by Kim Jong-pil after he separated from the DLP in a serious political conflict. With his victory, Korea achieved the first peaceful power transfer since liberation in 1945.

The regional party system initially started from the four-party system through the 1988 legislative election. However, it was sometimes a three-party system, as in the 1992, 1996, and 2016 legislative elections. The regional party system was frozen in place with the Democratic Party's (DP) political stronghold in the Jeolla provinces and the Grand National Party's (GNP) stronghold in North Gyeongsang Province.

The political consequence of the institutionalised regional party system was the freezing of the regional cleavages that structured party competition. Not all social cleavages translated into political splits (Sartori 1969). After Lipset and Rokkan's pioneering work (1967), Bartolini and Mair (1990) specified the three steps for structuring political cleavages: interest orientation, cultural and ideological orientation, and organisational manifestation. To institutionalise political conflict, it is necessary for political parties to first mobilise distinct group identities. When new cleavages emerge after the party system is frozen, it is not easy to politicise the new divide (Zielinski 2002), and Korea's experience of democratisation is a representative example of the potential challenges.

As discussed earlier, the June Uprising in 1987 that sparked democratisation proceeded in two stages: a citizens' protest that led to the 29 June Declaration and the Great Workers'

Struggle from July to September, the latter being the most massive labour strike since liberation. With the democratic opening, the demand for wages increased, the freedom of unions exploded, and it was an important issue whether the new political system would incorporate a socioeconomic agenda. However, the authoritarian–democratic cleavage was transformed into a regional cleavage through the two founding elections, and the socioeconomic issues raised in the second stage of democratisation with the Great Workers' Struggle failed to gain political representation in the already mobilised regional cleavage.

With the institutionalisation of the regional cleavage, Korean voters were mobilised along regional lines. To activate the latent class cleavage, it is necessary to mobilise labour through cross-pressure along class lines. During the thirty years after democratisation, there were significant efforts to politically mobilise workers, but they were not strong enough to cross the barrier of regionalism, except in some notable cases.

Since the Constitutional Court's decision invalidating the one-vote mixed electoral system (the way of distributing the proportional representative seats) ahead of the 2004 legislative election, the progressive party has been able to capture some seats every legislative election. However, most of the seats the progressive party has won have been through party-list votes.[13] There have been five legislative elections and three presidential elections since the 2004 legislative election, but most labour and low-income voters in Korea still do not vote based on their class or social status. For instance, the non-regular worker cleavage as an exemplary case of insiders and outsiders became one of the most salient labour issues, but it was not a salient issue at the political cleavage level. Even though the Justice Party (JP), the successor of the United Progressive Party (UPP), declared publicly in 2018 that another name for the JP was 'the party of non-regular workers',[14] the majority of non-regular workers still voted for conservative party candidates in the nineteenth presidential election in 2017.

The regional political party system that has dominated Korean politics for the past thirty years, called the cartel party system, has delayed the emergence of new political parties (Jang 2003; Katz and Peter 1995). Korea's democracy, regarded as one of the most successful democracies, thus does not represent significant conflicts in the social area, particularly regarding socioeconomic issues. Supposing that democracy is an institutional representation of conflict in the social area; this means that one of the most successful democracies is paradoxically unsuccessful with respect to one of the most fundamental functions of democracy.

5. Consequences of Conservative Democratisation

The process of democratisation in Korea was not a process of completely reforming the authoritarian system, but rather focused on democratising leadership turnover.

Democratisation was determined by negotiations between the authoritarian incumbent and political elites with political origins in the authoritarian regime of Park Chung-hee, excluding civil society. The 87 system, which was born as a result of democratisation, was a centralised, single-term presidential system combined with a majority style electoral system. Moreover, this system was combined with a regional political system dominated by influential political leaders. This system was a cartel system of the existing political elites, which built high barriers to entry for emerging political forces. This system has been further strengthened while Korea has consolidated democracy through successful three-time regime change over the past thirty years.

What are the consequences of conservative democratisation? Over the past thirty years, the 1987 system has been strengthened as a cartel system. As a result, the representative system has been biased. Let's look at the composition of the National Assembly from the thirteenth National Assembly to the most recent twenty first National Assembly (total number of the representative, 2,688). The most overrepresented age group was the 50s. The ratio of those in their fifties,, was almost half of the total representative (1328, 49.78%). University graduates constituted over 95 per cent. The overrepresentation of male college graduates in their fifties was overwhelming. On the contrary, among the representatives elected over same period. The proportion of women was only 10.04 per cent (268). Also, the youth (the 20s) are significantly underrepresented. The number of the representative in their 20s was only 4 out of 2688 over the same period.[15]

The issue of youth representatives is an important one that reflects the reality of the democratisation process in South Korea and the normative dimension of representing minorities. South Korea was a society with open social mobility with high economic growth when the baby boom generation (born 1952–1963), which is now retiring, played a leading role. At this time, South Korean citizens were able to ascend to the middle class through education as a stepping stone (in South Korean idiom, 'A dragon rises from a small stream'). Democratisation in South Korea overlapped with an unprecedented financial crisis. In overcoming the economic crisis, an economic downturn began in earnest, and economic inequality rapidly increased. Moreover, this era of low growth and deepening inequality was also characterised by rapid ageing and a low birth rate. These social structural changes brought about a decline in social mobility. Fairness is currently the most critical issue among Korean youth, whose threshold for entry into society has risen.[16]

Since democratisation, underrepresentation of the youth and overrepresentation of those in their fifties has been a persistent phenomenon. In the latest 2020 legislative election, compared to the proportion of the electorate (18.1 per cent, 7.95 million votes), the number of youth (those in their twenties and under) represented in the National Assembly is just two out the total 300 members (only 0.6 per cent). The situation does not improve much even if we expand the youth demographic to those in their thirties. Compared to the proportion of votes they received (699 million, 15.9 per cent), the number of representatives in their thirties is just eleven (3.6 per cent). As of the end of 2020, the level of youth representation in South Korea is also deficient compared to other Organisation for Economic Co-operation and Development

(OECD) countries. If we look at the ratio of parliamentary members under thirty in OECD countries, South Korea ranks twenty-third.

Underrepresentation of the youth does not only mean there are very few representatives in their twenties and thirties. One way to assess youth representation in collective representation beyond demographic representation is to evaluate legislative activity representing the youth. Bills on youth issues passed from the sixteenth (2000–2004) to twentieth (2016–2020) National Assemblies do not account for even 0. 01 per cent of the total number of cases. Let us discuss this in more detail. Only 8 bills out of 12,114 passed are related to youth issues during this period.

The critical point is that the National Assembly has not improved the underdevelopment of youth representation during the advance of South Korean democracy. In every election, major political parties have tried to win support from young voters. The youth have been nothing more than targets for getting votes. The political cartel structure based on the collusion of the major political parties has served as a high entry barrier for young people.

The failure of youth representation has a socioeconomic consequence. In South Korea, poverty among the elderly has become an important social issue, but poverty among young people is not an issue. In the democratisation process, youth poverty has not been alleviated but has intensified. The poverty rate for single-youth households rose from 16.7 per cent in 2006 to 21.2 per cent in 2014.

This situation has also significantly influenced fairness perceptions at the individual level. Intergenerational fairness has an essential bearing on support for democracy, which is still weak, despite successful democratisation. According to the fourth Asian Barometer Survey, more than half of the baby boomers (50.87 per cent), who were the protagonists of the high-growth era, had a positive perception of mobility between generations. The negative perception rate was only 27.75 per cent. On the other hand, in the eco-generation (born 1979–1992), who are the children of the baby boom generation, positive perception rate decreased to 36.90 per cent and negative perception rate increased to 32.07 per cent (Kim and Choi 2017).

6. Conclusion

South Korea celebrated the thirtieth anniversary of democratisation in 2017. At the same time, it experienced the unprecedented Candlelight Uprising, in which the power of a total of 17 million citizens finally achieved the impeachment of the corrupt President Park Geun-hye. Over the thirty years since democratisation in 1987, South Korea has successfully institutionalised democracy; during this period, the country has completed three government turnovers without suspension of the constitutional system. These past thirty years of democracy in South Korea, however, have a dual character.

The fierce resistance of students and civil society triggered the democratisation process in Korea in 1987. However, the political pact between the old political elites who played a central role in the Park Chung-hee regime institutionalised the democratic transition. The 1987 system, which was created through negotiations between political elites to the exclusion of civil society's influence, functioned as a political cartel among the conservative political elite. At its core, the centralised presidential system of 1987 combined with the majoritarian style electoral system led to a highly coveted presidency on the one hand, while serving as a high barrier to new political forces on the other. Moreover, the regional political system structured during democratisation has been a significant obstacle for transforming new social issues into political cleavages during the thirty years of democratisation. One of the notable consequences of this cartel system has been the underrepresentation of South Korea's minority populations.

One of the significant consequences of this system is the underdevelopment of youth representation and an explosion of fairness discourse. Democracy does not mean a cycle of elite rotation. The democratisation of democracy must begin for South Korean democracy, which started a new cycle after the 2016–17 Candlelight Uprising, to become a system that reflects many citizens' preferences.

Notes

1. See https://www.systemicpeace.org/polityproject.html, accessed 6 August 2021.
2. The scores in the two fields are again divided into a 7-point scale, as free (1.0–2.5), partly free (3.0–5.0), or not free (5.5–7.0). A country's freedom rating is calculated by averaging these two scores (https://freedomhouse.org/), accessed 6 August 2021.
3. The Economist Group, a leading British media organisation, has released democracy indexes since 2006 through its research institute, the Economist Intelligence Unit. The democracy index incorporates six criteria: election process, pluralism, government function, political participation, political culture, and civil liberty. Based on their scores in these categories, countries are classified as a 'full democracy', 'flawed democracy', 'hybrid regime', or 'authoritarian regime', (https://www.eiu.com/topic/democracy-index), accessed 6 August 2021.
4. This was also true of the other two stages. Chun Doo-hwan's government supported many politicians who were bound by political regulation ahead of the 12 February legislative election and who created the New Democratic Party (NDP). The NDP, guided by Kim Dae-jung and Kim Young-sam, became the largest opposition party, with sixty-seven seats and 29.3 per cent of valid votes. Even during confrontations, the authoritarian regime actively confronted political unrest using strategies such as concessions (promising not to object to direct elections on 30 April 1985), splitting (the chairman of the NDP's initiative regarding the conditional acceptance of the parliamentary system), and containment (the 13 April measure to protect the Constitution).
5. There are two perspectives on the nature of the Great Workers' Struggle: that it was a temporary struggle for the right to live or that it was the popular starting point for the radical transformation movement. However, the fight was an extension of the June Uprising. It

was a struggle for political democratisation that sought to expand democracy beyond the realm of politics to the workplace (Roh 2012: 188).
6. There has been much debate over the nature of the so-called 1987 regime, a political system created by the June Uprising of 1987: The 87 system has been conceptualised as a constitutional system based on the characteristics of the 1987 Constitution (Park M. 2005), as a labour system based on the characteristics of labour-management relations (Roh 2010), as a democratic system due to the fact that it signified democratisation (Yun 2005; Cho 2013), and as a regional political party system based on the characteristics of the party system (Park 2006; Son 2017).
7. Civil society represented by the National Coalition for Democratic Constitution (NCDC) was very inactive during the constitutional reform. The NCDC released its guidelines for constitutional amendments two months after the 29 June Declaration (4 August 1987). However, the reform process was subordinated to electoral strategy. In the discussions of the amendments, the different parts of society presented a variety of opinions on the direction of the constitution. For instance, the workers' commission for a democratic constitution presented five points: (1) a complete guarantee of basic labour rights; (2) guaranteeing the maximum basic rights of the people; (3) specifying the right of resistance; (4) granting voting rights to adults aged eighteen and older; and (5) clarifying the divided state and the will for independent and peaceful unification. However, the actors in the constitutional reform process did not seriously consider the claims of civil society (Kim 2006).
8. The four parties arrived at the five-year, single-term presidency after a political tug-of-war. The authoritarian incumbent DJP preferred a six-year single term, whereas the opposition UDP wanted to introduce a two-term presidency with a vice-president.
9. To prevent amendments for long-term rule, as had occurred with the 'amendment for re-election for the third term (*samseon gaeheon*) of the Third Republic and the 'amendment with rounding off to the nearest integer' (*sasa oip gaeheon*) of the First Republic, the Constitution was amended to make efforts to extend the term of the presidency ineffective (Article 128[2]). To limit the president's authority, the amendments included deleting the president's rights to take emergency measures and to dissolve the National Assembly.
10. The scope of workers with limited collective action rights was limited to major defence industries (Article 33). Social security regulations specified the object of protection and stipulated social security obligations for women, the elderly, and adolescents.
11. The Constitutional Court is in charge of adjudicating a law's unconstitutionality, impeachment trials, dissolving political parties, judging power disputes, and adjudicating constitutional complaints (Article 111). Compared with the Constitution of the Fifth Republic, the ninth constitutional amendment in 1987 contributed to establishing procedural democracy by enhancing fundamental rights, strengthening the National Assembly's powers, and introducing the direct election of the president.
12. Along with the disproportionate seat ratio between the district and proportional levels (224 vs 75), the method of assigning proportional seats still gave a large bonus to the largest party. Half of the proportional seats go to the ruling party, while the remaining half are distributed among the political parties according to the ratio of the number of seats won by district.
13. A notable exception was the 2012 (nineteenth) legislative election, where the United Progressive Party earned seven seats at the constituency level because of joint nominations with the Democratic Party.

14. See http://www.justice21.org/newhome/board/board_view.html?num=103845, accessed 6 August 2021.
15. Author's own calculation based on National Election Commission Data (https://www.nec.go.kr/site/nec/main.do).
16. Many surveys on the perceptions of fairness and equal opportunity suggest that Korean citizens no longer believe Korean society is dynamic or characterised by equal opportunities. For example, in a recent public opinion poll (Cho 2019), almost all (90.1 per cent) of the respondents perceived that Korea was 'a hereditary society', where wealth and social status are handed down to the next generation through socioeconomic background. Moreover, more than four-fifths (84.7 per cent) responded that such a phenomenon is worsening. Likewise, 82 per cent agreed with the statement that 'It is difficult to climb the ladder of class even if an individual makes an effort.'

Bibliography

Asian Barometer Survey. http://www.asianbarometer.org/survey

Bartolini, S., and Mair, P. (1990), *Identity, Competition and Electoral Availability* (Colchester: ECPR Press).

Cho, H.-Y. (2013), '"Sudong hyeongmyeongjeok minjuhwa cheje" roseo ui 87-nyeon cheje, bokhapjeok mosun, gyunyeol, jeonhwan e daehayeo: 87-nyeon cheje, 97-nyeon cheje, poseuteu minjuhwa cheje' [On the Complex Contradictions, Cleavages, and Transformation of the 1987 Regime as a 'Passive-Revolution-Type Democratisation Regime': The 1987 Regime, 1997 Regime, and Post-Democratisation Regime], *Minju sahoe wa jeongchaek yeongu* 24, 137–171.

Centre for Systemic Peace, https://www.systemicpeace.org/polityproject.html, accessed 6 August 2021.

Choi, J.-J., (2002). *Minjuhwa ihu ui minjujuui* [Democracy after democratisation]. Seoul: Humanitaseu.

Choi J.-J. (2004), 'Seomun' [Introduction], in Maravall José María and Adam. Przeworski, eds, *Minjujuui wa beob ui jibae* [*Democracy and the Rule of the Law*], trans. from English by A. Gyu-nam, S. Ho-chang et al. (Seoul: Humanitaseu), 9–70.

Cho, U.-B. (2019). 'gugmin 10myeong jung 9myeong hangug-eun seseubsahoe ' ['9 out of 10 people Korea is a hereditary society], *Sisanjournal*,9, September, https://www.sisajournal.com/news/articleView.html?idxno=190763, accessed 15 March 2021.

Chun, D.-H. (2017), *Chun Du-hwan hoegorok: Cheongwadae sijeol* [*Chun Du-hwan's Memoirs, Vol. 2: The Blue House Era*] (Republic of Korea: Jajak namusup).

Dahl, R. (1971), *Polyarchy: Participation and Opposition* (Newhaven, CT: Yale University Press).

Democracy Index 2020, https://www.eiu.com/topic/democracy-index, accessed 6 August 2021. https://freedomhouse.org.

Fishman, R. M. (2017), 'How Civil Society Matters in Democratization: Setting the Boundaries of Post-Transition Political Inclusion', *Comparative Politics* 49(3), 391–409.

Guo, S., and Stradiotto, G. (2014), *Democratic Transitions: Modes and Outcomes* (London and New York: Routledge).

Huntington, S. P. (1991), *The Third Wave: Democratization in the Late Twentieth Century* (Norman, OK: University of Oklahoma Press).

Im, H.-B. (Hyug Baeg Im) (1990), 'Hanguk eseo ui minjuhwa gwajeong bunseok: jeollyakjeok seontaek iron eul jungsim euro' [An Analysis of the Democratic Transition Process in South Korea], *Hanguk jeonchihak hoebo* 24(1), 51–79.

Im, H.-B. (Hyug Baeg Im) (2014), *Bidongsiseong ui dongsiseong: Hanguk geundae jeonchi ui daejungjeok sigan* [*Simultaneity of the Non-Simultaneous: The Popular Temporality of Modern Korean Politics*] (Seoul: Goryeo daehakkyo chulpanbu).

Im, H.-B. (Im Hyeok-baek) (2020), *Democratization and Democracy in South Korea, 1960-Present* (Singapore: Palgrave Macmillan).

Jang, H. (2003), 'Kareutel jeongdang cheje ui hyeongseong gwa baljeon: minjuhwa ihu Hanguk ui gyeongu' [The Formation and Development of the Cartel Party System: The Case of Korea since Democratisation], *Hanguk gwa gukje jeongchi* 19(4), 2–59.

Kang, S-G(2017), '6.29 seon-eon 8gaehang-ui uimiwa jinjeon-e daehan pyeong-ga' [Assessment of the meaning and progress of the eight clauses of the 6.29 Declaration] in W.Kang, ed. '6.29 seon-eongwa hangug minjujuui, [6.29 Declaration and Korean Democracy] (Seoul :Purungil).

Kang, U.-J. (WooJin, Kang) (2017), '87-nyeon cheje wa chotbul simin hyeongmyeong: Hanguk minjujuui ui jeonhwan' [The 1987 Political System and the 2017 Candlelight Citizen Revolution: Transformation of Korean Democracy], *Jeongchi bipyeong* 10(1), 47–86.

Kang W.-T. (2017), '87-nyeon heonbeop ui gaeheon gwajeong gwa sidaejeok hamui' [How the Constitution Was Revised in 1987 and the Historical Implications], *Yeoksa bipyeong* 119, 12–37.

Katz, R., and Peter, M. (1995), 'Changing Models of Party Organization and Party Democracy: The Emergence of the Cartel Party', *Party Politics* 1(1), 5–28.

Kim, D.-Y. (2006), '87-nyeon gaeheon hyeopsang gwa gungmin undong bonbu ui jeongchi haengwi' [Negotiation over the 1987 Constitutional Amendment and the Political Activity of the NCDC], *Jeongsin munhwa yeongu* 29(1), 276–301.

Kim, J.-W., (2021), 'Joeda, namseong, daejol, 50-dae, gwayeon geudeul i dangsin ui ipjang e seo jul kka' [Altogether, Men, College Graduates, 50s, Will They Stand in Your Position?], *Kyeonghyang sinmun*, 1 January, http://news.khan.co.kr/kh_news/khan_art_view.html?art_id=202101270600025, accessed 6 August 2021.

Kim, S.-I. (1992), *Chun Du-hwan sidae yukseong jeungeon* [*Testimonies on Chun Du-hwan's Upbringing*] (Republic of Korea: Joseon ilbosa).

Kim, T.-W., and Choi, J.-Y. (2017). 'Cheongnyeon Bingonsiltae' [Who is Poorer among Young People], *Bogeonbogjipoleom* 244, 6–19.

Korean Barometer Survey.: http://www.koreabarometer.org/

Lipset, M. S., and Rokkan, S. (1967), 'Cleavage Structures, Party Systems and Voter Alignments: An Introduction', in M. S. Lipset and S. Rokkan, eds, *Party Systems and Voter Alignments: Cross-National Perspectives* (New York: Free Press), 1–67.

Mainwaring, S., and Bizzarro, F. (2019). 'The Fates Of Third-Wave Democracies', *Journal of Democracy* 30(1), 99–113.

Mazzoleni, O., and Mueller, S., eds (2016), *Regionalist Parties in Western Europe: Dimensions of Success* (London: Taylor and Francis).

Munck, G. L., and Carol, S. L. (1997), 'Modes of Transition and Democratization: South America and Eastern Europe in Comparative Perspective', *Comparative Politics* 29(3), 343–362.

O'Donnell, G., and Schmitter, P. (1986), *Transitions from Authoritarian Rule: Tentative Conclusions about Uncertain Democracies* (Baltimore, MD: The Johns Hopkins University Press).

Park, C.-E. (2005), *Bareun yeoksa reul wihan jeungeon 1: 5-gong, 6-gong, 3-Gim sidae ui jeongchi bisa* [*Testimony for a Correct History, Vol. 1: Secret History of the Fifth and Sixth Republics and the Three Kims Era*] (Seoul: Randeom hauseu jungang).

Park, M.-R. (2005), '87-nyeon heonjeong cheje gaehyeok gwa Hanguk minjujuui: mueot ul, wae, otteotke bakkul geot inga' [Reform of the 1987 Constitutional System and Democracy in Korea: What, Why, and How to Change], *Changjak gwa bipyeong* 33(4), 34–51.

Park, S.-H. (2006), 'Hanguk ui "87-nyeon cheje": minjuhwa ihu Hanguk jeongdang cheje ui gujo wa byeonhwa' [Korea's '1987 System': The Structure and Change of the Party System in Korea after Democratisation], *Asea yeongu* 49(2), 7–41.

Roh, J.-G. (2010), 'Hanguk minjuhwa ui seonggwa wa hangye: minjuhwa 20-nyeon gwa nodong sahoe ui minjuhwa' [Fruits and Limitations of Democratisation in Korea: Twenty Years of Democratisation and the Democratisation of Labour Society in Korea], *Giyeok gwa jeonmang* 22, 37–63.

Roh, J.-G. (2012), '87-nyeon nodongjadae tujaeng ui yeoksajeok uiui wa hyeonjaejeok uimi' [A Study of the 1987 Great Labor Struggle and Its Historical and Contemporary Significance], *Gyeongje wa sahoe* 96, 178–209.

Roh, T.-W. (2011), *No Tae-u hoegorok: minjujuui wa na ui yeojeong 1* [*Roh Tae-woo's Memoirs, Vol. 1: National Democratisation and My Destiny*] (Seoul: Joseon nyuseu peureseu).

Sartori, G. (1969), 'From the Sociology of Politics to Political Sociology', *Government and Opposition* 4(2), 195–214.

Share, D., and Mainwaring, S. (1986), 'Transitions through Transaction: Democratization in Brazil and Spain', in W. Selcher, ed., *Political Liberalization in Brazil: Dynamics, Dilemmas and Future Prospects* (Boulder, CO: Westview), 175–215.

Schumpeter, J., (1942), *Capitalism, Socialism and Democracy* (New York: Harper and Brothers).

Son, H.-C. (2017), *Chotbul hyeongmyeong gwa 2017-nyeon cheje* [*The Candlelight Revolution and the 2017 System*] (Seoul: Seogang daehakkyo chulpanbu).

Yun, S.-C. (2005), '87-nyeon cheje ui jeongchijihyeong gwa gwaje' [Political Terrain and Tasks of the 87 System], *Changjak gwa bipyeong* 33(4), 52–76.

Zielinski, J. (2002), 'Translating Social Cleavages into Party Systems: The Significance of New Democracies', *World Politics* 54(2), 184–211.

CHAPTER 7

THE DEVELOPMENTAL STATE

MEREDITH WOO

1. DEFINING THE DEVELOPMENTAL STATE

MAX Weber defined the state as an entity with a monopoly on violence, capable of compelling compliance within a demarcated territory. Such state is developmental when it is concerned with economic growth and capable of implementing policies to promote it, often with the aid of what could be termed 'industrial policy'. In that sense, the developmental state can occur anywhere, as it did in continental Europe following formation of national states.

In Northeast Asia, the concept of the developmental state originates in the study of Japanese economic development. In *MITI and the Japanese Miracle*, Chalmers Johnson dubbed the Japanese state a 'capitalist developmental state' to underscore its success with long-term plans and industrial policy while remaining market-orientated, unlike socialist states. He argued that the Japanese capitalist developmental state traces its origin to the pre-war years, and in both pre-war and post-war incarnations its ideology was based on nationalism (Johnson 1982). With the replication of the Japanese miracle in South Korea, Taiwan, and Singapore, the concept was abbreviated to 'developmental state' but the idea that nationalism undergirds economic planning and mobilisation and that bureaucracy is at the centre of the coalition that includes the political parties and business remained intact (Johnson 1999).

Even before Johnson's work on the Japanese political economy was published, there were economic monographs that emphasised the role of state interventionism in Korean economic growth. The most notable was by LeRoy Jones and Sakong Il (1970), illustrating the role of economic bureaucracy in 'guiding' Korea's nascent business sector and fostering entrepreneurship. Two decades later, Alice Amsden (1989) published an account, entitled *Asia's Next Giant*, which validated their argument and tipped the hat in the direction of South Korea's economic policymakers. Another important work appeared in 1994, entitled *The Political Economy of Industrial Policy*. It was written by Ha-Joon Chang (1994), a Cambridge economist who scrutinised the actual practice of economic policymaking in South Korea and distilled from it the general tenets of industrial policy that could be applied elsewhere in the developing world. These works were animated by the debate on the cause of the East Asian 'miracle', whether it was due to free trade and free market (as 'orthodox' economists were wont to argue) or due to government interventionism (as the above 'revisionist' economists tended to argue). This was a debate of some consequence, aimed at the hearts and minds of policymakers in the developing world. If these economists were correct in their analysis of the South Korean economic growth, arguably one of the fastest in the world, the nostrum of market liberalism for promoting capitalist growth would be thrown into doubt, and with it, the prospect for globalism and international trade.

In my own work, *Race to the Swift: State and Finance in Korean Industrialization*, I provided historical and political context to these economic arguments, and in doing so, traced the evolution of the developmental state in South Korea (Woo 1991). In this chapter, I borrow from that work, and first discuss the historical context of the Northeast Asian developmental state. This is critical for helping us to understand whether the South Korean experience is *sui generis* or replicable in different historical contexts. Then I will discuss the politics of the developmental state, centring on the role of nationalism in economic mobilisation, repression, and international security that profoundly shaped the experience of the Korean nation in modern times. This will be followed with a discussion of economic policies in the years before the liberalisation and democratisation in South Korea. The discussion in this chapter is focused on the period of heavy industrialisation in South Korea (the 1970s), as it provides in the starkest way possible the South Korean archetype of the developmental state.

2. The Origins of the Korean Developmental State

Traditional Korea was governed by an agrarian bureaucracy, in a suzerain relationship with China that persisted through much of its history. When the last of the traditional dynasty collapsed, Korea joined the world capitalist system as a full-blown colony of Japan.

The colonial period (1910–1945) proved catastrophic in many ways. Politically, it eventually led to the division of the country, with the northern and southern halves under sponsorship of the victors of the Second World War. Economically, the course of its growth became tightly integrated to a regional economy designed and led by Japan. Whether understood in terms of a regional division of labour, or dovetailing with the product cycle, the Korean industrial structure ended up articulated with that of Japan.

Japan's empire, unlike those of most European nations, was regional and contiguous. The compass of Japan's strategic concern was in concentric circles radiating from the homelands: the 'cordon of sovereignty' encompassing territory vital to the nation's survival and under formal occupation, and the 'cordon of advantages', an outer limit of informal Japanese domination, seen as necessary to protect and guarantee the inner line (Jansen 1968).

In the first half of the colonial rule, Korea was a classic colonial economy showing uneven development. It was exploited as a breadbasket for Japan, with its worth measured by its ability to provide agricultural commodities to Japan. Imitating the same regional trade structure that Germany had imposed on its trading partners prior to the First World War, Japan sought to keep Korea as an agricultural backwater, a receptacle for Japan's manufactured goods, and it actively sought to dampen any efforts at industrialisation in Korea. In both German and Japanese cases, there was remarkable coherence in planning and execution of this policy.

The 1930s brought about an epochal change, however. As the result of the rapidly fluctuating international environment, including the boycott of Japanese products by other nations through tariffs and quotas, Japan came to pursue autonomous development, to create a self-sufficient economy within its bloc of influence. This delinking from the liberal world economy proceeded with the abandonment of the gold standard and the adoption of a control-based monetary system. It protected the domestic economy from the ravages of international economy and global depression, allowed for fiscal expansion at home through easy money, and made possible the promotion of exports through devaluation.

As Japan invaded Manchuria in 1931, it rapidly expanded war-related heavy industries, and Korea, as an entrepot between Manchuria and Japan as a natural supplier of an abundant variety of mineral resources, cheap labour, and hydroelectricity, was one of the logical locations for the crash industrialisation programme. In the 1930s, the real growth of Korea's manufacturing production and value added would average over 10 per cent per annum (Woo 1991: 19–42).

The colonial government intervened in the economy extensively, taking upon itself the leading role in creating the spurt of industrialisation. The government share of capital formation in Korea was consistently high, becoming more than half of total investment during 1930, and declining slightly as the Japanese zaibatsu began moving into colonial Korea.

In order to attract Japanese industries to Korea, the colonial government offered the guarantee of political stability, the state investment in infrastructure necessary for industrialisation, and other financial incentives. For the newer zaibatsu willing to invest in Korea, the government provided capital through the Industrial Bank of Japan (IBJ). The IBJ had been created in 1900 to meet the demands of long-term capital. By the 1930s, it was financing government-sponsored munitions and overseas projects, heading syndicates distributing and absorbing issues of the South Manchurian Railway Company and others. After 1937, it handled a large part of the financing of the new zaibatsu.

In a relatively short period of time, the grip of zaibatsu groups on the Korean economy became tight and concentrated, constituting, by 1940, some three-quarters of the total capital investment. The leading groups included Mitsubishi, Mitsui, Nichitsu,

Asano, Mori, Riken, Sumitomo, and Yasuda. The most noteworthy was Japan Nitrogen Fertilizer Company—Nichitsu for short—of the Noguchi interest. It became a de facto 'industrial ruler' of Korea, accounting for 35 per cent of Japanese direct investment in Korea by 1945. Nichitsu was the second largest chemical complex in the world, and its Korean plant was particularly profitable—more so than its counterpart in Japan proper.

Economic mobilisation of this magnitude was accompanied by a ferocious repression, both in Japan proper and its colonies. But political repression was more brutal in Korea than elsewhere because the populace was notoriously resistant to the Japanese rule. Consequently, Japan's military was forced to deploy two of its best divisions in Korea on permanent basis, and to widely distribute its gendarmerie. The extent of state repression is well documented, from the chilling details of massacres to harsh labour controls, to the unleashing of a classic police state for the politics of forced conformity: obliteration of the Korean national identity, language, surnames, the institution of emperor and Shinto worship, and so on.

If the political requisite for rapid industrialisation and sovereign security favours the emergence of an authoritarian regime, that would explain, in part, the similarity between the colonial form of corporatism/authoritarianism and the South Korean military dictatorship in the 1970s. The most useful memory for the latter industrialisers was that the colonial industrialisation pattern *worked*, and its success was based on close collaboration between the state and big business, and on the building of economies of scale.

The 1930s bequeathed a set of patterns, a model, that could be a silent companion of South Korean development, the parenthetical unspoken force that brings home the truth that people make their own history, but not in the circumstances of their choosing.

3. National Division and the Politics of Growth

With the ending of the Second World War, Korea was divided in half, with South Korea first governed by the US military government (1945–1948), and for the next twelve years, by the government of Rhee Syngman. North Korea was occupied briefly by the Soviet Union for a period of a year, then turned over by 1946 to the regime led by Kim Il-sung. South Korea was a Cold War 'client' state, with a political system where autocracy commingled with party politics and semi-fascist mobilisation, thriving on a system-wide corruption, but it still carried the US caché of liberal democracy.

South Korea was dubbed a 'forward defence state' in the Cold War, and a de facto Truman doctrine country, placed in tandem with Greece and Turkey. Thus, it was supported almost entirely through US direct aid, which, by the end of the 1950s was equivalent to 70 per cent of South Korea's domestic revenue. On top of this, the US military aid was always higher than the economic aid. In the financial year 1959, for instance, South Korea received more than $325 million in military aid, higher than $259 million for all of Europe, $226 million for Taiwan, $246 million for Turkey, $118 million for Greece, and $83 million for all of Latin America (Woo 1991: 48).

To reduce the burden of supporting South Korea as a client state, the United States pressurised it to normalise relations with Japan and re-enter a trade relationship with it. The centrepiece of the United States' East Asian policy was Japan, after all, and in the US conception, the quickest way to revive both Japan and South Korea, especially after the Korean War (1950–1953), was to revive the old, pre-war structure of regional trade, with South Korea serving as a market for Japanese manufactured goods.

Rhee Syngman understood this logic, and he fought tooth and nail against it. Rhee saw his country not as an economic appendix of the Japanese recovery, but as an independent and soon-to-be self-sufficient nation, if only enough US resources could be pumped into the economy. Rhee balked especially at the US attempt to coordinate the aid programme for all of East Asia, showering aid on South Korea, but simultaneously forcing the South Koreans to use it to procure goods from Japan. Instead of trade liberalisation, South Korea in the 1950s opted for import-substitution industrialisation (ISI), supported through direct foreign aid. ISI refers to a trade and economic policy that seeks to replace foreign imports with domestic production, to foster national industrialisation. In reality, however, ISI often intensified import, as production of domestic goods required equipment and parts that had to be procured abroad.

Eventually, the United States slashed the aid, which went from the all-time high of $383 million in the 1950s to $222 million by 1959. It also forced a stringent economic stabilisation on Rhee Syngman's government to rein in inflation by rapidly reducing government spending. The economy went into a recession, investment from the private sector did not materialise, and unemployment soared. Widespread political protests put an end to Rhee's regime in 1960 (Woo 1991: 72).

The 1950s was an interesting prelude to the full-blown version of the South Korean developmental state that followed it. If South Korea's dependence on aid and import substitution did not serve as a good template for what followed, the nationalism that undergirded Rhee's policies and his ability to leverage the nation's geopolitical position to its advantage certainly was. The South Korean developmental state was always conceived as a response to the existential threat to the nation, a state formation that was capable of fostering strong military and strong economy in as short a time as possible.

The nationalist logic of this developmental state only intensified over the next three decades. Even as US aid declined through the end of the 1950s and early 1960s, two things transpired to give South Korea a break: the Vietnam War and the rapprochement with Japan.

South Korea's participation in the Vietnam War brought enhanced US military assistance. When the first South Korean troops were dispatched in 1965, US military assistance, which had been 4.9 per cent of the South Korean gross national product (GNP), rose to 7.2 per cent. Between 1965 and 1970, US payment to South Korea was more than a billion US dollars.

More important than the dollar amount associated with Vietnam was the importance of Vietnam as the first export market for South Korea's industrial products. Whereas

South Korean exports to the United States and Japan remained labour-intensive goods such as textiles and plastic goods, wigs, and plywood, Vietnam absorbed a stunning 94 per cent in the total Korean steel export, 52 per cent in transportation equipment, and 40 per cent in non-electric machinery. In the end, Vietnam marked the coming of age for some of South Korea's largest conglomerates, such as Hyundai and Hanjin (the South Korean airlines group). The Vietnam War was not only a cornucopia of large invisible earnings and immense US assistance, but an incubator of new industries before testing the fires of international competition (Woo 1991: 94).

The rapprochement with Japan occurred with the signing of the 'normalization treaty'. With this event, South Korea was to receive $300 million in grants, $200 million in government loans, and $300 million in commercial credit from Japan. The total, $800 million, was a large sum for a country whose entire exports in 1964 amounted to $200 million. Again, the amount matters less than the use to which it was put. Notwithstanding the provision in the 1965 settlement that $300 million was to be used exclusively for agricultural development and importation of industrial materials from Japan, the South Korean government quickly directed it to creating the Pohang steel complex (today, one of the world's largest steel makers). The $200 million in government loans was used for investment in social infrastructure, including power plants, railroads, irrigation networks, and communication facilities. The commercial credit went into financing plants exports from Japan, such as power facilities, textile production machinery, and transportation equipment. In other words, the financial pay-out for the normalisation went a long way to jump-start South Korea's heavy industrialisation (Woo 1991: 87).

Without much notice or celebration that marked the regional economic integration efforts in Latin America and Europe, what eventuated was the investiture of a dual and complementary hegemony of Japan and the United States—one that South Korea used to its advantage.

With this regional security regime in place, external loans quickly began flowing in. Combined with the institution of 'sovereign risk', low-cost foreign capital, approved and guaranteed by the government, became the most coveted prize for business, which was more than willing to deposit the 'commission' for foreign loans into the coffers of the dominant party and perhaps government officials. This was one way where the financial policies espoused by the government cemented further the relationship between big business and government and the ruling party. Thus, by the end of the 1960s, the three indispensable conditions for development could be found in South Korea: a global economic structure that accommodated and welcomed an upstart, a developmental state that could exploit its external conditions and harness its grip on domestic sectors, and finally a hardworking and increasingly confident business sector. This was a formidable mosaic for economic growth; for democracy, however, it was none too auspicious.

By the early 1970s, the outward-leaning South Korean economy abruptly retreated inwards. In the days of the Vietnam War, when the South Korean soldiers substituted for Americans, the United States repeatedly assured South Koreans their security lock, stock, and barrel. It was not so under Richard Nixon. Just about every aspect of Nixon's global design affected South Korea. The Nixon doctrine sought to reduce the US payment deficits through heavy cuts in military spending abroad and sharing the imperial burden with reginal economic powers (in this case, Japan). It also sought to rectify the US trade deficit through import surcharge and rising protectionism, which deeply affected South Korea. The end of the gold standard and the institution of floating rates, followed by dollar devaluations, also had the effect of throwing South Korean planning off-kilter. It was these issues, along with infiltration of North Korean guerrillas into the South, and the 1973 oil shock, that help us to understand the challenges to which the developmental state which emerged full-blown in the 1970s was a response.

The new US military strategy moved away from the two-and-a-half war strategy to a one-and-a-half one. The former meant initial defence of Western Europe against the Soviet attack, *plus* a sustained defence of South Korea and/or Southeast Asia against an all-out Chinese attack, *plus* meeting a contingency elsewhere. In the latter, the second category—defence of South Korea against China—was simply dropped. This revision was a logical response to the Sino–Soviet split, to the fact that one-third of the Soviet and one-half of the Chinese military forces were now stacked on the Sino–Soviet border. If the Sino–Soviet bloc were no more, there was no reason—beyond the bureaucratic pork-barrelling—to fund military programmes based on an old Cold War assumption. The first place, besides Indochina, where the axe of the Nixon doctrine fell was South Korea. By the middle of 1971, some 20,000 US soldiers had been removed, with the rest to be phased out over the next five years. Seoul had little to say in the decision, having lost its trump card once the United States had determined upon Vietnam disengagement.

US protectionism, like the troop withdrawal, was not completely unexpected. South Korean leadership knew that Richard Nixon was indebted to the cotton growers and textile interests in the South, and also that he had to do something about the balance-of-payment deficit. Still, the protectionist measures affected South Korea seriously. Textiles constituted one-third of total South Korean manufacturing and 38 per cent of total exports. It also employed 32 per cent of the manufacturing population. Thus, the US protectionism threatened not just the South Korean textile industry, but also the entire South Korean economy (Woo 1991: 126).

Likewise, the quadrupling of petroleum prices was a disaster. It wreaked economic havoc, as it did in other nations bereft of sufficient energy sources and gave an existential shock to South Korea. There was a security angle here, as well. North Korea had plenty of energy reserves, a point that Seoul had chosen to ignore as long as the oil flow was cheap and plentiful. While South Korea depended on oil for most of its energy consumption, North Korea possessed great hydroelectric and fossil fuel reserves (greater in per capita terms than France). From the colonial time on, North Korea had always had excellent hydroelectric reserves, owing to its excellent geomorphological condition. To compound the problem, Pyongyang was on better terms with the Arabs, with North Korean pilots stationed in Egypt, and North Korean missile technicians in Syria. Seoul, on the other hand, was pro-Israel.

The South Korean government responded to the challenge by taking draconian measures. It removed all vestiges of liberal democracy and purged from the political system inevitable uncertainties that emanate from elections. For nearly two decades from this point on, South Korea remained in the grip of a largely authoritarian state that brooked little dissent from the populace.

The saving grace to this anti-communist and growth-orientated state was its bureaucracy, which remained professional and meritocratic. It is the constancy of this professional and expert bureaucracy that provided legitimacy to a regime that had not been legitimised through electoral means, and resilience when it was brittle by virtue of being authoritarian. The professionalism and meritocracy of South Korea's bureaucracy also set it apart from the Latin American 'bureaucratic authoritarianism' that prevailed in places like Brazil and other parts of Latin America through the 1970s. The origins of this phenomenon are multiple. Traditional Korea had been a centralised agrarian state, and for five centuries preceding the colonisation by Japan, a Confucian state that venerated officialdom, which could be obtained only through decades of learning and disciplined scholarship. On top of this long tradition, the Japanese imposed a modern bureaucracy, which was itself an adaptation from those in western countries, particularly France, Germany, and the United States. When Korea was liberated, the tradition of this modern—and hybrid—bureaucracy continued on, recruiting the best and brightest through examinations that only the most qualified few could pass.

The most important of the bureaucracy was the Economic Planning Board, which was an omnibus economic ministry in charge of most important areas of the economy in order to enable coordinated economic planning. It was from the confines of this agency that the successful five-year plans, which almost always surpassed the targets, were issued and implemented. These multiyear plans formed the bone of what we have come to know as industrial policy. In the 1970s, as the state took an authoritarian turn, the focus was on developing a heavy industrial capacity to make the economy more self-sufficient and comprehensive. The ambition was to turn South Korea, in the span of one decade, from the final processor of export goods to one of the world's major exporters of steel, ships, and other producer goods. The development of basic industries also held the promise of a vibrant defence industry, to end the reliance on US largess in weaponry and various attendant political inconveniences (such as human rights). And all this accompanied by a massive popular mobilisation to reduce the urban/rural gap—a potpourri of rural self-help and basic needs.

4. Industrial Policies

In the early 1970s, six industries—steel, chemical, metal, machine-building, shipbuilding, and electronics—were targeted for rapid growth, as objects of intense government scrutiny and development. One of the conspicuous features in this effort was an ambition to create a large industrial complex with 'state-of-the-art' production facilities for each target industry: the Yosu-Yochon complex for petrochemicals, Changwon for machine-building, Pohang for steel, Okpo for shipbuilding, the Kumi complex for electronics, and finally, Onsan for the nonferrous metal industry. The state would procure these industrial bases from farmers, bulldoze the land, install infrastructures (roads, harbours, water and electricity, etc.), and force-draft relevant industries with fiscal/financial sweeteners and exemptions on commodity and customs taxes on imported capital goods.

The projected economies of scale were breath-taking, and reflected the political obsession of the authoritarian regime. Every new plant had to be one of the best and the largest in the world and boasted as such, the quickest ever built, or the most efficient ever operated. This is the political culture of what Alexander Gerschenkron (1946) called 'late development': intense competitiveness vis-à-vis the outside, a collective sense of precariousness at home.

The production of producer goods had to substitute for imports *at the same time* that it had to be exported. The risk was large: if the markets for new exports could not be found, then enormous waste, idle capacity, unemployment, and financial problems would follow. In the end, South Korea proved successful, becoming the avatar of 'late development' in the European mould. This crusade for comprehensive and heavy industrialization was not without its detractors, the most important ones being international economic development agencies, such as the International Monetary Fund (IMF) and the World Bank, which believed that the government must reconsider its priorities and continue to privilege the textile industry as the most important industry in South Korea. After all, textiles still employed nearly one-third of manufacturing employment, churning out nearly one-half of total exports. These misgivings notwithstanding, South Korea's heavy industrialisation plan exceeded the outcome projected in 1973 and was completed by the end of the decade.

Integrated steel mills were the symbol of national prowess, and the government wanted something akin to a national champion that could be considered the best in the world. When the Pohang Steel Mill began its operation in 1973, it was really the first time that South Korea had an integrated steel mill that churned out iron, steel, and rolled products all at once. In ten years, South Korea's annual overall steelmaking capacity multiplied fourteenfold. This was the result of the government's profound commitment: between 1975 and 1982, 40 per cent of all loans to the heavy industrial sector went to steel. This success required constantly expanding demand for iron and steel, generated by a rapidly growing economy. The state carefully nurtured steel-consuming (construction and metal) and machine (transport, electrical) industries, which grew the fastest among all manufacturing sectors, emerging as predominant export industries by the end of the 1970s (Woo 1991: 118–147).

Shipbuilding guzzles thick steel plates, and therefore it is likely to grow big with the steel industry. In Europe, shipbuilding trailed after steel and naval expansion. The remarkable fact about the South Korean example, however, is that massive development in shipbuilding was carefully and simultaneously calibrated with that in steel, to take advantage of external economies.

Pushing shipbuilding took considerable courage, and it had two interesting features which resembled the earlier Japanese experience. One was deep state involvement through fiscal, financial, and managerial means to maximise economic and defence effects. The state would intervene, match, and mediate between the industry's customers and suppliers, select transportation companies and ocean liners, and even determine for the shipbuilders the type of ship and the length of time required to build it. Another was the notion of 'systemised' shipbuilding, whereby a coterie of small and medium-sized shipbuilders and other subcontractors would coexist with, and supply parts to, large shipbuilders. Shipbuilding, too, was a notable success and, within a decade of its establishment, went on to capture more than one-fifth of all new orders in the world market.

Chemical industry in South Korea was built, literally, from scratch. It was an industry that was both appropriate and inappropriate to South Korea. It was appropriate in that it is the pre-eminent industry of 'self-reliance', substituting synthetics for naturally occurring substances. It was inappropriate, however, in that it was capital intensive with minimal employment effect. It was also an industry that was difficult to establish and operate without foreign equity participation and technical assistance. Not a single fertiliser plant, not a single petrochemical complex, was a product solely of South Korean capital and know-how. All seven of the fertiliser plants that were built by the end of the 1970s were either foreign creations or joint ventures, and the roster had names like McGraw Hydrocarbon, Tennessee Valley Authority, the Swift Consortium, Gulf, Mitsui, Bechtel, and Agrico. In petrochemicals, the Ulsan Petrochemical complex was in partnership with Gulf, and the Yochon complex was in partnership with Mitsui. By 1978, foreign investment in chemicals and petroleum refining accounted for 40 per cent of the value of the entire stock of foreign investment. It was an oddity in a country that favoured foreign loans over foreign investment.

By the end of the 1970s, the output from the chemical sector was some 92 per cent over a decade before. As in steel and shipping, progress occurred through extremely rapid compression. For instance, import dependence of synthetic fibres went from 94 per cent to 10 per cent in that time period, while the degree of export dependence went from nil to 75 per cent (Woo 1991: 141).

Machine-building is at the core of the defence industry. The Changwon machine-building industrial complex is a huge hollow hugged by a harbour and as far away from the demilitarised zone (DMZ) as economically feasible. Big manufacturing immediately moved into the complex, and when the project was completed, Changwon, along with other industrial complexes, formed a sprawling industrial belt in the southern part of South Korea.

The South Korean government was determined to 'Koreanize' machine-building, satisfying domestic demand with domestic products to the greatest extent possible, and at the same time, increasing exports of machinery. The centrepiece of this effort was the automobile industry which, to produce vehicles, requires no fewer than 2,500 parts, mostly sophisticated manufactured components. Automobile production is a central force in any heavy industrialisation effort, consuming substantial quantities of steel, aluminium, glass, rubber, etc., not to mention other spill-over effects, such as the industry's creation of demand for extensive distribution and service networks. The success of the automobile industry owes in no small part to the government effort. Once the decision was made to nurture the automotive industry, the state exercised stringent controls through its domestic content programme, which meant localisation of functional items such as engines, transmissions, and axles. This is how the global automobile giants like Hyundai and Kia got their start.

Electronics is the last of the five industries that South Korea's developmental state promoted. Unlike the four other industries discussed above, the electronics industry is a *deus ex machina* for the upstarts of the late twentieth century—like Taiwan and South Korea—because it so neatly fills the lacuna between the light and heavy phases of industrialisation. The electronics industry was seized upon during the First Five-Year Plan, as South Korea's 'strategic export industry', along with textiles. This was due to 'international subcontracting', a form of manufacturing most often associated with the electronics industries in Taiwan and South Korea, spawned through the Japanese utilisation of cheap and competent labour nearby.

Once the electronics industry got moving, the government adopted a more comprehensive measure to 'rationalise' the industry—to create a complementary relationship between international subcontracting and domestic firms. In the early 1970s, the state concentrated the industry in one huge complex to facilitate communications and technological transfer: the Kumi Electronics Complex, situated along the Seoul–Busan expressway, was singled out as the mainstay of the '$10 Billion Exports by 1980' campaign, and the Ministry of Commerce ensured its success through a package of incentives and palliatives for the domestic and foreign companies finding new domiciles in Kumi. Buoyed by Japanese investment, the electronics industry met its quota in the campaign.

To become world class, however, the electronics industry needed more than the garden-variety government incentives. In order to obtain 'technological leapfrogging' and keep beating out competitors in an industry with a quick product cycle, where existing technologies become obsolete overnight, South Koreans had to invest heavily in training scientists and technicians, and increase its research and development (R&D). The results have been extraordinary, with a national champion such as Samsung Electronics eventually becoming one of the world's most consequential electronics firm.

In 1972, President Park Chung-hee complained of a democratic distemper in South Korea. 'While the affairs of the state are publicly debated and decided through the ballot box here, the North Koreans are of one mind, obsessed with making guns, mortars, and tanks' (Woo 1991: 147). Soon, out went the ballot boxes, and South Korea became of one mind, like its northern brethren, concentrating on building basic industries that were indispensable for defence. By the end of the decade, South Korea was capable of manufacturing, notwithstanding US protests, M-16 rifles, M-60 machine guns, M-48 tanks, model 500 helicopters, 'fast boats', medium- and long-range land-to-land missiles, and fighter aircraft.

The South Korean 'industrial deepening' of the 1970s was unthinkable apart from the security threat, real and perceived, from outside. And the timing makes little sense without paying attention to the decline in US security commitment that seemingly left South Korea out in the cold. The importance of the global security issue is really what set

South Korea apart from the Latin American version of the 'industrial deepening', which had been orchestrated in the absence of a Cold War security threat.

5. The Developmental State, Finance, and Big Business

The industrial deepening effort was a success. South Korea's GNP grew on average 11 per cent each year from 1973 to 1978, an outstanding achievement, even in the annals of the twentieth century's most prodigious economic performances. It was also this period that gave us a model of the South Korean political economy. By mediating enormous amounts of financial resources, both foreign loan and domestic resources, the state obtained both the autonomy and the capacity to shape the market, firms, and society at large. Here, we describe the mechanism for the industrialisation that we described in section 4. 'Industrial Policies'.

The resources for South Korea's industrialisation came largely from outside, in the form of foreign loans, to satisfy the investment ambition, which ran as much as one-third of the GNP by the end of the 1970s. In that time period, heavy industry absorbed more than three-quarters of the total investment in manufacturing. Government targets were often fulfilled earlier than planned. By contrast, the actual investment in light industry was less than one-half the initial projected investment. Machine-building surpassed the initial projection by a wide margin and investment in the chemical industry also outpaced the projection.

The main goal of South Korea's finance was to haemorrhage as much capital as possible into the heavy industrialisation programme. To that end, the government set financial prices at an artificial low to subsidise import-substitution of heavy chemical and export industries. It inevitably led to a bifurcation of the financial market. Business and government savings, and foreign capital, financed heavy industries. A large part of household savings stayed in the private or 'curb' market to finance the rest of the economy, including small and medium enterprises and consumers.

The average cost of all loans—banks, foreign, nonbank financial intermediaries, bonds—for export industries was almost always cheaper than that for industries producing for domestic consumption, and loans for heavy industries were significantly lower than that for light industries. The bank loans were always below the GNP deflator. The average real cost of bank loans throughout the decade was *minus* 6.7 per cent, for the informal or the 'curb' market was always positive, well above inflation. The average cost of borrowing in the curb was about 18.5 per cent. The difference in average between the two markets was, then, more than twenty-five percentage points.

The South Korean government also used 'policy loans' to promote heavy industrialisation. In some sense, all bank credits might be considered policy loans in South Korea. They were really business subsidies, given the interest rate differentials, and their allocation was scrutinised by the state. There were three routes to credits for those willing to invest in heavy industry. One was through the banking system: the Bank of Korea (BOK) rediscount, funds for specialised banks, and directed loans. The second source of policy loans was fiscal, taken out of the state budget. The third was the National Investment Fund (NIF). Policy loans accounted for nearly one-half of total domestic credit in the late 1970s. Of all policy loans, export credits and national investment loans were most significant, and they were plentiful for those who could prove their mettle through their sales volume abroad. National investment loans were not as plentiful, but were created with the express purpose of financing heavy and chemical industries, but enough to manoeuvre the Chaebol into these industries (Woo 1991: 1448–1475).

The political economy of this bifurcated financial system was illiberal, undemocratic, and statist. The ubiquitous curb, a vital part of the nation's economic life, was outside the protection of, yet at the mercy of, the state, which retained for itself the prerogative to shake up, freeze, and destroy the private money market, as needed. In an otherwise thriving capitalist nation, the formal financial sector remained backward. Every bank in the nation was owned and controlled by the state. Essentially, bankers were bureaucrats and not businessmen, and they extended loans to those favoured by the state. In doing so, they thought in terms of the GNP growth target set by the state, and not in terms of profit. The monetary authority—BOK—forfeited what little autonomy it might have had before the industrial push. In its stead, it was the Ministry of Finance that directed monetary policies: the Economic Planning Board to oversee bank budgets, and the Ministry of Commerce to influence the flow of export and other policy loans.

From the early 1970s on, bank loans became subsidies for the chosen—the entrepreneurs who had already proven their mettle through good export records, the risk takers who entered into heavy and chemical industries, and the faithful who plunged into the untried sea of international competition with new products, relying on the state's god offices to rescue them. It was really these entrepreneurs who made the big push possible, the drive for heavy and chemical industrialisation and industrial maturation.

To join the hallowed chosen few, enterprises had to be big, but to remain chosen, they had to be gigantic. Size was an effective deterrent against default—something that would threaten the economic stability of the country, forcing the government into the role of the lender of last resort. The importance of size in this regard cannot be overemphasised, since highly leveraged firms live with the constant spectre of default. It was for this reason that the big business in South Korea was often described as being 'octopus-like'. But the tentacles of the big business gripped not only the economy, but also the state as well: big state and big business would have to sink or swim together. A credit-based financial system mediated by an interventionist authoritarian state became the basis of the developmental state in South Korea. And when this financial system underwent liberalisation, the developmental state also came undone.

South Korea's big business is called the *Chaebol*. The Chaebol is a family-owned and managed group of companies that exercises monopolistic or oligopolistic control in product lines and industries. The conventional way to differentiate the Chaebol from its Japanese counterpart, the pre-war zaibatsu, is to note the conspicuous absence of a banking institution at the core of the former. Some business historians argue, however, that it was the general trading companies that formed the core of the pre-war zaibatsu. In South Korea, general trading companies have also acted as the core of a number of large Chaebol groups, mimicking the structures of, say, pre-war Mitsui and Mitsubishi. Even so, South Korea's general trading firms had no financial clout apart from the state, and the Chaebol groups did not possess banks that could back up their trading firms. In lieu of a group-affiliated bank, then, the state mediated the flow of domestic and foreign capital to the Chaebol and supervised its operations through a designated bank, whose role might be likened to that of the German banks prior to the First World War. The growth of the Chaebol was thus predicated on state provision of industrial capital.

Whenever credit allocation shows a bias for size, it sets in motion a powerful tendency towards market concentration. The extraordinary concentration of domestic credit in the Chaebol was such that towards the end of the 1970s, some 137 Chaebol claimed 70 per cent of total bank and 50 per cent of total financial institution loans outstanding (Woo 1991: 175). Such credit concentration and corporate debt leverage was extremely destabilising for the economy in times of global recession and slacking exports. Even in good times, huge non-performing loans, accumulated through the years, cast a thick pall over the health of the banking system. By the 1980s, the sum of non-performing loans in the banking sector came to be a good one-fifth or one-sixth of total domestic credit. This was the South Korean version of what the US political scientist Theodore Lowi (1979) called 'permanent receivership', meaning that institutions large enough to be a significant factor in the community get their stability underwritten. To deal with the situation, the government resorted to indirect taxation through inflation, as well as indirect taxation. Occasionally, the government grabbed the bull by the horns and forcibly 'reorganised' the troubled industry. The number of the Chaebol participants could be winnowed down to a few profitable ones through a state fiat ordering merger. This was called 'controlled competition', and happened in times of crisis, including most recently during the Asian Financial Crisis of 1997–1998.

The Chaebol in South Korea was born as a private agency of public purpose. Park had eradicated the distinction between public and private when he pumped resources into the Chaebol as national champions and the muscle of the industrialisation push. By the end of the decade, the chickens were coming home to roost.

6. Conclusion

The developmental state in South Korea is best understood in the context of international security, as is its demise. The industrialisation push (in the form that it took) was over not because it was a failure, but because it was a success. It was dismantled because its mission was largely completed. The industrialisation push, which had its origin in the Nixon doctrine and its apotheosis during President Carter's human rights crusade, which deeply rattled the government in South Korea, had been a nationalist response to the vicissitudes in 'big power politics' as the South Koreans were wont to say. By the end of the 1970s, however, the United States had reversed its policy towards East Asia, including South Korea. President Carter recanted his earlier plan to pull all US troops out of South Korea, as well as his earlier pledge to ship out all nuclear weapons from South Korea that had shielded it from North Korea.

This new policy towards East Asia, inaugurated in the later part of the Carter administration and consolidated in the Reagan era, sought to counter the Soviets in the Far East through tight US economic and security ties with Japan, South Korea, and in the aftermath of the normalisation of relations, the People's Republic of China. The logic of this sort of regional consolidation led to a swift US embrace and support of the new dictatorship that came to preside over South Korea for much of the 1980s. Japan was no less forthcoming, infusing, at US prodding, billions of dollars in financial aid to the new regime.

With the security context rapidly shifting, the rationale for the developmental state was not as robust as it once was. Finance was the lynchpin for the developmental state in South Korea, and financial liberalisation in South Korea also meant that the state would no longer have the leverage that it once yielded. Liberalising finance in South Korea took a long time, and it had four components: internationalisation, privatisation, deregulation, and capital market development. Internationalisation of the financial market meant that foreigners would enter banking, insurance, and capital markets to compete with domestic institutions, granted as a quid pro quo for South Korea's entry into foreign financial markets. To compete at the world level, South Korean financial firms had to behave like capitalists and not bureaucrats, thinking profit and not control. That meant the privatisation of banks in South Korea. But as banks cannot thrive in situations of financial repression (which does not reward financial intermediaries well), the finance would have to be deregulated, ceilings on interest rates lifted, the practice of policy loans abandoned, and return on financial assets made positive so that saving and financial intermediating could become profitable. The high cost of capital thus issued would finally lead the Chaebol to find other sources of financing, which, combined with the growing surplus in current accounts, resulted in the blossoming of the capital market. In this way, internationalisation, privatisation, financial deregulation, and development of the capital market formed inseparable aspects of financial liberalisation.

For the state, the implication was colossal. Dictatorship may have lasted in South Korea for another ten or more years since the end of the heavy industrialisation push, but the developmental state that coupled political repression with the industrial outcome was unravelling with the implementation of financial liberalisation, which started in earnest in the early 1980s, culminating with the Asian Financial Crisis of 1997–1998.

The path of financial liberalisation has been tentative and halting, with two steps forward and one step back, but over time, it closed the era when the state nursed big business from the cradle. It ended the era of the developmental state in South Korea as the world knew it. It also heralded a new era of capitalism, now spearheaded by an effective regulatory state, democratic polity, and world-class entrepreneurs, who are capable of withstanding the pressures of global competition and prevailing.

Bibliography

Amsden, A. (1989), *Asia's Next Giant* (New York: Oxford University Press).

Chang, H.-J. (1994), *The Political Economy of Industrial Policy* (New York: St. Martin's Press).

Gerschenkron, A. (1946), *Economic Backwardness in Historical Perspective* (Cambridge: Harvard University Press).

Jansen, M. (1968), 'Modernization and Foreign Policy in Meiji Japan', in R. Ward, ed., *Political Development in Modern Japan* (Princeton, NJ: Princeton University Press), pp.149–188.

Johnson, C. (1982), *MITI and the Japanese Miracle*. (Stanford, CA: Stanford University Press).

Johnson, C. (1999), 'The Developmental State: Odyssey of a Concept', in M. Woo-Cumings, ed., *The Developmental State* (Ithaca, NY: Cornell University Press), pp.32–60.

Jones, L. P., and Sakong Il(1970), *Government, Business and Entrepreneurship in Economic Development: The Korean Case*. (Cambridge, CA: Harvard University Press).

Lowi, T. (1979), *The End of Liberalism: The Second Republic of the United States*. (New York: Norton).

Woo, J.-E. (1991), *Race to the Swift: State and Finance in Korean Industrialization*. (New York: Columbia University Press).

CHAPTER 8

CHAEBOL

SANG-YOUNG RHYU

1. INTRODUCTION

AMONG South Korean scholars and non-South Korean scholars studying the country, Chaebol is one of the most fascinating topics. The Oxford dictionary defines 'Chaebol' as 'a large family-owned business community in South Korea', but this definition connotes various categories and concepts according to one's perspective. 'Chaebol' is also the term that features most frequently when discussing the South Korean economy and has become an indispensable word when analysing political phenomena in South Korea, such as democracy and political power. Before the 1997 Asian Financial Crisis, interest in Chaebols was primarily for their role as leaders in the development of the South Korean economy. Since the crisis, the focus has shifted to reform of the South Korean political economy and Chaebols' role in it. Indeed, Chaebols serve as genes deeply imprinted on the structural characteristics and historical origins of all sectors, including politics, society, and culture, as well as the economy and business management in South Korea.

Chaebol is a very contentious word in South Korea, both practically and theoretically. The light and shadow of Chaebols' influence on the South Korean economy contrast sharply, and the assets and liabilities that they left to South Korean politics and society seemed irreconcilable in the past. However, thanks to economic reforms and institutional change under pressure from democratisation and globalisation, the Chaebol system is transforming into one that reduces Chaebols' debts to South Korean society, while increasing assets. How have Chaebols grown and through what mechanism do they operate? What impacts has the Chaebol system had on South Korea's political economy, and how is the situation evolving? This chapter seeks objective and balanced answers to these questions, bringing quantitative data to bear on them, as well as analysing the arrangement of and changes to key economic institutions.

The chapter is arranged as follows. The second section briefly outlines diverse views, arguments, and assessments of Chaebols. Faced with the fact that the assessment of Chaebols greatly depends on how they are viewed and approached, this theoretical outline will allow a full, balanced portrayal of Chaebols. The third section tracks the birth and growth process of Chaebols. Section four analyses the political dynamics surrounding Chaebol reform. In particular, the fierce political debates among stakeholders surrounding Chaebol reform and institutional change that have been going on since the 1997 Asian Financial Crisis are summarised. The fifth section briefly analyses and forecasts the results of innovation displayed by Chaebols in the era of globalisation and infinite competition and the final section concludes with a summary of the key arguments in this chapter, along with theoretical implications for the sustainability and future of Chaebols.

2. Contending Perspectives on South Korean Chaebols

The theoretical debates and political wrangling currently under way in South Korean society stem from a mixed view of the historical context and current role of the Chaebols. These views reflect the three dilemmas that South Korean society, as well as the Chaebols, face. First, the evaluation of and position on reforming Chaebols completely changes depending on whether a person values (a) the Chaebols' political history; or (b) their economic achievements. The former stresses that the wealth accumulated by Chaebols is not that of shareholders alone, but also counts as assets of the South Korean people as a whole, as well as among a wider group of stakeholders because the Chaebols have grown thanks to the government's financial and institutional support since the early 1960s. The latter, on the other hand, stresses the logic that regardless of history, current high economic performance is due to Chaebols' efforts and innovation, and thus all achievements should be attributed to shareholders and companies (Park 2011). Second, high political distrust and high economic confidence in Chaebols have long coexisted in the political debates over Chaebol reform. Frequent collusive ties between politics and business and corruption cases, combined with worsening economic inequality, are spurring political distrust in and criticism of Chaebols. Contrasting voices of economic confidence and praise for Chaebols are growing as their international competitiveness increases and Chaebols' economic contribution to the South Korean economy expands. Third, with regard to Chaebols' future direction and role in South Korean society, different strategies for reform are presented, depending on whether they value technological innovation by business or demand corporate social responsibility and justice. Whereas the former suggests the voluntary discipline of Chaebols, which allows market principles and free competition to promote technological innovation in businesses, the latter, to enhance the social responsibility and sustainability of Chaebols, calls for strict government regulation and social monitoring. Depending on how one views these three aspects, how to both evaluate and reform Chaebols diverges greatly, creating a complex debate.

Meanwhile, the assessment of Chaebols is largely expressed using one of three metaphors: angels, demons, and necessary evils. These metaphors represent an epistemological question surrounding the status and role of Chaebols in South Korea's political economy. The framing of Chaebols as angels to South Korea was dominant during the authoritarian era and lasted until just before the 1997 Asian Financial Crisis. The narrative was that they were national champions who led South Korea's rapid economic growth, the miracle on the Han River, and contributed to South Korea escaping poverty. Park Chung-hee's developmentalist authoritarian regime and its preferential treatment of Chaebols were generally accepted by the public, as a case like South Korea was rare in the human history of industrialisation, in that it successfully industrialised and escaped poverty in a short period of time. The outbreak of the Asian Financial Crisis in 1997 triggered a change in the appraisal of Chaebols from angels to demons. With Chaebols' inefficiency and opacity pointed out as the main causes of the economic crisis, they were criticised as being the evil that left pain and dark shadows looming over the South Korean economy. In addition, considering the early 1960s in South Korea, the Chaebol system can be framed as a necessary evil. South Korea was impoverished, lacking the market or institutions needed for economic development. Chaebols, although they ignored democratic procedures and institutions, strategically allocated limited resources to engender the economic prosperity that South Korea currently enjoys. Following this view, a compromise reform strategy is proposed that will maintain Chaebols' strengths while also minimising their shortcomings.

These opposing views and assessments of Chaebols are not irrelevant to the scope of approaches to analysing them (Lim 2012). First of all, from the view that Chaebols are purely economic actors operating solely in the market, South Korea's Chaebols are the result of a perfectly rational choice and efficient allocation of resources. Both the success and failure of Chaebols are the result of market principles and free competition; the opacity or inefficiency of Chaebols may actually be the result of limitations of the system (Hwang 2002). In addition, government intervention and regulation will only lead to distortions in the market. Second, one might consider Chaebols as political hegemons operating in the political market rather than as actors in the economic market. According to this approach, the power of Chaebols does not come from the power of the market but from the political power that Chaebols control. This view sees the South Korean economy as one in which politicians—including the president—reign, while Chaebols rule. The visible hands of Chaebols, not the invisible hands of the market, operate the workings of the South Korean political economy. The idea of Chaebols as political hegemons is substantiated by two observations: first, the political economic power of Chaebols has repeatedly been at work in major elections and political events during the authoritarian era; and second, the Chaebol system operates as a real force that cannot be ignored even by democratically elected political power. Finally, emphasising organisational efficiency would narrow the scope of analysis to Chaebols as organisations of their own. This approach focuses on the structure and operations of Chaebols and the Chaebol system as an organisation, as well as associated phenomena and transaction costs. The Chaebols in South Korea came to form a unique business network structure in order to survive the initial conditions of low development in South Korea. The unique entrepreneurship of Chaebol founders shaped this process. Their opaque corporate governance is designed to minimise agent costs, and vertical and horizontal integration can be understood as Chaebols' survival strategy to reduce transaction costs amid the government's strange regulations and misalignment of institutions (Jwa 2002).

3. THE HISTORY OF CHAEBOL GROWTH AND GOVERNMENT POLICY

Chaebols have taken the lead in the growth of the South Korean economy, while also reaping the benefits of success. Chaebols have been able to grow rapidly, thanks to their cooperative relations with the Park Chung-hee regime, which employed a developmental state strategy. While direct and strong government intervention and control of the market have become commonplace, this institutional and policy environment has served as a foundation for the growth of Chaebols (Amsden 1992). The Chaebols, which actively utilised the national strategy and industrial policies of the Park Chung-hee regime, were able to grow both quantitatively and qualitatively in markets both in and out of South Korea. They grew in size, became more technologically advanced, and gained status in the international market. Regardless of the various criticisms, it is hard to deny that Chaebols have contributed greatly to South Korea's economic modernisation and industrialisation through this process.

South Korea's per capita income (GNI) increased from US$82 in 1961 to US$32,115 in 2019. The annual economic growth rate of South Korea averaged 10.03 per cent from 1961, when industrialisation began in earnest, to 1979, when the Park Chung-hee era ended. The growth rate averaged 8.64 per cent from 1980 to 1997, when the Asian Financial Crisis hit South Korea. South Korea's exports rose from US$100 million in 1964 to US$542.2 billion as of 2019. In 2018, South Korea became the seventh country in the world to exceed US$30,000 per capita income with a population greater than 50 million, joining the 30–50 club designated by the Organisation for Economic Co-operation and Development (OECD) as an indicator of economic prowess. These records indicate that South Korea successfully grew its economy in a short period of time at a rapid pace (Song 2003). This journey of economic growth, which began in the ruins of the Korean War, has always been attributed to the government's effective economic policies, the economic performance of large corporations, and the symbiotic government–business relationship (Kim 1994; Grinberg 2014).

The Chaebols in South Korea were established after the Korean War, which started in 1950. They started to grow rapidly in the early 1960s with the support of the Park Chung-hee regime's industrialisation strategy. Some studies place the origins of South Korean Chaebols in the Japanese colonial period and argue that continuity exists between businesses that were established then and Chaebols (Eckert 2016). However, today's major Chaebols were established before and after the Korean War. For example, Hyundai Engineering & Construction Co., the precursor to the Hyundai Group, was established in 1947 and grew in the wake of the Korean War and the subsequent years by contracting the construction of military facilities for US troops stationed in South Korea. Samsung Merchant, the precursor to the Samsung Group, was founded in 1938. What is now the Samsung C&T Corporation, the leading corporation of the group, was established in 1951. CheilJedang Industrial Co., the first manufacturer in the Samsung Group, was founded in 1953, and Cheil Industries Inc. was founded in 1954. All of these grew thanks to the explosive special demands of the Korean War and subsequent reconstruction projects (Rhyu 2005). However, the fully fledged growth of Chaebols began in the early 1960s with the Park Chung-hee regime's industrialisation strategy and Five-Year Economic Development Plans (Kim 1997).

Shortly after the military coup in May 1961, Park Chung-hee indicted the existing conglomerates as fraudsters and fined them a huge amount. However, he soon established a new ruling coalition by selecting them as partners for South Korea's modernisation and industrialisation. Through this, Park Chung-hee was personally able to strengthen his political power base, and South Korea gained a national economic foundation and entrepreneurial spirit for government-led industrialisation. In July 1961, the Federation of Korean Industries (FKI) was formed, with fourteen entrepreneurs under the leadership Lee Byung-chul, the chairman of the Samsung Group. The FKI proposed a large-scale industrial complex and a rapid industrialisation strategy through foreign loans to Park Chung-hee's military government (Kim 1997). After that, cooperative and strategic government–business relations led by the developmental state and Chaebols came to dominate South Korea's political economy, at least until the 1997 Asian Financial Crisis.

The South Korean government adopted a developmental state model and a rapid growth strategy to expedite modernisation and industrialisation in the early 1960s. President Park Chung-hee's personal background of growth out of poverty, his character, his education at the Manchuria Military Academy under Japanese colonial occupation, and the Cold War order all served as the backdrop for the Park Chung-hee government to learn about Japan's developmental state model and apply it to South Korea (Eckert 2016). The South Korean government adopted the concept of *Bugukgangbyeong*, meaning 'Rich Nation, Strong Army', which was the motto of the 1868 Meiji Restoration in Japan, for nationalistic mobilisation and industrialisation strategies. The Economic Planning Board was formed as a pilot agency in 1961 to plan, implement, and evaluate all economic policies under Park Chung-hee's strong mandate and to strategically allocate resources for the common purpose of economic growth (Kim 1994). In this process, the planned economy and policy effectiveness, in which state intervention was the norm, were more important than a free market rationale and price mechanisms. At that time, rapid capital accumulation and strategic allocation through government intervention were deemed more necessary for South Korea than free market principles and efficient allocation of resources. Under this policy concept, various industrial policies were implemented, and Chaebols emerged as national champions for rapid growth and an economic partner of the authoritarian regime.

The Five-Year Economic Development Plans, which began in 1962 and lasted for four phases until 1982, served as the policy background for bringing about South Korea's economic growth and for Chaebols to grow into key players in the South Korean economy. The original plan for the first phase of the Five-Year Economic Development Plan pursued an import substitution industrialisation strategy that prioritised agricultural development, but it failed to achieve successful results due to lack of funds and excessive goals. In 1964, under pressure from the United States, the first phase of the Five-Year Economic Development Plan was revised to a more realistic export-oriented strategy based on neoclassicism (Haggard 1990). The shift to an export-driven policy served as another occasion for the South Korean government and Chaebols to form a cooperative relationship. The government encouraged businesses to actively engage in long-term, large-scale investments by providing them with financial benefits through policy financing and indirect financing through banks. The South Korean government implemented active policies to attract foreign-invested companies as well because domestic capital alone was not enough to achieve its goals.

South Korean government introduced the Foreign Capital Inducement Act for the first time in 1960. However, the total export volume of South Korea was below US$100 million, the size of the companies was still small, and their production capacity was very weak. Therefore, it was almost impossible for South Korean companies to raise investment funds from overseas financial institutions. To overcome this, in 1962 the government helped attract foreign investments and loans by introducing a system under which the government guaranteed private companies' debts when raising funds from overseas. This system resulted in the government creating new credit and markets; it was one of the representative systems of a developmental state, one with a state-driven developmental strategy. In 1966, the consolidated new Foreign Capital Act was enacted to introduce policies to aggressively attract foreign capital into South Korea. In addition, in order to promote exports and attract foreign investment, the South Korean government implemented a policy to block labour movements within foreign-invested companies in 1970, which was reflected in domestic companies, helping them to perform stable projects with minimal production costs (Ahn 2008). The growth of Chaebols was sustained by government-interventionist policymaking and industrial policies that excluded labour, at least until democratisation in 1987.

The Ministry of Commerce and Industry systematically implemented export promotion policies beginning in 1964, which included a 50 per cent reduction in corporate and income taxes on the export income and export activities of businesses that earn revenue in foreign currencies, exemption from import duties on raw materials for export, and support for export financing with low interest. Thanks to these policies, the South Korean economy was able to achieve its export targets of US$500 million in 1968 and US$700 million in 1969. This policy of 'Building a Nation through Exports' had supported the rapid growth of Chaebols and strengthened their competitiveness in overseas markets (Kim 1994). With the shift of economic strategy from import substitution to an export orientation, resources and incentives were provided according to export performance, which resulted in Chaebols engaging in competition on the basis of performance, further leading to a reduction in the possibility of inefficient allocation of resources according to political interests and in the scale of unproductive rents for the economy as a whole.

However, in the early 1970s, the South Korean economy soon faced limitations in executing trade and labour-intensive industrialisation strategies, which amplified the need to upgrade its industrial structure to a capital-intensive and technology-intensive one, as well as to strengthen its export industry. Park Chung-hee's declaration of heavy and chemical industrialisation (HCI), which was announced on 12 January 1973, provided another opportunity for Chaebols to technically strengthen their competitiveness and grow quantitatively. The government selected six strategic industries to focus on: steel making, electronics, machinery, chemicals, shipbuilding, and non-ferrous metal industries. It implemented a plan to increase the ratio of HCIs in the industrial structure from 35.2 per cent in 1971 to 51 per cent in 1981. In December 1973, the government established the National Investment Fund (NIF) to finance long-term investment in HCIs, estimated at around $9.6 billion. The NIF interest rate was set at 9.0 per cent, whereas the prevailing three-year interest rate on bank loans was 15.5 per cent. Government-controlled banks also supported the HCI drive by providing policy-oriented loans with favourable terms. This was a dramatic departure from the second half of the 1960s. To promote HCIs, the government essentially had to secure economies of scale, make massive complementary investments, and develop skilled labour with the requisite technological skills. Instead of relying on market mechanisms, South Korea sought to address coordination and innovation externalities through integrated, forward-looking plans, even as it tried to aim for international competitiveness from the outset under the slogan of 'the exportization of all industries' (Lim 2012: 77–78).

Prior to pursuing HCI, on 3 August 1972, President Park Chung-hee issued an 'emergency order on economic stability and growth' to freeze all bonds and private loans held by large companies and forcefully converted them into investments, which was crucial evidence of the symbiotic relationship between the Park Chung-hee government and Chaebols. The move was proposed by the FKI and was implemented by Park Chung-hee to prevent large conglomerates from going bankrupt. Subsequently, by pulling underground financing into institutionalised and legal financing and enacting the Public Corporation Inducement Law, the government intended to relieve the debt burden and financial expenses for businesses and resolve the financial crisis of the South Korean economy (Haggard and Moon 1993). This order was a violation of private property rights and a distortion of the market, but it was an institutional measure that supported state capitalism and the developmental state strategy pursued by Park Chung-hee, and it resulted in the rapid growth of large corporation groups. Also, anecdotes that Park Chung-hee had frequently shared opinions with Chung Ju-yung, the Hyundai Group chairman, and Lee Byung-chul, the Samsung Group chairman, on large national projects since the 1960s—such as infrastructure developments, heavy chemical industrialisation, and construction projects in the Middle East—are well known (Kim 1994). South Korea became visible on the global stage as one of the newly industrialising countries and the South Korean Chaebols gained international recognition and the term

'Chaebol' itself began to appear in 1972 in English dictionaries, defined by Merriam-Webster as 'a family-controlled industrial conglomerate in South Korea'.

In the 1980s, beginning with the inauguration of the Chun Doo-hwan government, South Korean Chaebols were able to grow in a more institutionalised environment. Amid the international trend of neo-conservatism, neo-liberalism, and internationalisation, Chaebols concentrated their efforts on becoming competitive players in the global market, and the business-friendly environment continued regardless of the political power change. The antitrust law introduced in late 1980 marked a new beginning in the relationship between the government and Chaebols, but it can also be said that the institutional environment has become a more stable and reasonable one for Chaebols. The market environment during the Chun Doo-hwan regime, such as stabilisation, structural adjustment, and the three lows—low interest rates, low oil prices, and a weak US dollar—was favourable to large conglomerates, even in international terms. Such an environment served as a chance for Chaebols to grow in quality (Haggard and Moon 1993). In addition, the introduction of the Industrial Development Act in 1986 was a momentum for government policy to shift from direct and discretionary intervention over industrial policies to more rational and market-conforming ones. The 1987 democratisation and the explosion of the labour movement also called for the reform of Chaebols and served as a critical moment for the rise in political and economic costs, which had previously been curbed. However, despite many changes in the composition of the thirty largest conglomerates following the 1997 Asian Financial Crisis and the 2008 Global Crash, South Korea's large conglomerates have continued to grow, and their international competitiveness has increased without much interruption.

The growth of Chaebols is also reflected in the share of combined assets of Chaebols and their sales in South Korea's gross domestic product (GDP). In fact, the concentration of economic power by Chaebols and the growth of large corporations has been one of the strongest characteristics of the South Korean economy since 1960. According to Figure 8.1, the total portion of assets in South Korea's GDP of the thirty largest business groups

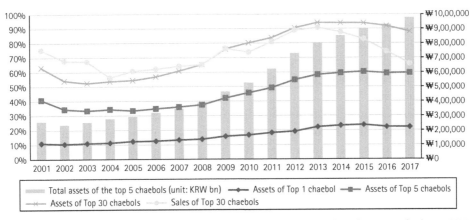

FIGURE 8.1: Changes in the proportion of the thirty largest Chaebols' total assets and sales to GDP

Source: Compiled by author and based on the data from Park (2017), 13-20.

increased from 63.1 per cent (480 billion KRW) in 2001 to 91.78 per cent (1,435,574 billion KRW) in 2016. This means that the thirty largest business groups had a higher growth rate in their combined assets than South Korea's GDP growth rate (Park 2017: 16). In addition, the thirty largest business groups accounted for a high percentage of sales nationally, from 477,742 billion KRW (75.21 per cent of total sales) in 2001 to 1,163,519 billion KRW (74.39 per cent) in 2016. When considered in light of the major products of large business groups and both domestic and foreign market conditions, sales totalled an even higher proportion, as in 2013, when they accounted for 90.62 per cent of total sales.[1] Thus, the growth of large business groups also means that the concentration of economic power by the Chaebols has intensified. As Figure 8.1 indicates, the five largest conglomerates in South Korea have accrued a disproportionate amount of assets and ratio in GDP relative to all other major companies. This trend sheds light on the bipolarisation of economic power between the five largest conglomerates and the rest of the major companies among the largest thirty groups. This has raised political and social concerns about the possible harm caused by the concentration of economic power and has resulted in increasing calls for Chaebol reform. In addition, it demonstrates that the style of regulating Chaebols primarily on the basis of size has been rendered obsolete.

4. The Political Economy of Chaebol Reform

After the Park Chung-hee regime, each administration, whether conservative or progressive, promised Chaebol reform as one of its core policies and attempted to present a fresh Chaebol policy distinct from that of previous governments. Chaebol reform has been a very effective issue for stirring up political attention. All administrations have tried to strengthen the foundation of their political economic power and clarify the administration's identity in regard to Chaebol policy by either promoting the economy through supporting Chaebols or regulating Chaebols and improving social justice. So has Chaebol reform succeeded or failed in South Korea? Did economic reforms spur change in Chaebols, and what are the reasons for this change (or lack of change)? Following the perspectives discussed in the section 'Contending perspectives on South Korean Chaebols', these questions come to different answers.

South Korea's competition policy is one of the most controversial policies among those concerned with Chaebol reform. From its enactment on 31 December 1980 until December 2020, the Monopoly Regulation and Fair Trade Act, which serves as the core institution dealing with Chaebol reform and competition policy in South Korea, has been amended as many as sixty-nine times. Having been frequently amended, this policy has also been very politically sensitive. The contents of the act reflect the current nature of relations between government and business, and its history sums up the evolutionary trajectory of capitalism in South Korea (Jwa 2002; Lim 2010).

The democratisation of South Korea in 1987 and the 1997 Asian Financial Crisis served as dual pressures that triggered economic reform in South Korea and resulted in extensive institutional change and Chaebol reform. During the 1997 economic crisis, nineteen out of the thirty largest business groups were liquidated. However, an interesting paradox remains in competition policy. First, while the initial purpose of competition policy was to protect small and medium-sized enterprises and to restrain the concentration of economic power by large conglomerates, as time passed, the Chaebols gained an even stronger concentration of economic power. Second, even though South Korea's competition policy has been strengthened to increase regulations on large businesses, the policy is generally not viewed as successful. As competition policy was reinforced, so was the concentration of economic power by large business groups. In particular, the ratio of the market controlled by the thirty largest business groups rose sharply, comprising almost 90 per cent in terms of asset size or sales (see Figure 8.1), concurrent with ongoing polarisation within the thirty largest groups that has served to provide criteria for regulation. Although corporate governance reforms have progressed in earnest, such trends remain unchanged. Why is this so? It is a paradox of competition policy and a dilemma to be solved in South Korea.

The South Korean government introduced a policy to constrain economic concentration, starting with the first amendment of the Fair Trade Act in December 1986. This includes restrictions on the establishment of holding companies, prohibition on cross-shareholding, prohibition on debt guarantees for affiliates, restrictions on the total amount of investment, and the designation of large enterprise groups. Later, the government persistently increased the intensity of Chaebol regulations, maintaining its goal of reducing economic concentration (Rhyu 2019).

Chaebol reform was fiercely pushed forward after the 1997 Asian Financial Crisis. The external pressure was intensified by International Monetary Fund (IMF) conditionality. Public opinion also labelled Chaebols as largely responsible for the economic crisis. The Chaebols had to accept the pressures for drastic reforms. During the financial crisis, the Kim Dae-jung administration strongly pursued reforms to improve the accountability and transparency of Chaebols' corporate governance structure (Haggard et al. 2003). As detailed in Table 8.1, a variety of reforms were implemented piecewise over a short time period.

Such reform was possible thanks to a policy coalition that formed with international pressure, and civil society groups with anti-Chaebol sentiments under the pro-reform leadership of the Kim Dae-jung administration. Furthermore, the style of reform changed from the previous mode of direct and arbitrary government intervention to one that worked through financial institutions, market, and economic policies. Such reforms acted as momentum for change away from the developmental state system that fuelled South Korea's economic growth, as neoliberal reforms were advanced in the aftermath of the 1997 Asian Financial Crisis. South Korean institutional change,

Table 8.1: Key principles for Chaebol reform after the Asian Financial Crisis

	Stages of reform	Principles
1	*Five tasks* (Feb 1998)	- Improvement of management transparency - Abolition of cross-debt guarantees - Capital structure improvement - Inducement of concentration on core business - Strengthening of managers' and majority shareholders' accountability
2	*Three new additional tasks* (Aug 1999)	- Restraint of circular-shareholding and unfair internal transactions between affiliates belonging to the same conglomerate - Separation of the financial industry from other service and manufacturing industries - Prevention of major shareholders' ad hoc bequeathal of stocks to their siblings
3	*Second-stage reform* (Feb 2000)	- Establishment of profit-oriented managerial practices - Revision of the force-out system of failed or hopeless companies - Establishment of a managerial system in which managers take full responsibility for operational and financial results - Formation of a virtuous circle among small and medium-sized, venture and large companies

particularly the series of Chaebol reforms that progressed after the 1997 Asian Financial Crisis, was fast in speed and broad in scope, the pattern was very abrupt and drastic, and external pressure and the state are seen to have played the biggest role.

The Moon Jae-in administration focused on eradicating deep-seated unfair practices by overhauling corporate governance and emphasising voluntary compliance by Chaebols. Corporate reforms have been carried out to strengthen the powers of minority shareholders and to eradicate business malpractices within the same group, such as excessive and unfair allocation of contracts to family-owned affiliates, which was customarily accepted in the past. Legal efforts have also been made to correct the anachronistic culture of Chaebol families, which can be seen in the Korean Air 'nut rage' incident.[2] In addition, a representative institutional investor, the National Pension Service, introduced a stewardship code to enhance the transparency and accountability of large conglomerates. The Samsung case, which is currently facing a litigation process due to involvement in the Park Geun-hye administration's corruption case, is another case that reflects the calls for reform of customarily accepted malpractices that are repeatedly committed by Chaebols (Rhyu 2018).

Considering only the structure of large conglomerates in an international perspective, South Korea is not the only country with large conglomerates such as Chaebols. The term 'Chaebol' originates from Japan's *zaibatsu*, and Japan's large conglomerate system remains intact. Also, large conglomerates or holding companies that have similar structures are common in Europe and the United States. Japan allows direct cross-shareholding within a single corporate group, and there is no regulation on ownership structure. Furthermore, Japan's major conglomerates take up a large portion of the entire Japanese economy. With globalisation pressures, large conglomerates in Japan are shifting from hierarchical to network organizations. However, the traditional conglomerate structure has been preserved. Europe generally maintains a policy of strengthening the control of large conglomerates to protect domestic companies from the threat of merger and acquisition by foreign companies. Germany's business groups form cross-sharing relations with banks and a pyramidal shareholding structure within a single group. Sweden allows major shareholders to hold multiple-voting rights and recognises a pyramidal shareholding structure, as well.[3] In general, most of European countries maintains large conglomerates with pyramidal shareholding structure, cross-shareholding, and multiple-voting rights, and it does not have regulations limiting ownership structures (Lee and Lee 2014). Furthermore, these companies comprise a higher portion of the national economy than do Chaebols in South Korea.

Then what caused the difference between these countries and South Korea in their policies towards and social perception of large conglomerates? It is difficult to get an answer without looking at the unique political economic character of South Korean capitalism and Chaebols. These include tangible and intangible political and social debt relations resulting from government support of Chaebols and the negative image that emerged amid long-term opaque and irrational government–business relations. Furthermore, various regulatory policies that focus on economic concentration, low social acceptance of shareholder capitalism (Rhyu 2010), the structure of South Korean politics whereby politicians hold more political power than capitalists, and the cultural nature of accepting that the government and politics hold more authority are all unique aspects of the South Korean context.

The South Korean economic system is now in the process of transition from the developmental state model to the globalised and democratic post-developmental state model. Global market rule and market players, including Chaebols, have started to promote property rights, rule of law, and shareholder capitalism. However, the South Korean society and government are still under the long legacy of strong government intervention, rule of politics, and stakeholder capitalism. South Korea has introduced the competition policy that values the protection of players rather than the protection of process. The assumption underlying the political culture that 'big is bad' persists in South Korean society, thereby compelling the country's government to continue implementing the traditional style of regulating Chaebols on the basis of size. As a result, certain systems such as multiple-voting shares or super-voting shares, which have been introduced in other advanced economies, cannot conceivably be adopted by South Korea. Notwithstanding the government's strong regulations, corruption scandals involving the informal politics between the country's government and Chaebols persist. All things considered, then, South Korean Chaebols, along with the unique approach by the government to regulate them, will likely not subside in the near future.

5. Innovation and Global Competitiveness of South Korean Chaebols

Chaebols in South Korean domestic politics are controversial and Janus-faced. However, in the global market, South Korea's large conglomerate groups are highly innovative and competitive. Here, Chaebols are not political hegemons but global corporations that have high international competitiveness. They are efficient and flexible organisations and are just market players that provide high-quality products and services to international consumers. South Korea's large conglomerates are large-scale investors in the world market and procurers of funds from the global capital market. Here, the corporate organisation of large business groups is no longer Chaebols with traditional hierarchical character but rather corporations with a flexible business network. Also, their role as competitive individual businesses becomes more important than their role as business groups.

For example, after Samsung Electronics entered the semiconductor industry in 1974, it became the number one company in the memory semiconductor sector in 2010. In 2011, it became the top manufacturer in global smartphone market shares. Samsung Electronics was also ranked at the top internationally in annual operating income in 2017. Hyundai Motors, which was established in 1967 and first started to export automobiles to the US market in 1986, ranked fifth among global manufacturers in the number of vehicles produced in 2010. Hyundai Motors, focusing on quality management, became one of the top 100 companies according to brand value in 2005 and has maintained high international reputation and competitiveness since then (Rhyu 2015: 64–72). The number of South Korean businesses listed in the *Fortune Global 500* increased from eight in 1995 to sixteen in 2019, and the ranking of the top five Chaebols is steadily rising, as visualised in Figure 8.2.

The major competitors of top Chaebols are large, global multinational corporations, and most of their profits also come from the overseas market. In the case of Samsung Electronics, 80 per cent of net profit comes from the overseas market. Market forces have grown stronger and large innovative companies have become more competitive due to economic reform and globalisation. The legal system always follows the reality of the market. Furthermore, large businesses no longer develop via government support. They do not want their corporate costs to increase due to non-economic factors incurred by politics and the government. And it is a reality that equal opportunities might no longer be able to guarantee fairness or social justice because the playground is so tilted. Moreover,

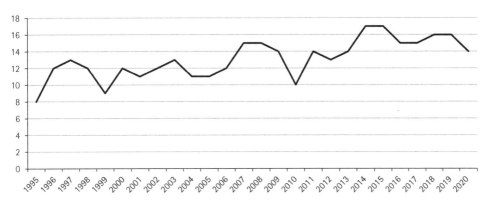

FIGURE 8.2: Number of South Korean companies listed in *Fortune Global 500*
Source: Compiled by author from *Fortune* homepage at https://fortune.com/global500/, accessed 6 August 2021.

the government cannot play the role of a strict watchdog spontaneously in situations which require help from large businesses to achieve economic growth and innovation.

6. Conclusion

The success of industrial policies and government intervention led to the growth of Chaebols. However, this success means that partnership between government and businesses, as was common in the past, is now unnecessary. Such a paradox is the same for both the government and Chaebols. The government is demanding new reform for Chaebols and Chaebols are demanding a new role in and policy from the government. This pain of rebirth began with democratisation in 1987 and the 1997 Asian Financial Crisis and continues today. Under the pressures of globalisation and democratisation, South Korea's developmental state and Chaebols are all going through the process of evolution and reform. Now South Korean society and the global market are demanding that the government provide more rational and market-conforming economic policies and that the Chaebols offer for more transparency and accountability. As democracy continues to consolidate and globalisation progresses, the relationship between the government and Chaebols will become more rational and transparent. The sustainability and future of Chaebols will depend on how innovative they are in the global market and the degree to which they can enhance social trust in South Korea.

Notes

1. It is not accurate to use GDP-based statistics for analysis of the economic concentration of Chaebols in economics. This is because the total amount of assets is stock variable, which evaluates accumulated results from the past on the basis of current results, and GDP is flow

variable as the sum of added value produced domestically throughout the year. However, the Fair Trade Commission in South Korea uses this standard. In this chapter, the data are interpreted as one piece of evidence of the growth trend of Chaebols rather than as a measure of the concentration of economic power.
2. On 5 December 2014, at JFK International Airport in New York City, an altercation broke out between Cho Hyun-Ah—the daughter of the chairman of Korean Air (KAL)—and two KAL Air flight cabin crew. In brief, two cabin crew served macadamia nuts in a bag as opposed to a porcelain bowl to Cho, one of whom Cho then ordered off the plane. Understandably, KAL was heavily criticised on behalf of Cho's actions. With respect to the legal implications of this event, she was found guilty in a South Korean court for obstructing aviation safety. Altogether, this scandal has given rise to a nationwide discourse on the issue of *gapjil*—a Korean term for the feudalistic and hierarchical behaviour and culture perpetuated by those in power seeking to maintain their dominance over their underlings.
3. A company's founders, executives, or other large shareholders may be assigned a class of common stock that has multiple-voting rights. Multiple-voting shares give major company insiders greater control over the company's voting rights, its board, and corporate actions. These super-voting shares can be a powerful defence against hostile takeovers.

Bibliography

Ahn, C. Y. (2008), 'New Direction of Korea's Foreign Direct Investment Policy in the Multi-Track FTA Era: Inducement and Aftercare Services', OECD Global Forum on International Investment OECD Investment Division, www.oecd.org/investment/gfi-7, accessed 6 August 2021.

Amsden, A. H. (1992), *Asia's Next Giant: South Korea and Late Industrialization* (New York: Oxford University Press).

Eckert, C. J. (2016), *Park Chung Hee and Modern Korea: The Roots of Militarism, 1866–1945* (Cambridge: Belknap Press of Harvard University Press).

Fair Trade Commission, 'Statistics', Homepage, https://www.ftc.go.kr/eng/index.do, accessed 6 August 2021.

Grinberg, N. (2014), 'From Miracle to Crisis and Back: The Political Economy of South Korean Long-Term Development', *Journal of Contemporary Asia* 44(4), 711–734.

Haggard, S. (1990), *Pathways from the Periphery: The Politics of Growth in the Newly Industrializing Countries* (Ithaca, NY: Cornell University Press).

Haggard, S., and Moon, C. I. (1993), 'The State, Politics, and Economic Development in Postwar South Korea', in K. Hagen, ed, *State and Society in Contemporary Korea* (Ithaca, NY and London: Cornell University Press), 51–93.

Haggard, S., Lim, W., and Kim, E., eds (2003). *Economic Crisis and Corporate Restructuring in Korea: Reforming the Chaebol* (Cambridge: Cambridge University Press).

Hwang, I. (2002), 'Chaebol Structure, Diversification and Performance', in Z. Rhee and E. Chang, eds, *Korean Business and Management: The Reality and the Vision* (Seoul: Hollym), 171–203.

Jwa, S. H. (2002), *The Evolution of Large Corporations in Korea: A New Institutional Economics Perspectives of the Chaebol* (Cheltenham: Edward Elgar).

Kim, C. Y. (1994), *Policymaking on the Front Lines: Memoirs of a Korean Practitioner, 1945–1979* (Washington, DC: The World Bank).

Kim, E. M. (1997), *Big Business, Strong State* (Albany, NY: State University of New York Press).

Lee, W., and Lee, B. (2014), *Yureopjuyoguk gieopjipdanui soyujibaegujo* [*The Ownership and Control Structure of European 6 Countries and Their Conglomerates: Status and Implications*] (Seoul: Korean Economic Research Institute).

Lim, H. (2010), 'The Transformation of Developmental State and Economic Reform in Korea', *Journal of Contemporary Asia* 40(2), 188–210.

Lim, W. (2012), 'Chaebol and Industrial Policy in Korea', *Asian Economic Policy Review* 7(June), 69–86.

Park, S. (2017), *Gyeongjeryeokjipjung haesoreul wihan jeongchaekgwaje* [*Policy Task to Reduce Economic Power Concentration*] (Seoul: Research Center for Market and Government at Seoul National University).

Park, S. R. (2011), *Hangukgieobui seongjanggwa seonggwa 2010* [*The Growth and Performance of Korean Enterprises 2010*] (Seoul: Korean Economic Research Institute).

Rhyu, S. Y. (2005), 'The Origins of Korean Chaebols and Their Roots in the Korean War', *Korean Journal of International Relations* 45(5), 203–230.

Rhyu, S. Y. (2010), 'Institutionalizing Property Rights in Korean Capitalism: A Case Study on the Listing of the Samsung Life', in J. Mo, ed., *The Rule of Law in South Korea* (Stanford, CA: Hoover Institution Press), 159–188.

Rhyu, S. Y. (2015), *The Spirit of Korean Development* (Seoul: Yonsei University Press).

Rhyu, S. Y. (2018), 'Moon Jae-in and the Politics of Reform in South Korea', *Global Asia* 13(3), 26–32.

Rhyu, S. Y. (2019), 'Policy Ideas and Interest Alignment in the Process of Institutional Change in Chaebol Reform', in S. Lee, and S.Y. Rhyu, eds, *The Political Economy of Change and Continuity in Korea: Twenty Years after the Crisis* (New York: Springer), 15–47.

Song, B. N. (2003), *The Rise of Korean Economy* (New York: Oxford University Press).

CHAPTER 9

NATIONALISM

JUNGMIN SEO

1. INTRODUCTION

When students of politics outside the Korean Peninsula study South Korean political history, they soon learn a few keywords, such as *Japanese colonialism*, *national division*, *Korean War*, *industrialisation*, and *democratisation*, through which the turbulent political experiences of the South Korean people are characterised. Nationalism is tightly associated with each keyword and an indispensable part of the South Korean political sphere today. However, textbooks on (South) Korean politics rarely include nationalism as a main chapter or properly emphasise the role of nationalism in Korean political history. The lack of nationalism in political analyses of South Korea does not mean that political scientists are ignorant or neglectful of the significance of nationalism in South Korean political development. Yet, the very strong and hegemonic nature of Korean nationalism has been taken for granted; it has been regarded as a fixed background of Korean political history by those scholars who recognise nationalism as an important factor in South Korean political development but often fail to appreciate the dynamic, chimerical nature of nationalism in South Korea.

Korean nationalism is unique and influential in both domestic politics and foreign policies. Academic works on (South) Korean politics frequently mention ethnic homogeneity, the existence of historical states for thousands of years, common language, and cultural heritage to emphasise the role of nationalism in contemporary South Korea. Nevertheless, this chapter does not aim to characterise Korean nationalism as a particular entity, as shown in popular discourses that contrast and compare Korean national characteristics with Japanese or Chinese national characteristics. A simple, unidimensional description of a specific nationalism can easily fall into essentialism, and in some extreme cases, racism. Some scholars moderately characterise Korean nationalism as 'ethnic', while implying the desirability of developing into 'civic' nationalism (Shin 2006). Yet, the binary of ethnic and civic nationalism is also rooted in the ethnocentrism of Western scholars, who saw nationalism in the East and postcolonial societies as a 'less civilised', dangerous phenomenon while also regarding nationalism in Western European history as positive and desirable historical forces that lead to political stability and democracy (Brubaker 1999). Nationalism is a set of vague and multifarious political discourses, not a concrete political programme or ideology that envisions a specific type of political community (Duara 1997). Hence, it is difficult to determine whether nationalism in a specific society is particularly violent or harmonious. Political violence and civic harmony under the name of nationalism are not the inherent characteristics of nationalism but the result of specific associations between nationalism and other socioeconomic and political elements such as poverty, civil society, militarism, and colonial experiences.

This chapter utilises the constructivist definition of nationalism that considers a nation a cultural artefact or an 'imagined community', a term coined by Benedict Anderson (2016). The existence of historical states for over two millennia, a uniquely homogeneous ethnic composition, and a well-defined linguistic and cultural community in the Korean Peninsula make both Koreans and non-Koreans believe that the Korean nation, along with Chinese and Japanese nations that have similar résumés, is an unusual political community that cannot be questioned or deconstructed, unlike other nations in Europe or postcolonial societies that are usually believed to be modern products. Nevertheless, nationalism as a political belief that a national community with equality among members and exclusiveness in determining membership should be the sole criteria for modern sovereignty was a novel idea in East Asia until the encroachment of Western imperialism in the nineteenth century (Duara 1997; Tanaka 1993). Though we might have a number of different definitions regarding what a nation is, nationalism as a political desire to make a modern and sovereign nation state in Korea and East Asia was a modern phenomenon that resulted from the penetration of the global discourses of nation and nationalism. From this perspective, the aim of this chapter is to delineate and discuss not necessarily 'Korean nationalism', but rather 'nationalism in South Korea', while not essentialising (South) Korean people and society but contemplating the complex interactions between nationalism and numerous historical and political events.

2. COLONIALISM AND NATIONALISM IN KOREA

Korea's entrance to the modern world, which was dominated by Western imperialism, was not voluntary but was forced by the Japanese Empire in 1876. The *Ganghwa* Treaty between Joseon and Japan was Joseon's first international treaty in the modern sense and, at the same time, an unequal treaty, characterised by extraterritoriality, forced opening of trade ports, and the granting of the rights to the Japanese to freely navigate and measure Korean seas (Cumings 2005: 102). Following the *Ganghwa* Treaty, a number of similar treaties were signed between Korea and Western imperial powers, and Korea entered into the modern world on unequal terms, while leaving the unequal international system it had been engaged in, the Sino-centric tributary system. By winning two major wars in East Asia, the First Sino-Japanese War (1894–1895) and the Russo-Japanese War (1904–1905), Japan was able to join the league of empires and annex Korea in 1910 without external opposition, but with substantial resistance from Korean elites, who were slowly but substantially embracing the cardinal tenet of modern nationalism, a nation's sovereignty in the international arena.

In postcolonial societies, memories of colonial experiences and experiences of struggles against imperialism are the main sources of nationalism that becomes the key element of political legitimacy (Barrington 2006). It is very common that leaders of anti-colonial struggles later become political leaders of decolonised nations. Yet, it is important to note that Korean colonial experiences have a few characteristics that contributed to the extraordinarily strong nationalistic discourses in postcolonial Korean society. First, the Korean Peninsula was colonised by a neighbour, Japan, which had long been regarded as an inferior entity in the Confucian world order from the perspective of traditional Korean elites. Hence, unlike the global expansion of colonialism in the image of the binary of the 'civilised' West and the 'uncivilised' colonies, Korean elites understood the forced annexation in 1910 as the predominance of barbarism over classical civilisation. Second, it is very important to note that Korea was colonised by a non-Western 'junior' imperial power. Whereas the British Empire was the model and universal imperial power in the nineteenth century, the Japanese Empire was a latecomer that had barely escaped from the semicolonial conditions imposed by the unequal treaties with the Western powers. From the perspective of Korean intellectuals who had started to understand the global history of capitalism and imperialism, Korean modernisation and the nation-making process were just one step behind Japanese achievements since the Meiji Restoration in 1868.

Third, and finally, Korean nationalism and Japanese imperialism were co-constitutive in the sense that Korean nationalism evolved essentially as anti-colonialism and Japanese imperialism became fully fledged by establishing its prime colony, Korea (Duus 1995). Unlike Western colonialism, which heavily relied upon indigenous elites to control its vast colonies, the Japanese Empire created a vast colonial state apparatus in Korea that penetrated into the grassroots of Korean society while constructing modern administrative, educational, and economic institutions. The Japanese Empire was not only interested in extracting human and natural resources from the Korean Peninsula, but was also very eager to produce well-disciplined, productive colonial subjects who would be beneficial to further expansion of the Empire without being granted citizenry rights. With over three-quarters of a million Japanese settlers in Korea, Japanese colonial rule was unusually comprehensive compared to British rule in India or French rule in Indochina (Uchida 2014; Young 1999).

Nationalism as intellectual discourse and political doctrine had been well introduced to Koran elites since the late nineteenth century when young Korean elites were exposed to the world via government-sponsored overseas educational programmes or newly available foreign literature in Korea. Yet, it is notable that nationalism as a modern political imagination penetrated colonial Korean society under Japanese rule (Em 2013). For instance, the March First Movement in 1919, which was regarded as the biggest anti-colonial protest, was triggered by the death of King Gojong who reigned over Joseon from 1863 to 1907. The protest lasted for two months with over a million participants and resulted in the establishment of the Provisional Government of the Republic of Korea in Shanghai, which was recognised as the origin of the current South Korean state by the constitution of the Republic of Korea in use today. In 1919, the death of King Gojong enraged hundreds of thousands of ordinary people in Korea. Yet, twenty-six years later, when the Japanese were defeated in the Second World War and colonial rule was ended, there was no single political party that claimed themselves 'royalist' among hundreds of political parties registered to the United States Army Military Government in Korea (1945–1948). Nationalism was the predominant discourse in post-liberation Korean society and royal legitimacy had entirely evaporated.

During Japanese colonial rule, while the state was stolen, the stateless Korean nation became an alternative locus for national existence and the primary target of political loyalty among the colonial population (Schmid 2002: 175). In this sense, though modern Korean nationalism was born through the efforts of Korean intellectuals in the late Joseon Dynasty, it was colonial rule that made Korean nationalism the hegemonic political discourse among ordinary Koreans in accordance with the Japanese colonial state's effort to penetrate into the grassroots of colonial society. There is no doubt that ordinary Koreans suffered under harsh and brutal Japanese colonial rule. However, Japan, as the forerunner of modernisation in East Asia, deeply impressed both independence activists and pro-Japanese collaborators at the same time (Eckert 2016). They had studied, emulated, or even envied the Japanese nation-making process, industrialisation, and cultural modernity since the Meiji Restoration. The primary mission of Korean nationalism under colonial rule was to overcome Japanese colonialism by learning from the enemy, Japan, and by looking for the better ideological and cultural source of modernity, the West.

3. Division, the Korean War, and Nationalism

The sense of incompleteness is the most important driving force of nationalism. Nation as an imagined community, therefore, endlessly produces internal and external others as critical threats to national purity. Nationalistic regimes, therefore, invoke public fear of infiltration of alien elements. In a Germany under Nazi control, the Jewish population, communists, Romani people, and other minorities became the victims of such provoked fear. In Japan, ethnic Koreans and ethnic Chinese have been discriminated against and feared for decades. Territorial loss, both real and imagined, is an equally important element of perceived national incompleteness. Irredentism based on ancient histories is ubiquitous in any nationalistic movement. The sense of territorial incompleteness became the key agenda of international politics in East Asia, as shown in the disputes over Senkaku/Diaoyudao between Japan and China, Dokdo/Takeshima between Korea and Japan, the Spratly Islands between China and Southeast Asian countries, and the Kuril Islands/the Northern Territories between Russia and Japan.

Compared with all the examples suggested above, the strongest example of the sense of national incompleteness is national division. For Germany, national division was forced as the result of the country's catastrophic defeat in the Second World War, but was resolved as the Cold War ended. For Ireland, its division is the legacy of British settler colonialism and religious disputes. The ideological struggles between Kuomintang and the Chinese Communist Party resulted in the presence of two Chinese states, the People's Republic of China on the mainland and the Republic of China in Taiwan; the former dominates the latter and legitimately represents both Chinas in international society. The division of Vietnam was also a legacy of colonialism but was ultimately solved by the forceful annexation of South Vietnam by North Vietnam. It is not difficult to imagine that national division left deep scars among ordinary people in those divided nations with separated families, sufferings from fratricidal civil wars, and, consequently, long-lasting hostility inside the national community. Of all examples of national division, the experiences and consequences of national division on the Korean Peninsula can be easily regarded as the worst and the most painful, as discussed below.

National division was largely a consequence of the emerging Cold War in East Asia. The Korean Peninsula was hastily divided into two parts for the convenience of the United States and the Soviet Union to disarm Japanese troops on the Peninsula. At the end of the Second World War, American military leadership drew a line on the thirty-eighth parallel and decided to let the Soviets disarm and control north of the line, and likewise for the Americans in the South. At that time, the Korean people understood the arrangement as a temporary one for the convenience of the Allied Forces and few questioned why Korea, a victim of Japanese colonialism, and not Japan, the culprit of the Pacific War, was being divided. Once the Peninsula was divided into two, both Americans and Soviets were eager to establish a regime that was strategically beneficial to themselves and started to intervene in the domestic politics of South and North Korea. The ideological struggles among Koreans intensified and the thirty-eighth parallel transformed from a convenient tactical line to a line that divided ideology, society, economy, and politics. There are a few different interpretations regarding the reasons for the division, as some emphasise international elements and others domestic ideological fissures inherent in Korean society (Cumings 1981; Stueck 1995). Yet, the drastic transformation of the thirty-eighth parallel between 1945 and 1948 from a temporary tactical boundary line to the unbreakable border between two political entities, South Korea and North Korea, was entirely unpredicted and unimaginable when Korea was liberated from Japanese colonial rule on 15 August 1945.

In a strict sense, the Korean people have never lived under a unified modern nation state, though they had lived under pre-modern dynasties that unified the Peninsula for centuries. The Joseon Dynasty that fell under Japanese colonialism was a pre-modern, feudal dynasty. Immediately after the liberation, the temporal division of South and North resulted in the births of two states, the Republic of Korea (South) and the Democratic People's Republic of Korea (North) in 1948. Though national division was a political reality, the two Koreas did not accept it. That both Koreas inscribed in their Constitutions that their territory and population cover the entire Peninsula resulted in the awkward situation that neither of them could govern half of the population and territory defined in their Constitutions; according to their Constitutions, the other half of their land and people were unconstitutionally occupied by rebels.

The Korean War from June 1950 to July 1953 was intensive and devastating, with around four million deaths, about half of them civilians (Cumings 2011: 35). It was fratricidal, not just in a metaphoric sense but in reality, as thousands of brothers and sisters had to fight against each other from opposite sides of the battleground. Meanwhile, the Korean War was inevitable because the seed of the war had already been embedded in the Constitutions of each state: recovery of illegitimately occupied territory by—legally speaking—rebel entities would be the prime political responsibility of any political leader. Nevertheless, the Constitutions were not the immediate cause of the war but the representation of the war-prone political and ideological arrangements in postcolonial (South) Korean society.

The primary tenet of nationalism is the principle of 'one nation, one state'. When European empires were disintegrated as the result of the two world wars, the cause of political struggle was the situation of 'many nations in one state', in which a dominant nationality tried to sustain its empire, while subordinating nationalities looked for their own independence. When a nation is divided to establish two states, the most important question that arises in the struggle between the two states is this: who has the right to represent the nation? When two states emerged on the Korean Peninsula in 1948, each state had to represent the entire nation. To do so, each had to delegitimise the other's claim for the right to represent the nation. The political leaders, especially Syngman Rhee, the first president of South Korea and a well-known Christian, vilified communist ideology for being a poison to national purity. Communism was regarded as foreign infiltration, and the leadership of Kim Il-sung in North Korea was nothing but a consequence of the Soviet project to dominate the world with communism. North Koreans, on the contrary, reified Kim Il-sung's anti-Japanese guerrilla warfare against Japanese troops in Manchuria in the 1930s as the root of the North Korean regime (Suh 1988). With nationalism based on anti-colonialism at the core of its regime legitimacy, North Korea vilified South Korea as the puppet of American imperialism and the descendant of pro-Japanese collaborators. The hatred and mistrust between North and South were, therefore, ontological from their very beginning, since the presence of the other itself was the biggest threat to each Korea.

The Korean War that started on 25 June 1950, was a sudden attack from the North for which the South was entirely unprepared. However, by observing the political situations on the Peninsula between 1948 and 1950, particularly their discursive, rhetorical, and structural dimensions, one can see that the war was inevitable. The Cold War was emerging and consolidating borderlines between two superpowers. The two Koreas were becoming the vanguards of the Cold War in East Asia. Both North and South were condemning each other. Official and public calls for immediate actions, including military options, for national unification were predominant across the Peninsula. Under the dictatorial leadership of Kim Il-sung, North Korean public discourses were all centred around the notion of 'national liberation', meaning liberating people in the South from US imperialism. In the South, 'National Unification' and 'March North' were common slogans for official and unofficial gatherings. The fervent calls for national unification by both sides were unsurprising because the official division through the establishment of two states happened when nationalistic fever among the populace was highest in the freshly decolonised Korean society.

The Korean War did not solve but made permanent the national question of division. By becoming a truly international war in which dozens of countries directly and indirectly participated with troops, medical supplies, or financial aid, it contributed to splitting the world into two camps, one centred around the United States and the other around the Soviet Union. If the Korean War was triggered by the emerging Cold War, it also completed the Cold War, given that it ended without a clear winner but with a clear-cut division of 'us' and 'them' across the world (Hajimu 2015). Simultaneously, the Korean War concretised national division as the newly drawn demilitarised zone in the middle of the Peninsula became not only the dividing line between the two Koreas but also the very front line of the Cold War in East Asia. National division then became a question that could not be solved without considering international geopolitics. Furthermore, with the unusually high number of civilian deaths resulting from military brutalities under noncombative situations that comprised nearly half of the total deaths during the Korean War, the memories of the atrocities committed by both sides against innocent civilians during the war made the hatred between the two Koreas not only political and ideological, but also a deeply emotional affair that has been profoundly ingrained in individual and familial psyches, as frequently expressed even today by senior protesters in South Korea, who have been adamantly against recent government policies of reconciliation towards North Korea. In this way, the Korean War made the sense of incompleteness the gravest emotional and psychological component in the narrative of Korean nationalism.

4. The Making of National Subjects

Anti-colonial nationalism is certainly a state-seeking movement that tries to repel imperial power to become an equal member of a world that, since the beginning of the age of nationalism, has been seen as a constellation of sovereign nation states (Jansen and Osterhammel 2017; Getachew 2019). Then, once a nation state is established, the state has to produce national subjects who are disciplined and loyal. Conventional political science often overlooks the dynamic interactions between state and nation in the nation-making process. As a consequence of many different events such as a world war, the disintegration of a multi-ethnic state through civil wars or separation movements, and a global tendency towards decolonisation, a nation state can be established by a group of ardent nationalist leaders. However, declaring and being recognised as an independent nation state is one thing, and turning a group of people in a given territory into national subjects is another. As Eugene Weber's masterpiece, *Peasants into Frenchmen: The Modernization of Rural France, 1870–1914*, published in 1976, meticulously delineated, a nation state has to nationalise its population by achieving a certain level of patriotism, standardised language, shared history, public memory, and so on. The population within the national boundary has to be disciplined and educated so that it can be, either rhetorically or in reality, the master of the nation state.

Just like many other postcolonial nation states, the South Korean state in the 1950s was dictatorial but fragmented, underdeveloped, and powerless (Moon and Rhyu 1999); it did not have the capacity to effectively produce national subjects. The slogans and rhetoric for nation and nationalism were prevalent in society. Yet, state power was maintained by surveillance, political campaigns, and terror, rather than by nationalistically invoked voluntarism, largely due to the limits of state capacity of the newly independent postcolonial state that had experienced a devastating war. The massive state projects that could create national subjects were possible when Park Chung-hee, a general who graduated from a Japanese military academy in the 1930s, became the national leader through a military coup in 1961. Through a series of such projects that paralleled his better-known achievement, the state-led economic developments in the 1960s and 1970s (Kim and Vogel 2011), Park Chung-hee ingrained the discourses of nation and nationalism in every corner of South Korean society.

In 1968, Park Chung-hee promulgated the National Charter of Education, which starts with the following sentence: 'We have been born into this land with the historic mission of regenerating the nation' (Yoo 1969: 5). The deeply nationalistic text of three short paragraphs that conflates individual ethics and national ethics was circulated to every school in the country; memorising and reciting the whole text became an important routine for all school children, who were often subject to physical punishment in school when they failed to memorise it all (Shin 2005). While the National Charter of Education imbued the historical mission of regenerating the nation to the young generation, the *Saemaul* (New Village) Movement that started from 1970 called for public remorse for the laziness and feudal habits of the rural population and, at the same time, the awakening of South Korean rural societies so that they could be modern and self-reliant (Han 2004). South Korean urban residents were organised into about thirty households as '*ban*' units and urged to gather once a month since 1974. The *ban* meetings were nationally synchronised and organised by the Ministry of Internal Affairs (Seo and Kim 2015).

In addition to the major projects listed above, the South Korean state in the 1960s and 1970s invested huge effort and resources to discipline and organise the fragmented society in a highly authoritarian, militarised, and nationalistic fashion (Koo 2001; Moon 2005). Those state policies can be characterised as a number of different but overlapping concepts such as bureaucratic authoritarianism, militarism, dictatorship, or even fascism. Yet such policies, however repressive they had been, undoubtedly produced disciplined and nationalistic modern national subjects. As seen in the next section, 'Revenge of the past', the repeated reification of the Korean nation as the ultimate target of political loyalty under the authoritarian regime made South Korean society not only collectivistic and ethnocentric, but also, ironically, capable of challenging the authoritarian state in the name of the nation.

5. Revenge of the Past: Nationalism and Progressive Politics in South Korea

A stereotypical image of South Korean democratisation in the 1980s is the decades-long confrontation between authoritarian regimes and emerging civil society (Kim 2000), symbolised by the 19 April Uprising in 1960 against the Rhee Syngman government, the Pusan-Masan Uprising in 1979 against the Park Chung-hee regime, and the Gwangju Democratic Movement in May 1980 against the Chun Doo-hwan government. Yet, compared with their precedents, the democratic movements in the 1980s, especially those of the South Korean college students, were quite distinct due to their anti-imperialistic and nationalistic discourses.

Whereas state-led nationalism under the Yushin regime legitimised the authoritarian South Korean state as the saviour of the nation from backward feudalism embedded in ordinary citizens, student activists in the 1980s called for liberation of the Korean nation from the ruthless dictators who had collaborated with Japanese colonialism and then were collaborating with American imperialism. The dominant faction among student activists, the so-called National Liberation Faction, cultivated nationalistic sentiments among college students by invoking the critical national question, 'Who divided the nation?', whereas the anti-communist South Korean government had long inculcated the question of who started the Korean War. The latter question was simply about North Korean responsibility for starting the devastating war. Yet, the former question of 'Who divided the nation?' raised by student activists in the early 1980s fundamentally vitiated the hierarchy of the South Korean state and the Korean nation. For the students, the South Korean state was not the saviour of the nation, as the Park Chung-hee regime had sincerely propagated, but an untrustworthy agent of colonial and imperial powers that perpetuated national division. Hence, the resistance against the authoritarian government was not just struggle over democracy but also national redemption (Seo 2009).

In terms of discursive structure and grammar, the student activists of the 1980s inherited more from the authoritarian regime under which they received primary and secondary education than from the remote democratisation discourses in the 1960s and 1970s (Seo 2009: 127). Anti-communist slogans of the Rhee Syngman regime or the pro-democracy movements until the 1980s were both ahistorical in the sense that neither dangerous communists nor an ideal democratic society were located in the progression of history. On the contrary, the Park Chung-hee regime's notion of the state as the national saviour and the 1980s student activists' assertion of national redemption both presume the decay of the nation that had been prosperous at one time. The structured nostalgia that presumed an imagined past of a nation in its ideal stage (Herzfeld 1996) was the basic discursive grammar for both the authoritarian regime in the 1970s and the student activists in the 1980s.

Though not all of the democratic activists in the 1980s were radical anti-American nationalists, the successful democratisation in 1987 resulted in a long-term consequence in South Korean politics: the appropriation of nationalistic language by the left-wing and progressive politics. The leaders of the student activists in the 1980s began to enter the field of formal politics in the 1990s, as they were proactively recruited by established political parties that desperately needed the fresh, democratic images of those young leaders. Since then, nationalistic agendas such as national unification policies, the Comfort Women (the Women Drafted for Military Sexual Slavery by Japan) issue, and national history education have been mostly dominated by left-wing and progressive politicians, whereas the conservative parties tend to shy away from those issues and focus on economic growth. The association of left-wing and progressive politics and nationalism is not uncommon in postcolonial societies, as anti-colonialism in Africa and Asia had close relationships with the Soviet-led Communist International, or Comintern (1919–1943), which supported anti-colonial struggles around the world to counter Western European imperial powers. Yet, in postcolonial South Korea, the politics of nationalism evolved in a dynamic way as state nationalism, which was the tool of authoritarian rules, and succumbed to the progressive politics that delegitimised the secular state by upholding nation as the ultimate target of political loyalty. From the democratisation of South Korean society in 1987 to the end of the century, being nationalistic in South Korea meant being politically progressive. Korean nationalism, however, started to lose its hegemonic status due to two main factors, as I discuss in the following section.

6. Korean Nationalism in the Age of Democratic Consolidation and Globalisation

Nationalism is still a dominating political discourse in South Korean society in the sense that no political power can win public support while denying the sacrosanct status of nationalistic missions such as national unification, commemoration of national sufferings under colonial rule, or the preservation and promotion of Korean language and script.

Its status is now under constant attack from different directions, especially from democratic consolidation and globalisation.

The event of democratisation in South Korea in 1987 achieved democratic institutional arrangements such as a democratic Constitution, fair elections for public offices, and freedom of speech. Many political scientists noticed that South Korea also consolidated its democracy in a relatively short period of time by eliminating chances of the return of authoritarian rule by blocking South Korean military's involvement in politics, repeated normal altercation between ruling parties, and popular support for a democratic system (Diamond and Shin 2000). Yet, the penetration of democratic practices and values such as individual autonomy, gender equality, and respect for minority rights across a certain society requires a significant amount of time. South Korean society is still struggling to deepen its young democracy.

As a renowned South Korean sociologist stated, democratic struggle in South Korea has transformed from a normal majority's (people's) struggle against an abnormal minority (military regime) to an abnormal minorities' (social minorities') resistance against the normal majority in South Korean society (Cho 2004). Democratisation and the subsequent expansion of citizenry rights in South Korea allowed social minorities who used to live within the national community but remained largely hidden in public discourse—such groups as *hwagyo* (ethnic Chinese in South Korea), LGBTQ persons, the disabled, and the so-called mixed-blood kids who were born between South Koreans and foreigners, especially between US GIs and South Korean women—to claim their political and social rights (Seol and Seo 2014). Korean nationalism that, like any other nationalism, has been built upon the notions of ethnic purity, family-oriented gender roles, and a productive body (Mosse 1985; Duara 2003) has been discriminating against those minorities and making them invisible from public discourse. Collective movements by those seemingly less national citizens have been blocked by the authoritarian regimes (Seol and Seo 2014: 13). Demands of those minorities for their citizenry rights after democratisation inherently vitiate the basic tenets of nationalism. For instance, the Queer Cultural Festival that started in 2000 at the centre of Seoul, the capital city, threatens not only the cultural conservatives in South Korean society, but also the basic structure of the nationalistic imagination of a community that is firmly grounded in the notion of a 'normal' family (Choi and Seo 2020).

Since the 1990s, like the rest of the world, South Korea has joined the tide of globalisation. Though globalisation refers to many different phenomena, such as free flow of capital across national borders and a revolution in telecommunication by the internet, it also signifies the age of international migration (Castles et al. 2013). Globalisation prompted the emergence of newcomers who came to South Korea for various reasons. The close economic ties between South Korea and China triggered the incoming of roughly a million Korean Chinese who emigrated from Korea to China during the late Joseon Dynasty and Japanese colonial rule. From Southeast Asia and Central Asia, hundreds of thousands of migrant workers came to South Korea, which started to suffer from a labour shortage in the late 1990s. International marriage, especially between rural South Korean men and Southeast Asian women, drastically increased from the early 2000s and had significant impacts upon the demographic composition of South Korean rural communities (Seol and Seo 2014; Lee 2019).

The emergence of minorities, each of whom faces a different degree of social and legal acceptance, is reshaping Korean nationalism. Given that outright rejection of those minorities in the Korean national community is unrealistic and politically and morally undesirable, Korean nationalism has to accommodate social, political, and demographic changes caused by the emergence of nonconventional South Korean populations. Some argue that the concept of the Korean nation is moving towards 'hierarchical nationhood' that does not rely on the notion of the binary of 'us and them' but on social and cultural stratification that is measured by the degree of 'Koreanness' (Seol and Seo 2014; Seol and Skrentny 2009). Some argue that a new nationalism that does not rely on Korean ethnic identity is on the rise in South Korean society (Campbell 2016). Though it is not easy to conclude how Korean nationalism is moving today, it is quite certain that Korean nationalism as it used to be cannot be sustained. It may evolve into a new type of nationalism that still monopolises the political discourse of South Korea. Or it may diminish into a factional ideology vis-à-vis other political values, as seen in European countries. Indeed, it is not unimaginable that South Korean society even moves towards a new kind of 'imagined community' that leaves the notion of nation and nationalism anachronic. However, any change of Korean nationalism would be tortuous and painful to Korean people, who have lived through the whole modernisation process with an exceptionally strong sense of national unity.

7. Conclusion

Nationalism is a very difficult concept to utilise in political analyses. A highly abstract and multifarious concept, it cannot be easily used as an independent or dependent variable in social science. Yet, it is also difficult to understand political actors' behaviours, either individual or collective, without considering the role of nationalism, especially in South Korea, where nationalism has historically shaped the ideological realms. For instance, the diplomatic conflicts between South Korea and Japan over historical issues such as history textbooks, compensation for Korean forced labour under Japanese colonial rule, or the Women Drafted for Military Sexual Slavery by Japan cannot be easily explained by conventional power politics because both South Korea and Japan share similar security concerns over North Korean nuclear threats and the rise of China as a superpower. Some would suggest that South Korea and Japan are making unnecessary diplomatic tensions over nonessential and emotional issues at the expense of national interest. Yet, those issues can be the very core ontological issues because nationalism has long been an integral part of a South Korean world view that informs what national interest is.

Bibliography

Anderson, B. (2016), *Imagined Communities: Reflections on the Origin and Spread of Nationalism* (New York: Verso).

Barrington, L. W., ed. (2006), *After Independence: Making and Protecting the Nation in Postcolonial and Postcommunist States* (Ann Arbor, MI: University of Michigan Press).

Brubaker, R. (1999), 'The Manichean Myth: Rethinking the Distinction between 'Civic' and 'Ethnic' Nationalism", in H. Kriesi, K. Armington, H. Siegrist, and A. Wimmer, eds, *Nation and National Identity: The European Experience in Perspective* (Zurich: Verlag Rüegger), 55–71.

Campbell, E. (2016), *South Korea's New Nationalism: The End of 'One Korea'?* (Boulder, CO: First Forum Press).

Castles, S., De Haas, H., and Miller, M. J. (2013), *The Age of Migration: International Population Movements in the Modern World* (New York: Guilford Press).

Cho, H.-Y. (2004), *Bijeongsangseonge daehan jeohangeseo jeongsangseonge daehan jeohangeuro* [*From Resistance against Abnormalities to Resistance against Normalcy*] (Seoul: Arke).

Choi, S., and Seo, J. (2020), 'Practicing Agency by Performing Vulnerability: Sexual Minorities at the Queer Culture Festival in Korea', *Journal of Asian Sociology* 49, 501–525.

Cumings, B. (1981), *The Origins of the Korean War, Vol. 1: Liberation and the Emergence of Separate Regimes, 1945–1947* (Princeton, NJ: Princeton University Press).

Cumings, B. (2005), *Korea's Place in the Sun: A Modern History*, rev. edn (New York: W. W. Norton).

Cumings, B. (2011), *The Korean War: A History* (New York: Modern Library).

Diamond, L. J., and Shin, D. C. eds (2000), *Institutional Reform and Democratic Consolidation in Korea* (Stanford, CA: Stanford University Press).

Duara, P. (1997), *Rescuing History from the Nation: Questioning Narratives of Modern China* (Chicago, IL: University of Chicago Press).

Duara, P. (2003), *Sovereignty and Authenticity: Manchukuo and the East Asian Modern* (New York: Rowman & Littlefield).

Duus, P. (1995), *The Abacus and the Sword: The Japanese Penetration of Korea, 1895–1910* (Berkeley, CA: University of California Press).

Eckert, C. J. (2016), *Park Chung Hee and Modern Korea: The Roots of Militarism, 1866–1945* (Cambridge, MA: Harvard University Press).

Em, H. (2013), *The Great Enterprise: Sovereignty and Historiography in Modern Korea* (Durham, NC: Duke University Press).

Getachew, A. (2019), *Worldmaking after Empire: The Rise and Fall of Self-Determination* (Princeton, NJ: Princeton University Press).

Hajimu, M. (2015), *Cold War Crucible: The Korean Conflict and the Postwar World* (Cambridge, MA: Harvard University Press).

Han, S. M. (2004), 'The New Community Movement: Park Chung Hee and the Making of State Populism in Korea', *Pacific Affairs* 77, 69–93.

Herzfeld, M. (1996), *Cultural Intimacy: Social Poetics in the Nation-State* (New York: Routledge).

Jansen, J. C., and Osterhammel, J. (2017), *Decolonization: A Short History* (Princeton, NJ: Princeton University Press).

Kim, B. K., and Vogel, E. F., eds (2011), *The Park Chung Hee Era: The Transformation of South Korea* (Cambridge, MA: Harvard University Press).

Kim, S. H. (2000), *The Politics of Democratization in Korea: The Role of Civil Society* (Pittsburgh, PA: University of Pittsburgh Press).

Koo, H. (2001), *Korean Workers: The Culture and Politics of Class Formation* (Ithaca, NY: Cornell University Press).

Lee, B. (2019), 'Immigrants' Integration Policies and Two Patterns of Governance in Korea and Japan', *Korean Journal of International Migration* 7, 57–84.

Moon, C. I., and Rhyu, S. Y. (1999), "Overdeveloped" State and the Political Development in the 1950s: A Reinterpretation', *Asian Perspective* 23, 179–203.

Moon, S. (2005), *Militarized Modernity and Gendered Citizenship in South Korea* (Durham, NC: Duke University Press).

Mosse, G. L. (1985). *Nationalism and Sexuality: Middle-Class Morality and Sexual Norms in Modern Europe* (Madison, WI: University of Wisconsin Press).

Schmid, A. (2002), *Korea between Empires, 1895–1919* (New York: Columbia University Press).

Seo, J. (2009), 'Using the Enemy's Vocabularies: Rethinking the Origins of Student Anti-State Nationalism in 1980s Korea', *Review of Korean Studies* 12, 125–146.

Seo, J., and Kim, S. (2015), 'Civil Society under Authoritarian Rule: Bansanghoe and Extraordinary Everyday-ness in Korean Neighborhoods', *Korea Journal* 55, 59–85.

Seol, D. H., and Seo, J. (2014), 'Dynamics of Ethnic Nationalism and Hierarchical Nationhood: Korean Nation and Its Otherness since the Late 1980s', *Korea Journal* 54, 5–33.

Seol, D. H., and Skrentny, J. D. (2009), 'Ethnic Return Migration and Hierarchical Nationhood: Korean Chinese Foreign Workers in South Korea', *Ethnicities* 9, 147–174.

Shin. G. (2006), *Ethnic Nationalism in Korea: Genealogy, Politics, and Legacy* (Stanford, CA: Stanford University Press).

Shin J. B. (2005), *Gukmin gyoyuk heonjang inyeom ui guhyeon gwa guksa mit dodeokgwa gyoyuk gwajong ui gaepyeon (1968–1994)* [Realization of the National Charter of Education Ideology and Revisions of Curriculums in History and Moral Education (1968–1994)], *Yeoksa munje yeongu* [Critical Studies on Modern Korean History] 15, 205–239.

Stueck, W. (1995), *The Korean War: An International History* (Princeton, NJ: Princeton University Press).

Suh, D. (1988), *Kim Il Sung: The North Korean Leader* (New York: Columbia University Press).

Tanaka, S. (1993), *Japan's Orient: Rendering Pasts into History* (Berkeley, CA: University of California Press).

Uchida, J. (2014), *Brokers of Empire: Japanese Settler Colonialism in Korea, 1876–1945* (Cambridge, MA: Harvard University Press).

Weber, E. (1976), *Peasants into Frenchmen: The Modernization of Rural France, 1870–1914* (Stanford: CA: Stanford University Press).

Yoo, H. J. (1969), 'The Charter of National Education', *Korea Journal* 9(8), 4–7.

Young, L. (1999), *Japanese Total Empire: Manchuria and the Culture of Wartime Imperialism* (Berkeley, CA: University of California Press).

PART 3
POLITICAL INSTITUTIONS

CHAPTER 10

CONSTITUTIONAL POLITICS

WON-TAEK KANG

1. Making the Constitution

Following independence in 1945, the Korean Peninsula was divided. The Soviet military forces ruled the northern part of the Korean Peninsula and the US military forces controlled its southern part. By 1948, North Korea had become a communist system, and South Korea adopted liberal democracy. In South Korea, a parliamentary election was held in May 1948 to build a separate state. It is noteworthy that there was a wide agreement to make the new nation 'a republic'. This is rather surprising, given the fact that Korea had been a monarchy. Kings as well as queens of several dynasties had ruled the Korean Peninsula for thousands of years before it was colonised by Japan in 1910.

Many political leaders involved in the independence movement from Japan in the early twentieth century, with few exceptions, preferred the new nation to be a republic. The Provisional Government, which acted from abroad in China for the independence struggle beginning in 1919, also considered the polity of the 'independent' homeland to be a republic. This was due to deep-seated distrust and disappointment in the previous dynasty. The Joseon Dynasty did not properly preserve the country and fell into a colony. The Xinhai Revolution in China, which destroyed the Qing Dynasty and established the Republic of China in 1911, also influenced the leaders of the independence movement.

In December 1945, the United States and the Soviet Union decided to hold a five-year trusteeship over the Korean Peninsula. The US–Soviet Joint Commission was set up to discuss the specifics of the trusteeship. But fierce opposition from right-wing forces in the South over trusteeship and confrontation between the United States and the Soviet Union blocked the progress of the Joint Commission. With the collapse of the Joint Commission, it was impossible to form a unified government over the entire Korean Peninsula. The establishment of separate governments was inevitable in the North and the South, respectively, and the founding election for the National Assembly was held on 10 May 1948 in the South. The first National Assembly had a two-year term, and was known as 'the Constitutional National Assembly' for its key role in enacting the Constitution (Shin 2001: 298).

In fact, the first National Assembly not only had to enact a Constitution, but also had to form a government in accordance with that Constitution. In the United States, the Constitution was first enacted at the Constitutional Convention in Philadelphia, and according to that Constitution, members of Congress and the president were elected later. In contrast, as the Constitutional National Assembly was responsible for both constitution-making and government formation, political considerations of major leaders and political parties could be inevitably involved in the process of forming the Constitution.

Between 1945 and 1948, extensive discussions on the contents of the Constitution took place in South Korea, and the proposals discussed at that time were also reflected in the constitution-making process of the National Assembly. Shortly after the National Assembly was convened on 31 May 1948, it set up a special committee for drafting the Constitution. The constitutional committee first proposed a draft constitution based on the parliamentary system. The parliamentary system was the preferred form of government of the Korean Democratic Party (KDP) (*Hanmindang*) (Kang 2019: 2–7). The KDP won a large number of seats in the National Assembly, but there was no popular leader within the party nationwide. Some influential members of the constitutional committee belonged to the KDP. The proposed contents were very similar to those of other parliamentary democracies. The prime minister would be practically responsible for state affairs and the president would be the symbolic supreme leader. The National Assembly was to be a bicameral system and the low house had the power of vote-of-no-confidence against the Cabinet. The president, who would be elected at a joint meeting of the two houses, could dissolve the lower house. The prime minister was to be appointed by the president and approved by the lower house.

However, the KDP's intentions faced strong opposition. Rhee Syngman was the most popular political leader at the time. He had lived in the United States for a long time, and received a doctorate in political science from Princeton University. He wanted to be a powerful national leader who could reign over all political factions.

Rhee insisted on adopting a presidential system. At first, the KDP refused, but when Rhee issued a political ultimatum, it was forced to accept his demand. Rhee declared that he would not cooperate in the formation of the government unless his demand for the introduction of a presidential system was accepted. The KDP could no longer reject Rhee's demand. Nationalist rightist and centrist parties, as well as leftist parties, refused to participate in the 1948 election, claiming that it would solidify the division of the Korean Peninsula. Under these circumstances, if Rhee, who was then highly respected nationwide, did not participate in the government, it could have depleted the political legitimacy of a new state.

The proposed parliamentary system was revised into a presidential system at the last minute. But the final product was a kind of compromise. The final constitution was based on the presidential system, as Rhee demanded, but at the same time many elements of the parliamentary system survived. In other words, the final form of government was a mixture of a presidential system and a parliamentary system.

The president's right to dissolve the National Assembly and the legislature's right to a vote of no confidence, which are key elements of the Cabinet system, were removed. The president and vice-president were allowed to serve up to two four-year terms. However, the post of prime minister was not removed, and the president appointed the prime minister, with the consent of the National Assembly. The executive had the authority to submit legislation and budget proposals to the National Assembly. It also allowed lawmakers to concurrently hold ministerial posts. The Cabinet Meeting was set up as a collective decision-making body and important matters concerning state affairs carried out by the president had to be in writing, with the documents must be signed by the prime minister and related ministers. These provisions were intended to keep the president in check so that he or she could not make arbitrary decisions. It is noteworthy that such provisions were included in the original draft on the basis of the Cabinet system. Besides, the president and vice-president were each elected in the National Assembly, not by popular vote. Given that the basic principle of the presidential system is the independence of the legislature and the executive, this indirect election of the president and prime minister is a different feature from the US presidential system.

As such, the Korean presidential system was created through a completely different historical process from that of the United States. The final Constitution was the result of political compromise between Rhee and the KDP. The intended presidential system was not a strong presidential system. Some elements of the Cabinet system were left in the constitution-making process. This was because the KDP envisioned a president who could be systematically checked by the Cabinet (Suh 2012: 259). However, the original intention of the constitution drafters was not properly preserved. Since then, the power of the president was uninterruptedly strengthened by authoritarian rulers such as Rhee Syngman, Park Chung-hee, and Chun Doo-hwan.

2. The Strengthening of the Presidential Power and the Rise of Authoritarianism (1952–1980)

The Constitution, enacted in 1948, was revised nine times. Except for three revisions, all were related to the strengthening of presidential power or extending presidential term limits.

The first constitutional amendment was made in 1952. Rhee Syngman wanted to extend his time in office, but he could not gain the support of a majority of the National Assembly. At that time, the Constitution required the president to be elected by the National Assembly. Instead, Rhee tried to amend the Constitution so that the president would be elected by popular vote. However, the National Assembly, which had the power to revise the Constitution, vehemently opposed such attempts. On 28 November 1951, Rhee submitted to the National Assembly a bill to amend the Constitution, which called for popularly electing the president and a bicameral legislature. When the National Assembly voted on it, the bill was rejected with 19 votes in favour, 143 against, and one abstention. The results of the vote clearly showed that Rhee's support within the National Assembly was extremely slim. Rhee also learned that the constitutional amendment was not possible with the support from the lawmakers (Shim 2017: 83–87).

Instead, Rhee decided coercively to carry out his plan. Taking advantage of the outgoing Korean War, President Rhee declared martial law. He also mobilised political hoodlums to stage protests against the opposition. The day after declaring martial law, the military police arrested ten lawmakers on charges of being involved in the International Communist Movement. Under the menacing guard of armed police and soldiers who had surrounded the parliamentary building, the amendment bill was passed with 163 votes in favour, no votes against, and 3 abstentions on 4 July 1952. Rhee had forcefully suppressed the National Assembly and carried out his will. Just a month after the passage of the constitutional amendment, a presidential election was held on 5 August, and Rhee was re-elected president by an overwhelming margin. However, it set an undesirable precedent for the forced revision of the Constitution to extend the president's power. The military was also mobilised for political purposes. This was the starting point of the distortion of liberal democracy that lasted for the next thirty-five years (Kang 2015: 29).

The second constitutional amendment was another of Rhee's ploys to extend his time in office. The Constitution, revised in 1952, allowed only up to two terms. In 1954, Rhee attempted to revise the Constitution to abolish the term limit. Rhee first had to secure enough lawmakers to revise the Constitution. To that end, Rhee and the ruling Liberal Party cheated in the 1954 parliamentary elections. Above all, the police were blatantly involved in the election. As a result of the election, the ruling Liberal Party won 114 of the 203 seats, while the main opposition party won 15. The remaining seats were all independents. Rhee bribed and intimidated some of the independent lawmakers into joining the Liberal Party. On 20 November 1954, the National Assembly voted on the constitutional amendment. The key point of the revision was to abolish presidential term limits only for the first president, that is only for Rhee (Kang 2015: 30–38). However, the vote in the National Assembly produced unexpected results. While 136 votes were required for constitutional amendment, only 135 votes were in favour. Rejection was declared. However, Rhee and the Liberal Party decided to overturn the result by raising absurd and unreasonable arguments.

Two-thirds of the 203 legislators for constitutional amendment was mathematically 135.33. The ruling party claimed that the amendment had passed because 135, not 136, was the closest number to 135.33. Such a ridiculous claim was validated, despite fierce resistance from the opposition parties, and Rhee was cleared to be the president indefinitely.

Public discontent with President Rhee increased significantly, as he forcibly amended the Constitution for long-term rule and ruled the country arbitrarily. Indeed, support for the opposition parties rose in the 1956 presidential elections. With the sudden death of the main opposition candidate, Shin Ik-hee, just a week before the election, Rhee was easily re-elected president, but his vote rate dropped significantly. Furthermore, in the vice-presidential election, the opposition candidate, Chang Myun, was elected. It showed that the people's dissatisfaction with Rhee's authoritarian rule had reached a serious level.

As the 1960 presidential elections approached in such an unfavourable atmosphere, Rhee and the ruling party attempted to carry out widespread and massive election irregularities (Kang 2015: 51–69). The interior minister, Choi In-Kyu, formulated fraudulent election plans a few months before the election, and even trained officials on how to implement them. On Election Day, election fraud was carried out as planned, and the 1960 presidential elections became the worst in terms of election irregularities. Mass protests led by students, intellectuals, and journalists took place nationwide. The anger and resistance of the people was so strong that the Rhee Syngman regime could not withstand it. President Rhee eventually had to step down and went into exile in the United States.

With the fall of the First Republic, the Constitution was amended. In response to Rhee's dictatorship, the new Constitution provided for a parliamentary system. This third constitutional amendment, which, unlike before, was done in a democratic way (Kang 2019: 11–13). In the new Constitution, the prime minister was the head of the administration, who was responsible for state affairs. The president became the symbolic supreme leader of national unity. Parliament had two houses; the low house had a term of four years and the upper house's tenure was six years, requiring that half of the seats needed to be newly elected every three years. In addition, the Constitutional Court was set up, and the political neutrality of the police was declared. The heads of local governments had to be elected by local residents.

In November 1960, another minor constitutional amendment was made to allow retroactive punishment. When the Second Republic was established, the Democratic Party won a landslide election victory. However, punishment for those who committed election irregularities or corruption under the previous administration had not been properly carried out. Those who committed serious crimes were acquitted or given only minor sentences. As the angry public strongly protested the moves with great discontent, the Democratic Party administration had to make a constitutional amendment centred on retroactive legislation that could punish them (Han 1983: 138–146).

However, the Second Republic did not survive long. On 16 May 1961, a military coup led by General Park Chung-hee took place. Normal political activities were banned and direct military rule lasted for two-and-a-half years. A new Constitution was made during this period. The coup leaders revived the presidential system and made it strong. After the Supreme Council of National Reconstruction headed by several military leaders promulgated the new Constitution in November 1962, it was finalised by a national referendum on 17 December 1962. The Constitution prior to the coup required the National Assembly's approval to amend the Constitution, but the military did not follow the rules and decided by a referendum.

Under the new Constitution, the president was elected by popular vote and was allowed to serve up to two four-year terms. The vice-presidency was abolished and the previous bicameral system was changed to a unicameral system. It retained the position of prime minister. The administration kept the authority to submit legislation and budget proposals. Moreover, the constitutional amendment made it more difficult than before. A constitutional amendment required not only more than two-thirds consent of the legislators, but also the passage of a referendum. With the fifth constitutional amendment, the Third Republic was launched. It is noteworthy that although the coup seems to have destroyed the existing political system, the main elements of the newly adopted Constitution were not fundamentally different from before (Kang 2019: 13–14); that is, although the coup leaders revised the Constitution almost entirely, the nature of a hybrid political system made by the Constitutional Assembly in 1948 remained almost the same.

Park Chung-hee ran for president in 1963, but won by only a narrow margin (Kang 2019: 181–183). The difference in votes with the major opposition candidate was only about 150,000 votes. Four years later, however, he easily won the 1967 presidential election. With the effect of economic growth, support for Park Chung-hee increased significantly, particularly in urban areas, compared to four years prior. According to the constitutional provisions he made, the presidential election in 1967 was the last election in which he could run. However, like Rhee Syngman, Park Chung-hee also sought to extend his term.

Park Chung-hee followed a path similar to that of Rhee Syngman. In order to amend the Constitution, the draft had to be passed in the National Assembly before the referendum. To this end, Park Chung-hee committed serious election fraud in the 1967 National Assembly election. During the election campaign, money and gifts were widely offered to voters, and violence and smear campaigns were used. Public officials boldly intervened in the election (Kang 2015: 82–96). In that election, the ruling Democratic Republican Party (DRP) won 130 seats, far more than the 117 seats required to pass a constitutional amendment. The main opposition party, the New Democratic Party (NDP), won only forty-four seats. After the election, strong protests occurred nationwide, but Park Chung-hee secured the legislative seats necessary for the amendment.

In September 1969, a constitutional amendment was attempted to enable Park Chung-hee's third term. Opposition parties, as well as citizens and students, strongly resisted this attempt. Moreover, there was also disagreement within the ruling party over Park Chung-hee's attempt to extend his power. Some lawmakers within the ruling party believed that Kim Jong-pil, who was the mastermind of the coup, should become the next president. Park forcefully suppressed them. To avoid the opposition's strong resistance, the ruling party passed the constitutional amendment in the middle of the night as if it were a military operation. The constitutional amendment was passed in an exclusive meeting in which only the ruling party members were allowed entry. Opposition lawmakers were not even informed of where and when to vote.

After the constitutional amendment, the 1971 presidential election was held. The electoral competition between Park Chung-hee and Kim Dae-jung, the candidate of the NDP, was tense. Park Chung-hee had a very tough election. At the end of the presidential campaign, Park Chung-hee declared, 'This is the last time I ask you to vote for me' (Kang 2019: 186–190). Finally, Park Chung-hee was elected president for the third time, but the margin of votes with Kim Dae-jung was not significant. In the National Assembly elections held shortly after the presidential election, the ruling party also fared badly. The ruling DRP won 48.8 per cent of the vote, while the opposition NDP won 48.4 per cent. In terms of the number of seats, the DRP won 113 while the NDP won 89. The opposition party secured far more seats than the sixty-nine needed to prevent constitutional amendments from passing in the National Assembly. Now another constitutional amendment to extend Park Chung-hee's rule seemed impossible. In fact, many people, including even the ruling party lawmakers, thought Park would no longer run.

However, upsetting everyone's expectations, Park set up the most comprehensive and coercive political system to extend his power. On 17 October 1972, Park Chung-hee undertook his boldest and most blatant attempt to secure power for life. He declared emergency martial law and disbanded the National Assembly. Park actually conducted another coup. The seventh constitutional amendment established a political system for Park Chung-hee's life-long dictatorship. Although the president had to be elected indirectly by delegates, this procedure was effectively meaningless. With the establishment of the Yushin regime, Park no longer needed to ask voters to vote for him, as he promised during the 1971 election. Park effectively eliminated the normal electoral procedures.

One-third of the National Assembly was appointed by the president (Kang 2019: 18–22). All court judges, including the chief justice, were also appointed by the president. Essentially, all legislative, executive, and judicial powers were concentrated in the hands of the president. In order to reduce the number of elections, the terms of office for the president and National Assembly increased from four to six years. The president was able to issue emergency measures, under which civil liberties and rights could be severely restricted. Neither slander nor criticism of the president was allowed. Freedom of speech and expression and freedom of assembly were thoroughly suppressed. And these emergency measures were not subject to judicial review. Park Chung-hee issued nine emergency measures under this Constitution, and the ninth emergency measure encompassed the most repressive and undemocratic measures to complete the dictatorship. Liberal democracy virtually disappeared under the so-called Yushin (often translated as 'revitalising') regime.

This dictatorship suddenly collapsed in October 1979 when Park Chung-hee was assassinated by his close aide. After Park Chung-hee's death, Choi Kyu-ha, then prime minister, became president according to the process laid out in the Yushin Constitution. Anticipation of a 'Seoul Spring', or a movement to restore democracy, was high, but a military faction led by Chun Doo-hwan launched another coup (Kang 2019: 22–26). After seizing power through a coup, Chun Doo-hwan forced President Choi to step down and became president himself. Since then, Chun again revised the Constitution. This was the eighth constitutional amendment.

The president's term of office was seven years and only allowed a single term. Similar to the Yushin Constitution, the president was required to be elected indirectly by delegates. Nominally, competition between candidates was allowed, but in reality it was a mere token event. The president's nomination of one-third of the lawmakers under the Yushin Constitution was abolished. However, the election law gave the largest party two-thirds of the proportional seats, making it easy for the ruling party to secure a majority of seats. In addition, most of the repressive devices designed by the Yushin Constitution were maintained. Moreover, the Chun Doo-hwan regime created not only the ruling party, but also the opposition parties. They created two 'satellite' opposition parties. The party system was artificially manufactured to serve their political purposes.

The Chun Doo-hwan regime revised the Constitution, but in fact, it was not fundamentally different from the Yushin Constitution. It was essentially an extension of the Yushin regime. With the birth of the Fifth Republic, the 'Yushin regime without Park Chung-hee' was created.

3. Democratisation and the Constitutional Reform

The Chun Doo-hwan regime faced very fierce resistance from citizens and students from the beginning. The Chun regime suppressed their protests by force, and caused numerous casualties especially in Gwangju. Despite such oppression, resistance and protests against the authoritarian regime continued.

In 1983, significant demands for democratisation began with the hunger strike of Kim Young-sam, a former leader of the opposition NDP. Kim Young-sam's hunger strikes brought together again the opposition forces that split in 1980 in the 'Seoul Spring'. In 1984, they formed a political organisation called the 'Council for the Promotion of Democracy (CPD)' and prepared for the National Assembly election, scheduled for the following year (Kang 2019: 348–357).

Just before the 1985 National Assembly election, the former opposition forces formed a party called the New Korean Democratic Party (NKDP). During the election campaign, they proposed a constitutional amendment which would restore direct presidential elections, criticising the current presidential electoral system as 'gymnasium elections'. The way delegates, who had effectively no political choice, gathered together in a spacious indoor gymnasium to elect a president was sarcastically called 'a gymnasium election'. The NKDP, led by outstanding opposition leaders Kim Young-sam and Kim Dae-jung, emerged as the leading opposition party in that election, defeating the satellite opposition parties. And from February 1986, the NKDP as well as the CPD intensely launched a campaign for constitutional amendment. Their key requirement was constitutional reform for a popularly elected president.

However, the Chun Doo-hwan regime had no intention of revising the Constitution. Their justification was that debates about constitutional amendments would be allowed only after the successful hosting of the Seoul Olympics in 1988. But the nationwide campaign for constitutional amendment gained huge support from the public. At the same time, this successful campaign put considerable pressure on the Chun Doo-hwan regime.

In April 1986, in response to public pressure, President Chun Doo-hwan met with opposition leaders, and they agreed to form a special committee for constitutional reform in the National Assembly. However, while the opposition NKDP demanded the popularly elected presidential system, the ruling Democratic Justice Party (DJP) insisted on the introduction of a parliamentary system. Considering the current election law, which was clearly in favour of the ruling party, the opposition party would have only a slim chance of taking power under a Cabinet system. Eventually, the two parties failed to reach an agreement, and the special parliamentary committee on constitutional amendment was also suspended in 1986.

However, the pro-democracy movement reached its peak in 1987. Millions of citizens took to the streets demanding democratisation. The demand for democratisation was summed up as a call for a constitutional reform of the 'popularly elected presidential system'. On 29 June 1987, the Chun Doo-hwan regime finally surrendered to the massive resistance and accepted the demand for constitutional amendment. Roh Tae-woo, the presidential candidate of the ruling DJP, declared his acceptance of demands for a constitutional revision. Roh also said the ruling and opposition parties should agree to revise the Constitution as soon as possible to ensure free and fair competition. As such, South Korea's democratisation came as a compromise between pro-democracy movement forces and the authoritarian regime. Thus, the amendment to the new Constitution was also carried out by discussions between the two political forces (Kang 2017).

Approximately one month after the 29 June Declaration of democratisation, the ruling DJP and the opposition party organised an 'eight-member political talk' as a channel to negotiate a constitutional amendment. Four members represented the ruling party and the other four belonged to the main opposition party, which was renamed the Unification Democratic Party (UDP). However, two out of four members of the UDP belonged to Kim Young-sam's faction, and the other two represented the Kim Dae-jung faction (Kang 2017: 1–18). All major issues related to the revision of the constitution were discussed in this 'eight-member political talk'. Therefore, the revision of the Constitution was not led by the National Assembly, but was actually led by three political leaders, Roh Tae-woo, Kim Young-sam, and Kim Dae-jung. The 'political talk' proceeded very efficiently and reached an agreement on most issues in almost a month.

The National Assembly reconvened the Special Committee on Constitutional Reform, which was formed in 1986. The Special Committee on the Constitutional Amendment of the National Assembly made a draft based on the agreements at the 'eight-member meetings'. This revised Constitution passed the plenary session of the National Assembly on 12 October 1987, and it was finalised through a referendum two weeks later. In the referendum, 93.1 per cent of voters approved the new Constitution. The turnout rate was 78.2 per cent. It was the ninth constitutional amendment. The constitutional amendment in 1987 was made through discussions and agreements between vying political powers.

It took only a month-and-a-half to revise the Constitution, which was a very short time, and there are several reasons why this happened. First of all, the constitutional amendment process was led by only the three major political leaders: Roh Tae-woo, Kim Young-sam, and Kim Dae-jung. Moreover, as the eight-member political talks, which represented the three leaders, were held behind closed doors, frank and free discussion and transactions were possible without being conscious of the public or the media. Compromises could be reached quickly. As the 29 June Declaration meant an agreement between the two political forces on the key issue of a system of direct presidential elections, other issues were actually of secondary importance (Kang 2017: 16–27). The main concern of the people was also focused primarily on that issue.

Sometimes differences in opinions occurred. An example was related to the president's term of office. The ruling DJP proposed a six-year, single-term presidential system. By contrast, the UDP proposed a four-year, two-term president with a vice-president. However, the president's term of office was finally set as a single term of five years, and the vice-presidential system was not adopted. The single-term presidency reflected incumbent President Chun Doo-hwan's will. Chun thought that completing his term of office as a single term 'contributed' to South Korea's political development. This is because until then no president had ended his tenure after a single term. Chun insisted that the successor, 'emulating him', should serve a single term. Roh Tae-woo once considered the four-year, two-term president as in the United States. However, Chun was still the sitting president and the leader of the ruling DJP. The DJP proposed a six-year term, but Kim Young-sam and Kim Dae-jung opposed it. The two Kims wanted the most favourable environment for them to become president. The president's term of office was set at five years, not six years, to reduce the time for new challenges, even if they lost an election.

Meanwhile, the UDP proposed the introduction of the vice-presidential system. The vice-presidential system was an unacceptable proposal for the DJP. With two leading candidates in the opposition party, Kim Young-sam and Kim Dae-jung, the introduction of the vice-presidential system enabled both men to run as running mates for the president and vice-president. The DJP wanted to split the two Kims and make them run independently. However, neither Kim Young-sam nor Kim Dae-jung, both with strong ambitions to become president, seriously considered the possibility of becoming a vice-presidential candidate at all. As such, the political interests of not only Roh Tae-woo, Kim Young-sam, and Kim Dae-jung, but also Chun Doo-hwan's preferences together led to the creation of the five-year, single-term presidential system, the most important framework of the 1987 Constitution.

Another reason why the Constitution was easily agreed upon was that there existed 'an answer that all parties could accept'. Key political leaders such as Kim Young-sam and Kim Dae-jung understood democratisation as a 'return to the political order before the Yushin regime was established' (Kang 2017: 24). In other words, they thought that democratisation meant a return to the Third Republic, where political competition regularly occurred. Because of this perception, whenever disagreements arose, except for on a few key issues, they used the revised Constitution provisions in 1962 as the basis of their judgement.

This process of constitutional revision leads us to realise the important characteristics of South Korea's democratisation. Democratisation in South Korea was never a 'revolution'. Some of the pro-democracy forces argued for radical change not only in the political order, but also in the economic–social order. However, democratisation was limited to the restoration of procedural democracy, as symbolised by the slogan of 'the introduction of the popularly elected president'. In particular, Kim Young-sam and Kim Dae-jung, who led the democratisation movement, believed that if procedural democracy was restored, they had a high possibility of taking power.

One of the interesting features of the Park Chung-hee period before the Yushin regime is the dynamics of electoral politics. Even before the Yushin regime, it cannot be said that Korean politics in the Third Republic had a high level of democracy. After the coup in 1961 toppled the democratically elected government, Park Chung-hee established the Third Republic. As noted, elections during this period were not conducted in a very fair and democratic way. State agencies systematically and extensively intervened in elections, and, in particular, the Korean Central Intelligence Agency, the police, and local administrative organisations blatantly endeavoured to secure support for the ruling party. In addition, in rural areas, the distribution of money and goods by administrative and party organisations was also rampant. However, during the Third Republic, elections were competitive. For example, in the 1963 presidential election, the margin of votes between Park Chung-hee and Yun Bo-seon, the main opponent, was merely 156,000 votes. In the 1971 presidential election, when Kim Dae-jung was the candidate for the NDP, the difference between Park and Kim was 940,000 votes. In fact, the dynamics of electoral politics occurred even under the Yushin regime. In the National Assembly election in 1978, the opposition NDP slightly outpaced the ruling DRP in terms of votes. Although the opposition party could not win more seats, the 1978 general election showed that electoral politics remained competitive even under the most repressive political environment. From these experiences, Kim Young-sam and Kim Dae-jung came to believe that they could win if free and fair elections were guaranteed.

This is why the establishment of a fair and free presidential election system was most important in the process of amending the Constitution in 1987, and other issues were generally regarded as 'trivial'. The fact that the Constitution modelled by major political forces was the Constitution of the Third Republic before the Yushin regime is also deeply related to the experiences of Kim Young-sam and Kim Dae-jung.

Among other things, it is important to note the establishment of the Constitutional Court in the 1987 Constitution. In fact, the Constitutional Court was established in the Second Republic, but the Constitution of the Third Republic abolished it. The 1962 Constitution required the Supreme Court to adjudicate the constitutionality of statutes, dissolve political parties, and judge election lawsuits without establishing a separate Constitutional Court, and impeachment trials were to be conducted by an impeachment trial committee (Kang 2017: 27–30).

During the negotiations in 1987, the issue of the constitutional judgments was relatively neglected not only by Roh Tae-woo but also by Kim Young-sam and Kim Dae-jung. At the time, the opposition party paid more attention to the procedure of selecting

Supreme Court judges than the establishment of a separate Constitutional Court. The opposition party preferred to establish a selection committee to recommend the chief justice or Supreme Court judges to the president. Until then, the president had appointed the chief justice.

However, the role of President Chun Doo-hwan was important in establishing an independent Constitutional Court. Chun opposed the Supreme Court's authority to dissolve political parties. He was concerned that if granted this power, the court would be forced to intervene in partisan conflicts. In response to Chun's opinion, the ruling DJP sought a new alternative, which was the introduction of the Constitutional Court. However, the opposition party initially disagreed with the DJP's proposal. The opposition party later agreed to establish an independent Constitutional Court if the DJP accepted a condition that the ordinary people could file a constitutional complaint to the Constitutional Court. The opposition party also suggested that it would agree with the ruling party's proposal for the president to appoint the chief justice and justices of the Supreme Court with the consent of the National Assembly, if the DJP accepted their proposal of constitutional complaints.

However, the establishment of an independent Constitutional Court could possibly conflict with the interests of the Supreme Court. However, the chief justice at the time did not object to the establishment of the Constitutional Court. The reason for this was the bitter memory of political retaliation against the Supreme Court in relation to its interpretation of a military-related clause of the State Compensation Act as unconstitutional under the Park Chung-hee regime in 1971. The Constitution of the Third Republic stipulated the right to claim state compensation, and in the case of soldiers and military personnel, the right to claim state compensation was restricted. The Supreme Court, which had the right to adjudicate on the constitutionality of statutes, decided that this clause was unconstitutional. This was the only constitutional review during the Third Republic. The Park Chung-hee regime was dissatisfied with the ruling and attempted to take retaliatory measures against some judges. Later, the justices of the Supreme Court involved were forced to leave the Court. Because of these negative memories, the chief justice was reluctant for the Supreme Court to deal with constitutional issues. Through this process, an independent Constitutional Court was established by agreement between the opposing parties. The Constitutional Court was given five powers: (1) adjudication of the constitutionality of statutes; (2) impeachment of high-ranking government officials, including the president; (3) dissolution of political parties; (4) resolving competence disputes between government institutions, central government, and/or local government; and (5) ruling on constitutional complaints.

The Constitutional Court has since played a very active role in major political or social issues. The Constitutional Court, along with the popularly elected presidential system, was considered the most important products of the 1987 constitutional revision. So far, the Constitutional Court has exercised all authorities granted, including two rulings on the impeachment of presidents and one ruling to dissolve a party. The role of the Constitutional Court has become very influential in South Korean politics.

4. CONCLUSION

The Constitution, revised along with democratisation in 1987, has remained unchanged ever since. The current Constitution is the longest surviving Constitution in Korean political history. Since 1987, South Korean democracy has made considerable progress. A system of checks and balances has been established and civil liberties and human rights have been enhanced. In terms of electoral democracy, seven presidents have been elected over the course of more than thirty years through a legitimate process, and three peaceful power changes have occurred. Fair and free elections have been widely accepted as 'the only game in town'. The most important aspect of the 1987 Constitution was the restoration of procedural democracy, and South Korean politics has successfully maintained that goal over the past thirty years. Besides, South Korea has overcome political crises such as the impeachment of the presidents peacefully through constitutional procedures without experiencing massive unrest, social turmoil, or instability. South Korea has achieved democratic consolidation. Constitutional politics, established in 1987, has been stable for more than three decades.

In recent years, demands for another constitutional amendment have often been raised. This is because of the limitations of the current Constitution. As mentioned earlier in the section on 'Democratisation and the constitutional reform', the 1987 Constitution was modelled on the 1962 Constitution. In other words, the revision of the Constitution in 1987 was not future-oriented but rather a return to the pre-Yushin political order. Today, the 1987 constitution does not fit well with democratised and diversified South Korean society. In addition, since the restoration of procedural democracy was a primary concern in 1987, the power of the so-called imperial president, which was uninterruptedly strengthened over the long period of authoritarian regimes, was not properly reviewed. The need to decentralise the authority and power of the central government is another reason for another constitutional reform. The five-year, single-term presidential system also poses serious problems in terms of the continuity of key national policies However, attempts to amend the Constitution so far have been unsuccessful. As the limitations and problems of the 1987 Constitution are clear, demands for another constitutional reform will continue to emerge.

BIBLIOGRAPHY

Han, S. J. (1983), *Je 2 Gonghwaguk kwa Hangukey Minjujuey* [*The Second Republic and the Korean Democracy*] (Seoul: Jongnoseojeok).

Kang, W. T. (2015), *Daehangmingug minjuhwa iyagi* [*The Political History of Korean Democratisation*] (Seoul: National Museum of Korean Contemporary History).

Kang, W. T. (2017), '1987nyeon heonbeobey gaejeong guajeonggwa sidaejeok hamey' [How the Constitution was Revised in 1987], *Critical Review of History* 119, 12–37.

Kang, W. T. (2019), *Hangug Jeongchiron* [*Understanding Korean Politics*], 2nd edn (Seoul: Pakyoungsa).

Shim, J. Y. (2017), *Hanguk Jeongdang Jeongchisa* [*The History of Korean Party Politics*] (Seoul: Baeksanseodang).

Shin, B. R. (2001), *Hanguk Bundansa Yeongu* [*A Study of Korea's Division History*] (Seoul: Hanul).

Suh, H. K. (2012), *Daehanmingug heonbeobey tansaeng* [*The Birth of the South Korean Constitution*] (Seoul: Changbi).

CHAPTER 11

LEGISLATIVE POLITICS

BYOUNG KWON SOHN

1. INTRODUCTION

UNDER the Constitution of the Sixth Republic, South Korea is counted among the countries with a presidential form of government. The president, both the chief executive and the head of state, is directly elected, and cannot serve more than one five-year term. The Constitution also separately stipulates the National Assembly as another central institution, ensuring the general principle of dual legitimacy which most presidential forms of government embody. Under the current election law, the unicameral National Assembly is composed of members both directly elected in individual districts across the nation and those who gain seats through a proportional voting system.

Since South Korean democratisation in 1987, the National Assembly has endeavoured to increase its political power vis-à-vis the president and the executive branch. The number of members' bills has gradually increased since the thirteenth National Assembly, which was the first Assembly of the Sixth Republic. In addition, the regular legislative session for the inspection of governmental offices was resurrected beginning with the thirteenth National Assembly. Moreover, the National Assembly adopted the Law on Confirmation Hearings in 2000 to hold more systematic confirmation hearings over the governmental personnel nominated by the president. The National Assembly also established affiliated research organisations, such as the National Assembly Research Service and the National Assembly Budget Office, in 2007 and 2003, respectively.

Despite these efforts on the part of the National Assembly, the public has not evaluated this institution highly. The general public has viewed the workings of the National Assembly simply as falling short and even wasteful, sensing that members betray the public good for their own individual and partisan benefits. Inter-party deadlock in the Assembly has almost become routinised, exhausting the public with partisan bickering in Yeouido, an island in the Han River in Seoul, where the National Assembly building is located. More often than not, the National Assembly is decried as an 'animal parliament' (*dongmulgukoe*) because members of each party do not hesitate to physically wrestle with each other for the benefit of their own party. When the National Assembly does not deliver timely laws due to partisan bickering, it is criticised as a 'vegetable parliament' (*singmulgukoe*) for its extreme unproductiveness. All this negative public sentiment towards the National Assembly makes it necessary to delve into what is wrong with its internal workings, and to which institutional and behavioural defects these problems should be ascribed.

Against this background, this chapter explores the main characteristics of the National Assembly by focusing on the standing committees and the parliamentary parties, which are the two leading actors in the South Korean legislative setting. Given this objective, this chapter starts by providing a historical overview of the National Assembly's development, and then describes the main characteristics of the National Assembly under the current Sixth Republic in the following section. Next, the chapter reviews the feature traits of the National Assembly by highlighting the key functions of the standing committees and then the major roles played by the parliamentary parties. In the final section, a diagnosis of the nature of the National Assembly legislative process is provided in terms of a consensual versus majoritarian dichotomy.

2. Overview of the National Assembly History

The National Assembly came into being on 31 May 1948, almost three years after the US military initiated an interim administration over South Korea following its independence from Japanese imperial rule on 15 August 1945. As a result of the first parliamentary election held across the part of the Korean Peninsula south of the thirty-eighth parallel on 10 May 1948, a fresh cohort of 198 members of the historic first National Assembly were elected, 85 of them as independents (Korean National Assembly 2021a, 2021b).[1] As a unicameral body, the first National Assembly, which is often called 'the Constitutional Assembly' (*Jeheongukoe*), enacted the nation's fundamental laws shaping the newly born Republic, including the Constitutional Law, the National Assembly Law, the Government Organization Law, and other major laws required for meeting the new born nation's basic needs (Kim 2001: 121–129).

As the parliamentary elections proceeded throughout the First Republic (1948–1960), a two-party system emerged as a prototype of South Korean party politics within the National Assembly. A series of pairs of mutually opposing parties arose and receded during this early Republic, including such dyads as the ruling Liberty Party (*Jayudang*) and the leading opposition Democratic National Party (*Mingukdang*), and later the Liberty Party and the major opposition Democratic Party (*Minjudang*). Along with the two-party system, presidential dominance over legislative politics gradually took hold, as the first Korean president Rhee Syngman began to wield overwhelming power over the legislative (Paik 1991; Shim 2009: 51–109; Korean National Assembly 2021b). The Cold War atmosphere surrounding the Korean Peninsula helped President Rhee to remain powerful and supreme in party politics by exploiting 'red-scare' tactics against his political opponents.

When the Second Republic (1960–1961) came along after President Rhee stepped down following 'the April 19 Revolution', the National Assembly began to operate under the parliamentary form of government for the first time. As a corollary, the National Assembly was expected to be the central forum for democratic political deliberation. The tragedy, however, was that the Second Republic was too short-lived to fulfil this anticipation, and crumbled following a military coup led by General Park Chung-hee (Shim 2009: 111–150).

Breaking his own promise to return to the military as soon as social order was restored, General Park ran in the fifth presidential election in 1963, and was elected president by defeating Yun Bo-seon, who was both the leader of the Democratic Politics Party (*Mineongdang*) and the president of the Second Republic. The beginning of the Third Republic (1963–1972) marked another threshold of the historical trajectory of the National Assembly in that the executive-dominated legislative process resumed under the semi-authoritarian presidential system of the Third Republic (Oh 2004; Sohn 2018: 169–184).

In designing the new republic, the Supreme Council of National Reconstruction (*Gukgajaegeonchoegohoeui*), which was the Park-led military council established after the 1961 coup, abhorred the legislative processes, which were time-consuming and floor-dominated. So it amended the National Assembly Law in order to expedite legislative process in the new National Assembly soon to be launched in 1963; that is, the Supreme Council amended the National Assembly Law for the purpose of making standing committees the central organs of legislation. As it turned out later, the newly adopted committee-centred legislative process was only a façade to cover up the Park government's desire to allow executive bills to rapidly pass through parliament. By tactfully resorting to the standing committees, where the ruling Republican Party (*Gonghwadang*) was always in the majority and monopolised the chairpersonship, Park's government could enact government bills as quickly as possible. This new norm of legislative efficiency finally replaced the norm of democratic deliberation. In line with this, writing on the role orientations of National Assembly members in the late 1960s and the early 1970s, a time which mostly falls within this Third Republic, Kim and Woo (1975: 281) conclude that 'compromise, accommodation, or conciliation does not appear to be an important part of the legislative norms in the National Assembly'.

Finally, the National Assembly legislative process during the Fourth and Fifth authoritarian Republics (1972–1979, 1980–1987) was so dictated by the super-majority ruling parties, the Republican Party and the Democratic Justice Party (*Minjeongdang*), respectively, that the voices of the opposition parties were muted. The status of the National Assembly was reduced to a rubber stamp submissively endorsing the government proposals, while its role of representing the people was ignored or minimised at best (Yoo 2018: 300–304). Besides, South Korean voters were not able to directly elect their president. Their basic political rights were severely restrained. And pro-democratisation rallies and student street protests were brutally suppressed by the police (Sohn 2018: 185–209). Unfortunately, even after the end of the Fourth Republic triggered by the assassination of President Park, authoritarian rule continued, this time being succeeded by a new cohort of politicised military officers headed by General Chun Doo-hwan. The dictatorial regime of the Fifth Republic came to an end only after the political liberalisation in 1986 and the vehement pro-democratisation protests in June 1987 (Han 2016: 337–342).

Once South Korean politics got back on the democratic track, thanks to the successful pro-democratisation movement in 1987, the newly adopted Constitution of the Sixth Republic (1987–present) restored voters' right to directly elect the president, which was a long-awaited political achievement for South Korean citizens. Moreover, the new Constitution strengthened the power of the National Assembly vis-à-vis the president by depriving him of the power to dissolve the parliament. It also granted the legislature the power to confirm the prime minister, the chief justice of the Supreme Court, and other top-ranking government personnel nominated by the president, and allowed the National Assembly to regularly inspect and audit governmental offices (Sohn 2018: 210–216; Yoo 2018: 304–314).

Among other things, the thirteenth National Assembly (1988–1992) needs to be emphasised for several reasons. First of all, the thirteenth Assembly was important in that it was launched under a divided government, meaning that the ruling Democratic Justice Party failed to obtain a majority of the parliamentary seats, and that the legislative politics was on the verge of deadlock (Yoo 2006: 72–73). In other words, President Roh Tae-woo, who, thanks to his military background and role in the previous authoritarian regime, was elected the first president of the Sixth Republic amid splits in the opposition camp, could not move forward without the support of any one of the opposition parties.

On top of that, the thirteenth National Assembly was also remarkable in that it established several important precedents that subsequent Assemblies were supposed to follow. Among other things, parties in the National Assembly agreed to an informal norm that the chairs of the standing committees should be distributed among the parties in proportion to the seats each party gained (Kim 2001: 304; Yoo 2006: 83–88; Ka 2010: 140–141). This new norm of proportional chairpersonship was an outcome forced upon the ruling Democratic Justice Party by the opposition party leaders, who were often called the 'three Kims'—Kim Dae-jung, Kim Young-sam, and Kim Jong-pil—in the context of the unprecedented divided government.

Finally, the thirteenth National Assembly also mattered in that it ushered in a new legislative era in which a 'system of legislative consultation' was first established. In contrast to the legislative practices and procedures of the past authoritarian days, the thirteenth National Assembly and the following Assemblies were supposed to proceed on the basis of consultation between the speaker of the National Assembly and party leaders, on the one hand, and among the party leaders, on the other hand (Yoo 2006: 81–82; Jeon 2018: 209–211). In a nut shell, the unprecedented political environment of the divided government ended up producing a consultative mode of legislative decision-making, preventing the ruling party from monopolising legislative powers.

3. THE MAIN CHARACTERISTICS OF THE LEGISLATIVE PROCESS IN THE NATIONAL ASSEMBLY IN THE SIXTH REPUBLIC

No doubt the National Assembly has been regarded as one of the pillar constitutional institutions in South Korean politics, as well as in the political context of the Sixth Republic. Regardless of the public's evaluation of the National Assembly, all political parties in South Korea strain to gain as many seats as possible in the legislature, since their political influence should be proved in terms of the number of Assemblymen they keep in line in the parliament. Moreover, when granted the status of a 'parliamentary group' by procuring the stipulated number of seats per the National Assembly Law, the party will have many institutional privileges, such as the right to speak on the floor and governmental financial subsidies.

With respect to the number of terms members may serve, both the National Assembly Law and the Election Law do not impose any limit; that is, incumbents are allowed to run for the Assembly without having to worry about term limits. The absence of term limits, however, does not automatically guarantee an incumbency advantage in the next election. Since the nomination processes are highly centralised within political parties, party leaders tend not to nominate disloyal incumbents. They also usually do not nominate incumbents and may sweep away members on a massive scale when they need to rebrand their unpopular party image. In this way, incumbents may sometimes suffer disadvantages.

As is the case with most parliamentary democracies, the National Assembly is also expected to make laws, represent constituencies, and check and monitor the president and the executive body. Historically speaking, most major bills have been proposed by the executive, and that remains a normal pattern (Park 1998). However, it also needs to be pointed out that the frequency of bill introduction by members has increased with the onset of the Sixth Republic when compared to the National Assemblies of the past authoritarian Fifth Republic. For example, during the sessions of the eleventh (1981–1985) and twelfth (1985–1988) National Assemblies, 202 and 211 member bills were introduced, respectively. In contrast, during the thirteenth (1988–1992), the fourteenth (1992–1996), and the fifteenth (1996–2000) National Assemblies, the numbers of bills introduced by members were 570, 321, and 1,144, respectively.

Nevertheless, the passage rate of the executive bills is usually more than double that of bills offered by members. For example, the passage rates of 'executive bills' during the fourteenth and fifteenth National Assemblies were 92 per cent and 82 per cent, respectively, while those of 'member bills' were 37 per cent and 40 per cent each

(Gukoesamucheo [National Assembly Secretariat] 2000: 508–512). In this sense, it would not be widely off the mark to say that the executive still leads the National Assembly in the legislative process.

When members propose bills and amendments, they do so primarily to make their own mark in the legislative process, or to symbolically show that they are tending to the interests of their party and constituencies, or the organised interests who support them. Members are particularly keen to heed the interests of constituents, holding regular meetings with local voters and reporting on their legislative activities. Since one important goal is getting re-elected and re-election depends upon constituents' evaluations, constituency services are crucial for members if they intend to run again (Yoon 2010: 325–330; Park 2020: 124–125, 132–134).

Finally, members find it important to monitor and check the policies and workings of the executive branch, including those of the president. This part of legislative function tends to be emphasised more by opposition parties rather than the ruling party (Jang 2020: 158–159). This is particularly the case as presidential democracies imitate parliamentarian practices in their actual workings (Choi 2010: 281). Opposition parties in the Assembly endeavour to reveal to the public the policy mistakes as well as the political corruption and scandals of the president and the executive. In line with this, the annual legislative session for the inspection of government offices has never been conducted without intense brawls between the ruling party and the opposition parties (Jang 2020: 163–164). Against this broad background, the main features of the National Assembly committees and parties will be described in the following subsections.

3.1 Characteristics and Defects of the Standing Committee System

According to the National Assembly Law, the standing committee system is comprised of both standing and special committees. On the whole, most of the major committees in the National Assembly are permanent standing committees, while a few special committees are established to work for a designated period of time. One exception among these special committees, however, is the Special Committee on Budget and Accounts, which is a special but permanent committee.

All standing committees, including the Special Committee on Budget and Accounts, have at least one subcommittee to scrutinise and mark up bills. The standing and permanent special committees in the current twenty-first National Assembly, which began in May 2020, are shown in Table 11.1.

One interesting fact to note is that most standing committees are organised in a fashion in which the jurisdiction of each committee corresponds to the functions of its Cabinet counterpart(s) and other government agencies in the executive branch. In line with this pattern, most of the seventeen standing committees of the twenty-first

Table 11.1: Standing committees in the twenty-first South Korean National Assembly

Committee	No. of members	No. of ruling Democratic Party members	No. of opposition People Power Party members	No. of non-parliamentary group members
National Assembly Management Committee	28	16	10	2
Legislation and Judiciary Committee	18	11	6	1
National Policy Committee	24	14	8	2
Economy and Finance Committee	26	15	9	2
Education Committee	16	9	6	1
Science, ICT, Broadcasting, and Communications Committee	20	12	7	1
Foreign Affairs and Unification	21	11	7	3
National Defence Committee	17	10	6	1
Public Administration and Security Committee	22	13	8	1
Culture, Sports, and Tourism Committee	16	8	6	2
Agriculture, Food, Rural Affairs, Oceans, and Fisheries Committee	19	11	8	0
Trade, Industry, Energy, SMEs, and Startups Committee	30	18	10	2
Health and Welfare Committee	24	15	7	2
Environment and Labour Committee	16	9	5	2
Land, Infrastructure, and Transport Committee	30	18	10	2
Intelligence Committee	12	8	4	0
Gender Equality and Family Committee	17	10	6	1
Special Committee on Budget and Accounts	50	29	17	4

Source: https://www.assembly.go.kr/assm/assemact/committee/committee01/assmCommittee/committeeUserList.do, accessed 7 August 2021.

National Assembly, with a few exceptions, generally correspond to the Cabinet-level ministry (or ministries) and other governmental organisations. As the names and organisation of the ministries in the executive branch change, therefore, those of the committees in the National Assembly also change in tandem; that is, whenever a new government proposes to the National Assembly a new organisational plan in the form of the Government Organization Law, the National Assembly usually passes it, and subsequently amends its own National Assembly Law in order to reflect the ministry changes into the standing committee system.

The partisan make-up of committee chairpersonship and membership is determined in proportion to the percentage of the seats each party gains in the parliamentary election; that is, the majority party, whether the governing party or not, cannot monopolise the chairs of the committees. It has usually been the case that during the first session of every new National Assembly, party leaders go through a series of negotiations, sometimes lengthy and intense, over how to distribute the committee chairs.[2]

As mentioned above, the legislative process in the National Assembly since the Third Republic has been centred on standing committees rather than on the floor. According to students of comparative legislature, the status of standing committees is usually associated with the policymaking power of legislatures. For example, Mezey (1979: 21–44) shows that while the policymaking power of standing committees is modest in 'reactive' legislatures, the standing committees in 'active' legislatures exert strong influence in making government policies. Loewenberg and Patterson (1979: 210) also note that a weaker committee system has less influence on policy, although their work is not exclusively focused on comparing standing committees across countries. In addition, Lees and Shaw (1979: 4), in comparing legislatures across countries, specifically focus on the nature and functions of 'committees' in the belief that the committees are the place 'where the vital decisional and deliberative interactions occur within organizations'.

It cannot be denied that standing committees in the South Korean National Assembly also play an important role in the legislative process. First, all bills must proceed through standing committees to reach the floor for voting, meaning that the standing committees are the gatekeepers of parliamentary procedure. Without being reported out by a standing committee, bills, whether they are members' or executive bills, cannot proceed further. Second, the standing committees are virtually the first stage where the pros and cons of the bill are argued, amendments to the bills are proposed, and the compromises are tentatively reached (Jeon 2010a: 190–195).

Notwithstanding the committee centrality in the National Assembly, the standing committee system is not that effective in many respects, for several reasons. First of all, committee specialisation is not institutionalised in the National Assembly, and that means the term of committee membership is both relatively short and very unstable. In fact, the relatively short two-year term of committee membership was designed to facilitate membership circulation across committees so that a member may alternately be on prestigious committees and on other less valuable committees (Park 1996: 333–336). As a result, committee members do not have enough time to develop policy expertise.

Furthermore, committee membership within even that short term is not guaranteed, making it further difficult for committee members to accumulate specialty. In other words, the high rate of committee membership turnover is not simply due to the two-year term of committee membership. It is also due to the fact that a member can change committees within the two-year term with the permission of party leadership. As a result, the average committee turnover rates of the eleventh, twelfth, thirteenth, and fourteenth National Assemblies were 51.6 per cent, 44.8 per cent, 51.2 per cent, and 58.4 per cent, respectively (Park 1996: 335). With these frequents shifts of committee membership, the National Assembly has rarely been given the opportunity to institutionalise itself.

As a corollary, the seniority norm is not well established for the selection of committee chairs. To make matters worse, the parliamentary election is characterised by a very high turnover rate, depriving incumbents of the chance to return to the committee to which they formerly belonged. In addition, committee assignment does not necessarily proceed by taking the member's career or expertise into consideration. It is rather a politicised process in one sense or another, meaning that party loyalty may influence the process. To the extent that the National Assembly committee assignment process is more or less politically driven and that the roles and jurisdictions of committees are not seriously considered in the recruiting of committee members, the institutionalisation of the National Assembly still has a long way to go. If we are to agree with the argument of Polsby (1968: 145) who states that one characteristic of an institutionalised organisation, such as the US Congress, is that it implements a 'division of labour in which roles are specified' and has 'regularized patterns of recruitment of roles', there is little doubt that the National Assembly falls far short. Thus, the so-called interest–advocacy–accommodation hypothesis proposed by Shepsle (1978) cannot be applied to the National Assembly committee assignment process, since it is not carried out in a way to represent geographically oriented local interests.

As described above, the standing committee system in the National Assembly is not capable of playing a strong policymaking role. Despite the organisational centrality of standing committees, the low level of committee institutionalisation, the underdeveloped committee assignment process, and the frequent committee membership turnover all prevent standing committees from matching the penetrating influence of the executive. Put simply, the National Assembly standing committees show many characteristics found in the standing committees of 'marginal legislatures' in that the committees in marginal legislatures are characterised by 'the lack of policy expertise, the fluidity of committee membership, and the absence of competent professional staff' (Mezey 1979: 118).

3.2 The Predominant Position of Legislative Parties

In addition to standing committees, the parliamentary parties are another important actor in the National Assembly. In most cases, parliamentary parties affect their members in the legislative arena through party leaders and the party caucus. In the National Assembly, each party usually has one 'floor leader' (*wonnaedaepyo*), one senior deputy floor leader, and several deputies. The floor leader is elected by the party caucus, and the deputy floor leaders, including the senior deputy, are selected by the party's floor leader from among the members of the party (The Minjoo Party 2021a; The People Power Party 2021a).

Among other things, party leadership directs the members by deciding on the official party line ahead of votes on controversial bills (Jeon 2014: 201), and plans legislative and procedural strategies, both in the committee and on the floor. In the case of the ruling party, party leaders make every ardent effort to enact the bills proposed by the executive branch or favoured by the president. Moreover, party leaders also assign standing committee seats to their party members (Park and Jeon 2019: 60), and interact with the leaders of other parties during the legislative session as situation develops.

On the other hand, the party caucus is the supreme organisation composed of the entire membership of the party in the Assembly (The Minjoo Party 2021b; The People Power Party 2021b). As a plenary forum for all members of the party, it provides members an opportunity to deliver their opinion to the party leadership and their peers. Some assertive members occasionally challenge the party leaders' directives rather than simply endorsing the guidelines and voting cues imposed by them. In most cases, however, the party caucus strengthens the party leadership with respect to voting and legislative strategies, thus legitimising and finalising the party's official positions in the legislative process. It does so particularly when the president stands behind the party leadership.

There is no doubt, therefore, that political parties in the National Assembly play a preponderant role in managing legislative affairs, and party loyalty can explain many aspects of members' legislative behaviour. The predominant status of parliamentary parties can be confirmed by several facts. First of all, party affiliation of a member is a robust predictor of his voting behaviour. Even after controlling for other major variables such as ideology, constituency characteristics, committee membership, and seniority, party membership proves to be the most powerful factor in predicting members' voting patterns (Lee 2005: 203, 206; Jeon 2006; Moon 2011: 31, 33–34).

Second, the official party position on a particular vote, usually called '*dangnon*' in Korean, is so strict and intolerant that no member can break with it without taking the huge risk of being severely rebuked by party leadership. As a matter of fact, once the official position of the party is taken on a series of votes, the members of the party have to adhere to it. Otherwise, the defecting member is sure to be harshly criticised and may even be forced to leave the party (Park 2010: 256–260).

Finally, members of the party in the Assembly should obey the party's legislative directives if they intend to run for re-election. This is primarily because party leadership virtually monopolises the nominating procedure for parliamentary elections. It is commonplace, at least within major parties, that the nomination procedure is highly centralised in the hands of the party leadership. Although a separate and independent party nomination committee is set up, the will of the party leadership, including the

Table 11.2: Level of partisan polarisation in the seventeenth to twentieth South Korean National Assemblies

National Assembly	Name of the liberal party	Party ideology score	Name of the conservative party	Party ideology score	Ideology score difference between two parties
Seventeenth National Assembly	Unified Democratic Party	−21.4	Grand National Party	27.6	49.0
Eighteenth National Assembly	Democratic Unified Party	−31.8	Saenuri Party	18.4	50.2
Nineteenth National Assembly	The Minjoo Party	−28.1	Saenuri Party	23.9	52.0
Twentieth National Assembly	The Minjoo Party	−24.7	Liberty Korea Party	29.5	54.2

Source: https://www.chosun.com/site/data/html_dir/2018/01/08/2018010800257.html, accessed 7 August 2021.

president in the case of the ruling party, weighs heavily on the minds of the members of the party nomination committee. Well aware of this, the members of the Assembly dare not even imagine defecting from the official party line (Jeon 2010b: 120).

One important fact to note is that the legislative procedure dominated by the party gets more and more polarised as the ideological distance between the two major opposing parties widens. The ever-increasing inter-party polarisation in the National Assembly is well captured in Table 11.2.

As shown in Table 11.2, the ideological distance between the two major parties has increased quite significantly from the seventeenth National Assembly to the twentieth National Assembly. Ideological distance began at 49.0 in the seventeenth Assembly and has since jumped to 54.2 in the twentieth Assembly. The increased distance suggests that inter-party compromise on legislative affairs will get harder to achieve in the future.

With regards to the origin of this steep partisan ideological polarisation, it is widely agreed that it began in the seventeenth National Assembly. The freshman cohort of the National Assembly was from the so-called 386-generation, so named because most of them were born in the 1960s, entered college in the 1980s during the authoritarian Fifth Republic, and were in their thirties when elected. Most of them, too, were the members of the progressive Uri Party (*Yeollinuridang*) led by President Roh Moo-hyun, and were highly ideological and supportive of Roh's policies (Sohn 2004; Yoon 2004). With many of these activist-turned-legislators participating in parliamentary sessions, the National Assembly began to show incessant deadlock and highly conflictual modes of decision-making (Sohn 2018: 246–248).

The increasing partisan polarisation of a highly ideological nature makes inter-party compromise in the National Assembly extremely hard to achieve, and, as a result, inter-party deadlock has become a commonplace phenomenon rather than an exception. As a corollary, partisanship and confrontation in the legislative process have been routinised (Chung 2008: 79–83; Sohn and Ka 2008: 95–96). The traditional American-style 'to get along, go along' norm has rarely been observed among the members of opposing parties.

To summarise, the level of inter-party cooperation is extremely low, and legislative productivity of the National Assembly is rarely satisfactory. Since each party sees the other as a potential adversary rather than a legislative partner, bridging the gap between the opposing parties and finding common ground is much easier said than done. In particular, partisan deadlock grows worse when the president pushes his own policy agenda of a highly controversial nature through the National Assembly.

4. Conclusion

As explained, the thirteenth National Assembly started with the inter-party consultative system. Although the consultative system was an outcome enforced upon the then governing Democratic Justice Party under the unprecedented divided government, the spirit of consultative legislative management has been believed to operate in today's National Assembly.

In a sense, the consultative system was a unique outcome brought about by the moderate multiparty system shaped during the three Kims' era of the late 1980s and most of 1990s. As the multiparty system grew into an easily anticipated outcome in both presidential and parliamentary elections, it became much rarer than before that a single majority party could emerge and dominate the legislative process. In this unique political context, the consultative system was gradually taken for granted as time passed. And once such a path was paved in the National Assembly, the majority party, conservative or progressive, regarded sharing committee chairs with the minority parties as the norm, and the consultative mode could survive, at least in spirit. Consequently, the majority party's attempts for unilateral management of legislative affairs have faced frequent public criticism in that such practice was seen as an attempt to revert to the old authoritarian days.

Aware of these backlashes against arbitrary modes of legislative management, the majority party has sought a consensual outcome with minority parties unless some inevitabilities prevented it, even when it can force its will to prevail through floor voting. The spirit of seeking consensus among legislative parties materialised again during discussions on the amendment of the National Assembly Law in the last days of the eighteenth National Assembly in 2012. The amended legislation, which is commonly called 'the National Assembly Advancement Law' (*Gukoeseonjinhwabeop*), was intended to penalise physical confrontation in legislative sessions, among other things. More importantly, it was also designed to protect minority party rights by permitting the filibuster and by strictly delimiting 'the speaker's right to impose a deadline for committee deliberation over a bill' (*Jikgwonsangjeong*), or curbing the speaker's arbitrary power to discharge a bill out of the committee of jurisdiction if it fails to report it out by a designated time.

Despite its own efforts to seek legislative consensus through the consultative system, however, the National Assembly has suffered chronic partisan confrontation, and it still does in the current twenty-first National Assembly. In fact, partisan confrontation in the National Assembly has become even more severe after the impeachment of President Park Geun-hye and the subsequent inauguration of President Moon Jae-in 2017. As the inter-party ideological distance between the two leading parties, conservative and progressive, diverged almost irrevocably, deal-making through political compromise has become extremely hard to achieve. Regardless of conservatives or progressives, the leaders of the ruling party tend almost blindly to follow the directives of the president, depriving themselves of manoeuvring space to compromise with the major opposition party (or parties) of different ideological bents. In contrast, the major opposition party, in its turn, regards it as virtually the norm to challenge the ruling party as strongly and frequently as possible. In this mode of legislative decision-making, deliberation within committees and subcommittees are all strewn with partisan brawling, virtually nullifying the spirit of the National Assembly Advancement Law.

Truly, nobody doubts that the constitutional and political power of the National Assembly has been tremendously enhanced since the democratisation, compared to that during the past authoritarian days. Moreover, the National Assembly itself has strained to improve its performance when faced with public rebuke, correcting procedural deficiencies and organisational defects of the institution. Almost all speakers, as well as the leaders of all parties, insist on the imperative of inter-party legislative co-operation for delivering public goods, claiming that reaching consensus through mutual consultation is the best way to recover the public's trust.

The actual workings within the National Assembly, however, are still tainted by chronic inter-party conflicts and mutual criticism; that is, whenever a party obtains majority party status following a parliamentary election, it feels a strong urge to push its will through the legislature. This urge of the majority party gets particularly forceful when it comes to the bills the president badly wants to see passed with maximum speed.

In summary, the National Assembly has consistently sought inter-party cooperation based on mutual consultation since the thirteenth parliament. The National Assembly itself knows well that the goal of consensus-building through inter-party consultation is not easy to achieve, but it has tried to do this, nevertheless. Nowadays, however, the spirit of inter-party consultation has grown weaker and weaker as the parties tend to regard other parties not as competitors but as adversaries. The accelerating polarisation among voters, exemplified by the syndrome of partisan fandom, too, makes legislative compromise even harder to achieve. As a result, the majoritarian mode of decision-making does now seem to prevail over the inter-party consensus-building in the actual workings of the National Assembly. This pattern will continue for some time, as long as the two major parties with opposite ideological foundations are not willing to learn how to live together.

Notes

1. Despite the whole membership of 200, the Constitutional National Assembly started with 198 members, for the 2 elections in Bukjeju (Northern Jeju Island) were delayed to 10 May 1949 due to the 4.3 Incident in 1948.
2. However, we need to note the exceptional case of the twenty-first National Assembly. As this National Assembly began to take shape, extreme conflict-ridden inter-party negotiations erupted over the chairpersonship of the Judiciary Committee, a crucial committee in the flow of bills. Sensing that the ruling Minjoo Party would not concede this chair, the Liberty Korea Party, the then leading opposition party, refused to accept any chairpersonship whatsoever. As a result, the Minjoo Party took all the chairs.

Bibliography

Choi, J.-Y. (2010), 'Gukoewa daetongnyeong' [The National Assembly and the President], in Uihoejeongchiyeonguhoe [Legislative Politics Research Group], ed., *Hangung gukoewa jeongchigwajeong* [*Korean National Assembly: Its Political Process*] (Seoul: Oreum), 263–288.

Chung, J.-M. (2008), 'Saengsanjeong gukoeunyeongeul wihan daetongnyeong-gukoe gwangyewa jeongdang' [Productive Legislature and Presidential–Legislative Relationship in Korea], *Korean Party Studies Review* 7(1), 77–102.

Gukoesamucheo [National Assembly Secretariat] (2000), *Uijeongjaryojip: Jeheongukoe–Je15dae gukoe* [*Legislative Data of the National Assembly: Constitutional National Assembly–the Fifteenth National Assembly*] (Seoul: Hangukkeompyuteoinswae(ju)) [Korean Computer Printing Co.]).

Han, J.-T. (2016), 'Je5gonghwagung sigiui minjuhwaundong' [The Democratization Movement during the Fifth Republic], in M. Shin, ed., *Hangugui minjuhwawa minjuhwaundong: seonggonggwa jwajeol* [*The Democratization and Democratization Movement in Korea: The Success and Failure*] (Seoul: Hanul), 324–384.

Jang, S.-J. (2020), 'Gukoeui haengjeongbu gamsi min gamdok' [The National Assembly's Monitoring and Oversight of the Executive Branch], in B. Sohn, S. Ka, K. Park et al., *Gukoe yeoreobogi: hangung gukoeui jedowa haengtae* [*National Assembly Inside Out: Institutions and Practices of the Korean National Assembly*] (Seoul: Oreum), 157–171.

Jeon, J.-Y. (2006), 'Gukoeuiwonui galdeungjeong tupyohaengtae bunseok: je16dae gukoe jeonjapyogyeoreul jungsimeuro' [A Study of Members' Conflictual Voting Behavior in the 16th Korean National Assembly], *Korean Political Science Review* 40(1), 47–70.

Jeon, J.-Y. (2010a), 'Gukoe ipbeopgwajeong' [The Legislative Process of the National Assembly], in Uihoejeongchiyeonguhoe [Legislative Politics Research Group], ed., *Hangung gukoewa jeongchigwajeong* [*Korean National Assembly: Its Political Process*] (Seoul: Oreum), 181–208.

Jeon, J.-Y. (2010b), 'Je18dae gukoe wonnaejeongdangui jeongdangeungjipseong bunseok' [Party Cohesion of the Eighteenth National Assembly], *Korean Party Studies Review* 9(2), 119–139.

Jeon, J.-Y. (2014), 'Gukoe wonnaejidobuui ipbeobyeonghyangnyeong bunseok' [The Keys to Legislative Success in the National Assembly of Korea: The Role of Committee Leadership], *Korean Party Studies Review* 13(2), 193–218.

Jeon, J.-Y. (2018), 'Gukoeuijangui gwonhangwa yeokal: jedoui geunwongwa yeoksajeong byeonhwa' [The Powers and Roles of the National Assembly Speaker: Institutional

Origin and Historical Changes], in B. Sohn, S. Ka, J. Jeon, J. Cho, K. Park, and S. Yoo, *Daehanmingung gukoejedoui hyeongseonggwa byeonhwa* [*The Formation and Change of the Institutions in the Korean National Assembly*] (Seoul: Purungil), 167–221.

Ka, S.-J. (2010), 'Gukoe wonguseong' [Legislative Leadership Selection of the National Assembly], in Uihoejeongchiyeonguhoe [Legislative Politics Research Group], ed., *Hangung gukoewa jeongchigwajeong* [*Korean National Assembly: Its Political Process*] (Seoul: Oreum), 131–154.

Kim, C. L., and Woo, B. (1975), 'Political Representation in the Korean National Assembly', in G. R. Boynton and C. L. Kim, eds, *Legislative Systems in Developing Countries* (Durham, NC: Duke University Press), 261–286.

Kim, H.-W. (2001), *Hangukgukoeron* [*The Korean National Assembly*] (Seoul: Eulyoo Munhwasa).

Korean National Assembly (2021a), 'Yeokdae gukoesogae' [Introducing Successive National Assemblies], https://www.assembly.go.kr/views/cms/assm/assembly/asshistory/asshistory0101.jsp, accessed 7 August 2021.

Korean National Assembly (2021b), 'Jeongdangbyeol uiseong min deukpyohyeonhwang' [Party Seats and National Votes Percentage], https://www.assembly.go.kr/views/cms/assm/assembly/asshistory/asshistory0103.jsp, accessed 7 August 2021.

Lee, H.-W. (2005), 'Gukoeuiwonui pyogyeol yoin bunseok: jeongdang,inyeom geurigo jiyeokgu' [Analysis of Member's Voting Behaviour in the Sixteenth Korean Assembly], *Korea and World Politics* 21(3), 187–218.

Lees, J. D., and Shaw, M. (1979), 'Introduction', in J. D. Lees and M. Shaw, eds, *Committees in Legislatures: A Comparative Analysis* (Durham, NC: Duke University Press), 3–10.

Loewenberg, G., and Patterson, S. C. (1979), *Comparing Legislatures* (Boston, MA: Little, Brown and Company).

Mezey, M. L. (1979), *Comparative Legislatures* (Durham, NC: Duke University Press).

Moon, W.-J. (2011), 'Dadangjeeseoui dangpapyogyeolgwa jeongdangchungseongdo: 17dae min 18dae jeonbangukoe bunseok' [Party Voting and Party Loyalty in Multiparty Party Systems: An Analysis of Roll Call Data from the Seventeenth and the Early Eighteenth National Assemblies], *Korean Journal of Legislative Studies* 17(2), 5–40.

Oh, C.-H. (2004), 'Je3gonghwagung jeongchichejeui yuhyeong gwanhan yeongu' [A Study on the Regime Type of Korea's Third Republic], *Korean Political Science Review* 25(1), 143–165.

Paik, Y.-C. (1991), 'Je1gonghwagugui uihoejeongchie gwanhan yeongu: uihoewa haengjeongbugwangyereul jungsimeuro' [A Study on the Congressional Politics in the First Republic of Korea: With Special Reference to the Executive–Legislative Relationship], *Korean Political Science Review* 25(1), 133–158.

Park, C.-P. (1996), 'Hanmiil 3guk uihoeui jeonmunseong chukjeokgujoe daehan bigyoyeongu' [A Comparative Study on the Specialization of the Legislatures among the USA, Japan, and Korea], *Korean Political Science Review* 30(4), 321–342.

Park, C.-M. (1998), 'Haengjeongbuui ipbeopbu jibae: byeonhwawa jisok' [Executive Predominance over Legislature: Change and Continuity], *Korean Journal of Legislative Studies* 4(2), 6–29.

Park, K.-M. (2010), 'Gukoewa jeongdang' [The National Assembly and the Party], in Uihoejeongchiyeonguhoe [Legislative Politics Research Group], ed., *Hangung gukoewa jeongchigwajeong* [*Korean National Assembly: Its Political Process*] (Seoul: Oreum), 237–261.

Park, K.-M. (2020), 'Gukoeuiwonui uijeonghwaldong' [The Legislative Activities of the Members of the National Assembly], in B. Sohn, S. Ka, K. Park et al., *Gukoe yeoreobogi: hangung gukoeui jedowa haengtae* [*National Assembly Inside Out: Institutions and Practices of the Korean National Assembly*] (Seoul: Oreum), 123–137.

Park, K.-M., and Jeon, J.-Y. (2019), 'Hangung jeongdangui jidobuwa dangnaeminjujuui: je19dae gukoe jeonbangiui saenuridanggwa minjutonghapdang' [Party Leaders and Intra-Party Democracy: Saenuri Party and the Democratic United Party in the Nineteenth National Assembly], *Journal of Parliamentary Research* 14(1), 47–71.

Polsby, N. W. (1968), 'The Institutionalization of the U.S. House of Representatives', *American Political Science Review* 62(1), 144–168.

Shepsle, K. A. (1978), *Giant Zigsaw Puzzle: Democratic Committee Assignments in the Modern House* (Chicago, IL: The University of Chicago Press).

Shim, J.-Y. (2009), *Hangung jeongdangjeongchisa: wigiwa tonghabui jeongchi* [*Korean Party History: Politics of Crisis and Integration*] (Seoul: Paiksan Publishing House).

Sohn, B. K. (2004), '17dae choseonuiwondeurui uijeonghwaldong pyeongga' [Characteristics of the Freshmen Representatives in the National Assembly Activities], *Korean Journal of Legislative Studies* 10(2), 85–109.

Sohn, B. K., (2018), 'Hangukyeong baljeongukgaui jeongchijedo' [Political Institutions of the Korean Developmental State], in B. Sohn and S. Park, *Hangukyeong baljeongukgaui gukgainyeomgwa jeongchijedo* (*National Ideology and Political Institutions of the Korean Developmental State*] (Seoul: Ingansarang), 143–273.

Sohn, B. K., and Ka, S. (2008), 'Galdeungui hyeonsilgwa habuie daehan somang: gukoe unyeong min uisagyeoljeong bangsige daehan 17dae gukoeuiwondeurui insik [Conflicts in Reality and Desire for Consensus], *Journal of Korean Politics* 17(1), 87–109.

The Minjoo Party (2021a), 'Wonnaegigu: wonnaedaepyo' [Parliamentary Organization: Floor Leader], https://theminjoo.kr/introduce/rule/const, accessed 7 August 2021.

The Minjoo Party (2021b), 'Wonnaegigu: uiwonchonghoe' [Parliamentary Organization: Party Caucus], https://theminjoo.kr/introduce/rule/const, accessed 7 August 2021.

The People Power Party (2021a), 'Wonnaegigu: wonnaedaepyo' [Parliamentary Organization: Floor Leader], http://www.peoplepowerparty.kr/renewal/about/constitution_view.do?bbsId=PCo_000000000070098, accessed 7 August 2021.

The People Power Party (2021b), 'Wonnaegigu: uiwonchonghoe' [Parliamentary Organization: Party Caucus], http://www.peoplepowerparty.kr/renewal/about/constitution_view.do?bbsId=PCo_000000000070098, accessed 7 August 2021.

Yoo, B.-K. (2006), *Galdeunggwa tahyeobui jeongchi: minjuhwa ihu hanguguihoejeongchiui baljeon* [*Politics of Conflict and Compromise: Development of Korean Parliamentary Politics since Democratization*] (Seoul: Oreum).

Yoo, S.-J. (2018), 'Gukoeui haengjeongbu gyeonjebangsik: jedojeong yeonwongwa hyeongseong geurigo byeonhwa' [The Checks of the National Assembly against the Executive: the Institutional Origin, Formation, and Change], in B. Sohn, S. Ka, J. Jeon, J. Cho, K. Park, and S. Yoo, *Daehanmingung gukoejedoui hyeongseonggwa byeonhwa* [*The Formation and Change of the Institutions in the Korean National Assembly*] (Seoul: Purungil), 273–319.

Yoon, J.-B. (2004), '17dae choseonuiwondeurui sahoe, gyeongjejeong baegyeong' [A Profile of Members of the Seventeenth National Assembly], *Korean Journal of Legislative Studies* 10(2), 59–84.

Yoon, J.-B. (2010), 'Gukoewa jiyeokgu' [The National Assembly and the Constituencies], in Uihoejeongchiyeonguhoe [Legislative Politics Research Group], ed., *Hangung gukoewa jeongchigwajeong* [*Korean National Assembly: Its Political Process*] (Seoul: Oreum), 315–344.

CHAPTER 12

EXECUTIVE POLITICS

JONGKON LEE

1. INTRODUCTION

ACCORDING to David Easton (1965: 149), politics is the authoritative allocation of values. In democratic countries, the authority to distribute valuable resources is basically delegated to legislative branches whose members are elected by constituents. In South Korean politics, however, the distribution authority was totally consolidated in the hands of the executive branch, at least by 1979. At the time of liberation from Japanese colonial rule in 1945, South Korea had a considerable number of political and economic problems. Due to the long Japanese occupation and the Korean War, the private economy did not have the ability to grow on its own.[1] Under these economic circumstances, many people with higher education preferred to have jobs in government institutions rather than in private companies. After entering public office, they grew into professional bureaucrats by gaining administrative experience and increasing their expertise in policymaking. This trend became stronger, especially with the enactment of the State Public Officials Act (*Gukgagongmuwonbeop*) in 1949 and the implementation of the administrative exams to select high-ranking civil servants (*haengjeonggosi*). Moreover, South Korea adopted a presidential system in the First Constitution, and early presidents such as Rhee Syngman and Park Chung-hee had long maintained unchallenged power. The high-quality workforce supply and the strong authority of the chief executives enabled the executive branch and its affiliated bureaucrats to exert great influence on national policy decisions. The lawmakers of the National Assembly, on the other hand, did not have sufficient expertise to match the professional bureaucrats. As a result, a policy environment was created in which policy decisions were made centred on professional bureaucrats instead of lawmakers. In particular, since the biggest problem facing South Korea at the time was economic development, the bureaucratic agency tasked with devising economic policies—especially, the Economic Planning Board (EPB; *Gyeongjegihoikwon*) of the 1960s and 1970s—maintained significant policymaking authority.

However, the size of the South Korean economy had grown and the foreign trade structure grew complicated in the 1970s, making it difficult for the professional bureaucrats to plan everything. High-quality manpower still flowed into the administration even in this period, but as the economy developed and society diversified, the executive branch became unable to solve all of society's problems. On the other hand, private companies began to grow and became self-sustaining during that period, which led to calls for a market economy rather than the state-planned economy. The economic downturn in the late 1970s led to rapid progress in discussions on market opening and liberalisation of foreign trade. As a result, in the 1980s and 1990s, many administrative reforms to state-led economic policies were implemented, one by one. Many government regulations were abolished, and economic planning centred on the EPB weakened. Also, as various social demands that had been suppressed during the economic growth period erupted beginning in the 1980s, social policy ministries grew significantly and the inter-ministerial power relations within the executive branch became more balanced.

In the 2000s, there was a great change in the political power of the president and the National Assembly, which greatly affected the authority of bureaucrats to make policy decisions. Despite the end of the military regime with the inauguration of President Kim Young-sam in 1993, the presidents of the 1990s (i.e. Kim Young-sam and Kim Dae-jung) still wielded enormous political influence. In contrast, Roh Moo-hyun, the president elected in 2002, did not belong to the mainstream faction of his party (the Millennium Democratic Party), and his influence over the National Assembly was also not significant. The National Assembly even proposed his impeachment in 2004 for failing to maintain political neutrality. The case proved that the president's authority had been greatly reduced compared to the past, although the impeachment attempt itself failed. Contrary to the decline in presidential power, the National Assembly grew remarkably, and powerful lawmakers entered the presidential Cabinet and began to direct the administration. These political trends were maintained throughout the 2000s and 2010s; Presidents Lee Myung-bak and Park Geun-hye could not take full control of their party, and President Park Geun-hye was even impeached during her term. The fall in presidential power and the rise in the power of the National Assembly harmed the authority of bureaucrats to make policy decisions. Admittedly, even in this period, several state-led plans were still in place, including the Four Major Rivers Project and the Three-Year Plan for Economic Innovation. However, the National Assembly actively intervened in the planning process and continued to raise questions during implementation, again forcing plans to be revised several times. Bureaucrats in the executive branch still play a big role in national policy decisions, but their influence on policymaking has decreased significantly compared to the past.

2. The Beginning of South Korean Executive Politics

The Republic of Korea (South Korea) experienced the Korean War between 1950 and 1953 after its independence in 1945. As a result, it experienced considerable economic difficulties.

According to Chung (1956: 225), '[South Korea] faces grave economic difficulties. The limitations imposed by the Japanese have been succeeded by the division of the country, the general destruction incurred by the Korean War, and the attendant dislocation of the population, which has further disorganized the economy'. Thus, major political forces of the late 1940s, including the Representative Democratic Council of South Korea (*Namjoseon daehangukmin daepyo minjuuiwon*) led by Rhee Syngman aimed to develop the economy based on state-led economic plans (Choi 2008: 182–183). In 1948, the First Constitution of South Korea also emphasised the development of the national economy and stipulated that foreign trade should be kept under state control. To oversee economic planning, the Rhee administration established the Planning Administration (*gihoikcheo*) in 1948, and reorganised the agency in 1955 to create the Ministry of Reconstruction (*buheungbu*). However, the state-led economic development plan was not properly implemented in the 1950s. The outbreak of the Korean War seriously destroyed the remaining industrial facilities, resulting in a sharp decline in production. As a result, the South Korean government had no choice but to rely on foreign aid economically. In particular, US aid accounted for about 70 per cent of total imports and 75 per cent of total fixed capital formation (Haggard et al. 1991: 852). Figure 12.1 shows a significant increase in the amount of grant from the United States Agency for International Development (USAID) in the mid-1950s. Thus, it was not easy for South Korea to manage the funds as they wished without reflecting US intentions (Choi 2008: 179). Moreover, President Rhee, who was a strict anti-communist, opposed the idea of a state-led economic plan (Lee 1999: 265). Therefore, in the 1950s, the main tasks of economic planning agencies such as the Planning Administration and the Ministry of Reconstruction were limited to negotiations with the United States on the amount and conditions of the aid and the management of the aid funds (Choi 2008: 203–204).

Despite the limitations on the South Korean administration's discretion, the foundation of South Korean executive politics was forged at this time. During this period, there

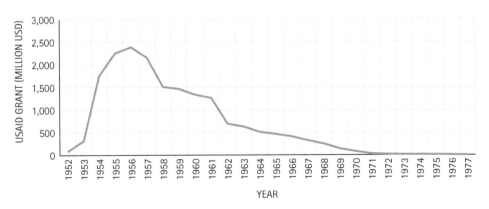

FIGURE 12.1: USAID grants to the Republic of Korea

Note: USAID grant (millions of Constant 2018 US dollars)
Source: USAID's US Overseas Loans & Grants reports, https://foreignassistance.gov/reports, accessed 8 August 2021.

was little growth in the private sector compared to the bureaucratic system that had existed since the Japanese colonial period (Kim 1991: 104–110). Thus, highly educated people began to serve in government organisations rather than in the private sector. In particular, the high-ranking civil service exam, first implemented in 1950, became an important channel for young and highly educated people to enter the bureaucracy. Although the political growth of those who passed the civil service exam was not yet significant before the 1960s (Koo 2009: 155), they gradually grew to take central positions in the policymaking process of the South Korean administration. For example, Kim Hak-ryul, who passed the first high-ranking civil service exam in 1950, became the minister of the EPB in 1969, and was essentially in charge of the entire South Korean economy.

3. The Executive for Economic Development: 1961–1979

Park Chung-hee, who gained power through a military coup in 1961, established the Supreme Council for National Reconstruction (*gukgajaegeonchoigohoiui*), the highest governing body that took control of the legislative, administrative, and judicial powers. Then, he inaugurated the Third Republic and took office as president in 1963. Even though state power became divided into three branches, this was only nominal. The political power of the Park Chung-hee administration overwhelmed other government branches. In other words, administrative supremacy was firmly established. Figure 12.2 shows the passage rate and number of bills in the South Korean National Assembly. From the first National Assembly to the fourth National Assembly, which were convened while Rhee Syngman was president, bills introduced by the executive branch as well as legislators were not actively promoted. In contrast, from the sixth National Assembly (1963–1967) to the ninth National Assembly (1973–1979), in which President Park Chung-hee led South Korean politics, not only the number of executive-introduced bills but also their passage rate increased significantly (see Table 12.1). The figures indicate that bureaucratic policymaking prevailed in the 1960s and 1970s. However, the political legitimacy of the administration was not high because President Park won power through a military coup. Therefore, the Park administration needed to raise its political legitimacy through economic growth and pushed ahead with the administration-led economic plans in earnest.

The Park administration set up the EPB two months after the coup to make the administrative system more efficient and hierarchical for long-term economic planning, and upgraded the EPB to a deputy prime minister-level agency in 1963. However, professional bureaucrats at the EPB did not have enough influence to determine the main direction of national policy in the early 1960s. In the years after the military coup, more than 60 per cent of ministers and vice-ministers were appointed from the military, and major policy decisions were also up to them (Kim and Kang 2017: 122–124).

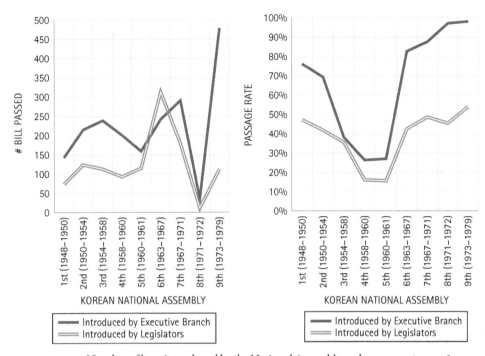

FIGURE 12.2: Number of laws introduced by the National Assembly and passage rates, 1948–1979

Source: South Korean National Assembly Bill Information System, https://likms.assembly.go.kr/bill/main.do, accessed 8 August 2021.

Table 12.1: Park Chung-hee administration's Five-Year Economic Development Plans

Five-Year Plans	Major project of interest	EPB minister
First (1962–1966)	Infrastructure construction (e.g. railroad, power plant, etc.)	Kim Yu-taek (12/1963–5/1964) Chang Ki-young (5/1964–10/1967)
Second (1967–1971)	Laying the foundation for heavy industry (e.g. steel and petrochemical industry)	Park Chung-hoon (10/1967–6/1969) Kim Hak-ryul (6/1969–1/1972)
Third (1972–1976)	Heavy Chemical Industry Drive (e.g. electronics, shipbuilding, machinery, petrochemicals, and non-ferrous metals)	Tae Wan-son (1/1972–9/1974) Nam Deock-u (9/1974–12/1978)
Fourth (1977–1981)	Technological innovation (e.g. electronic technology)	Shin Hyeon-hwak (12/1978–12/1979)

Note: The name of the Fourth Plan was changed to the Five-Year Economic and Social Development Plan. The word 'social' was newly included to reflect diversified social needs.

However, the administrators from the military failed to produce notable results in the policy areas that required professional knowledge, especially economic issues. In particular, the First Five-Year Economic Development Plan was unsuccessful in its early stages. In the early days of the plan between 1962 and 1964, the Park administration focused on expanding domestic demand and replacing imports by developing agriculture and building basic industries. However, it was not implemented as originally expected due to problems such as the depletion of foreign exchange and agricultural output reduction. Nevertheless, EPB Minister Kim Yu-taek, who was not from the military, was unable to revise the policy direction of the plan (Joo 1998: 19).[2] He was politically subordinate to Prime Minister Song Yo-chan, who had served in the military, and his henchman, Deputy Minister of EPB Song Jeong-beom, thus failed to implement his policy initiatives (Kim 2020: 90–92).[3] Even after Song Yo-chan stepped down in 1962, Minister Kim Yu-taek failed to show strong leadership on economic policy decisions.

As economic performance lagged, the Park Chung-hee administration, which had to gain political legitimacy through economic development, made changes to the EPB. President Park appointed Chang Ki-young, a non-military figure who had served as vice-president at the Bank of Korea, as the new EPB head and gave him full control over economic policies. Chang transformed existing economic plans into export-oriented policies centred on light industry. This policy revision was very successful, leading to high-level economic growth. In 1964, South Korea's exports surpassed $100 million for the first time, and since then, exports grew by more than 40 per cent every year, surpassing $200 million in 1966 and $300 million in 1967. Chang also began working on the Second Five-Year Economic Development Plan with Kim Hak-ryul, the vice-minister of the EPB.[4] The EPB led by Minister Chang not only designed economic plans, but also actively intervened in the realisation of the plans. The agency led the construction of infrastructures such as Gyeongbu Expressway, a highway between the two largest cities in South Korea Seoul and Busan, and the establishment of state-owned heavy industry enterprises such as Pohang Iron and Steel Company (POSCO; *pohangjecheol*). As Minister Chang's influence on policymaking grew and he began to voice opposition to presidential policy, President Park replaced Chang in 1967 and appointed a former military official, Park Chung-hoon, as EPB minister (Joo 1998: 43–44; Hwang 2011: 220–227). However, the new minister could not make sufficient progress in economic planning. The construction of petrochemical complexes and POSCO were key projects of the Second Five-Year Economic Development Plan, but the EPB, led by Minister Park, failed to lead the projects successfully (Nishino 2015: 62–63). The investment in the Ulsan Petrochemical Industry Complex was insignificant, and the establishment of POSCO was also on the verge of being suspended due to a lack of funds. The inflation rate was also not properly controlled. Since economic plans were not appropriately implemented, President Park appointed a professional bureaucrat to lead the EPB again. Kim Hak-ryul, who served as vice-minister of EPB under Minister Chang Ki-young, took charge of the national economy from 1969 to 1972 as the EPB minister. A professional bureaucrat who had worked at the Ministry of Finance (*jaemubu*) and the EPB, Kim Hak-ryul successfully led the Second Five-Year Economic Development

Plan, including the construction of POSCO, with the full support of President Park (Kim 2020: 200–212). For example, South Korea's gross domestic product (GDP) per capita, which was less than $100 by the early 1960s, rose to around $300 in the early 1970s. The remarkable economic growth produced by professional bureaucrats ensured the legitimacy of bureaucratic-led policy decisions throughout the 1960s and 1970s.

South Korea's economy grew in size and international exchanges increased in the 1970s, and the need for bureaucrats with more professional knowledge increased. In particular, the first oil crisis, which caused trade deficits and inflation indexes to soar, raised the need to make economic policies based on professional knowledge. As a result, the Park administration appointed scholars who had acquired professional knowledge in academia to high-ranking positions. For example, Nam Deok-u, who worked at the Bank of Korea in the 1950s and served as an economics professor at Sogang University in the 1960s, was named the new head of the EPB in 1974. To alleviate the economic crisis, Nam and the EPB utilised a strategy to actively participate in Middle East construction projects to overcome the foreign exchange crisis (Joo 1998: 127–132). For example, the agency prepared the Act on Promotion of Overseas Construction (*Haeoigeonseol chokjinbeop*) in cooperation with the Ministry of Construction (*Geonseolbu*) to support companies that sought contracts for overseas construction projects. Moreover, the EPB continued to pursue the export-driven growth policy of the Park Chung-hee administration, achieving $10 billion in exports and $1,000 in GDP per capita. The EPB's strategies were sufficiently effective and, as a result, bureaucratic-led policymaking practices were also maintained for a while longer.

4. THE EXECUTIVE UNDER ADMINISTRATIVE REFORM: 1980–2002

Even after the death of President Park Chung-hee in 1979, bureaucrat-led national policy decisions continued, and economic priorities were maintained as well. President Chun Doo-hwan, who gained power through the 12 December Military Insurrection, lacked political legitimacy.[5] Thus, similar to President Park Chung-hee, he tried to overcome it through economic development. However, the political, economic, and social situations of 1980, and even the international atmosphere were different from those of the previous period. These changes meant that the EPB-led economic plans were no longer valid and that significant reform of existing administrative practices was needed.

Compared to the 1960s and 1970s, the size of South Korea's economy has greatly increased. For instance, South Korea's per capita GDP was $79.46 in 1960, but it grew more than twenty times as big to $1,714.10 in 1980. As the size of the economy grew, it became increasingly difficult for the EPB to formulate an economic plan in consideration of all variables, and the need for administrative reform was raised. Thus, opinions on administrative reform began to emerge from within the bureaucracy. For example, some of the EPB bureaucrats such as Kim Jae-ik (Director General for Planning; *gihoikgukjang*) and Kang Kyeong-sik (Deputy Minister of Planning; *gihoikchagwanbo*) began to argue for a market-orientated national economy rather than a state-led economic system in the 1970s. However, it was not easy for them to reform the EPB-led administrative practices in the period, due to opposition from other EPB bureaucrats, including Minister Nam Deok-u, who had led the export-driven economic growth (Nam et al. 2003: 97–101). Efforts to change the state-led economic growth policy began to take shape, as Kim Jae-ik moved to the position of Senior Presidential Secretary for Economic Affairs in 1980, and Kang Kyeong-sik was appointed as the finance minister in 1982. They promoted economic policies centred on market economy ideals and liberalisation of international trade, and EPB Minister Shin Byeong-hyeon supported their policies by promoting economic stabilisation instead of national growth.

The international atmosphere also intensified this trend. As neoliberalist economic policies were prevalent in the United States and the United Kingdom in the early 1980s, the Jeon administration began to ease government regulations to stimulate the market economy. The administration set up a committee under the prime minister to improve factors hindering growth and development (*Seongjangbaljeon jeohaeyoin gaeseon simuiwiwonhoi*), and bureaucrats and civilian experts alike participated in the committee to reduce government intervention in the market economy. Likewise, in the 1990s, President Kim Young-sam established the Commission for Administrative Reform (*Haengjeongsoisin wiwonhoi*) under the direct control of the president, and its composition consisted only of civilian members, excluding government officials. The commission was active from April 1993 to February 1998, reviewed 22,917 regulation cases, and proposed administrative reform for 1,680 of them (Commission for Administrative Reform 1998: 39–43). South Korea's foreign exchange crisis in 1997 accelerated administrative reform. To overcome the crisis, restructuring was implemented across all areas of the country, and government administration was no exception. Kim Dae-jung, who was elected president in the year of the financial crisis, promoted administrative reform based on the idea of New Public Management. For example, the Regulatory Reform Committee (*gyujegaehyeokuiwonhoi*) was created for deregulation. The Committee abolished 5,430 of the total 11,125 regulations in 1998, the first year of its establishment, and 503 of the remaining regulations in 1999 (Regulatory Reform Committee 2003: 500-501). It continued to improve various regulations even after 2000. In addition, the Planning and Budget Committee (*gihoikyesanuiwonhoi*; later, promoted to the Ministry of Planning and Budget in 1999) was also established to strongly promote administrative reforms such as privatisation of public enterprises and consignment to the private sector.

In the course of these reforms, several state-owned enterprises, such as South Korea Heavy Industries and Construction and Daehan Oil Pipeline Corporation, were privatised, including POSCO, which symbolised the period of state-led industrialisation in the 1960s and 1970s (Kim 2001: 90–92). About two decades of administrative reforms gradually weakened the influence of bureaucrats on policymaking.

Reflecting the atmosphere of economic and social liberalisation, the Five-Year Economic Development Plan, which had been the most important achievement of bureaucratic decision-making in the 1960s and 1970s, was also reformed. The main focus of the plan shifted from promoting exports and fostering heavy and chemical industries to increasing industrial competitiveness through technological innovation and economic liberalisation (Suh 2007: 21-24). As a result, several ministries related to the objective emerged in the 1980s. For example, the Ministry of Communication (*Chesinbu*), which had been a small ministry in charge of postal service, grew into a central ministry for technological reform. The ministry established companies such as South Korea Telecommunications Authority and Data Communication Corporation of South Korea to liberalise the telecommunication business and promoted liberalisation in telephone ownership and public telephone networks.[6] The budget of the ministry was less than 5 per cent of the total government budget in the 1970s, but its budget grew significantly to more than 15 per cent in the 1980s (Jung and Kum 2014: 65).

Furthermore, social liberalisation diversified public demands for labour rights, welfare, and social development, and the Five-Year Plan also began to reflect these demands. In reality, the name of the economic development plan contained the words 'social development' from the Fourth to Sixth Plans, as seen in Table 12.2. In this atmosphere, the Ministry of Health and Social Affairs, which had little presence in the 1960s and 1970s, began to grow significantly in the 1980s (Jung and Kum 2014: 65) and became one of the most influential ministries of the 2000s (Oh 2007: 267). Not only have the existing ministries become more influential, but several social policy ministries have been newly established in response to various public demands. For example, the Ministry of Labour was established in 1981; the Environmental Agency (*Hwangyeongcheong*), which was

Table 12.2: Five-Year Economic and Social Development Plans in the 1980s and 1990s

Five-Year Plans	Objective	Major project of economic interest
Fifth (1982–1986)	Social development with stability, efficiency, and balance	Technology-intensive industries (e.g. televisions, videocassette recorders, and semiconductor-related products)
Sixth (1987–1991)	Economic advancement and promotion of national welfare based on efficiency and equity	Science and technology by raising the ratio of research and development investment
New Economy Five-Year Plan (1993–1997)	Economic and social advancement for the twenty-first century and the reunification of South Korea	High-technology industries (e.g. microelectronics, fine chemicals, bioengineering, optics, and aerospace)

created in 1980, was promoted to the Ministry of the Environment (*Hwangyeongbu*) in 1990; and the Ministry of Gender Equality was newly established in 2001. The name of the Ministry of Health and Social Affairs was also changed to the Ministry of Health and Welfare in 1994, emphasising the need for 'welfare' policies.

Following this trend, the ratio of legislative bills submitted by the executive branch also changed. Until the 1970s, laws related to financial and economic planning were significantly higher in proportion in government bills, but since the 1980s the proportion of social policy-related bills (e.g. welfare, health, labour rights, environmental protection, and gender issues) has increased significantly (see Figure 12.3). On the other hand, the EPB, which led the growth-orientated economic plan, was abolished in 1994 when it was merged with the Ministry of Finance, and the Five-Year Plans also came to an end in 1997. This does not mean that the influence of economy-related ministries has completely disappeared. The Ministry of Economy and Finance (*Gihoikjaejeongbu*), which took over the EPB, was still the most influential, even in the 2010s (Oh 2018: 158). However, since the 1980s, administrative reforms have been carried out to liberalise the market and realise social policies, and in the process, the influence of the EPB (and the Ministry of Economy and Finance), which had served as the general manager of South Korea, was greatly reduced.

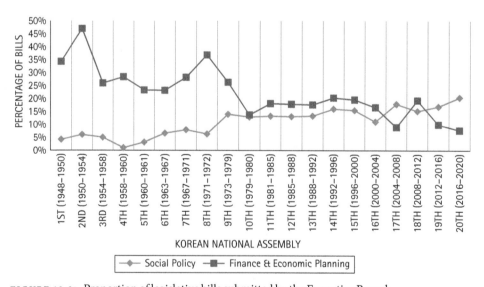

FIGURE 12.3: Proportion of legislative bills submitted by the Executive Branch

Note: Based on the number of bills dealt with by the National Assembly's committees on financial and economic planning and social policies. Since social policy is unclear in scope, only the bills reviewed by the National Assembly committees dealing with welfare, health, labour, environmental protection, and gender issues were compiled as social policy bills into the graph.

Source: South Korean National Assembly Bill Information System, https://likms.assembly.go.kr/bill/main.do, accessed 8 August 2021.

5. The Executive in the Era of Democratisation: 2003–Present

Political democratisation has further weakened bureaucratic policymaking. In the 2002 presidential election, the two major candidates were Roh Moo-hyun of the Millennium Democratic Party and Lee Hoe-chang of the Grand National Party. They were neither from the military, like Park Chung-hee, Chun Doo-hwan, and Roh Tae-woo, nor were they party leaders until the mid-1990s. Prior to the 2002 presidential election, South Korean politics was dominated by several military-turned-politicians and a few big-name politicians called the 'three Kims', that is, Kim Young-sam, Kim Dae-jung, and Kim Jong-pil. Only a few of these figures could be presidential candidates, and competition in the primaries was practically meaningless. Even after being elected president, they maintained an administrative-orientated national decision-making system based on their strong political power. However, their influence, which had been maintained for decades, began to diminish little by little in the 1990s. With the inauguration of a civilian government after President Kim Young-sam was elected in 1992, the influence of politicians from the military has been limited.[7] The era of the three Kims also ended in 2003, as President Kim Dae-jung's term of office ended.

In the 1980s and the 1990s, presidential candidate selection processes were nothing more than a formality in which the candidates of each party had been virtually already determined. However, with the end of the 'three Kims' era in the 2000s, presidential candidates began to be chosen through party primaries. With actual competition taking place, various factions have emerged within single parties. As a result, even after being elected, the president cannot fully control the lawmakers of his or her own party (Choi and Koo 2017: 22–26). The president's grip on the National Assembly has been reduced, and the executive branch has also been unable to monopolise policy decisions unlike in the past. Lawmakers continued to question the administration's policies, and the number of cases in which lawmakers themselves presented bills without relying on government proposals began to increase rapidly. Moreover, since the 2000s, it has become highly difficult for the presidential party to hold a stable majority in the National Assembly, further accelerating legislative checks on the administration (Kim 2005: 272–278).

Bureaucratic power in South Korea has been steadily declining since the 1980s due to social diversification and the reduction of presidential power. Instead, the National Assembly began to emerge as a major policymaking institution in the 2000s and 2010s. For example, Figure 12.4 shows that the proportion of the bills submitted by lawmakers to the National Assembly has risen sharply compared to those submitted by the administration. Likewise, Figure 12.5 indicates that the number of laws passed through the National Assembly has also increased compared executive legislation

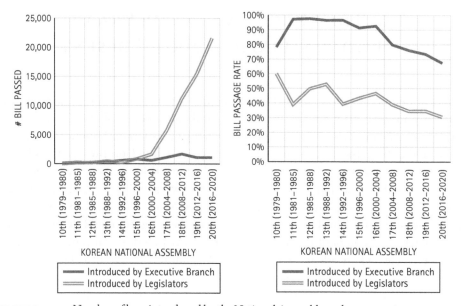

FIGURE 12.4: Number of laws introduced by the National Assembly and passage rates, 1979–2020

Source: Korean National Assembly Bill Information System, https://likms.assembly.go.kr/bill/main.do, accessed 8 August 2021.

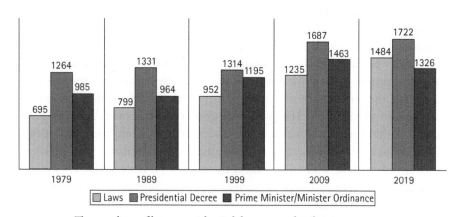

FIGURE 12.5: The numbers of laws, presidential decrees, and ordinances

Source: Ministry of Government Legislation, http://www.moleg.go.kr/lawinfo/status/announcementReport, accessed 8 August 2021.

(i.e. presidential decrees and prime minister/minister ordinances). Although the passage rate of bills introduced by the executive branch remains higher than that of lawmakers, it has been significantly lower than in the past, when it exceeded 90 per cent. As the political power of the National Assembly and political parties gets stronger during the post-democratisation period, the influence of bureaucrats on policymaking is gradually decreasing. Moreover, this trend is expected to continue in the 2020s.

6. Conclusion

In South Korea, the executive has played a major role in national policy decisions since at least the 1960s. Especially in the 1960s and 1970s, South Korean society was very simple and economic development was the only national goal. As a result, President Park Chung-hee had considerable political power. In this political environment, the administration monopolised the direction of national policy. In particular, the EPB, which was in charge of economic development plans, played the role of general manager of South Korea.

In the 1980s and 1990s, as the export-orientated economic growth policy lost its effectiveness, the presidents of the period (i.e. Chun Doo-hwan, Roh Tae-woo, Kim Young-sam, and Kim Dae-jung) initiated their own administrative reforms to realise the objectives of market liberalisation, deregulation, and internationalisation. Several commissions for regulatory reform were established, and numerous deregulation measures were proposed and reviewed. Consequently, numerous government regulations have been eased during this period, and the EPB's state-led economic policies have also been largely shifted to market-orientated ones. Moreover, as the economy grew and social needs diversified, the public's desire for social liberalisation also greatly increased. Under the economic and social climate of liberalisation, the EPB's policymaking authority was greatly diminished. The Five-Year Economic Development Plan, which used to symbolise administration-led economic growth, also ended in 1997. In contrast, ministries dealing with issues such as welfare, health, labour rights, and environmental protection were newly established or promoted, and there was a significant increase in the number of statutes handled by the ministries.

In the 2000s, with the end of the military dictatorship and the end of the 'three Kims' era, the president's grip on political parties and the National Assembly weakened. In contrast, political democratisation provided more political power to the National Assembly. Lawmakers began to propose numerous bills on their own without checking with the administration. A significant increase in the number of bills proposed by lawmakers has been witnessed, especially since the seventeenth National Assembly (2004–2008). In addition, influential politicians who have long been active in the National Assembly were appointed prime minister in the 2000s, making it easier for the National Assembly to keep the administration in check. Admittedly, as of 2020, the administration's policymaking function cannot be said to be weak. Large-scale projects, such as the Four Major Rivers Project, were also led by the administration in the 2000s. Nevertheless, compared to the past, the executive branch's political influence on policymaking has been significantly reduced relative to the political growth of the National Assembly.

Notes

1. By 1962, South Korea's nominal GDP per capita was less than $100. In 1957, South Korea's nominal per capita GDP stood at $73.00, far lower than Japan's $331.31 and that of the United States at $2,769.
2. Kim Yu-taek was a professional bureaucrat who had already served as the director of the finance office (*ijaegukjang*) under the Ministry of Finance, vice-minister of finance and governor of the Bank of Korea during the Rhee Syngman administration.
3. Kim was appointed to head the EPB three times in a short period from July 1961 to May 1964, with an average term of only about six months. Kim was a reputable bureaucrat with expertise, but he was unable to maintain his post for long due to the political influence of those from the military.
4. The plan included building a self-reliant economy in South Korea and increasing the proportion of heavy and chemical industries to light industries.
5. After forcing President Choi Kyu-hah to resign, Chun Doo-hwan took office through indirect elections in 1980.
6. Several technocrats such as Oh Myung, who served as Vice-Minister (5/1981–7/1987) and Minister (7/1987–12/1988) of the Ministry of Communication, led the administrative reforms.
7. President Kim Yeoug-sam disbanded Hanahoi (a private organisation of those who graduated from the Korean Military Academy) that had politically supported politicians from the military, including Chun Doo-hwan and Roh Tae-woo.

Bibliography

Choi, J.-Y., and Koo, B.-S. (2017), 'Dangnae pabeolui teukseonggwa pabeol gan galdeungyangsang: hannaradang/saenuridangeul jungsimeuro' [Characteristics of Party Factions and Patterns of Factional Conflicts: An Analysis of Factions in the Two Conservative Parties in the Korean National Assembly], *Dongseoyeongu (East and West Studies)* 29, 1–28.

Choi, S.-O. (2008), '1950nyeondae gyehoikgiguui seolripgwa gaepyeon: jojik mit gineungbyeonhwareul jungsimeuro' [The Establishment and Reorganization of Korean Planning Agency in 1950s], *Gyeongjaesahak [Review of Economic History]* 45, 179–208.

Chung, K.-C. (1956), *Korea Tomorrow: Land of the Morning Calm* (New York: Macmillan).

Commission for Administrative Reform (1998), *Hangjeongsoisinbaekseo 4 [Administrative Reform White Paper 4]* (Seoul: Commission for Administrative Reform).

Easton, D. (1965), *A System Analysis of Political Life* (New York: John Wiley & Sons).

Haggard, S., Kim, B.-K., and Moon, C.-I. (1991) 'The Transition to Export-led Growth in South Korea: 1954–1966', *Journal of Asian Studies* 50, 850–873.

Hwang, B.-T. (2011), *Park Chung-hee Paradigm: gyeongjegihoikwon gwajangi bon Park Chung-hee daetongryeong [Park Chung-hee Paradigm: President Park Chung-hee Observed by the Director of the Economic Planning Board]* (Seoul: Chosun News Press).

Joo, T.-S. (1998), *Gyeongje mot sallimyeon gambanggandaei: hangukui gyeongjebuchongli, geu inmulgwa jeongchaek [If the Economy Fails to Revive, You Will Go to Jail: Korea's EPB Ministers, the People and Their Policies]* (Seoul: Jungang M&B).

Jung, C.-H., and Kum, H.-S. (2014), 'Bucheobyeol yesane geungeohan urinara yesanbyeondongyului teukseongbunseok: 1966nyeon-2006nyeon ilbanhoigyeyesaneul jungsimeuro' [An Analysis of the Budget Variation Rate in South Korea: Focused on the

General Accounting Budgets of 1966–2006', *Hanguk haengjunghakhoibo* [*Korean Public Administration Review*] 48, 55–80.

Kim, I.-K., and Kang, W.-T. (2017), 'Park Chung-hee Junggwoneun "gunbu" jibaechejeyeotna: gun chulsin jungchielriteu chungwoneul jungsimeuro' [Was the Park Chung-Hee Rule a Military Regime: Focusing on the Political Elite from the Military], *Hangukgwa gukjejungchi* [*Korea and World Politics*] 33, 101–135.

Kim, J.-S. (2020), *Nae Abeojiui kkum: chilsun gija adeuli jeonhaneun 40dae buchongri Kim Hak-ryul iyagi* [*My Father's Dream: The Story of Kim Hak-ryul, Deputy Prime Minister in His 40s, Delivered by the Son of a 70-Year-Old Journalist*] (Seoul: Denstory).

Kim, J.-K. (2001), 'Kim Dae-jung jeongbuui gonggieop minyeonghwajeongchaeke daehan pyeongga' [Privatization for Whom?: An Examination of the Current Government's Privatization Policy, 1998–2000', *Haengjeongnonchong* [*Korean Journal of Public Administration*] 39, 83–111.

Kim, Y.-H. (2005), 'Hangukui daetongryeongje heonjeongjilseoui bulanjeong yoin bunseok bunjeomjeongbuwa daetongryeong-gukhweganui daerip' [An Analysis of South Korean Presidential System's Political Instability—Extreme Confrontations between National Assembly and President under the Divided Government], *Gukjejeongchiyeongu* [*Journal of International Relations*] 8, 261–288.

Kim, Y.-M. (1991), 'Rhee Syngman Junggwonui heungmanggwa geu jeongchisajeok uimi' [The Characteristics and Demise of the Rhee Regime], *Hanguk jungchihakhoibo* [*Korean Political Science Review*] 25, 103–132.

Koo, H.-W. (2009), 'Baljeongukga, baetaedoin jayulseong, geurigo jedoronjeok hamui: Rhee Syngman jungbu, Park Chung-hee jungbu, Chun Du-hwan jungbuui saneophwa jeongchaekeul jungsimeuro' [Developing Countries, Embedded Autonomy, and Institutional Implications: The Industrialization Policies of the Rhee Syngman Administration, the Park Chung-hee Administration, and the Chun Doo-hwan Administration], *Hanguk sahoiwa hangjungyeongu* [*Korean Society and Public Administration*] 20, 145–178.

Lee, K.-H. (1999), *Gyeongje geundaehwaui sumeun iyagi: gukga janggi gyeongjegaebal ipanjaui hoigorok* [*The Hidden Story of Economic Modernization: Memoirs of a Long-Term Economic Development Planner*] (Seoul: Voicepub).

Nam, D.-W., Krause, K. B., Kang, K.-S. et al. (2003), *80nyeondae gyeongjegaehyeokgwa Kim Jae-ik suseok* [*Economic Reform in the Eighties and Presidential Secretary Kim Jae-ik*] (Seoul: Samsung Gyeongjeyeonguso).

Nishino, J. (2015), 'Hanil gyeongje hyeopryeok gwangyeui sijakgwa jedohwa gwajeong' [Early Stage of Bilateral Economic Cooperation and the Process of Institutionalization], *Ilbonbipyeong* [*Korean Journal of Japanese Studies*] 12, 50–71.

Oh, J.-R. (2007), *Hangukui gwanryoje gwonryeokgujo: jindangwa cheobang* [*Korean Bureaucratic Power Structure: Diagnosis and Prescription*] (Seoul: Korean Study Information).

Oh, J.-R. (2018), 'Gwanryoje gwonryeok cheukjeong: Park Geun Hye jeongbu jungangjeongbureul jungsimeuro' [Measuring Bureaucratic Power: Focusing on the Central Administration Agencies in Korea], *Hanguk haengjunghakhoibo* [*Korean Public Administration Review*] 52, 139–166.

Regulatory Reform Committee (2003), *Gyuje gaehyeok baekseo 5* [*Regulatory Reform White Paper 5*] (Seoul: Regulatory Reform Committee).

Suh, J.-H. (2007), 'Overview of Korea's Development Process until 1997', in J.-H. Suh and D. H. C. Chen, eds, *Korea as a Knowledge Economy: Evolutionary Process and Lessons Learned* (Washington. DC: World Bank Institute and Korea Development Institute) 17–46.

CHAPTER 13

JUDICIAL POLITICS

DONGWOOK CHA

1. INTRODUCTION

THIS chapter aims to explain the meaning, function, and role of the judiciary in the South Korean political process. However, compared to other state agencies, it is difficult to relate the courts to politics in the political arena. This is because, even considering political and social differences around the world, it is believed that courts should not be influenced by politics, and even in South Korea until the 1990s, the judiciary had been extremely reluctant to engage in political affairs. Rather, courts were criticised for playing no role in situations where human rights were violated by political power. However, the attitude of the court, which mainly dealt with civil and criminal legal disputes, began to change.

The South Korean Constitutional Court, newly established in 1987, began issuing politically controversial rulings in the early 2000s, and recently the South Korean Supreme Court and lower courts have begun to issue public judicial rulings which incite the need to analyse the judges' political intentions. For instance, on 15 July 2020, the fifth civil division of the Seoul High Court reversed the precedent that greatly limited the scope of the government's liability for the damages caused by the Yusin dictatorship's emergency measures in the mid-1970s. That precedent was set under former Chief Justice Yang Seung-tae in 2015, during the presidency of Park Geun-hye. According to the precedent, the Yusin regime's emergency measures were not subject to judicial review because it was a political decision made at the highest level. In 2020, however, the High Court ruled that, even if the plaintiff failed to prove the illegal behaviours, such as illegal detention and cruel acts, including torture, during the investigation, the state is responsible for damages because the emergency measures themselves, the legal basis for the investigation, are illegal.

Most of the South Korean Supreme Court rulings that limit the scope of responsibility for the state's past actions were reached during the presidencies of Lee Myung-bak and Park Geun-hye, which are widely viewed as conservative administrations. However, under the new Supreme Court led by the Chief Justice Kim Myeong-soo appointed by President Moon Jae-in, located on the other side of the ideological spectrum from his two predecessors, lower court judges have attempted to reverse the precedents set by the previous Supreme Court. If the Court's precedent can be changed based on the political ideology of a new administration, how should it be understood in the context of the constitutional order of judicial independence?

Judicial independence is essential for protecting people's rights and freedoms. In any healthy democratic system, judges should not be subject to political pressure from the other two branches or from private or partisan interests. Only when judicial independence is guaranteed can the court make objective and neutral rulings.

How can we characterise the role of the court in a political system? Traditional theories of judicial review have persistently searched for neutral or principled ground as the only legitimate bases for judicial decisions and have rejected any political motive in judicial decision-making. An idealised picture of an apolitical institution—court—driven by the traditional concept of law is that the members of the institution must have disinterested and objective standards and pursue the goal of impartial justice under law. The persistence of the myth of judicial objectivity tends to infuse the debate with orthodox neutralist arguments, which conceals individual judges' value preferences.

Since law is an important political resource, however, courts are capable of significant redistribution of values in the polity. And merely an introductory survey of this process would demonstrate that judges have not been shy in using this power to achieve particular goals. Particularly, the power of judicial review has been viewed as the most politically controversial power held by judges because its exercise demolishes boundaries that allegedly separate things 'political' from things 'judicial' (Shapiro and Sweet 2002: 142).

When the authoritarian regime collapsed in 1987 after three decades, the victorious political forces in South Korea rushed to transform their country into a liberal constitutional democracy. The Constitution was quickly revised, and in the process an unfamiliar new institution was created: the South Korean Constitutional Court—a tribunal composed of judges with the power to overturn legislative enactments and executive orders if they were found inconsistent with the highest law in the country, the Constitution.

The South Korean Constitutional Court has often aroused resentment and opposition from powerful political elements in society. It has frequently had to say no to the legislature, the executive branch, or powerful private entities. Actually, a very large proportion of high-profile cases brought to the Constitutional Court involved intense political controversies. Many grew out of power struggles between opposing political forces in society (Cha 2006). Indeed, politics envelops almost every aspect of the Constitutional Court, including the way the justices of the Constitutional Court are selected, the individuals and institutions who have access to the Court, the cases the Court hears, and the reactions to its decisions. Does this mean that the South Korean Constitutional Court is a political institution by nature and that its decisions are inherently political decisions?

2. Political Understanding of Judicial Power

In a democratic polity, the dominant characterisation of a court as legal institution leads to the general belief in judicial objectivity and neutrality. The belief makes it a sin for judges to let their value preferences influence judicial deliberations. However, there is an opposing perspective that, since law is an important political resource, courts may be compelled to authorise significant redistribution of values in a society. In the course of settling disputes in accordance with existing law, courts often have no choice but to make new rules. It is this policymaking function, much more than dispute resolution, which places the judiciary at the centre of controversy.

The South Korean Constitutional Court was created outside of the hierarchical system of the ordinary courts consisting of the South Korean Supreme Court and the lower courts. The South Korean Supreme Court hears appeals of judgments or rulings rendered by the Appellate Courts and is vested with the authority for judicial administration. In contrast, the South Korean Constitutional Court exclusively exercises constitutional review. Ordinary courts are substantially barred from so doing, though they may refer constitutional questions to the Constitutional Court.

The rationales for granting a special court the exclusive power of judicial review are as follows: first, it strengthens the independence of the ordinary courts by taking the constitutional review of statutes away from ordinary courts so that the ordinary courts can be free from the political influences of lawmakers; second, the special court's efficiency and expediency secures effective protection of human rights and the Constitution because the power of judicial review is concentrated in an independent court and exercised under a unitary procedure (Epstein et al. 2001: 20–27; Ginsburg 2003: 35–42).

In other words, the Constitutional Court was given the mission of actively exercising the power of judicial review that was difficult for ordinary courts to exercise, faithfully playing the role of guardian of human rights, and thus securing the independence of ordinary courts as well as the Constitutional Court itself. So, to what extent can we defend the legitimacy of the expansion of judicial review, which has been accused of having a counter-majoritarian nature?

The power of judicial review by an independent judiciary is a necessary condition for judicial activism. The political activism of the judiciary has become an extremely relevant issue in contemporary democratic regimes even though many believe that judicial policymaking conflicts with the very essence of a democratic polity. Although judicial activism is a multifaceted concept, a definition of judicial activism upon which many agree is the court's tendency to expand the scope of its power and its roles even if it falls in direct conflict with the legislative and/or executive branches.

According to Bickel (1986: 16, 21), 'judicial review is a counter-majoritarian force in our system' because 'judicial review expresses a form of distrust of the legislature'. Linz (1978) even argues that courts can contribute to the breakdown of democracy. This can occur, according to him, as the loss of cohesion in regime-supporting coalition parties causes highly conflictive issues to be moved from the arena of partisan politics to the arena of allegedly neutral powers like the judiciary (Linz 1978: 37, 69). At base, Linz (1978)'s argument is in line with that of a multitude of critics of judicial policy-making, who argue that having important policy matters decided by non-majoritarian institutions like courts is inherently undemocratic and damaging to the legitimacy and effectiveness of majoritarian institutions like legislatures and elected executives (Tate 1997:143–150). So, is the power of judicial review nothing but a bad omen?

Interestingly, Robert Dahl (1957) argued that judicial review is not counter-majoritarian in a practical sense. He suggested that judicial power, at least exercised by the United States Supreme Court, is best seen as a legitimising force; it places a stamp of approval on broad policy proclivities already set out by Congress and the president. Far from being the guarantor of individual and minority rights that it is often said to be, the Court actually joins what Dahl (1957) calls the current 'law-making majority' in helping it to rule. The Court tends to adopt policies that are generally consistent with the policy preference of this ruling coalition of interests. When the ruling coalition is not united or is indifferent on certain policy issues, the Court can move in with important policies of its own. But at best, such policies are likely to be consistent with the general political philosophy of the governing coalition (Dahl 1957: 279–295).

In a slightly different vein, Rosenberg (1991) focuses on the limited role and power of the United States Supreme Court in the US political context. Rosenberg (1991) argues that court decisions are neither necessary nor sufficient for producing significant social reform. He begins by positioning two contrasting views of judicially induced change, which he calls the 'dynamic court view' and the 'constrained court view'. The dynamic court view holds that US courts have produced, can produce, and do produce dramatic social change. The constrained court view, however, echoes Hamilton et al. (2012)'s 'least dangerous branch' prediction—that having the power of neither the purse nor the sword, and surrounded by the more powerful democratically elected branches, judicial power is felt mainly along the edges of policymaking, with only minimal or indirect impact on social change. After an exhaustive examination of a wealth of empirical evidence in the areas of racial segregation in education, abortion and other women's rights, environmental regulation, reapportionment, and criminal law, Rosenberg (1991) concludes that the constrained court view more closely approximates the role of the courts in the US political system. While courts can be effective producers of significant social reform, this occurs only when a great deal of change has already been made (Rosenberg 1991).

This type of political understanding of judicial power started with the emergence of US legal realism. Within the legal academy, legal realists dispatched traditional mechanistic and formalistic conceptions of law and instead emphasised the creativity found in judging. An important consequence of the legal realist movement was that law could no longer be understood in isolation but now had to be considered in light of larger political, economic, and social background structures (Llewellyn 1930: 431–465; Posner 1987: 761–780; Fried 1988: 331).

By combining the premise of legal realism and the methodology developed by the behaviouralists in political science, a group of researchers started focusing on the background, attitudes, and ideological preferences of individual justices rather than on the nature of the Court as an institution and its significance for the political system. Empirical analyses that connect judges' decisions to attributes such as their socio-economic, educational, or professional backgrounds rest on a similar picture of political actors as calculators advancing preferences or interests. The exemplar of this approach is the 'attitudinal model' pioneered by the work of C. Herman Pritchett (1948) and developed by Jeffrey Segal and Harold Spaeth (1993).

It is true that, in contrast to other political institutions, the US Supreme Court has an organisational structure that prefers an individual level of analysis because the US Supreme Court as an institution is characterised by 'the absence of formal hierarchies among justices, their equal access to relevant information, and their ability to participate as individuals' (Gillman and Clayton 1999: 2). However, Segal and Spaeth limited their model to explaining behaviour only in the US Supreme Court and only to decisions on the merits because of the Court's unique institutional position. They recognised that 'because the Supreme Court sits atop the judicial hierarchy, and because in the type of cases that reach the Supreme Court legal factors such as text, intent, and precedent are typically ambiguous, justices are free to make decisions based on their personal policy preferences' (Segal and Spaeth 1993: 973).

This finding that the US Supreme Court's unique institutional context functioned as a facilitating condition for judicial activism by freeing the justices from external political constraints to pursue their own value preferences is probably one of the most important contributions of the attitudinal model (Segal 1999: 237). However, this 'attitudinal model' has only limited explanatory power for the South Korean Constitutional Court because the backgrounds, attitudes, and ideological preferences of individual justices of the South Korean Constitutional Court do not work well as explanatory variables regarding the Court's unexpected judicial activism. Considering the individual characteristics of the Court's members, most notably their conservative make-up, many scholars and jurists in South Korea are sceptical about the possibility that the functions and role of the Court would expand. The justices showed no differences from past judges and prosecutors in terms of their ideology and passive attitudes towards new initiatives on constitutional policymaking. Surprisingly, the justices of the Constitutional Court have been very active and pushed the Court in a liberal direction. From the institution's inception, it has strongly demanded the protection of the basic rights promulgated in the South Korean Constitution.

3. The Institutional Structure of the South Korean Courts

Traditionally, the South Korean conception of the role of a judge had been influenced far more by German tradition than by American thinking. Faced with the prospect of being called upon to resolve highly controversial constitutional questions, most of the sitting justices of the South Korean Supreme Court seemed to be reluctant to take responsibility for constitutional review (West and Yoon 1992: 76). The disinclination of the Supreme Court to take a leading role in defining the content of 'constitutionalism' was attributed to scepticism about 'judicial activism'. As a consequence of the 1987 June 10th Democratisation Uprising, the South Korean Constitutional Court—a separate, new, independent highest court—was granted the power of judicial review, while the South Korean Supreme Court would remain as the other national High Court within the judicial hierarchy for legal issues other than constitutional issues.

Under the present Constitution, the South Korean Constitutional Court has the broadest jurisdiction. Article 111 of the South Korean Constitution and Article 2 of the Constitutional Court Act (hereinafter CCA) provides that the South Korean Constitutional Court shall have jurisdiction over the following issues: (a) constitutionality of statutes upon the request of ordinary courts; (b) impeachment; (c) dissolution of political parties; (d) competence disputes between state agencies, between a state agency and a local government, or between local governments; and (e) constitutional complaints.

In theory, these powers place the Constitutional Court on an equal status with the legislative and executive branches. All of these powers enable the Court to strike a balance between the powers of the other branches. Jurisdiction over impeachment gives the Court a restraining power over the excesses of government officials and suggests that, at least in theory, no official, no matter how powerful, is above the law. Jurisdiction over the dissolution of political parties gives the Court power over the legislative branch in part. The power to adjudicate questions of intra-governmental competence disputes is also important in that it establishes the Court as the arbiter of power conflicts among the various organs of the other branches of government. In spite of the significance of those three powers, the two core jurisdictions of the Constitutional Court are its power to adjudicate the constitutionality of statutes and constitutional complaints.

The Constitutional Court's jurisdiction over the judicial review of the constitutionality of statutes, in principle, is mandatory, like that of the German Constitutional Court, and not discretionary like the certiorari jurisdiction of the US Supreme Court. Its power to review the constitutionality of legislation, however, is both passive and relatively narrow. While the power to review provides a necessary check on the unrestrained power of the legislative branch, it does not afford the Court the maximum leeway to take on an activist role because it still must wait for constitutional questions to be referred to it from lower courts.

Unlike the German system of abstract judicial review, where not only the courts but also the other branches of the government can refer constitutional questions for final adjudication, under the South Korean system only the courts have this power. Thus, compared with the German Federal Constitutional Court, the South Korean Constitutional Court depends far more on the rest of the judiciary to define its role (Lim 1999: 123).

The frequency with which requests are referred to the Constitutional Court depends to a considerable extent on whether the regular courts are disposed to grant a strong presumption of constitutionality to legislation. A request for referral will be denied if the court primarily determines that the law is constitutional, even though a party argues to the contrary. If a party raises a constitutional question in a civil or criminal trial, but the court declines to refer it to the Constitutional Court, there is an alternative that the party may resort to a direct petition to the Constitutional Court under CCA art. 68(2).

As mentioned earlier, the South Korean judiciary consists of two courts. One is the Constitutional Court, which deals only with constitutional disputes, and the other is the ordinary court organisation, which deals with all other legal disputes, with the Supreme Court at its peak.

The ordinary courts in South Korea are organised in a unitary system of three levels. At the lowest level, district courts and family courts are subdivided into single judge and collegiate trial divisions, also containing appellate divisions which hear appeals of cases decided by single judges. At the middle level, High Courts hear appeals from administrative agency decisions and from collegiate divisions of district courts. At the highest level, the Supreme Court hears appeals from High Courts and appellate divisions of district and family courts (see the Court Organization Act).

The South Korean Supreme Court consists of a chief justice and thirteen justices. It has exclusive jurisdiction over the validity of the presidential election and National Assembly elections. The Constitution vests in the Supreme Court the authority for judicial administration as well as the power to establish regulations regarding the internal discipline of the courts, the administration of judicial affairs, and trial procedures. This power is exercised by the Justices' Council, which consists of all the justices of the Supreme Court. Following the civil law tradition, a decision of the Supreme Court does not have the binding force of a precedent in subsequent cases of a similar nature. The interpretation of a law rendered in a particular case by the Supreme Court, however, does have a binding effect on the lower courts when the case is remanded.

The Constitutional Court is created outside of the hierarchical system of the Supreme Court and the lower courts. Formally, the two High Courts have mutually independent jurisdictions. From the perspective of the bench of the Supreme Court, however, the Constitutional Court can be easily regarded as an unnecessary extra organ that can usurp the Supreme Court's power. While the Supreme Court has the power to decide which cases get referred to the Constitutional Court, this never gives the Supreme Court total control over the Constitutional Court's docket since a very large percentage of the cases adjudicated by the Constitutional Court come to it by way of direct constitutional complaints. Even though the Supreme Court officially has considerable ability to control the Constitutional Court through its power to nominate three out of the nine Constitutional Court justices, the Constitutional Court justices are appointed by the president upon nomination by various institutions. Three Constitutional Court justices are nominated by the National Assembly, three are nominated by the chief justice of the Supreme Court, and three may be appointed by the president themselves. The head of the Constitutional Court is appointed by the president from among the justices, with the consent of the National Assembly.

The Supreme Court thus controls the Constitutional Court to some degree, given that the number of cases the Constitutional Court hears and some of the Constitutional Court justices are selected by the Supreme Court. Nevertheless, the Constitutional Court has historically had a great degree of independence from the Supreme Court.

4. Theoretical Discussion on the Role of Courts in South Korean Politics

Although recently questions have been frequently raised about political bias in ordinary court rulings in South Korea, it is the Constitutional Court which has always been at the centre of political controversy. This is because many of the constitutional disputes start from political disputes, and the political forces that have caused such political disputes do not find a solution in the realm of politics and, eventually, bring their case to the Constitutional Court, increasingly hoping that the Constitutional Court will make a strongly binding judgment that everyone should follow as to who is right and who is wrong by using the authority of the final interpreter of the Constitution (Cha 2016).

Actually, a very large proportion of the cases brought for decision to the Constitutional Court involved intense political controversies. This does not mean that the decisions of the South Korean Constitutional Court are political. Political decisions are different from legal or judicial decisions. Political decisions require no justification or explanation as legal decisions do. Political decisions are not correct or incorrect in any objective sense (Schwartz 2000: 4).

On the contrary, the Constitutional Court has to persuade society that its decisions were based not on partisan political considerations but on neutral, objective law, even when the issue in dispute obviously had highly contentious political origins and consequences. It has to transform public policy disputes into questions of constitutional interpretation that could be decided by texts, procedures, principles, and rules that are generally accepted as legal and not political. Nevertheless, it is not surprising that the South Korean Constitutional Court and individual justices have been constantly subject to attack for being political or biased.

On the one hand, the bedrock preconditions for the success of this constitutional tribunal are independence and impartiality from the dominant political power, from the appointing authority, and from outside pressures of all kinds. Without independence and impartiality and public faith in the existence of those qualities, the Court cannot become an authority whose orders are to be obeyed and an effective promoter of the rule of law since the ultimate power of the Court depends on maintaining the myth of judicial objectivity. To put it another way, it is important for the Court to remain aloof from the partisanship and daily political and social turbulence that often surround many of the issues with which it deals.

On the other hand, the Constitutional Court's power of constitutional review helps to define the paths along which the political system of South Korea develops. Because the Constitution fixes the rules of the political game, constitutional litigation as a policymaking initiative attracts competing political parties, individuals, and groups who have interests in moving policy away from the status quo and those who seek to insulate policies that favour them from reform-minded legislators. Therefore, there is no reason to think that judicial review will not incrementally extend its influence to all main arenas of policymaking in the polity.

In this sense, the South Korean Constitutional Court can be identified as a political institution not because the justices of the Court act like elected policymakers who consciously advanced policy preferences or constituent interests but because the justices' deliberation and rulings are one part of the process for constructing political values and their legal interpretations are often influenced by particular political contexts. By the way, if the Constitutional Court tries to use its supreme authority over constitutional interpretation to uphold the Constitution as highest principle in regulating the realm of politics, the most important issue that must be encountered and overcome is its own institutional legitimacy.

The use of judicial power to fulfil its mission mainly depends on the judiciary's institutional legitimacy. The role played by the judiciary depends on the general setting of the political system. In a regime where its executive power is, at least in principle, stronger and more decisive, and thus more capable of responding to political demands, the potential for judicial action is correspondingly reduced (Cooter and Ginsberg 1996: 295–313; Spiller 1996: 477–515; Pederzoli and Guarnier 1997: 260).

If liberal values become diffused in the political culture (e.g. a greater awareness of individual political rights) and there is a lack of consolidated rules for the democratic game in a highly divided setting, more judicial activism is likely to occur. As social rifts become more severe, political polarisation becomes more prominent. While no political group can gain enough electoral support to be a dominant ruling party or coalition, the court becomes perceived as the most reliable civil institution in the country. When legislative and executive powers are polarised, the court accumulates more institutional power. The more the political setting becomes polarised, the more institutional power the court gains. As a result, it may endeavour to consolidate a hegemonic position (Barzilai 1997: 196). Nevertheless, judicial power is highly contingent on the acceptance of other policymakers. Judges who wish to see their policy preferences realised have to make strategic calculations about the views of other colleagues on the bench, legislators, administrators, and other political actors.

5. Recent Cases Regarding the Role of Courts in South Korean Politics

Judicial activism strengthens the court's status as a guardian of human rights while the court's fighting against human rights violations by other state agencies is very likely to affect courts' institutional building (Epstein et al. 2001). However, if the tradition of an independent judiciary is lacking, the court should be careful when being judicially active because, in those cases, courts have yet to build up reservoirs of public and political support from which to draw when confronted with threats. The relative lack of legitimacy and support may be a function of a general and long-held suspicion of judges, who are generally believed to have not been neutral and have been subordinate to political power (Gibson et al. 1998: 343–358). In an environment ripe with distrust of judges, in order to build up sufficient public support and political capital, courts need to be careful to avoid cases and decisions that would provoke noncompliance by other institutions of governance and resort to safer areas of individual rights jurisprudence.

In the case of the South Korean Constitutional Court, on the one hand, the high rate of decisions striking down laws as unconstitutional shows that the Court has been able to overcome its passivity in relation to the other branches of government. On the other hand, it may imply that the Court has overstepped its role as a judicial institution under separation of powers by resorting to excessively broad interpretation. Although the Constitutional Court justices will not always choose to substitute their own policy judgement for that of others, they are in a good position to assert themselves in policymaking against, or in competition with, the legislative and executive branches. In addition, under the condition that the public respects judicial rulings and this public support works as an important judicial resource, the Constitutional Court has shown a tendency to make politically active decisions relying on prevailing public opinion.

The cases introduced here are the ones to which at least a minority of the academic community has raised disagreements, citing flaws in the process of reasoning and the conclusions, even though the Constitutional Court has exercised the authority granted by the Constitution. Another common feature of these cases is that they have won the absolute support of public opinion.

The recent hotly debated case concerning the role of the Constitutional Court in the face of extreme political disputes was the impeachment of the president (Kim 2018). Since the Constitutional Court's jurisdiction to impeach the president is granted by the Constitution, it cannot be said that the Constitutional Court has exceeded the scope of its authority. However, questions continue to be raised over whether it is politically reasonable for Constitutional Court justices to dismiss a president elected directly by the people. Because the impeached president Park Geun-hye seriously lost the people's trust and an absolute majority of people were in favour of her impeachment, the voice of critics of the decision was not well heard. However, questions about the Constitutional

Court's impeachment authority which are not on the surface now may come to the surface later.

The case proceeded as follows. On 10 March 2017, the Constitutional Court unanimously approved the National Assembly's December 2016 impeachment motion against President Park Geun-hye. Park's approval ratings had fallen to 4 per cent after a huge corruption scandal broke out in October 2016 revealing that Park relied too much on her long-time friend, Choi Soon-sil, who was not a public official to manage state affairs. Choi was also thought to have used the president's trust to manipulate state affairs (Lim 2017).

The four central claims in the impeachment passed by the National Assembly are as follows: (a) the abuse of power in demotion of civil servants; (b) Park's infringement on the freedom of speech/press by pressurising for the president of a newspaper critical of the regime to be dismissed; (c) the duty to protect the right to life and to faithfully carry out presidential responsibilities; (d) the abuse of power in granting political power to Choi Soon-sil. The Court only recognised as legitimate for the purposes of impeachment the fourth claim, the abuse of power to benefit Choi Soon-sil (Lim 2017). The Court explained the reason for the ruling as follows:

> The respondent [Park] also abused the authority delegated by the citizens for personal purposes.... The President, ... must exercise such power legitimately in accordance with the Constitution and law; and must disclose the performance of official duties in a transparent manner to enable appraisal by the public, ... However, the respondent allowed Choi [Soon-sil] to intervene in state affairs while keeping this a complete secret. Suspicions were raised on several occasions, ... but each time the respondent denied this, simply condemning them as mere suspicions instead.... The respondent made insincere apologies to the public and failed to keep her word, instead of endeavouring to regain the trust of the people with regard to her breaches of the Constitution and law.... In conclusion, the respondent's acts of violating the Constitution and law are a betrayal of the people's confidence, and should be deemed as grave violations of the law that are unpardonable from the perspective of protecting the Constitution. Since the negative impact and influence on the constitutional order brought about by the respondent's violations of the law are serious, we believe that the benefits of protecting the Constitution by removing the respondent from office, who has been directly vested with democratic legitimacy by the people, overwhelmingly outweigh the national loss that would be incurred by the removal of the President.
>
> (Hun-Na1 2017)

The key points of the ruling can be summarised as follows: Park's acts of violating the Constitution and law are a betrayal of the public trust, thereby leading the Court to conclude that the benefits of upholding the Constitution overwhelms the cost of political turmoil resulting from the removal of the president (Lim 2017). The decision made Park the first president in South Korean history to be ousted by the judiciary. The Court dispelled concerns that its conservative ideology would affect the ruling.

The next case involving the dissolution of a political party also raises similar issues to the impeachment trial. Although the power of the court to order the disbandment of a political party is also an authority granted by the Constitution, it is politically feasible for the fate of a political party to be determined by the people through elections. Thus, the question has yet to be resolved whether it is in line with democratic principles for unelected constitutional judges to force a political party, having received enough support to have a seat in parliament, to be dissolved.

The case proceeded as follows. On 5 November 2013, the government filed a claim with the Constitutional Court to dissolve the Unified Progressive Party (UPP). At the same time, the government applied for a court injunction to suspend activities of the UPP during the trial. UPP had five seats in the National Assembly. The government's petition was prompted by the arrest of several UPP members for plotting a rebellion in 2013. Seven members were eventually convicted of plotting to overthrow the South Korean government in cooperation with North Korea. The Minister of Justice claimed that dissolution of the UPP and removal of UPP members from the National Assembly was justified on the grounds that the objective of the UPP, including its platform, is based on North Korea's socialism, which is against South Korea's fundamental democratic order. The government stated before the Court in its final argument that the UPP had attempted to establish a pro-communist government to realise North Korean-style socialism. On the contrary, the UPP refuted the government's accusation by saying that it only wanted greater reconciliation with the North. During the trial, both UPP supporters and its opponents held demonstrations, shouting slogans and waving signs (Lee 2014).

The Constitutional Court decided to dissolve the respondent (the UPP) and strip its affiliated lawmakers of their National Assembly seats on the grounds that its objectives and activities are against the fundamental democratic order under the Constitution. Eight out of nine justices agreed to accept the government's petition to disband the UPP and to forfeit its seats in parliament and ban an equivalent party from forming (SNU Law Research Institute 2015).

Since its creation in 1988, the South Korean Constitutional Court has successfully introduced into the South Korean political system a new dimension of constitutional review and has substantially helped the democratic transition in South Korea. Nevertheless, currently, the South Korean Constitutional Court is facing unprecedented political and social pressures from highly polarised political forces.

If there is a lack of consolidated rules of the democratic game in a highly divided setting, more judicial activism is likely to occur. As social rifts become more severe, political polarisation becomes more prominent. While no political group can gain electoral support enough to be a dominant ruling party or coalition, the court becomes perceived as the most reliable civil institution in the country. When legislative and executive powers are polarised, the court accumulates more institutional power. Thus, the political deadlock in a highly divided setting is likely to be the major structural stimulus for increasing judicial activism because the polarised setting allows judges to vote sincerely without constraints from the legislature and the executive.

6. Conclusion

The current South Korean Constitution divides judicial power into two courts. The two High Courts are separate in terms of jurisdiction but equal in terms of status, in accordance with a separate constitutional article. Article 107(1) of the South Korean Constitution provides that, when the constitutionality of a law is at issue in trial, the Supreme Court shall request a decision of the Constitutional Court and shall judge according to the decision thereof. At the same time, Article 107(2) provides that the Supreme Court shall have the power to make a final review of the constitutionality or legality of administrative decrees, regulations, or actions when their constitutionality or legality is at issue in a trial.

South Korea's two highest courts once disputed who has the final power to examine the unconstitutionality of an executive order, although the Constitution clearly states that each jurisdiction is distinct. The Constitution stipulates that the Supreme Court has the final authority to examine whether an executive order is unconstitutional, but the Constitutional Court has brought about a jurisdictional dispute because the final authority in interpreting the Constitution is in the Constitutional Court. Now the debate has subsided, but it could recur at any time. The motive for the debate was, after all, the question of who was the boss in the Korean judicial system.

Recently, there has been a growing tendency in South Korea to seek a solution to political disputes in the two courts. This phenomenon was triggered by public concern that the representative system of South Korea has shown itself incapable of politically solving diverse economic and social problems in South Korean society. Therefore, the South Korean public has begun to turn their eyes towards the courts, hoping that the two highest courts exercise their supreme judicial power to solve those problems. The South Korean public has started to consider the judiciary as an effective means for social engineering.

In any system of divided powers, there must be a disinterested institution to referee conflicts over the division of power. In South Korea, this task was initially assigned to the Constitutional Court, and the Supreme Court and lower courts began to join the mission. The power of judicial review is a double-edged sword. On the one hand, if exercised courageously—but prudently—to defend the rights of politically and economically disadvantaged segments of the population or to hold the line against abuses of power, it could enhance constitutionalism in transitional and consolidating phases of democratisation. On the other hand, judicial review could easily become a formidable instrument for legitimating interests of existing political and economic elites.

Recently, concerns have been raised in South Korea about the judicialisation of politics and the politicisation of the judiciary. The judicialisation of politics refers to a phenomenon in which politicians cannot resolve disputes in the political arena in a political way but package them into legal disputes and ask the court to resolve them. This is proof that politicians do not communicate with each other anymore. The politicisation of the judiciary has led to a series of situations in which some judges reveal their individual political views and suspected politically biases through social media and in other forums, and their rulings are suspected to be political rulings. This phenomenon will undermine the institutional legitimacy of the judicial system. If this happens, the settlement of disputes by an equitable third party will no longer be expected, and social settlement of all disputes can be perceived as a political division.

From the perspective of the US academic community discussing the judiciary in the political context, the current situation facing South Korea's judiciary may seem natural. However, I think that the United States' and South Korea's judiciaries should have different degrees of caution in their relevance to politics. Judicial independence in the United States has been well maintained, to the degree that some believe that judges in the United States have gone too far in some cases. Therefore, public trust in the court is stronger than in any other country. Even if the court makes a politically controversial ruling, people believe that it is the court's own political position, not representing or subordinating to any political force. However, South Korean courts are not yet an institution in which the people's trust has been solidified through a long history like in the United States. The court's rulings are interpreted as favouring one political force, and those who oppose the rulings do not try to understand the reasoning process of the rulings and instead demand impeachment of the judge.

To discuss the judiciary in its function and role in the political context, strong judicial independence should be the premise, and judges should let their political values permeate the ruling, keeping the public's trust in the judiciary from faltering. In doing so, South Korean judges lack experience. It cannot be concluded that it is wrong for a judge's political values to influence the judgment. If there is a judge who understands politics as dividing sides and giving one side an advantage, the judge must be excluded from the trial on a politically significant issue. However, if a judge understands that politics is the distribution of social resources based on values shared by the majority of the people through negotiation and compromise, the judge will make a reasonable and acceptable ruling on issues of political significance. Proper political education is more urgent than ever for South Korean judges.

Bibliography

Barzilai, G. (1997), 'Between the Rule of Law and the Laws of the Ruler: The Supreme Court in Israeli Legal Culture,' *International Social Science Journal* 152, 193–208.

Bickel, A. M. (1986), *The Least Dangerous Branch: The Supreme Court at the Bar of Politics*, 2nd edn (New Haven, CT: Yale University Press).

Cha, D. (2006), 'wi-hŏn-pŏp-lyul-sim-sa-che-to-ŭi min-chu-chŏk chŏng-tang-sŏng-e kwan-han ko-ch'al: tae-ŭi-che min-chu-chu-ŭi ha-e-sŏ-ŭi hŏn-pŏp-chae-p'an-che-to-ŭi p'il-yo-sŏng-kwa che-to-chŏk kae-sŏn-pang-an-e kwan-han chae-kŏm-t'o', *chŏng-pu-hak-yŏn-ku* 12, 161–195.

Cha, D. (2016), 'chŏng-ch'i-ŭi sa-pŏp-hwa-e tae-han hŏn-pŏp-chae-p'an-so-ŭi ch'aek-im kuk-hoe-ŭi-wŏn-kwa kuk-hoe-ŭi-chang kan kwŏn-han-chaeng-ŭi sa-kŏn-ŭl chung-sim-ŭ-lo', han-kuk-chŏng-tang-hak-hoe-po 15, 69–103.

Cooter, R. D., and Ginsberg, T. (1996), 'Comparative Judicial Discretion: An Empirical Test of Economic Models', *International Review of Law and Economics* 16, 295–313.

Dahl, R. (1957), 'Decision-Making in a Democracy: The Supreme Court as a National Policy-Maker', *Journal of Public Law* 6, 279–295.

Epstein, L., Knight, J., and Shvetsova, O. (2001), 'The Role of Constitutional Courts in the Establishment and Maintenance of Democratic System of Government', *Law and Society Review* 35, 117–163.

Fried, C. (1988), 'Jurisprudential Responses to Legal Realism', *Cornell Law Review* 73, 331–367.

Gibson, J. L., Caldeira, G. A., and Baird, V. A. (1998), 'On the Legitimacy of National High Courts', *American Political Science Review* 92, 343–358.

Gillman, H., and Clayton, C. W. (1999), 'Beyond Judicial Attitudes: Institutional Approaches to Supreme Court Decision-Making', in C. W. Clayton and H. Gillman, eds, *Supreme Court Decision-Making: New Institutionalist Approaches* (Chicago, IL: University of Chicago Press), 1–12.

Ginsburg, T. (2003), *Judicial Review in New Democracies: Constitutional Courts in Asian Cases* (Cambridge: Cambridge University Press).

Hamilton, A., Madison J., Jay J., and Beeman, R. (2012), *The Federalist Papers*, 1st edn (Penguin Books) 138–149.

Hun-Na1 (2017), 10 March, http://search.ccourt.go.kr/ths/pr/eng_pr0101_E1.do?seq=1&cname=%EC%98%81%EB%AC%B8%ED%8C%90%EB%A1%80&eventNum=48728&eventNo=2016%ED%97%8C%EB%82%981&pubFlag=0&cId=010400, accessed 10 April 2022.

Kim, J. W. (2018), 'Korean Constitutional Court and Constitutionalism in Policy Dynamics: Focusing on Presidential Impeachment', *Constitutional Review* 4(2), 222–248.

Lee, H. (2014), 'The Erosion of Democracy in South Korea: The Dissolution of the Unified Progressive Party and the Incarceration of Lee Seok-ki', *The Asia-Pacific Journal: Japan Focus* 12(5), 1–12.

Lim, H. S. (2017), 'A Closer Look at the Korean Constitutional Court's Ruling on Park Geun-hye's Impeachment', *Yale Journal of International Law*, 18 May, https://www.yjil.yale.edu/a-closer-look-at-the-korean-constitutional-courts-ruling-on-park-geun-hyes-impeachment/, accessed 10 April 2022.

Lim, J. (1999), 'A Comparative Study of the Constitutional Adjudication Systems of the U.S., Germany and Korea', *Tulsa Journal of Comparative and International Law* 6, 123–162.

Linz, J. J. (1978), 'Crisis, Breakdown, and Reequilibration', in J. J. Linz and A. Stephan, eds, *The Breakdown of Democratic Regimes* (Baltimore, MD: Johns Hopkins University Press), 3–124.

Llewellyn, K. N. (1930), 'A Realistic Jurisprudence—The Next Step', *Columbia Law Review* 30, 431–465.

SNU Law Research Institute (2015), 'Notable cases: Notable Constitutional Court Cases: Constitutional Law', *Journal of Korean Law* 15(1), 259–282, https://s-space.snu.ac.kr/bitstream/10371/97156/1/11_Notable%20Cases%201_%ec%b4%88%ea%b5%90.pdf, accessed 10 April 2022.

Pederzoli, P., and Guarnier, C. (1997), 'Italy: A Case of Judicial Democracy?', *International Social Science Journal* 152, 253–270.

Posner, R. A. (1987), 'The Decline of Law as an Autonomous Discipline: 1962–1987', *Harvard Law Review* 100, 761–780.
Pritchett, C. H. (1948), *The Roosevelt Court* (Chicago, IL: University of Chicago Press).
Rosenberg, G. N. (1991), *The Hollow Hope: Can Courts Bring about Social Change?* (Chicago, IL: University of Chicago Press).
Schwartz, H. (2000), *The Struggle for Constitutional Justice in Post-Communist Europe* (Chicago, IL: The University of Chicago Press).
Segal, J. A. (1999), 'Supreme Court Deference to Congress: An Examination of the Marksist Model', in C. W. Clayton and H. Gillman (eds), *Supreme Court Decision-Making: New Institutionalist Approaches* (Chicago, IL: University of Chicago Press), 237–253.
Segal, J. A., and Spaeth, H. J. (1993), *The Supreme Court and the Attitudinal Model* (Cambridge: Cambridge University Press).
Shapiro, M., and Stone Sweet, A. (2002), *On Law, Politics, and Judicialization* (New York: Oxford University Press).
Spiller, P. T. (1996), 'A Positive Political Theory of Regulatory Instruments: Contracts, Administrative Law or Regulatory Specificity?', *USC Law Review* 69, 477–515.
Tate, N. C. (1997), 'Introduction: Democracy and Law—New Developments in Theory and Analysis,' *International Social Science Journal* 152, 143–150.
West, J. M., and Yoon, D. K. 1992. 'The Constitutional Court of the Republic of Korea: Transforming the Jurisprudence of the Vortex,' *American Journal of Comparative Law* 40, 73–119.

PART 4

PARTIES AND ELECTIONS

CHAPTER 14

PARTIES AND PARTY SYSTEMS

SUNGHACK LIM

1. INTRODUCTION

WE are all familiar with Schattschneider's noted assertion, 'The political parties created democracy and modern democracy is unthinkable save in terms of the parties' (Schattschneider 1942: 1). Political parties have been instrumental in linking civil society to democratic governance. Parties represent people by responding to, articulating, and aggregating the various interests in society, and these interests are translated into a policy agenda. They perform not only the function of representing people, but also of making themselves accountable for their activities through free and fair electoral systems. Therefore, political parties are a bare necessity of modern democracy.

Political parties are found in most counties, democratic or authoritarian, and in most democracies, old or new. The way political parties connect with citizens and gain their support, how they elect candidates, how they organise, and the goals they pursue may be different, but they connect civil society and government and play a vital role in shaping the democratic process. Thus, democratic transition specialists stress that the survival and success of new democracies depends on party system institutionalisation (PSI).

PSI is understood in terms of the stability in the rules and nature of inter-party competition, the development of firm roots in society, the acceptance of parties and the electoral system as legitimate, and so on. Party systems in new democracies are, by and large, unsettled because parties are less embedded in society, not recognised as rightful and necessary actors, and electoral volatility is high. Therefore, PSI has repeatedly been acknowledged as a critical factor for measuring the quality and consolidation of democracy (Mainwaring et al. 2006).

Since the late 1980s, South Korea has established democratic rules and institutions to protect the political freedom and civil rights of its citizens following its experience with brutal authoritarian regimes. In this process, political parties built democratic institutions and have been recognised as necessary actors for democratic governance. Although electoral democracy has taken root in South Korea, its road towards strong PSI is far from complete. The characteristics of the South Korean political party system, including non-ideological regional factionalism, personality-based party organisation, and growing electoral volatility due to party changes, has contributed to weak PSI (Hermanns 2009).

However, South Korea was the first third-wave democracy in East Asia to achieve a peaceful power transfer to an opposition party in 1997, and, up to the present, there have been two more power transfers. This means South Korea has become a fully fledged consolidated democracy. Although reform is necessary for the party system to be more stable, accountable, and responsive for democratic deepening, the question that remains is how was South Korea's new democracy able to move forward to consolidation without strong PSI?

In this chapter, I first briefly introduce the main characteristics of parties and the political system in South Korea. The development and change of these unique characteristics are a result of two critical events. One is the democratisation in 1987 and another is the major political reform in 2004. The basic characteristics of South Korea's parties and party system developed right after democratisation. The phenomenon known as 'three Kims politics', which had a substantive impact during this period, will be discussed in detail. Finally, the possibility of change to the parties and party system will be discussed. In particular, the impact of the political reforms on parties and the party system in 2004 will be examined.

2. The Characteristics of South Korean Political Parties and the Party System

The main characteristics of South Korean parties and the party system, including non-ideological party roots in society, personality-based party organisation, and high electoral volatility, manifested themselves in a series of presidential elections. Figure 14.1, which displays candidates' vote share by region, their party, and presidential candidates of the five presidential elections after democratisation, illustrates unambiguously all three points. First, South Korea can be characterised by strong regionalism in election returns. The country can in general be split into eastern and western regions based on support for candidates, and partisan support, especially in the southeast and southwest regions, seems to be firmly consolidated. The southeast (Yeongnam) supports conservative candidates, whereas the southwest (Honam) supports liberals.[1] This region-based voting behaviour is showing signs of weakening little by little, but it is still the most important factor in South Korean politics.

Looking at the major candidates in presidential elections, the omnipresence of the so-called 'three Kims' can be seen up to the 1997 presidential election. Kim Dae-jung (DJ) ran for president in the 1987, 1992, and 1997 elections and was finally elected in 1997.[2] Kim Young-sam (YS) ran for president in 1987 and 1992 and was elected in 1992. During the three Kims' era, parties were personal instruments for getting charismatic leaders elected in the presidential election.

Electoral volatility is one of the elements of PSI which indicates the degree of inter-party competition. It measures the net difference in the percentage of votes earned or lost by each party from one election to the next. Lower electoral volatility means a stable party system. According to Hyun (2011), the average rate of electoral volatility from the 1988 general election to the 2010 election was 29.4 per cent. In 1992, the rate increased to 37.4 per cent because there was a big merger among three parties to form the Democratic Liberal Party (DLP). DJ was a presidential candidate for three different parties (the People's Democratic Party [PDP] in 1987, the Democratic Party [DP] in 1992, and the National Congress Party [NCP] in 1997). This high electoral volatility is attributed to the parties' mergers, splits, or name changes for the three Kims' convenience.

Figure 14.1 also demonstrates two more characteristics of South Korean parties and the party system. First, there are four prominent colours, which indicate regional turf in which each candidate and party dominate. Since the 1992 presidential election, the number of colours has diminished from four to two. In other words, the party system has changed from a multiparty system to a two-party (sometimes 2.5-party) system.[3] Three parties decided to merge to form the Democratic Liberal Party (DLP) right before the 1992 presidential election, which created the rivalry between the southwest and southeast region, as well as between the conservative and liberal ideologies. Since then, two major parties, occasionally with an additional smaller party striving for negotiating group status, have dominated South Korean politics.

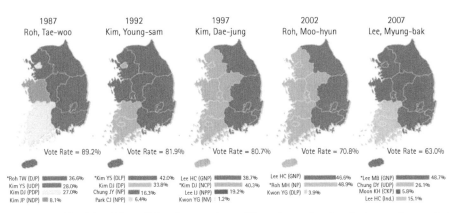

FIGURE 14.1: Presidential candidates' percentage of the votes and regional winners from 1987 to 2007. Presidential winners are marked by asterisks

Source: Song et al. (2014: 598).

Two peaceful power transfers from ruling to opposition party can be found in 1997 and 2007 in Figure 14.1. In 1997, the area covered in green representing the liberal candidate Kim Dae-jung expanded to most of the West of South Korea to win the election. He became the first opposition candidate to become president, as well as the first president from the southwest region of the country. In 2007, nearly the entire county is covered in blue, save the southwest, signifying the victory of the conservative candidate Lee Myung-bak. This second power transfer meant that South Korea had passed Huntington's two turnover test of democratic consolidation (Huntington 1991). The third power transfer, which is not included in Figure 14.1, happened in 2017, when Moon Jae-in, the candidate of the liberal party, won. After President Park Geun-hye was impeached by the National Assembly and the Constitutional Court, a peaceful power transition was once again carried out.

To summarise the above, South Korean political parties and the party system are characterised by a low PSI level, and the party system has changed from a multiparty system to a two-party system. There were three successful power transfers, which means elections function as an important mechanism for political decisions.

3. The Causes of the Two-Party System and Weakly Institutionalised Parties

Parties in South Korea originally functioned as electoral machines for the three Kims and a regional party system dominated South Korean politics, which led to a weak PSI score. This unique development of political parties and the party system was due to not only South Korean specificity, but also to the parties' response to the changing political environment. The historical legacy of socio-economic development, the institution-building process, prominent political leaders, and political institutions themselves have influenced the parties and the interaction between them.

3.1 Historical Legacy

Hicken and Kuhonta (2011) emphasise historical legacies as a critical variable affecting current levels of PSI. In Asia, the immediate postwar period was an important time of development for institutionalised party systems. Party politics in the authoritarian era, the political and economic structure, and the mode of implementation of democratisation imposed structural restrictions on the political landscape afterwards. South Korea's international and domestic political factors also had a profound influence on the development of political parties and the party system. One reason for weak PSI in new democracies is that party development was frequently intruded upon during long periods of authoritarian rule. This made it impossible and unnecessary for political parties to invest in party organisations and procedures (Lee 2009). The personalised political party structure that persisted throughout the authoritarian era and the weak link between parties and civil society were incredibly unfavourable to the growth of institutionalised political parties. The vast organisation of bureaucracy and the executive office of the president, which developed during the era of the developmental state, have led the direction and execution of policies, and the role of the ruling party or opposition party became often secondary (Jaung 2018).

Choi (2012) asserts that the main reason for the stagnation and decline of South Korean democracy after democratisation is that the political representation system has become fixed on conservative competition without reflecting the needs and changes of society. Cold War anti-communism has imprisoned South Korea's political party system in an ideologically conservative framework. Through the experiences of the division of South and North Korea and the Korean War, party politics were bound to represent only conservative ideologies for a long time. Political parties tried to maintain their existing conservative supporters and strove to appeal to other conservatives by transforming themselves into catch-all parties.[4] As a result, the ideological spectrum of the party system was limited and narrowed.

The type of democratic transition is also very important because it has a profound influence on the formation and settlement of political institutions. The transition to democracy can be seen as a result of the interaction between the regime-maintaining and regime-opposing forces. South Korea is a typical case of pact democratisation, or democratisation through negotiations among the opposing forces. Therefore, the authoritarian legacy has remained to some extent intact, even though political competition was restored and civil society became politically active. This is another reason why political parties and the party system are conservative (Im 1996). Historical legacies such as the intrusion of authoritarian rule, weak linkages between parties and civil society, Cold War anti-communism, and pact democratisation had contributed to the development of personalised political party structure, as well as to party competition only within the conservative spectrum.

3.2 The Three Kims' Politics and Regionalism

The term 'three Kims' refers to YS, DJ, and Kim Jong-pil (JP), all of whom had been politically predominant in South Korean politics from the 1970s to the 2000s. All three leaders share the same surname 'Kim', the most popular surname in South Korea. Three Kims politics substantially began when each ran for the presidential election in 1987. YS served as the fourteenth president from 1993 to 1998, and DJ served as the fifteenth president from 1998 to 2003. JP served as prime minister from 1971 to 1975, and from 1998 to 2000. The Three Kims era finally ended when JP retired from politics after his party's devastating defeat during the general election in 2004.

The importance of three Kims politics can be said to be threefold. First, as the most significant politicians before and after democratisation, they had tremendous influence in all aspects of South Korean politics for a long time. They were superstars that always appeared at important moments in South Korean politics. Second, political parties worked as machines to help the three Kims win the presidency. Their political parties resembled the cadre and personalised party models and operated in a hierarchical and centralised manner around the leader. Third, politics based on so-called regionalism took root and became the principal political cleavage (Im 1996; Chung 2002).

The three Kims played an important role in all areas of South Korean politics. DJ and YS were opposition leaders who fought for democracy. They played a pivotal role in overthrowing the authoritarian regime. On the other hand, JP, as a co-leader of the military coup, played an important role in establishing and maintaining Park Chung-hee's military regime. Ahead of the thirteenth presidential election, DJ and YS failed to unify under a single banner, and eventually both ran in the presidential election. JP also ran in 1987, and the presidential election that year was a four-way race with the three Kims and Roh Tae-woo, the presidential candidate of the authoritarian successor party Democratic Justice Party (DJP) (Yi 2009). The failure to agree on a single candidate between YS and DJ and the shortage of political funds and organisation capacity of the three Kims gave an advantage to Roh, who finally won the thirteenth presidential election.

The three parties created by the three Kims for the 1987 presidential election and the authoritarian successor party competed in the subsequent general election in 1988. A four-party system was formed and each party received absolute support from their respective leaders' home region. The ruling party, the DJP, secured the most seats but failed to form a majority in the National Assembly, which led to a divided government. President Roh, who wanted to administrate state affairs by overcoming the divided government, YS, who thought that securing conservative support and securing sufficient political was a key to winning the next presidential election, and JP, who thought he could take power through a parliamentary system later, agreed to ally. In the end, YS became the candidate of the newly created party which formed via a three-party merger (the so-called Grand Conservatives Coalition) and won the fourteenth presidential election in 1992 (Kang 2019: 199–200).

Since then, a two-party system has evolved between the conservatives based in the southeast region and the liberals based in the southwest region. Just before the fifteenth presidential election, DJ formed a coalition with JP, the so-called DJP Alliance. DJ won the presidential election in 1997 and appointed JP as prime minister (Kang 2019: 201). Finally, the three Kims era ended when JP retired from politics in 2004.

3.2.1. *Party*

Political parties had virtually functioned as electoral machines to achieve the three Kims' political ambitions. Hellmann describes South Korea as a 'partyless' democracy because political parties only function for the interests of party leaders and thus have failed to become independent political actors (Hellmann 2014). Parties' split, merged, or were newly created repeatedly according to the political interests of the three Kims, preventing party institutionalisation. The three Kims, who received absolute support in their home regions, ruled over their political parties by controlling the nominations of candidates for public office. Since being nominated meant being elected in the districts of the three Kims' home regions, the candidates had no choice but to be loyal to the three Kims. This was a key factor in sustaining the personalised party structure.

Another mechanism of a personalised party system is the party leader's control over political funds. After democratisation, the political funding system was also improved and provided adequate institutions to raise political funds for both the ruling and opposition parties. Although the system was improved compared to the past, illegal political funding remained a problem. Parties eventually had to reach out for external support due to the increasing cost of campaigns. External support, which was often unofficial and illegal in terms of amount and transparency, became a hotbed of corruption. Therefore, in the early stage of democracy, political funding was mainly acquired through informal and illegal channels rather than official channels, and was concentrated in the hands of the three Kims. They were able to control their political parties by distributing political funds to their followers in exchange for loyalty (Lim 2018).

3.2.2 *Regionalism*

South Korea is typically considered to be one of the world's most homogenous countries. But South Korea is also characterised by deep regionalism. Figure 14.1 illustrates this deep regionalism, especially in the 1987 presidential election, in which the three Kims and Roh were able to re-establish their own party by securing support from their distinctive home regions. Regionalism strengthened in the following 1988 general election. The three Kims opened the era of regional politics by building their forces based on regions.

The results of the 1988 general elections in terms of region were as follows: DJ's Peace Democratic Party took thirty-six out of thirty-seven seats in Honam, Roh's DJP took twenty-five out of twenty-nine in Daegu and Gyeongbuk province, and YS's Unification Democratic Party took twenty-three out of thirty-seven in Busan and Gyeongnam province. In the Chungcheong area, JP's New Democratic Republican Party won fifteen out of twenty-seven seats. As regionalism settled in, the candidates grew accustomed to using regionalism for campaigning rather than ideology and policy differentiation.

The political rivalry between the four regions gradually turned into a confrontation between two regions, Yeongnam and Honam. The Grand Conservative Coalition between the Yeongnam and Chungcheong regions in 1992 alienated the Honam region and this reinforced regional antagonism between Yeongnam and Honam. Later, in 1997, another coalition between Honam and the Chungcheong region (the DJP coalition) bolstered this pattern of regional competition. As a result, the initial four-party system gradually transformed into a two-party (or 2.5-party) system. Figure 14.1 tells this tale. Regionalism has prevented voters from voting based on a rational calculation of candidates. Widespread voting based on personality and region, as well as the weak relationship between parties and ideology, has contributed to weak PSI.

3.2.3 *Political Institutions*

The type of democratisation has a great influence on the formation of democratic institutions. Pact democratisation by major political forces has contributed to creating a political system that is relatively advantageous to existing political parties. The fundamentally majoritarian electoral system was introduced in 1988. At the time, it was considered a reform. The multi-member constituencies system used during the authoritarian regime was a system in which two or more members are elected as representatives from one constituency. The two-member constituencies system was introduced because it could strengthen the vested interests of the ruling party. It was advantageous for the ruling party because it could win one seat even in urban areas where opposition parties dominated, and two ruling party candidates could be elected in rural areas. Another reason was that it was easy for the ruling party to gain a majority by dividing the opposition party through increasing the likelihood of electing a minor party candidate. Therefore, during the democratic transition, YS and DJ strongly demanded electoral reform and the creation of a single-member constituencies system (Sim 2009: 373–375). It was also the three Kims' political calculation that this system gave an advantage to parties having strong regional support.

As a result, the initial four-party system gradually transformed into a two-party or 2.5-party system. Eventually, two major political parties, based in Yeongnam and Honam, developed and maintained 'hostile symbiosis'. A proportional representation system was also introduced. In the 1988 general election, the number of districts increased significantly to 224, and the number of proportional seats was expanded to 75 seats, one-third of the district seats. However, it is a mistake to think that the expansion of proportional seats would be favourable to minority parties. In the name of political stability, the electoral law introduced in 1988 regulated that the dominant party obtain half of the proportional seats (Kang 2019: 209).

Therefore, the South Korean party system can be considered a two-party system as well as a conservative cartel party system. Katz and Mair (1995), who introduced this new type of party organisation model, argue that the major characteristics of a cartel party system are the increasing state subsidies to political parties and inter-party collaboration to elevate the entry barriers against new or minor parties. By providing themselves with the advantage of state subsidies and collaborating, major parties prevent new or minor parties from being competitive in elections, which leads to the cartelisation of the party system. Most political scientists in South Korea agree that a cartelised party system has evolved since the 1987 democratisation (Kwak 2001; Jaung 2003). Major parties have seriously competed in elections, but cooperated to increase state subsidies to themselves and block the entry of new parties (Lim 2011). These at once personalised-cadre and cartelised parties generated the two-party, cartelised party system in the end (Kim 2015). In terms of their party organisation model, it is almost impossible to identify South Korean parties as one model because they have attributes of the cadre, catch-all, and cartel party models.

4. CHANGES TO PARTIES AND THE PARTY SYSTEM

South Korean political parties and the party system faced new challenges in the early 2000s when the three Kims retired from politics. The existing hierarchical and personalised parties became more decentralised and democratic through internal democratic reforms. However, democratic reform within the parties was a daunting challenge to a new democracy. Even the political parties in advanced democracies where party politics institutionalised from early on face difficulties due to decreases in the number of party members and the weakening of the party's identity among voters due to post-industrial industrialisation. South Korean parties' tasks included not only dealing with the same challenges that advanced democracies face, but also liquidating the deep-rooted politics of the three Kims.

A few minor reforms have been implemented after democratisation, but major parties were reluctant to take any meaningful measures. However, a series of political money scandals by presidential candidates uncovered after the 2002 presidential election left no option for political parties but to implement reform measures. Public distrust in political parties and politicians was too severe to be ignored. The Association for Political Reforms was created through joint cooperation between academia and non-governmental organisations (NGOs) (Siminsahoeundongjeongbosenteo 2006: 451–452). Fortunately, bills incorporating policies suggested mostly by the Association were passed in 2004. The reform was intended to create a break from the old-style 'three Kims' politics and to institutionalise the political party system.

Political reforms focused on two aspects: internal party reform and party system reform (Kim 2008). First, internal reforms focused on getting rid of the three Kims' monopoly on nomination and exclusive control of political funds which enabled them to control the party. Party decisions are still made top-down by high-ranking officials or members of the National Assembly, but high-ranking officials are now democratically elected by party members. This top-down decision-making structure was focused on producing as many winning candidates as possible. Eventually, the organisation and decision-making process of parties became more decentralised and open to the public. Major parties even allowed a more open nomination process, in which the average citizens, who are not party members, can participate.

Due to weak ideological connections, election campaigns either appealed to emotional regionalism or clientelistic networks, which required a large sum of political funds. The district party chapter, the so-called money-eating hippo, was abolished. This measure was justified by the need to break away from machine politics, decrease the demand for political funds, and make parties more open and democratic. The previous expensive campaigns to mobilise constituents by district party chapters has been changed to mass media-orientated election campaigns that cost less (Lim 2018).

As the proportion of voters from younger generations, who are unaffected by the regional biases, grows, it has become difficult for political parties to mobilise voters. These difficulties were aggravated by the abolition of the district party chapter and lack of political funds. The rapid change in the media environment brought about a change in the way parties communicate with voters. Voters can easily obtain information on politics and elections through a variety of media sources. As the political role of the media has grown to the extent that the media has enormous influence on the candidates' chances of winning the election, many politicians have begun using mass media-orientated campaign strategies rather than seeking to mobilise voters through party organisations (Park 2012).

In this respect, though not in full form, South Korean political parties share characteristics of the electoral-professional party model to a considerable degree. Since the reform in 2004, the typical characteristics of the electoral-professional party, such as more stress on issues and personalised leadership, the central role of professional specialised tasks, and appeal to the opinion electorate during elections (Panebianco 1988: 264), can be easily found (Park 2012).

The second reform intended to ease problems caused by the cartelised party system through transforming regional-based party competition patterns into ideological and policy competition and revitalising minor parties (Lim 2011). Electoral reforms have been repeatedly advocated because the electoral system, mainly based on a plurality rule, provides systematic advantages to major parties with regional bases. The electoral system was changed in March 2004 to initiate these reforms. The one-person, two-vote system, in which the voters vote for one candidate in their district and one party in a party list vote, was implemented to increase the level of proportionality. The Democratic Labour Party, a left-wing minority party, won 13 per cent of the party list vote and sent eight proportional representatives to the National Assembly, along with two more representatives who won their respective district races. However, the number of seats allocated for proportional representatives has decreased since the 2004 general election. Only 18 per cent of the total seat is allocated to proportional seats, which is very low in comparison with Organisation for Economic Co-operation and Development (OECD) countries. Despite the reform, one of the main characteristics of the cartelised party system which makes it difficult for minority parties to enter remains almost intact.

In terms of political funding, government subsidies make up a large part of a party's finances, so the cartel party system seems to be preserved. However, the expansion of government subsidies for parties in South Korea is quite different from the West. First, subsidies kept increasing immediately after democratisation, but stabilised eventually. The reason why government subsidies became the most important source of income for South Korean parties is the ban on company and organisation donations and the abolishment of the Central Party's Political Fundraising Association rather than the continued increase of subsidies. As the revenue from donations sharply decreased, the proportion of subsidies increased relatively. Second, if the cartelised party system were active, it could have prevented such measures, which would have been a huge financial blow to the large political parties. However, in the end, the parties were forced to accept these reforms due to deteriorating public opinion about the political fund scandal. Third, in the case of the West, the transition to cartel parties was a response to decreased party income, which was a result of weakened support and loyalty among party members. However, major parties in South Korea were never mass parties that relied heavily on party membership fees, even before the advent of the cartel party (Kang 2009: 126). Therefore, in terms of subsidies, the cartelised party system in South Korea is not an appropriate concept to explain the organisational change and response of South Korean parties.

These changes can also be evaluated in terms of PSI. Mainwaring et al. (2006) focus on two dimensions of PSI: party roots in society and the stability of interparty competition. First, in the more institutionalised systems, parties are strongly rooted in society so that voters are robustly attached to parties. Programmatic or ideological linkages help to serve as a shortcut for voters' electoral decisions. Second, in more institutionalised systems, there is substantial stability in patterns of party competition, which can be measured by electoral volatility.

In South Korea, strong party roots in society have not been able to be developed because regionalism, not ideology, serves as a shortcut for electoral decisions. However, there are some signs of regionalism gradually weakening. The 1997 presidential election was a decisive moment in weakening regionalism. With the election of the first Honam president, the sense of alienation caused by Youngnam's political domination has been to some extent resolved, and socio-economic discrimination against Honam people has decreased.

After the three Kims retired from politics, the emergence of new social cleavages further weakened regionalism. The younger generations especially are more interested in post-industrialisation issues such as quality of life, human rights, practical issues, and so on, and are no longer imprisoned by regionalism (Chung 2002). Therefore, the ideological and generational cleavages have become deep enough to undermine the robust regional cleavage since the 2004 general election (Choi and Cho 2005; Kim et al. 2008). According to the Party Polarisation Index, which measures party system polarisation based on voter perceptions of party positions, polarisation in South Korea dropped to 0.70 in the 2000 election, after DJ colluded with the conservative party to win the election, but rebounded to 3.55 in the 2004 election (Dalton 2008: 907–908).

After the DJ administration implemented a North Korea-friendly policy, the so-called Sunshine Policy, a sharp ideological conflict arose. The conservatives opposed the policy, labelling it appeasement towards North Korea, whereas the liberals supported the Sunshine Policy. Contrasting views on North Korea intensified due to its overlapping with regional bases. Honam supported the Sunshine Policy, whereas Yeongnam opposed it. As regions and ideologies overlapped, ideological and policy differences on other issues between political parties became clearer. One study contends that there is a certain interaction at the level of the party voter as well as the voter government in terms of ideological positions of the political parties. And issues which parties highlight during campaigns are reflected in budget planning (Hyun 2011). Therefore, despite the fact that regionalism is still the most important factor in voter decisions, the ideological linkage between parties and voters seems to be strengthening.

According to the second dimension of PSI, frequent splits and mergers, as well as the creation of new parties in South Korea, have had a negative impact on the stability of interparty competition. This has increased electoral volatility, which refers to the degree of change in voting behaviour between elections. According to Mainwaring et al. (2006: 208), the electoral volatility mean of the South Korean general election from 1988 to 2000 was 24.6. Of the thirty-eight countries surveyed, the average of South Korea was close to the median, which is higher than that of old democracy, but lower than that of the new democracy. However, a conservative two-party system based on regional cleavage had been frozen to some extent. Croissant and Völkel (2012: 259) argue that the South Korean party system seems 'to be paradoxically stabilizing in a situation of protracted under-institutionalisation, as both cases combine more or less stable party system patterns with weak institutionalisation'. The stability of interparty competition has been maintained despite moderate electoral volatility.

According to one study (Roh and Lee 2019) using the concept of 'internal bloc volatility', despite the frequent change of party names and splits and mergers of parties, voters' support for the political party representing their preferred ideological axis remains strong. Internal bloc volatility is measured by the ideological cleavage line divided into blocks of parties rather than individual party organisations (Bartolini and Mair 1990). In terms of the ideological division between conservatism and liberalism in South Korea, internal bloc volatility means election volatility across the ideological bloc by calculating the total number of votes of political parties in the same ideological bloc. As a result, it was found that the volatility between blocks after democratisation was stable at a level similar to that of the Western advanced countries, and South Korean political parties have been changing within the same ideological framework despite frequent mergers and splits. In terms of internal bloc volatility, the South Korean political party system can be evaluated as stable. Hellmann (2014) also demonstrates that political parties in South Korea have stabilised interparty competition through programmatic linkages, even though they were unable to establish a formal organisational base.

If new concepts and methodologies are applied especially in terms of electoral volatility, South Korean PSI is not that weak and gradually improves to the level of advanced democracies unlike previous studies. It can be said that this gradually improving PSI has had a good effect on the development and consolidation of democracy. Jin (1995: 59) argues that 'a strong inclination toward a two-party system, a decreasing ratio of independent candidates, a decreasing divergence of voting trends between rural and urban residents and an increasing legislative role' are positive signs of increasing institutionalisation. This overall success of democratic progress reveals that peaceful power transfers from the ruling party to an opposition party through a free and fair presidential election created an auspicious environment for political institutions to mature in South Korea (Hahm et al. 2013).

5. Conclusion

In the development of South Korean democracy, political parties have always played a vital role. Political parties were created, split, and merged according to the political leader's needs, but it has represented the public's interest at critical political junctures. During the democratic transition and consolidation, parties became an indispensable part of democratic governance.

South Korean political parties are faced with three difficulties, including overcoming the legacy of the past authoritarian era, solving problems associated with 'three Kims' politics, and at the same time coping with the decline of the party that the rest of world is also experiencing. Because the political environment of South Korea was and is quite different from the West, the development of political parties and the party system was and is quite different in terms of the process and results. Therefore, it is problematic to uncritically apply Western models of the sequential and linear evolution based on Western experiences (Randall et al. 2002; Kang 2009; Han 2020). Since South Korean political parties are still in a fluid and amorphous stage, they are only hodge-podge parties which have elements of many models of political party organisation, including those of the mass party, catch-all party, cartel party, and electoral-professional party (Kim 2008). The reason, characteristics, and degree of the cartelised party system are also quite different from those of the West. In the case of PSI, it was confirmed in this chapter that the evaluation may differ if a new approach and concepts are applied. Even well-established party systems in the West with high PSI show party instability and their electoral volatility from election to election is more erratic (Drummond 2006). Revision of the concept and application of PSI seems necessary (Luna 2014). Through more comprehensive research and a new conceptualisation of parties and the party system of South Korean democracy, a new theory about the role and influence of parties in maintaining and consolidating democracy should be developed.

Notes

1. In terms of political cleavage, mostly two ideological camps have infused the formation of the South Korean party system. One is the conservatives, who upheld the value of economic growth and anti-communism. The other is the liberals, who demanded political liberalisation during the authoritarian regimes. This cleavage has also intertwined with regional bases. The third one, the progressives, advocating pro-labour policies, managed to emerge in the formal political realm after the introduction of new electoral system in 2004.
2. In South Korea, the three Kims, given their lofty political stature, are typically referred to by using the initials of their given names. Therefore Kim Young-sam is called 'YS', Kim Dae-jung is referred to as 'DJ', and Kim Jong-pil is called 'JP'.
3. The South Korean party system has consistently been a two-party system (Hellmann 2014: 60). The average effective number of elective parties and the effective number of

parliamentary parties since the thirteenth assembly are 3.55 and 2.59, respectively. These figures are almost the same as other plurality two-party systems (see Chapter 16 of this volume).
4. Choi regards both the conservative and liberals as conservative because they have ignored a major ideological cleavage between capital and labour. The fact that established conservatives and liberals prevented the pro-labour force from being a meaningful political actor shows characteristics of the cartel party.

Bibliography

1. Literature written in Korea

Choi, J.-J. (2005), 'Minjuhwaihuui minjujuui' [Democracy after Democratization] (Seoul: Humanitas).

Choi, J. Y., and Cho, J. (2005), 'Jiyeokgyunyeorui byeonhwa ganeungseonge daehan gyeongheomjeok gochal' [Regional Cleavage in Korea Disappearing?], *Korean Political Science Review* 39(3), 375–394.

Hyun, J. H. (2011), 'Minjuhwa ihu jeongdangjeongchi: jeongdang, yugwonja geurigo jeongbu' [Party Politics after Democratization: Political Parties, Voters and Government], *Journal of Korean Politics* 20(3), 81–108.

Jaung, H. (2003), 'Kareutel jeongdangchejeui hyeongseonggwa baljeon: Minjuhwa ihu hangugui gyeongu' [The Rise of Carter Party System in Democratic Korea], *Korea and World Politics* 19(4), 2–59.

Jaung, H. (2018), 'Jeongchaekjeongdangui buchimgwa hanguk minjujuui 30nyeon' [The Rise and Fall of Policy-Based Parties in Korean Democracy], *Korean Party Studies Review* 17(3), 5–33.

Kang, W.-T. (2009), 'Hanguk jeongdang yeongue daehan bipanjeok geomto: Jeongdang jojik yuhyeongeul jungsimeuro' [A Review of Research Trends of South Korea's Political Parties], *Korean Party Studies Review* 8(2), 119–141.

Kang, W.-T. (2019), *Hanguk jeongchiron* [Understanding Korean Politics], 2nd edn (Seoul: Bagyeongsa).

Kim, J. S. (2015), 'Juyo jeongdangui jigudang jojikgwa unyeonge daehan siljeung bunseok: Jigudang pyeji ijeon jipapjaryoreul jungsimeuro' [How Political Parties Organize and Fund Local Party Chapters before the Enactment of the 2004 Political Party Act], *Korean Party Studies Review* 14(3), 5–39.

Kim, Y.-H. (2008), 'Choegeun hanguk jeongdangui gaehyeokjochie daehan pyeongga' [An Evaluation on Recent Party Reforms in South Korea], *Korean Party Studies Review* 7(1), 195–210.

Kwak, J. Y. (2001), 'Hanguk jeongdangchegyeui minjuhwa: Jeongdang-gukgagan gwangyereul jungsimeuro' [A New Perspective on Democratization of the Korean Party System: Party–State Relationship since 1987], *Korean Journal of Legislative Studies* 7(1), 34–62.

Lim, S. (2018), 'Hanguk jeongdangui jaewongujo byeonhwawa minjujuui' [The Structural Change of Party Finance and Democracy in Korea], *Korean Party Studies Review* 17(2), 61–91.

Park, K. (2012), 'Hanguk jeongdangmodere gwanhan tamsaekjeok yeongu: Minjuhwa ihu chongseonui seongeogyeongjaengeul jungsimeuro' [An Exploratory Study on Party Models in South Korea: The Electoral Competitions in General Elections after Democratization], *Korean Party Studies Review* 11(1), 31–57.

Roh, G.-W., and Lee, H.-W. (2019), 'Minjuhwa ihu hanguk jeongdangchegyeneun buranjeonghanga?: Yuhyo jeongdang suwa seongeo yudongseong sebunhwareul jungsimeuro' [Is the Korean Party System Unstable after Democratization?: Focusing on the Effective Number of Parties and Electoral Volatility Indexes], *Korean Party Studies Review* 18(4), 5–35.

Sim, J. (2009), *Hanguk jeongdangjeongchisa* [Political History of Korean Political Parties] (Seoul: Baeksanseodang).

Siminsahoeundongjeongbosenteo (2006), *Hanguksiminsahoeyeongam 2005* [Korean Civil Society Yearbook 2005] (Seoul: siminui sinmunsa).

Yi, D. W. (2009), 'Hanguk jeongchibaljeongwa jeongchijidojaui yeokal: Kim Dae Joong, Kim Young Sam, Kim Jong Pil eul jungsimeuro' [Roles of Political Leaders with Development of Korea Politics: Focusing on Kim Dae Joong, Kim Young Sam and Kim Jong Pil], *Region and World* 33(1), 251–277.

2. Literature written in English

Bartolini, S., and Mair, P. (1990), *Identity, Competition, and Electoral Availability* (Cambridge: Cambridge University Press).

Choi, J. J. (2012), *Democracy after Democratization: The Korean Experience* (Stanford, CA: Shorenstein Asia-Pacific Research Centre).

Chung, J. M. (2002), 'Party-System Change in Post-Democratization Korea: A Partisan Realignment Perspective', *Korea Observer* 33(1), 47–65.

Croissant, A., and P. Völkel (2012), 'Party System Types and Party System Institutionalization: Comparing New Democracies in East and Southeast Asia', *Party Politics* 18(2), 235–265.

Dalton, R. J. (2008), 'The Quantity and the Quality of Party Systems: Party System Polarization, Its Measurement, and Its Consequences', *Comparative Political Studies* 41(7), 899–920.

Drummond, A. J. (2006), 'Electoral Volatility and Party Decline in Western Democracies: 1970–1995', *Political Studies* 54(3), 628–647.

Hahm, S. D., Jung, K., and Kim, D. (2013), 'Peaceful Power Transfers or Successions and Democratic Consolidation in South Korea', *Korean Social Science Journal* 40(1), 53–64.

Han, J. (2020), 'How Does Party Organization Develop beyond Clientelism in New Democracies? Evidence from South Korea, 1992–2016', *Contemporary Politics*, https://doi.org/10.1080/13569775.2020.1862444.

Hellmann, O. (2014), 'Party System Institutionalization without Parties: Evidence from Korea', *Journal of East Asian Studies* 14(1), 53–84.

Hermanns, H. (2009), 'Political Parties in South Korea and Taiwan after Twenty Years of Democratization', *Pacific Focus* 24(2), 205–224.

Hicken, A. and Kuhonta, E. (2011), 'Shadows from the Past: Party System Institutionalization in Asia', *Comparative Political Studies* 44(5), 572–597.

Huntington, S. (1991), *The Third Wave: Democratisation in the Late Twentieth Century* (Norman, OK: University of Oklahoma Press).

Im, H. B. (1996), 'Opportunities and Constraints to Democratic Consolidation in South Korea', *Korea Journal of Population and Development* 25(2), 181–216.

Jin, Y. (1995), 'Testing Political Party Institutionalisation: A Theory and Practice', *Journal of Political and Military Sociology* 23(1), 43–65.

Katz, R. and Mair, P. (1995), 'Changing Models of Party Organization and Party Democracy: The Emergence of the Cartel Party', *Party Politics* 1(1), 5–28.

Kim, H. M., Choi, J. Y. and Cho, J. (2008), 'Changing Cleavage Structure in New Democracies: An Empirical Analysis of Political Cleavages in Korea', *Electoral Studies* 27(1), 136–150.

Lee, Y. (2009), 'Democracy without Parties? Political Parties and Social Movements for Democratic Representation in Korea', *Korea Observer* 40(1), 27–52.

Lim, S. (2011), 'Political Parties and Party System in Korea after Democratisation: Cartelized Party System and Oscillations between Two Models', in F. L. Liang and W. Hofmeister, eds, *Political Parties, Party Systems and Democratisation in East Asia* (Singapore: World Scientific Publishing Co.), 211–241.

Luna, P. (2014). 'Party System Institutionalisation: Do We Need a New Concept?', *Studies in Comparative International Development* 49(4), 403–425.

Mainwaring, S. and Torcal, M. (2006), 'Party System Institutionalisation and Party System Theory after the Third Wave of Democratization', in R. Katz et al., ed., *Handbook of Party Politics* (London: Sage Publications', 204–227).

Panebianco, A. (1988), *Political Parties: Organisation and Power* (Cambridge: Cambridge University Press).

Randall, V., and Svåsand, L. (2002), 'Introduction: The Contribution of Parties to Democracy and Democratic Consolidation', *Democratisation* 9(3), 1–10.

Schattschneider, E. E. (1942), *Party Government* (New York: Holt, Rinehart and Winston).

Song, T. S., M.S. Yang, and C. S. Kim, (2014), 'The Saemangeum Reclamation Project and Politics of Regionalism in South Korea', *Ocean and Coastal Management* 102(PB), 594–603.

CHAPTER 15

MINORITY REPRESENTATION

KYUNGMEE PARK

1. INTRODUCTION

How representatives respond to citizens politically is important for the success of representative democracy (Pitkin 1967). However, newly emerged or marginal issues out of the political mainstream are seldom represented in the political sphere. In this vein, it is not surprising that minority issues such as gender, migration, and generation do not receive the attention of political parties and assemblies.

Interest regarding political minorities in South Korea has yet to grow past the early stage. The 1987 democratisation movement provided opportunities to reform the political corruption of the authoritarian period; however, the issue of political reform was more significant than minority representation. Minority representation, which had been excluded from political arguments until recent times, began to be discussed after the accomplishment of democratic consolidation, but is yet to be sufficiently addressed.

This interest in political minorities stems from the expectation that improving minority representation will transform the political realm of South Korea. Gender studies have indicated that raising the composition of legislatures to 30 per cent female lawmakers (i.e. the critical point) can fundamentally transform the political spectrum (Dahlerup 1988). In 1995, the United Nations Commission on the Status of Women recommended gender quota systems, stating that the percentage of women lawmakers in legislatures should at minimum be 30 per cent. However, parliamentary research regarding New Zealand has shown that even if the percentage of female lawmakers does not reach 30 per cent, the parliamentary processes can still be affected (Grey 2002).

This study found that if the percentage of female lawmakers exceeds 15 per cent, the female members can form a collective voice. These studies have commonly suggested that increases in the number of political minorities, including women, can help minorities to influence political processes.

Minority representation is low in South Korea. The percentage of women lawmakers remains insufficient to fundamentally transform the political realm, and the debate regarding migrant and generational representation remains merely symbolic. Moreover, there was only one migrant representative, and the issue of generational representation has only recently emerged. In the first general election after democratisation in 1987, the proportion of female members was 2 per cent, whereas, as of 2020, this number has increased by approximately ten times to 19 per cent, now exceeding 15 per cent.

Political cleavage has served as a factor hindering the improvement of minority representation. In the debate regarding *democracy versus anti-democracy*, the influence of *regionalism* has been dominant; voters tend to support politicians who were born or raised in their region, as well as parties that have roots in their home regions. The regional identity of candidates and political parties has been more important than their policies or political orientation in voting decisions.

However, after the economic recessions in 1997 and 2008, the cleavages of democracy versus anti-democracy and regionalism have weakened. These two economic crises have highlighted policy issues, such as that of gender, welfare, and generational representation. In particular, due to the controversy regarding the provision of free meals to students in 2000, welfare policies emerged as a crucial issue. Political parties aiming to win elections had little choice but to amend party constitutions and campaign promises to ensure that they include these new issues. More recently, in the 2017 presidential impeachment process, younger people supported the impeachment, while older generations opposed it. This triggered the emergence of generational issues. Over the years, the legislative processes of the National Assembly have begun to reflect these minority issues.

This chapter explores how political minority issues have been discussed in the electoral candidate nomination processes and the legislative process of the National Assembly in South Korea. First, political cleavages are discussed as a structural factor wherein political minorities cannot be represented. Second, we investigate the changes after democratisation in how political parties consider political minorities and their nomination. Third, the representativeness and political behaviour of political minorities in the National Assembly are explored. Finally, the representation of political minorities and the significance of enhanced representativeness in South Korean politics are discussed.

2. Political Cleavage, Minority Representation, and Political Systems

The 1987 democratisation movement served to highlight the cleavage of democracy versus anti-democracy, thereby ending the long military rule. People participated in massive rallies and protests to demand the abolition of indirect presidential elections, which led to the president being elected in a gym, as well as constitutional reform, including a system that would allow direct election of the president. The military government had little choice but to accept these demands, as they faced significant pressure from civil society. Free political competitions began in earnest, starting with the thirteenth presidential election in December 1987 and the thirteenth general election in April 1988.

Although the old military ruling clique, with victories in the presidential and general elections, could stay in power, it did not achieve landslide victories. Under the cleavage of democracy versus anti-democracy, political forces were divided into the conservative forces supporting the old ruling clique and the progressive forces supporting new politics. The thirteenth National Assembly, wherein the opposition parties held the majority of seats, established various special committees for eradicating the illegalities and corruption of the military government and promoted diverse political reforms. In the debates regarding democracy versus anti-democracy, the discussion of minority representation was sidelined.

Voters' support for regional representation was unequivocal because economic development had been focused on the Yeongnam region (the Southeast region) (Lee and Park 2011). The prevailing perception was that the long-time military ruling forces from the Yeongnam region were focused on economic development only in the metropolitan areas and Yeongnam. Therefore, voters from other regions, who were eager to develop their own areas, supported candidates and political parties with roots in their regions. As a result, patterns of regional voting prominently reinforced regional cleavages, while overlapping with the cleavage of democracy versus anti-democracy. The 1997 East Asian economic recession led to increased interest in the provision of social safety nets for those from socially weaker groups in society. However, while focusing on corporate restructuring and economic recovery, the issue of minority representation remained in the background.

Reforming the political system to better include gender representation as one political minority was first discussed after the recommendation of the gender quota system of 30 per cent by the United Nations Commission on the Status of Women in 1995 (cf. United Nations 1995). First, the revised election law in March 2002 specified that all political parties should nominate female candidates as part of their proportional representation lists in the local elections. The election law, which was revised in August 2005, specified the percentage of nominations for female candidates in Article 47(3) and 47(4): 50 per cent of proportional representation candidates for general elections and local elections, and 30 per cent of district representation candidates for electoral districts. In particular, this gender representation system was stabilised institutionally by introducing the zipper system, which insists that only women are nominated for 'odd' number positions on parties' proportional seats list in Article 47(3). The election law has been enforced by invalidating the registration of proportional representation candidates when a party does not follow the nomination proportion and the order of female candidates for proportional seats lists (cf. Article 52(2) of the election law). However, in the case of candidates' nomination for electoral districts, sanctions are not imposed even if the specified percentage is not achieved (cf. Park 2012; Jeon 2013).

On the other hand, political interest regarding migrants was insufficient for establishing a political system which includes them. The increase in international marriages in the 2000s led to increased interest in multicultural families. To ensure social integration, helping married migrants and their children adjust to South Korean society and providing them with educational opportunities became crucial tasks (Jang 2017; Min and Oh 2017). Since the law on multicultural families was first submitted to the National Assembly in May 2007, a total of sixty-nine bills have been proposed thus far, among which only eleven bills have passed (cf. Law and Bills on The National Assembly of the Republic of Korea homepage). As political minorities, migrants face high barriers to becoming members of the National Assembly. Jasmine Lee—a member of the nineteenth National Assembly (2012–2016)—is the only migrant representative in the history of the National Assembly; no other migrants have ever entered the National Assembly.

Generational representation is the most recent issue in terms of minority representation (cf. Park et al. 2018). Issues regarding generational representation emerged during the 2012 presidential election from debates about welfare policies conducted between the progressives and the conservatives regarding *selectivism* versus *universalism*. The conservatives claim that selectivism loses widespread appeal when it is used to restrictively provide welfare benefits to those in the lower-income bracket, based on their conditions and needs. Universalism, which focuses on distributing benefits to all people, has become the dominant paradigm (cf. Shin 2012; Park et al. 2018). Under universalism, not only the socially disadvantaged groups, but all citizens can become welfare recipients.

Candidates and political parties attempting to procure electoral victories are forced to consider the different types of welfare services that are required for each generation. Since the 2012 presidential election, governments have implemented welfare policies for each generation, based on their life cycle. As youth issues attracted national attention, awareness regarding the need for youth representation has increased, and political parties are also becoming interested in nominating young people in the general elections.

In South Korea, gender representation has improved significantly compared to the low interest in migrants and generational representation. According to electoral prospects, debates regarding migrants and generational representation without institutional systems to enforce their entry into the political system continue to be considered as marginal issues by political parties. However, based on the gender quota system, women who have built social and political careers have also entered the National Assembly. Despite the use of this institutional system, gender representation in South Korea is ranked 117th among countries included in the 2020 Inter-Parliamentary Union statistics.

3. Party Nomination for Political Minorities

The electoral system is one factor restricting minority representation (cf. Kim 2007, 2020). For a total of 253 out of 300 seats (84.3 per cent), the candidates who receive the majority of votes based on a first-past-the-post system are elected, whereas 47 seats (15.7 per cent) are elected in the closed proportional lists created by political parties (Article 21(1) in the election law). In this electoral system, political minorities are unlikely to win nominations because parties attempt to increase the number of seats by nominating candidates with positive reputations who are well known among voters. On the other hand, a proportional seat is used for political minorities nominated by the parties aiming to create a reform-centred image that includes considerations regarding political minorities. To improve the party image, parties have recently revised their party constitutions and codes, which also affected candidate nomination processes for elections.

First, the changes in government policies were introduced to tackle gender issues. Gender issues began to be earnestly discussed after the establishment of the Ministry of Gender Equality in 2001. Gender policies have been expanded to include family, child, and youth policies among other issues, and the name of this organisation was changed to the Ministry of Gender Equality and Family in 2005. Over the years, gender issues began to be reflected in the electoral strategies and campaign promises of political parties (Kim 2013). After the introduction of the gender quota system and the revision of the election law, activists from women's organisations who had diverse political experiences were nominated by political parties (Oh et al. 2005).

On the other hand, the issue of migrant representation has not been highlighted (Jang 2017). Although different administrations have established and operated multicultural policies, these policies have not been enforced from the perspective of political parties. They have nominated migrants merely as symbolic figures. Jasmine Lee, who served as the representative for the migrants, was elected on the proportional seat list in the nineteenth general election and remained active in the National Assembly for a period of four years. Eight years later, she became a proportional candidate for a third party in the twenty-first general election of 2020, but she failed to win. With the exception of Jasmine Lee, there have been no cases of migrant representation in the National Assembly.

The fact that Jasmine Lee has been the only migrant representative implies that migration issues are considered marginal issues in the party nomination processes. The nomination of migrants who lack popularity, compared with other candidates, would likely entail high risk for political parties, given the fierce competitions of district elections. Therefore, political parties only consider migrants for a proportional seat if they want to convey a reform-centred image to voters.

In contrast, the issue of generational representation has emerged more recently. This issue has been reflected in government policies after welfare issues were highlighted in campaign promises in the 2000s. The unstable economic situation caused by two economic recessions led to increased awareness about the need for social safety nets. These welfare policies were required to help the elderly who lost their jobs due to corporate restructuring, as well as retired older people. In addition, employment support policies were required to help younger people who faced a shortage of job opportunities. Marriage support and childcare policies also became crucial to addressing reduced marriage and birth rates. In addition to these changes in government policies, the two economic recessions impacted the campaign promises of political parties to gain political support from diverse generations (Lim 2015). Moreover, the 2017 presidential impeachment widened the generational gap. Younger generations were active in the Candlelight rallies to support impeachment, while the older generations attended the so-called *Taegeukgi* rallies, dubbed so because many attendees waved the Korean national flag, to oppose it.

Gender representation has improved due to these government policies, as well as changes in political parties. Table 15.1 presents the percentage of nominated candidates based on gender in the general elections. The percentage of female candidates was only 0.7 per cent before democratisation (1948–1986); however, this number increased by approximately ten times to 10.7 per cent after democratisation. Moreover, female representation has remained at approximately 1/100th of that of male candidates (89.3 per cent).

On some level, democratisation has contributed to the improvement of gender representation. At the beginning of democratisation, female candidates constituted only 1.9 per cent of the total candidates in the four general elections; however, this percentage had almost doubled from that of the percentage before democratisation (0.7 per cent). The percentage of female candidates was 1.3 per cent in the thirteenth general election (1988); 1.8 per cent in the fourteenth general election (1992); decreased to 1.5 per cent in the fifteenth general election (1996); and increased to 3.2 per cent in the sixteenth general election (2000).

The number of female candidates significantly increased after the gender quota system was applied in the seventeenth election (2004). In five general elections, including the seventeenth general election, female candidates increased to 17.0 per cent. The percentage of female candidates was 11.5 per cent in the seventeenth general election (2004); 16.5 per cent in the eighteenth general election (2008); 13.0 per cent in the nineteenth general election (2012); 15.5 per cent in the twentieth general election (2016); and increased to 26.7 per cent in the recent twenty-first general election (2020). The percentage of female candidates increased by eleven times compared with that of the general elections conducted without the gender quota system. The percentage of female candidates in the twenty-first general election was approximately twenty-five times higher than that of the thirteenth general election, which was the first election after democratisation, and approximately two times higher than that of the seventeenth general election, wherein the gender quota system was first introduced. Although

Table 15.1: Candidates by gender (unit: persons)

			Female	Male	Total
Non-democratic period			75	10,806	10,881
			0.7%	99.3%	100.0%
Democratic period	Without gender quotas system	13th	14	1,029	1,043
			1.3%	98.7%	100.0%
		14th	19	1,032	1,051
			1.8%	98.2%	100.0%
		15th	21	1,365	1,386
			1.5%	98.5%	100.0%
		16th	33	1,005	1,038
			3.2%	96.8%	100.0%
		Total	87	4,431	4,518
			1.9%	98.1%	100.0%
	With gender quotas system	17th	156	1,200	1,356
			11.5%	88.5%	100.0%
		18th	215	1,086	1,301
			16.5%	83.5%	100.0%
		19th	142	948	1,090
			13.0%	87.0%	100.0%
		20th	173	919	1,092
			15.8%	84.2%	100.0%
		21st	374	1,028	1,402
			26.7%	73.3%	100.0%
		Total	1,060	5,181	6,241
			17.0%	83.0%	100.0%
	Total		1,147	9,612	10,759
			10.7%	89.3%	100.0%

Source: ROK National Election Commission homepage (http://info.nec.go.kr/main/showDocument.xhtml?electionId=0000000000&topMenuId=CP&secondMenuId=CPRI06), accessed 22 November 2021.

gender representation in the National Assembly of South Korea has improved, it is now just slightly above the critical point determined for New Zealand (15 per cent) (Grey 2002).

The percentage of female candidates is low because gender representation is a marginal issue in party nominations (Park 2008; Jeon 2005; Yoo 2012). Political parties frequently alter candidacy to ensure that it remains advantageous for them and helps them to achieve electoral victories. Although they announce nomination criteria and schedules, including the qualification terms for the candidates, the party leadership often directly nominates its electoral candidates; this act is known as 'strategic nomination'. In the seventeenth general election, wherein nominations based on intra-party candidate elections were widespread, only 20–30 per cent of candidates in electoral districts were elected by intra-party candidate races, whereas the rest were directly appointed by the leaders of these political parties (Jeon 2005).

The electoral nomination by the leaders of political parties may provide an opportunity for female candidates to be nominated and win against male candidates (Kim 2009) because it can be difficult for female candidates to win in the electoral race, wherein male candidates are more likely to dominate. Therefore, political parties have established female-friendly provisions to improve gender representation. Two approaches are used to help elect female candidates as district candidates (Yoo 2012): one such approach is to provide women who are second in the intra-party races with an opportunity to surpass the first candidate by adding 20 per cent to the percentage of affirmative votes; the second approach is to set a target percentage (e.g. 30 per cent) for female candidates nominated for the electoral districts.

The Political Fund Act is also a crucial factor for ensuring that political parties comply with the gender quota system (Park 2012; Jeon 2013). If political parties do not nominate a specific percentage of female candidates in the local elections, the government subsidies provided to them will be reduced by applying Article 52(2) of the election law. In the first (1994) and second (1998) local elections, wherein no gender quota system was introduced, female candidates comprised 2.3 per cent of the total candidates in both elections. In the third local election (2002), wherein the gender quota system began to be applied partially, the percentage of female candidates increased to 3.6 per cent. In the seventh local election (2018), wherein the gender quota system was applied fully, this percentage increased significantly to 18.2 per cent.

On the other hand, migration and generational issues do not tend to be included in the nomination criteria of political parties because political parties are interested in the extent to which the two issues are reflected in their campaign promises. Political parties pay close attention only to the number of seats by nominating candidates who are likely to win the election. This may occur because the candidate's age (i.e. generational representation) is not a crucial issue determining the party nomination.

Table 15.2 presents the number and percentage of candidates based on age group. In the general elections conducted before democratisation, candidates in their forties (39.7 per cent) comprised the highest percentage of candidates, whereas those in their fifties (24.4 per cent) and thirties (24.1 per cent) ran at similar percentages. In the general elections conducted after democratisation, differences were more noted: candidates in their fifties represented the highest percentage of candidates with 40.1 per cent, followed by 29.7 per cent candidates in their forties, 18.2 per cent candidates in their sixties or older, 10.3 per cent candidates in their thirties, and 1.8 per cent of candidates in their twenties.

Table 15.2: Candidates by age group (unit: persons)

		25–29	30s	40s	50s	60s	Total
Non-democratic period		466	2,672	4,400	2,706	831	11,075
		4.2%	24.1%	39.7%	24.4%	7.6%	100.0%
Democratic period	13th	22	130	430	384	77	1,043
		2.1%	12.5%	41.2%	36.8%	7.4%	100.0%
	14th	25	143	289	495	99	1,051
		2.4%	13.6%	27.5%	47.1%	9.4%	100.0%
	15th	7	199	388	596	196	1,386
		0.5%	14.4%	28.0%	43.0%	14.1%	100.0%
	16th	35	134	308	334	227	1,038
		3.3%	12.9%	29.7%	32.2%	21.9%	100.0%
	17th	12	164	524	396	260	1,356
		0.9%	12.1%	38.6%	29.2%	19.2%	100.0%
	18th	17	151	483	447	203	1,301
		1.3%	11.6%	37.1%	34.4%	15.6%	100.0%
	19th	18	36	289	498	249	1,090
		1.7%	3.3%	26.5%	45.7%	22.8%	100.0%
	20th	26	61	233	524	248	1,092
		2.4%	5.6%	21.3%	48.0%	22.7%	100.0%
	21st	27	87	249	638	401	1,402
		1.9%	6.2%	17.8%	45.5%	28.6%	100.0%
	Total	189	1,105	3,193	4,312	1,960	10,759
		1.8%	10.3%	29.7%	40.1%	18.2%	100.0%

Source: ROK National Election Commission.

These changes in the percentage of candidates by age group reflect the changes in the demographic composition. In 2000, South Korea became an 'ageing society', wherein the percentage of people aged sixty-five years or older was 7 per cent or higher of the total population. In 2017, the country became an 'aged society' with more than 14 per cent of the total population constituting people aged sixty-five or older.[1] The age group of candidates for general elections also changed. After the thirteenth general election, the percentage of candidates aged above sixty years continued to increase, whereas that of candidates in their twenties decreased. Candidates in their twenties, 2.1 per cent of the total candidates in the thirteenth general election, were only 0.5 per cent of candidates in the fifteenth general election, then 2.4 per cent in the twentieth general election and 1.9 per cent in the twenty-first general election. By comparison, the percentage of candidates aged above sixty years was 7.4 per cent in the thirteenth general election, 21.9

per cent in the sixteenth general election (approximately three times higher), and 28.6 per cent in the twenty-first general election.

A noteworthy point is that the percentage of candidates in their fifties decreased and those in their forties increased relatively in the thirteenth, sixteenth, seventeenth, and eighteenth general elections. These changes were closely related to the demand in each period for political reform to move forward from the past. First, in the thirteenth election, political parties were more interested in nominating new faces with reformative images, compared with politicians related to the military regime.[2] In the sixteenth general election, a stronger demand for political reform had taken root. Civic groups hit their stride in their anti-nomination campaign to disrupt the nomination and election of some incumbent lawmakers and politicians, thus affecting party nominations. Eventually, among the 115 persons targeted by the civic groups in the anti-nomination campaign, 59 failed to be elected. However, the leaders of civic groups who led this 'civil disobedience' were punished for their illegal electoral campaigns.

The changes in the percentages of the age groups of candidates in the seventeenth and eighteenth general elections were closely related to the impeachment and approval ratings of President Roh Moo-hyun (2003–2007). The seventeenth general election was conducted shortly after the presidential impeachment by the sixteenth National Assembly, wherein the opposition party occupied a majority. The opposition party passed the presidential impeachment bill for violating obligations related to political neutrality. Many citizens conducted large-scale Candlelight rallies every day at Gwanghwamun Square in central Seoul opposing impeachment (cf. Lee et al. 2017; Park 2020). In the seventeenth general election, held a month after the presidential impeachment bill was passed, public opinion against the presidential impeachment affected party nominations. Political parties felt it a political liability to nominate incumbent lawmakers who had passed the presidential impeachment bill. Public opinion criticising the opposition party that led to impeachment ended with the victory of the ruling party, which occupied 50.8 per cent of the seats in the seventeenth National Assembly.

However, the decline of Roh Moo-hyun's presidential approval rating affected party nominations in the eighteenth general election. President Roh's approval rating fell to 5.7 per cent in 2007 (Joongang-ilbo 2006), which was the lowest approval rating of all presidents. Members of the ruling party attempted to erase the relevance of the president by deserting their political colours and forming a new party, thus leading parties to nominate new faces to highlight their reform-centred images.

Amid these rapid political changes, political parties attempted to nominate younger candidates with positive reputations to emphasise their reformative image. As a result, political rookies in their forties were nominated as electoral candidates. However, during the period of political stability, many opportunities were presented for incumbent lawmakers to run for re-election, which increased the age range of the candidates.

4. The Behaviour of Political Minorities in the National Assembly

Although parties and governments have become increasingly interested in minority representation, minorities are still a minority in the National Assembly. As shown in Table 15.3, despite the increase in the number of women incumbents, this percentage remains less than 30 per cent, which is the critical point that can fundamentally transform the political realm. The percentage of female members, which was only 1.9 per cent before democratisation, increased from 2.0 per cent in the thirteenth National Assembly to 19.0 per cent in the twenty-first National Assembly.

The gender quota system increased the percentage of female members in the National Assemblies to 15.7 per cent, approximately five times higher than the percentage before the introduction of the gender quota system. In the sixteenth National Assembly, before the introduction of the gender quota system, the percentage of women incumbent members increased to 6.4 per cent, but this percentage was very small. However, starting from the seventeenth National Assembly, wherein the gender quota system was introduced, the proportion of women exceeded 10 per cent. The percentage of female members in the seventeenth National Assembly was 13 per cent, approximately two times higher than that of the sixteenth National Assembly, and 6.5 times higher than that of the thirteenth National Assembly. After the introduction of the gender quota system, this percentage increased to 13.7 per cent in the eighteenth National Assembly, 15.7 per cent in the nineteenth National Assembly and 17.0 per cent in the twentieth National Assembly. In the twenty-first National Assembly, which started in May 2020, the percentage of female members was the highest thus far at 19.0 per cent, but it remained below the global gender equality average of 25.1 per cent (Inter-Parliamentary Union 2020).

This increase in female members affected the ideological distribution of the National Assembly. In the seventeenth National Assembly, wherein the gender quota system was first applied, the ideology of the female members differed from that of male members in each party (Kim et al. 2007). In a measure of ideology on a 0–10 scale, with 0 being the most progressive, female members (2.91) of the progressive parties were more progressive compared with the male members of the same party (4.5). In addition, female members (6.2) of the conservative parties were more conservative compared with their male counterparts (5.95). Female members were more ideologically extreme than male members of the same parties. However, in the twentieth general election, female candidates in both parties were more conservative compared with the male candidates (Park et al. 2016). This differed from the propensity of female lawmakers in the United States and United Kingdom, who were more progressive, compared with their male counterparts, regardless of party membership (Thomas 1994; Norris and Lovenduski 1995).

Table 15.3: Members in the national assemblies by gender (unit: persons)

			Female	Male	Total
Non-democratic period			50	2,552	2,602
			11.9%	88.1%	100.0%
Democratic period	Without gender quotas system	13th	6	293	299
			2.0%	98.0%	100.0%
		14th	4	295	299
			1.3%	98.7%	100.0%
		15th	11	288	299
			3.7%	96.3%	100.0%
		16th	19	280	299
			6.4%	93.6%	100.0%
		Total	40	1,156	1,196
			3.3%	96.7%	100.0%
	With gender quotas system	17th	39	260	299
			13.0%	87.0%	100.0%
		18th	41	258	299
			13.7%	86.3%	100.0%
		19th	47	253	300
			15.7%	84.3%	100.0%
		20th	51	249	300
			17.0%	83.0%	100.0%
		21st	57	243	300
			19.0%	81.0%	100.0%
		Total	235	1,263	1,498
			15.7%	84.3%	100.0%
	Total		275	2,419	2,694
			10.2%	89.8%	100.0%

Source: ROK National Election Commission.

In addition, the increase in the number of female lawmakers led to changes in the legislative processes of the National Assembly. In the seventeenth National Assembly, female members were increasingly active in legislative activities and standing committees, which comprised a high percentage of female members, and had a tendency to pass bills related to gender issues (Kim 2011). Unlike male members who were interested in policies focused on the elderly, female members actively proposed bills regarding gender and welfare (Kim et al. 2007; Jeon and Kwak 2017). In other words, gender-based differences were noted in the legislative processes. This tendency is similar to those noted in the New Zealand Parliament, wherein a collective effect was achieved when female lawmakers accounted for 14.4 per cent of the total candidates (Grey 2002).

Some studies have also suggested that gender-based differences do not exist in the National Assembly. In the seventeenth and eighteenth National Assemblies, women incumbents of the conservative party were not friendly to gender-related legislation, and only those with experience in civic groups expressed their support for such bills (Kwon 2015; Jeon and Kwak 2017). The attitudes of female members towards gender-related legislation differ based on the parties to which they belong or their individual careers, and no gender-based differences have been noted between female and male lawmakers. In the nineteenth National Assembly, wherein the percentage of female incumbents was above 15 per cent, gender-based differences were unclear (Park and Jin 2017).

In the nineteenth National Assembly, with only one migrant representative, political interest in migration-related laws was not high. The need for increased migration representation is only identified by the political activities of Jasmine Lee. During her four-year term, she was active in the National Assembly and proposed 686 bills. Among them, she was involved in proposing 644 bills and tabled 42 bills as the chief sponsor. Of the 42 bills she proposed, many were related to migrants, women, and the youth, and 16 (38.1 per cent) of them were reflected in governmental policies.

Female lawmakers were more interested in migration issues, compared with male lawmakers. In the seventeenth National Assembly, women incumbents were active in proposing the Multicultural Families Support Act and the Foreign Workers Employment Act (Min and Oh 2017). In addition, in the eighteenth and nineteenth National Assemblies, female members actively initiated the Multicultural Families Support Act (Jang 2017).

In addition, the issue of generational representation has yet to be sufficiently addressed in the National Assembly. As shown in Table 15.4, after democratisation, the percentage of incumbents in their fifties (49.8 per cent) surpassed the critical point of 30 per cent. Members in their forties (25.4 per cent) and those in their sixties (21.0 per cent) shared a similar percentage; only a few members were in their thirties (3.7 per cent) and twenties (0.1 per cent). People who wish to become political candidates must be above twenty-five years of age. Young adults in their twenties and thirties do not have sufficient time to build their political careers and be elected as members of the National Assemblies.

This age profile is closely related to the electoral characteristics of South Korea, wherein approximately one-half of the incumbent lawmakers are defeated in every election. In the twenty-first general election that was conducted in 2020, 115 incumbent lawmakers (38.3 per cent) won re-election and only 149 incumbents (49.5 per cent), including the aforementioned 115 incumbent lawmakers, won a second term or more. The remaining 151 incumbents (50.3 per cent) are all first-time lawmakers. In South Korea, wherein the change rate of members of the National Assembly is high, political parties seek to win elections with high support rates by nominating well-known

Table 15.4: Members in the national assemblies by age group (unit: persons)

		25–29	30s	40s	50s	60s	Total
Non-democratic period		12	346	992	620	185	2,155
		0.5%	16.1%	46.0%	28.8%	8.6%	100.0%
Democratic period	13th	1	17	111	138	32	299
		0.3%	5.7%	37.1%	46.2%	10.7%	100.0%
	14th	0	8	70	179	42	299
		0.0%	2.7%	23.4%	59.9%	14.0%	100.0%
	15th	0	10	69	162	58	299
		0.0%	3.3%	23.1%	54.2%	19.4%	100.0%
	16th	0	13	65	106	89	273
		0.0%	4.8%	23.8%	38.8%	32.6%	100.0%
	17th	0	23	106	121	49	299
		0.0%	7.6%	35.5%	40.5%	16.4%	100.0%
	18th	0	7	88	142	62	299
		0.0%	2.3%	29.5%	47.5%	20.7%	100.0%
	19th	0	9	80	142	69	300
		0.0%	3.0%	26.7%	47.3%	23.0%	100.0%
	20th	1	2	50	161	86	300
		0.3%	0.6%	16.7%	53.7%	28.7%	100.0%
	21st	2	11	38	177	72	300
		0.6%	3.7%	12.7%	59.0%	24.0%	100.0%
	Total	4	100	677	1,328	559	2,668
		0.1%	3.7%	25.4%	49.8%	21.0%	100.0%

Source: ROK National Election Commission.

political rookies. As a result, they are interested in nominating candidates in their fifties, who have built their social reputation and careers.

However, the percentage of candidates in their fifties was low in the thirteenth and seventeenth National Assemblies. In contrast, the percentage of the incumbents in their forties exceeded 30 per cent in both the thirteenth (37.1 per cent) and seventeenth (35.5 per cent) National Assemblies, and, as a result, the influence of younger people relatively increased. The reason for the increase in candidates in their forties was related to political changes because many candidates who were related to the military government were defeated electorally and new faces were elected in the thirteenth National Assembly. In addition, in the seventeenth National Assembly, the opposition party's incumbents who supported Roh Moo-hyun's impeachment were defeated, and new politicians in their forties who had been nominated by the ruling party received the advantage in the electoral campaign.

In the National Assembly, wherein a significant number of candidates are in their fifties, some differences based on age groups were noted in the attitudes towards the legislative processes (Seo and Park 2009; Lee 2016). Younger lawmakers were increasingly active in proposing new legislation. In addition, young first-term lawmakers are active in proposing legislation focused on the issues of political minorities, such as multicultural families and the employment of migrant workers (Min and Oh 2017).

However, the older generation is relatively passive towards bill proposals, yet has more significant impact on the legislative processes. The bills proposed by senior members are increasingly likely to be passed at standing committees and plenary sessions, compared to that of young and junior members (Oh 2014). Senior members also have a significant impact in terms of passing contentious bills, primarily due to the fact that party leaders are typically aged over fifty and they are leading their parties and candidate nominations in the next elections. Therefore, incumbent lawmakers are forced to consider the nomination process and their re-election prospects, and thus follow the party platform and the decision of party leaders in the processes of dealing with contentious bills.

In recent years, generational representation has emerged as a political variable due to generational conflicts surrounding welfare policies because the controversy regarding welfare recipients has increased as the government welfare services have expanded. Elderly people are in favour of welfare spending, whereas younger people, who have to wait for a long time before they can receive welfare benefits, do not actively support such policies (Park et al. 2018). Younger people, who refer to themselves as the *sampo* generation (the generation that has given up on courtship, marriage, and childbirth), do not approve extending the age of retirement or the old-age pension, while supporting youth allowances. On the other hand, the retired old people have negative perceptions regarding the younger people's attitudes towards employment and culture. In this situation, political parties led by the elderly age group tend to nominate young candidates to receive support from the younger generation.

5. Conclusion

After democratisation, political minorities began to receive attention; however, this did not affect their status as political minorities. Only gender representation has improved to a significant extent. The gender quota system has significantly contributed to enhancing gender representation through the nomination of female candidates. However, migrants have yet to be considered as a subject for social integration, and their representation has remained at a merely symbolic level. Issues regarding generational representation have emerged in an effort to resolve generational conflicts, and have affected the legislative processes of the National Assembly and the political decisions of governments.

To improve minority representation, the introduction of appropriate political systems is required. Gender representation, driven by the gender quota system, has led to changes in the legislative processes of the National Assembly. The gender quota system forces parties to nominate female candidates by establishing the nomination criteria to provide women with privileges. Although the percentage of female candidates has remained below 30 per cent, the critical point, the status of female politicians has been considerably elevated in the political arena.

For migrants who do not have institutional systems to improve their representation, the policy decisions that reflect the multicultural environment in South Korean society are required. The number of married migrants increases by approximately 150,000 every year, and the number of foreigners staying in South Korea continues to increase (Statistics Korea homepage 2020). The increased number of migrants has weakened the South Korean people's exclusive attitude towards foreigners in South Korean society, which is homogenous, and has thus led to increased acceptance towards migrants and diverse cultures. Awareness regarding multicultural policies and foreign employment policies is high. However, on the political side, migrant representation is discussed marginally, at a merely symbolic level.

Generational representation has recently emerged as a political issue, and its importance is expected to increase. It is deeply related to the fact that changes in industrial structure caused by technological development have dismantled the employment system, thereby resulting in increased economic anxiety. The generational conflict regarding the question 'For whom is limited government finance intended to be spent?' is affecting the government's policy decisions. The younger generation demands welfare budgets for various youth-centric issues, such as employment, marriage, and parenting, whereas the older generation has expressed the need for economic stability and medical services after retirement. As different generations demand different kinds of financial support, they are coming into conflict with one another, based on differences in their political orientation. Rallies with divergent opinions conducted at Gwanghwamun Square have highlighted the significance of perceptions regarding the generational gap.

In South Korea and its consolidated democratic system, minority representation has been not debated in the political realm in earnest. The reasons why gender, migrants, and generational issues must be addressed, as well as how to discuss them, are yet to be tackled in the political arena. Political parties have treated these issues merely as campaign promises and policies; they are not yet seriously discussed. However, in the future, interest regarding minority representation is expected to increase, and social consensus on this will help to further develop South Korean democracy.

Notes

1. Life expectancy increased to 62.3 years in 1970, 66.2 years in 1980, 71.7 years in 1990, 70.6 years in 2000, and 80.2 years in 2010. According to the recent census of 2018, life expectancy was 82.7 years old.
2. The younger generation was active during democratisation. The 'Sampallyuk saedae (386 Generation)' was the representative generation during democratisation. The name 'Sampallyuk saedae' is based on their age (thirties), the decade during which they attended

university (the 1980s), and the decade during which they were born (the 1960s). They are now called the 'Opallyuk saedae (586 Generation)' because they are currently in their fifties.

Bibliography

Dahlerup, D. (1988), 'From a Small to a Large Minority'. *Scandinavian Political Studies* 11(4), 275–298.

Grey, S. (2002), 'Does Size Matter?', *Parliamentary Affairs* 55(1), 19–29.

Inter-Parliamentary Union (2020), 'Global and Regional Averages of Women in National Parliaments', http://archive.ipu.org/wmn-e/world-arc.htm, accessed 22 November 2021.

Jang, I. (2017), 'Ijujeongchaek-ui ibeophyeonhyeohwang bal-uija teukseong' [The Current Situation of Migration Policy and Characteristics of Proposer], *Contemporary Society and Multiculture* 7(1), 48–76.

Jeon, Y. (2005), 'Hubogongcheongwajeong-ui minjuhwa-wa keu jeonchijeok gyeolgwa' [Democratisation of Candidate Selection in Korean Parties and Its Implication], *Korean Political Science Review* 39(2), 217–236.

Jeon, J. (2013), 'Kukheo-uiwon yeoseonghaldangjea chaetaek-ui jeongchijeok dongin bunseok' [Political Dynamics of Adopting Gender Quota in Korea], *Korean Politics Studies* 22(1), 29–52.

Jeon, J., and Kwak, J. (2017), 'Kukwe-uiwon-ui jeongchaekjjeok gwansim-ui seongcha bunseok' [Gender Gap of Parliamentary Members' Policy Interest], *Korean Politics Studies* 26(2), 105–127.

Joongang-ilbo (2006), 'Roh daetongryon jijido, yeokdae daetongryong joong choiak girok' [The Support Rate of President Roh, the Lowest Record among All Presidents], https://news.joins.com/article/2529271, accessed 22 November 2021.

Kim, H. C. (2007), 'Honhabsik seongeojaedofo-ui byunwha-wa jeongchijeok hyokwa' [A Comparative Analysis in New Zealand, Japan and S. Korea], *Civil Society & NGO* 5(1), 205–240.

Kim, M. (2009), '18dae chongseon-e natanan yeoseongjeongchi-in-ui chung-won' [The Recruitment of Female Politicians in the 18th Congressional Election], *Social Science Studies* 17(1), 50–82.

Kim, M. (2011), 'Hanguk kukwe-uiwon-ui jeongchae-useonsun-wi-e natanan gender cha-" [The Gender Difference in Policy Priorities of South Korean Legislators], *Korean Politics Studies* 20(3), 109–136.

Kim, E. (2013), '2010 jibangseongeo-e natanan yeoseonggong-yak bunseok' [An Analysis on the Manifest on Women in the 2010 Local Election], *Journal of Legislative Studies* 40, 5–35.

Kim, H. C., (2020), 'Joonyeondongjea biraedaepyojea-ui jeongchijeok hyokwa' [The Political Effects of the Semi-Mixed Member Proportional Representation System in Korea], *The Korean Area Studies Review* 38(2), 79–100.

Kim, W., Lee, H., and Kim, E. K. (2007), 'Yeoseong-ui-won-i gukwereul byeonhwasikineunga?' [Do Women Change the National Assembly?], *Korean Party Studies Review* 6(1), 27–54.

Kwon, S. H. (2015), 'Yeoseongjeonchaek beob-an-e daehan je17·18dae kukwe-uiwon tupyohangtae bunseok' [Differences of Legislative Voting Behaviour in Women's Policy Bills], *Korean Women's Studies* 31(4), 331–366.

Lee, H. S. (2016), 'Uiwondeul-e beob-an bal-ui hangtae bunseok' [Explaining Korean Representatives' Sponsorship Behavior], *Dispute Resolution Studies Review* 14(1), 161–188.

Lee, K. Y., and Park, K. (2011), 'Jiyeokbaljeongwa ji-yeokjeok jeongdangtupyo' [Regional Development and Regional Party Voting], *Social Science Studies* 19(2), 138–171.

Lee, H., Lee, J., and Seo, B. (2017), '"Chotbul" "Matbul" jipheo-e daehan taedo-wa 19dae daeseon' [Effects of the Attitudes toward the Candlelight Protest and the Counter-Protest on Voting Behaviour in the 2017 Presidential Election], *Journal of Contemporary Politics* 10(2): 43–75.

Lim, Y. (2015), 'Jeongdangjeongchi-wa hanguk bokjijeongchi—ui jeonwan' [Party Competition in Pension Reform and Transformation of Welfare Politics in South Korea], *Korean Party Studies Review* 14(1), 5–35.

Min, T. E., and Oh, H. J. (2017), 'Hanguk damunhwa-eu ibbeophyeonwang' [Legislators Bills on Multicultural Policy in the National Assembly], *Journal of Multicultural Society* 10(1), 97–125.

Norris, P., and Lovenduski, J. (1995), *Political Recruitment* (Cambridge: Cambridge University Press).

Oh, H. J. (2014), 'Beop-an-e ttareun jeongdangwa sang-im-wi-wonhwe-ui ibbeop yeonghangryeok' [Influence of Party and Standing Committees on Law-Making Decision in Korean National Assembly], *Korean Party Studies Review* 13(1), 155–180.

Oh, M., Kim, K., and Kim, M. (2005), 'Hanguk jeongdang-ui yeoseonggukhwe huboja gongcheongwa hanguk-ui yeoseongjeongchi' [Female Candidate Nomination by Political Parties in South Korea], *Korean Political Science Review* 39(2), 369–397.

Park, K. (2008), '18dae chongseon-ui gongchungwa jeongdangjojik' [Party Nomination and Organization in the 18th General Election], *Korean Party Studies Review* 7(2), 41–63.

Park, K. (2012), 'Yeoseonghaldangjea-ui jeokyong yoin yeongu' [An Exploratory Study on the Factors of Gender-Quotas Application], *Legislative Review* 18(3), 73–101.

Park, K. (2020), '2017nyeon tanhackjeonkuk ihoo seadae byunwhawa jeongdanchaeje' [Generational Change and Party System after the 2017 Presidential Impeachment], *Journal of Social Science* 46(3), 1–25.

Park, S., and Jin, Y. (2017), 'Gukhwe yeoseong-ui-won-ui yeoseong gwanryeon uije-e daehan tupyohangtae' [Voting Behavior of Women Legislators on Women-Related Bills], *21st Century Political Science Review* 27(2), 111–136.

Park, Y., Kim, M., Park, W., Kang, S., and Koo, B. S. (2016), 'Je20dae gukhwe-ui-won dangseonja mit huboja-ui inyeomseonghangkwa jeongchaektaedo' [Ideology and Policy Positions of the Candidates and the Elects in the 20th Korean National Assembly], *Legislative Review* 22(3), 118–158.

Park, K., Sohn, B. K., Jeong, H., and Yoo, S. (2018), 'Hanguk bokjijedo jiji-ui sedaebyeol cha-" [Generational Differences in Korean Welfare Institutions Supports], *Dispute Resolution Studies Review* 16(2), 71–98.

Pitkin, H. F. (1967), *The Concept of Representation* (Berkeley, CA: University of California Press).

Seo, H., and Park, K. (2009), '17dae gukhwe ui-wonbal-ui bup-an-ui gagyeol yo-in bukseok' [An Analysis on Passage of the Legislators' Bills], *Korean Political Science Review* 43(2), 89–111.

Shin, K. Y. (2012), 'Hyundae hankook-ui bokjijeongchiwa bokjidamron' [The Welfare Politics and Welfare Discourse in Contemporary Korea], *Economy & Society* 95, 39–66.

Statistics Korea homepage. (2020). Available from: https://kosis.kr/statisticsList/statisticsListIndex.do?menuId=M_01_01&vwcd=MT_ZTITLE&parmTabId=M_01_01&outLink=Y&entrType=, accessed 22 November 2021.

The National Assembly of the Republic of Korea homepage, https://likms.assembly.go.kr/bill/main.do, accessed 22 November 2021.

Thomas, S. (1994), *How Women Legislate* (New York: Oxford University Press).

United Nations (1995), 'Report of the Fourth World Conference on Women', Beijing, 4–15 September.

Yoo, S. (2012), '19dae chongseongwa yeoseong daepyoseong' [19th Congressional Election and Gender Representation], *East and West Studies* 24(3), 207–229.

CHAPTER 16

ELECTIONS AND ELECTORAL SYSTEMS

WOOJIN MOON

1. INTRODUCTION

THIS chapter explains how the electoral system in South Korea has formed into a two-party-dominated system and identifies the elements that prevent a third party from winning seat shares proportional to its vote share. Although South Korea has adopted a variant of a parallel voting system that combines single-member district seats and proportional representation seats, the South Korean electoral system is not much different from a plurality system because the district seats account for more than 80 per cent of the total seats. Due to the paucity of proportional representation seats, even if a third party wins around 10 per cent of the vote, its maximum seat share amounts to only two per cent of the total seats.

The South Korean electoral system generates campaign strategies similar to those that arise in the typical plurality system. Given that the plurality system involves electing only one candidate from a district, candidates need to appeal to overarching values or interests. Instead of presenting clear and articulate policies, they focus on fabricating and advertising images of themselves as politicians that can boost the regional or national economy, as well as deliver regional benefits and constituency services. Negative campaigning and mudslinging have also pervaded. When a candidate needs to present an ideological policy position, they try to convert their policy into valances that appear to benefit as many people as possible.

There are two major political issues over which political parties compete and citizens make voting decisions. Unlike most Western European countries, redistributive issues have not been salient in South Korea. Although redistributive issues have recently become more salient (see Chapter 18), electoral competition has long revolved around inter-Korean issues. The socio-economic status of citizens does not significantly affect their political attitudes and partisan support. Instead, citizens are divided more by generation, as different generations have been exposed to different levels of anti-communism. Regional voting is another feature that characterises electoral competition in South Korea. The lack of party system polarisation has caused regionalism to be a factor in citizens' voting decisions.

This chapter is organised as follows. In the following section, the changes to the electoral system and how they affected the formation of the two-party-dominant system are explained. Next, this chapter addresses the characteristic features of political parties' campaign strategies and the voting behaviour of citizens. In the penultimate section, the causes of regional voting and its variations in terms of party system polarisation are introduced, before the final section concludes the chapter.

2. Electoral Systems and Party Systems

After its democratisation, South Korea adopted a parallel voting system, which combined single-member district (SMD) seats and proportional representation (PR) seats. As presented in Table 16.1, the electoral system went through several reforms in attempts to improve proportionality. The 1988 general election to select the thirteenth National Assembly was held under a system that elected 224 SMD members and 75 PR members. In this system, each voter casted a single vote for a district candidate, and 75 PR seats were allocated according to the district seat share of each party that won at least five district seats. To help the largest party secure a majority, this system assigned 50 per cent of the PR seats to the party that won a plurality of the vote.

Although the provision for advantaging the plurality party was repealed, beginning with the fourteenth National Assembly election, South Korean electoral systems have had several elements that have contributed to reinforcing the two-party system. The electoral systems used for the thirteenth and fourteenth assembly elections allocated seats based on seat share (Kim and Chang 2017). Because there is no chance for a small party to win a seat if it does not have concentrated support within a district or multiple districts, its seat share is lower than its vote share. Thus, the method of allocating PR seats based on district seat share provides small parties with a very low chance of winning a PR seat.

In the parallel voting system used in the general elections of 1996 and 2000 for the fifteenth and sixteenth National Assemblies, respectively, the allocation method based on seat share was repealed (Kim and Chang 2017). Starting with the fifteenth National Assembly election, PR seats were allocated according to the district vote share of each party that won at least five district seats or 3 per cent of the total district votes (Kim and Chang 2017). However, the voting rule that only allowed each voter to cast one vote for a district candidate remained intact (Kim and Chang 2017). Because voters know that the chance for a small party candidate to win an SMD seat is almost nil, they strategically support a major party candidate, so as not to waste their votes. Therefore, the resulting district vote share of a small party is lower than its actual support. Thus,

Table 16.1: Electoral systems of South Korea since 1987

Assembly	PR seats/total seats	Legal threshold	Allocation method	Other rules
21st (2020)	47/300	Vote share of at least 3 per cent	Party list vote share	Mixed member semi-PR system First stage: allocate seats to each party by (list vote share × 300 − district seats)/2; total seats to be allocated in the first stage are adjusted to thirty seats Second stage: (list vote share × 17) Third stage: sum the two types of seats obtained in the two stages
17th (2004)–20th (2016)	20th: 47/299 19th: 54/299 18th: 54/300 17th: 56/300	At least five seats or vote share of at least 3 per cent	Party list vote share	Parallel two-vote system
15th (1996)–16th (2000)	16th: 46/273 15th: 46/299	At least five seats or vote share of at least 5 per cent	District vote share	Parallel one-vote system One seat to the party with 3–5 per cent of vote share
14th (1992)	62/299	At least five seats	District seat share	Parallel one-vote system One seat to the party with more than 3 per cent of vote share
13th (1988)	75/299	At least five seats	District seat share	Parallel one-vote system Winning party premium 50 per cent of seats to the plurality party with less than 50 per cent of vote share

the parallel one-vote systems that allocated seats disadvantaged small parties. Even worse for small parties was the decrease in the number of PR seats in the fifteenth and sixteenth general elections. The proportion of PR seats decreased from 25.1 per cent in the thirteenth National Assembly to 16.9 per cent in the sixteenth National Assembly. Thus, the new electoral rules did not improve the chances for small parties to win seats.

On 19 July 2001, the Constitutional Court ruled that allocating PR seats based on district vote share is unconstitutional because the allocation of PR seats according to district vote shares without holding a separate PR election violates the principle of direct representation (Kim and Chang 2017). Starting with the seventeenth National Assembly election in 2004, each voter cast two votes: one for a candidate and the other for a party. In this system, PR seats are allocated based on the party list vote share to parties that won more than five seats or 3 per cent of the total district votes (Kim and Chang 2017). The new system gives small parties a greater chance to win PR seats than the old systems. Voters now support the party they prefer in party list voting, or even divide their votes to support a small party. Under this system, the Democratic Labor Party (DLP) was able to win ten seats, thus ending the South Korean party configuration in which there was no main leftist party.

However, the new electoral system remained highly advantageous to the two major parties. The number of PR seats shrank from fifty-six to forty-seven under the new system. Because the number of PR seats was too small compared to that of SMD seats, seat allocation under the new system was highly disproportionate. Given that the number of PR seats was only forty-seven, a list vote share of 10 per cent enabled a small party to win a maximum of five seats, which represents less than 2 per cent of the total seats. In the seventeenth National Assembly election, the DLP only won 3.3 per cent of the total seats, despite winning 12.9 per cent of the list votes.

In recognition of the fact that the electoral system remained biased towards the two major parties, the DLP consistently demanded electoral reform to increase the proportionality of the electoral system. The Justice Party (JP), a descendent of the DLP, insisted upon the adoption of the mixed-member PR system used in Germany (Moon 2020). In December 2019, the ruling Democratic Party of Korea (DPK), the JP, and small splinter parties from the centrist People Party passed an electoral reform bill to adopt a mixed-member, semi-PR system (Moon 2020). During the negotiation process, the coalition partners initially agreed upon increasing the number of PR seats to seventy-five (Moon 2020). However, the new system ultimately left the composition of the two types of seats intact: 253 SMD seats versus 47 PR seats. The previous legal threshold of 3 per cent of party list votes was maintained (Moon 2020).

As demonstrated in Table 16.1, the new hybrid system uses an unintuitive multi-stage allocation method. In the first stage, party i's first stage list seat share (L_i) is computed by multiplying party i's list vote share to the total of 300 seats, then subtracting the number of district seats (D_i) from L_i. If $D_i > L_i$ the party receives no PR seat. Thus, a major party that performs strongly in the SMD election could receive no PR seats in this stage. The list votes cast to the major party will be wasted if the party wins no PR seats. By contrast, this method is advantageous for small parties that fail to win a district seat because D_i is 0 for these parties. In the second stage, P_i is computed by dividing $(L_i - D_i)$ by 2. In the third stage, if $\sum_{i=1}^{n} P_i$ is greater than 30, multiply P_i by some number α such that $\sum_{i=1}^{n} \alpha P_i$ is 30. The reason for the third-stage adjustment is to leave seventeen PR seats to be allocated to the large parties that did not receive any PR seats in the first stage. Finally, in the fourth stage, the remaining seventeen seats are allocated according to each party's list vote share.

The Unified Future Party (UFP), the major opposition party, opposed this reform because they were concerned that it could cause them to lose several seats to small parties (Moon 2020). The UFP proclaimed that if the new system were to be adopted, it would create a satellite party that put forth candidates only for the PR seats. When the new system was adopted, the UFP followed through on this promise by forming the Future Korea Party (FKP). The DPK criticised the UFP's creation of this satellite party, but it followed the same strategy by creating its own satellite party, Civil Together (CT). The DPK and the UFP candidates only ran in single-member districts, while their satellite parties, the FKP and CT, put forward candidates only for the PR seats.

Before the DPK made its satellite party, the JP hoped to take advantage of the new system by winning the party list votes of the DPK supporters, who would strategically support the JP with the knowledge that their list votes for the DPK could be wasted under the new system (Moon 2020). However, the JP's hope was shattered by the DPK's creation of the satellite party that absorbed the DPK supporters' strategic votes that were expected to be cast for the JP. South Korean voters, who had grown tired of stalemates in the twentieth National Assembly, delivered unexpected levels of support to the DPK. The government party ended up winning a landslide victory, taking 180 of 300 seats; the JP could not increase its number of seats by even one. The allocation of the seats under the new electoral system turned out to be the same as that of the previous parallel voting system. Ironically, the new system, which was designed to foster the development of a multiparty system, ultimately reinforced the two-party system in the twenty-first National Assembly.

If the two major parties had not created satellite parties, the JP would have won more than ten seats because the JP won 9.8 per cent of the list votes. Assuming that the number of district seats won by the two major parties would not change without their satellite parties, the JP would have won twelve seats if it obtained about 10 per cent of the list votes. For the JP to win the status of a 'negotiation group' with twenty seats,[1] it must garner at least 20 per cent of the list votes. However, it is not feasible for the JP to win 20 per cent of the list votes because this would require at least 10 per cent of the DPK voters to strategically support the JP. Given that there exist other liberal parties that hold similar ideological positions to the DPK, the DPK supporters' strategic votes are expected to be dispersed to several parties. Unless the number of PR seats is considerably increased, the probability that the new system can create a multiparty system is low.

Figure 16.1 displays the effective number of elective parties (ENEP) and the effective number of parliamentary parties (ENPP). The average ENEP and ENPP since the thirteenth assembly are 3.55 and 2.59, respectively. Given that the average ENEP and ENPP of democracies with a plurality system are, respectively, 3.30 and 2.40 (Powell 2000), South Korea's electoral system yields an almost equivalent number of parties as a plurality system. Figure 16.1 does not show an increasing pattern for ENEP or ENPP, despite the fact that there have been several electoral reforms aiming to improve proportionality. The reason for the maintenance of the two-party system is that there has been no substantial change in electoral rules. Each rule change to improve proportionality is offset by some change in another rule to protect the advantage of the major parties. For example, when the major parties adopted a more proportional allocation method, they also decreased the number of PR seats to compensate for their loss of seats from the change in allocation method.

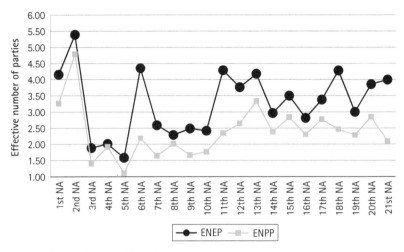

FIGURE 16.1: The effective number of parties

Note: 'NA' in the figure is the abbreviation for the National Assembly election.

3. Campaign Strategies and Voters' Political Attitudes

Stokes (1963) categorises political issues into two types: position issues and valence issues. Position issues, exemplified by the degree of government intervention in the economy, 'involve advocacy of government actions from a set of alternatives over which a distribution of voter preferences is defined' (Stokes 1963: 373). Meanwhile, valence issues 'involve the linking of the parties with some condition that is positively or negatively valued by the electorate' (Stokes 1963: 373). Incumbents thrive in campaigns focusing on their positive valences, such as personal performance, experience, and services, whereas challengers capitalise on exploiting the incumbent's negative valences, such as poor performance, neglect of the district, or personal lapses.

In most West European countries, the most salient position issues have been redistributive issues, such as welfare expansion or tax increases (Huber and Inglehart 1995). However, inter-Korean issues have dominated redistributive issues in South Korea due to the division between North and South Korea, the experience of the Korean War, and forty years of authoritarian rule, during which the population was indoctrinated with anti-communist ideology (Moon 2018a). Following democratisation, the conservative parties continued to appeal to anticommunist sentiment, preventing other issues from becoming more salient (Moon 2018a). President Kim Dae-jung presented the 'Sunshine Policy' to soften North Korea's attitudes towards the South by encouraging interaction with and economic assistance to North Korea (Moon 2018a). Inter-Korean summits in 2000 and 2007 greatly weakened the anti-communist fervour during the liberal regimes. However, the deterioration of inter-Korean relations after these regimes, the development of nuclear weapons by North Korea, and the conservative regimes' use of McCarthyism in a renewed 'Red Scare' restored anti-communist sentiment (Moon 2018a).

Figure 16.2 shows South Korean people's preferences regarding the inter-Korean relationship and welfare expansion. The black solid line represents the proportion of citizens who oppose humanitarian aid to North Korea, while the black dashed line represents the proportion of citizens who support such aid. The two lines show that the two types of citizens were evenly divided when President Roh Moo-hyun was elected in the sixteenth election. However, conservative citizens opposing aid continued to outnumber liberal citizens, except for during the seventh local election, which was held 23 days after President Moon Jae-in and North Korea state chairman Kim Jong-un met in a historic summit in 2018. However, the good feelings towards North Korea did not last long. Two years later in 2020, hawks over inter-Korean issues again outnumbered doves. Figure 16.2 also displays the distribution of preferences regarding welfare issues. The grey solid line represents the proportion of citizens who oppose welfare expansion, whereas the proportion of welfare expansion supporters is indicated by the grey dashed line. The figure shows that liberal preferences have always outnumbered conservative preferences on welfare issues.

Given that the preferences over the two issues are asymmetrically distributed, the campaign strategies of the two major parties should differ. Specifically, it is advantageous for the conservative party to target inter-Korean issues, while it is beneficial for the liberal party to highlight welfare issues. The conservative parties have attempted to bring inter-Korean issues to the forefront and conjuring up a 'Red Scare' has been a

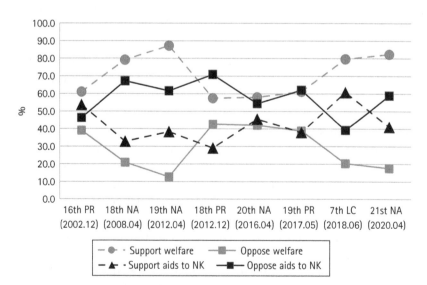

FIGURE 16.2: Citizens' preferences on the two major issues in South Korea (%)

Note: Voters' opinions during the seventeenth PR election are not included because the data are not available.

typical campaign strategy. However, the liberal party did not actively attempt to make welfare issues salient until the 2010 local elections, in which the liberal opposition party pledged universal and free social welfare (Yang 2020: 430).

'NA', 'PR' and 'LC' in the figure are the respective abbreviations for National Assembly, presidential and local elections.

The liberal party was unable to make welfare issues a prominent part of its campaign agenda for several reasons. In a plurality system in which districts elect a single candidate, candidates must garner as many votes as possible. Thus, the plurality system motivates candidates to avoid position issues that can alienate voters. Instead, candidates focus on valence issues that constituents commonly like. In South Korea, candidates typically advertise their ability to develop the national or regional economy or provide their district with constituency services, while highlighting their connections with powerful leaders. School ties, regional ties, family ties, and personal traits such as integrity, legislative experience, and educational background are the most common valences on which candidates try to capitalise.

When candidates need to put position issues on the campaign agenda, they attempt to convert these position issues into valence issues. International issues can easily be transformed into valence issues because it is easy to fabricate a framework of internal friends versus external foes. Because inter-Korean issues are related to national security, the issues can effectively divide friends and foes. People are more likely to rally around security issues than economic issues because the former is perceived as a matter of life and death, while the latter is perceived as a matter of pursuing a better life.[2] The conservative party has often pushed the liberal party into a corner by asking them to clarify whether North Korea is a friend or a foe. It has also attempted to exploit the 'Red Scare' tactic by exaggerating the chance of a nuclear attack by North Korea.

By contrast, converting welfare policies into a valence issue is more difficult than doing so for inter-Korean issues because it is more difficult to identify an external foe with welfare policies. Nevertheless, the conservative and liberal parties have, respectively, set up their frameworks to convert welfare policies into valence issues: trickle-down or waterfall economics for the conservative parties versus trickle-up or fountain economics for the liberal parties. The former, based on supply-side economics, posits that reducing taxes on businesses and the wealthy would stimulate business investment in the short term and benefit society at large in the long term. The latter, based on Keynesian economics, states that policies that benefit the middle class and the working class will boost the productivity of society at large, and that the benefit will 'trickle up' to the wealthy. In trickle-down economics, welfare reduction is suggested to benefit all, whereas in trickle-up economics, welfare expansion is expected to make everybody better off. In the United States, the Republican Party has advocated for the former, whereas the Democratic Party has advocated for the latter (Moon 2018a).

In South Korea, Lee Myung-bak, a successful former businessman and Seoul mayor, promoted trickle-down economics during the campaign for the seventeenth presidential election in 2007 (Moon 2018a). He attacked the two previous liberal governments with slogans, accusing them of amateurism that caused ten years of economic recession. He successfully revived the authoritarian regime's developmentalist ideology that economic development is more important than economic equality (Moon 2018a). The conservative Grand National Party (GNP) pointed to Venezuela as a case in which welfare populism destroyed the economy. Under these circumstances, bringing up welfare issues would have been risky for the liberal party at that time.

Lee Myung-bak proposed the 747 Plan that pledged 7 per cent economic growth, raising the per capita gross domestic product (GDP) to US $40,000 and making Korea the world's seventh-largest economy. His campaign strategy focusing on economic growth worked well. Lee won a landslide victory, despite the emergence of the BBK scandal during the campaign.[3] The Lee administration repealed the gross real estate holding tax and reduced both income and corporate tax rates. However, the trickle-down effect was not realised. His administration recorded a GDP growth rate of 3.2 per cent, the lowest since democratisation.[4] Lee's policies based on trickle-down economics led South Korea to have 'the second-largest income gap among OECD [Organisation for Economic Co-operation and Development] member states, next only to the United States' (Yang 2020: 430). The growing income inequality provided circumstances in which not only liberal, but also conservative parties needed to capitalise on welfare issues.

Both the liberal and conservative parties pledged to provide greater social welfare in the eighteenth presidential election in 2012. The conservative Saenuri Party (SP) candidate, Park Geun-hye, pledged to provide universal social welfare benefits, including an increase in the monthly basic old-age pension benefit, free health care for four major diseases, and free childcare for all children aged five or under (Yang 2020: 430). Worrying that the rich would complain about this welfare expansion, the SP did not forget the strategy of converting welfare issues into valence issues. The Saenuri Party scrupulously dubbed its welfare programmes economic 'democratisation' to add a positive connotation. Park Geun-hye leveraged nostalgia for the administration of her father, Park Chung-hee, whom most South Koreans believe contributed substantially to the remarkable economic development that occurred during his reign. She took full advantage of the halo effect revolving around her father and won the eighteenth presidential election.

However, President Park could not keep her promises regarding universal welfare programmes due to the financial crunch (Yang 2020). She also suffered from poor economic performance. Park's government marked a new record for the lowest GDP growth rate since democratisation, with a rate of 3.0 per cent (Moon 2018a). The economic downturn that occurred during the administrations of two consecutive conservative governments disillusioned many Koreans, who had believed that conservative rule would be beneficial for the economy. The liberal Democratic Party of Korea (DPK) attacked this poor economic performance in the twentieth assembly election in 2016 with the catchphrase, 'The problem is the economy!'

The final blow to Park and her SP came with the Choi Sun-sil scandal that occurred in late 2016. This caused Koreans to stop believing that the conservatives were strong in terms of security. Many Koreans had previously supported conservative parties due to this belief, despite feeling that the conservatives were corrupt. However, many Koreans were shocked by the Choi Sun-sil scandal, which revealed that their president was a puppet directed by a con woman, and they realised that their beliefs were unsubstantiated.

Before the Choi Sun-sil scandal broke, Moon Jae-in initially moved cautiously ahead of the campaign for the nineteenth presidential election. However, after the Choi Sun-sil scandal broke, Moon's camp adopted a more aggressive campaign strategy. He pledged to clean up 'accumulated evils' to restore justice in the country. Moon attempted to obviate his opponents from conjuring up the Red Scare by calling the conservative SP a group that provided fake security. He also proposed audacious welfare programmes, which included subsidies for childcare, basic pensions for the elderly, expansion of national health insurance, medical support for dementia patients, and the provision of public rental houses for young people, newly-weds, and ordinary people who did not own homes. He also highlighted job creation as a top priority and pledged to decrease wage gaps between conglomerates and small firms, as well as discrimination against irregular workers.

The South Korean electorate's evaluation of the two major parties' valences changed dramatically after the Choi Sun-sil scandal. The conservatives had long built an image of a party that was strong on the economy and national security. However, they forfeited their long-held advantages on these valences. Table 16.2 displays public opinion regarding the most salient issues at the time of the election, as well as evaluations of the two major parties' valences since the eighteenth assembly election in 2008. Until the nineteenth assembly election held before the Choi Sun-sil scandal, the most urgent problem was considered to be economic growth, but this changed to unemployment in the nineteenth presidential election in 2017, then to economic inequality in the seventh local and twenty-first assembly elections held after the scandal.

Until the twentieth assembly election of 2016, the conservative parties (the GNP and its descendant SP) were thought to be the ones who could better solve economic and security problems compared to their liberal counterparts (Moon 2018a). However, in the seventh local election, where the liberal DPK swept fourteen of seventeen metropolitan mayoral and gubernatorial elections, more than 60 per cent of the survey respondents believed that the liberal DPK could do better not only in reducing economic inequality, but also in keeping the country secure (Moon 2018b). The distrust of the conservative party (the UFP, a descendant of the SP) deepened further in the twenty-first assembly election of 2020, in which the DPK won a landslide victory, taking 180 of 300 seats. The post-election survey revealed that more than 90 per cent of the survey respondents evaluated the DPK's security and economic competence to be better than that of the UFP (Korea Research 2020).

Table 16.2: Opinions about crucial issues and evaluations of the two major parties' valences (%)

The 18th assembly election survey (2004)
The party that can solve the most important political problem

GNP (conservative)	UDP (liberal)	PPL (conservative)	DLP (leftist)
55.7	19.3	6.0	5.1

The 19th assembly election survey (2008)
The most urgent problem to be solved

Economic growth	Welfare expansion	Political reform	Educational reform
40.7	22.8	15.5	7.6

The party that can solve the most urgent problem

Saenuri (conservative)	DUP (liberal)	UPP (leftist)	LFP (conservative)
51.8	36.4	9.3	1.2

The 20th assembly election survey (2012)
The party that can solve the economic problem

Saenuri (conservative)	DPK (liberal)	PP (centrist)	JP (leftist)
43.7	32.8	22.1	1.4

The party that can solve the security problem

Saenuri (conservative)	DPK (liberal)	PP (centrist)	JP (leftist)
53.1	33.1	12.6	1.1

The 19th presidential election survey (2017)
The most urgent problem to be solved

Unemployment	Price	National security	Welfare
40.0	13.6	10.3	9.3

The 7th local election survey (2018)
The more urgent problem between national security and income inequality

National security	Economic inequality
36.1	63.9

The proportion of voters evaluating the liberal DPK's valences better than the conservative LPK

National security	Reducing inequality
62.7	77.1

The 21st assembly election survey (2020)
The more urgent problem between national security and income inequality

National security	Economic inequality
38.2	61.8

The proportion of voters evaluating the liberal DPK's valences better than the conservative UFP

National security	Reducing inequality
95.6	98.5

4. Regional Voting and Generational Conflict

While two major position issues (inter-Korean and welfare issues) and two major valence issues (security and economic competence) have long played significant roles in Korean elections, regionalism is a feature that has characterised electoral competition in South Korea after democratisation. Previous studies offered different interpretations regarding the cause of regionalism; these included interpretations of regionalism in terms of communitarian culture (Choi and Lee 1980), political mobilisation (Sohn 1997), a rational choice of voters (Cho 2000), regional identity (Lee 1998), regional antagonism (Jhee 2015), in-group favouritism and out-group antipathy (Yoon 2019), a reflection of ideological conflict (Choi 1991), and a combined effect of ideological and regional components (Moon 2005).

Scholars have also disagreed about whether regional conflict overlaps with ideological conflict. The early studies on regional voting argued that the two types of conflicts are independent from each other, based on their finding that there are no significant ideological differences among the people of Honam and Youngnam, the southwest and southeast regions of South Korea, respectively, the two regions of South Korea in which regional voting patterns remain strong (Kang 2003; Lee 1998). However, more recent studies found that ideology and regional conflicts indeed overlap (Baek et al. 2003; Hur 2019; Moon 2005; 2018a). According to Moon (2005), regional voting consists of ideological and regional components. First, Honam and Yeongnam residents support their regional party because of the ideological congruence between their ideologies and that of their party. Second, residents of the two regions support their regional party because they have the prospective 'expectation that their regional party would improve the political and economic conditions of the region' and the retrospective 'feeling of relative deprivation that the party of a rival region has taken regional benefits away from them' (Moon 2005: 585).

Scholars explain Honam people's liberal ideology in terms of their experiences of economic discrimination and political oppression by the military regimes (Choi 1991; Moon 2005). First, President Park Chung-hee's discriminatory policies alienated the people of Honam economically. Second, the massacre of Gwangju citizens by the military forces of Chun Doo-hwan on 17 May 1980 left indelible scars on the Honam people. Hwang (1996) distinguished Honam regionalism from Yeongnam regionalism by suggesting that while Honam regionalism resulted from resistance to authoritarianism, Yeongnam regionalism arose from the desire to maintain its economic and political hegemony.

Cognitive dissonance theory can explain the persistence of political attitudes of people from Honam and Yeongnam. According to this theory, people who experience internal inconsistency tend to make changes to justify their beliefs by avoiding circumstances and contradictory information that is likely to increase the magnitude of the cognitive dissonance. In politics, once people find a political leader to admire, they tend to identify their ideology and policy preferences with those of the leader. When people are faced with contradictory information about their political beliefs, they resist the information and look for new information that instead reinforces their beliefs. In other words, a voter's ideology is an outcome of the rationalisation of their political choices (Lee and Hur 2010). Honam people, who respected the liberal Kim Dae-jung, developed a liberal ideology, whereas Yeongnam people, who supported authoritarian and conservative presidents for years, reinforced their conservative ideology to rationalise their political choices.

However, the ideological disparity between the two regions cannot by itself explain the considerable gap between regional and national support of regional parties. For example, the difference in the proportion of liberal voters between Honam and the nation has ranged from zero percentage points in the fifteenth presidential in 1997 election to 44.4 percentage points in the seventeenth assembly election in 2004 (Moon 2018a). However, the gap between regional and national support of the regional party representing Honam has ranged from 21.2 percentage points in the nineteenth assembly election in 2023 to 54.0 percentage points in the fifteenth presidential election. Thus, Honam people have voted disproportionately for their regional party, considering their ideological composition. Moon (2005: 589) called this support the 'regional component' of regional voting, distinguishing it from the 'ideological component' (extra ideological vote base).

Moon (2018a) found that regional voting becomes intensified when the party of a rival region seizes power, whereas it is weakened when a regional party does. Based on this finding, Moon (2018a) claims that relative deprivation is a stronger incentive for regional voting than expectation of regional benefits. While the people of Chungcheong or Gangwon provinces would have the feeling of relative deprivation, people in these regions only cast regional votes when they have a powerful political leader who is popular enough to challenge the major two-party candidates.

Regional voting in Chungcheong or Gangwon provinces has occurred several times. When Kim Jong-pil from Chungcheong formed the New Democratic Republican Party (NDRP) for the thirteenth assembly election in 1988 and the United Liberal Democrats (ULD) for the fifteenth assembly election in 1996, the NDRP and ULD won 26.5 percentage points and 34.7 percentage points, respectively, in extra support from Chungcheong. When Jeong Joo-young from Gangwon, the chief executive officer (CEO) of Hyundai company, ran for the fourteenth presidential election in 1992, he won 17.8 percentage points in extra support from his region. However, the regional voting in Chungcheong or Gangwon is not as strong as that of Honam or Youngnam because the ideological component of Chungcheong or Gangwon is not as large as that of Honam or Yeongnam.

Scholars have also paid attention to variations in regional voting. Figure 16.3 shows the change in regional voting in South Korea; the values on the y-axis represent the average differences between the regional and national vote shares of regional parties. Before democratisation, regional voting only appeared in the seventh presidential

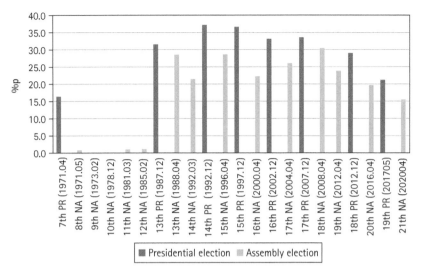

FIGURE 16.3: The averages of extra vote shares that regional parties won from their regions (%)

election in 1971, in which a strong political leader, Kim Dae-jung from Honam, emerged to compete against President Park Chung-hee from Yeongnam. In this election, the Democratic Republican Party stoked regionalism. Lee Hyo-sang, the National Assembly Speaker at that time, appealed to Daegu voters to vote for Park Chung-hee to maintain the hegemony of the 'Yeongnam Regime' against the challenge from the people of Honam (*Dong-A Ilbo* 2000).

However, regional voting did not appear in the subsequent elections held before democratisation. Regional voting re-emerged abruptly after democratisation and remained constant throughout the post-democratisation period. The figure also shows that regional voting has been systematically stronger in presidential elections than in assembly elections. The interpretations of regionalism in terms of various predispositions such as regional identity, antagonism, or favouritism have had difficulty explaining why such predispositions became suddenly intensified after democratisation, and why they have been stronger in presidential elections than in assembly elections.

Empirical studies have presented different findings about the variations in regional voting. Some scholars have suggested that regionalism is weakening (Choi and Cho 2005; Kang 2010; Lee 2011). By contrast, Lee and Park (2011: 158) argue that 'regionalism in South Korean elections is likely to remain strong'. Jhee (2015) found that regional antagonism decreased during the Kim Dae-jung administration, but slightly intensified during that of Lee Myung-bak. Kim (2010) also finds that regional voting did not change throughout the thirteenth, fourteenth, and fifteenth presidential elections. Yoon (2017) claims that the regional conflict between the Yeongnam and Honam regions has transformed into conflict between the Daegu-Gyeongbuk and Honam regions.

However, more important than simply observing such variation in regionalism is theoretically explaining why it varies. Moon (2005; 2018a) offers a theory that explains the variation in regional voting in terms of party system polarisation. He argued that as political parties' ideological positions became less distinguishable after democratisation, it became easier for the parties to sway ideological voting decisions by offering regional benefits. Before democratisation, the South Korean party system was polarised, with the two major parties diverging from each other based on a cleavage of authoritarianism versus democratisation (Moon 2018a). Once this cleavage disappeared after democratisation, voters saw little difference between the parties that converged along a newly formed conservative–liberal ideological spectrum (Moon 2018a). Seeing little ideological differences among the parties, voters chose to support the parties formed by their regional leaders.

Moon (2018a) presents empirical findings that support the negative relationship between regional voting and the polarisation of the party system. Moon (2018a) measures the ideological positions of the parties by using post-election surveys going back to the seventeenth assembly election in 2004. Figure 16.3 includes two recent elections that were not included in Moon's study, which analysed cases until the twentieth assembly election. Post-election survey measures for the ideological positions of the two major parties in the two subsequent elections reveal that the ideological gaps have become even more divergent since the nineteenth assembly election. Figure 16.3 shows that regional voting has concurrently decreased further since the nineteenth assembly election.

5. Conclusion

This chapter has examined the effects of electoral systems on the formation of the two-party system in South Korea. The major institutional factor that has prevented the emergence of a multiparty system is the imbalance between the number of district seats and the number of PR seats. It has long been argued that a multiparty system would prevent a concentration of power in the majority governing party. Although a mixed-member, semi-proportional system was adopted in the twenty-first assembly election in 2020, the JP, the third party, failed to increase its number of seats because the major parties formed satellite parties. Most South Koreans have demanded that the mixed-member, semi-proportional system be repealed and replaced with a more proportional system to generate a multiparty system.

However, it is not clear whether the major parties will adopt a new system that is advantageous to small parties. The adoption of a semi-proportional system itself was possible because the governing Democratic Party of Korea (DPK) conceded to small parties to earn their cooperation in exchange for their support of the DPK's long-desired prosecution reform bill. Given that the DPK won a supermajority of seats in the twenty-first assembly election, the party does not have any incentive to adopt an electoral system that is more advantageous to small parties.

In this chapter, it has been shown that inter-Korean issues have been more salient than redistributive issues in South Korean elections. However, in recent elections, redistributive issues have gained more attention, as more voters want to expand social welfare and reduce income inequality. In addition, the policy difference between the two major parties has become more salient as the Moon Jae-in administration has pursued more aggressive welfare reforms. In response to this, Kim Jong-in, head of the emergency committee of the main opposition United Future Party (UFP), suggested the introduction of universal basic income by arguing that 'the goal of politics is to maximise economic freedom to buy a loaf of bread'.

Given that Park Geun-hye was elected president largely due to her movement towards the left to incorporate voters at the centre, and that the UFP's shocking defeat in the twenty-first assembly election largely resulted from its movement to the extreme right, Kim Jong-in's move towards the left will likely help the UFP recover power. Indeed, the rate of support for the UFP exceeded that for the DPK on 14 August 2020 for the first time since the impeachment of Park Geun-hye on 10 March 2017. However, the failure of redistributive issues to emerge as a salient issue was due to the very slight difference between the redistributive policies of the parties. Thus, if the UFP moves towards the left on the redistributive policy dimension, a decrease in policy difference could make redistributive issues less salient. Moreover, if the DPK and the UFP become closer in terms of redistributive and inter-Korean issues, the role of valence issues, including regionalism, will increase both in political parties' campaign strategies and in citizens' voting decisions.

Notes

1. The status of a 'negotiation group' is given to each party with at least twenty legislators. Negotiation groups are entitled to a variety of privileges, including chairpersonship of a standing committee, a greater amount of state funding, and participation in consultation meetings of floor leaders to decide the assembly's legislative agenda.
2. Hibbs (2000) called voting based on security issues 'peace voting' and voting based on economic issues 'bread voting'. He found that the growth of real disposable personal income and the cumulative numbers of US military personnel killed in the Korean and Vietnamese wars entirely determined the aggregate votes in the post-war presidential elections.
3. The BBK scandal consisted of an allegation about Lee's involvement with the manipulation of stock prices by Kim Kyung-joon, the director of an investment firm, who created shell companies and spread false rumours about the pending acquisition of these companies by foreign investors; the allegation was found to be true.
4. The economic growth rates for the previous governments were 9.06 per cent (No Tae-wu), 5.61 per cent (Kim Young-sam), 8.05 per cent (Kim Dae-jung), and 4.48 per cent (No Mu-hyeon).

References

Baek, J., Cho, J., and Cho, S., (2003), 'Jiyeokjuui, geuligo 2002 nyeon daetonglyeong seongeo' (Ideology, Regionalism, and the 2002 Korean Presidential Election), *Guka Jeonlyak (National Strategy)* 9(4), 139–168.

Cho, K. (2000), *Jiyeokjuui seongeowa hablijeok Yugeonja* (*Regional Voting and Rational Voters*) (Seoul: Nanam).

Choi, J. (1991), 'Jibae ideollogiloseoui jiyeokjuuiui yeokhal' (The Role of Regionalism as a Ruling Ideology), in J. Kim and J. Choi, eds, *Jiyeokjuui Yeongu* (*Studies of Regionalism*), 30–39 (Seoul: Hakminsa).

Choi, S., and Lee C. (1980), 'Environment, Policy and Electoral Participation: A Comparison of Urban and Rural Areas', in C. Kim, ed., *Political Participation in Korea*, 165–180 (Santa Barbara, CA: ABC-Clio Press).

Choi, J., and Cho, J. (2005), 'Jiyeok gyunyeolui byeonhwa ganeungseonge daehan gyeongheomjeog gochal' (Is Regional Cleavage in Korea Disappearing?), *Hanguk Jeongchi Hakhoebo* (*Korean Political Science Review*) 39(3), 375–394.

Dong-A Ilbo (2000), 'Jiyeokgamjeong bigeuksa' (Tragic History of Regional Antagonism), March 03.

Hibbs, D. A. (2000), 'Bread and Peace Voting in U.S. Presidential Elections', *Public Choice* 104, 149–180.

Huber, J., and Inglehart, R. (1995), 'Expert Interpretations of Party Space and Party Locations in 42 Societies', *Party Politics* 1(1), 73–111.

Hur, S. (2019), 'Jiyeok gyunyeoleun eotteohge gyunyeol doeneunga?' (Changing Regional Voting Behavior of Korean Voters?), *Hyeondae Jeongchi Yeongu* (*Journal of Contemporary Politics*) 12(2), 5–37.

Hwang, T. (1996), 'Hankukui Jiyeok Paewonjeon Sahoigujowa jiyeok hyeokmyeongui gujo' (The Structure of Regional Hegemony and the Logic of Regional Revolution), in H. J. Yeonguhwo, ed., *Jeonchi Bipyeong* (*Political Critique*), 75–130 (Seoul: Asia Moonhwasa).

Jhee, B. (2015), 'Minjuhwa ihu jiyeok gamjeongui byeonhwawa wonin' (Changes in Regional Antagonism and Its Causes in Korea after Democratization), *Hanguk Jeongdang Hakhwobo* (*Korean Party Studies Review*) 14(1), 63–91.

Kang, W. (2003), *Hangukui seongeo jeongchi* (*Electoral Politics in South Korea*) (Seoul: Pureungil).

Kang, W. (2010), *Hangukui seongeo jeongchiui beonhwawa jisok* (*The Change and Continuity in Electoral Politics in South Korea*) (Pajoo: Nanam).

Kim, J. (2010), 'Hanguk jiyeokjuuiui byeonhwa' (The Change of Korean Regionalism), *Hyeondae Jeongchi Yeongu* (*Journal of Contemporary Politics*) 3(2), 89–114.

Kim, Y., and Chang S. (2017), 'Daehanminguk seongeojedo byeoncheonsa' (History of Changes in Korean Electoral Rules), *Hyeondaesa Gwangjang* (*Forum for Contemporary History*) 10, 10–40.

Korea Research (2020), *2020 Hankuk research 9cha jeonggijosa* (*2020 Korea Research: The 9th Regular Rurvey*) (Seoul: Korea Research).

Lee, K. (1998), *Hangukui Seongeowa Jiyeokjuui* (*Elections in Korea and Regionalism*) (Seoul: Oreum).

Lee, K. (2011), *Hanguiinui tupyo haengtae* (*Voting Behavior of Koreans*) (Seoul: Humanitas).

Lee, K., and Park. J. (2011), 'Jiyeokmin hogamdoga jeongdang jijie michineun yeonghyang' (Effects of Regional Feelings upon the Party Support in Korea), *Hangukgwa Gukjejeongchi* (*Korea and World Politics*) 27(3), 131–158.

Lee, N., and Hur, S. (2010), 'Haprijeokin yugwonjainga, haprihwahaneun yugwonjainga?' (Are Voters Rational or Rationalizing?), *Hanguk Jeongch Hakwobo* (*Korean Political Science Review*) 44(2), 45–67.

Moon, W. (2005), 'Decomposition of Regional Voting in South Korea: Ideological Conflicts and Regional Benefits', *Party Politics* 11(5), 579–599.

Moon, W. (2018a), *Hanguk minjujuuiui jakdong mechanism* (*The Working Mechanism of Korean Democracy*) (Seoul: Korea University Press).

Moon, W. (2018b), '6·13 Jibangseongeoeseo natanan du juyojeongdange daehan taedowa deobuleominjudang jiji bunseok' (An Analysis of Attitudes towards the Two Major Political Parties and Electoral Support for the Democratic Party in the 7th Local Elections), *Euijeong Nonchong* (*Journal of Parliamentary Research*) 13(2), 5–29.

Moon, W. (2020). 'Dadangcheje Daetongryungjeeseoui ipbupjeok hyeoprukgwa jeongchijedo' (Legislative Cooperation in Multiparty Presidentialism), *Hanguk Jeongchi Yeongu* (*Journal of Korean Politics*) 29(3), 93–122.

Powell, G. B. Jr (2000), *Elections as Instruments of Democracy* (New Haven, NJ: Yale University Press).

Sohn, H. (1997), *Byeonhwangiui Hanguk Jeongchi* (*Korean Politics in a Transitional Era*) (Seoul: Changjakwa Bipyungsa).

Stokes, Donald E. (1963), 'Spatial Models of Party Competition', *American Political Science Review* 57, 368–377.

Yang, J. (2020), 'Korean Social Welfare Politics', in C. Moon and M. Moon, eds, *Routledge Handbook of Korean Politics and Public Administration*, 420–434 (New York: Taylor and Francis).

Yoon, J. (2017), 'Gyochapryeokgwa jiyeokjuui tupyoui byeonhwa' (Cross-Pressure and the Change of Regional Voting), *Hanguk Jeongdang Hakhwobo* (*Korean Party Studies Review*) 16(3), 5–45.

Yoon, K. (2019), 'Jiyeok gyuyeolui yujiwa byeonhwa' (Persistence and Change of Regional Cleavage)', *Hangukgwa Gukjejeongchi* (*Korea and World Politics*) 35(2), 35–64.

CHAPTER 17

POLITICAL COMMUNICATION

HAN SOO LEE

1. Introduction

THIS chapter introduces political communication in South Korea by focusing on electoral campaigns. Political communication is involved in all political relationships when it is defined as 'a constitutive process that produces and reproduces shared meaning' (Craig 1999: 125). In particular, political scientists are interested in how messages are exchanged between political actors and how the process affects them, which is well observed in campaigns. Political parties, candidates, and voters send messages through various communication channels during election periods. We can thus paint a picture of political communication in South Korea by exploring campaign communication. To introduce campaign communication in South Korea, this chapter briefly reviews the evolution of campaign communication tools and their influences on elections.

Campaign communication has evolved from face-to-face communication to online communication in South Korea. Information and communication technology (ICT) has changed campaign communication. Politicians actively adopt and utilise new communication tools. New media, such as websites, smartphones, and social media, can affect campaign styles. The most recently introduced campaign communication tools are social media services, such as Twitter, Facebook, and YouTube. An important question, then, is how do new media affect campaign styles and strategies?

This chapter also examines the effects of new media on political behaviour by focusing on voter turnout and vote choice. In South Korea, social media initially attracted the public attention for its impact on voter turnout. People uploaded pictures verifying their participation in voting on their social media and encouraged the participation of others. Political scientists are certainly interested in the influence of new media on vote choice, and it is an interesting and important question as to whether or not using new media leads to support for certain candidates or parties.

2. A Brief History of Campaign Communication in South Korea

In general, campaign communication has evolved from face-to-face interaction, to communication via mass media outlets, and then to online communication (Norris 2000). The first national election in South Korea was the Constitutional Assembly Election on 10 May 1948. Since then, mass rallies had been a conventional method of campaigning until television replaced it. Candidates and political parties mobilised large crowds for campaigns. With party activists and members, they stumped around the country to earn votes. Before the revision of the election law in 1997, it was common to see huge crowds listening to candidates' speeches in big open spaces, such as school grounds. Candidates tried to show off their popularity by mobilising as many people to attend rallies as possible. The mass media reported on campaign rallies, and citizens may have assessed candidates' popularity according to the size of each rally.

Although mass rallies were the main campaign tool for candidates and parties, scholars and civic organisations criticised the method as a major source of electoral fraud and plutocracy (Kim et al. 2011). Politicians also seemed to understand the inefficiency of using mass rallies for campaigning. In addition, the mood of democracy required political reforms, including to electoral institutions. The presidential election law was revised in 1987, and the revised law allowed TV debates. In the 1987 presidential election, a press organisation invited one candidate at a time to talk about issues in front of TV cameras, which was recorded and broadcast for the first time in South Korea. It was a discussion between reporters and a candidate, but not a live debate between candidates. The first TV debates between candidates were held for the 1991 local elections. In 1992, the National Assembly revised the presidential election law again, reducing the number of mass rallies allowed while campaigning and allowing TV advertisements. Furthermore, in 1997, the fifteenth National Assembly prohibited outdoor mass rallies and encouraged mass media campaign by allowing more TV advertisements, speeches, debates, and so on.

These institutional changes certainly influenced campaign communication. Candidates and parties since then have focused more on utilising mass media for campaigning. Kang (1999) concludes that TV emerged as the most influential campaign tool in the 1997 presidential election. The first televised presidential debates between candidates were held ahead of the 1997 election, and the rating was over 50 per cent. The 1997 presidential election can be seen as the first 'TV election' in South Korea (Kang 1999). TV is, of course, still one of the major information sources for voters. According to survey results during the 2020 general elections, about 25 per cent of citizens responded that they obtained most political information through TV (Lee et al. 2020).

Campaigns, however, continued to change with the advent of ICT. The internet seems to have rapidly replaced other communication tools as the preferred method of campaign communication. The revision of the election law in 1997 already allowed for online campaigning. In particular, the 2002 presidential election is regarded as the first 'internet election' (Yun 2003). During the election period, candidates created websites and used them to spread information, connect online and offline organisations, and raise campaign money (Lee 2012). According to Yun (2003), who studies the effects of the internet on the 2002 presidential election, it is clear that Roh Moo-hyun more successfully utilised the internet for campaigning compared to his opponents, although it is difficult to assert that the internet was decisive in his victory.

Unlike the 2002 presidential election, however, the online campaign was not so influential in the 2007 presidential election, even though the internet environment had improved greatly (Chang 2008; Yun 2008). Yun (2008) indicates three reasons why online campaigning was not so influential in the 2007 presidential election. First, voters did not pay much attention to the election compared to the previous one. In fact, Lee Myung-bak had led the race for about a year and won the election by more than a 20 per cent margin. In addition, candidates and parties learned the importance of online campaigning from the 2002 presidential election. Hence, in the 2007 presidential election, all major candidates campaigned online. Second, since online campaigns had been salient and controversial in the previous election, the National Election Commission put more regulations on online campaign activities and rigorously punished related violations during the 2007 presidential election period. Finally, candidates' online campaign strategies were not so effective in this election. Even though the ICT and communication environment had improved tremendously, candidates' online campaign strategies did not change accordingly. Most candidates used new media to simply spread information, rather than to communicate with voters.

Mentioning social media, such as Facebook and Twitter, is inevitable when discussing online political campaigning. The emergence of social media changed people's communication patterns. In addition, as more people started to use smartphones, social media became a major communication tool among individuals. Today, citizens obtain and share information through social media. Candidates and parties seem to understand the value of social media as a communication tool and use them for political campaigns (Jungherr 2016). In the 2008 US presidential election, Barak Obama successfully utilised social media for his campaign (Gerodimos and Justinussen 2015). Donald Trump sent campaign messages and announced policies through Twitter.

In South Korea, candidates started utilising social media in the 2010 local elections (Kum 2011). During these elections, celebrities and citizens posted pictures verifying that they had voted on their social network sites, such as Facebook. According to Lee, Seo, and Kim (2012), voters posted their turnout pictures on social media to persuade others to vote as well as to express themselves. In fact, Yun (2013) argues that the voter turnout rates increased in the 2010 local elections partially because of the voter participation campaign on social media.

Scholars (Lee 2012; Yun 2014) indicate that the 2011 Seoul mayoral by-election is the first election in which political candidates used social media actively. Candidates tried to communicate with their constituents by posting pictures on Facebook and Instagram and sending Twitter messages (Lee et al. 2012). Since then, social media have been playing a significant role in campaign communication.

The first social media presidential election in South Korea is considered to be the 2012 presidential election. On 29 December 2011, the South Korean Supreme Court ruled that it was unconstitutional to prohibit expressing political support for a candidate on social media. In 2012, about 25 million people were using smartphones, and there were about 6.4 million Twitter users and about 7 million Facebook users (Kang et al. 2012). Thus, the environment for social media campaigns was established as the 2012 presidential election neared. Candidates and parties also observed some effects of social media on political behaviour in the 2011 Seoul mayoral by-election.[1] This brings us to the question of how politicians are using new media during campaigns today.

3. New Media and Political Campaign: How Politicians Use Them

Today, many people communicate through social media and search for and spread information online. If voters obtain information online, candidates and parties need to campaign online as well. Moreover, compared to traditional methods, online communication methods have several advantages related to political campaigning (Bimber and Davis 2003). First, by using online communication tools, candidates can send more information instantly, cheaply, anytime, and anywhere. They can construct campaign websites and provide a variety of information. Moreover, candidates can instantly respond to their opponents' messages through social media. Second, online communication makes it possible to provide relevant information to targeted voters. Analysing voters' online information search patterns, candidates can show specific policy proposals about which voters are interested. Third, using online communication tools, candidates can receive feedback about their campaign, and even talk with voters directly. Finally, unlike traditional media, online media can transmit text, audio, and video information simultaneously. Candidates can thus post text messages with video clips using online media.

In general, online communication provides various methods for campaigning. However, not all candidates or parties benefit equally from the improved communication environment. Rash (1997) argues that small parties are more likely to benefit from the development of ICT because online communication tools are cheaper and more extensive than conventional communication tools. Hence, even small parties without enough resources can campaign effectively by using online communication tools. However, Davis (1999) cautions that major parties utilise online communication tools better because they have more resources and experience.

In addition, online communication tools can affect the method of campaigning. As mentioned earlier, using online communication tools, candidates can discuss issues and policy proposals directly with voters. Hence, some argue that online communication tends to facilitate public discourse during election periods (Hague and Loader 1999). On the contrary, Davis (1999) insists that candidates and parties use online communication tools to mobilise voters, rather than to communicate with them.

How, then, do candidates and parties use online communication tools in South Korea? Certainly not all candidates and parties utilise online communication tools actively and successfully. How candidates use the tools depends on their campaign strategies. According to prior research (Foot and Schneider 2006; Lilleker et al. 2011), candidates and parties utilise new media to provide information for voters, link voters to other voters, groups, and websites, interact with/between voters, and mobilise voters. Successful campaigns can make voters feel more engaged in politics and connected to one another. Eventually, by doing so, candidates and parties can earn public support and win elections.

As mentioned previously, the 2002 presidential election is considered the first internet election in South Korea. Of course, this does not mean that online communication tools were first used by candidates in the election. Rather, the internet emerged as a key campaign communication tool in the election. Yun (2003) finds that Roh Moo-hyun successfully utilised his website for mobilisation.

The beginning of Roh's online campaign can be traced back to the 2000 general election. Roh ran for a National Assembly seat in Busan. Even though his party offered a relatively safe seat to him, Roh refused the offer and decided to go to a competitive district in order to break down political regionalism. However, Roh lost the election, and his supporters formed an organisation, 'Roh-Sa-Mo'[2] on his homepage[3] after the election. The organisation was the first of its kind formed online. Roh's supporters expanded their activities online, and also offline. They discussed public issues and suggested policy proposals online. As a result, before the 2002 election, the size of 'Roh-Sa-Mo' had increased to around 70,000 members (Yun 2003).

Roh's online campaign was successful in terms of raising campaign contributions too. Utilising the internet, Roh raised campaign money based on individual contributions. Voters could donate campaign money via multiple methods on his homepage, and Roh was able to raise over 7 billion KRW from about 200,000 supporters (Yun 2003). In sum, it is possible to evaluate Roh's online campaign as being more successful than his opponents, particularly in terms of mobilising supporters (Yun 2003).

Candidates' efforts to mobilise voters online are also observed in general elections. According to Kim (2004), compared to the 2000 congressional elections, in the 2004 congressional elections more candidates opened and utilised websites for campaigning. Kim (2004) analyses candidates' websites based on how the website menus are constructed. The results show that most candidates used their homepages to provide information such as their campaign news/schedule and policy proposals. More than 90 per cent of candidates constructed a bulletin board (or discussion) platform in the 2004 election. About 63 per cent of homepages included a function for accepting campaign contributions.

The results imply that candidates open campaign websites in order to mobilise supporters and discuss their proposals. However, candidates only responded to about 15 per cent of voters' messages (Kim 2004). In other words, even though online campaign tools have some advantages for civic discussion, candidates do not actively use it. In addition, major party candidates operated campaign websites more than minor party or independent candidates. These results are similar to those of Kamarck (2002), who examined campaign websites during the 1998 and 2000 US elections.

In addition to websites, candidates and parties use social media for political campaigning. During the 2012 presidential election, both Park Geun-hye and Moon Jae-in operated multiple online campaign tools, such as official websites, blogs, Twitter, Facebook, and KakaoTalk.[4] In particular, Park Geun-hye was keen to utilise social media more because the party evaluated that Na Kyung-won, of the Hannara Party,[5] lost the Seoul mayoral by-election in 2011 because of the successful social media campaign by Park Won-sun.[6]

Park Geun-hye mainly used social media to spread information. The Saenuri Party election workers interacted with voters through social media by responding to their comments (Kum 2014). However, Park rarely sent messages to people herself and rarely directly interacted with voters through social media. Compared to Park, Moon actively utilised social media by frequently sending messages and responded to voters' comments himself (Park and Cho 2013). Despite this effort, however, Moon lost the 2012 election. Without using new media, no one can win an election today; but using new media well does not guarantee victory.

In the 2017 presidential election, most candidates actively used social media. For instance, they enthusiastically put video clips on YouTube, sent messages through Twitter, and uploaded pictures on Facebook. However, according to Kim (2018), compared to other candidates, Moon focused more on real-time, direct communication with voters via social media. For example, Moon opened more live streaming channels on Facebook and interacted with voters while streaming. Also, it is noteworthy that Moon utilised social media for a relatively long time before the election. Kim (2018) argues that live streaming and continued online communication with voters contributed to Moon's victory in the 2017 election.

In general, candidates and parties utilise online communication tools by focusing on spreading information and mobilising voters in South Korea. Compared to minor parties and candidates, major parties and candidates more successfully use online communication tools for their campaign. In the early stages of online campaigning in South Korea, left-wing parties seemed to campaign online more successfully, but the distinction has since disappeared. Today, major parties and candidates understand the importance of new media and organise special teams for online campaigning. In fact, according to Chang and Lew (2013), managing social media campaigns significantly affects election results. However, despite the prediction that online communication tools will facilitate civic discussion during election periods, candidates do not actively make use of social media to interact and engage in discussions with voters.

4. New Media and Political Participation

As mentioned in section 2 'A Brief History of Campaign Communication in South Korea', social media first drew attention in terms of politics in South Korea for the possible boost it provided in voter turnout. Some scholars (Katz and Rice 2002; Negroponte 1995; Grossman 1995) argue that new media increases political participation. Political participation involves some costs, such as searching for information and understanding issues. Thanks to the development of ICT, people can search for political information more conveniently, meaning that the cost of political participation decreases. Theoretically, the likelihood of citizens participating in politics increases if they obtain election and campaign information more easily and quickly. In addition, voters can discuss issues online, contributing to an increase in political interest and participation (Negroponte 1995).

In contrast, others are sceptical about the positive impact of new media on political participation. They argue that new media simply reflect reality; that is, the development of ICT will not diminish inequality in political participation (Davis 1999; Davis and Owen 1998). People who have more resources, such as time, money, and knowledge, tend to have better access to technology. Certainly, people who have more resources are more likely to participate in politics. Hence, the digital divide will strengthen inequality in political participation (Norris 2001).

Moreover, the development of ICT may cause polarisation in political participation. Since there are more channels, people who are not interested in politics can isolate themselves from politics easily, while politically interested voters can consume a lot of political information. For instance, those uninterested in politics can watch entertainment programmes all day long, while politically interested voters can watch only news programmes. Interested voters may become more politically knowledgeable, and the uninterested will become less politically knowledgeable (Bennett and Iyengar 2008). This can affect political participation and cause polarisation in participation.

How, then, are new media affecting political participation in South Korea? According to one study exploring Twitter messages during the 2010 local elections, the most frequent messages (about 24.2 per cent) the day before the election were about encouraging voter turnout (Shin and Woo 2011). It is common to see some messages encouraging participation through social media during elections in South Korea. One may speculate that these messages positively affect voting and participation in South Korea. In fact, according to survey results on the 2012 general election, about 39.4 per cent of voters say that they have some experience of participating in politics through social media (Yun 2013). However, in order to verify the influence of new media on political participation, including on voter turnout, we need more systematic, empirical evidence.

Political participation can be categorised into conventional participation, such as turning out to vote, and non-conventional participation, such as attending demonstrations. When investigating the effects of new media on political participation, some (Kim and Yun 2004) focus on conventional participation, and others (Sung et al. 2007; Ko and Song 2010) deal with non-conventional participation as well. On the other hand, it is possible to categorise political participation into online and offline participation. Signing online petitions can be an example of online political participation, while turning out to vote is an example of offline political participation. Online and offline political participation can affect each other (Shim 2012). Here, the focus is on political participation during elections.

Since the 2002 presidential election, political scientists have studied the effects of new media on political participation in South Korea (Chang 2014; Cho 2011; Kim and Yun 2004; Song and Min 2009; Yun 2013). There are somewhat mixed results regarding the influences of new media on political participation during election periods. Some scholars (Chang 2014; Chung and Cho 2004; Kim and Yun 2004; Song and Min 2009) argue that new media positively affect political participation. For instance, estimating the effects of online activities on political participation in the 2004 general election, Kim and Yun (2004) find that voters who visit party/candidate homepages are more likely to turn out to vote.

Unlike Kim and Yun (2004), Song and Min (2009) measure online activities as searching and spreading campaign information and putting comments on candidates' websites in the 2008 general election. According to them, searching online for information on candidates' policies significantly and positively correlates with individual turnout decisions. Additionally, individuals who spread campaign information online are more likely to turn out to vote. However, voters who search for personal information on candidates are less likely to turn out to vote. The dissonant results require further explanation and study. Moreover, if politically interested voters tend to search for information online, political interest is the key variable explaining political participation, rather than the action of searching for information online.

The use of new media can be measured in multiple ways. Kim, Kim, and Kim (2011) measure in terms of how much time voters use new media, how often they write messages or comments on social network sites, and how often they search for political information through new media. According to their results, citizens who spend more time using social media and more frequently search for political information through social media are less likely to participate in politics offline; that is, the use of new media can even reduce offline political participation.

However, they show that people who actively express their political opinions through social media are more likely to participate in politics online (signing online petitions) and to participate in politics offline (discussing politics with friends and joining in protests) (Kim et al. 2011); that is, people who are politically active online are also politically active offline. Shim (2012) also argues that people who express their political opinions online are more likely to turn out to vote. However, these results do not clearly show whether or not online activities themselves directly influence political participation.

Sung et al. (2007) measure online activities in terms of consuming online news. They argue that individuals who more frequently consume news online tend to participate in politics online and offline. However, it can be controversial whether or not online news consumption is a proper measure of online activities to estimate the effects of new media on political participation. Berman and Weitzner (1997) argue that new media can facilitate political participation because these platforms allow people to discuss issues, exchange opinions, and form issue groups more conveniently. Therefore, consuming news online may not properly measure the effects of new media on political participation. Also, according to their results (Sung et al. 2007), as voters consume newspaper and TV news more frequently, they are also more likely to participate in politics offline and online. In other words, these results show that people who consume news more often are more likely to participate in politics in general.

By measuring online activities in terms of frequency using new media, Cho (2011) reveals that the use of social media does not significantly increase offline political participation but does increase online political participation. For instance, people who more frequently visit social network sites are more likely to participate in online political discussions, but they are not more or less likely to take part in political protests or rallies. Furthermore, voters who search for political information through new media are not more or less likely to participate in offline politics compared to those who get political information from traditional media. Similarly, Chang (2014) shows that the amount of social media usage and voters' credibility of information from social media do not explain individual voter turnout. The results generally show that new media do not facilitate offline political participation.

While analysing Twitter messages and users during the 2012 general election, Yun (2013) discovered that the amount of social media use does not significantly explain individual turnout decisions. Neither do Twitter users' various activities, such as the number of messages and the simple act of 'following' significantly relate to turning out to vote. However, voters who follow politicians on Twitter are more likely to vote. Politically interested voters tend to follow politicians on Twitter and vote. In fact, Yun (2013) shows that voters who use Twitter for political purposes are more likely to vote.

The insignificant effects of new media on offline political participation can be caused by the fact that they vary across different groups. For instance, young people are more familiar with new ICT and use social media more frequently. Hence, it is plausible to assume that new media can affect political participation among the young. Prior research investigating the effects of new media on political participation among young South Korean adults shows that the use of social media tends to facilitate political efficacy but does not significantly affect voter turnout (Lee and Kim 2012; Hong 2011). These results are somewhat similar to some studies in the United States (Baumgartner and Morris 2010; Hargittai and Shaw 2013; Vitak et al. 2011). They generally show that using social network sites, such as Facebook, can increase social capital, particularly among young people. However, it is not certain whether or not new media directly facilitate political participation, such as voter turnout (Baumgartner and Morris 2010).

In sum, the results regarding the effects of new media on political participation in South Korea are mixed and show some puzzles. It looks certain that the use of social media is associated with online political participation. According to previous studies

(Chang 2014; Cho 2011), voters who frequently use new media are politically active online. Furthermore, scholars show that people who are politically active online tend to be politically active offline (Kim et al. 2011; Shim 2012). It logically follows that people who frequently use new media should show a higher level of offline political participation. However, the positive association between new media use and offline political participation is not salient. Even a significant negative relationship between the amount of new media use and conventional political participation is found (Kim et al. 2011). A more systematic, comprehensive analysis is required to understand the relationships between new media use, online participation, and offline participation.

Another question to resolve is the path between political interest and online and offline political participation. As mentioned earlier, people who are politically active online tend to be interested in elections already. Hence, they are more likely to turn out to vote. In other words, we need more evidence that social media use brings about interest and participation in politics (Norris 2000). The use of new media may condition the effects of political interest or social capital on political participation (Choi 2016).

5. New Media and Vote Choice

With the influence of new media on political participation, political scientists have been interested in the effects of new media on vote choice. For instance, does the use of social media lead to the support of a certain candidate or party in South Korea? Theoretically, media use can affect vote choice. Media use is associated with obtaining information, and information affects behaviour. For instance, if a voter consistently consumes news from a politically slanted media outlet, they are likely to be affected by the information from the media outlet and vote for a candidate according to the information (Dilliplane 2014).

More specifically, using online and offline media can affect political preferences and vote choice distinctively. One of the characteristics of new media is variety. Compared to the past, there are many more channels and information sources. Citizens can select information sources that provide news that matches their political preferences. For instance, conservatives can watch conservative YouTube channels and share the information through Facebook. Eventually, conservatives tend to become more conservative and liberals tend to become more liberal (Sunstein 2001).

In addition, information carried by online and offline media can be different even though it is about the same issue. Above all, issues have multiple facets and can be framed by information providers and carriers. If there are more information providers and carriers online, more frames around issues are likely to be produced online. Furthermore, more disinformation (so-called fake news) is now made and spread online (Zimmermann and Kohring 2020). Individuals can produce 'news' without fact checking and spread it through social media. Such disinformation and framed information can affect voters, but not all individuals are affected by incoming information.

Voters care about the accuracy of incoming information, but also tend to accept incoming information corresponding to their political preferences (Kunda 1990). In sum, it is plausible to speculate that voters who receive political information consistently, mainly from online media, tend to show more polarised political preferences and choices than their counterparts.

So, do new media users show different political preferences and choices in South Korea? According to Yun (2013) based on a study of Twitter use in the 2012 general election, voters who read more Twitter messages written by candidates and follow well-known Twitterians are more likely to vote for progressive party candidates. However, as he mentioned, the results are likely to be caused by the fact that well-known Twitterians were generally progressive during the 2012 election. Also, reading candidates' Twitter messages is likely to be guided by voters' political predispositions. In contrast, the amount of time spent using the internet and social network services does not explain vote choice in his analysis; that is, based on the results, it is difficult to assert that new media use affects vote choice.

Studying the relationships between the use of social network services and political behaviour in the 2012 presidential election, Chang (2014) argues that the use of social media does not significantly explain individual vote choice and party support. Other empirical studies also show similar results (Choi et al. 2013; Chung 2014). In sum, while controlling for pre-existing political preferences, the use of new media does not, independently, significantly explain individual vote choice and party support in South Korea.

6. Conclusion

This chapter introduced political communication by focusing on campaign communication. The evolution of campaign communication is associated with communication tools. Up until the 1997 presidential election, mass rallies were the main campaign method. The 1997 presidential election is considered to be the first TV election in South Korea. Since the 2002 presidential election, online communication tools have played a significant role in campaigning.

Today, no candidate can win an election without using online communication tools in South Korea. Candidates mainly use online communication tools to mobilise resources and voters, rather than to discuss policies. Not all candidates successfully manage online campaigns, but a successful online campaign does not guarantee winning an election.

The influence of new media on South Korean voters is yet unclear. The use of new media tends to positively correlate with political participation online, and online political participation is associated with offline political participation. However, the use of new media neither significantly nor consistently explains offline political participation and individual vote choice.

Notes

1. Although many expected that the 2012 general election would be the first social media election, the effects of social media were not so meaningful in the election (Lee 2012).
2. The meaning is 'a group of people who love Roh Moo-hyun'.
3. www.knowhow.or.kr, accessed 22 November 2021. Officially, the homepage opened on 17 May 2000 (Yun 2003). Now this is the homepage of the Rohmoohyun Foundation.
4. KakaoTalk is a free instant messaging application. According to Kum (2014), basically almost all citizens who own smartphones use KakaoTalk in South Korea.
5. Later, they changed the name to the Saenuri Party.
6. In the election, although an independent, all opposition parties supported Park Won-sun and he was the sole candidate to face the ruling party nominee.

Bibliography

Baumgartner, J. C., and Morris, J. S. (2010), 'Social Networking Web Sites and Political Engagement of Young Adults', *Social Science Computer Review* 28(1), 24–44.

Bennett, W. L., and Iyengar, S. (2008), 'A New Era of Minimal Effects? The Changing Foundations of Political Communication', *Journal of Communication* 58(4), 707–731.

Berman, J., and Weitzner, D. J. (1997), 'Technology and Democracy', *Social Research* 64(3), 1313–1319.

Bimber, B., and Davis, R. (2003), *Campaigning Online: The Internet in U.S. Elections*. (Oxford: Oxford University Press).

Chang, W. (2008), 'Inteonetgwa seon-geokaempein: 17dae daeseon UCC hwaryongeul jungsimeuro' [Internet and Electoral Campaign: Focusing on Utilizing the UCC of the 17th Presidential Election], *Korean Political Science Review* 42(2), 171–201.

Chang, W. (2014), 'Sosyeolleteuwokeu kaempeingwa yugwonja chamyeo hyogwa: 18dae daeseonui gyeongheomjeok bunseok' [Social Network Campaign and Electoral Participation Effect: Empirical Analysis of the 18th Presidential Election in Korea], *Korean Journal of Area Studies* 32(3), 37–55.

Chang, W., and Lew, S. (2013), 'Sosyeolleteuwokeu kaempeinui jeongchijeok hyogwa: 19dae chongseonui teuwiteo bikdeiteo bunseok' [The Political Effect of the Social Network Campaign: Tweeter Big Data Analysis of the 19th National Election], *Korean Political Science Review* 47(4), 93–112.

Cho, J. (2011), 'Jeongbohwaga jeongchichamyeoe michineun hyogwa: Gyeongheomjeok bunseok' [An Empirical Analysis on the Relationship between the Development of ICTs and Political Participation], *Korean Political Science Review* 45(5), 273–296.

Choi, J. (2016), 'SNS iyonggwa jeongchichamyeo: Jeongchijeok sahoejabon-gwa jeongbo mit orakchugu donggiui jojeoldoen maegaehyogwareul jungsimeuro' [The Effects of SNS Use on Political Participation: Focusing on the Moderated Mediation Effects of Politically Relevant Social Capital and Motivations], *Korean Journal of Journalism & Communication Studies* 60(5), 123–144.

Choi, M., Lee, H., and Kim, W. (2013), 'Tupyojaui hubo jiji byeonhwawa midieo taedo byeonhwa: Je18dae daetongnyeongseon-geo paeneol yeon-gu' [The Voters' Changes in the Candidate Supports and the Media Attitudes: A Panel Study of the 18th Presidential Election Voters], *Journal of Communication Science* 13(3), 627–660.

Chung, I. (2014), 'Seongeo maeche yuhyeonggwa tupyogyeoljeong yoine daehan yeon-gu: 6.2 jibangseon-geo, 4.11 chongseon, 12.19 daetongnyeong seon-geo bigyo' [The Impact of Social Media on the Voters' Candidate Choice Factors: The Analysis of Social Media in the 6.4 Busan Local Election], *Locality & Communication* 18(4), 239–278.

Chung, Y., and Cho, S. D. (2004), 'Hanguk netijeunui juyo guseonggwa jeongchijeok teukseong: 17dae chongseoneul jungsimeuro' [A Research on Socioeconomic and Political Features of Korean Netizen: Focusing the Case of the 17th National Congressional Election], *National Strategy* 10(3), 117–146.

Craig, R. T. (1999), 'Communication Theory as a Field', *Communication Theory* 9(2), 119–161.

Davis, R. (1999), *The Web of Politics: The Internet's Impact on the American Political System* (New York: Oxford University Press).

Davis, R., and Owen, D. (1998), *New Media and American Politics* (New York: Oxford University Press).

Dilliplane, S. (2014), 'Activation, Conversion, or Reinforcement? The Impact of Partisan News Exposure on Vote Choice', *American Journal of Political Science* 58(1), 79–94.

Foot, K. A., and Schneider, S. M. (2006), *Web Campaigning* (London: MIT Press).

Gerodimos, R., and Justinussen, J. (2015), 'Obama's 2012 Facebook Campaign: Political Communication in the Age of the Like Button', *Journal of Information Technology & Politics* 12(2), 113–132.

Grossman, L. (1995), *The Electronic Republic* (London: Penguin).

Hague, B. N., and Loader, B. D. (1999), *Digital Democracy* (New York: Routledge).

Hargittai, E., and Shaw, A. (2013), 'Digitally Savvy Citizenship: The Role of Internet Skills and Engagement in Young Adults' Political Participation around the 2008 Presidential Election', *Journal of Broadcasting & Electronic Media* 57(2), 115–134.

Hong, W. (2011), 'Mueosi daehaksaeng-eul tupyohage hayeonneun-ga? 10.26 bogwolseon-georeul tonghae salpyeobon daehaksaeng tupyouiji hyeongseong-e daehan yeon-gu' [What Made College Students Vote in the 10.26 By-Election?], *Journal of Political Communication* 23, 327–359.

Jungherr, A. (2016), 'Twitter Use in Election Campaigns: A Systematic Literature Review', *Journal of Information Technology & Politics* 13(1), 72–91.

Kamarck, E. C. (2002), 'Political Campaigning on the Internet: Business as Usual?, in E. C. Kamarck and J. S. Nye, eds, *Governance.com: Democracy in the Information Age*, 81–103 (Washington D.C.: Brookings Institution Press).

Kang, W. (1999), 'Yugwonjaui seontaekgwa TV seongeoundongui hyogwa' [Voter Choice and the Effects of TV Election Campaign], *Journal of Korean Politics* 8, 155–174.

Kang, W., Yun, S., Cho, H., and Lee, S. (2012), *SNSreul hwaryonghan jeongchihongbo yeongu* [A Study on Political Advertisement using SNS] (Seoul: Korea Press Foundation).

Katz, J. E., and Rice, R. E. (2002), *Social Consequences of Internet Use: Access, Involvement, and Interaction* (Cambridge, MA: MIT Press).

Kim, S., Kim, Y., and Kim, J. (2011), 'Wep(Web) gisul baljeondangyebyeol iyongjaui jeongchichamyeo haengtae yeongu' [A Study of Web 1.0–3.0 Technologies and New Political Participations], *Journal of Communication Science* 11(4), 103–137.

Kim, S. T., Kim, Y. J., Choi, H. G., and Kim, H. J. (2011), 'Nyumidieoreul tonghan sotong chaeneorui hwakjanggwa jeongchichamyeo byeonhwa yeon-gu: inteonetgwa sosyeolmidieoreul jumokamyeo' [Communication Channel Expansion and Political Participation: Focusing on the Internet and Social Media], *Peace Studies* 19(1), 5–38.

Kim, Y. C. (2004), 'Je17dae chongseongwa inteonet hompeijireul iyonghan seon-geoundong: seon-geoundong-yuhyeonggwa netijeunchamyeoreul jungsimeuro' [Internet Campaign in the 17th National Assembly Election: Types of the Internet Campaign and Netizen's Participation], *21st Century Political Science Review* 14(2), 75–96.

Kim, Y. C., and Yun, S. (2004), 'Je17dae chongseoneseo inteonesui yeonghyangnyeok bunseok: seongeogwansimdowa tupyocheomyeoreul jungsimeuro' [The Influence of the Internet on the Electoral Concern and Voting Participation in the 17th National Assembly election], *Korean Political Science Review* 38(5), 197–216.

Kim, Y. H. (2018), 'Je 19 dae daeseon hubojaui sosyeolmidieo iyong donghyanggwa teukjing' [Presidential Candidates' Trends and Characteristics of Social Media Use], *Issue and Point* 1406, 1–4.

Ko, K, and Song, H. (2010), 'Inteonet hang-uiwa jeongchichamyeo, geurigo minjujeok hamui: 2008nyeon chotbulsiwi sarye' [Protest Using the Internet, Political Participation and Its Democratic Implications: The Case of the 2008 Candlelight Protest in Korea], *Journal of Democracy and Human Rights* 10(3), 233–269.

Kum, H. (2011), 'Jeongchiinui sns hwaryong: Jeongchijeok sotong doguroseoui teuwiteo' [Utilization of SNS in Congress: Twitter as a Political Communication Mechanism], *Korean Party Studies Review* 10(2), 189–220.

Kum, H. (2014), '18dae daetongnyeong hubodeurui nyumidieo seon-geojeollyak pyeongga' [Evaluation of Candidates' New Media Campaign Strategies for the 18th Presidential Election in Korea], *21st Century Political Science Review* 24(1), 121–143.

Kunda, Z. (1990), 'The Case of Motivated Reasoning', *Psychological Bulleti.* 108, 480–498.

Lee, M., Seo, H. J., and Kim, H. (2012), 'Tupyoinjeungsyat Bunseok Jagipyohyeon-gwa Seoldeugui Keomyunikeisyeon' [Why Do People Post the Mentions with Their Picture of Voting on Twitter?], *Korean Journal of Journalism & Communication Studies* 56(6), 246–277.

Lee, S., and Kim, D. (2012), 'Sosyeolmidieoui jeongchijeok iyongi yugwonjadeurui jeongchi chamyeo uidoe michineun yeonghyang yeongu' [The Impact of Using Social Media with Political Purposes on the Intention of Political Participation of Social Media Users], *Journal of Public Relations* 16(1), 78–111.

Lee, S. Y. (2012), '4.11 chongseon-gwa sosyeol neteuwokeu jeongchikaempein: Chongseon hubojaui teuwiteo seon-geokaempeineul jungsimeuro' [Social Network Campaign in the 19th Korean Assembly Elections], *21st Century Political Science Review* 22(3), 287–312.

Lee, S. Y., Park, Y. H., Lee, H. S., and Lim, Y. J. (2020), *Analyzing the Effects of TV Debates in the 21st National Assembly Election* (Seoul: Korean Political Science Association).

Lilleker, D. G., Koc-Michalska, K., Schweitzer, E. J., Jacunski, M., Jackson, N., and Vedel, T. (2011), 'Informing, Engaging, Mobilizing or Interacting: Searching for a European Model of Web Campaigning', *European Journal of Communication* 26(3), 195–213.

Negroponte, N. (1995), *Being Digital* (New York: Knopf).

Norris, P. (2000), *A Virtuous Circle: Political Communications in Postindustrial Societies* (Cambridge: Cambridge University Press).

Norris, P. (2001), *Digital Divide: Civic Engagement, Information Poverty, and the Internet Worldwide* (Cambridge: Cambridge University Press).

Pariser, E. (2011), *The Filter Bubble: What the Internet Is Hiding from You* (London: Penguin).

Park, C., and Cho, J. (2013), 'SNSui jeongchijeok dongwongineunge gwanhan bipanjeok gochal: 18dae daeseoneseo teuwiteoreul jungsimeuro' [A Critical Review of Twitter Political Mobilization Effect], *Korean Party Studies Review* 12(2), 187–220.

Rash, W. Jr (1997), *Politics on the Nets: Wiring the Political Process* (New York: W. H. Freeman).
Shim, H. (2012), 'Sosyeolmidieoui jeongchichamyeo hyogwae gwanhan yeon-gu: Jugwanjeok gyubeomgwa dongnyujipdanamnyeogeul jungsimeuro' [The Effect of Social Media Use on Political Participation: Focusing on the Subjective Norm and Peer-Group Pressure], *Communication Theories* 8(3), 6–52.
Shin, H., and Woo, J. (2011), 'Teuwiteoeseo ireonaneun jeongchijeok damnonhwaldonge daehan tamsaekjeok yeongu: 2010nyeon 62 jibangseongeogwallyeon teuwitgeul naeyong bunseogeul jungsimeuro' [An Exploratory Study on Twitter as a Sphere of Political Discussion], *Media & Society* 19(3), 45–76.
Song, K. J., and Min, H. (2009), 'Inteonet jeongchijeongbo sanghojagyonggwa jeongchichamyeo: 18dae chongseon netijeun seolmunjosareul jungsimeuro' [The Internet Political Information Interactivity and Political Participation], *21st Century Political Science Review* 19(1), 71–91.
Sung, D., Yang, S., Kim, Y., and Lim, S. (2007), 'On-opeurain jeongchichamyeoe daehan midieo yeonghyangnyeok bigyo yeongu: Nyuseuiyong midieoe ttareun suyongja sebunhwareul jungsimeuro' [A Comparative Study on the Media Effects about On-Off line Political Participation: Focus on the Audiences' Fragmentation According to the Use of News Media], *Journal of Cybercommunication Academic Society* 24, 5–50.
Sunstein, C. R. (2001), *Echo Chambers: Bush v. Gore, Impeachment, and Beyond* (Princeton, NJ: Princeton University Press).
Vitak, J., Zube, P., Smock, A., Carr, C. T., Ellison, N., and Lampe, C. (2011), 'It's Complicated: Facebook Users' Political Participation in the 2008 Election', *Cyberspychology, Behavior, and Social Networking* 14(3), 107–114.
Yun, S. (2003), '16dae daetongnyeongseongeowa inteonesui yeonghyangnyeok' [2002 Presidential Election in South Korea and the Effects of the Internet], *Korean Political Science Review* 37(3), 71–87.
Yun, S. (2008), '17dae daeseone natanan ollain seongeoundongui teukseonggwa hangye' [Why the Online Election Campaign Failed in the 2007 Presidential Election]. *Korean Political Science Review* 42(2), 71–87.
Yun, S. (2013), 'Teuwiteoui jeongchijeok hwaryongi tupyohaengtaee michineun yeonghyang: 19dae chongseon saryereul jungsimeuro' [Political Use of Tweet and Its Impact on Voting Behavior: The 19th National Assembly Election], *21st Century Political Science Review.* 23(3), 225–245.
Yun, S. (2014), 'Nyumidieo hwaksangwa seongeoui byeonhwa' [The Proliferation of New Media and Change in Election], *Studies of Broadcasting Culture* 26(2), 67–92.
Zimmermann, F., and Kohring, M. (2020), 'Mistrust, Disinforming News, and Vote Choice: A Panel Survey on the Origins and Consequences of Believing Disinformation in the 2017 German Parliamentary Election', *Political Communication* 37, 215–237.

CHAPTER 18

NEW ISSUE POLITICS

SEUNG-JIN JANG

1. INTRODUCTION

It has long been believed that not many issues were contested in South Korean politics. Under a series of authoritarian regimes, South Korean politics was all about being for or against democratisation. Since democratisation was achieved in 1987, South Korean politics has been dominated by a small number of political parties, whose support bases were largely defined by geographical regions, with little issue content. Since the 2000s, although a new cleavage emerged across generational differences in political ideology, political disagreements have been predominantly defined by a narrow set of political issues related to North–South Korean relations and reunification.

However, the first sign of change came when, in 2008, several hundred thousand ordinary citizens participated in Candlelight demonstrations protesting the resumption of importation of US beef products (suspected of causing 'mad cow disease'). Throughout a series of demonstrations, public opposition gradually expanded to such issues as educational reforms and privatisation of public enterprises. The Seoul mayoral by-election in 2010 was another milestone. The sitting mayor of Seoul, who opposed the city-wide introduction of a free school lunch programme, resigned after he lost in a local referendum and the issue quickly evolved into more general issues of social welfare. Two years later, the issue of economic democratisation stood out as an important campaign issue in the eighteenth Presidential election. Afterwards, politicians and voters began to discuss a wide range of issues, many of which had never been salient in South Korean politics.

This chapter reviews some of the new issues that have—or may potentially—become salient in South Korean politics, and what the public thinks of them. Of course, the list of new issues is selective and far from exhaustive. The issues covered here are simply those that, based on the literature on South Korean politics and society over the past decade, seem to be noteworthy in understanding contemporary and near-future South Korean politics.

2. Economic Issues: Welfare and Redistribution

South Korea has long been barren ground for economic issues to play significant roles in political competitions. It has maintained a small welfare state with limited redistribution intervention by the government. Distributive interests of organised workers were violently suppressed by authoritarian governments or co-opted by collective bargaining at the company level for wage increase, corporate welfare, and job security (Yang 2013). The single-member district plurality system set a high hurdle for newly formed leftist parties, which in turn enabled mainstream parties to keep related issues off the political agenda.

However, the financial crisis in 1997 shook this ground profoundly. Many South Koreans experienced severe economic hardship, and the South Korean economy entered a phase of structural low growth. Economic inequality increased rapidly, with corresponding decreases in social mobility. Public demands for welfare and expansion of the social safety net soared, and, in this respect, it was not a coincidence that the issue of a free school lunch programme became salient in the Seoul mayoral by-election in 2010. Elected officials began to take positions on these issues and to have a different voice. For example, Kang et al. (2020) and Park et al. (2016) show that, since the eighteenth National Assembly in 2008, members of the two major political parties have taken clearly distinctive positions on economic issues, such as welfare increase, regulation of big business, privatisation of health care, and public funding for childcare, while differences on political issues still persist.

These changes have triggered a large literature on South Koreans' attitudes towards welfare and redistribution. Earlier studies found that South Koreans had highly inconsistent and fragmented welfare attitudes and that no significant class differences could be found in their attitudes (e.g. Kim and Yeo 2011). However, more recent data show that a person's income and assets have begun to exert significant and systemic effects on preferences on welfare and redistribution (Kim and Kwon 2017; Lee et al. 2018; Yeo and Kim 2015).

Table 18.1, which is based on data from the 2016 Korean General Social Survey (KGSS), displays the contour of welfare attitudes among South Koreans. The majority of respondents supported welfare expansion as well as tax increases to afford it. More importantly, support for tax increases tends to be higher as we move to the respondents who express stronger support for welfare expansion. In the sense that people who want welfare expansion are also willing to pay more tax to financially afford it, the pattern in Table 18.1 indicates that welfare attitudes among South Koreans have become more consistent than before.

Another point to be noted is that South Koreans' welfare attitudes are also differentiated by age group, as younger generations are more likely to support government intervention to reduce inequality and poverty than older ones (Kim and Roh 2017). This is

Table 18.1: Welfare attitudes among South Koreans (%, N = 1,042)

	Tax increase to expand social welfare			
	Agree	Neither agree nor disagree	Disagree	Total
The government should provide welfare at the maximum level	14.68	4.22	5.09	23.99
↑	16.70	8.45	4.51	29.65
	10.08	6.33	5.57	21.98
↓	6.72	3.65	3.65	14.01
The government should provide minimum assistance as needed	3.55	1.44	5.37	10.36
Total	51.73	24.09	24.18	100

Source: Korean General Social Survey, 2016.

important because, since the 2000s, a person's age has become a key factor influencing their political ideology and vote choices. The fact that preferences on welfare and redistribution are also differentiated by age group implies that these issues may have become an integral dimension which defines the progressive–conservative political ideology spectrum in South Korean politics.

In fact, Table 18.2 shows that, depending on political ideology, South Korean voters display considerable differences in policy preferences not only on political issues (which have been believed to predominantly, if not solely, determine political ideology in South Korean politics), but also on economic issues. Differences between progressives and conservatives are still greater on political issues than on economic issues. In addition, progressives and conservatives are not so different from each other in magnitude, yet are statistically significantly different on some economic issues, such as tax increases on high-income earners and privatisation of public enterprises. However, it is undeniable that ideological splits in South Korean politics now occur in multiple dimensions and economic issues compose one of them.

One may argue that the importance of economic issues in recent South Korean politics implies the possibility of a new political cleavage rising between the haves and have-nots. In fact, there are some studies that present empirical evidence of stratification of vote choices and policy preferences across economic status (Jang 2013; Lee 2014a; Lee and Kwon 2016; Lee and You 2019). The conventional wisdom in South Korean politics that low-income voters tend to vote for conservative parties and candidates—so-called class-betrayal voting—largely disappears once we control for the fact that low-income voters are concentrated among the old, who make overwhelmingly conservative choices (Cheon and Shin 2014; Kang 2013; Lee and You 2019).

Table 18.2: Political and economic issue preferences by political ideology (%, N = 1,016)

	Political ideology		
	Progressive	Moderate	Conservative
Strengthening South Korean–US Alliance			
Agree	54.66	54.45	73.08
Neither agree nor disagree	31.37	37.43	22.44
Disagree	13.98	8.12	4.49
Abolishment of National Security Law			
Agree	34.37	17.54	18.91
Neither agree nor disagree	31.37	43.98	32.69
Disagree	34.16	38.48	48.40
Normalisation of Gaeseong industrial complex			
Agree	49.69	37.17	33.65
Neither agree nor disagree	25.78	36.65	31.09
Disagree	24.53	26.18	35.26
Priority of welfare over economic development			
Agree	43.17	36.65	30.45
Neither agree nor disagree	28.88	34.03	33.65
Disagree	27.95	29.32	35.90
Discretion of business over contingent workers			
Agree	16.46	18.42	23.72
Neither agree nor disagree	6.15	29.74	29.17
Disagree	67.39	51.84	47.12
Tax increase of high-income earners			
Agree	84.47	78.27	76.60
Neither agree nor disagree	11.80	17.28	12.18
Disagree	3.73	4.45	11.22
Privatisation of public enterprises			
Agree	20.19	20.16	23.72
Neither agree nor disagree	17.70	33.77	33.01
Disagree	62.11	46.07	43.27

Source: Korean General Social Survey, 2016.

However, the saliency of economic issues should not be overstated. For the cleavage between the haves and have-nots to become salient, it must be the case that individuals with a similar age make different political choices depending on their economic status; however, there is little evidence that a person's income brings such heterogeneity within the same age group (Kim and Lee 2020). Studies that argue otherwise tend to focus on alternative measures of economic status such as education, wealth (or their combination with income), and subjective class consciousness. If income makes a difference, it is limited to the period when income inequality is rising (Lee and Kwon 2016). Above all, regardless of the measures of a person's economic status, variations in South Koreans' political ideology and vote choices across them are still not as salient as across a person's age or region of residence.

Therefore, the advent of class cleavage in South Korean politics remains in the realm of possibility. The key variable here will be how the state of economic inequality changes. If economic inequality continues to increase and the prospect of social mobility keeps shrinking, voters in the same age group or region will re-sort themselves into different prescriptions for improving the distribution of economic resources and opportunities in South Korean society. Then, the rise of a new cleavage between the haves and have-nots—along with the current one between the young and the old—will not be a remote possibility.

3. Gender Issues

In established democracies, it is often the case that gender does not explain much variation in political behaviour. In the past, it was argued that women might be less interested in, less knowledgeable about, and less participatory in politics than men. When they did participate, women tended to vote for conservative parties, if not simply follow their spouses' decisions. However, the expansion of women's opportunities for higher education and professional jobs, changes in perceptions—and practices to a lesser extent—of gender roles in the family and workplace, and the rise of feminism and gender consciousness have encouraged women to take more active and independent roles in politics, and thus diminished gender differences in political engagement.

Nowadays, women turn out to vote in most elections at a rate comparable with men, though some degree of disparity still persists in second-order elections and in non-institutional forms of participation (Burns et al. 2001). On the other hand, the 'traditional' gender gap has been replaced by the 'modern' gender gap in many western democracies (Inglehart and Norris 2000). Because women tend to be less economically well off and more likely to have caring responsibilities than men, women are generally on the left of men in their policy preferences and vote choices (Abendschön and Steinmetz 2014; Alvarez and McCaffery 2003; Bergh 2007; Box-Steffensmeier et al. 2004; Howell and Day 2000; Iversen and Rosenbluth 2006; Manza and Brooks 1998).

3.1 The Gender Gap in South Korea

South Korea has been known for its strong patriarchal culture with Confucian traditions, which makes it questionable whether the traditional gender gap has been similarly

Table 18.3: Turnout rates in recent elections by gender (%)

	Presidential elections			National Assembly elections			Nationwide local elections		
	2007	2012	2017	2008	2012	2016	2010	2014	2018
Male	63.3	74.8	76.2	48.4	55.7	58.8	55.1	57.2	59.9
Female	63.1	76.4	77.3	44.3	53.1	57.4	54.7	57.2	61.2

Source: Republic of Korea National Election Commission.

replaced by the modern one in South Korea as it has in many western societies. In fact, many studies on the gender gap in South Korea have shown that the traditional gender gap is still prevalent. Though overall turnout rates in elections are not significantly different between male and female voters (see Table 18.3), until recently, individual-level survey data show that female voters are still relatively less interested in and less psychologically engaged in politics (Koo 2019; Lee 2013). For example, according to the 2016 KGSS, 58.9 per cent of female respondents said that they were not very, or not at all, interested in politics (as opposed to 38.9 per cent of male respondents) and 25.2 per cent of female respondents did not support any particular political party (as opposed to 22.3 per cent of male respondents).

On the other hand, despite the persistence of the traditional gender gap, a few studies report evidence of the emergence of the modern gender gap in South Korea. It is no longer the case that female voters are more conservative than male voters in their political orientations, vote choices, and evaluations of female candidates (Lee 2013; Lee 2014a). South Korean women may still not be particularly progressive compared to men. Figure 18.1 displays the percentages of male and female respondents whose political ideology is conservative or progressive over time. Until the late 2000s, South Korean women were on average more conservative than men because there were significantly less ideologically progressive women. However, in the 2010s, the difference in political ideology between the genders has sharply reduced as an increasing number of women have embraced progressive ideology.

If we focus on younger generations of South Koreans, it may seem more evident that the modern gender gap is emergent in South Korea. It is well known that women in their late twenties and thirties consistently turn out to vote at higher rates than their male counterparts (Koo 2019; Koo et al. 2015). Studies also find that, among youth, women have more progressive views than men on issues of North Korea and reunification (Koo and Choi 2019) and are more likely to support progressive parties and candidates (Kim and Lee 2020). However, with the rapid transformation in social structure over a short period of time, there are still greater differences in political attitudes between the younger and older generations of women than between men and women in the same generation (Park 2020). Therefore, it is premature to say that young South Korean men and women are distinctive from each other in any politically

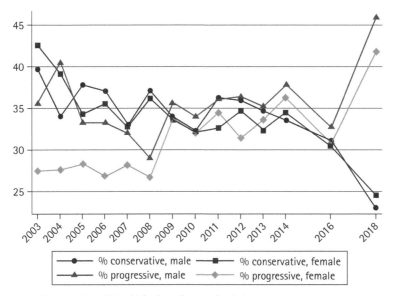

FIGURE 18.1: Changes in political ideology by gender (%)

Source: Korean General Social Survey, 2003–2018.

significant way and thus that the South Korean society is witnessing the rise of a new social cleavage based on gender.

3.2 The Emergence of Gender Conflicts

Since the mid-2010s, gender has gained new political significance in South Korean society. The rise of so-called Me Too movements and a series of hate crimes and (alleged) sexual abuse cases against women have made gender inequality and women's grievances salient in public discourses. Unreasonable expressions of hatred towards the opposite sex are rampant online, and a large number of ordinary women organised offline sit-ins protesting against gender discrimination. It seems that South Korean society is now divided by gender and that gender conflicts have become one of the most serious problems to be addressed.

However, in spite of the impression that one may get from recent media reports, gender is still not the most salient basis of social conflict in South Korea. According to the Korean Social Integration Surveys (KSIS), conducted annually by the Korea Institute of Public Administration (KIPA), South Koreans think that the most serious conflicts in South Korean society are ideological ones between progressives and the conservatives, followed closely by economic ones between the haves and the have-nots. Figure 18.2 shows that in 2019, 87.4 per cent of respondents believed that ideological conflicts are somewhat or very serious, and 82 per cent believed that economic conflicts are. On the other hand, 54.7 per cent of respondents believed that gender

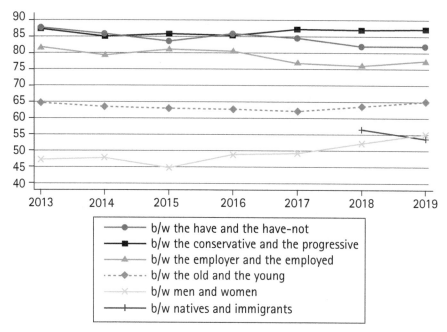

FIGURE 18.2: Salience of different types of social conflicts in Korea (%)

Note: Data show the percentage of respondents who believed that the given conflicts are somewhat or very serious.

Source: Korean Social Integration Surveys, 2013–2019.

conflicts between men and women are somewhat or very serious. Of course, it is undeniable that the salience of gender conflicts has increased during the 2010s. However, many South Koreans still believe that other types of social conflicts are more serious than gender conflicts.

While the salience of gender conflicts has not reached the level of other social conflicts, especially those of a socio-economic nature, this does not mean that people are not concerned with gender relations in South Korean society. For example, Figure 18.3 shows the percentages of respondents who believe that gender relations in South Korea are somewhat or very unfair, divided by a person's gender and age group. A couple of things are noticeable from the results. First, an increasing number of South Koreans believe that men and women are not treated fairly. Second, a person's gender and age make significant differences in perceptions of gender relations in South Korea: women and the young are more sensitive to unfair treatment between genders than men and the old. Last, and probably most importantly, the difference between age groups has recently been replaced by one between genders, and in 2019, South Korean men in their twenties and thirties more resemble older men than they do women of their age. In other words, gender relations can potentially be an issue that divides men and women, cross-cutting generations that have traditionally defined political cleavages in South Korea.

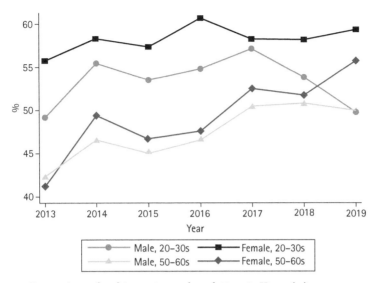

FIGURE 18.3: Perceptions of unfairness in gender relations in Korea (%)

Note: Data show the percentage of respondents who believed that gender relations in Korea are somewhat or very unfair.

Source: Korean Social Integration Surveys, 2013–2019.

What do South Koreans then think of more specific aspects of gender relations? Table 18.4 shows how respondents of the KGSS in 2018 answered a series of questions regarding gender stereotypes and women's roles in South Korean society. The results are somewhat contradictory to what Figure 18.3 may indicate. With respect to what gender relations should look like in South Korea, men in their twenties and thirties have opinions more similar with women of their age than with older-aged men. What Figure 18.3 and Table 18.3 together show is as follows: many young South Korean men are like their female counterparts in normatively believing that men and women should be treated equally, thus in being relatively free from the traditional patriarchal culture. However, they are different from young women in their perceptions of whether women are actually discriminated against—therefore, by extension, in need of some remedial measures—in South Korean society.

In a similar regard, the KGSS in 2016 featured an interesting experiment. Respondents, randomly divided into two groups, are offered a list of groups that are said to be discriminated against in South Korean society. A baseline list, offered to the control group, includes the following five groups: immigrant workers, people from Jeolla province, disabled persons, sexual minorities, and conscientious objectors. The treatment group receives the same list with the addition of a sixth group, women. Respondents are asked to indicate how many groups they think are not being discriminated against so that they do not need protection at the governmental level. As two groups are offered with the same list with the exception of women, a significant difference between the average responses among the treatment group and the control group attests to what respondents

Table 18.4: Opinions on gender relations in Korea (%, N = 1,028)

	Male All	Male 20s–30s	Male 50s–60s	Female All	Female 20s–30s	Female 50s–60s
The things that husbands and wives should do in family life must be distinguished						
Strongly/fairly/somewhat agree	26.2	11.0	36.1	26.3	8.1	40.3
Neither agree nor disagree	21.5	20.3	21.3	16.6	16.1	16.8
Strongly/fairly/somewhat disagree	52.4	68.7	42.6	57.1	75.8	42.9
Husband's job is to earn money and wife's job is to look after the home and family						
Strongly/fairly/somewhat agree	26.5	8.6	40.0	26.4	6.7	36.8
Neither agree nor disagree	24.7	22.7	25.2	18.0	16.8	20.3
Strongly/fairly/somewhat disagree	48.8	68.7	34.8	55.6	76.5	42.9
It is more important for a wife to help her husband's career than to pursue her own career						
Strongly/fairly/somewhat agree	36.6	12.3	55.8	41.1	14.8	60.6
Neither agree nor disagree	20.1	18.4	19.5	14.8	10.7	15.5
Strongly/fairly/somewhat disagree	43.3	69.3	24.7	44.1	74.5	23.9
What women really want are a family and children, although they like to work too						
Strongly/fairly/somewhat agree	37.1	16.0	53.9	44.1	14.8	61.0
Neither agree nor disagree	28.3	33.7	23.5	18.7	15.4	18.4
Strongly/fairly/somewhat disagree	34.6	50.3	22.6	37.2	69.8	20.6

Source: Korean General Social Survey, 2018.

think of women's status in South Korean society. By only answering the total number of social groups, rather than specifying which, this 'list experiment' is a good technique to uncover a person's true thoughts on sensitive items.

Figure 18.4 shows the results of the list experiment across a person's gender and age group. Among male respondents in their twenties and thirties, as well as among males who are fifty or older, the treatment group scores statistically higher average responses than the control group. On the other hand, among female respondents, irrespective of their age, the differences in average responses between the treatment group and the control group failed to reach a statistical significance at the 95 per cent confidence level. In other words, young South Korean men are likely to disagree that women are victims of severe discrimination and thus in need of governmental protection and compensation.

Few can deny the fact that gender disparities and discrimination against women still persist in South Korean society: The World Economic Forum ranks South Korea 108th out of 153 countries in its Global Gender Gap Report 2020. Out of 300 members of the National Assembly elected in 2020, there are only 57 female members (19 per cent). And the gender wage gap in South Korea is the highest among Organisation for Economic Co-operation and Development (OECD) countries at 32.5 per cent in 2019, with only

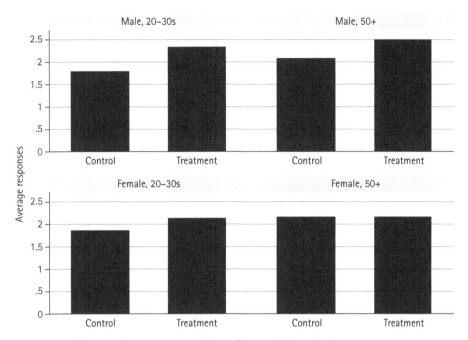

FIGURE 18.4: List experiment on perceptions of women's status in Korea

Source: Korean General Social Survey, 2016.

about 10 per cent of all managerial positions being held by women. Then, why are many young male South Koreans, who are willing to embrace the ideal of gender equality, reluctant to acknowledge the objective reality and give only lukewarm support for public policies to address gender inequalities? One possible answer lies in how they perceive social and economic structures of South Korean society and their prospects for status mobility in it. The South Korean media often reports on the severe competition young South Koreans have to go through in striving for higher education and better jobs, which in turn leads them to be excessively meritocratic. This may result in them being critical of any measures that violate strictly procedural equality, even for the purpose of achieving substantive equality, including in gender relations. However, no scientific research so far has been done to test this hypothesis, which may be a key to understanding the possibility that the issue of gender will become a new salient cleavage in South Korean politics.

4. The Issue of Immigration

According to the Ministry of the Interior and Safety (MOIS), the foreign-born population in South Korea amounted to over 2 million in 2018, which was more than twice that in 2008. The foreign-born population now comprises about 4 per cent of the total population in South Korea; though still not being high in absolute terms, its rapid increase is unparalleled to that of the native population. In addition, while migrant workers still occupy the largest share of the foreign-born population (32 per cent), female marriage immigrants and foreign-national Koreans—who tend to enter with the purpose of long-term residence—have increased to a much greater and faster extent, and thus diversified the foreign-born population in South Korea. Combining with the trend of declining fertility and population aging, immigrants are henceforth expected to play more significant roles in the South Korean economy and society, which naturally leads to the increasing political saliency of related issues.

4.1 Attitudes towards Immigration and Immigrants

In spite of—or due to—the increasing number of immigrants in South Korean society, the majority of South Koreans are still not particularly hospitable to them. In the 2018 KGSS, 43.6 per cent of respondents answered that the number of foreign workers should be decreased, while only 17.2 per cent said their number should be increased. Similarly, 31.7 per cent of respondents answered that the number of women marriage immigrants should be decreased, while 21.5 per cent said their number should be increased. In fact, compared to ten years ago, percentages of KGSS respondents who oppose the inflow of immigrants have declined (see Table 18.5). However, it is also true that a greater number of South Koreans are still reluctant to accept, rather than welcome, new immigrants.

One of the reasons why many South Koreans are not welcoming newcomers with open arms should have to do with how immigrants are perceived to affect the South Korean economy and society. According to the survey of Korean attitudes and values, commissioned by the Ministry of Culture, Sports, and Tourism (MCST) in 2016, South Koreans hold not so positive—if not altogether negative—views about the consequences of immigration. However, major concerns that South Koreans have on immigration are not of an economic nature. A greater number of South Koreans raise concerns that immigrants may increase crime rates and harm the social integrity and cultural unity of the nation than those who are concerned with economic ramifications. In other words,

Table 18.5: South Koreans' attitudes towards inflow of immigrants (%)

	Foreign workers		Female marriage immigrants	
	2008	2018	2008	2018
Should increase greatly/some	20.2	17.2	22.0	21.5
Should stay the same	26.6	36.9	28.5	41.9
Should decrease greatly/some	50.5	43.6	46.3	31.7

Note: Numbers do not add up to 100 due to 'don't know' or no opinion.
Source: Korean General Social Survey, 2008 and 2018.

Table 18.6: South Koreans' attitudes towards consequences of immigration (%)

	(Strongly) agree	Neither agree nor disagree	(Strongly) Disagree
Foreign workers take jobs away from native Koreans	32.8	34.8	32.4
Foreign workers drain, rather than contribute to, the national wealth	35.3	38.4	26.3
Immigrants cause the increase of crime rates	49.0	34.6	16.4
Accepting people with diverse national origins harms the national unity	39.7	44.9	15.3
Legal immigrants should have the same rights as native Koreans	54.9	32.5	12.6
Regardless of parents' national origins, a person born in South Korea should have the right to citizenship	46.4	35.3	18.3

Source: MCST Survey of Korean Attitudes and Values, 2016.

while recognising the economic benefits of immigration, many South Koreans have considerable reservations about the advent of a multicultural society (Jang 2010; Yoon 2016). Interestingly, however, Table 18.6 also shows that South Koreans are relatively tolerant of granting legal rights to immigrants in spite of reservations about their social integration.

What, then, explains South Koreans' attitudes towards the entrance and integration of immigrants to South Korean society? Most studies agree that economic self-interests do not have much explanatory power. Instead, those South Koreans who believe that immigrants undermine the longstanding cultural unity of South Korea are more likely to embrace exclusive definitions of the national in-group, to oppose an increase in numbers of immigrants, and to be critical of the integration of immigrants into South Korean society (Chang 2019; Ha and Jang 2015; Hahn et al. 2013; Jang 2010; Jo 2011; Min 2013). When the economy matters, it is the socio-tropic evaluations of the national economy, rather than the pocketbook evaluations of individual financial situations, that influence South Korean attitudes towards immigration.

Among other determinants of South Korean attitudes towards immigration, it is noticeable that the effect of political ideology is somewhat limited. This is in part because the issue of immigration and multiculturalism has not yet become a salient issue that aligns South Korean voters along the ideological or partisan divide. Major political parties do not clearly distinguish themselves from each other in their votes on immigration and multicultural policies in the National Assembly (Seol and Jeon 2016). Except in a small number of areas with a large number of immigrants, many South Koreans still perceive the issue of immigration as a distant one, with little relevance to their personal or political choices. However, as the number of immigrants continues to increase, it is natural to expect that issues of how to accommodate and incorporate these newcomers will become more and more salient in South Korean politics.

4.2 Attitudes towards North Korean Defectors

In addition to immigrants in general, there is a particular group of newcomers to South Korea with unique backgrounds: North Korean defectors. Since the famine in the late 1990s, increasing numbers of North Koreans have decided to leave the country for South Korea. According to the Ministry of Unification, the annual number of North Korean defectors entering South Korea was less than 1,000 in the 1990s, but consistently increased to 2,000–3,000 between 2006 and 2011. Since 2012, the number of North Korean defectors entering South Korea in a given year decreased to an average of about 1,300, and 1,047 North Korean were admitted in 2019. Currently, about 30,000 North Korean defectors in total reside in South Korea.

North Korean defectors have a special political and social status in South Korea, which distinguishes them from other immigrants and refugees from other countries. Though they are viewed as political asylum seekers in South Korea, they are not legally recognised as refugees. As the South Korean Constitution does not recognise North Korea as an independent state, North Korean defectors are not legally considered to have fled their country of origin, but simply to have moved within Korean territory. In addition, as South and North Korea had shared a history as a single political community with a common ancestry and homogeneous culture for more than 1,000 years, North Korean defectors are not ethnically, linguistically, and culturally distinctive from South Koreans in a significant manner.

Given the special status of North Korean defectors, it is interesting that South Koreans do not have positive attitudes towards North Korean defectors, even less so than towards immigrants in general. Figure 18.5 shows the percentage of KSIS respondents who are willing to form an intimate relationship (as a spouse or close friend) or casual relationships (as a co-worker or neighbour) with immigrants and North Korean defectors. Over the years, South Koreans are consistently more willing to form intimate or casual relationships rather with immigrants than with North Korean defectors. In other words, in spite of their similarities in ethnicity, language, and culture, South Koreans feel a greater social distance from North Korean defectors than from other immigrants. In fact, these feelings of social distance are mutual, as many North Korean defectors have had a hard time adjusting to South Korean society and expressed emotional distance or isolation from South Koreans (Kim and Jang 2007).

The reason that South Koreans do not have particularly positive attitudes towards North Korean defectors may be that the political division of the Korean Peninsula for the past seven decades and the concomitant differences in economic and social systems between the two Koreas have led South Koreans to regard North Koreans as a different out-group, who are not distinguishable from other immigrants (Ha and Jang 2016). In fact, those factors that affect South Koreans' attitudes towards immigrants have similar influences on their attitudes towards North Korean defectors (Ha and Jang 2016; Kim et al. 2018). Furthermore, attitudes towards North Korean defectors are inevitably linked to how one thinks of North Korea and its relationships with South Korea (Kim et al.

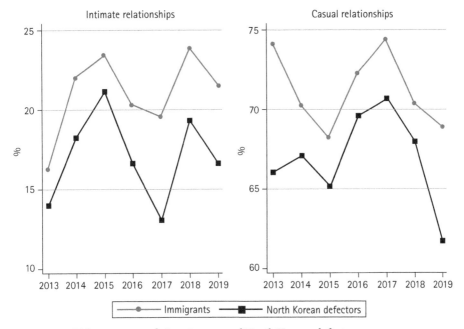

FIGURE 18.5: Tolerance towards immigrants and North Korean defectors

Note: Data show the percentage of respondents who are willing to form intimate (spouse or close friend) and casual (co-worker or neighbour) relationships with immigrants and North Korean defectors.

Source: Korean Social Integration Surveys, 2013–2019.

2018; Kwon and Song 2015). As a result, in contrast to the issue of immigration, which has not yet become a salient political issue, a person's ideological disposition permeates their attitudes towards North Korean defectors, with those with conservative ideology feeling greater social distance from North Korean defectors.

5. Conclusion

Have the issues reviewed in this chapter—welfare and redistribution, gender, and immigration—changed South Korean politics in a significant way? At least so far, the answer is 'not so much'. The political salience of economic issues has certainly increased, and they are now one of the staples on which major political parties and candidates cannot but take positions in electoral campaigns. However, their impacts are still limited if we consider to what extent a person's economic status or preferences on economic issues, controlling for other characteristics, drive political ideology and vote choices in South Korea. Though South Koreans recently seem to be more concerned about the issues of gender or immigration, controversies around these issues are confined to the social realm and have not yet come to the political fore. In addition, the political salience of the issues of gender and immigration is not constant, depending on the occurrence of exogenous events.

Nevertheless, the issues reviewed here show that South Korean politics is no longer simply monopolised by the issue-less regional divide or by a single set of political issues concerning North–South Korea relations. Different issues have moved in and out of public attention and political competitions have taken place on many different fronts. While some of those issues are new, others are older, but in a new form. This diversification of issue content in South Korean politics indicates the dynamism of this still young democracy.

Bibliography

Abendschön, S., and Steinmetz, S. (2014), 'The Gender Gap in Voting Revisited: Women's Party Preferences in a European Context', *Social Politics: International Studies in Gender, State & Society* 21(2), 315–344.

Alvarez, R. M., and McCaffery, E. J. (2003), 'Are There Sex Differences in Fiscal Political Preferences?', *Political Research Quarterly* 56(1), 5–17.

Bergh, J. (2007), 'Explaining the Gender Gap: A Cross-National Analysis of Gender Differences in Voting', *Journal of Elections, Public Opinion and Parties* 17(3), 235–261.

Box-Steffensmeier, J. M., De Boef, S., and Lin, T. M. (2004), 'The Dynamics of the Partisan Gender Gap', *American Political Science Review* 98(3), 515–528.

Burns, N., Schlozman, K. L., and Verba, S. (2001), *The Private Roots of Public Action: Gender, Equality, and Political Participation* (Cambridge, MA: Harvard University Press).

Chang, H. I. (2019), 'Public Attitudes toward Immigration Policies in South Korea', *Asian Journal of Political Science* 27(2), 190–210.

Cheon, B. Y., and Shin, J. W. (2014), 'Jeosodeukcheungilsurok bosujeongdangeul jijihaneunga? hangukeseo gyecheungbyeol jeongdang jijiwa jeongchaek taedo, 2003–2012' [Are Low Incomes More Likely to Be Political Conservative? Party Support and Policy Attitudes by Income in South Korea, 2003–2012], *Journal of Korean Social Trend and Perspective* 91, 9–51.

Ha, S. E., and Jang, S. J. (2015), 'Immigration, Threat Perception, and National Identity: Evidence from South Korea', *International Journal of Intercultural Relations* 44, 53–62.

Ha, S. E., and Jang, S. J. (2016), 'National Identity in a Divided Nation: South Koreans' Attitudes toward North Korean Defectors and the Reunification of two Koreas', *International Journal of Intercultural Relations* 55, 109–119.

Hahn, K. S., Park, S. J., Lee, H., and Lee, H. L. (2013), 'Hangukinui chin-baniminjeok taedo: gaeinseonho pyeonhyanggwa naejaejeok injong taedoui yeonghyang' [Koreans' Attitudes toward Immigration: Person Positivity Bias and the Effects of Implicit Racial Preferences], *Media & Society* 21(3), 107–144.

Howell, S. E., and Day, C. L. (2000), 'Complexities of the Gender Gap', *Journal of Politics* 62(3), 858–874.

Inglehart, R., and Norris, P. (2000), 'The Developmental Theory of the Gender Gap: Women's and Men's Voting Behavior in Global Perspective', *International Political Science Review* 21(4), 441–463.

Iversen, T., and Rosenbluth, F. (2006), 'The Political Economy of Gender: Explaining Cross-National Variation in the Gender Division of Labor and the Gender Voting Gap', *American Journal of Political Science* 50(1), 1–19.

Jang, S. J. (2010), 'Damunhwajuuie daehan hangukindeului taedo: gyeongjejeok ihaegwangyewa gukga jeongcheseongeul jungsimeuro' [Multiculturalism among Koreans: The Role of Economic Self-Interests and National Identities], *Koran Political Science Review* 44(3), 97–119.

Jang, S. J. (2013), '2012nyeon yangdae seongeoeseo natanan gyecheunggyunyeolui ganeungseonggwa hangye' [The 2012 Elections and the Possibility (and Limitation) of Class Cleavage], *Korean Political Science Review* 47(4), 51–70.

Jo, J. I. (2011), 'Nuga wae yeoseonggyeolhoniminjadeulgwa saengsangineungjik geullojadeului yuip jeunggaleul bandaehaneunga: munhwajeok wihyeopbyeoningwa gyeongjejeok wihyeopbyeoninui yeonghyangnyeok bunseokeul jungsimeuro' [Determinants of Korean Political Attitudes toward International Marriage Immigrants and Low-Skilled Migrants], *Koran Political Science Review* 45(2), 281–305.

Kang, W. C., Koo, B. S., Lee, J. M., and Jung, J. (2020), 'Je21dae gukhweuiwon inyeomseonghyanggwa jeongchaek taedo' [Ideology and Policy Positions of the Elect in the 21st Korean National Assembly Election], *Journal of Legislative Studies* 26(3), 37–83.

Kang, W. T. (2013), 'Hanguk seongeoeseoui 'gyegeup baeban tupyo'wa sahwe gyecheung' ["Class betrayal voting" in South Korean elections], *Korean Party Studies Review* 12(3), 5–28.

Kim, G. D., and Lee, J. M. (2020), 'Sedaegyunyeolui imyeom: sedae nae ijilseonge daehan yeongu' [We Are Not the Same: Heterogeneity within Political Cohorts in South Korea], *Korean Political Science Revie.* 54(4), 135–165.

Kim, G. D., Kim, H. B., Jung, J. D., Oh, K. Y., Eom, K. Y., and Lee, J. M. (2018), 'Bukhanitaljumine daehan hangukindeului taedo: sangjingjeongchiirongwa gyeongjeiikironeul iyonghan sigyeyeol bunseok' [South Korean Attitudes toward North Korean Refugees: A Perspective of Symbolic Politics and Economic Interests], *Korea and World Politics* 34(2), 1–36.

Kim, H. G., and Kwon, H. Y. (2017), 'Budongsangwa bokjigukga: jasan, buchae, geurigo bokjitaedo' [House and the Welfare State: Assets, Debts, and Attitudes toward Welfare Policy], *Korean Political Science Review* 51(1), 261–285.

Kim, J. U., and Jang, D. J. (2007), 'Aliens among brothers? The Status and Perception of North Korean Refugees in South Korea', *Asian Perspective* 31(2), 5–22.

Kim, Y. S., and Roh, J. (2017), 'Bokjitaedoe iteseoui sedaehyogwa' [Cohorts and Welfare Attitudes in South Korea], *Korean Party Studies Review* 16(3), 109–142.

Kim, Y. S., and Yeo, E. (2011), 'Hangukinui bokjitaedo: bigyegeupseonggwa biilgwanseong munjeleul jungsimeuro' [Koreans' Welfare Attitude: Focusing on the Inconsistency and Insignificance of Class Differences in Welfare Attitude], *Economy and Society* 91. 211–240.

Koo, B. S. (2019), 'Traditional Gender Gap in a Modernized Society: Gender Dynamics in Voter Turnout in Korea', *Asian Women* 35(1), 19–45.

Koo, B. S., and Choi, J. Y. (2019), 'Byeonhwahaneun hanbando hwangyeonghaeseoui uri gukminui tongilinsik bunseok: hyeondaejeok seongcha, gukga jabusim, tongilhyoyong insik' [An Analysis of Public Perception of Unification in a Changing Security Environment around the Korean Peninsula: Modern Gender Gap, National Pride and Perceived Utility of Unification], *Oughtopia* 34(1), 43–75.

Koo, B. S., Yoon, S. J., and Choi, J. Y. (2015), '20-30dae namnyeo yugwonja tupyoyului seongbyeol yeokjeon hyeonsange gwanhan peojeul' [A Puzzle of Reverse Gender Gap in Young Korean Voter Turnout], *Korean Party Studies Review* 14(2), 115–140.

Kwon, S. H., and Song, Y. H. (2015), 'Pileul nanun hyeongje, iutboda mothan chincheok?: bukhanitaljumine daehan namhanjuminui sahwejeok georigamgwa gyeoljeongyoin, 2007-2014' [Blood Brothers or Distant Relatives? Determinants of Individuals' Social Distance toward North Koreans in South Korea, 2007-2014], *Oughtopia*. 30(2), 123-160.

Lee, C. S., Hwang, I. H., and Lim, H. (2018), 'Hanguk bokjigukgaui sahwegyeongjejeok gicho: jasan bulpyeongdeung, boheomyokgu, bokji seonhodo, 2007-2016' [The Socio-Economic Foundations of the Korean Welfare State: Asset Inequality, Insurance Motives, and Social Policy Preferences, 2007-2016], *Korean Political Science Review* 52(5), 1-30.

Lee, H. K., and Kwon, H. Y. (2016), 'Hangukui bulpyeongdeunggwa jeongchiseonhoui gyecheunghwa' [Inequality and Income Stratification of Voter Preferences in Korea], *Korean Political Science Review* 50(5), 89-108.

Lee, S. Y. (2013), '2012 Hanguk yeoseong yugwonjaui jeongchijeok jeonghyanggwa tupyohaengtae' [Political Orientation, Attitude and Electoral Behavior of the 2012 Korean Female Voters], *Korean Political Science Review* 47(5), 255-276.

Lee, W. (2014a), 'Seonggwa sedaeui jeongchigyeongje' [Political Economy of Gender and Generation in Korea], *Korean Journal of Public Finance* 7(4), 1-40.

Lee, Y. (2014b), '2000nyeondae ihu hanguk sahwe gyecheunggyunyeol gujoui deungjang' [The Formation of the Class Cleavage Structure in South Korea: Focusing on the Presidential Elections since 2002],. *Korean Political Science Review* 48(4), 249-270.

Lee, Y., and You, J. S. (2019), 'Is Class Voting Emergent in Korea?', *Journal of East Asian Studies* 19(2), 197-213.

Manza, J., and Brooks, C. (1998), 'The Gender Gap in U.S. Presidential Elections: When? Why? implications?', *American Journal of Sociology* 103(5), 1235-1266.

Min, T. E. (2013), 'Sangjingjeongchiirongwa gyeongjeiikironeuro bon hangukinui iminja taedo' [Korean Attitudes toward Immigrants: The Product of Symbolic Politics and Economic Interests], *Korean Journal of International Studies* 53(2), 215-247.

Park, S. (2020), 'Jendeo nae sedaegyeokchainga, sedae nae jendeogyeokchainga?: cheongnyeon yeoseongui jagipyeonggainyeomgwa jeongchaektaedo bunseok' [Generational Gap in Gender, or Gender Gap in Generation? An Analysis of Ideology and Policy Attitude of Young Females], *Korean Party Studies Review* 19(2), 5-36.

Park, Y. H., Kim, M. S., Park, W. H., Kang, S. G., and Koo, B S. (2016), 'Je20dae gukhweuiwonseongu dangseonja mit hubojaui inyeomseonghyanggwa jeongchaektaedo' [Ideology and Policy Positions of the Candidates and the Elects in the 20th Korean National Assembly Election], *Korean Journal of Legislative Studies* 22(3), 117-157.

Seol, D. H., and Jeon, J. Y. (2016), 'Gukhweui iminjeongchaek gyeoljeonggwa jeongdangjeongchi: je18dae gukhweleul jungsimeuro' [Party Politics in Immigration Policy Making], *Korea and World Politics* 32(2), 137-172.

Yang, J. J. (2013), 'Parochial Welfare Politics and the Small Welfare State in South Korea', *Comparative Politics* 45(4), 457-475.

Yeo, E., and Kim, Y. S. (2015), 'Hangukui junggancheungeun eotteon bokjigukgaleul wonhaneunga? Junggancheungui bokjitaedowa bokjigukga jeonmangeui hamui' [What Welfare State Does the Korean Middle Class Want? The Welfare Attitude of the Middle Class and Its Implications for the Prospect of the Welfare State in Korea], *Korean Political Science Review* 49(4), 335-362.

Yoon, I. J. (2016), 'Damunhwa sosujae daehan gukmininsikui jihyeonggwa byeonhwa' [Characteristics and Changes of Koreans' Perceptions of Multicultural Minorities], *Journal of Diaspora Studies* 10(1), 125-154.

PART 5

CIVIL SOCIETY

CHAPTER 19

SOCIAL MOVEMENTS

Developments and Structural Changes after Democratisation

JIN-WOOK SHIN

1. INTRODUCTION

THIS chapter describes the changes and characteristics of South Korean social movements since democratisation in 1987 from a historical and structural point of view. Although South Korea experienced many political upheavals and tragedies, including war, dictatorship, and state violence, South Korean society has achieved significant success in developing democracy and civil society since the 1990s.

Social movement was one of the driving forces for institutional and cultural change in South Korea. Not only democratisation movements, but also social movements with different issues, goals, and constituents led the growth of autonomous civil society under authoritarian rule and contributed to the collapse of dictatorship (Katsiaficas 2012). Furthermore, social movement has been one of the most influential forces since the transition to democracy, raising agendas for reform, diagnosing problems, presenting alternatives, and organising actions (Kim 2006; Kim 2000).

However, more than thirty years have passed since democratisation; thus, it is necessary to thoroughly examine whether continuous progress has been made in terms of the growth of civil society organisations and the generalisation of citizen participation, even after the 2000s. In addition, to understand the dynamics of today's South Korean politics and society, it is of great importance to clarify what transformations the configuration of the macrostructure of social movements has undergone since democratisation (Shin 2020a).

This chapter provides an overview and analysis of the long-term trends and macrostructural features of civil society, social movements, and protest action in South Korea after democratisation. In the second section, a basic conceptual clarification is provided, before going into the main subject. In the third section, a brief history of South Korean social movements under authoritarian regimes is outlined, and the growth of civil society and changes in protest behaviour is described. In the fourth and fifth sections, the transformation of the macrostructure of social movements in South Korea is explained with three key words: differentiation, decentralisation, and ideological division. In the sixth section, South Koreans' participation in civil society organisations and political activism is evaluated from the perspective of international comparison. The final section discusses the theoretical and political implications of the changes in South Korean social movements.

2. Conceptual Clarification

Before entering the historical–empirical discussion, I will first offer a concise clarification of the meaning of the three most important concepts used in this chapter: social movements, protest, and civil society. The three concepts often point to different aspects of the same phenomenon, but we need to analytically distinguish them to clearly capture the complex reality.

First, the term *social movement* is understood here as a particular type of collective action 'which represents preferences for changing some elements of the social structure and/or reward distribution of a society' (McCarthy and Zald 1977: 1217). However, it is not just an instrument to achieve the goals, but also develops 'a culture, ... and a new scheme of life' (Blumer 1951: 199). Furthermore, it is not just temporary action, but an 'organized, sustained ... challenge to authorities, powerholders, or cultural beliefs and practices' (Goodwin and Jasper 2009: 4).

Second, social movements often include elements of protest. The concept of *protest* can be defined as 'any kind of group activities carried out by nonstate actors designed to express and enact dissent publicly' (Rucht 1998: 30). Protest in that sense can be a particular moment of social movements, but in other cases it may be temporary, ambiguous in goals and identities, and lacking sustainable bases. Therefore, it is important to observe carefully whether, and how much, a certain protest event is part of, or develops into, social movement.

Third, social movement is the most active component of civil society, but it cannot be assumed that social movements simply reflect the conditions of civil society in a broader sense. The modern notion of *civil society* refers to spheres of individual freedom and interests, as well as spheres of intermediary associations and local communities (Ehrenberg 1999). Such voluntary associations of individuals cover a wide variety of phenomena, including non-profit/non-governmental organisations (NGOs), trade unions, cooperatives, local communities, and Sunday football clubs, as well as social movements. Social movements may be rooted in the soil of abundant civil society associations, but sometimes they may be nothing but islands in a desolate civil society environment.

Based on the above conceptual relationship, this chapter primarily focuses on the changes and structural features of South Korean social movements, but relates them to the broader context of civil society, on the one hand, and the more concrete events and processes of protest action, on the other.

3. Civil Society before and after Democratisation

3.1 The Growth of Resistant Civil Society under Authoritarian Regimes

South Korea was under authoritarian rule for nearly forty years until democratisation in 1987, but under dictatorship, a resistant civil society developed amid 'protest dialectics' (Chang 2015) between the repressive state and pro-democracy movements. Therefore, a recurrent confrontation between a 'strong state and contentious society' (Koo 1993) has been one of the driving forces that moved the dynamics of South Korean politics.

From the 1960s to the 1980s, various social movements (including those from the religious, student, labour, and women's sectors) grew together within a broader solidarity against dictatorship and state violence. The ideas, symbols, organisations, participants and their networks, and shared memories of these movements have had a strong and long-standing impact upon South Korean social movements since democratisation.

In the religious sector, priests and laymen have been engaged in social activism since the 1960s, but they became more active under the military dictatorships in the 1970s and through the 1980s. Almost all religious faiths, including Protestants, Catholics, and Buddhists, acted together to fight for democracy, human rights of workers and poor people, peace on the Korean Peninsula, and the spread of democratic and pluralistic culture (Chang 1998; Kang 2000).

The movements of university students were the most threatening force to the dictatorial regime. The students had already played a crucial role in the struggle for democracy since the 1960s, but it was in the 1980s that they took the lead in social movements and political activism in South Korea. With the military massacre in Gwangju in 1980, the student movements radicalised their ideologies and action methods and made a great effort to strengthen their organisational infrastructure (Shin and Hwang 2003).

The labour movements have been constantly suppressed by the state and the employers since the establishment of the Republic of Korea, but in the 1970s, an independent labour movement called the *minjunojo undong* (Democratic Trade Union Movement) was launched to form unions, protect workers' rights, and oppose the authoritarian government (Asia Monitor Resource Centre 1988; Ogle 1990). The main participants were young women working at light-industry companies in the manufacturing sector, fighting against disrespect and violence by male managers, as well as disastrous labour conditions and low wages (Koo 2001).

In other areas, too, social movements had developed since the 1980s as part of the democratisation movement. For example, movements for women's rights, female workers' movements, and women's associations for democracy grew during this period (Kim and Kim 2014). In addition, environmental movements developed on the basis of class perspectives, focusing on the health-and-safety issues of workers and residents in the industrial areas (Koo 1996).

From a structural point of view, the social movements under dictatorship can be understood as reactions to the rapid capitalist industrialisation driven by the authoritarian state and labour-repressive capital. Although these movements were in an extremely hostile political environment, they could develop their own ideologies, culture, and agency, based on strong community and backed up by moral support from the society. Nevertheless, under the condition that citizenship rights were largely restricted by the state, there were fundamental limitations to the growth of autonomous civil society comprising ordinary citizens.

3.2 The Persistent Growth of Civil Society after Democratisation

Democratisation brought great change to the environment of civil society and social movements. The autonomous and legally guaranteed spheres of political action have expanded, widening the scope of action and the possibilities of finding allies within institutional sectors. Governments, political parties, and the media have become more open towards the participation and challenges of the citizens (Cho 2000; Kim 2006).

However, it is necessary to examine whether civil society in South Korea only temporarily expanded immediately after democratisation and then fell into stagnation or whether democracy allowed and encouraged civil society to continue to grow and mature in the longer term. There are claims that South Korean civil society declined as party democracy progressed and former movement leaders advanced into politics (Choi 2020), but such a view stems from confusing the decline of 'particular' movement groups such as large-scale NGOs and trade unions with a 'general' trend of South Korean civil society as a whole, while neglecting the significant growth at the grassroots and local level and the macrostructural transformation of civil society since the 2000s.

It is useful to look at three basic aspects (i.e. the number of civil society organisations, the frequency of assemblies and demonstrations, and the trends of illegal and violent protest events) before moving on to the macrostructural

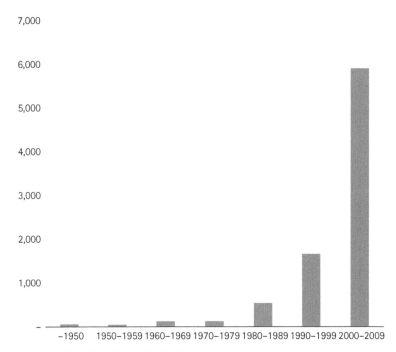

FIGURE 19.1: Number of newly established civil society organisations, 1950–2009
Source: Encyclopaedia of Korean Civil Associations; adapted from Kong and Lim (2016: 51).

transformations and the local civil society activities in sections 4 'The Sectorial Differentiation of Social Movements' and 5 'Decentralization and Ideological Division of Social Movements', respectively.

First, the number of newly established civil society organisations has increased, a clear trend since the 1990s, which soared more steeply after the 2000s. As Figure 19.1 shows, the number of new organisations in civil society grew from 538 in the 1980s to 1,662 in the 1990s and jumped to 5,902 in the 2000s. In other words, democratisation did not just trigger a temporary explosion of civil society, but became the foundation for an accelerated growth of the associational life of the citizens. Section 5.3 'Newly Emerging Social Movements since the 2010s' makes evident that such civil society growth extended to the local level in the 2010s.

Meanwhile, after the first power change to a liberal-progressive government in 1998, the frequency of protests skyrocketed, but it began to stabilise by 2003 and has maintained a certain level thereafter. According to Figure 19.2, the annual frequency of assemblies and demonstrations soared from 9,729 in 1997 to 34,138 in 2002, but remained around 10,000 from 2003 to 2019.

More importantly, the frequency of illegal and violent protest has declined sharply. Such a trend stood out during the period of the liberal-progressive governments of President Kim Dae-jung (1998–2003) and President Roh Moo-hyun (2003–2008), but the tendency did not reverse later under the conservative governments of President

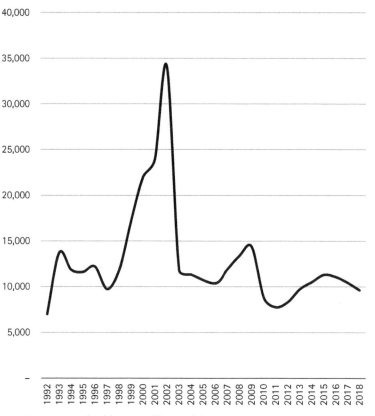

FIGURE 19.2: Frequency of public assemblies and demonstrations, 1992–2019

Source: Korean National Police Agency (2020a), 'Frequency of Public Assemblies and Demonstrations', white paper. http://index.go.kr/potal/stts/idxMain/selectPoSttsIdxSearch.do?idx_cd=1613, accessed 27 December 2020.

Lee Myung-bak (2008–2013) and President Park Geun-hye (2013–2017). As Figure 19.3 shows, there were more than 800 illegal and violent protests per year by the mid-1990s, but the number fell below 100 in the 2000s and approached nearly zero in 2019.

Comparing the situation before and after democratisation reveals a clear contrast. Table 19.1 shows that under dictatorship, the number of protests was relatively low due to political suppression, but there were frequent violent confrontations between public authorities and the protesters. In contrast, in a democratic system, the number of protests and their participants were much higher than in the past, but illegal and violent events plummeted.

Along with the general trends of the growth of civil society, significant changes have taken place in the macrostructure of social movements. Among them, the three most significant changes were (a) the *differentiation* of social movements into independent issue areas, including labour, women, environment, peace, political reform, economic justice, human rights, and education; (b) the *decentralisation* of the communication and

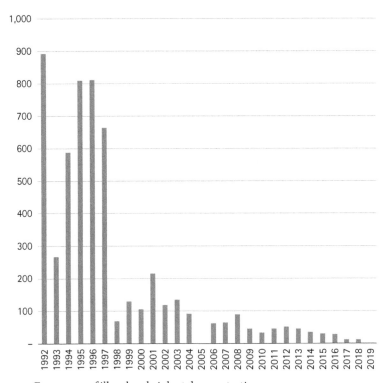

FIGURE 19.3: Frequency of illegal and violent demonstrations, 1992–2019

Source: Korean National Police Agency (2020b), 'Statistics on the Status for Illegal and Violent Demonstrations', white paper. http://index.go.kr/potal/stts/idxMain/selectPoSttsIdxSearch.do?idx_cd=1613, accessed 27 December 2020.

Table 19.1: Protest behaviour before and after democratisation

	1980s	2000s
Number of illegal and violent protest events	1,163	5,902
Number of public assemblies and demonstrations	4,148	153,333
Percentage of illegal and violent events	28%	4%

Sources: Korean National Police Agency, 'Number of Protest Events and the Illegal and Violent Protests', white paper. http://index.go.kr/potal/stts/idxMain/selectPoSttsIdxSearch.do?idx_cd=1613, accessed 27 December 2020 and Hong (2017: 198).

mobilisation structure, as well as the networks of social movements at the macro level; and (c) the ideological *division* of civil society in general and social movements in particular, intensifying the contention between the movement groups pursuing conflicting values and reform agendas. Sections 4 and 5 describe these structural transformations of social movements.

4. The Sectorial Differentiation of Social Movements

4.1 From Unity to Diversity

Democratisation of the political system led not only to the quantitative growth of civil society organisations but also to their differentiation into diverse issue areas (Cho et al. 2012; Shin and Chang 2011). After the great common enemy of dictatorship disappeared, the emphasis of social movements working on different problem areas gradually shifted away from unity towards diversity.

During the period from the late 1980s to the mid-1990s, the first major differentiation occurred: the distinction between *minjung undong* and *shimin undong*. The *minjung* is a concept of collectivity articulated in the context of the protest movements of the 1970s and the 1980s, the meaning of which embraces all kinds of oppressed, marginalised, and discriminated social groups, including workers, farmers, poor people, women, migrants, and the disabled (Lee 2007; Wells 1995). However, the *minjung undong* (people's movements) mainly referred to class-based social movements, such as labour, farmers', and poor people's movements. The word *shimin*, on the other hand, had long been used to refer to urban residents, but after democratisation it began to be used with political implications. The *shimin undong* (citizens' movements) reflected such semantic changes. The demarcation line between the people's and the citizens' movements is often not clear, but the fact that such a conceptual distinction became popular in the 1990s was a sign that South Korean social movements were rapidly being differentiated.

A large part of the people's movements had the perception that there was 'no change' in capitalism and class inequalities even after democratisation, such that radical struggles were needed continuously. In fact, labour movements were often suppressed by employers, but politicians were reluctant to legislate to protect workers. On the other hand, the citizens' movements emphasised 'change'; they believed that many things had changed since democratisation and that the movement should change accordingly. They believed that in a democratised political environment, concrete reform should be the primary goal of the movement, even if the prospects of structural change are preserved. They also preferred legal, non-violent, and moderate methods of action to attract as much empathy from the citizens as possible (Lim 2000).

In addition, both *minjung* and *shimin* movements were further differentiated into different issue areas; for example, labour, peasant, urban poor, political reform, economic justice, environment, gender, education, peace, human rights, consumer rights, and social welfare. These movements shared great values such as democracy, equality, and pluralism at the abstract level, but their primary interests and goals were different, and they sometimes had conflicting philosophies and worldviews. In other words, the differentiation of social movements meant not simply the separation of organisational networks, but more importantly, a new moral and strategical relationship among movements (Shin 2020b: 171–176).

4.2 The Uneven Development of Citizens' Movements and Labour Movements

The citizens' movements that contributed greatly to changing the South Korean social movements in the 1990s had distinct characteristics that clearly distinguished them from the democratisation movements during the authoritarian era. Among other things, the tendencies towards diversification, institutionalisation, and professionalism have special importance.

First, regarding goals, the citizens' movements did not presuppose the priority of a single goal such as democracy or workers' liberation, nor did they insist on the centrality of a specific group such as the proletariat. Instead, they pursued 'solidarity in diversity', drawing positive response from the middle-class citizens in a democratised political environment. While attaching value to all aspirations for change, the citizens' movements were able to grow rapidly with the participation and support of citizens.

Second, in terms of the means of action, the citizens' movements stressed solving problems and realising alternatives through institutional channels such as the court, parliament, government, and media. They cooperated with the media to raise issues, influenced legislation in cooperation with their allies in political parties, and put pressure on government bureaucrats to implement reform policies. Although campaigns on the street were still important means of action, they were linked to strategies that focused on more institutionalised channels.

Third, the movement activists became more and more professional. Although the number of citizens engaged in political and social activism had risen, those who played a substantial role in the movement activities were those with professional competencies. They were experienced activists, scholars, experts, and lawyers in each field, and journalists who conveyed the claims and activities of the movements to the public sphere.

Citizens' movements have achieved numerous policy innovations and institutional reforms. From the 1990s to the mid-2000s, a lot of reform legislation took place either at the initiative of the movement organisations or in cooperation with the government and political parties. These reforms covered a wide variety of agendas, such as human rights, environment, gender, social welfare, and health care. In that context, the citizens' movements of the 1990s were even evaluated as having performed the function of a 'quasi-party' and 'delegation of representation' under the condition of underdevelopment of party politics right after democratisation (Cho 2000).

However, in the areas where the conflict of class interests was intense, social movements still had to fight many difficulties. Although freedom of expression, speech, thought, and association of the middle class greatly expanded, the self-organisation and collective action of workers were still oppressed by the company, and the government and political parties often were passive about correcting the extreme power imbalance between capital and labour (Lee 2011).

In this environment, workers in large corporations succeeded in achieving a considerable degree of employment security and income levels through radical struggles, but many workers who wanted to follow that path failed to cross the threshold of even minimal collective action. As Figure 19.4 shows, the frequency and number of participants of labour disputes grew sharply over the three years from 1987 to 1989, but with the sophistication of employers' strategies and the gradual segmentation of the labour market, many peripheral workers faced greater difficulties in achieving united action.

Workers' organisational resources were also temporarily strengthened after democratisation, but then declined steadily. From 1987 to 1989, the number of trade unions increased considerably, but the unionisation rates continued to decrease from the early 1990s and have remained at only 10 per cent since the 2000s. Although the unionisation rate has risen since 2017, when the Moon Jae-in administration took office, it is unclear whether this trend will continue under the conservative Yoon Seok-yeol administration, which began in 2022. Moreover, because most of the unionised workers today have regular

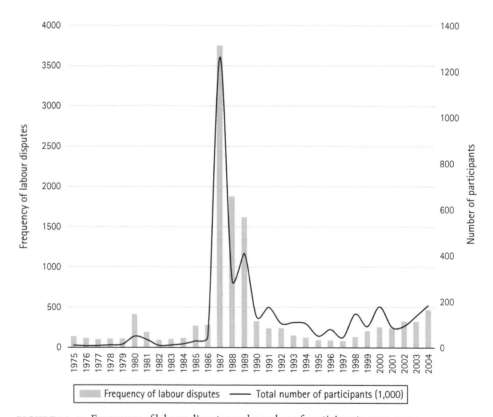

FIGURE 19.4: Frequency of labour disputes and number of participants, 1975–2004

Source: Ministry of Employment and Labour, 'Statistics of Labour Disputes'. http://index.go.kr/potal/main/EachDtlPageDetail.do?idx_cd=1512, accessed 24 May 2006.

employment status in large companies, union membership is an important source of institutional division of the labour market, along with company size and employment status. Against this background, the protest action and organised movements of workers located on the periphery of the labour market have become increasingly active since the 2010s. I return to this issue in section 5.3 'Newly Emerging Social Movements since the 2010s'.

5. Decentralisation and Ideological Division of Social Movements

5.1 The 'Candlelight Protest' and the Rise of Networked Social Movements

Some important new trends in South Korean citizen politics and social movements emerged with the beginning of the twenty-first century. The scale and political impact of spontaneous protest actions by the citizens who are networked using information technologies grew rapidly. Consequently, the structure of the social movement ecology became more and more decentralised, and the relative status of the existing movement organisations was reduced accordingly.

In the early 2000s, a new kind of large-scale protest action called the 'Candlelight protest' became the most popular and influential form of citizens' political expression and participation. In the Candlelight protest, a large-scale action with participants often numbering in the hundreds of thousands, even more than a million, was not uncommon; the composition of the gathering varied greatly in many respects, including age, gender, occupation, and prior experience with protest action. Participants were skilled in using new information and communication technologies to share information, exchange opinions, and discuss strategies. Many of them were independent from political parties and formal movement organisations, but wanted to exert a direct influence upon institutional politics and the government's policy decisions (Jho 2008; Lee 2009; Lee 2013).

Furthermore, Candlelight protests shook the dichotomies that had been taken for granted in the study of social movements. Most of the participants did not follow an organisational strategy but acted in a very orderly manner; they claimed to be unrelated to politics but showed great enthusiasm for politics; most of them were not members of a movement organisation, but they had sophisticated skills of protest not unlike experienced activists; and they emphasised expression itself, rather than achieving a concrete goal, but they could exercise a great political influence by the act of expression.

Such large-scale Candlelight protests have had a profound impact upon South Korean politics and government policies. For example, in 2008, in a four-month Candlelight protest against the US–South Korea agreement on the import of US beef products and the government's neoliberal policies, the approval rating of President Lee Myung-bak dropped to a single digit; several ministers resigned; and the ruling party had to either abandon or postpone much of its original policy plan. A more dramatic event occurred during the time of President Park Geun-hye. Starting in the autumn of 2016 and lasting half a year, the Candlelight movement protested President Park's abuse of power; in response, the National Assembly impeached the president on 9 December 2016, and the Constitutional Court decided to approve the impeachment on 10 March 2017 (Lee et al. 2010; Dudden 2017; Shin 2020b).

What is interesting is that when the waves of protest subsided, the participants of Candlelight protests tended to return to private life, rather than join or establish a social movement organisation. However, in today's information society, the private world includes many online public forums, political discourses, and communication processes on public issues. These scattered and fragmented potentials for political participation in everyday life, which Alberto Melucci called 'submerged networks' (Melucci 1989), quickly rise to the surface of politics when people encounter another triggering issue. This is a new way of sustaining the vitality of citizens' political activism in South Korea in the twenty-first century.

5.2 The Left–Right Division of the Field of Social Movements

Another notable change after the mid-2000s was the proliferation of conservative organisations and right-wing movements. The spread of the right-wing movements began in response to the strengthening of progressive forces after democratisation. As former leftist leaders and activists of radical social movements moved to the centre of political power and the conservative party fell into a crisis, right-wing movements with the purpose of rebuilding the conservative hegemony emerged from the mid-2000s. The most active groups among them were the New Right movements led by intellectuals, journalists, and businessmen, and the far-right activism led by conservative Christians, veteran organisations, and 'anti-communist' activist groups.

The South Korean New Right symbolised the conservative establishments, a characteristic contrasting with the often subversive and anti-elitist pretensions of many European right-wing forces. The South Korean New Right tried to combine an anti-leftist offensive with discourses which were friendly to business, market, and private property. Meanwhile, the far-right groups, which were politically highly active and often violent, amplified and revitalised the legacy of the dictatorship. Their Red-Scare, totalitarian discourses, and militaristic uniforms and rituals were taken from decades before (Fiori and Kim 2018; Shin 2015).

Conservative groups and right-wing movements which rapidly spread from the mid-2000s became influential forces in South Korean society within a short period of time. After the conservative government seized power in 2008, the vitality of these organisations as a social movement soon weakened. However, since the impeachment of President Park Geun-hye in 2017, not only have the far-right movements rapidly proliferated, but their ideologies, language, arguments, and behaviour have all become far more radical than in the 2000s (Yang 2020).

If the symbol of progressive protests was a 'candlelight', the key symbol for organising the ideological identity and consolidating the solidarity of the recent right-wing protesters is the *'taegeukgi'*, the name of the South Korean national flag. Right-wing protesters, also known as the *'taegeukgi* brigade', have been regularly engaged in large-scale protests called *'taegeukgi* rallies' in downtown Seoul since the end of 2016. In the 2000s, the radical right-wing force comprised a small number of their organisations' members, whereas the crowd at the *'taegeukgi* rallies' sometimes reached tens of thousands. Although they have leaders and organisations, the underlying structure of communication and mobilisation is decentralised and closely related to the new technologies of the Information Age. Ironically, many features of the growing far-right movements in South Korea resemble those of the Candlelight protest, despite the sharp contrast between the two in ideological and political terms (Cho and Lee 2021).

5.3 Newly Emerging Social Movements since the 2010s

New streams of social movements and other civil society activities, which may lead to significant changes in South Korean politics and society in the future, have gradually spread since the 2010s. Prime examples are civil society groups in local grassroots spaces; a new generation of feminist and sexual minorities movements; and the precarious workers' movements, especially by the youth.

These emerging social movements emphasise the experience and voices of the people directly involved in social problems; mobilisation on the basis of an individual's self-motivation; and a horizontal, open communication structure. They also tend to reject bureaucratic efficiency and elitist movements led by prominent leaders and keep their distance from large-scale movement organisations and political parties. Moreover, they sometimes break with conventional ways of distinguishing progressives and conservatives, and do not conform to the mainstream of South Korean social movements since democratisation.

To begin with, what should be made clear about the recent trends in South Korean civil society is that although social movement activities have become increasingly spontaneous and unorganised since the 2000s, the overall organisational foundation of civil society has not weakened at all. In fact, the number of non-profit organisations has continued to increase and, particularly, the expansion of organisations operating at the local level have led the general trend. According to Figure 19.5, the number of national non-profit organisations increased modestly during the 2010s, whereas the number of regional non-profits surged from 9,570 in 2012 to 13,014 in 2019.

Thus, even if the influence of the large-scale movement organisations that led the growth of citizens' movements in the 1990s has weakened in recent years, it does not imply the organisational weakening and loss of vitality of civil society in general. On the

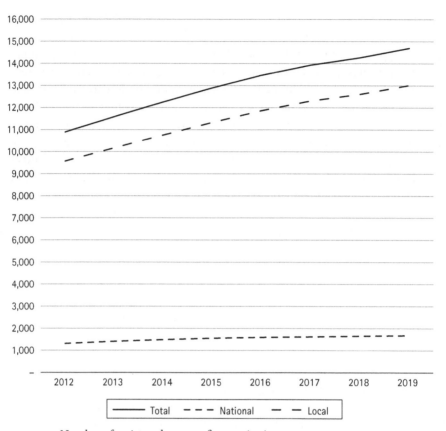

FIGURE 19.5: Number of registered non-profit organisations, 2012–2019

Source: Ministry of the Interior and Safety, 'Statistics on the Registered Non-Profit Organisations'. http://index.go.kr/potal/main/EachDtlPageDetail.do?idx_cd=2856, accessed 29 November 2019.

contrary, civil society organisations with local bases, especially cooperatives, community movements, social enterprises, and social service groups, have increased significantly since the 2010s.

Such changes took place along with the vitalisation of local politics in the wake of the 2010 and 2014 local elections. Today, many local governments support local communities and social movements, and the local civil society organisations take part in the process of policy planning, decision-making, and implementation through diverse institutions of cooperative governance (Hong et al. 2018; S. Kim 2017; Kong and Lim 2016).

Along with the quiet changes taking place in grassroots civil society, more visible and provocative changes are also under way. The first examples to mention are the new generation of feminist and sexual minorities movements. Participants of these movements want to fight sexual violence, discrimination, and human rights violations without delegating their voices to pre-existing women's movement organisations and political parties. Committed activists of the new feminist movements, called 'young young feminists', emphasise the subjectivity of 'the person involved' more radically than the 'young feminists' of the 2000s (Yun 2020).

The #MeToo campaigns in South Korea led to a series of sensational political events, including arrests, suicides, and resignations of the most influential politicians. Political parties are now under strong pressure to increase their gender awareness and to offer policy alternatives. All these facts show how profoundly the recent 'feminism reboot' is shaking the grammar of institutional politics (Hasunuma and Shin 2019). Since South Korea's gender inequality is the worst among democratic societies by many indicators, it is expected that the new feminist movements driven by young women will continue to redefine moral standards and reshape the rules of the game in South Korean politics.

Another notable trend since the 2010s is a series of new labour movements that can be called the non-regular workers' movements or, more generally, the precarious workers' movements. In South Korea, the process of labour market segmentation began in the 1990s, but especially after the Asian Financial Crisis in 1997, the expansion of the non-regular employment sector became a big social problem (Shin 2013). As a response to such structural changes, the struggle of non-regular workers has continued since the 2000s. Although they were seriously lacking in what Eric Olin Wright called 'structural power' and 'associative power' (Wright 2000), they are finding ways to overcome such limitations through solidarity with civil society actors (Lee and Lee 2017).

In the development of the emerging movements of precarious workers, young workers play a particular role. They established general trade unions which have the character of a social movement organisation as well, greatly expanding membership and social influence within a short time. Examples are the Youth Community Union and Alba Union, which represent the interests of youth precarious workers (Yang and Chae 2020). The changes in civil society and social movements since the 2010s, as described above, are still actively progressing, and thus have the potential to deeply transform South Korean politics, society, and culture in the future.

6. Political Activism in South Korea: An International Comparison

Having described the quantitative and structural changes in South Korean civil society and social movements after democratisation, this section evaluates the degree to which South Korean citizens participate in civil society's non-profit organisations and political activism in comparison with other advanced democratic societies or post-authoritarian societies.

One of the basic ways to compare the scale of participation in civil societies is to measure the proportion of participants among the total population. Scholars have often evaluated that although South Korea social movements are active and influential, civil society participation by ordinary citizens is considerably weaker in comparison with advanced democracies. However, such an evaluation does not reflect the remarkable changes since the 2000s.

As we can see in Figure 19.6, which illustrates the results of the World Values Survey, civil society participation in South Korea was negligible in the 1980s, but it increased significantly after democratisation and, in the 2000s, became much higher than that of Japan in many areas. More importantly, whereas many Western countries saw a significant decline in civil society participation during the 2000s, South Korea maintained or increased steadily in all areas, significantly narrowing the gap with the West.

Also, in an international comparison of citizens' participation in political action, South Koreans are quite active. Figure 19.7 shows the sum of response rates of 'Have done' and 'Might do' in political action and online political action, using the data from the World Values Survey Wave 7 (2017–2020), and compares nine countries that have survey results for all indicators. Although participation in South Korea is generally weaker than that in Western democracies in many respects, South Koreans are more active than citizens of any other countries in online political action to organise political activities, events, and protests.

When compared with post-authoritarian countries (Argentina, Brazil, Greece, Taiwan, and South Korea), South Koreans are the most involved in online politics. In other respects, the degree of participation of South Koreans is the second highest among the five countries compared. Japanese citizens are more engaged than South Koreans in relatively moderate activities such as petitions, whereas South Koreans are more active than the Japanese in the remaining three fields of action.

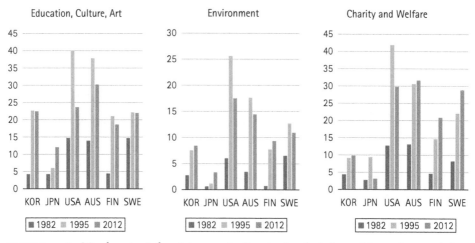

FIGURE 19.6: Members in civil society organisations in six selected countries, 1982–2012 (%)

Notes: KOR: South Korea; JPN: Japan; US: United States; AUS: Australia; FIN: Finland; SWE: Sweden.

Source: World Values Survey 1982, 1995, 2012; adapted from Joo (2017: 360).

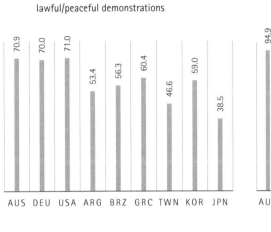
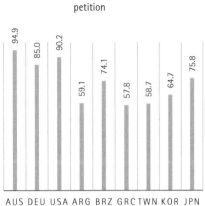
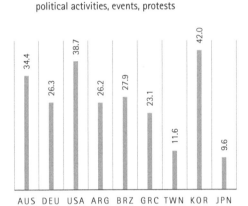
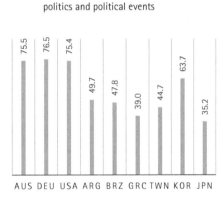

FIGURE 19.7: Citizens' political action in nine selected countries, 2017–2020 (%)

Notes: AUS: Australia; DEU: Germany; USA: United States; ARG: Argentina; BRZ: Brazil; GRC: Greece; TWN: Taiwan; KOR: South Korea; JPN: Japan.

Source: World Values Survey Wave 7 (2017–2020). https://www.worldvaluessurvey.org/WVSContents.jsp, accessed 28 December 2020.

7. Conclusion

I would like to conclude this chapter by describing the theoretical and practical implications of the aforementioned changes and structural features of South Korean social movements and civil society after the democratisation of the political system in 1987.

First, regarding the relationship between democratisation and social movements, the latter not only greatly contributed to ending the dictatorship, but also the ideas, constituents, and organisations of the former continued to play a big role in developing progressive movements after democratisation. Conversely, democratisation did not just temporarily trigger the expansion of civil society, but in the long term became the basis for the growth of the organisational foundation of civil society, citizens' participation, and the development of civic culture. The task for the future is how to incorporate such new civil society actors and voices into a new democratic framework.

Second, regarding the status of social movements in society, it seems that South Korea is gradually approaching what social movement researchers call 'social movement society' (Meyer and Tarrow 1998). In South Korea, the number of movement participants, the number of civil society organisations, and the influence of social movements upon institutional politics continued to grow after democratisation. In addition, social movements increasingly mobilise the institutionalised means of action, while they are recognised by institutional sectors as a normal part and a powerful actor of society. Therefore, the government and political parties now need to communicate more with actors of civil society and social movements and include them in the political process to effectively respond to discontent and demands from society.

Third, in terms of the macrostructure of social movements, the most significant was the increase in structural complexity in the ecosystem of social movements. The field of social movements in South Korea today is characterised by the cross-cutting and interpenetration of several structural tendencies, including sectoral differentiation, decentralisation, ideological division, and the rise of several new streams. Therefore, social movements in South Korea must act and interact in a much more complicated and changeable relationship with one another than in the past. Now, all attempts to define the nature of '*the* South Korean civil society' or '*the* South Korean social movements' as a monolithic entity cannot properly understand and evaluate the multilayered and intersecting reality.

Bibliography

Asia Monitor Resource Centre (1988), *Min-ju No-jo. South Korea's New Trade Unions: The Struggle for Free Trade Unions* (Hong Kong: Asia Monitor Resource Centre).
Blumer, H. (1951), 'Collective Behavior', in A. McClurg Lee, ed., *New Outline of the Principles of Sociology*, 199–220 (New York: Barnes and Noble).
Chang, P. Y. (2015), *Protest Dialectics. State Repression and South Korea's Democracy Movement, 1970–1979* (Stanford, CA: Stanford University Press).
Chang, Y.-S. (1998), 'The Progressive Christian Church and Democracy in South Korea', *Journal of Church and State* 40, 437–465.
Cho, H.-Y. (2000), 'Democratic Transition and Changes in South Korean NGOs', *Korea Journal* 40(2), 275–304.
Cho, H.-Y., Aeria, A., and Hur, S.-W. (2012), *From Unity to Multiplicities. Social Movement Transformation and Democratization in Asia* (Petaling Jaya, Malaysia: SIRD).
Cho, S., and Lee, J. (2021), 'Waving Israeli Flags at Right-Wing Christian Rallies in South Korea', *Journal of Contemporary Asia* 51(3), 496–515.

Choi, J. J. (2020), 'The Democratic State Engulfing Civil Society: The Ironies of Korean Democracy', *Korean Studies* 34, 1–24.

Dudden, A. (2017), 'Revolution by Candlelight: How South Koreans Toppled a Government', *Dissent* 64(4), 86–92.

Ehrenberg, J. (1999), *Civil Society. The Critical History of an Idea* (New York: New York University Press).

Fiori, A., and Kim, S. (2018), 'Civil Society and Democracy in South Korea: A Reassessment', in Y. Kim, ed., *Korea's Quest for Economic Democratization*, 141–170 (Cham: Palgrave Macmillan).

Goodwin, J., and Jasper, J. M., eds (2009), *Rethinking Social Movements: Structure, Meaning, and Emotion* (Lanham, MD: Rowman & Littlefield).

Hasunuma, L., and Shin, K. (2019), '#MeToo in Japan and South Korea: #WeToo, #WithYou', *Journal of Women, Politics & Policy* 40(1), 97–111.

Hong, S.-T. (2017), 'Sahoeundong-ui pongnyeokseong gujohwa: eogap-gwa jeohang-ui pongnyeokjeok sanghojagyong, 1960–1987' (Structured Violence of Social Movements in South Korea: Violent Interaction of Repression and Protest, 1960–1987), *Economy and Society* 115, 183–211.

Hong, S.-T., Cheon, H., and Lee, M.-J. (2018), 'Social Conditions of Village Democracy in South Korea', *Development and Society* 47(1), 85–117.

Jho, W. (2008), 'The Transformation of Cyberactivism and Democratic Governance in South Korea: The Role of Technology, Civil Society, and Institution', *Korea Observer* 40(2), 337–368.

Joo, S.-S. (2017), *History of South Korean Civil Society, 1987–2017* (Seoul: Hakminsa).

Kang, I.-C. (2000), 'Religion and the Democratization Movement', *Korea Journal* 40(2), 225–247.

Katsiaficas, G. (2012), *Asia's Unknown Uprisings. Volume 1: South Korean Social Movements in the 20th Century* (Oakland, CA: PM Press).

Kim, D.-C. (2006), 'Growth and Crisis of the South Korean Citizens' Movement', *Korea Journal* 46(2), 99–128.

Kim, J. (2017), '#iamafeminist as the "Mother Tag": Feminist Identification and Activism against Misogyny on Twitter in South Korea', *Feminist Media Studies* 17(5), 804–820.

Kim, S. (2017), 'From Protest to Collaboration: The Evolution of the Community Movements amid Sociopolitical Transformation in South Korea', *Urban Studies* 54(16), 3806–3825.

Kim, S.-K., and Kim, K. (2014), *The South Korean Women's Movement and the State: Bargaining for Change* (London: Routledge).

Kim, S. (2000), *Democratization in South Korea: The Role of Civil Society* (Pittsburgh, PA: University of Pittsburgh Press).

Kong, S.-K., and Lim, H.-C. (2016), *Hanguk Shiminsahoe-reul Geurida* (*Drawing the Landscape of Civil Society in South Korea*) (Seoul: Jininjin).

Koo, D.-W. (1996), 'The Structural Change of the South Korean Environmental Movement', *Korean Journal of Population and Development* 25(1), 155–180.

Koo, H. (1993), 'Strong State and Contentious Society', in H. Koo, ed., *State and Society in Contemporary Korea*, 231–249 (Ithaca, NY: Cornell University Press).

Koo, H. (2001), *Korean Workers: The Culture and Politics of Class Formation* (Ithaca, NY: Cornell University Press).

Korean National Police Agency (2020a), 'Frequency of Public Assemblies and Demonstrations', white paper. http://index.go.kr/potal/stts/idxMain/selectPoSttsIdxSearch.do?idx_cd=1613, accessed 27 December 2020.

Korean National Police Agency (2020b), 'Statistics on the Status for Illegal and Violent Demonstrations', white paper. http://index.go.kr/potal/stts/idxMain/selectPoSttsIdxSearch.do?idx_cd=1613, accessed 27 December 2020.

Korean National Police Agency, 'Number of Protest Events and the Illegal and Violent Protests', white paper. http://index.go.kr/potal/stts/idxMain/selectPoSttsIdxSearch.do?idx_cd=1613, accessed 27 December 2020.

Lee, B.-H. (2011), 'Labour Solidarity in the Era of Neoliberal Globalization', *Development and Society* 40(2), 319–334.

Lee, B.-H., and Lee, S. S.-Y. (2017), 'Winning Conditions of Precarious Workers' Struggles: A Reflection Based on Case Studies from South Korea', *Industrial Relations* 72(3), 524–550.

Lee, H.-W. (2009), 'Political Implications of Candle Light Protests in South Korea', *Korea Observer* 40(3), 495–526.

Lee, J. (2013), 'The Netizen Movement: A New Wave in the Social Movements of South Korea', in H.-Y. Cho, L. Surendra and H.-J. Cho, eds, *Contemporary South Korean Society. A Critical Perspective*, 123–142 (London: Routledge).

Lee, N. (2007), *The Making of Minjung: Democracy and the Politics of Representation in South Korea* (Ithaca, NY: Cornell University Press).

Lee, S.-O., Kim, S.-J., and Wainwright, J. (2010), 'Mad Cow Militancy: Neoliberal Hegemony and Social Resistance in South Korea', *Political Geography* 29, 359–369.

Lim, H.-S. (2000), 'Historical Development of Civil Social Movements in Korea: Trajectories and Issues', *Korea Journal* 40, 5–25.

McCarthy, J. D., and Zald, M. N. (1977), 'Resource Mobilization and Social Movements: A Partial Theory', *American Journal of Sociology* 82(6), 1212–1241.

Melucci, A. (1989), *Nomads of the Present: Social Movements and Individual Needs in Contemporary Society* (London: Hutchinson Radius).

Meyer, D. S., and Tarrow, S. (1998), *The Social Movement Society: Contentious Politics for a New Century* (Oxford: Rowman & Littlefield).

Ministry of Employment and Labour, 'Statistics of Labour Disputes'. http://index.go.kr/potal/main/EachDtlPageDetail.do?idx_cd=1512, accessed 24 May 2006.

Ministry of the Interior and Safety, 'Statistics on the Registered Non-Profit Organisations'. http://index.go.kr/potal/main/EachDtlPageDetail.do?idx_cd=2856, accessed 29 November 2019.

Ogle, G. E. (1990), *South Korea. Dissent within the Economic Miracle* (London: Zed Books).

Rucht, D. (1998), 'The Structure and Culture of Collective Protest in Germany since 1950', in D. S. Mayer and S. Tarro, eds, *The Social Movement Society*, 29–57 (Lanham, MD: Rowman & Littlefield).

Shin, G.-W., and Chang, P. Y., eds (2011), *South Korean Social Movements: From Democracy to Civil Society* (London: Routledge).

Shin, G.-W., and Hwang, K. M., eds (2003), *Contentious Kwangju. The May 18 Uprising in Korea's Past and Present* (Oxford: Rowman & Littlefield).

Shin, J.-W. (2015), 'Ideological Conflicts within Civil Society and Korean Democracy in Trouble', in E.-J. Lee and H. B. Mosler, eds, *Civil Society on the Move: Transition and Transfer in Germany and South Korea*, 73–92 (Frankfurt am Main: Peter Lang).

Shin, J.-W. (2020a), 'Changing Patterns of South Korean Social Movements, 1960s–2010s: Testimony, Firebombs, Lawsuit, and Candlelight', in D. Chiavacci, S. Grano, and J. Obinger, eds, *Civil Society and the State in Post High-Growth East Asia*, 239–268 (Amsterdam: Amsterdam University Press).

Shin, J.-W. (2020b), 'The Winding Path of Democratization and the Transformation of Citizen Politics in South Korea, 1987–2017', in H. B. Mosler, ed., *South Korea's Democracy Challenge: Political System, Political Economy, and Political Society*, 157–183 (Berlin: Peter Lang).

Shin, K.-Y. (2013), 'Economic Crisis, Neoliberal Reforms, and the Rise of Precarious Work in South Korea', *American Behavioral Scientist* 57(3), 335–353.

Wells, K. M., ed. (1995), *South Korea's Minjung Movement. The Culture and Politics of Dissidence* (Honolulu: University of Hawaii Press).

World Values Survey Wave 7 (2017–2020). https://www.worldvaluessurvey.org/WVSContents.jsp, accessed 28 December 2020.

Wright, E. O. (2000), 'Working-Class Power, Capitalist-Class Interests, and Class Compromise', *American Journal of Sociology* 105(4), 957–1002.

Yang, M. (2020), 'Defending "Liberal Democracy"? Why Older South Koreans Took to the Streets against the 2016–17 Candlelight Protests', *Mobilization* 25(3), 365–382.

Yang, K., and Chae, Y. J. (2020), 'Organizing the Young Precariat in South Korea: A Case Study of the Youth Community Union', *Journal of Industrial Relations* 62(1), 58–80.

Yun, J.-Y. (2020), 'Feminist Net-Activism as a New Type of Actor-Network that Creates Feminist Citizenship', *Asian Women* 36(4), 45–65.

CHAPTER 20

INTEREST GROUP POLITICS

YOOJIN LIM AND YEONHO LEE

1. Introduction

INTEREST groups are organised in order to influence public policy by sharing common interests. They have played an important role as political actors, actively participating in the policymaking process because exerting influence or pressure on government is critical for interest groups to achieve their goals (Berry 1984: 5; Key 1958: 21; Truman 1971: 33; Wilson 1973). Interest groups are also referred to as *pressure groups* in that they exert various forms of pressure to promote the interests of the group in the process of policymaking.

In a democratic political system that accepts the diversity of a society, different interests of its members are also freely expressed. Due to the lack of information and the distortion of election politics, however, political parties in charge of 'input' in the political process (Easton 1957) face limitations in representing or reflecting the demands of a particular group in a society. Therefore, interest groups have emerged to fill the gap in the policymaking process. In a democratic society, interest groups play an important role in putting the demands, together with political parties, into the political process.

Interest groups are different from political parties (Key 1958: 22). First, interest groups, as advocates of special interests in a society, exert influence over policymaking, whereas political parties aim to take control of their own government to decide and execute policies. In other words, interest groups are associations that strive for decision and execution of specific public policies without attempting to nominate candidates for office, participate in election campaigns, or take full control of the government (Schattschneider 1942: 187–188). Second, interest groups pursue narrowly focused special interests, unlike political parties which aggregate the general interests to formulate policies for the whole country. Third, interest groups pursue their own special interests behind the scenes, whereas political parties are operated on the basis of policies and party platforms that are open to public.

In this regard, interest group politics indicates that various interest groups existing in a society exert influence on legislative process as well as on the policymaking and enforcement process in order to realise their interests. Thus, the more developed and diversified a society is, the more likely that diverse interest groups actively pursue their own special interests. Various conflicts in a society have direct correlation with people's demands. So, these interests are concentrated on interest groups and put into the political process in the course of institutionalising voluntary and daily political participation.

There are two perspectives on the impact of interest group politics on society in general. First, interest group politics undermines democracy because it reduces social stability. These arguments put great emphasis on its nature, which advocates exclusive interests and sees interest groups as a form of faction. In the early days of the United States, James Madison warned of the evils of factions, emphasising that humans tend to oppress one another, rather than cooperate in pursuing a common good (Berry 1999). Similarly, Olson (1982: 47) also argued from a neoclassical economic perspective, stating that special interest groups reduce efficiency and total returns and may even disrupt the political life of the society in which they operate. In other words, they point out that interest group politics are accompanied by political and economic side effects, as interest groups pursue selfish and biased interests.

On the other hand, interest groups were regarded as a natural phenomenon that appears in the course of development and democracy. In particular, liberal democracy guarantees freedom of association and expression, which means that interest groups seeking special interests are indispensable. Alexis de Tocqueville (1956 [1835]) had praised American interest group politics as 'art of association'. Interest group politics can decentralise power by maintaining and expressing various social cleavages, ultimately preventing policy decisions from shifting to extreme ends on a spectrum of different social interests (Lee 2001: 25). Therefore, revitalisation and growth of interest groups are important in the development of democracy. Interest group politics and democracy are closely related in that democracy can be practiced under the condition in which social forces are centred and balanced with national power.

Until recently, there has been a strong tendency in South Korea to recognise the collective action of interest groups as unfair to national interests and the public interest (Jung 2011: 7). Rather than evaluating the roles of interest groups in South Korea, this chapter seeks to provide an overview of interest groups, explore the changes in interest group politics in terms of democratisation and, finally, draw implications for the deepening of democracy in South Korea. This chapter consists of the following. First, it briefly analyses the landscape of interest groups. Next, it looks historically at the democratisation and changes in interest group politics in South Korea. Finally, the chapter reviews the changes in interest group politics and suggest the implications in terms of deepening democracy of South Korea

2. The Landscape of Interest Groups in South Korea

Interest groups have emerged in the form of 'associative interest groups' in the industrialisation process since the 1960s. Under the authoritarian regimes, interest groups were established by government support or coercion and mobilised for the purpose of fulfilling the national development goals. However, after democratisation in 1987, the scope of activities of interest groups gradually expanded and diversified into various social issues so as to pursue public interests. We seek to understand the landscape of interest group politics by distinguishing the types of representative interest groups and overviewing their development process in South Korea.

2.1 Labour Unions

Korea's two biggest labour unions are the *Hankuk Nochong* (Federation of Korean Trade Unions) (FKTU), and the *Minju Nochong* (Korean Confederation of Trade Unions) (KCTU). The FKTU was founded in March 1946 as the Federation of Labour Unions for the Promotion of Independence and was reorganised as the General Federation of Korean Trade Unions in April 1954, and finally renamed the Federation of Korean Trade Unions in November 1960. Neither multiple labour unions nor a national union federation were allowed until the Trade Union and Labour Relation Adjustment Act was revised in 1997. Under these circumstances, the FKTU has represented the interests of workers as the only peak organisation officially authorised under the authoritarian government. However, the FKTU went through a more involuntary progress than an autonomous one, staying within the scope of limited activities imposed by state sponsorship and engagement. Thus, it was rather subordinate to the authoritarian government, without its own ideology or class consciousness (Yoon and Kim 1989: 79).

Meanwhile, the KCTU was a progressive labour organisation launched in 1995 for the purpose of social reform and the political empowerment of workers. It was finally legalised in November 1999. Contrary to the conservative and restrictive labour movement of the FKTU even after democratisation in 1987, the KCTU, along with other social movement groups, led the struggle for social reform and further sought the political power of the labour class. The KCTU was able to achieve such progress as a result of militant unionism through challenge against the authoritarian regime that suppressed autonomous labour movements. Since then, the KCTU actively looked for ways to further secure its identity and expand its size through more active strikes and struggles (Lee 1997: 72).

Since the legalisation of the KCTU in 1999, the two labour unions have been competing against each other in South Korea, taking differentiated political lines. The

KCTU has pursued the political power of the working class from the beginning of its formation, nominating candidates for elections at each level. However, rather than making efforts to pursue independent political power, the FKTU ran its organisation under the auspices of the government, such as its chairman acting as a member of the ruling authoritarian government. For example, the KCTU demonstrated the possibility of becoming a major political power for the working class by organising People's Victory 21 during the 1997 presidential election, even before its legalisation (Shin 2011: 46–47). Eventually, in the seventeenth National Assembly election in 2004, the Korean Democratic Labour Party emerged as a third party. On the other hand, in the case of the FKTU, its former officials have been appointed as members of the ruling party or key members of the conservative governments. Furthermore, in the fifteenth general election in 1996, the former FKTU chairman ran as a candidate for the ruling conservative party (Kim, Y. 1997b: 117–118).

Recently, these two labour organisations have seen a shift in the balance of power: a weakening of the FKTU and a strengthening of the KCTU. The FKTU, the only legitimate organisation until 1997, had 1,021,134 union members in 1996, more than double the KCTU membership (418,154 when launched in 1999). However, the FKTU has been declining since a number of unions changed their umbrella organisation from the FKTU to the KCTU (Shin 2011: 45). As of December 2018, the KCTU had 968,035 (41.5 per cent) members, exceeding that of the FKTU, which had only 932,991 (40 per cent) members, and has finally established itself as the biggest labour organisation in terms of membership for the first time in twenty-three years (Lee, Y. 2019).

2.2 Economic Organisations

Economic organisations representing business interests in South Korea include the *Jeongyeongryeon* (Federation of Korean Industries) (FKI), the *Daehansangui* (Korea Chamber of Commerce and Industry) (KCCI), the *Hangukmuyeokhyeophoe* (Korea International Trade Association) (KITA), the *Jungsogieopjunganghoe* (Korea Federation of Small and Medium Business) (KBIZ), and the *Gyeongchong* (Korea Employers Federation) (KEF), which have developed in line with the history of economic development in the country.

First of all, the FKI was launched in 1961 as the Korea Businessmen's Association and renamed the Federation of Korean Industries in 1968. The FKI has served as an organisation exclusively representing the interests of large business groups (Chaebols). For example, it aims to affect economic policies and promote internationalisation of the Korean economy in order to nurture a free market and sound national economy. Because it is based on an unbalanced growth strategy, South Korea's economic growth strategy has disproportionately favoured large companies. According to Figure 20.1, the members of the FKI rapidly rose in number from 178 in 1970 to 247 and 415 in 1975 and 1979, respectively. As a result, Chaebols' interests were more dominant in economic policies during the Park Chung-hee government. This created a circular structure,

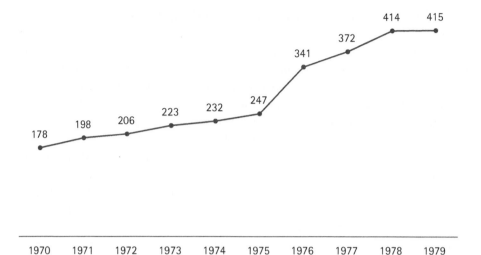

FIGURE 20.1: Changes in the numbers of members of the FKI under the Park Chung-hee government, 1970–1979

Source: Federation of Korean Industries (each year); Bae (2001).

which further strengthened the FKI's position to realise Chaebols' interests in terms of national economic decisions, even after the 1987 democratisation (Hwang 1997: 80–81). Despite its efforts to reform, however, the FKI faces an existential crisis. Its status as a leading economic organisation in South Korea has been sharply weakened. All four major Chaebols, including Samsung, Hyundai Motor, SK, and LG, left in 2017, after it was involved in the 'Choi Soon-sil scandal'. As a result, the FKI's profit took a major downturn. Total business revenue was 45.6 billion KRW in 2018, down 32.3 per cent from 67.4 billion KRW in 2017, which is less than half of revenue in 2016 (93.6 billion KRW) before the four major Chaebols left the FKI. Its revenue from membership fee also plunged to 40.8 billion KRW in 2016, 11.3 billion KRW in 2017, and 8.3 billion KRW in 2018 (Han 2019).

Second, the Korea Chamber of Commerce and Industry (KCCI) is a legal private economic organisation established under the Chamber of Commerce Act of 1952. It was modelled after the Hansung Chamber of Commerce and Industry, which was established in 1884, and is a pivotal institution that serves as a bridge between the government and the business community. The KCCI takes charge of a comprehensive economic organisation, with members from both commercial and industrial enterprises, including large and small businesses in all sectors. With seventy-three regional chambers of commerce and industry, it divides the districts across the country and promotes the improvement and development of commerce and industry in each administrative district. In the past, it maintained a lower status than other economic organisations, such as the FKI. Recently, however, due to the weakening of the FKI, the KCCI became the most representative organisation in South Korea (Kim 2020: 300).

Third, the Korea Enterprises Federation (KEF) was established in 1970 in order to establish industrial peace and achieve economic development through efficient corporate management and establishment of rational labour–management relationship. Since then, the government has begun to prepare long-term measures on labour–management issues by collecting opinions from different management circles in order to improve joint interests in the management sector. In particular, the KEF aims to build a harmonious labour–capital relationship through dialogue based on mutual respect and trust, rather than confrontation and conflict between classes (Lee 2010: 125).

Finally, the Korea Federation of Small and Medium Business (KBIZ) was established in 1962 and renamed in April 2006. The KBIZ is in charge of stabilising the management of small- and medium-sized enterprises (SMEs), securing markets for products, promoting international cooperation and exports, supporting cooperatives and mutually beneficial cooperation between large enterprises and SMEs, supporting local SMEs, and implementing a deduction system for small businesses and its owners. As of 2018, a total of 658,949 companies were members of 609 local unions, which is 18.6 per cent of all SMEs (Korea Federation of Small and Medium Business [KBIZ] 2018).

2.3 Professional Organisations

A *professional organisation* is an association that enhances special interests of experts performing specific functions on the basis of professional knowledge accumulated through long-term training. It also performs public service activities, such as the pursuit of collective interests, including the improvement of the members' welfare and status, as well as social services related to specialised fields (Kim, W. 1997: 142).

Professional organisations are interest groups in that they primarily protect and improve the welfare of their members, but there are some features that distinguish them from other interest groups. First of all, professional organisations can join only if they have certain qualifications to work in a specific field. They must receive education and training to acquire specialised knowledge and also be recognised as an expert by government. Therefore, it can be said that the number of members of professional organisations are regulated by the state. Second, professional organisations are expected to participate in various activities for social public goods. This is because professional organisations have been established by laws that control the activities of professionals. In this regard, the legal basis for their establishment prioritises public interest activities (Park 2001: 418–419).

Most representative professional organisations in South Korea include the following: the Korean Bar Association, the Korean Medical Association, the Korean Pharmaceutical Association, and the Korean Teachers and Education Workers Union.

The Korean Bar Association was established in 1950 under the Law of Lawyers enacted in 1949. On behalf of its members, the Korean Bar Association seeks to improve the welfare of lawyers, such as limiting the number of people allowed to pass bar examinations. On the other hand, as a group of legal experts, it also stipulates the role for public interest, including advocating for basic human rights and establishing a democratic basic order and pro bono affairs (Park 2001: 418). The Korean Bar Association greatly contributed to South Korea's democratisation under the authoritarian regime by insisting on the revision and abolition of undemocratic laws and by enacting and proposing laws to accelerate the democratisation process (Lee 2010: 136). In addition, since the late 1980s, the Korean Bar Association has played a pivotal role in protecting democracy, exerting more active efforts to protect human rights, realising social justice, and improving the legal system (Kim, W. 1997: 150).

The history of the Korean Medical Association dates back to as early as 15 November 1908, when the Korean Medical Affairs Research Society was founded. After the establishment of the Korean government in 1948, it changed its name to the Korean Medical Science Association and began its original role and activities as a medical organisation, and finally changed its name to the Korean Medical Association in 1995. After that, the name was changed to Chosun Medical Association in 1947 and the organisation pursued its original role as a group of medical doctors. It was renamed again as the Korean Medical Association in 1995 (Kim, W. 1997: 152). The Korean Medical Association carries out health-care-related public service activities, including improvement of social welfare and national health promotion, along with the aim of improving the welfare of all Korean doctors (Park 2001: 418).

2.4 Public Interest Groups

After democratisation, there was a boom of new civic organisations in South Korea. It was even referred to as 'the explosion of civil society' (Kang 2018: 375). In the process, a new type of civic organisation emerged that had not been seen in the past. Examples include the *Gyeongsilryeon* (Citizens' Coalition for Economic Justice) (CCEJ) in 1987, the *Hwangyeongyeonhap* (Korean Federation for Environmental Movement) (KFEM) in 1993, and the *Chamyeoyeondae* (People's Solidarity for Participatory Democracy) (PSPD) in 1994. At first glance, these civic organisations are not in line with the characteristics of interest groups in traditional definitions: the pursuit of special interests of members, the voluntary participation of members and the operation and activities of groups by professional staff who are not volunteers, and involuntary and compulsory membership (Joo 2004; Park 2001).

However, a new type of civic organisation that emerged during democratisation can be understood as 'associational' interest groups for the following two reasons (Almond and Powell 1978). First, they have formal professional staff, rules, and procedures agreed upon by members, while sharing specific purposes. Second, this type of organisation can be considered as a political actor that injects collective interests into the political process through various methods. It should be noted that the nature of the interests sought by these civic organisations is not that of a special interest that only works selectively for its members. Rather, they should be seen as public interests such as human rights, social justice, and the environment (Berry 1999). In this regard, this chapter includes a new type of civic association that has been pursuing the public interest in the context of South Korea.

The Citizens' Coalition for Economic Justice (CCEJ) was established on 8 July 1987, with the aim to improve democratic welfarism and economic justice though a method of peaceful and professional movement (Kim 1996: 278). The CCEJ launched a different level of civic activism from the past, with post-class 'citizens' as the main body, seeking gradual development within the capitalist system, rather than pursuing a drastic change (Park 1999: 232). As a result, the view of the CCEJ in the early days was not all that friendly. The government and businesses viewed the CCEJ as an anti-government opposition group, while many civic activists criticised it for undermining the cause of the civic movement. However, the CCEJ gradually gained public support by launching various movements in non-violent, peaceful, reasonable, and legitimate ways (Park 1997: 180).

People's Solidarity for Participatory Democracy (PSPD) was founded on 10 September 1994, in order to monitor state power, present specific policies and alternatives, and build a participatory democratic society in which freedom, justice, human rights, and welfare are properly realised through practical civic actions. The PSPD has ruled out government intervention since the beginning of its establishment, including not receiving financial support from the government. Also, the PSPD continued its active solidarity and partnership with progressive social groups (Park 1997: 189). This was possible because the PSPD put in efforts to inherit and develop the tradition of the existing democratic movement. It should be noted that unlike the CCEJ's pursuit of a new form of civic movement, the PSPD maintained a critical stance on the existing democratic movement (Park 2001: 200–201).

The Korean Federation for Environmental Movement (KFEM) began on 2 April 1993, when eight regional environmental associations initiated a nationwide environmental movement. Now the KFEM has grown beyond the realm of environmental activist. Its activities have expanded to raising issues through monitoring environmental policies in the implementation stage, hosting environmental campaigns, setting policy agendas, proposing policy alternatives, and deliberating policy alternatives (Ha 2008).

3. Democratisation and Changes in Interest Group Politics

3.1 Before the Democratisation of 1987: Responsive Dependence on State Power

South Korea's interest groups have been quite crippled since the early stages of formation and throughout the authoritarian past. In the stage of the 'explosion of political participation', interest groups were either a means for political elites to take advantage of the organisation's power and influence or a result of a leadership struggle within a single ideological group. Thus, interest groups were pressurised by politics, rather than exerting pressure on it. On top of that, many of these groups were viewed as a political and social mechanism serving government purposes and as a deformed figure subordinate to an authoritarian government (Jung, Y.-K. 1995: 122–124).

As social structures were differentiated with rapid industrialisation in the 1960s, interest groups in the modern sense appeared in South Korea. For instance, the FKI, the association of businessmen, and the FKTU, the representative body of workers, were formed at this time. Nevertheless, both the FKI and the FKTU were linked with the military regime, rather than reflecting the demands of businesses and labour. Thus, interest groups played a role as both a channel for monopoly and a tool for state control. In addition, they were limited from freely deciding and executing their own agendas beyond the state apparatus. In particular, the authoritarian state used different strategies according to the nature of interest groups. For example, for business groups such as the FKI, the authoritarian government applied an inclusionary policy to exert indirect control and mutual cooperation; whereas, an exclusionary policy of direct control and opposition was promoted to workers' organisations such as the FKTU. Under such conditions, interest groups were subject to state control and were merely social intermediaries for political mobilisation. As long as the authoritarian leadership lasted, interest groups appeared to be in the form of government-affiliated organisations in South Korea (Chang 1985: 135).

Prior to the democratisation in 1987, South Korea's strong authoritarian state had exerted extreme influence on interest group politics in two ways. First, the strong authoritarian regime carried out a secretive policymaking process without consulting anyone, including the ruling party. This imperial presidentialism that controlled both political parties and the executive was maintained for a long time. Most policy decisions were monopolised by a few political elites or technocrats, resulting in a greater power and one extremely concentrated in the executive branch (Yoon and Kim 1989: 72). As a result, interest groups did not have any means to express their own demands and contact channels to communicate with the executive (Ahn 1971). Y. Kim (1990: 254–255) showed that both business and labour organisations were focused on lobbying the government during this period. He explains that it was partly due to the overwhelming dominance of the authoritarian government, but it also had to do with the lack of congressional authority and the limited role of political parties. In other words, authoritarianism accelerated the 'governmentarisation' of interest groups.

Second, the monopoly over scarce resources by the authoritarian government allowed preferential treatment of selective industries, resulting in the domination of industries by a few big businesses. In this process, big businesses merely served as the state's tool for national economic development, failing to check and balance against the state power as independent organisations (Chang 1996: 290). For example, the Park Chung-hee government provided a vast amount of government subsidies to leading industries in the process of transitioning to heavy chemical industrialisation and provided policy finance to alleviate the risks to be faced. Rather than using the FKI as a channel, the government induced the Chaebols to participate in heavy chemical industrialisation by directly interacting with them. The Conference on Export Expansion and the Special Meeting on the Coordination of Heavy and Chemical Industries are the most representative examples (Bae 2001: 28–29). As the government's profit distributions were in a form of selective preferential treatment for individual companies, it became even more difficult to seek any other forms of collective association. Accordingly, Chaebols focused on special interests through informal contacts with power elites, rather than reflecting their groups or businesses (Ahn 1971: 110).

3.2 After Democratisation of 1987: Competitive Pluralism

After the democratisation in 1987, interest group politics fundamentally changed. Their field of activities, organisational process, and influence rapidly grew. As the state's repressive control over civil society was eased and the liberalisation of society progressed, numerous new interest groups emerged (Jung, Y.-S. 1995: 126). Out of a total of 9,467 civic groups published in the *Overview of Private Organisations of 1997*, an analysis of 3,200 organisations whose year of establishment are known illustrates that civic organisations continued to increase after democratisation. Table 20.1 shows that as of 1997, 55.8 per cent of all civic groups were established after the democratisation in 1987 (Yeom 2002: 116–117).

During this period, interest groups also began to exert influence on various social issues as the content of interests changed (Kim, Y. 1997a: 68–69). Instead of being broad and abstract, specific interests-driven organisations were created, such as the Korea Street Vendors Confederation and the National Alliance of Squatters and Evictees. In addition, interest groups dealing with similar agendas were organised against the monopolised interest representation established under the corporatist authoritarian system (You 2020). 'Homogeneous interest groups' emerged to maintain the competition through mutual conflict and cooperation within the same realm of civil society (Lee 2001). These interest groups have been expressing various interests by showing cooperative or conflicting aspects of specialised issues, while maintaining a competitive relationship. For example, the Korean Teachers and Education Workers was newly formed as a rival to the Korean Federation of Teachers' Association (Jung, Y.-K. 1995: 126).

Table 20.1: Establishment of South Korean civic organisations (as of 1997)

Establishment	Before 1960	1961–1970	1971–1979	1980–1986	1987–1989	1990–1992	1992–1996
Percentage	7.7	10.3	11.0	15.0	14.4	17.7%	23.7

Source: Yeom (2002).

At the same time, many public interest groups were nationally organised and began to exert greater influence in the policymaking process (Yeom 2002: 119). These groups sought general public interests, such as social and economic justice, consumer protection, and environmental preservation, rather than pursuing specific interests (Kim 2000; Koo 2002). Examples include the CCEJ, the PSPD, and the KFEM. The CCEJ exerts influence on economic policies, including the public ownership of land, real-name financial systems, and the decentralisation of economic power concentrated in Chaebols. The PSPD took the lead in making Chaebols' corporate structure more transparent through the minority shareholder movement. It also led other active civic participationm such as monitoring of lawmakers' parliamentary activities to prevent corruption (Chae 2016: 1098–1099).

Moreover, the government has established a system to actively support civic organisations, including public interest groups. The Act on Registration of Social Organisations of 1961 enacted by the authoritarian government had long regulated the establishment of social organisations by imposing registration obligations on all social organisations with very few exceptions, while allowing them to be deregistered by the authority. However, in January 1994, the Act on Reporting Social Organisations deleted the provision for registration (Article 3) and the cancellation of registration by the registration authority. This allowed social organisations to free themselves from state control and secure a considerable level of autonomy (Jung, Y.-S. 1995: 106). In addition, the Assistance for Non-Profit, Non-governmental Organisation Act enacted in 2000 shifted the role of the government from domination to support of interest groups. Civic organisations were further activated as it became possible for them to receive government support if the following were met: to be registered with either the central or local government for more than one year, to have more than 100 members, and not to be established to support a particular political party or to spread a creed of any special religion (Kang 2018: 378).

Post-democratisation interest group politics shows interest articulation as a collective action, including strikes and demonstrations. After the democratisation in 1987, the frequency and intensity of political protests declined sharply, but conflicts between interest groups seeking special interests have intensified (Jung, Y.-S. 1995: 14). Unlike the government's sluggish and ineffective response to conflicts between special interest groups, public interest groups have made significant contributions when conflicts arise among them (You 2020: 68–69). For example, under the Kim Young-sam government, when the Korean Medical Association and the Korean Pharmaceutical Association were at odds over the right to make herbal medicines, it was the CCEJ that mediated the dispute (Park 2001: 294–304). Under the Kim Dae-jung government, the CCEJ played a significant role in reconciling the conflict between the Korean Medical Association and the Korean Pharmaceutical Association over the division of medicine and in getting the Korean Medical Association to finally accept the government guideline (Park 2001: 423–427).

The role and the status of the legislature and political parties as communication channels for interest groups remained secondary even after democratisation in South

Korea. This was partly due to the authoritarian legacy of the developmental state in South Korea. But more importantly, it was mainly due to the lack of a system to link the activities of interest groups with political parties and the low institutionalisation of political parties (Jung 2011: 13). Thus, public interest groups had to play a similar role to that of the political parties, taking charge of interest aggregation and articulation. Especially in the 1990s, when political parties lacked policymaking expertise, these public interest groups played the role of 'interest aggregation' that political parties should have carried out. In the 1992 presidential election, for example, the CCEJ derived fifty-four reform agendas which were promoted by the Kim Young-sam government, such as the real-name finance transaction system, the freedom of information law, the administrative capital law, and campaign finance reform. In addition, campaigns of the minority shareholder by PSPD and Chaebol reform by the CCEJ were also reflected in the Kim Dae-jung government (You 2020: 68).

3.3 Democracy after the Democratisation in the 2010s: Conflictual Pluralism

The number of interest groups has been increasing ever since 2010, as the diversification of society has accelerated due to the deepening of democracy and the progress of the fourth industrial revolution. Interest groups aimed at pursuing private interests are directly related to their group members. As interest groups become more diversified and subdivided with the emergence of homogeneous interest groups, competition among them can lead to social conflicts. The competition by any means to survive is sometimes driven to 'extreme pluralism' (Im 1999: 83–84). For example, in 2020 the Korean Medical Association opposed the establishment of a public medical university and the expansion of public medical centres; furthermore, it continued the collective suspension of, and refusal to apply for, the national exam of medical students. This was an example of the pursuit of sectarian and selfish interests, while ignoring a public function of national health widely recognised among Korean citizens.

After 2010, interest group politics began to change. Interest groups have begun to recognise the National Assembly and political parties as important means of interest articulation. There are still institutional restrictions that do not allow donations of political funds to political parties and candidates for public office, but interest groups are pushing for specific political activities through the establishment of a new party and the promotion of proportional representation. For example, the Korea Federation of Micro Enterprise supported the creation of the Small Commercial and Industrial Owner's Party in the twenty-first general election in 2020. The Korean Medical Association launched a campaign to join a political party as a member to articulate their special interests in the policymaking process (Goh 2019).

One of the most important examples for conflictual interest group politics since 2010 has been the strike by the Korean Taxi Workers' Union against the car-sharing service. During the taxi industry's strike on car-sharing services in 2018, two taxi drivers chose tragic deaths (Lee, H. 2019). In addition, the taxi industry held a rally in front of the National Assembly and started to target the National Assembly as a channel of interest articulation. One example of this is the Korea National Joint Conference of Taxi Associations putting up a large banner saying, 'Let's Politicise!' and calling for a legislation to ban all illegal passenger transportation.

4. Conclusion

In the process of industrialisation of the developmental state, conflicts of interest tend to intensify, and, as a consequence, interest groups have further diversified. In particular, interest groups that grew quantitatively and qualitatively through democratisation in the 1980s actively invested various interests into the political process that were suppressed during the authoritarian era. In addition, new public interest groups that have emerged with the growth of civil society since the 1990s have brought about the revitalisation of interest group politics and contributed greatly to the political development of South Korea,

There were changes in interest group politics in South Korea after the 1987 democratisation. First, the democratisation weakened the state's coercive control and increased autonomy in the civil society, leading to a decline of interest groups that functioned as a political mobilisation mechanism under the unilateral protection of, and control by, the authoritarian government. Furthermore, various interest groups were formed to reflect their special interests in the legislation and implementation process. As a result, conflict between interest groups increased as their interest articulation erupted rapidly.

Second, in terms of a mode of activities, conflicts between interest groups and between interest groups and government have increased. Protests and campaigns on different social and economic issues became more frequent, which had previously been suppressed by the state's oppressive control during the authoritarian era. Conflicts between interest groups and the government have emerged to protect their special interest when their collective interests have been violated in the course of the government's policymaking or enforcement. At the same time, these conflicts are becoming more complicated, sometimes with the creation of two or more interest groups within the same socio-economic agenda.

Nevertheless, the existence of legal regulations prohibiting political participation of interest groups in South Korea still hinders the vitalisation of interest group politics. For example, the Political Fund Act still prohibits corporations and organisations from donating political funds, and there is no official lobbying system for interest groups to participate in the operations of the National Assembly. Therefore, institutional reform is required to allow interest groups to freely engage in political activities such as making political donations, supporting specific candidates, and issuing evaluations of politicians during the election campaign. In addition, the relationship between interest groups and the National Assembly should be institutionalised in order to resolve interest conflicts, including homogeneous interest groups and public interest groups. Such changes will contribute to building a legitimate basis for different interest groups to inject their own interests in the policymaking process in a more transparent way.

In order for interest group politics to continue to develop, an effective conflict coordination system is required to mediate the interest conflict that may arise in the process of expressing various interests. Such a conflict management system would have to take into account the following factors: self-regulation of conflicts between interest groups, activation of a permanent body for exchange of opinions between the government and interest groups, institutionalisation of the conflict mediation system, and so on. This would contribute to the development of democracy in South Korea.

Bibliography

Ahn, H. (1971), 'Hanguk haengjeonggwajeongui iik tuipe gwanhan yeongu' (Input of Interest in the Korean Administration Process), *Korean Journal of Public Administration* 9(1), 104–120.

Almond, G., and Powell, B. (1978), *Comparative Politics: System, Process and Policy* (Boston, MA: Little, Brown & Co.).

Bae, E. (2001), 'Gwonwijuui jeongchichejehaui jeongbuwa gyeongje iikjipdan gwangye' (The Relationship between Government and Economic Interest Groups in the Authoritarian Political Regimes), *Korean Public Administration Review* 35(2), 19–39.

Berry, J. M. (1984), *The Interest Group Society* (Boston, MA: Little, Brown & Co.).

Berry, J. M. (1999), *The New Liberalism: The Rising Power of Citizen Groups* (Washington, DC: Brookings Institute Press).

Chae, J. (2016), 'Hanguk simindancheui giwongwa jeongae geurigo gwaje' (The Origins and Development of Korea Civil Society and Challenges), *Journal of Humanities and Social Science* 7(6), 1089–1111.

Chang, D. (1985), 'Saneophwawa iikjipdan' (Industrialisation and Interest Groups), *Korean Political Science Review* 19, 61–75.

Chang, D. (1996), 'Hangukui iikjipdan'(Interest Groups in South Korea), in J. Min et al., eds, *Hangukeui jeongchi* (*Korean Politics*), 285–310 (Seoul: Nanam).

de Tocqueville, A. (1956 [1835]), *Democracy in America* (New York: Penguin).

Easton, D. (1957), 'An Approach to the Analysis of Political Systems', *World Politics* 9(3), 383–400.

Federation of Korean Industries (FKI) (1991), *Jeongyeongryeon 30-nyeonsa* (*Thirty Years of the Federation of Korean Industries*) (Seoul: FKI).

Goh, E. (2019), 'Chongseon apdugo. Iikdanche jeongchiseryeokhwa jaengeoleum' (A Quick Step for Politicization of Interest Groups Ahead of the 21st General Election), *Hankyung*, 18 December, https://www.hankyung.com/politics/article/2019121866201, accessed 30 November 2021.

Ha, M. (2008), 'Jojikui jeongdangseong insik, frame guseong, geurigo seongjang' (Organisations' Legitimacy Perception, Frame Construction, and Growth), *Korean Review of Organizational Studies* 5(2), 217–265.

Han, D. (2019), 'Jaegye daebyeonin, jeongyeongryeon wigi. Sadae geurup taltoehago Jeongbuneun passing' (The FKI, a Business Spokesman, Faced a Crisis. The Four Major

Chaebols Left and the Government Bypassed It), *Chosun Ilbo*, 31 March, https://biz.chosun.com/site/data/html_dir/2019/03/30/2019033000021.html?utm_source=urlcopy&utm_medium=share&utm_campaign=biz, accessed 30 November 2021.

Hwang, J. (1997), 'Sayongja danche' (Employers' organisations), in Y. Kim, ed., *Iikjipdan Jeongchiwa Iik Galdeung* (*Interest Group Politics and Interest Conflicts*), 78–103 (Seoul: Hanwool).

Im, H. (1999), 'From Affiliation to Association: The Challenge of Democratic Consolidation in Korean Industrial Relations', in D. McNamara, ed., *Corporatism and Korean Capitalism*, 159–181 (London: Routledge).

Joo, S. (2004), *NGOwa Siminsahoe* (*NGO and the Civil Society*) (Seoul: Hanyang University Press).

Jung, S. (2011), 'Hangukui minjuhwawa iikjeongchiui byeonhwawa yeonsokseonge daehan yeongu' (Changes and Continuities of the Interest Group Politics in Korean Democratization)', *Korean Party Studies Review* 10(1), 5–30.

Jung, Y.-K. (1995), 'Iikjipdanui baljeongwa yeokhal' (Development of Interest Groups and Its Roles), in B. Ahn et al., eds, *Gukga, Siminsahoe, Jeongchiminjuhwa* (*State, Civil Society and Political Democratisation*), 119–156 (Seoul: Hanwool).

Jung, Y.-S. (1995), 'Gukga-siminsahoe gwangyeui beopjeok jedojeok gochal' (Legal and Institutional Consideration of the State–Society Relationship), in B. Ahn et al., eds, *Gukga, Siminsahoe, Jeongchiminjuhwa* (*State, Civil Society and Political Democratisation*), 94–118 (Seoul: Hanwool).

Kang, W. (2018), *Hanguk Jeongchiron* (*Understanding Korean Politics*) (Seoul: PY Books).

Key, V. O. (1958), *Politics, Parties and Pressure Groups* (New York: Thomas Y. Crowell).

Kim, S. (2000), *The Politics of Democratisation in Korea: The Role of Civil Society* (Pittsburgh, PA: University of Pittsburgh Press).

Kim, W. (1997), 'Jeonmunjik danche' (Professional Organisations), in Y. Kim, ed., *Iikjipdan Jeongchiwa Iik Galdeung* (*Interest Group Politics and Interest Conflicts*), 140–164 (Seoul: Hanwool).

Kim, Y. (1990), *Hanguk Iikjipdangwa Minjujeongchibaljeon* (*Interest Groups and Development of Democracy in Korea*) (Seoul: Daewangsa).

Kim, Y. (1996), 'Hanguke isseoseo iikjipdangwa siminsahoe' (Interest Groups and Civic Society in Korea), *Journal of Democratic Civic Education* 1, 269–286.

Kim, Y. (1997a), 'Hanguk iikjipdanui baljeongwajeong' (Development of Interest Groups in Korea), in Y. Kim, ed., *Iikjipdan Jeongchiwa Iik Galdeung* (*Interest Group Politics and Interest Conflicts*), 65–77 (Seoul: Hanwool).

Kim, Y. (1997b), 'Nodongja danche' (Labour Unions), in Y. Kim, ed., *Iikjipdan Jeongchiwa Iik Galdeung* (*Interest Group Politics and Interest Conflicts*), 104–139 (Seoul: Hanwool).

Kim, Y. (2020), *Jesaui Mulgyeolgwa Hangukjeongchiui Gwaje* (*The Fourth Wave and Tasks in Korean Politics*) (Seoul: PY Books).

Koo, H. (2002), 'Civil Society and Democracy in South Korea', *The Good Society* 11(1), 40–45.

Korea Federation of Small and Medium Business (KBIZ) (2018), '2018 nyeon Jungsogieop Hyeonhwang' (Current Status of Small and Medium Business in 2018), https://www.kbiz.or.kr/, accessed 30 November 2021.

Lee, H. (2019), 'Haeneomgin carpool galdeunge tto "jeongbu jikjeop naseoya"' (The Government Should Step into the Carpool Conflict That Has Passed the Year), *Money Today*, 10 January, https://news.mt.co.kr/mtview.php?no=2019011011175241588, accessed 30 November 2021.

Lee, J. (2001), '21-segi iikjipdanjeongchiui jeongae: Saeroun dojeongwa geukbokgwaje' (The Development of Interest Group Politics in the 21st Century), *Journal of Asiatic Studies* 44(1), 1–31.
Lee, J. (2010), *Iikjipdan jeongchi* (*Interest Group Politics*) (Goyang: Ingansarang).
Lee, W. (1997), 'Nodongundongui yangdaeseryeok: Hanguk nochonggwa Minju nochong' (The Two Major Labour Movements in Korea: FKTU and KCTU), *Journal of Korean Social Trends and Perspectives* 35, 54–79.
Lee, Y. (2019), 'Minju nochong johapwonsu hanguk nochong cheot chuwol. 23-nyeonmane jeil nochong deunggeuk' (The Number of Members of the KCTU Overtook the FKTU for the First Time in 23 Years, and Became the Largest Confederation of Trade Unions in South Korea), *Yonhap News*, 25 December, https://www.yna.co.kr/view/AKR20191224120300004, accessed 30 November 2021
Olson, M. (1982), *The Rise and Decline of Nations* (New Haven, CT: Yale University Press).
Park, K. (1997), 'Sahoe ilban danche' (Social Organization), in Y. Kim, ed., *Iikjipdan Jeongchiwa Iik Galdeung* (*Interest Group Politics and Interest Conflicts*), 165–196 (Seoul: Hanwool).
Park, S. (1999), 'Simindanchewa jeongbuganui gyeonje hyeopryeokui byeonjeungbeopjeok johwa mosaek' (Dialectical Harmony between Civic Organisations and Government), *Korean Public Administration Quarterly* 11(1), 31–49.
Park, S. (2001), *NGOwa Hyeondae Sahoe* (*NGOs and Modern Society*) (Seoul: Arche).
Schattschneider, E. E. (1942), *Party Government* (New York: Farrar and Rinehart).
Shin, K. (2011), 'Minjuhwa ihuui minjujuuiwa nodongundong: Hangukui sarye' (Democracy and Labour Movement after Democratisation in South Korea), *Journal of Social Science* 50(1), 37–70.
Truman, D. (1971), *The Governmental Process* (New York: Alfred A. Knopf).
Wilson, J. Q. (1973), *Political Organisations* (New York: Basic Books).
Yeom, J. (2002), 'Hanguk simindancheui seongjanggwa nyugeobeoneonseuui ganeungseong' (Development of Civic Organisation and Possibilities of New Governance in Korea), *Journal of Asiatic Studies* 45(3), 113–147.
Yoon, H., and Kim, Y. (1989), 'Hanguk iikjipdanui jeongchi chamyeoe daehan yeongu' (A Study on Political Participation of the Interest Groups in Korea), *Korean Political Science Review* 23(1), 39–80.
You, J. (2020), 'Political Process: Election, Interest Group Politics and Mass Media', in C. Moon and M. Moon, eds, *Routledge Handbook of Korean Politics and Public Administration*, 59–76 (London: Routledge).

CHAPTER 21

LABOUR UNION ACTIVISM

SOONMEE KWON

1. Introduction

In the advanced capitalist states of the West, the movement for the working class to politically represent its interests led to the formation of independent working-class parties that were distinguished from liberal parties in the late nineteenth and early twentieth centuries. These labour parties, in addition to national and industry-wide unions, made it possible for the interests of Western labour activism to be reflected in public policymaking. In contrast, South Korean workers have had neither an encompassing union nor a strong party to articulate their collective voice, even after the collapse of the authoritarian regime.

The traditional explanation for this is the South Korean state's harsh oppression of labour. According to the statist perspective, South Korean workers were unable to organise into a 'class' due to political control and exclusion deriving from the authoritarian state (Choi 1997). South Korean workers were mobilised for the goals of the developmental state. The repressive state imposed low wages and long working hours to realise the public good of export-driven economic growth, even after democratisation (Choi 1997; Roh 2010). It can be said that Korean workers lived a life of slavery in which they were completely deprived of the civil, political, and social rights defined by T. H. Marshall (1950). This approach also emphasises the structural and institutional environment, including anti-communist ideology, the national security law, and labour laws that hindered the organisation of the working class.

The statist perspective provides an important clue to understanding why the labour movement expanded immediately after democratisation only to suddenly contract in the 1990s. However, this view cannot fully explain the dynamics of the South Korean labour movement in the era of democratisation. Whereas South Korea's labour union activism is regarded as exhibiting 'late growth and premature stagnation' (Lim and Kim 1993), it has also shown an amazing resilience. Unlike advanced industrial countries such as the United Kingdom, the United States, Germany, Japan, and Sweden, where labour unions have been shrinking for decades, South Korea's union membership rate has remained almost unchanged since the mid-1990s. This is due to the growth of the Korean Confederation of Trade Unions (KCTU), a militant national umbrella union, and especially its expansion in the public sector. Membership in the KCTU has only recently begun to slightly outnumber that of its moderate rival, the Federation of Korean Trade Unions (FKTU). However, the KCTU led the South Korean labour movement even when it was much smaller than it is now. These points suggest that, although union size is an important power resource for unions, their direction and methodology are just as important (Shin 2011).

The alternative approach to explaining South Korean workers' low level of political empowerment points to problems with union leadership. According to Jangjip Choi (1993), South Korea's 'democracy without labour' is largely due not only to oppression of labour from above, but also to radical union leadership that refuses to recognise the importance of the elections and party politics institutionalised after the democratic transition of 1987. Studies on the crisis in labour union activism since the late 2000s have also stressed endogenous factors. For example, union leadership has not adequately responded to socio-economic changes such as the emergence of non-regular workers and the polarisation of the labour market. The labour movement has continued path-dependent behaviour that is orientated towards regular workers. For these reasons, it is important to simultaneously examine how the state has tried to suppress organised labour and how the leadership of the labour movement has reacted to that suppression.

This chapter is structured as follows: the second section describes the characteristics of the labour movement under the authoritarian regime. The third and fourth sections divide the labour union activism after democratisation into two critical periods on the basis of the degree of worker's industrial citizenship and political influences. The first period runs from 1987 to the first half of 1997, when militant labour union activism was in its infancy. The second phase runs from the second half of 1997 to the present, after South Korean society was battered by the Asian Financial Crisis. Finally, the conclusion briefly presents some implications of this study.

2. The Authoritarian State and Oppressive Labour Policies

The anti-communism of the Cold War provided a favourable environment for the emergence of authoritarian regimes in South Korea and prevented the formation of the working class in the 1950s. Under the right-wing administration of Rhee Syngman (1948–1960), the FKTU was the only legal union. The FKTU was organised from the top down with the support of the Rhee administration. Therefore, it functioned as a political machine to strengthen the power of Rhee's authoritarian regime (Kim 1995). The majority of the FKTU's leaders consisted of youth activists from the right wing rather than members of the working class. The FKTU became a stronghold of corrupt and factional union leaders.

In Choi's (1997) analysis of South Korean labour politics, the state elites curbed workers' wages and banned their political participation without giving them any policy incentives, unlike South American state corporatism. South Korean workers generally complied with the government's policy of 'growth first, distribution later'. President Park Chung-hee (1962–1979) revised the Trade Union Act in 1963 to require official approval for the establishment of unions and to prohibit multiple unions at both the national and workshop level. Unions were also strictly prohibited from engaging in political activities. In 1971, Park declared a national emergency to deprive the unions of the right to collective bargaining and action, a step that was further strengthened by the 1972 *Yushin* constitution.

This repressive approach was retained during the presidency of Chun Doo-hwan (1980–1988), who seized power through a coup in 1979. In particular, the Chun government limited union activities to the legal umbrella unions and the unions that had direct working relations with employers. He achieved this by inserting a clause into the Trade Union Act that prohibited intervention by 'third parties'. The purpose of this clause was to prevent anti-government labour activists, student activists, and civic groups from allying themselves with the working class. In so doing, the government sought to keep union activism within the boundaries of enterprise unionism.

Cracks began to appear in South Korean workers' long acquiescence after the death of Chun Tae-il. On 13 November 1970, Chun Tae-il, a twenty-two-year-old tailor at a small clothing store in the Cheonggye area of Seoul, immolated himself after leading a demonstration to protest against poor working conditions. The last slogans he shouted were 'Workers are not machines!' 'Observe the Labour Standards Act!' 'Don't let my death be in vain!' (Cho 2009). After his death, his mother and colleagues, joined by supportive university students, demanded that the Labour Office let workers form unions and improve working conditions (Chun 2017). That eventually led to the establishment of the Cheonggye Clothing Union, an independent labour union with 500 members. This union was an icon of the South Korean labour movement until it was forcibly disbanded by the Chun administration in 1981 (Choi 1997).

The death of Chun Tae-il kindled a sense of justice among many university students and some religious leaders and triggered their interest in labour issues, which had been neglected amid the focus on modernisation and economic development. It inspired student activists to jump directly into factories, while hiding their identity, or to ally with the labour movement. According to Yoo (2013), student activists found solidarity with labour activists in the 1970s and 1980s through such ideologies as anti-dictatorship, socialism, and people's democracy (*minjungjuui*). Groups supportive of the working class, such as the Young Catholic Workers and the Protestant group Urban Industrial Missions, became sympathetic to the labour movement. Small group activities provided by church groups elevated workers' class consciousness (Koo 2001). The independent trade union activism in the 1970s was largely based in the Seoul area because of the high concentration of pro-labour church groups in that area (Koo 2001).

South Korea reorientated its industrialisation strategy from light industry in the 1960s to heavy and chemical industry (HCI) in the 1970s, while actively seeking foreign direct investment. South Korea's leading industries today, such as automobiles, shipbuilding, electronics, and semiconductors, were built around this time. HCI companies were large in size, and most of their workers were men. However, those workers carried out few noteworthy labour actions except for a spontaneous action by Hyundai shipyard workers in 1974.

Throughout the 1970s, female workers played a prominent role in the labour movement. Female wage earners constituted 'a highly homogeneous group, characterised by their rural background, young age, single status, low educational attainment, and usually heavy burden of supporting their poor families' (Koo 2001: 36). South Korea's crucial labour actions in the 1970s occurred in labour-intensive light industry (especially textile factories), in which most workers were women. But these women's actions were thwarted by pro-business male managers, police interventions, or a combination of the two. The Confucian culture that was prevalent in South Korean society at that time exploited female workers by instilling familialism and subservience at the workplace and imposing unlimited loyalty to employers. Furthermore, the dominant discourse about union activism was that unions were a wasteful social 'disease', disrupted order, and were manipulated by 'the Reds' (Kim 2005).

So why were male workers quiescent during the 1970s? There are two explanations. One is that some of the large-scale HCI firms employing male workers were defined as defence industries in the 1970s, leading to strict regulation of labour disputes. Male workers there were forced to accept 'military-style control' for fear of losing their benefits under the military exemption system, which waived their mandatory military service (Kim 1988). The other explanation is that the cost of unionisation increases with scale, reflecting the Olsonian perspective (Olson 1971). According to Choi Jangjip (1997), a few courageous workers seeking to set up a union will have a harder time at a large business than a small one. More workers have to participate in decision-making at large businesses, which also manage their workforces more systematically.

3. The Great Workers' Struggle of 1987 and the Birth of Militant Union Activism

The democratisation movement in June 1987 succeeded in restoring procedural democracy and expanding political freedom in South Korea. Greater political freedom reduced the cost of collective actions among male workers in heavy industrial complexes. Labour disputes began in Ulsan—where affiliates of the Hyundai Chaebol

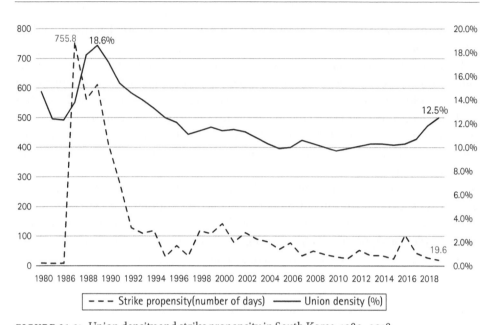

FIGURE 21.1: Union density and strike propensity in South Korea, 1980–2018

Note: Strike propensity measured by the number of working days lost due to strikes per 1,000 wage earners.

Source: Korea Labour Institute (2020).

(meaning a family-owned conglomerate) were concentrated—and soon spread throughout the country. As Figure 21.1 shows, the strike propensity jumped from 8.5 days in 1986 to 755.8 days in 1987. A total of 3,749 strikes took place in 1987, which was twice the total of the previous decade. The number of participants in the strike was 1.26 million, which was five times greater than total participants during the previous decade. Most of these actions took place during the three months from July to September 1987. Workers fought fiercely for economic demands such as democratic labour unions, wage hikes, and better working conditions. As a result of the Great Workers' Struggle, new unions were formed and union density rose from 12.3 per cent in 1986 to 18.6 per cent in 1989.

The Great Workers' Struggle was neither organised for political purposes nor guided by national leadership. Rather, it was spontaneous, with unorganised workers taking advantage of the government's relaxation of its rigid control of labour after the success of the uprising in June 1987 (Im 1994). The Great Workers' Struggle can be seen as an expression of accumulated discontent among workers who had been paid low wages and deprived of their basic rights for decades during Korea's industrialisation under an authoritarian regime. The Great Workers' Struggle also showed that the centre of gravity of the labour movement had shifted from female workers in light industry to male workers in heavy industry.

The new unions advanced from building regional coalitions to forming a national coalition through a series of campaigns to revise labour laws in the second half of 1988.

Democratic labour unions sought to abolish three harmful clauses in labour laws: a ban on multiple unions, a ban on third-party intervention, and compulsory arbitration on public utilities. In January 1990, the unions involved in this struggle organised into the *Chunnohyup* (Korea Trade Union Congress, KTUC). The KTUC was the prototype of the militant labour movement (Shin 2011), adopting the motto of 'the realisation of social equality'. However, the KTUC was designated an anti-state and illegal organisation by the Roh Tae-woo administration (1988–1993), which prohibited all its rallies, struggles, and events. The KTUC only lasted for five years but served as the forerunner of the KCTU, which came to symbolise South Korea's democratic labour unions.

As Dan (2020) points out, there are two reasons to regard the KTUC as a predecessor of the KCTU. First, the activities of the KTUC have influenced the identity of democratic union activism to this day. The KTUC resisted the deep-rooted ideology of labour–capital collusion and the state's unilateral control of the unions. It established the tradition of the democratic union movement, which used the slogan *nodonghaebang* ('labour emancipation') to represent workers' class identity, militancy, and orientation towards social revolution. Second, the KTUC clearly expressed the organisational and political goals of the democratic union movement. In terms of organisation, the union aimed to overcome enterprise unionism and to build an encompassing national centre based on industrial unionism; politically, it aimed to build a worker-led party differentiated from the liberal party.

Shocked by the Great Workers' Struggle and democratic union activism, the FKTU implemented internal reforms. Distancing itself from the authoritarian governments of the past, the FKTU resolved to reinvent itself as an independent national centre. As part of these reforms, it launched a political committee to articulate the various interests of workers to political parties and government agencies. The FKTU also attempted to change relations with employers, who were hostile to labour unions, and openly condemned employers' unfair labour practices. In contrast with the KTUC, the FKTU participated in a 'law-abiding struggle' to secure economic benefits for its members, and since late 1989, it has gradually approached the 'social consensus' model in line with its goal of strengthening participation in public policymaking and political activities (Choi et al. 1999).

Despite democratisation and workers' fierce struggles, industrial citizenship was at a standstill, and the authoritarian regime's impact on the working class still lingered via path-dependency. The revised labour laws of 1987 retained the basic framework of the authoritarian industrial relations of the past and only granted workers minimal rights of organisation, collective bargaining, and action. The laws maintained prohibitions on unions' political activities, multiple unions, and the intervention of third parties. Beginning in 1990, therefore, major unions, including the large manufacturing unions and white-collar unions such as the Korean Teachers and Educational Workers' Union (KTU), organised in 1989, convened each fall in the Joint Committee for the Ratification of International Labour Organisation (ILO) Fundamental Conventions and the Reform of the Trade Union Act in response to the Roh Tae-woo government's decision to seek membership in the ILO.

The KCTU was finally established in November 1995, composed of 862 enterprise unions and a total membership of 418,000 (about 25 per cent of all organised labour). The new national centre made an enormous effort to revise the existing labour laws, but its legal status was rejected by the Kim Young-sam administration (1993–1998) until November 1997. The government's reasoning was that the KCTU included unregistered unions.

Kim Young-sam, South Korea's first civilian president since democratisation, set globalisation as a top priority in managing state affairs. The Kim Young-sam administration liberalised the foreign exchange, financial, and capital markets, bowing to US pressure ahead of South Korea's entry into the Organisation of Economic Co-operation and Development (OECD) in 1996. To make the labour market more flexible, the government submitted a bill to the National Assembly that would revise the labour laws by deregulating employment and working hours, allowing the use of strike-breakers during strikes, and banning the payment of wages during strikes on the principle of 'no work, no pay'. The ruling party lawmakers sneaked into the National Assembly at dawn on 26 December 1996, and passed the bill before opposition lawmakers could intervene. The KCTU immediately held a press conference and organised a general strike. The KCTU's strike and demonstrations continued for more than a month. In the end, the Kim Young-sam administration decided to nullify the labour laws and reform them through an agreement between the ruling and opposition parties. The newly revised labour laws fell far short of the KCTU's expectations. They continued to allow the use of strike-breakers and the 'no work, no pay' principle during strikes and did not recognise government employees and teachers' right to organise. One important outcome of this struggle was that the KCTU acquired legitimacy. Other achievements were ending the prohibition of third-party intervention and recognising multiple unions above the corporate level; however, multiple unions at the corporate level were not legalised until July 2011.

After the 1987 Great Workers' Struggle, there were important changes in the labour movement in regard to ideology and leadership. Activists who had been part of the university student movement emerged as the leading cohort of the labour movement, guiding strikes and demonstrations at the regional and national levels. They considered the unification of fragmented labour unions and organisations a vital part of social transformation. Their ideological position on the labour activism was generally orientated towards revolutionary unionism, as opposed to reformist unionism (Lee 1988; Kim 1995). Around this time, South Korea's young intellectuals on the left went beyond anti-government ideas and began to arm themselves with socialist ideology. They were devoted to Marxism–Leninism or North Korea's *Juche* ideology. But after the fall of the Socialist bloc, socialist doctrine was criticised even within the progressive camp. Anti-regime and illegal underground organisations were no longer sustainable, due to public apathy as well as government oppression. Faced with this situation, radical labour activists of the younger generation sought legitimate and public political activities through the mechanisms of representative democracy.

Progressive groups attempted to build political parties for the lower and working classes several times after democratisation in 1987 and throughout the 1990s. However, all their attempts failed. One of the main reasons was that progressives were divided over the establishment of a working-class party and the direction of social transformation. Progressives were largely split into two camps. The first camp was National Liberation (NL), which followed North Korea's *Juche* ideology. NL supported a coalition of all democratic forces, tactically including liberals, on the way to the social transformation of South Korea and national reunification with North Korea. NL thought that the formation of a working-class party would only benefit the 'enemy' (i.e. the 'American imperialists' and their puppet conservative governments in South Korea) by dispersing the votes of the democratic electorate. The other camp was the People's Democracy (PD), which emphasised the need to build a working-class party that was distinct from both the liberal and conservative parties. PD criticised North Korean-style socialism and the Soviet socialist model and aimed for an idealistic socialist state that could overcome undemocratic tendencies, bureaucratic oppression, and economic inefficiency.

4. Consolidation of the Dual Labour Market and Political Marginalisation of Labour Union Activism after the Financial Crisis of 1997

Dualisation and fragmentation have been two of the most enduring characteristics of the South Korean labour market since the late 1990s (Kwon and Hong 2019). Although the unequal labour market began in the 1980s, it was aggravated by the 1997 financial crisis and has become an enduring problem since then. Wage inequality varies with the size of the firm, type of employment, and gender, but the most serious wage gap is the one associated with firm size. According to Roh (2021), as of 2019, the gross average monthly wages of workers with a contract of at least one year at small and medium-sized companies (with 5 to fewer than 500 employees) was only 59.4 per cent of wages at large companies (with 500 or more employees).

South Korea's bailout by the International Monetary Fund (IMF) between1997 and 2001 was a harbinger of the end of high growth and low unemployment and the beginning of the lasting phenomena of corporate restructuring and employment instability. The Kim Dae-jung administration (1998–2003), inaugurated in the midst of the financial crisis, aggressively pushed through neoliberal restructuring, including flexibilisation of the labour market, in line with IMF requirements (Kwon and Hong 2019). On the understanding that economic pain would be fairly divided among workers, capitalists, and the state, the KCTU and the FKTU reluctantly participated in tripartite dialogue to overcome the desperate financial crisis. Thus, in early February 1998, the first social pact was signed in South Korean labour politics. The core of this agreement was a political trade-off of labour market flexibilisation for workers' increased industrial and social rights (Park 2001). Organised labour accepted the introduction of large-scale layoffs and temporary agency work. In return, the government promised to protect labour unions' political activities in the private sector, permit the unionisation of teachers and civil servants, and strengthen the social security system for the involuntarily unemployed.

The social agreement of 1998 contradicted the traditional hypothesis that the organisational infrastructure of the unions (i.e. a high union density and a centralised bargaining structure) is critical for successfully reaching social pacts (Baccaro and Lim 2007; Yang 2010). The biggest driving force behind the class compromise of 1998 was social actors' intense fear and sense of crisis over the gloomy economic situation. Since then, the South Korean social dialogue system, called the Economic, Social and Labour Council, has been institutionalised as a presidential advisory body. The government takes the initiative at the Council, while the KCTU stays aloof. After the KCTU signed the social agreement in 1998, its leadership lost the confidence of delegates for supporting neoliberal labour market policies. Whether or not to participate in social dialogue has always been an important agenda item in the KCTU's internal politics. Since late 1998, most of the KCTU's factions and members have rejected social dialogue, which shows that the KCTU is dominated by hard-line activists.

The militant KCTU's repeated refusal to take part in social dialogue is one of the key reasons for the instability of industrial relations in South Korea. The strike propensity in South Korea is far higher than that of Japan and Taiwan, two East Asian countries that share its experience with economic development. The South Korean labour movement tends to prefer the hard-line route because there is less political room and fewer opportunities to articulate workers' collective interests. According to Lee Yoon-kyung (2006: 732), 'the president-centred political institutions in democratised Korea allowed little political permeability to organised unions demanding labour reform. The unions, being unable to effectively influence either the electoral space or the centralised policymaking process, have resorted to disruptive activities outside of institutionalised politics.'

Another important reason for intransigent labour union activism in South Korea is related to the radical ideology held by the major left-wing factions within the KCTU. These factions, which have a profound influence on rank-and-file members in the KCTU, still hold a rigidly anti-capitalist attitude, though this has faded somewhat in recent years (Kwon 2020). They are sceptical of the compatibility of capitalism and democracy in South Korea and subscribe to ideas that are ideologically rooted in either Marxism–Leninism or North Korea's *Juche* ideology. They tend to regard South Korean society as being far from a genuine democracy and South Korea's predatory capitalism as being incompatible with a generous welfare state, barring fundamental reform of the monopolistic Chaebol system. The leftists' pessimistic attitude towards South Korean democracy and capitalism led to a preference for collective actions by rank-and-file members over political compromises with capitalists or governments through the union leadership.

Since its foundation, the KCTU has pursued job security and wage equality for all workers. Enormous financial resources are required for full employment and income equality, resources that are no longer readily available in the period of welfare retrenchment in a post-industrial society (Iversen and Wren 1998). These goals would also require the large corporate union members to share their privileges through refraining from seeking wage increases or shortening working hours. Unfortunately, the unions at export-orientated conglomerates in South Korea lack the will to share their privileged status with outsiders. They tend to be satisfied with achieving economic prosperity through collective bargaining at the enterprise level, rather than pursuing class solidarity through industry-wide bargaining. Moreover, South Korea's welfare system is not based on universal citizenship, but on the principles of social insurance, under which benefits are linked to contributions. Since the individual's ability to contribute is determined by employment experience and status in the labour market, this social security system even has a regressive characteristic in terms of reproducing social inequality, rather than improving the distribution structure between the haves and have-nots (Yang 2005).

As shown in Figure 21.2, the share of South Korean wage earners who are non-standard workers as of 2020 reached 36 per cent according to Statistics Korea and 42 per cent according to the Korea Labour and Society Institute (KLSI). In the analysis of Statistics Korea, the percentage of non-regular workers increased sharply between 2002 and 2004, but has not changed significantly since then. On the other hand, KLSI analysis suggests that non-regular employment has been on a gradual decline after peaking in 2005. That decline can be seen as resulting from the regulations on the use of non-regular workers that have been implemented since 2007.

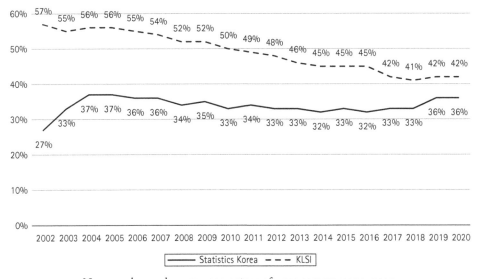

FIGURE 21.2: Non-regular workers as a percentage of wage earners, 2002–2020

Source: Kim (2020).

Of the two analyses of data on non-regular workers, unions trust the KLSI analysis more. Why is there such a large difference in the ratio of non-standard workers calculated by the two organisations, even though they are analysing the same data from the government survey of the economically active population? Statistics Korea estimates that only those who select one of seven employment types in the survey (contingent work, part-time work, temporary agency work, contract work, home-based work, on-call work, and dependent self-employment) are non-standard workers. But Kim Yoo Sun (2020), who led the KLSI's analysis, asserts that about 1.18 million temporary and daily workers (two of the most precarious types of employment) were omitted from the statistics of non-standard workers. Looking at working conditions, which are at the heart of the controversy about the number of non-regular workers, there are 490,000 low wage earners (those who earn less than two-thirds of the median wage) and 440,000 people earning less than the legal minimum hourly wage (8,590 won in 2020). A large percentage of these temporary and daily workers are married women (33 per cent) or poorly educated workers who did not graduate from middle school (17 per cent).

Labour market duality in South Korea is very serious. The average monthly wage of non-regular workers is only 55 per cent of that of regular workers (Statistics Korea 2020). Moreover, the social insurance systems were designed for regular workers, leading to the exclusion of non-regular workers and further exacerbating the problem of income polarisation.

As shown in Figure 21.3, most regular workers are covered by the social safety net, but the percentages of non-regular workers enrolled in the national pension, health insurance, and unemployment insurance schemes are less than half that of regular workers. Statistics Korea and Kim (2020) report similar patterns of social welfare disparity by employment type.

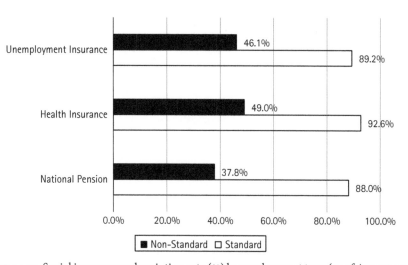

FIGURE 21.3: Social insurance subscription rate (%) by employment type (as of August 2020)

Note: National pension and health insurance only count employees at workplaces. Independent subscribers, beneficiaries, and dependents are excluded.

Source: Statistics Korea (2020).

The problems of labour market inequality emerged as one of the major issues of South Korean politics in the 2000s. Labour forces and leftist groups agreed with building a welfare state on the basis of universal citizenship. Nevertheless, the ideological cohesion of the South Korean labour movement has been weak, and the division between the FKTU and the KCTU has persisted. For example, the FKTU supports liberal parties, whereas the KCTU is allied with left-wing parties such as the Justice Party or the Progressive Party. Moreover, the ideological fragmentation of the KCTU is deeply related to a hegemonic struggle at both the workshop and national level (Kwon 2020). The centrifugal forces produced by union leaders competing to attain different political goals are one of the important factors that sustain the social and political isolation of labour union activism.

At the same time, South Korean capitalists have adopted more sophisticated tactics to undermine trade unions in the neoliberal era. For example, large-scale strikes in the workplace frequently resulted in dismissal of the strikers, or civil and criminal litigation against the strike leaders, including claims for financial damage. That has led to individualised forms of struggle outside the workplace. One example is the *gogongnongseong* ('sky protest'), a protest held at a high altitude, a new form of labour struggle that has increased since the 2000s (Lee 2019).

Sky protest is the last form of resistance available to South Korean workers when their grievances are unlikely to be resolved through traditional strikes mobilising rank-and-file union members. High towers, smokestacks, and Goliath cranes are the sort of places where desperate workers can voice their demands. Not only does this maximise public attention, but it also deters rapid arrest by the police. Recent sky protests have mainly been organised to demand employment security against unfair dismissals in the process of corporate restructuring. Some of the longest-lasting sky protests were held by Kim Jin-sook at Hanjin Heavy Industries in 2011 (309 days), Finetek union leaders in 2017–2019 (426 days), and Kim Yong-hee, a worker laid off by Samsung, in 2019–2020 (355 days). This type of struggle not only illustrates how vigorously the South Korean labour movement resists injustice but also symbolises the social and political isolation of militant union activism.

South Korea's dual labour market imposes a dilemma on the labour movement: whether or not to embrace outsiders. After taking office in 2017, President Moon Jae-in pledged to draw up a blueprint for an inclusive welfare society that would alleviate social polarisation and treat workers with respect (Kwon and Hong 2019). Given South Korea's centralised presidential system, the Moon administration's pro-labour attitude could aid efforts to expand workers' citizenship. But the Moon administration's pledges have gradually lost their lustre, and the COVID-19 pandemic of 2020/2021 has ultimately exacerbated instability in the labour market. Under these circumstances, South Korean organised labour has recently declared that it will fight to abolish all kinds of discrimination, guarantee basic labour rights to microenterprise workers and gig workers, and carry out structural reforms of the welfare system for the benefit of outsiders. It remains to be seen whether this will actually prove to be a turning point towards the kind of social movement unionism that would welcome outsiders into a labour union movement that has long been the domain of regular workers, mostly men, at conglomerates.

5. Conclusion

As we have seen in this chapter, the South Korean labour movement has suffered from both organisational and political weakness. Workers who organised prior to South Korea's democratisation were oppressed by the anti-communist authoritarian regime; that regime's policy of 'growth first, distribution later'; and institutionalised state violence. They were forced to endure backbreaking labour and degrading treatment in order to achieve the state's goals for industrial growth. Even amid these dark political times, courageous female workers in light industry occasionally attempted to set up independent labour unions to improve their working conditions. But corrupt union leaders, who were brainwashed with an anti-communist ideology, were complicit in government crackdowns on these independent labour unions.

The success of the struggle for democratisation in 1987 opened the floodgates for the labour movement. But because of the conservative nature of South Korea's democratisation, the citizenship of individual workers remained inadequate, and the government put off allowing labour unions to engage in political activities. The interests of the working class were systematically excluded from the party system. The growth potential of the labour movement was considerably limited by the fact that South Korea's democratisation occurred at almost the exact time that neoliberalism was spreading around the world (Shin 2011). Nevertheless, the conditions of the labour movement after democratisation should be regarded as a great improvement over the authoritarian era. Union leaders were granted much more autonomy over their activity than they had been in the past. The unions organised by these leaders were now able to make strategic choices between multiple options. Would they be enterprise unions or industrial unions? Would they take part in social dialogue or boycott it, maintaining their militant approach? Would they work with liberal parties to empower workers politically or would they build a separate party for the working class? Would a working-class party (assuming they established one) be ideologically focused on socialism or on nationalism?

After democratisation, the newly established independent unions banded together to form the KCTU, which served as a rival of the FKTU. The KCTU, today South Korea's largest trade union national centre, has pursued a militant strategy that is wedded with the fragmented enterprise bargaining system. The KCTU leadership did try to shift from enterprise unionism to industrial unionism, but most of its attempts failed because they conflicted with the preferences of unions at the conglomerates. The majority of labour unions sought to maximise their occupational welfare through collective actions at the enterprise level. Furthermore, the militant labour movement threw its support behind the establishment of a working-class party in the 2000s, but the movement remained extremely divided on an ideological level. This has three implications, which we will examine below.

First, even the independent labour unions that advocated a 'democratic labour movement' and 'the construction of an egalitarian society' were still firmly focused on labour market insiders, despite their lofty rhetoric. They were fairly reluctant to speak for the labour market outsiders who had most directly experienced the employment instability resulting from neoliberal labour reforms. That deviation from the labour movement's fundamental pursuit of social solidarity not only created a crisis of representation for the movement, but also limited the social and political empowerment of the working class.

Second, the labour movement's focus on insiders illustrates the power of enterprise unionism and its institutional inertia. A majority of unions in South Korea are formally organised above the enterprise level, but practically speaking, the authority for negotiations, strike actions, and union finances is still held by the leadership of enterprise unions. Enterprise unionism has been embedded since the authoritarian period, and labour and management favour it strongly, especially at conglomerates. By adopting a militant approach, while refraining from asking for the wage maximisation that would be needed for an industry-wide class compromise, labour unions at conglomerates can enjoy occupational welfare and wages at a higher level than other workers in the same industry. Conglomerate managers seek to keep labour unions inside the corporate fence, hoping to secure trained workers who are loyal to the company.

The final implication is the impact that South Korea's unique geopolitical situation has on labour politics. The reason that anti-unionism has persisted for so long, even after South Korea's democratisation, is that, amid the continuing military threat posed by North Korea, opposition to communism and to the Pyongyang regime gave South Korea's conservatives a convenient excuse for oppressing the combative labour movement. Labour unions who merely opposed government policies were thought to be plotting the overthrow of the capitalist system, tainting their reputation with the public. Unions were not allowed to engage in politics until 1998, and even that freedom has not been extended to individual teachers or public servants, or the unions to which they belong. Government and capital's hostile attitude towards democratic labour unions only reinforced confrontational labour relations and militant unionism. Anti-unionism has been particularly severe under conservative administrations, and that hostility made labour activists pessimistic that genuine democracy could be achieved in South Korea's capitalistic system without revolutionary change. Furthermore, conservative reactionaries' tendency to equate anti-communism and anti-unionism amid the ongoing division of the Korean Peninsula gave rise to a reaction of its own: Factions devoted to nationalism and unification of the peninsula became major political groups that exercise immense power over South Korea's labour movement.

BIBLIOGRAPHY

Baccaro, L., and Lim, S. (2007), 'Social Pacts as Coalitions of the Weak and Moderate: Ireland, Italy, and South Korea in Comparative Perspective', *European Journal of Industrial Relations* 13(1), 27–46.

Cho, Y. (2009), *Chun Tae-il pyeongjeon (The Biography of Chun Tae-il)* (Seoul: Chun Tae-il Ginyeomsaeophoe).

Choi, J. (1993) *Hangukminjujuui iron (The Theory of Democracy in South Korea)* (Seoul: Hangilsa).

Choi, J. (1997), *Hangugui nodongundonggwa gukga (The Labour Movement and the State in South Korea)* (Seoul: Nanam).

Choi, Y., Cho, H., and Yoo, B. (1999) *Hangugui nosagwangyewa nodongjeongchi I: 1987 nyeon ihu hangugui nodongundong (Industrial Relations and Labour Politics in South Korea I: South Korea's Labour Movement since 1987)* (Seoul: Korea Labour Institute).

Chun, S. (2017), *They Are Not Machines: Korean Women Workers and Their Fight for Democratic Trade Unionism in the 1970s* (London: Routledge).

Dan, B. (2020), 'Chunnohyup changnib 30junyeoneul majihayeo' (On the 30th Anniversary of the Foundation of the Korea Trade Union Congress), *Maeil nodong News*, 22 January.

Im, H. (1994), *Sijang, gukga, minjujuui: hanguk minjuhwawa jeongchiyeongje iron (Markets, States, and Democracy: South Korea's Democratic Transition and Theories of Political Economy)* (Seoul: Nanam).

Im, H. (2005), 'Hanguk jabonjuui seonggyeoggwa nosagwangye' (South Korean Capitalism and Industrial Relations), in S. Lim, Y. Choi, Y. Im, J. Park, B. Lee, and S. Lee, eds, *South Korea's Industrial Relations Model I*, 19–70 (Seoul: Korea Labour Institute).

Iversen, T., and Wren, A. (1998), 'Equality, Employment, and Budgetary Restraint: The Trilemma of the Service Economy', *World Politics* 50(4), 507–46.

Kim, D. (1995), *Hanguksahoe nodongja yeongu: 1987nyeon ihurul jungsimeuro (A Study on Workers in Korean Society: Focusing on the Period after 1987)* (Seoul: Yeoksawa bipyeong).

Kim, H. (1988), 'Hanguk dokjeomjabonui undonggwa nodonggwajeongui byeonhyeong' (The Monopoly Capitalism Movement and the Transformation of the Labour Process in South Korea), *Socioeconomic Review* 1, 41–90.

Kim, W. (2005), *Yeogong 1970, geuneodeului banyeoksa (Female Factory Workers, 1970: Their Counter-History)* (Seoul: Imagine).

Kim, Y. (2020), 'Bijeonggyujik gyumowa siltae: Tonggyecheong, gyeongjewhaldong-ingujosa bugajosa gyeolgwa' (The Volume and Reality of Non-Regular Workers: Supplementary Results of the Economically Active Population Survey in August 2020), KLSI's issue paper 139, 1–31.

Koo, H. (2001), *Korean Workers: The Culture and Politics of Class Formation* (Ithaca, NY: Cornell University Press).

Korea Labour Institute (2020), 'KLI Labour Statistics Archive', https://www.kli.re.kr/kli/selectBbsNttView.do?key=44&bbsNo=10&nttNo=134944&searchY=&searchCtgry=&searchDplcCtgry=&searchCnd=all&searchKrwd=&pageIndex=2&integrDeptCode=, accessed 30 November 2021.

Kwon, S. (2020), 'Why Welfare State Building Is of Secondary Importance to Leftists in Japan and South Korea', in J. J. Yang, ed., *The Small Welfare State: Rethinking Welfare in the US, Japan and South Korea*, 140–162 (Cheltenham: Edward Elgar).

Kwon, S., and Hong, I. (2019), 'Is South Korea as Leftist as It Gets? Labour Market Policy Reforms under the Moon Presidency', *Political Quarterly* 90(1), 81–88.

Lee, J. (1988), '80nyeondae nodongundongron jeongaegwajeongui ihaereul wihayeo' (Understanding the Development Process of Labour Movement Theories in the 1980s), in Korean Christian Industry Development Institute, ed., *The Ideology of the South Korean Labour Movement*, 212–306 (Seoul: Jeongamsa).

Lee, Y. (2006), 'Varieties of Labour Politics in Northeast Asian Democracies: Political Institutions and Union Activism in Korea and Taiwan', *Asian Survey* 46(5), 721–740.

Lee, Y. (2019), 'Neo-Liberal Methods of Labour Repression: Privatised Violence and Dispossessive Litigation in Korea', *Journal of Contemporary Asia* 51(1), 20–37.

Lim, H., and Kim, B. (1993), 'Minjuhwagwajeongeseoui gukga, jabon, nodonggwangyeui hangukjeok hyeonsil' (The Reality of the State, Capital and Labour Relations in the Process of Democratisation in South Korea), in J. Choi and H. Lim, eds, *Challenges from Civil Society*, 139–200 (Seoul: Nanam).

Marshall, T. H. (1950), *Citizenship and Social Class and Other Essays* (New York: Cambridge University Press).

Olson, M. (1971), *The Logic of Collective Action: Public Goods and the Theory of Groups* (Cambridge, MA: Harvard University Press).

Park, T. (2001), 'Hhangukeseo sahoehyeobyakjeongchiui chulhyeongwa geu bulanjeongseong yoin bunseok' (The Emergence of Concertation Politics and Its Instability in South Korea), *Korean Political Science Review* 34(4), 161–177.

Roh, J. (2010), 'Hangugui nodongjeongchiwa gukgapeurojekteu byeondong: Lee Myeong-bak jeongbuui nodongtongjejeollyak' (Labour Politics and the State Project in South Korea: The Case of the Lee Myung-bak Government), *Industrial Relations Study* 16(2), 1–32.

Roh, M. (2021), 'Dae-jungsogiobgan nodongsijang gyeokcha byeonhwa bunseok, 1999–2019' (Analysis on the Changes in the Labour Market Gaps between Large Enterprises and Small-Medium Enterprises, 1999–2019), *Small Business Focus* 21(4), 1–24.

Shin, K. (2011), 'Minjuhwa ihuui minjujuuiwa nodongundong: Hangugui sarye' (Democracy and the Labour Movement after Democratisation in South Korea), *Journal of Social Science* 50(1), 37–70.

Statistics Korea (2020), 'Supplementary Results of the Economically Active Population Survey by Employment Type in August 2020', Statistics Korea (kostat.go.kr), accessed 21 December 2020.

Yang, J. (2005), 'Hanguk daegieopjungsim gieopbyeol nodongundonggwa hanguk bokjigukgaui seonggyeok' (Corporate Unionism and Its Impact on the Korean Welfare State), *Korean Political Science Review* 39(3), 395–412.

Yang, J. (2010), 'Korean Social Concertation at the Crossroads: Consolidation or Deterioration?', *Asian Survey* 50(3), 449–473.

Yoo, G. (2013), '1970nyeondaewa 1980nyeondaeui haksaengundongyeongu: Haksaengundonggadeului nodongundong chamyeo yangsanggwa yeonghyang' (A Study of the Student Movement in the 1970s and 1980s: The Patterns and Effects of Student Activists' Participation in Labour Activism', *Memory and Future Vision* 29, 52–97.

CHAPTER 22

CITIZENS' SUPPORT FOR DEMOCRACY

YOUNGHO CHO

1. INTRODUCTION

SCHOLARS of political culture and democracy have debated whether the cultural reservoir for democracy has eroded around the world. Some scholars such as Robert Foa and Yasha Mounk (2016, 2017) posit a thesis of the end of the consolidation paradigm given that citizens have been away from democracy and have attached to authoritarianism in both old and new democracies. This thesis realistically breaks down the expectation that democracy would be sustainable once it reaches consolidation. Yet, other scholars disagree with the thesis and contend that support for democracy among global citizenries is still solid and its erosion is found in only some countries (Inglehart 2016; Norris 2017).

This scholarly debate has been associated with substantially concerning phenomena such as democratic backsliding and the rise of authoritarianism around the world. However, South Korea seems remote from this academic concern and growing literature of democratic deconsolidation. The main reason for the distance relates to the 2016–2017 Candlelight protest and its subsequent political changes. As comparative political scientists entered a debate on the global backsliding of democracy, the Candlelight protest suddenly took place to halt democratic deconsolidation experienced during the Lee Myung-bak and Park Geun-hye governments (2008–2017) and provided a moment in which South Korean democracy rebounded.

Because the Candlelight protest resulted in such dramatic changes as the downfall of Park Geun-hye from presidency to prison and the restoration of democracy, it is clear that the Candlelight protest saved South Korean democracy from retreat. However, what is not clear is whether it buttresses the legitimacy of democracy among ordinary citizens. While politicians, citizens, and scholars are proud of the Candlelight protest and its contribution to South Korean democracy, little is known about how the cultural foundation for democracy has changed over the past decades. Although a growing proportion of citizens around the world tend to withdraw support for democracy and prefer its authoritarian alternatives, few studies have historically examined whether South Korean citizens depart from this global trend or take part in the deconsolidation of their democracy.

Analysing the five waves of the World Values Survey from 1996 to 2018, it can be seen that support for democracy has steadily eroded and leanings towards non-democratic alternatives have increased among South Korean citizens. This downward trend did not stop even after the Candlelight protest, but has continued since. These results suggest that the Candlelight protest halted the democratic deconsolidation of the Lee Myung-bak and Park Geun-hye governments, but that such democratic rebound is likely to be a temporary moment because citizens' commitment to democracy has cooled. Furthermore, the results also indicate that the four decades of democratic practices have failed to inculcate democracy in the minds of Korean citizens and, rather, have contributed to disillusionment about democracy. Therefore, it is reasonable to conclude that deconsolidation of Korean democracy has already started and will be an enduring phenomenon.

2. Consolidation and Deconsolidation of South Korean Democracy

Democratic consolidation and deconsolidation are useful concepts because not all countries passing through regime transition reach a stable democracy. Indeed, only a small proportion of transitioning countries have been consolidated over the past two centuries; most of them have rejected one form of authoritarianism and ended up with another. Because democratic consolidation is not a one-way street, it is possible for transitioning countries to revert to authoritarianism and for consolidated democracies to deconsolidate. Many of the new democracies have recently experienced democratic deconsolidation, in which the quality of democracy deteriorates and authoritarian governance emerges even in the presence of democratic institutions.

South Korea has experienced democratic consolidation and deconsolidation since the 1987 regime transition. In particular, the country had undergone democratic deconsolidation under the Lee Myung-bak and Park Geun-hye governments before the Candlelight protest of 2016–2017, but South Korean democracy rebounded afterwards. Figure 22.1 shows a historical trend of the Varieties of Democracy (V-DEM) liberal democracy index since 1987. The V-DEM liberal democracy index combines two aspects of democracy: electoral (suffrage, elected officials, clean elections, and freedom of association and expression) and liberal (equality before the law, individual liberties, and judicial and legislative constraints on the executive). Thus, this index shows consolidation and deconsolidation of liberal democracy at the regime level.

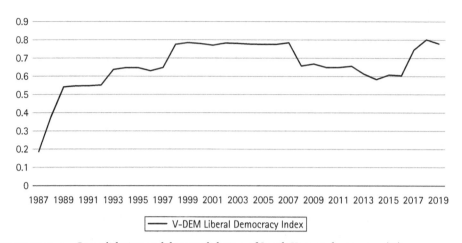

FIGURE 22.1: Consolidation and deconsolidation of South Korean democracy (%)

Source: The Varieties of Democracy Institute.

According to Figure 22.1, the historical trajectory of South Korean democracy has gone through four phases since 1987: consolidation, persistence, deconsolidation, and restoration. In the first phase, liberal democracy in South Korea continued to consolidate from 1987 to 2000. Although President Roh Tae-woo was elected from the military groups, his government (1988–1992) did not block democratic transition, but institutionalised presidential and legislative elections. As the first civilian president since Rhee Syngman (1948–1960), Kim Young-sam (1993–1997) instituted civilian supremacy over the military by disbanding a military clique (*Hanahoe*), whose members had been highly involved in the authoritarian past, and expanded democratic elections to all levels of government. In 1997, South Korea became the first East Asian democracy in which power was peacefully transferred to an opposition leader, Kim Dae-jung. The Kim Dae-jung government (1998–2002) advanced civil and political rights despite the 1997 Asian Financial Crisis. Assessing the democratic progress of the 1990s, Kim Byung-kook (2000: 53) wrote that 'electoral politics has become the only possible political game in town'.

In the second phase, the early and middle 2000s, South Korean democracy persisted as political representation was enlarged to include various ideological parties such as the Democratic Labour Party, whose principles were close to socialism and, thus, had been prohibited under the authoritarian past. After ten years of the progressive governments of Kim Dae-jung and Roh Moo-hyun, a traditional conservative party, the Grand National Party, returned to power through the 2007 national election, which suggested that South Korean democracy had passed Huntington's two-turnover test of democratic consolidation (1991: 267). On the basis of the enlargement of ideological representation and the passing of the two-turnover test, Hahm Chaibong (2008: 129) declared that 'South Korea's democracy is consolidated in the maximalist sense'.

However, South Korea experienced democratic deconsolidation before the Candlelight protest of 2016–2017. Lee Myung-bak was elected president from the conservative side in 2007 and Park Geun-hye succeeded him in 2012; their actions while in office indicated that South Korean democracy had waned. For example, freedom of expression and association were restricted and the Korean National Intelligence Service illegally interfered in the 2012 presidential election by manipulating public opinion online (Cho and Kim 2016). It was also revealed during the early period of the Candlelight protest that the Park Geun-hye government had blacklisted about 10,000 artists critical of her presidency (Shin 2018).

However, the Candlelight protest became a turning point, after which Korean democracy was restored, as evidenced in Figure 22.1. During late 2016, Korean mass media discovered that Park Geun-hye had allowed Choi Soon-sil, her personal confidante, who held no government position, to freely meddle in domestic and foreign policies, actions collectively called the 'Park Geun-hye and Choi Soon-sil scandal'. The Candlelight protest escalated during November 2016, when political parties hesitated and failed to pass the impeachment of President Park Geun-hye. The date of 3 December was the largest protest recorded in modern Korean history: 2.3 million citizens nationwide, including 1.9 million in Seoul, took to the streets and demanded the immediate impeachment and resignation of Park Geun-hye. Six months of continuous Candlelight rallies ended with Park's dramatic downfall from president to prisoner, after which a new government was elected and South Korean democracy rebounded.

Because the Candlelight protest stopped deconsolidation of South Korean democracy and enabled its restoration, scholars started to praise both the Candlelight protest and South Korean democracy. For example, Hong-koo Lee (2017), the former prime minister of Korea, praised 'South Korea as a beacon of Asian democracy' and Yascha Mounk (2018: 185) stated that the Candlelight protests 'can serve as inspiration to defenders of liberal democracy around the world'. Ha-joon Chang (2017) described in the *New York Times* that 'South Koreans worked a democratic miracle'. Finally, after editing a special issue of *Korea Journal* about the Candlelight protest and South Korean democracy, HeeMin Kim (2019: 15) concluded that 'we are optimistic about the future of democracy in Korea'.

Although these scholarly evaluations are insightful enough to provide temporary information about the state of democracy in South Korea, they are limited in assessing its consolidation and deconsolidation in a systematic way. The reasons are twofold. First, conceptually, these assessments of South Korean democracy narrowly focus on institutional dimensions of democratic health and, thus, fail to view democratic consolidation as multidimensional phenomena having both institutional and cultural aspects. As Rose et al. (1998: 8) aptly pointed out, 'if institutions are the "hardware" of democracy, then what people think about these institutions constitutes the "software" of democracy'. Second, little is known about whether the Candlelight protest temporarily halted deconsolidation of South Korean democracy or functioned as an important moment to deepen democracy. Likewise, it is an imperative task to examine whether democratic restoration is a short moment and democratic deconsolidation is a persistent trend in South Korea.

This study aims to assess deconsolidation of South Korean democracy from the perspective of ordinary citizens. By tracking citizens' support for democracy and authoritarian alternatives for the past two decades, this study sheds fresh light on the conditions and prospects for South Korean democracy.

3. Relevance and Conceptualisation of Democratic Support

To stabilise and advance, democracy requires democrats. In other words, democracy requires institutions, as well as cultural components which make these institutions work. These cultural components include social capital, liberal values, tolerance, mutual trust, postmaterialism, and belief in rule of law. Yet, one is clearly more fundamental than the rest in new democracies: public attitudes towards the legitimacy of democracy, such that citizens support democracy and reject its authoritarian alternatives (Rose et al. 1998; Svolik 2013).

There are reasons why public support for democracy is critically important in the dynamic politics of democratic transition and consolidation. Theoretically, unlike authoritarian forms of government, modern democracy allows citizens as the fundamental judges to elect its leaders and influence directions of national policies. Practically, new democracies of the non-Western world lack legacies and traditions of liberal and democratic politics and, thus, they suffer from a shortage of political capital to promote democratic change. In this unfavourable and uncertain environment, citizens' support for democracy constitutes the most valuable political capital that pro-democracy politicians can utilise to complete democratic transition and further democratic consolidation. On the contrary, when a substantial number of citizens are discontented with democratic politics and withdraw support for democracy, authoritarian forces are likely to grow and eventually initiate actions for democratic deconsolidation and backsliding (Svolik 2013). Accordingly, most scholars agree that citizens' support for democracy helps prevent democratic backsliding and deconsolidation (Dahl 1998; Foa and Mounk 2016; Rose et al. 1998).

What constitutes support for democracy and how does one measure it? Conceptually, support for democracy is a dynamic and sequential phenomenon with multiple dimensions and levels. Following Almond and Verba's tripartite model of civic culture (1963), democratic support has multiple dimensions including affective support for, cognitive understanding of, and behavioural commitment towards democracy. Support for democracy is a multilevel phenomenon because citizens simultaneously realign their commitment towards democracy as an ideal and as a practice (Rose et al. 1998). Democratic support is also dynamic in that it accompanies attachment to democracy on the one hand and detachment from authoritarianism on the other (Foa and Mounk

2016). Finally, support for democracy is sequential in that citizens agree with the demise of authoritarian rule first and then endorse the introduction of democratic institutions in the politics of democratic transition (Shin 2021). Likewise, new democracies can consolidate when ordinary people approve newly installed democratic institutions and stop considering authoritarian alternatives.

Over the past three decades, international and national research institutes have developed measures of democratic support and compared cross-national differences in democratic legitimacy. Nonetheless, despite scholarly consensus on the relevance of democratic support, there is a lack of agreement about its measures, and different surveys track citizen reactions to democratisation in different periods and phases. Regarding the case of South Korea, the Korea Barometer Survey investigated citizens' attitudes towards democracy from 1996 to 2010 and the Asian Barometer Survey has examined public opinion about democracy since 2003.

For this chapter, the World Values Survey (hereafter, WVS) was chosen because it has regularly examined support for democracy and authoritarianism over more than two decades since 1996. The five waves of the WVS were employed: 1996 (1,249 respondents), 2001 (1,214), 2005 (1,200), 2010 (1,200), and 2018 (1,245). The WVS asked what South Korean citizens thought about having democracy and two authoritarian rules (strongman and military) and allowed respondents to express this as a four-point Likert scale from *a very good* to *a very bad* way of governing this country.

These measures are useful in unravelling a sequential and dynamic pattern of regime support during the past decades for two reasons: (a) the two authoritarian rules are practical alternatives to democracy among South Korean citizens because strongman rule is spreading around the world and military rule is the specific regime they directly experienced before the 1987 democratic transition; (b) declining support for democracy and increasing support for authoritarianism constitute evidence of democratic deconsolidation because democratic institutions were settled during the mid-1990s. If an increasing number of South Koreans start to consider authoritarianism as a good way of governing the country while living under established democratic institutions, it indicates that democratic deconsolidation is under way. For simplicity, the four responses were dichotomised into binary types: support for democracy, strongman rule, and military rule.

4. Citizens' Support for Democracy and Authoritarianism in South Korea, 1996–2018

Has mass support for democracy increased or declined in South Korea? Have South Korean citizens realigned support for democracy and authoritarianism? What type of regime support is emerging as a dominant trend? What does the realignment of citizens' support for democracy and authoritarianism imply for the prospect of democracy in South Korea? These are imperative questions to evaluate the state of and prospects for democracy in South Korea. To answer these questions, three sequential steps are taken. First, the degree to which South Korean citizens have been supportive of democracy and authoritarianism over the past decades is examined. Second, a typology of regime supporters is constructed, and their changes in the varieties of regime supporters such as democrats, hybrids, and autocrats are tracked over time. Finally, the distributional changes of these types are investigated across different social segments, as well as time.

Figure 22.2 shows South Korean citizens' support for the three different regimes: democracy, strongman rule, and military rule. The striking upshot is that mass support for democracy declined from 85 per cent to 70 per cent in the period from 1996 to 2018, whereas the public's approval rates of strongman rule and military rule as good ways of governance have steadily increased from 32 per cent to 67 per cent and 5 per cent to 17 per cent, respectively, in the same period.

When one takes a close look at these trends, it is apparent that support for democracy and rejection of strongman rule were prevalent among more than two-thirds of South Koreans in 1996 and 2001. Moreover, rejection of military rule was overwhelmingly high (over 95 per cent) until 2010. However, waning support for democracy and waxing demand for strongman rule started in the early 2000s and escalated throughout the 2010s. Finally, about one in five South Koreans regarded military rule as a good governance model, and there are only three percentage points difference in support for democracy over strongman rule.

These results suggest a dramatic shift in public attachment to these three regimes. During the 1990s, when a series of democratic reforms were implemented to inspire presidential popularity, democracy was predominantly preferred as a good and desirable regime, and a majority of Koreans did not express nostalgia for the past authoritarian rule, showing their resolve against it. These cultural factors contributed to the

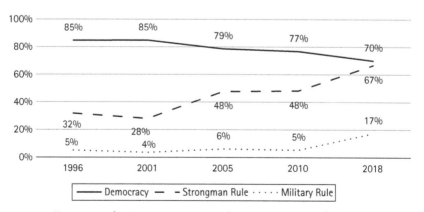

FIGURE 22.2: Trajectory of regime support in South Korea, 1996–2018 (%)

Source: World Values Survey.

dissolution of past authoritarian legacies and establishment of newly installed democratic institutions.

However, although South Korean citizens have continued to practice democratic institutions over the past decades, public confidence in democracy has failed to persist: three in ten no longer accept democracy as a good governance model. More worrisome is that an increasing number of the citizens have been open to both strongman rule and military rule as good ways of governing South Korea. When these findings are considered together, it is logical to conclude that the legitimacy of democracy is shallow, rather than solid and democracy conflicts with authoritarian rule in the minds of South Korean citizenry, although they live under established democratic institutions.

Comparative studies of regime support have reported the degree to which citizens endorse democracy over authoritarianism across countries and over time (Foa and Mounk 2016; Inglehart and Welzel 2005; Norris 2017). However, these studies are limited in determining the dynamic and sequential realignment of regime support in which citizens living in democracy start to prefer authoritarianism (Shin 2021). Thus, these studies fail to predict what kind of democratic deconsolidation takes place in new democracies.

There has been scholarly consensus that South Korean democratic institutions were settled in the late 1990s and democratic consolidation was attained at least at the institutional level in the mid-2000s (Hahm 2008; Kim 2000). If this consensus is correct and public demand for authoritarianism is related to deconsolidation of an already consolidated democracy, what direction of democratic deconsolidation is emergent in South Korea?

To answer these questions, a typology of regime supporters has been constructed using attitudes towards democracy, strongman rule, and military rule. The three dimensions, when combined together, can yield eight ideal types of regime supporters. The first type is *full democrats,* referring to those respondents who simultaneously support democracy and reject both strongman and military rules. These full democrats form a group directly upholding democracy in South Korea. The following three types are *hybrids* because they endorse both democracy and authoritarianism. The three types include *military rule hybrids, strongman rule hybrids,* and *full hybrids.* Likewise, there are three types of autocrats: *military autocrats* for those rejecting democracy and accepting military rule, *strongman autocrats* for those rejecting democracy and endorsing strongman rule, and *full autocrats* for those rejecting democracy and supporting both authoritarian rules. The final type is *apathets,* representing those who show no regime preferences. Apathets are alienated from and indifferent to the politics of democratic consolidation and deconsolidation.

If South Korean citizens have realigned their regime support, how has it changed over time? Figure 22.3 shows changes in the varieties of regime support between 1996 and 2018. As anticipated from Figure 22.2, the most significant change has taken place in full democrats, whose proportion has dropped from 58 per cent to 19 per cent. About two-thirds of the full democrats (29 per cent) have shifted their regime orientations away from democracy and towards authoritarianism over the past three decades. Where have they gone? The largest gain is found in those of hybrids. In particular, there are 16 per cent and 9 per cent increases in strongman rule hybrids and full hybrids, respectively. On the side of authoritarian types, strongman autocrats gained 8 per cent from 1996 to 2018. There are only minor changes of less than 4 per cent in the remaining types: military hybrids, military autocrats, full autocrats, and apathets.

Combined, these results indicate that hybrids have gained 26 per cent over the past decades, consequentially constituting the most prevalent group: 52 per cent of South Korean citizens. This group was a minority (26 per cent) in 1996, but outnumbered full democrats by a margin of 33 per cent in 2018. Autocrats comprised only 8 per cent in 1996, but they had increased to 18 per cent in 2018. Thus, it is apparent that hybridisation of democratic and authoritarian orientations has become a dominant phenomenon in the minds of South Korean citizens.

If hybridisation and autocratisation of regime support are associated with democratic deconsolidation, what direction have Korean citizens driven in terms of democratic deconsolidation? As signalled in Figure 22.2 and confirmed in Figure 22.3, while living with established democratic institutions, 52 per cent of South Korean citizens have advanced support for strongman rule. Whereas 38 per cent of South Koreans retain support for democracy, 14 per cent have abandoned democratic support and have embraced strongman rule as the most preferred regime type. These findings suggest that cultural deconsolidation of South Korean democracy has already set in, and the coming

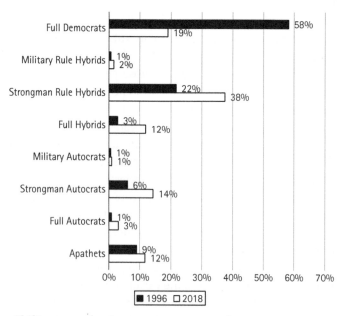

FIGURE 22.3: Shifting types of regime supporters, 1996 and 2018

Source: World Values Survey.

regime welcomed by a majority of citizens is likely to be strongman rule with democratic institutions, rather than military rule.

The final question remains to be answered: what social groups shoulder South Korean democracy and drive its hybridisation with strongman authoritarian rule? Recent scholars examining the trend of democratic support in the West have debated which social segments evince the erosion of democratic support. For example, Foa and Mounk (2016) found that democratic support has declined in the West, and young millennials and rich citizens are sceptical of democracy and most open to authoritarian alternatives. On the basis of the evidence, Foa and Mounk (2016) warned that scholars are overly confident that old consolidated democracies are unassailable and they fail to recognise signs of deconsolidation. Finally, Foa and Mounk (2017) declared the end of the consolidation paradigm.

On the other hand, not all scholars agree with them. In particular, Inglehart (2016) stated that declining support for democracy and increasing openness to non-democratic alternatives are not found across democracies but are apparent only in the United States. This debate sparked subsequent online exchange in the *Journal of Democracy*, with Norris (2017) and other scholars (Alexander and Welzel 2017; Voeten 2017) showing that the cultural foundation of democracy is solid and institutional backsliding of democracy is negligible in the West. Owing to their analyses, they judge that the thesis of democratic deconsolidation is by and large exaggerated.

This academic debate raises a question about who defends South Korean democracy and who drives its deconsolidation. To determine ordinary citizens of democratic consolidation and deconsolidation in South Korea, Three actor-centric theories of democratic development were chosen: elite competition, neo-modernisation, and political competition. First, drawing from Moore's famous statement about 'no bourgeoisie, no democracy' (1966), scholars of the elite competition theory contend that democracy is likely to advance as the rising economic class demands democracy and constrains the top incumbent elites of politics and economy (Ansel and Samuels 2014). Thus, a credible demand for democracy is expected to come from the upper and middle classes of Korea, rather than from those who remain poor.

Second, following Inglehart's initiative, scholars of the neo-modernisation theory have proposed the cultural theory of stable democracy, whereby social modernisation leads to democratic change as those with cognitive resources such as educational attainment and political interest are attached to democracy and detached from authoritarianism (Inglehart and Welzel 2005). This model indicates that college-educated citizens with political interest are supportive of democracy over authoritarianism.

Finally, building on Schattschneider's famous statement, 'the political parties created democracy' (1942), the political competition model presents the view that democratic change follows as existing political cleavages see opportunities from electoral and non-electoral methods to instigate political cleavages and mobilise supporters to maximise the parties' political interests (Ziblatt 2017). This model logically suggests that democratic support varies across two major cleavages of South Korean politics: ideological and generational.

To evaluate the shifting citizenship for the past decades, the focus is on two broad types of regime supporters (full democrats and hybrids) and examine how these two varied across the following six variables in 1996 and 2018: subjective social class, income, education, political interest, ideology, and generation. For a simple comparison, all the variables were transformed into binaries or ordinals.

What social groups have maintained sturdy support for democracy and what other groups turned to hybridisation of South Korean democracy? Table 22.1 reveals pessimistic results in that hybridisation of regime support is evident across all social and political groups between 1996 and 2008, whereas the proportion of full democrats has substantially declined in all groups. What is interesting is that the drop in the proportion of full democrats and the rise in that of hybrids are strong among those of the democratising actors identified by the recent actor-centric theories: upper-class and high-income groups, college-educated citizens with political interest, and ideologically progressive young generations. Democratic fervour has gradually disappeared and openness to authoritarianism has risen among the same groups. The proportions that are no longer full democrats are 48 per cent, 47 per cent, 50 per cent, 42 per cent, 44 per cent, and 40 per cent among the categories of the upper class, high income, college education, high political interest, progressive ideology, and young generation, respectively. The percentage increase in the hybrids ranges from 28 per cent in the young generation to 34 per cent in the college-educated and high-income groups. Finally, the full democrats are not distinguished across different social and political groups and they are overwhelmed by the hybrids in 2018.

These analytical results have theoretical and practical implications. Theoretically, as consistent with the expectations of the elite competition, neo-modernisation, and political competition models, these actors mounted democratic energy by supporting democracy and rejecting authoritarian alternatives in 1996. It appeared that political coalitions for democratisation were formed among those middle- and upper-class citizens with educational attainment and political interest, on the one hand, and those progressive young generations, on the other, in the 1990s. However, those variables of the actor-centric theories do not make differences between the full democrats and the hybrids in 2018, which raises a question about the validity of the recent actor-centric theories in explaining cultural politics of democratic deconsolidation in South Korea.

What practical implication do these results have about the state and prospects of South Korean democracy? The results suggest that authoritarian forces in Korea are in an offensive position, whereas democrats are in a defensive one. Although democratic institutions are present, hybridisation of democracy and authoritarianism is inevitable, as an increasing number of citizens have already withdrawn authentic support for democracy and consider strongman rule as a good governance model.

The strongman rule with democratic institutions is a real alternative model to liberal democracy around the world. Hugo Chávez in Venezuela, Recep Erdoğan in Turkey, and Viktor Orbán in Hungary rose to power through democratic elections, and then gradually subverted democracy. This type of democratic backsliding by executive takeovers tends to proceed as illiberal leaders sustain democratic institutions, but then abuse them

Table 22.1: Distribution of regime supporters between 1996 and 2018 (%)

	1996		2018		Difference	
	Full Democrats (A)	Hybrids (B)	Full Democrats (C)	Hybrids (D)	C–A	D–B
(Pooled)	58	25	19	51	–39	26
Subjective social class						
Lower	52	32	19	49	–33	17
Middle	58	24	20	51	–38	27
Upper	64	23	16	53	–48	30
Income						
Low	53	30	19	50	–34	20
Middle	64	19	21	49	–43	29
High	62	23	15	57	–47	34
Education						
High school and below	52	30	18	51	–34	21
College and above	69	17	20	51	–50	34
Political interest						
Low	55	29	20	50	–35	21
High	61	23	18	52	–42	30
Ideology						
Progressive	64	22	20	50	–44	28
Centre	58	27	18	50	–40	23
Conservative	52	28	19	54	–33	26
Generation, y						
39 and below	60	22	20	50	–40	28
40–54	59	26	19	52	–39	26
55 and above	46	38	18	51	–29	13

Source: World Values Survey.

to build non-democratic governance. The outcome is a new form of authoritarian rule, which Levitsky and Way (2010) called *competitive authoritarianism* and Zakaria (2003) termed *illiberal democracy*. These strong and illiberal leaders have combined authoritarian governance in substance and democratic institutions in form.

The competitive and strongman authoritarianism is not unfamiliar in modern Korean history. Rhee Syngman and Park Chung-hee before the 1972 martial constitution were exemplary leaders of competitive authoritarianism because they drove authoritarian rule while giving lip service to liberal democracy and manipulating democratic institutions such as elections, multiparty competition, and legislatures. Even under the Park Chung-hee and Chun Doo-hwan governments of 1972–1988, legislative elections did not stop, and these military leaders were elected presidents via electoral college. Moreover, all three dictators were statist leaders who attempted to represent the people of South Korea as a whole, stood above government branches, and accumulated political power in the name of achieving national goals such as an anti-communist agenda against North Korea and economic development against poverty. Thus, the past dictatorship of South Korea was closer to competitive and strongman authoritarianism than to closed military rule in which a military junta rules a country without allowing elections, opposition parties, and a legislature.

That a majority of the Korean citizens retain support for democracy but consider strongman rule as a good governance model offers three specific implications for the prospects of Korean democracy. One is that democratic institutions are not likely to break down in the foreseeable future because seven in ten citizens see democracy as a preferred system. Recent scholars of democratisation have raised a question about the democratic utility of democratic institutions (Zakaria 2003; Svolik 2019). According to them, elections and legislatures may not serve democratic advancement, although they are likely to improve enduring problems of authoritarian governance such as informational asymmetry, lack of credibility, and violent succession. Thus, it is possible that democratic institutions can continue without making democratic progress for the long term and democracy in South Korea is not likely to be exceptional.

The next implication is that against a backdrop of democratic institutions, the authoritarian style of governance will tend to continue. This hybridisation of democratic institutions and an authoritarian style of governance was evident during the Lee Myung-bak and Park Geun-hye governments, and it has been observed even in the Moon Jae-in government (Shin 2020). Because South Korean presidents are strong in authority in comparison with other branches, they tend to expand executive power to a maximum degree, rather than to practice the democratic principle of constrained and limited government; their attempts to mount and wield presidential power have resulted in constant struggles among political parties and social groups without elevating democratic standards. As Przeworski (1991: 9) aptly pointed out, democracy is consolidated and self-enforcing as the political stakes of taking government power decline and government leaders practice limited power. The principle of limited power is hard to practice, due to strong presidentialism as well as citizens' demand for strongman leadership in South Korea.

Finally, the steady erosion of democratic support would be a significant barrier to further democratic change because it no longer provides a sufficient amount of democratic capital which can be used to deepen the democratic quality of South Korea. Inevitably, Korean leaders would compromise between liberal norms of democracy and populist demands of ordinary people, which works against the systematic development of liberal democracy in South Korea.

Two questions arise from the analytical results about the cultural erosion of South Korean democracy: how did the Candlelight protest affect the prospect of Korean democracy? Is democratic breakdown possible in Korea? With regard to the first question, it is indisputable that the Candlelight protest halted democratic deconsolidation under the Lee Myung-bak and Park Geun-hye governments. What is not clear is whether the Candlelight protest can bring about further democratic changes. Because the WVS 7 was conducted eight months after the Candlelight protest officially ended in the vacancy election of May 2017, the results of the WVS 7 can be used to determine the democratic effects of the Candlelight protest on regime support in South Korea. According to Figures 22.2 and 22.3, public support for democracy over authoritarianism had been declining before and this downward trend continued after the Candlelight protest. Therefore, the Candlelight protest saved South Korean democracy not because of mass demand for democracy, but despite its decline. Although slogans about democracy and popular sovereignty poured out on the streets of Seoul and other cities, the democratic role of the Candlelight protest was defensive in that South Korean democracy has been restored to the level achieved before the Lee Myung-bak government. As a result, the long-term positive effect of the Candlelight protest is likely to be limited in deepening both democratic citizenship and South Korean democracy.

If the future of South Korean democracy is not bright, can it break down? This question relates to how the country's democracy would survive despite substantial erosion of its cultural foundation. The answer to this question requires further research beyond the scope of this chapter, but it is worthy of additional discussion. The recent literature of democratisation and democratic development commonly suggest that new democracies can survive due to four structural conditions (Levitsky and Way 2010; Inglehart and Welzel 2005; Levitsky and Ziblatt 2018). Internationally, democracies can last when they are close to democratic hegemons such as the United States and the European Union and foreign threat from authoritarian hegemons is not seriously detrimental. Politically, democracies tend not to break down where one political group is not sufficiently powerful enough to bend other groups. Socially, democracies can avoid breakdown when civil society external to the state apparatus is large and vibrant. Institutionally, democracies can be preserved when institutional and legal constraints on executive power are substantial.

When these structural conditions are considered together, it is evident that South Korean democracy will not break down in the near future. South Korea has been a bloody ally and imperative economic partner of the United States, the global democratic hegemon; and South Korea has maintained limited political connections with authoritarian neighbours such as China, Russia, and North Korea. Domestic influence of those authoritarian neighbours are so far restrained. Politically, South Korea's two rival parties have been based on regional, ideological, and generational cleavages in which one group does not allow the other to subvert existing institutions. As Dahl (1971: 16) posited a half century ago, democracy can last because the expected costs of suppression is simply high. As evident in the 2016–2017 Candlelight protest and the 2019 mass rallies in support of and opposed to Justice Minister Cho Kook, massive resistance, pro- or anti-government, is nearly impossible to stifle in South Korea. Moreover, civil society is large and the state sector is small in South Korea. For example, public sector employment as a percentage of the labour force was more than 25 per cent in Hungary in 2013, 40 per cent in Russia in 2011, and 50 per cent in China in 2012. On the other hand, public sector employment in South Korea was the lowest (8 per cent) among advanced countries in 2013 (Organisation for Economic Co-operation and Development 2015). Finally, one legal constraint on South Korean presidents is notable, although presidential power is strong over the legislative and judicial branches: South Korean presidents can serve only one term by constitution. Because of the term limit, South Korean presidents wield strong power only while in office; they are unable to accumulate political power sufficient to subvert democracy.

When these structural conditions and the cultural erosion of democratic support among mass citizens are considered together, one expects that South Korean democracy is likely to survive without making substantial progress. Two decades ago, Richard Rose and Doh-chull Shin (2001: 331) raised the possibility that Korean democracy would fall into 'a low-level equilibrium trap in which the inadequacies of elite are matched by low popular demands and expectations'. and incomplete democracy may persist indefinitely unless leaders abide by the rule of law and demonstrate liberal integrity. The overall results presented in this chapter determine that the incomplete democracy of South Korea has been locked into such a low-equilibrium trap.

5. Conclusion

Recent scholars have reported that the third wave of global democratisation is over and democratic backsliding is evident in some new democracies (Levitsky and Ziblatt 2018; Mounk 2018). International institutes such as Freedom House and Economic Intelligence have shown a consistent decline in the levels of civil liberties and political rights across new democracies. In line with this trend, comparative scholars have examined and debated the degree to which cultural deconsolidation of democracy has proceeded in old and new democracies (Foa and Mounk 2016, 2017; Norris 2017).

This chapter took a cultural perspective to examine deconsolidation of South Korean democracy and evaluate its conditions and prospects in a systematic manner. Analysing the WVS from 1996 to 2018, it was found that support for democracy has steadily eroded, whereas public openness to strongman rule and military rule has increased on a par. The cultural deconsolidation of Korean democracy had already been set in the early 2000s, and its current state is that full democrats are outpaced by hybrids two times over. Although democratic institutions are likely to persist, hybridisation of these institutions and authoritarian governance is likely to be a dominant feature of South Korean politics. A majority of the country's citizens do not seem to be aware of how dangerous strongman rule would be because they regard it as a good way of ruling the country. Therefore, South Korean democracy has fallen into a low-equilibrium trap as citizens' demand for democracy is low and elites, progressive or conservative, continue to violate rule of law, liberal integrity, and limited government (Rose and Shin 2001; Svolik 2013).

These are the costs of incomplete democracy, which entail political discontent and mass protests in South Korea.

To escape from this trap, Korean democracy needs to increase its numbers of full democrats who not only embrace democracy but also reject all types of authoritarian rule. In the politics of democratisation and democratic change, to end authoritarian rule and to construct liberal democracy are two different tasks. Having democratic institutions does not guarantee that they will work. South Korean politics has focused on the former but has lacked efforts to practice principles of liberal democracy and enhance democratic citizenship. Without improving democratic citizenship, democracy in South Korea will persist as incomplete, and ordinary citizens must pay the price for this.

Acknowledgement

This work was supported by the National Research Foundation of Korea (NRF-2022S1A3A2A02090384).

Bibliography

Alexander, A., and Welzel, C. (2017), 'The Myth of Deconsolidation. Online Exchange on Democratic Deconsolidation', *Journal of Democracy*, https://www.journalofdemocracy.org/online-exchange-democratic-deconsolidation/, accessed 22 November 2021.

Almond, G., and Verba, S. (1963), *The Civic Culture* (Princeton, NJ: Princeton University Press).

Ansell, B., and Samuels, D. (2014), *Inequality and Democratization* (New York: Cambridge University Press).

Chang, H. (2017), 'South Koreans Worked a Democratic Miracle', *New York Times*, 14 September, https://www.nytimes.com/2017/09/14/opinion/south-korea-social-mobility.html, accessed 22 November 2021.

Cho, Y., and Kim, Y. (2016), 'Procedural Justice and Perceived Electoral Integrity', *Democratization* 23(7), 1180–1197.

Dahl, R. (1971), *Polyarchy* (New Haven, CT: Yale University Press).

Dahl, R. (1998), *On Democracy* (New Haven, CT: Yale University Press).

Foa, R., and Mounk, Y. (2016), 'The Danger of Deconsolidation', *Journal of Democracy* 27(3), 5–17.

Foa, R., and Mounk, Y. (2017), 'The End of the Consolidation Paradigm', Journal of Democracy, https://www.journalofdemocracy.org/online-exchange-democratic-deconsolidation/, accessed 22 November 2021.

Hahm, C. (2008), 'South Korea's Miraculous Democracy', *Journal of Democracy* 19(3), 128–142.

Huntington, S. (1991), *The Third Wave* (Norman, OK: University of Oklahoma Press).

Inglehart, R. (2016), 'The Danger of Deconsolidation: How Much Should We Worry?', *Journal of Democracy* 27(3), 18–23.

Inglehart, R., and Welzel, C. (2005), *Modernization, Cultural Change, and Democracy* (New York: Cambridge University Press).

Lee, H. (2017), 'South Korea as a Beacon of Asian Democracy', *East Asia Institute Column*, 21 September 21.
Kim, B. K. (2000), 'Party Politics in South Korea's Democracy', in L. Diamond and B. K. Kim, eds, *Consolidating Democracy in South Korea* (Boulder, CO: Lynne Rienner Publishers), 53–85.
Kim, H. M. (2019), 'Corruption, Citizen Resistance, the Future of Democracy in Korea', *Korea Journal* 59(1), 5–15.
Levitsky, S., and Way, L. (2010), *Competitive Authoritarianism* (New York: Cambridge University Press).
Levitsky, S., and Ziblatt, D. (2018), *How Democracies Die* (Danvers, MA: Crown).
Moore, B. (1966), *Social Origins of Dictatorship and Democracy* (New York: Beacon Press).
Mounk, Y. (2018), *People Vs Democracy* (Cambridge, MA: Harvard University Press).
Norris, P. (2017), 'Is Western Democracy Backsliding?', Journal of Democracy, https://www.journalofdemocracy.org/online-exchange-democratic-deconsolidation/, accessed 22 November 2021.
Organization for Economic Co-operation and Development (OECD) (2015), *Government at a Glance* (Paris: OECD Publishing).
Przeworski, A. (1991), *Democracy and the Market* (New York: Cambridge University Press).
Rose, R., and Shin, D. (2001), 'Democratization Backwards', *British Journal of Political Science* 31(2), 331–354.
Rose, R., Mishler, W., and Haerpfer, C. (1998), *Democracy and Its Alternatives* (Baltimore, MD: Johns Hopkins University Press).
Schattschneider, E. (1942), *Party Government* (New York: Farrar & Rinehart).
Shin, D. (2018), 'The Deconsolidation of Liberal Democracy in Korea', *Korea Observer* 49(1), 107–136.
Shin, D. (2021), 'Democratic Deconsolidation in East Asia', *Democratization* 28(1), 142–160.
Shin, G. W. (2020), 'South Korea's Democratic Decay', *Journal of Democracy* 31(3), 100–114.
Svolik, M. (2013), 'Learning to Love Democracy', *American Journal of Political Science* 57(3), 685–702.
Svolik, M. (2019), 'Democracy as an Equilibrium', *Democratization* 26(1), 40–60.
Voeten, E. (2017), 'Are People Really Turning Away from Democracy?', *Journal of Democracy*, https://www.journalofdemocracy.org/online-exchange-democratic-deconsolidation/, accessed 22 November 2021.
Zakaria, F. (2003), *The Future of Freedom* (New York: W. W. Norton).
Ziblatt, D. (2017), *Conservative Parties and the Birth of Democracy* (New York: Cambridge University Press).

PART 6
CULTURE AND MEDIA

CHAPTER 23

CINEMA AND TELEVISION

HYANGJIN LEE

1. INTRODUCTION

'THE cinema and its audience have developed together' (Furhammar and Isaksson 1971: 7). Cinema and television exercised a significant influence on contemporary South Korean politics. At the same time, they are inevitably affected by political power at particular times. Cinema and television can give viewing pleasure to mass audiences. They can impress the viewers with dramatic stories conveying laughter, emotion, and catharsis. The media storytelling, reflecting on reality, can echo political oppression as an obligation in a passive way. It can also resist political oppression by drawing attention to contradictions in society from the perspective of the general public.

Storytelling is the prime communication method of the two media (Lacey 2000). From a traditional point of view, the storytelling styles of cinema and television are different from each other. In the early history of cinema, TV was considered as the main competitor threatening the film industry. For example, Andre Bazin said, 'TV is not an art' but he highly valued the intimacy of TV as a daily media which could change cinematic representation styles and viewing experiences (Bazin 2014). He looked for a collaboration and hybridisation of representational aesthetics as if anticipating the upcoming transmedia in the decades that followed. Indeed, as Walter Benjamin pointed out in his classic work, 'The Work of Art in the Age of Mechanical Reproduction', cinema itself also is a newly arrived art form, that is, the seventh art (Benjamin 2015).

The origins of cinema and television in Korean society followed a different path of development. The first Korean contacts of the two media were political propaganda of foreign occupation forces. The Japanese colonial powers were the agency of storytelling, deciding the purposes and contents of social narratives. Even after the liberation from Japan in 1945, the United States Army Military Government in Korea used the cinema for politicisation of the people to implant anti-communism as the state ideology. The first broadcasting station launched in South Korea was also the US military television

Armed Forces Korea Network (AFKN-TV), which Americanised the local film and media culture.

The 1980s democratic movements changed the political nature of the two media. The media freedom was recovered to voice political criticism of cinema and television in the 1990s. Democratisation accommodated the popularity of cinema and drama expanded to a global audience in the following decade. China Central Television (CCTV) aired Munhwa Broadcasting System (MBC)'s *What is Love* (1992) in 1997 to coin the term, '*hallyu*' (Korea Creative Content Agency (KOCCA) 2015: 4). It took three years to complete the necessary administrative procedures after the contract. However, its tremendous nationwide audience rating of 4 per cent resulted in South Korean television drama overcoming political barriers and directly communicating with Chinese viewers. Regarding its unprecedented popularity, diplomats commented that 'the fifty years of gap in Korea–China relations was filled with a drama' (KOCCA 2015: 5). In Japan, cinema transformed the Korean Wave into a political event. *Shiri* (Kang Je-gyu 1999) was released at 150 cinemas in January 2000. It ranked second in the Japanese box office for three consecutive weeks and attracted audiences of 1.3 million (Lee 2007: 362). Its extraordinary success as a foreign film provided a new strategy of South Korean cinema for Asian markets. Within a few years, it became a 'global minor' in Asia (Kim 2005: 90) and the second most popular foreign film after Hollywood in Japan (Lee 2007: 362). The Japanese Prime Minister Koizumi Junichiro exploited the Korean Wave to create his own public-friendly image and initiate *hallyu* South Korea-Japan relations (Lee 2013, 2017). He visited Pyongyang for the North Korea–Japan Summit in 2002 and 2004. During the 2004 South Korea–Japan Summit in Jeju, he performed in a media event sitting on the '*Shiri* bench' with President Roh Moo-hyun to remind television viewers of *Shiri*. He recollected that the film made him more aware of the tension between North and South Korea (*The Dong-A Ilbo* 2004b). Cinema and television are the leading agents of the Korean Wave and currents as the forerunners of transmedia global culture. From the perspective of TV viewers and cinema audiences, they have even become indistinguishable forms of transnational, transmedia contents, as they are viewed via various online or streaming services (Kim 2019).

Storytelling is a key attribute for the role of South Korean cinema and television as political criticism. Drama is the core genre of cinema and television programmes to the South Korean viewers (KOFIC 2019). The robust narrative structure utilises stories of war and colonialism, national division and military dictatorship, and democratisation movements experienced by the people. This narrative often exhibits a strong, persuasive power, not only to local, but also to global audiences. From this perspective, storytelling identifies the transmedia space of cinema and television, which have a significant influence on South Korean politics. It can, moreover, facilitate global understanding of South Korean politics through transmedia experiences.

Park Chan-wook's *Oldboy* (2003), the winner of the Grand Prix at the 2004 Cannes Film Festival and chosen for the BBC's 21st-century's 100 great films in 2016 (*BBC* 2016) caricatures the South Korean society after democratisation. The inserted TV screen features the news of the 2000 inter-Korean summit in Pyongyang and major political events mixed in with entertainment and general programmes, such as drama, music, sports, and variety shows for over fifteen years when the protagonist, Oh Dae-su, is trapped in a private prison. The penthouse of a high-rise building where Lee U-jin lived, and the basement where he confined Oh signifies the hierarchy of capitalist society. Television is the window through which Oh can see outside and beyond his present confines. Lee is the pinnacle of the food chain pyramid, which the state forces cannot reach. The dystopian images of South Korean society after democratisation on the screen convey a sense of irony and absurdity to the viewers, who are isolated from society and watch TV in their own room like Oh (Lee 2009).

Television drama's global visibility and its political implications have also been significant. The most noticeable advent was Korean Broadcasting System's (KBS's) *Winter Sonata* (2002) and the Yon sama boom in many global societies (Lee 2013). Similar to *Oldboy*, in which Oh Dae-su is named after Oedipus, *Winter Sonata* uses the Oedipus complex to introduce a birth secret, lost memories, a traffic accident, and blindness: all may be considered rather clichéd elements of melodrama. Fear of paternal murder and incest, the two oppressed taboos of a patriarchal society are potent metaphors of popular anxiety and criticism of inherited power and wealth (Lee 2013). These are portrayed as the main predators of capitalist society. In more recent years, as repeatedly appeared in Chaebols and lawyer dramas on global streaming services, such as Netflix, Hulu, and Amazon, the motif of the Oedipus complex evolves into the confrontation of two families symbolising two opposing classes. The sufferings of the younger generation and their resistance to the cartel of power groups serves to identify the hereditary status hierarchy system in contemporary capitalist society.

The coercive power of business and bureaucrat elites supported by lawyers, judges, and high-ranking police, are the common evils in bestseller Korean Wave dramas. Two 2019 TV series, *Crash Landing on You*, about a romantic love story of a South Korean heirless and a North Korean officer, and a period horror, *Kingdom*, widened global popularity of K-dramas. They provided popular criticism on crony capitalism and neoliberalism for the borderless viewers beyond Asia in a similar vein. The two works have enjoyed much global popularity. They communicate the fact that people still suffer due to the national division brought about by the Cold War system or the historical trauma of authoritarian military dictatorship.

The role of television as a storyteller is not limited to fiction. A number of 'high-impact' incidents may be seen as key pivotal media events (Dayan and Katz 1992): the vivid broadcasting of the 2014 Sewol ferry disaster and subsequent programmes continuously reporting the lives of the remaining families; the broadcasting of the 2016–2017 Candlelight protests at Seoul Plaza, leading to the impeachment of Park Geun-hye; and the 2018 inter-Korean summits. The latter two events were broadcast as a reality drama, reminding the viewers of the Red Devils at Seoul Plaza during the 2002 World Cup, and Kim Dae-jung and Kim Jong-il at Pyongyang during the 2000 inter-Korean summit, as a historical déjà vu. These dramatic manifestations transformed a political agenda into an emotive media event. The political controversy over the MBC's *PD Note* on the 2008 Candlelight protests against US beef is a good example (Kwak

2012: 95–96). Immediately after the conclusion of the South Korea–US beef import negotiation, it featured mad cow disease (vCJD), warning of the dangers of importing US beef into South Korea. Regarding the reports, government officers and conservative newspapers expressed concerns that 'television played a huge role in spreading made cow fears' (*The Chosunilbo* 2008). There were also accusations of ideological bias and false reports, lawsuits of importers, and criticism of MBC president Kim Jae-cheol. Kim was appointed by the Lee Myung-bak administration and his task was to identify actors and celebrities who supported the protests. The various social disputes tended to be concluded with the importers losing their legal cases in 2010. However, the 2017 Moon Jae-in government's appointment of MBC president Choi Seung-ho, the producer of the *PD Note* programmes reissued the disputable roles of television in South Korean politics in 2017 (*The JoongAng Ilbo* 2017b). Indeed, 'PD journalism' (Ko 2006) emphasised the importance of storytelling in regard to creativity and the power of visual effects. These potent elements were enough to shake the hegemonic foundation of the conservative government and further deepen the ideological conflicts between the people. In essence, media storytelling can change the political perceptions of the people and help them overcome the collective trauma of military dictatorships and pro-North Korean stigma. However, it also needs to be critically monitored by civil society.

Informed by the overview of cinema and television as a means of political communication outlined above, this chapter discusses the identity politics of cinema and television in democratic transitions of contemporary South Korean society. It examines the ways in which politics has influenced the social commentary tradition of the two media, and how the media criticism has affected the political perceptions of the people. The evaluation of institutional changes and political criticism of the two media aims to draw conclusions regarding the significance of cinema and television as storytellers of contemporary South Korean politics, as well as their inherent limitations.

2. Film Censorship and the Storytelling of Progressive Politics

'The Film Act' was finally abolished and 'the Film Promotion Act' was introduced in 1996. After censorship was eliminated, activist workers and students who used to be framed as having an 'anti-governmental, pro-North Korean character' returned as innocent victim-heroes of the democratisation movement on the screen. Jeon Tae-il in *A Single Spark* (Park Kwang-su 1995), and Park Jong-cheol and Lee Han-yeol in *1987 When the Day Comes* (Jang Joon-hwan 2017) are the screen memories of the three iconic youths. The year 2020 was the fiftieth anniversary of Jeon's death. He committed suicide through self-immolation, considering himself the victim of a harsh labour environment and inhumane treatment (Jeon 1998). Lee was killed by riot police during the demonstrations against the concealment of Park's torture-murder and democratic constitutional dispute in 1987. Their deaths sparked the June Uprising and the June 29th Declaration (Hong 2018).

The significant change after the abolition of censorship created a critical assessment of historical memories denied by the politics of the Cold War, regaining freedom of expression (Park 2002). The stories included a number of traumatic events: the victims of the Jeju 4.3 Uprising in 1947; the US military massacre during the Korean War; the thirty-one criminals trained for a secret mission to kill Kim Il-sung by Park's government in 1968, and civil revolutionary forces and their families during the 1980 Gwangju Uprising. These harrowing incidents are reconstructed on the screen. *Jiseul* (O Muel 2013), *Little Pond* (Lee Sang-woo 2009), *Silmido* (Kang Woo-suk 2004) and *A Taxi Driver* (Jang Hoon 2017) are the most memorable works. They accuse the state of gross irresponsibility, which ultimately caused prolonged historical trauma and painful memories inflicted on the victims.

Film censorship was enacted by Park Chung-hee's military regime, based on film policy during the Japanese forced occupation period. Park's administration tightly controlled freedom of expression from the industry to enforce mass production of propaganda films (Lee 2000). It used cinema to create an image of an 'anti-Communist, free democratic state'. It also demonised those who resisted military dictatorship as the enemy of 'the imagined national community'. After Park's regime promulgated the motion picture law in 1962, the film law and its constituting policies were revised four times in 1963, 1966, 1970, and 1973, respectively (Park 2002). In essence, the film policies were encapsulated in regulatory censorship and industrial restrictions. In fact, the state-operated film censorship during Park's regime was not much different from its North Korean counterpart, as Kim Il-sung advocated, in Lenin's often quoted statement, 'that of all the arts, the most important for us is the cinema' (Taylor 1983).

Interestingly, the first renaissance of South Korean cinema was in the 1960s, when state censorship was not completely in control (Lee 2019; Yecies and Shim 2012). The absurdity of film censorship in the l980s sparked a new revival in national cinema. The irony lies in the fact that it effectively brought about an ongoing power dynamic between political suppression and cultural resistance. Under Park and Chun Doo-hwan's military dictatorial rules, a number of film-makers were arrested for violating the National Security Act, and many films fell victim to pro-communist criminal charges (Lee 2016). Numerous films dealing with the suffering of the poor were banned or severely censored by the authorities. They were accused of provoking social unrest, anxiety, or class conflict. Moreover, it was claimed that they undermined the national image by exposing such social problems to foreign audiences. Yu Hun-mok's *Aimless Bullet* (1961), Lee Man-hui's *The Seven Female POW's* (1964) and Lee Jang-ho's *A Fine, Windy Day* (1980) are some of the most representative directors and works victimised by this vicious film censorship. A political satire, *Declaration of Fool* (Lee Jang-ho 1983) is 'the masterpiece' created by absurd film censorship itself (Lee 2019).

The 1987 democratisation movement saw the end of the state-controlled film censorship. In the late 1970s, social realism and experimental film traditions were revived by a group of young directors including Ha Gil-jong, Lee Jang-ho, and Kim Ho-sun, forming 'Visual Age', a youth film movement (Lee 2019; Yecies and Shim 2015). The film movement inspired university students and the next generation of film-makers, who were critical of mainstream cinema and studied the experimental aesthetics of German, French, and Latin American cinemas. Many of them were involved in politically provocative film-making throughout the 1980s and 1990s. Cinema was a part of the democratic forces (Progressive Media Movement Research Center Prism 2002). The core groups of 1980s national film movements joined the mainstream film industry. Several of them were at the forefront of progressive film culture and were active as critics and movement activists. Those who joined venture capital companies introduced a new type of film production and investment system, strengthening the industry's financial foundation. Through the structural changes of production and distribution, South Korean cinema recovered its local market share and saw a marked increase in audience popularity from 20.2 per cent in 1990 to 39.7 per cent in 1999 (Korean Film Council (KOFIC) 2001: 20). With the advent of the so-called 386 generation, South Korean cinema moved from the era of Chungmuro, the old mecca, to the era of Gangnam, a trendy emerging business area.

The driving force of recovery was the rise of New Korean Cinema in the 1990s (Stringer and Shin 2005; Paquet 2010). A high number of films, both artistically and commercially well received, were made by these younger-generation directors and producers. They successfully won back the local audiences and the attention of foreign markets. Films made by them revived social commentary tradition, stimulating public awareness and debates on the current issues. These included the democratic transition after compressed modernisation under the authoritarian government, and the popular demand on redistribution of wealth after the rapid economic growth driven by the state. The films also helped to articulate the democratic aspirations, endurance of political oppression, and the suffering due to economic hardship. This popular authorism became the driving force of contemporary South Korean cinema, resisting the dominance of Hollywood at home and abroad. It led the second renaissance in the 2000s, even despite the controversy regarding limiting screen quotas between South Korea and the United States as the result of the free trade agreement (FTA) in 2006–2007 (*Hankyoreh* 2006).

Political drama informed by popular authorism was the most representative genre in the 2000s, and invented the qualifier, 'a ten million film', (i.e. a film exceeding ten million viewers) (Lee 2016). The favourite themes of the 2000s South Korean-styled blockbuster are historical memories of war and colonialism, and prevailing genres are period and action thrillers. The screen memories criticise the government and business elites, who are incompetent in protecting the people from global capitalism and militaristic expansion. *Parasite*'s Palme d'Or award at the Cannes Film Festival in 2019 and four Oscar awards for Best Picture, Best Director, Best Original Screenplay, and Best International Feature in 2020 are a symbolic victory of South Korean popular authorism, the popular storytellers of politics and democratic society. It is the first non-English film to win Best Picture. Bong is considered a significant game changer in regard to global film markets, which were previously dominated and led by Hollywood (Lee 2020).

Contemporary South Korean cinema has now emerged as an alternative global cinema. Arguably, *Parasite*'s Bong, and *OldBoy* (2003)'s Park, and *Burning*'s (2018) Yi

Chang-dong, are some of the most representative popular auteur directors representing the progressive South Korean film culture to a global audience. Nevertheless, Presidents Lee and Park's administrations blacklisted fifty-two directors, including the three directors, with more than 100 individuals working in the film industry. Lee's administration ordered the National Intelligence Service to conduct a survey of 'the ideologically-biased film and broadcasting production and left wing directors and producers' immediately after the 2008 US beef candlelight protests (*Weekly Kyunghayng* 2017). From the conservative governments' stance, Park and Bong, two Cannes winners and Democratic Labour Party members were 'red' (*Hankyoreh* 2020). The political accusation went further: Hong Jun-pyo, the candidate of Liberty Korea Party in the May 2017 presidential election blamed that '"the left-wing code" denotes a ten million audience film' (*YTN Radio* 2017). Park's administration expanded the blacklist into 9,473 artists categorising them into three groups: supporters of Moon Jae-in; those of Park Won-sun, the 2011–2020 mayor of Seoul, and those who signed the *Sewolho* declaration (*The Korea Times* 2016). What emerges from these developments is that cinema appears to fulfil the key role as a critical storyteller of society and political influence (*Cinem21* 2017). It became a form of media forum featuring opposing forces of the conservative governments in the post-democratisation era.

3. Television Regulation and the Polarisation of Politics

The ideological contestation of television over politics was more dramatic. The 16 May military coup d'etat led by Park in 1961 was the direct background of the birth of state television in South Korea. The first television station HLKZ-TV started broadcasting in 1956 during Rhee Syngman's administration (Kang et al. 2007). After HLKZ-TV, the US-styled commercial broadcaster, was sold to the Korean Broadcasting System (KBS) in 1961, a number of public and private TV stations established a nationwide broadcasting network in the 1980s to witness the rapidly growing popularity of drama and sports broadcasting (Choi and Kang 2001). It also intensified the serious competition of audience ratings between the broadcasting stations. The era of television drama arrived once cinema completely lost its political persuasive power, and as a result of the popularity of apolitical entertainment in the 1970s. A new constitution, the Yushin system, was promulgated to launch the Fourth Republic by Park's regime in 1972. Consequently, the film industry was even more marginalised as television receivers were installed nationwide, leading to the rapidly growing popularity of television drama and comedy (Park et al. 1996).

However, Chun's regime implemented the press merger and abolition policy in November 1980. South Korea under Chun was a 'military society' (Cho 2015). He controlled television broadcasters as a public relations office, and forced the KBS to merge and acquire private stations, including the Tongyang Broadcasting Company, and to buy 65 per cent of the shares of MBC (Park et al. 1996: 209). In 1981, the number of TV sets exceeded 80 per cent of population access and colour broadcasting was fully implemented (Park et al 1996: 211). The programmes were also strictly controlled by the government. The viewers at that time referred to the primetime news as 'ttaengchun news', as they always began their reports with a report featuring Chun. Resisting his unprecedented media consolidation, various civil societies led campaigns to refuse KBS reception fee payment nationwide in 1985 and 1986 (Cheong 2012). Since then, television has become the ultimate site for those resisting political power to restore freedom of expression. The ideological content and manipulation over media policy in the pre-era of democratisation of South Korea may well reflect 'the oppressive relationship between the strong state and weak society' (Koo 1993; Choi 2012).

In this sense, the June 29th Declaration, a speech by Roh Tae-woo, the presidential candidate of the ruling party in 1987, was a turning point in television regulation history (Kwak 2012). It manifested that 'the government cannot and should not attempt to control the press'. In contrast to Chun, Roh used television to convince people of his promise to make concessions to opponents of the authoritarian military regime's oppressing democracy. The popular demand for democratisation and the United States' pressure on Chun's regime paid off. There was a declaration confirming the fact that Roh was voted in as president in December 1987. Roh promised the political satire of television and cinema *(The JoongAng Ilbo* 2020), but the political diversity provided by the government did not bring any significant deregulation of the industries (Kwak 2012). Public service broadcasting unions were established in 1988. MBC was separated from the KBS, and a new commercial broadcaster, the Seoul Broadcasting System created in 1990. Since democratisation, the political leaning of television broadcasters has been swayed by regime change. The new government appointed new presidents of public broadcasters. However, this pro-governmental leadership resulted in continuous trade union disputes and strikes, which have occurred twenty-two times in the thirty years since democratisation (Cho 2018). During the presidency of Lee and Park, the mass dismissal of reporters and production staff occurred (Kim 2017; *Hankyoreh* 2017). Under these circumstances, television drama communicated people's anxiety and discontent within a sharply polarised political discourse. This intensified the extreme confrontation between conservative governments and progressive unions (Cho 2018: 140). Indeed, television drama cannot be free from the commercialism gauged by audience ratings, but no longer needs to be subject to government intervention in terms of political leaning. As discussed below, entertaining moral stories offered by television in recent years to a greater extent depict a class society of utmost disparity ruled by neoliberalism. In this context, those with inherited wealth who are protected by corrupt politicians and lawyers are considered to be the ultimate form of evil. Even taking into account that the exaggerated representation is owing to the audience rating competitions, it can be said that criticism of television drama after democratisation is closer to the political leaning of a progressive camp.

The global popularity of TV drama as a representative genre of the Korean Wave is another significant change within the mitigation of political regulation. First, democratisation vitalised the outsourced production market through the introduction of the studio production system (Cho et al. 2012). The outsourced production compulsory programming policy was implemented in 1991. The government advocated a new policy aimed to resolve the monopoly of terrestrial broadcasters for the diversity of broadcasting contents and to improve the quality of programmes by enhancing competitiveness. In 2020, the ratio of compulsory outsourcing production of television broadcasters increased from 3 per cent to 16–35 per cent (Korean Foundation of International Cultural Exchange (KOFICE) 2020). Studio Dragon, the JTBC Studio, and Studio S became the most popular programme providers of South Korean drama for global streaming services (KOCCA 2019a).

Second, the linked operation of drama specialised cable channels and their sister production studios to co-produce and distribute with global streaming services. The first cable TV broadcasting started in 1995. In 2011, Lee's administration approved four generalist television channels operated by major newspaper companies: Chosun, Joongang, Donga, and Mail Business Newspaper (MBN). There were concerns about three highly circulated conservative newspapers' influence on broadcasting (Kim 2018). On the other hand, the increased number of cable channels has provided a variety of good-quality dramas without significant political leanings. Among them, tvN and OCN are leading specialised drama channels which are actively engaged in transnational co-production and distribution to expand their global audience (KOCCA 2019a).

Finally, we should pay attention to the contribution of global streaming services, such as Netflix, Wavve, or TVING. Half of the top ten ratings dramas in the Netflix Asian market in 2020 were South Korean dramas (*The Chosunilbo* 2021). In 2019, Netflix signed contracts with additional South Korean production and distribution companies (*The Times* 2020). *Crash Landing on You* (2019), *Itaewon Class* (2020), *Mr Sunshine* (2018), *Kingdom* (2019), and *Signal* (2016) are some of the top ten recommended by *The Times*. In this sense, the institutional and technical renovations have transformed South Korean drama into cutting-edge, trendy content for a global audience. The country's violent political history is a fascinating source material for these highly popular dramas.

4. Cinema and Political Criticism

In the 1990s, the government no longer openly denounced cinema's independence. The 1998 slogan for the cultural policy of the Kim Dae-jung government manifested to 'provide support, do not interfere-"arm's length principle"'. Even in considering the high value as 'soft power' (Lee 2017; Nye 2004; Nye and Kim 2019), non-intervention became a prerequisite condition for film policy. The blacklisting by Lee and Park's administrations, in this sense, was an apparent anachronic interference to disclose deep antagonism between the conservative governments and the industry, which revitalised through democratisation movements. *Poem* (Lee Chang-dong 2010), *The Attorney* (Yang Woo-suk 2013), *Another Promise* (Kim Tae-yoon 2013) and *Diving Bell: The Truth*

Shall Not Sink with Sewol (Lee Sang-ho and Ahn Hae-ryong 2014) are only a few among numerous works victimised by the blacklisting.

In contrast to television programmes provided by a mixed form of public and commercial broadcasters, cinema is firmly placed within the commercial domain. Chun's government introduced the 3S (Screen, Sex, and Sports) policy and colour-TV broadcasting to neutralise political criticism of cinema as a democratic force. In 1986, the military government abolished the import quota system (1956–1986), which was followed by the United International Pictures (UIP) direct distribution in 1988. The US pressure for free access in the South Korean distribution market became more tense during the progressive administration years. Roh's government eventually agreed with the United States to reduce the screen quota for the mandatory numbers of days for the South Korean film exhibition in 2007. Resisting the government's decision, the anti-screen-quota reduction campaigns appealed for popular support with nationalistic phrases: 'In order to crush the conspiracy of the United States and pro-American bureaucrats, it is the time for the people to really step out' (*Cine21* 2006). The campaign received considerable support, but equally generated much controversy regarding the fairness of the protectionist policy in terms of equity with other fields, in particular, farming and automotive industries for the FTA negotiation with the United States. Consequently, cinema had to face free-market competition led by neoliberal globalisation.

Appointing Lee Chang-dong as the Minister of Culture, Roh's administration led a number of actors and critics to enter politics. They were representative figures of Nosamo ('We Love Roh'), the first-ever political fan club formed in 2002 (Forster-Carter 2009). On the other hand, the reduction of the screen quota by US pressure undermined the ideological alliance between cinema and progressive governments (Lee 2016). The cinema's criticism exposed the growing public discontent regarding government incompetence. This was especially evident in the failure to cope with the indiscriminate advance of global capitalism in everyday life and the destructive influence of the US military expansion. Thematic concerns of the highest-grossing film genres were diversified in later years to convey their common criticism of the impotence of those in power, such as from action division dramas, *JSA* (Park Chan-wook 2000) and *Silmido* (Kang Woo-suk 2004) to a costume drama *The King and the Clown* (Lee Jun-ik 2005) and a monster thriller *The Host* (Bong Joon-ho 2006). This social commentary tradition differentiates South Korean cinema from the conservative mainstream film cultures in many other countries.

During this process, the industry coped with the radically changing environment to overcome the looming crisis. The industrial expansion, with the focused investment of 'a ten million film', facilitated political criticism as the best popular entertainment. Bong, arguably, the most successful political satirist represented the South Korean style blockbuster (Lee 2016; Lee 2020). *The Host* (Bong Joon-ho 2006) is a black comedy about a family trying to save a daughter from a monster living in the Han River polluted by the US military bases: 'the symbol of the rapid economic growth' succinctly articulates anti-global capitalism and anti-American sentiments. The dead girl, killed by the monstrous creature, and the family crying over her picture in the funeral scene remind the audience of the two school girls' deaths by a US military vehicle in 2012 (i.e. the Yangju Highway Incident), and the first Candlelight protests triggered by the incident. Kim Ki-duk, the director of *Spring, Summer, Autumn, Winter ... Spring* (2003) severely criticised the screen monopoly of *The Host*, determined and dictated by neoliberal market principles. His criticism is valid (Jin 2020). At the same time, it is undeniable that the political blockbusters led the recovery of national cinema. They raised the domestic market share up to 64.7 per cent in 2006, which almost took up the direct distribution of UIP, falling to 15.9 per cent in 1993 (KOCCA 2019b).

Lee and Park's administrations forced the cinema industry to distance itself from the ideologic orientation of the democratisation movement. CJ, one of the major production and distribution companies, made two blockbuster historical dramas, *Ode to My Father* (Yun Je-kyoon 2015) and *Operation Chromite* (John H. Lee 2016) for 'matching the code to alleviate President Park's uncomfortable feelings' (*Yonhap News Agency* 2017). The films could be interpreted as either stimulating patriotism or criticising chauvinistic marketing strategies. The films explored again the confronting views between the conservative and progressive forces on North Korea's military provocation and modern Korean history (*The JoongAng Ilbo* 2015). The highest-grossing work, *Roaring Currents* (Kim Han-min 2014) portraying naval battles of General Yi Sun-shin during the Japanese invasions of Korea (1592–1598) is another example. It was highly referred to by Park's administration, conveying her 'ruling philosophy' and idea of cinema, 'patriotism + creative economy' (*The JoongAng Ilbo* 2017c). On the other hand, the oppression of the Busan International Film Festival (BIFF) serves as an opposite paradigm. The BIFF, one of the biggest global film events, could not avoid confrontation with Park's administration. The premiere of *Diving Bell: The Truth Shall Not Sink with Sewol* in 2014 resulted in severe budget cuts and the forced resignation of the film festival's leadership.

'Moon Jae-in's cinema politics' (*The JoongAng Ilbo* 2017a) more often featured the president sobbing or laughing while watching a film at cinema. He was the first president who watched a film at BIFF. Watching *1987: When the Day Comes*, *Taxi Driver*, and *Masquerade* (Choo Chang-min 2016) made during the final years of Park's administration, he expressed his sympathy for the struggles of the victims of democratisation and President Roh. *Parasite* was actively promoted by his government and the opposition party to highlight cinema as an significant agent of South Korean politics (*Hankyoreh* 2020).

5. Drama and Political Criticism

By contrast to the ideological alliance between cinema and anti-government forces in the 1980s, political criticism of television drama began in earnest with democratisation. However, the habituality and everydayness of viewing practices can facilitate the viewer's sympathy in regard to criticism of politics and government embedded in seemingly apolitical stories. *Eyes of Dawn* (1991) was the first memorable work unfolding the unspoken stories of the Japanese military sexual slavery and forced conscription, and the Jeju 4.3 Uprising and massacre (Baek 2018). The collective memories were taboo subjects under the military governments of Park and Chun. *Sandglass* (1995) dramatises the brutality of military dictatorship, dealing with a series of political incidents including democratisation of labour union movements YH trade and Dongil textiles (Nam 1996), the violent oppression of opposition party leaders, the Samcheong re-education camp (a military detention centre for critics of Chun's regimes), and the Gwangju Uprising. Starting with *Taejo Wang Geon* (2001–2002), *The 5th Republic* (2005) and *Jumong* (2006–2007), television drama continued to manifest its criticism of historical military intervention.

President Roh Tae-woo stated in his 2004 speech that, 'the adhesion between politicians and businessmen' is 'the closed and privileged gangster culture deeply rooted in political power' (*The Dong-A Ilbo* 2004a). 'Money politics-corruption and cronyism' (Kang 2008: 3) witnessed the collusion of business and political elites, which was consolidated by the developmental military dictatorship. This legacy still exerts a strong influence on South Korean society. Regardless of genre, from melodrama, action comedy, romantic comedy, and mystery to sitcom, these absurdities were dealt with directly or indirectly. In particular, the 1990s drama series exploited government and business corruption to create a love triangle and family conflicts. The most influential works are *The First Love* (1996) and *Sandglass* (1995), with the highest and third highest viewer ratings, respectively (Lee 2014).

Political criticisms of recent works take a more liberal approach. *Itaewon Class* (2020) and *SKY Castle* (2018–2019), for example, deal with school violence and the irregularities to blame for the political alliance of inherited rich and powerful families. The drama series depicts school life as a miniature of real society, where class interests establish perpetrator-and-victim relations (Bourdieu 2010). The image of school bullying and its victims giving up resistance reminds many viewers of the '*sampo* or *Npo* generation', young people giving up essential things in their life, such as dating, marriage, and having children, owing to the extreme gap in the class society. The *sampo* generation theory highlights the structure of social inequality and the crisis in the labour market facing the young generation in the neoliberal order (Bang and Yu 2015).

Along with satire on class hierarchy, education-based discrimination, and school bulling, the popularity of legal drama dealing with the organised crimes of legal professions, bureaucrats and large corporations are also significant (Nam et al. 2019). The poetic justice elaborated by two Chaebol-lawyer drama series, *Stranger* (2017) and *Diary of a Prosecutor* (2019), effectively support this argument (Lee 2017). In the drama series, junior prosecutors and police officers accuse the Chaebols and politicians of organised crimes from an insider's point of view. The stories disclose the collusion of politics and capital as moral corruption from the subjective agent's point of view and the paradigm establishes the dichotomy of good and evil. It involves younger-generation criticism of older generations, who are the preferential groups of high growth under the developmental military dictatorship. The emotional, ideological detachment from the generation of democratisation implies the public disappointment of older-generation politics and government. It seems, however, that they are unable to eradicate inherent corruption within the system.

The rise of *minjung* (people) historical drama is another significant challenge, depicting the middle class, the commoners, and the outcasts such as doctors, merchants, court maids, or slaves as the true forces of historical change (Yang 2015). *Hur Jun* (1999–2000), *Sangdo* (2001–2002), *Jewel in the Palace* (2003–2004), *The King's Doctor* (2012–2013), and *The Slave Hunters* (2010), long-running Asian bestsellers, are representative of the early works. Despite the criticism of distortion, the stories of *minjung*, often overlooked by history, allow the portrayal of a class-divided society from the perspective of democracy. Within the subcategorised genres, such as fantasy, fusion, and faction (compounding fact and fiction) historical dramas, *minjung* represents the voices of ordinary citizens in present society. *Nokdu Flower* (2019) dealing with the 1894 Donghak peasant revolution, and *Mr Sunshine* (2018), an interclass love story of a Korean–American and a *yangban* (a traditional ruling class) woman who joined the Righteous Army, evince this current progression of historical drama.

6. Conclusion

'Entertainers and sports stars replace doctors and lawyers', stated the *Yonhap News Agency*'s news headline of a survey of 2018 teenagers' preferred jobs (*Yonhap News Agency* 2019). In another survey conducted by MBN in 2018, 70 per cent of 4,505 respondents (elementary, middle-, and high-school students) stated that they thought about being an entertainer as their future job (*MBN* 2018). The survey results suggest that cinema and television is the optimised media-scape to foster the younger generation's interest in politics, stimulating political debate, reform, and awareness by listening to their voices and reflecting their views through policy. For a future-orientated democratic society, the utmost significance of cinema and television is to raise and develop this multimedia generation as critical storytellers of politics. Diverse civil societies need to monitor and engage the media storytelling to consolidate the mutually influential relationship between the people and those in power.

Cinema and television after democratisation have had different relationships with politics. Television began to resist governmental intervention. Broadcasting unions were formed, and civil society led campaigns to refuse reception fee payments. Television drama's criticism of crony capitalism also greatly influenced the political perception of the viewers. Furthermore, the vitalisation of the outsource production market and the introduction of comprehensive channels has expanded the popularity of TV drama to global audiences. On the other hand, cinema joined the 1980s democratic forces to maintain its ideological alliance with the progressive governments until the reduction of the screen quota system threatened the industry's survival. The rise of South Korean-style blockbusters led by popular authorism successfully revived the industry to grow to a global minor cinema in the late 2000s.

Cinema and television have pursued popularity to secure its independence from government. The political engagement of the two medias has survived the decades of military dictatorship and its aftermath. In order to entertain a large audience reflecting various tastes, political drama should resist within the existing system and compromise with commercialism. Popular authorism is an effort to achieve commercial success and critical acclaim. At the same time, it is not easy to escape from the excesses of commercialism, since it aims to communicate the absurdity of class hierarchy to mainstream audiences.

Bibliography

Ahn, S.-J. (2011), *The Pusan International Film Festival, South Korean Cinema and Globalization* (Hong Kong: Hong Kong University Press).

Baek, D.-S. (2018), 'Representation of the Division of Korea in Television Dramas during the Democratic Transition', *Story & Image Telling* 15, 144–181.

Bang, H.-K., and Yu, S.-M. (2015), 'Korean Newspapers and Discourses on the Young Generation (From Silk Generation to Sampo Generation): Walking a Tightrope between Crisis Theory and the Theory of Hope', *Korean Journal of Journalism & Communication Studies* 59(2), 37–61.

Bazin, A. (2014), *André Bazin's New Media* (Oakland, CA: University of California Press).

BBC (2016), 'The 21st Century's 1000 Greatest Flms', 19 August.

Benjamin, W. (2015), *Illuminations* (London: Bodley Head).

Bourdieu, P. (2010), *Distinction* (Abingdon: Routledge).

Cine21 (2006), 'Filmmakers Are Angry at President Roh Moo-hyun's Remarks on Reducing Screen Quotas', 17 February.

Cine21 (2017), 'The Process of Implementing Blacklists in the Film Industry Revealed One After Another', 22 December.

Cho, H.-J. (2018), 'A Study on the Struggle for Professional Autonomy of the Public Service Broadcasting Unions in Korea', *Journal of Communication Research* 55(2), 112–168.

Cho, J.-S., Kim, D.-J., and Kim, D.-W. (2012), *Research and Analysis on the Independent Production and Content Market: Including of Alternative Research Frame and Policy Implication* (Seoul: Korea Communication Commission).

Cho, M.-G. (2015), *Korean Broadcasting and Regulations* (Seoul: Communication Books).

Choi, C.-B., and Kang, H.-D. (2001), *Our Broadcasting 100 Years* (Seoul: Hyunamsa).

Choi, J.-J. (2012), *Democracy after Democratization: The Korean Experience* (Stanford, CA: Shorenstein Asia-Pacific Research Center).

Dayan, D., and Katz, E. (1992), *Media Events: The Live Broadcasting of History* (Cambridge, MA: Harvard University Press).

Forster-Carter, A. (2009), 'Roh Moo-Hyun', *The Guardian*, 25 May.

Furhammar, L., and Isaksson, F. (1971), *Politics and Film* (London: Studio Vista).

Hankyoreh (2006), 'U.S. Makes Proposal on FTA Screen Quota Issue: Sources', 24 October.

Hankyoreh (2017), 'Dismissed MBC Journalists Return to Work', 12 December.

Hankyoreh (2020), 'Who Made Blacklist Bong Jun-ho … the Dead Wind of Korea Party's "Bong Marketing"', 20 December.

Hong, K.-S. (2018), 'June Democratization Uprising and Archive', *Archive In* 43(2), 34–43.

Kang Je-gyu (1999), *Shiri*.
Jeon, T.-Il (1998), *Do Not Let My Death Be in Vain* (Seoul: Dolbegae).
Jin, D. Y. (2020), *Transnational Korean Cinema: Cultural Politics, Film Genres, and Digital Technologies* (New Brunswick, NJ: Rutgers University Press).
Kang, D. C. (2008), *Crony Capitalis* m (Cambridge: Cambridge University Press).
Kang, M.-G., Baek, M.-S., and Choi, I.-S. (2007), 'American Cultural Cold War and the First Korean Television Station, HLKZ', *Korean Journal of Journalism and Communication Studies* 10, 5–33.
Kim, D. (2018), *Media Governance in Korea 1980-2017* (Cham: Palgrave Macmillan).
Kim, E.-Y. (2005), 'The SWOT Analysis of "Hallyu" and Developing Winning Strategies of Preserving Korean Films' Market in Asia', *Cinema Studies* 27, 89–110.
Kim, J. (2019), 'Korean Popular Cinema and Television in the Twenty-First Century: Parallax Views on Nation/Transnational Disjuncture', *Journal of Popular Film and Television* 47(1), 2–8.
Kim, S.-E. (2017), 'Dismissed Journalists of the "Post-Democratization" Era: Reconstituting the Trajectory of Press Control by Korean Political Regimes through the "Condensed" Life History of Dismissed Journalists', *Media and Society* 25(3), 221–328.
Ko, H.-Il (2006), 'A Study on the Differences between PD Journalism and Reporter Journalism: Mainly Focusing on the Connection between Organizational Cultures and Constructional Characteristics of the Investigative Programs', *Studies of Broadcasting Culture* 18(2), 161–192.
Korea Creative Content Agency (KOCCA (2015), 'The Korean Wave 20 Years', *Broadcasting Trend & Insight* 1, 4–15.
KOCCA (2019a), *2019 Broadcasting Industry White Paper* (Seoul: KOCCA).
KOCCA (2019b), *2019 Korean Film Industry Report* (Busan: KOFIC).
Korea Foundation of International Cultural Exchange (KOFICE) (Seoul: 2020), *Hallyu Now* 37, 17–23.
Korean Film Council (KOFIC) (2001), *Korean Film Industry Structure Analysis* (Seoul: KOFIC).
Korean Foundation for Intenational Cultural Exchange (2019), *Hallyu White Paper* (Seoul: KOFICE).
Koo, H. (1993), *State and Society in Contemporary Korea* (Ithaca, NY: Cornell University Press).
Korea JungAng Ilbo (2017), 'PD Note Was Not Guilty, but Not "True" Either', 21 December.
Kwak, K.-S. (2012), *Media and Democratic Transition in South Korea* (Abingdon: Routledge).
Lacey, N. (2000), *Narrative and Genre: Key Concepts in Media Studies* (London: Macmillan).
Lee, H. (2000), *Contemporary Korean Cinema: Identity, Culture and Politics* (Manchester: Manchester University Press).
Lee, H. (2009), 'The Shadow of Outlaw in Asian Noir: Hiroshima, Hong Kong and Seoul', in M. Bould, K. Glitre, and G. Tuck, eds, *Neo-Noir* (London and New York: Wallflower Press), 118–135.
Lee, H. (2013), 'Buying Youth: Japanese Fandom of the Korean Wave', in R. Siddle, ed., *Critical Readings on Ethnic Minorities and Multiculturalism in Japan* (Leiden: Brill), 1053–1073.
Lee, H. (2016), 'The "Division Blockbuster" in South Korea: The Evolution of Cinematic Representation of War and Division', in M. Berry and C. Sawada, eds, *Divided Lenses: Screen Memories of War in East Asia* (Hawaii: Hawaii University Press), 62–73.
Lee, H. (2017), 'The Korean Wave and Anti-Korean Sentiment in Japan: The Rise of a New Soft Power for a Cultural Minority', in T.-J. Yoon and D. Y. Jin, eds, *The Korean Wave: Evolution, Fandom, and Transnationality* (Lanham, MD: Lexington Books), 185–208.

Lee, H. (2019), '*Declaration of Idiot* (1983): Cinema of Censorship and an Accidental Masterpiece', in S. Lee, ed., *Rediscovering Korean Cinema* (Ann Arbor, MI: Michigan University Press), 215–232.

Lee, M.-H. (2007), 'Export of Korean Films in Japan: Focused on the Films Released between 2002 and 2006', *Journal of Communication & Information* 39(8), 355–384.

Lee, N. (2020), *The Films of Bong Joon Ho* (New Brunswick, NJ: Rutgers University Press).

Lee, Y.-D. (2014), *Film and Video Contents Production Dictionary* (Seoul: Communication Books).

Lee, Y.-M. (2017), '[TV] Uncovering the Enclosed Power-Type Corruption, *Whisper*, *Secret Forest*, *Manipulation*', *Hwanghae Review* 12, 353–360.

Maeil Broadcasting Network (MBN) (2018), '7 of 10 Teenagers "Dreamed of Being Entertainers"', 30 July.

Nam, M.-J., Jeong-hyun, B., and Su-kyung, O. (2019), 'Reconsideration of Education Fever, Meritocracy, and Educational Fairness: Focusing on the Discourse Analysis of Drama *Sky Castle*', *Study of Educational Sociology* 29(2), 137–167.

Nye, J. (2004), *Soft Power: The Means to Success in World Politics* (New York: Public Affairs).

Nye, J., and Kim, Y. (2019), 'Soft Power and the Korean Wave', in Y. Kim, ed., *South Korean Popular Culture and North Korea* (New York: Routledge), 41–53.

Paquet, D. (2010), *New Korean Cinema: Breaking the Waes (Short Cuts)* (New York: Columbia University Press).

Park, S.-G., and Paquet, D. (1996), 'Liberation 50 Years: Korean Press and Social Change', *Social Science and Policy Studies* 18(1), 157–237.

Park, S. H. (2002), 'Film Censorship and Political Legitimation in South Korea, 1987–1992', *Cinema Journal* 42(1), 120–138.

Progressive Media Movement Research Center Prism (2002), *A History of Film Movement* (Seoul: Seoul Publication Media).

Stringer, J., and Shin, C.-Y. (2005), *New Korean Cinema* (New York: New York University Press).

Taylor, R. (1983), 'A "Cinema for the Millions": Soviet Socialist Realism and the Problem of Film Comedy', *Journal of Contemporary History* 18(3), 439–461.

The Chosunilbo (2008), 'Parties Must Stop the Panic Bandwagon', 6 May.

The Chosunilbo (2021), 'The Most Watched Drama on Netflix in 2020?', 7 January.

The Dong-A Ilbo (2004a), 'Roh Says: "Let's End Political–Economic Adhesion"', 27 May.

The Dong-A Ilbo (2004b), '[Korea–Japan Summit] Koizumi "Watching Shiri to Feel Inter-Korean Tension"', 22 July.

The JoongAng Ilbo (2015), 'Ode to My Father and Park Geun-hye', 2 January.

The JoongAng Ilbo (2017a), 'Film before Promise, Moon Jae-in's Cinema Politics', 2 September.

The JoongAng Ilbo (2017b), 'PD Note Was Not Guilty, but Not "True" Either', 21 December.

The JoongAng Ilbo (2017c), 'What Kind of Film Have Presidents Watched . . . Instead of Popcorn, Go to the Cinema with the "Ruling Philosophy"', 14 August.

The JoongAng Ilbo (2020), 'Did Even during the 6th Republic . . . Situation Like Comedy Not Allowing Political Satire', 24 August.

The Korea Times (2016), 'Presidential Office Blacklisted 9,473 Artists for Political Reasons', 12 October.

The Times (2020), 'The 10 Best Korean Dramas to Watch on Netflix', 12 May.

Weekly Kyunghyang (2017), '[Focus] Search for Left-Wing Filmmakers, Who Are Actor and Director?', 26 September.

Yang, N. R. (2015), 'Strategic Storytelling Structure of 2000s Popular Korea Historical Film', *Journal of Culture Contents* 12, 199–240.

Yecies, B., and Shim, A.-G. (2012), 'Power of the Korean Film Producer: Park Chung Hee's Forgotten Film Cartel of the 1960s Golden Decade and Its Legacy', *Japan Focus* 10(3), 1–23.

Yecies, B., and Shim, A.-G. (2015), *The Changing Face of Korean Cinema: 1960 to 2015* (Abingdon: Routledge).

Yonhap News Agency (2017), 'CJ, Making *Ode to My Father* and *Operation Chromite* under the Pressure of President Park', 17 January.

Yonhap News Agency (2019), 'Teenager … Entertainers and Sports Stars than Doctors and Lawyers', 2 June.

YTN Radio (2017), 'Hong Jung-pyo Saying "Left-wing Code Denotes a Ten Million Audience Film"', 19 December.

CHAPTER 24

THE INTERNET AND SOCIAL MEDIA

DAL YONG JIN

1. INTRODUCTION

STARTING in the late 1990s, several new digital technologies, such as high-speed internet, social media, and smartphones, have transformed and reshaped South Korean politics in various ways, from elections, to political gatherings, to civic movements. Many people in South Korea, both politicians and citizens, have utilised these digital technologies to implement and further their political agendas. Although these digital technologies were created only one or two decades ago, their impacts on people's political activities have rapidly increased. Many candidates for various political activities, including several elections such as presidential elections and local council elections, have increasingly relied on these new technologies, and many citizens also use them to make their voices heard. Korea is one of the most wired countries in the world, and since young voters are tech-savvy and have lived with digital technologies instead of legacy media, it is crucial for politicians to appropriate digital technologies to attract more voters, in particular young voters.

This chapter examines the close relationships between the growth of digital technologies and South Korean politics. It analyses how the internet and social media have been influencing political messaging, voter behaviour, and the circulation of ideas in Korea, in which traditional media such as broadcasting and newspapers have played a major role in national politics since the early 2000s. It also explores how internet portals, such as Naver and Daum (now Kakao), and mobile messaging services, such as Kakao Talk and Line, which account for over 70 per cent and 90 per cent of their respective markets, shape the political conversation and can act as gatekeepers for the circulation of ideas. In particular, it investigates whether the growth of these new media technologies has influenced people's perceptions of politics and elections, which means that it discusses people's use of new media technologies in their political practices, in other words, whether people utilise them to organise and develop their political activities, as well as whether the shifting use of new media technologies has influenced their political behaviours in key elections. In order to discuss these issues, the rapid growth of new media technologies, which mainly started in the mid-1990s, is documented in the next section.

2. THE ROLES OF NEW MEDIA IN DIGITAL KOREA

Traditional media, such as network broadcasters like KBS, MBC, and SBS, and major newspapers, including *The Chosun Ilbo*, *The Dong-A Ilbo*, and *The JoongAng Ilbo*, have played a key role in South Korean politics. They have not only provided news and information on politicians, but have also influenced people's decisions during election periods. Consequently, these media outlets have faced several critiques from several civic communities in that major media corporations unethically attempt to select their preferable candidates as new presidents. The media originally did not act as 'a king maker', and they were respectful due to their major role as a cornerstone of the public sphere, referring to a space that facilitates 'critical public debate' to enable democratic practice, which is important mainly because communication between the nation state and the private realm is interconnected within the public sphere (Habermas 1989). The South Korean media have arguably been 'perceived as the instruments of public interest, gathering and contesting opinions, which in turn promote democracy in a modern society' (Song and Son 2017: 353). In other words, in South Korea, 'the media have been a key player in the unrelenting struggle for democratisation throughout the successive authoritarian military regimes. The media stood up against the regimes by questioning their legitimacy, and by criticising oppressive policies and undemocratic practices' (Shin 2005: 32). As such, the media have secured respect and trust from voters, and in general from South Korean people.

News reports have had profound effects on the formation of public opinion on various issues, including voters' attitudes towards political parties, political candidates, and campaign issues (Shin 2005: 32). South Koreans heavily relied on traditional media to learn about domestic politics until the late 1990s, when the internet had just started. In other words, the media have enjoyed tremendous privileges due to their power in South Korean society. Several conservative newspapers, including *The Chosun Ilbo*, were known as 'king makers', due to their influential institutional power in presidential elections. Three major conservative newspapers, including *The Chosun Ilbo*, *The JoongAng Ilbo*, and *The Dong-A Ilbo*, controlled over 70 per cent of the South Korean newspaper market in terms of subscriptions. The market share of these three major conservative newspapers increased from 71 per cent in December 2000 to 78 per cent in December 2004 (Ahn 2005). Based on this dominant market control, they exercised undeniable influence over the national public opinion, and they were widely believed to be guilty of manipulating political news reports (Huh 2005).

However, their institutional power has greatly decreased because of the emergence of digital media. Since the late 1990s, South Korea has rapidly changed its media environment due to the growth of new digital media, such as the internet, social media, and smartphones. Although many South Koreans still consume political news and information through traditional media, they have shifted their reliance to these digital media. As the general public acquires political news from digital media technologies, politicians and political parties had no choice but to transform their strategies and started to emphasise the significant role of new digital media. The public flooded the internet, challenging politicians on various political problems, and presidential elections in the early twenty-first century presented the public with a greater opportunity to increase their political participation and voice due to the internet (Huh 2005).

What is significant is that this shifting media environment in tandem with South Korean politics creates the role of media as an agenda setter. The changing media ecology surrounding digital media does not mean that digital media have entirely replaced traditional media. There are also several unexpected negative aspects in the digital age. Although the optimistic view emphasised the potential of digital media in disseminating political information and ideas faster yet in a less costly manner, and there was a high hope for a participatory democracy rejuvenated by cyber-activism (Rheingold 2003), the same digital media would bring forth the decline of civic engagement and the decay of the public sphere by detaching individuals from intimate interactions in their local communities (Putnam 2000, cited in Lim and Lee 2010), resulting in change in the public sphere. As Lim and Lee (2010: 244) argued, the explosion of digital media use in South Korea was deeply embedded in the country's political and economic structure, and South Korea was transformed into a digital media-rich society, and, at the same time, 'growing political participation and social movements energised the public sphere'.

Referencing several significant civic movements in tandem with digital media, including the 2002 Candlelight vigil (Kang 2009), this chapter mainly focuses on instructional politics relevant to major elections, including presidential, general, and local elections, mainly due to the increasing role of social media in various elections. As Shirky (2011: 28) points out:

> since the rise of the Internet in the early 1990s, the world's net worked population has grown from the low millions to the low billions. Over the same period, social media have become a fact of life for civil society worldwide, involving many actors regular citizens, activists, nongovernmental organizations, telecommunications firms, software providers, governments.

The following section, therefore, discusses the emergence of digital media and their shifting role in contemporary South Korean politics.

3. THE EMERGENCE OF DIGITAL MEDIA

South Korea has rapidly developed and advanced digital technologies as some of the most significant areas for its national economy and youth culture since the mid-1990s. As South Korea has advanced its broadband penetration since the late 1990s, South Korean digital technologies, such as mobile telecommunications, digital games, and social media, have become the hallmarks of South Korean society, symbolising digital Korea (Jin 2016a). Korea is a late comer to the internet age; however, the country has rapidly advanced other digital technologies, which deeply influence South Koreans' daily lives. As the Organisation for Economic Co-operation and Development (OECD) (2020: 92) identifies, 'Korea is a top player in emerging digital technologies, with an outstanding digital infrastructure and a dynamic ICT sector', and 'digital technologies offer opportunities to raise firms' productivity and the population's well-being'.

There are several primary dimensions that have contributed to the growth of digital Korea, including competition among corporations, including Chaebol, skilled and talented manpower, and rapid economic growth. Favourable government policies starting in the mid-1990s have also driven the growth of information and communication technologies (ICTs) for sustainable economic growth. Ever since then, South Korea's new economy has been based on ICTs and their contribution to the country's transformation into a digital society (Oh and Larson 2011). Of course, as Kwang Suk Lee (2011) aptly puts it, the rapid growth of ICT has been made possible mainly due to the nexus of the South Korean government and ICT corporations in building national infrastructure.

To begin with, the Korean government planned to transform the country towards a knowledge-based economy by setting up the Korea Information Infrastructure (KII) in March 1995. The government was well aware that 'the national digital network in use did not have the capacity to handle the vast amount of multimedia data that would be transmitted in the 21st century, and that Korea's future therefore depended on the implementation of an advanced information infrastructure'. The South Korean government also realised that 'the sharing of information was an essential element needed to raise competitiveness and citizens' quality of life and level of education, together with the rapid democratisation process that had put an end to 26 years of military dictatorship in 1987 and introduced direct presidential elections' (Yoon 2016: 46). The goal was to construct an advanced nationwide information infrastructure consisting of communications networks, internet services, application software, computers, and information products and services (Lee 2011; Jin 2016b). In the first phase of the KII project, the government attempted to lay the foundation for building a national information network, and later, the project advanced the use of information networks by encouraging individual and industrial end users. The ultimate goal was to interconnect the national information network, reaching out to the global network (Lee and Jung 1998: 62). The KII project aimed to build high-speed and high-capacity networks through market competition and private-sector investment, as well as government policies (Jin 2011; Lee 2011).

More specifically, the South Korean government has intensified its primary role as the funder and regulator in the ICT sector. By creating several supportive mechanisms through its legal and financial arms, the Kim Dae-jung government (1998–2003) and the Roh Moo-hyun government (2003–2008) continued the ICT-led economic policy, considering ICT as one of the most important driving forces to foster growth in the national economy (Jin 2016b). Two conservative regimes, Lee Myung-bak (2008–2013) and Park Geun-hye (2013–2017), also substantially initiated the growth of the digital Korea project. The Moon Jae-in government (2017–2022) even intensified its support to the growth of digital technologies, and therefore digital economy and culture.

As the most recent phenomenon, South Korea has advanced smartphone technologies and culture. Several Chaebols, including Samsung Electronics and LG Electronics, have developed and produced their own smartphones since 2009. South Korea has also advanced relevant applications, including instant mobile messengers, such as KaKao Talk and Line (Jin 2016b), pertinent to the smartphone. Based on these developments, 5G was introduced nationwide earlier than in any other country in the world. Within one year of 5G services' commercial introduction on 3 April 2019, the number of subscribers had almost reached six million, with high fibre-backhaul availability enabling fast adoption (OECD 2019). Korea's density of broadband fibre subscriptions is the highest OECD-wide (OECD 2020). The government's plan for innovative growth focuses on digital opportunities raised by the use of 5G, which brings three key advantages.

First, its higher speed allows for the transmission of large volumes of data, for instance, for virtual reality TV or hologramme calls. Second, its lower latency allows instant response, for example, for automatic and connected vehicles or Internet of Things (IoT) devices. Third, its hyperconnectivity allows for the simultaneous connection of numerous sensors and devices, as is needed in smart factories and smart cities. The government promotes numerous projects relying on 5G to increase competitiveness and innovation in industries (e.g. smart manufacturing, smart grids and smart health care) or to enhance quality of life by solving social problems with smart cities and homes (notably in Sejong), as well as smart roads and traffic systems. The expected effects include higher production, exports, and employment (The Presidential Committee on the 4th Industrial Revolution, 2017)

Likewise, the South Korean government has continued and intensified its role as a major actor in the realm of digital technologies. The government has initiated the digital Korea project due to the significance of the ICT markets for the national economy. As the South Korean economy has been established and grown through state-led developmentalism, meaning the South Korean government takes a top-down model in the development of national economy, the government continues its function while developing neoliberal globalisation (Jin 2016b). As the South Korean government has developed ICTs and related corporation-friendly policies, a few key ICT sectors, including broadband and mobile telecommunications, surged in the overall ICT market. In the mobile sector, a few transnational corporations have produced mobile phones—feature phones first, followed by smartphones—to become the top mobile device makers in the world. Naver and Daum have also become two major internet portals, which are some of the most significant symbols representing digital South Korea because South Koreans heavily rely on them for news, information, entertainment, and social network sites (Jin 2016b). Under favourable government ICT policies, these major corporations have turned out to be the major players in building digital Korea as users and producers. Of course, as South Korea has emerged as one of the leading ICT nations, many global ICT firms, including internet, social media, smartphone, and digital platform firms, such as Google, Yahoo, Dell, Sony, and Netflix, have vehemently invested in the South Korean market and increased their shares in the most networked digital society.

Digital Korea has not only transformed the national economy, but also politics and culture. While the government and ICT corporations have advanced digital technologies and infrastructure, many South Koreans heavily rely on ICTs for their daily activities and cultural lives. By fully utilising social media and digital platforms to enjoy cultural content, from K-pop to webtoons, South Koreans have greatly increased their use of and reliance on new digital technologies, such as the internet, social media, and smartphones, to organise their political activities and share their political opinions, which eventually influence their political decisions during major presidential and general elections.

4. The Shifting Role of Digital Media in South Korean Politics

4.1 The Internet and South Korean Politics

The first major political event in which digital technologies, in particular the internet, were heavily used and influenced people's political attitudes and actions was the 2002 presidential election. Roh Moo-hyun's victory in the 2002 election was arguably influenced by online media and the internet; therefore, politicians from then onwards have developed their political strategies in tandem with digital technologies. Back then, South Korea already led the world in the provision of broadband access. South Korea had a broadband penetration of 21.3 per 100 inhabitants as of December 2002, placing the country first in broadband penetration rates, followed by Hong Kong (14.6), Canada (11.5), Taiwan (9.4), and the United States (6.5) (International Telecommunication Union 2003). The broadband-enabled population skyrocketed from only 370,000 in 1999 to 10 million subscribers in October 2002 (Ministry of Information and Communication (MIC) 2002). This meant that late in 2002 more than 70 per cent of South Korean households were connected to high-speed internet (Ward 2003), and therefore, many South Koreans could easily access the internet with high speed anywhere and anytime. Based on the rapid growth of these infrastructural foundations, many South Korean politicians and the general public began to rely on the internet to learn about the 2002 presidential election.

What happened was that online news services began to emerge as an important source of news for many South Koreans, in particular youth and young adults, who were more distrustful about the news they got in traditional media. The outcome of the 2002 South Korean presidential election, which occurred on 19 December, pointed to a decline of influence in the nation's big three newspapers: *The Chosun Ilbo*, *The JoongAng Ilbo*, and *The Dong-A Ilbo*. These right-wing newspapers, which were all fervent supporters of Lee Hoi-chang, the opposition's presidential nominee, failed to wield significant influence in the 2002 presidential election (Rhee 2003). Many South Koreans already believed that major newspapers and broadcasters misinformed the public through biased articles and reporting and distortion of facts, better known as 'fake news' in contemporary society. In the midst of such stifling circumstances, frustrated young voters saw the internet as an outlet where they could spill out their diverse views and create a counter-agenda forum (Rhee 2003).

Two major critical junctures occurred right before the election. On the one hand, a few days before election day, when a North Korean ship carrying missile export cargo was stopped by the United States, the tension between South Korean and North Korea intensified. As usual, major newspapers and broadcasters quickly capitalised on their chance to sway the public support for Lee and played up this news. However, this time, it did not work because of the internet. Instead of relying on legacy media, younger voters went to find the news and posted messages on the online bulletin boards. The internet played a decisive role in the 2002 election (Rhee 2003).

On the other hand, on the night before election day, multimillionaire politician Jung Mongjoon, who had unified a single candidacy with Roh a few weeks before the election, suddenly withdrew his support of Roh Moo-hyun. Speculation was rampant that this sudden blow would cause Roh to lose the election. Young voters, again, went to the internet early on the morning of election day and posted messages such as 'Let's go vote!'. With these, they appealed to young netizens to go to the polls. According to exit polls, Roh was behind Lee by a margin of 1–2 per cent in the morning. However, a large influx of young voters who largely supported Roh poured into the voting booths in the afternoon. Consequently, from 2 p.m. on that day, exit polls reversed and Roh began to take the lead (Song 2002; Rhee 2003). Although it could not be said that the internet was the sole reason for Roh's victory, it was not deniable to admit the shifting media environment due to the increase in the internet use. In a nutshell, South Korean youth created a cyber-acropolis, a modern-day adaptation to the ancient Greek's direct participatory democracy (Song 2002; Rhee 2003).

One particular dimension for Roh's victory in tandem with digital media technologies was Nosamo ('People who love Roh Moo-hyun'), an internet-based group organised in 2000 as a fan club for the former president Roh, which played a major role. Nosamo was started by a few netizens at a PC bang (Internet café); however, it soon became a prominent political movement. In 2002, the group came into national prominence as an active force behind Roh's election to the presidency in a tight contest against the more established political figure of Lee Hoi-chang. This political breakthrough was recorded as one of the most significant contributions of digital media 'with a combination of the Internet and mobile phone-based communication' (Castells et al. 2009: 193). While the internet-based campaign had lasted for years, providing core political networks, it was the mobile phone that mobilised large numbers of young voters on election day and probably reversed the voting result being systematically utilised (Fulford 2003: 92, cited in Castells et al. 2009: 193–194). In fact, Nosamo is widely credited with mobilising the voters in the election, and its efforts included a mobile-phone campaign on election day to urge young voters to cast their ballots, which was not precedented:

> Koreans realized they had entered a new era after the last presidential elections. By 11 a.m. on Dec. 19, 2002, exit poll results showed that the iconoclastic Roh Moo Hyun, 56, a 2-to-1 favorite among youth, was losing the election. His supporters hit the chat rooms to drum up support. Within minutes more than 800,000 e-mails were sent to mobiles to urge supporters to go out and vote. Traditionally apathetic young voters surged to the polls and, by 2 p.m., Roh took the lead and went on to win the election. A man with little support from either the mainstream media or the nation's conglomerates sashayed into office on an Internet on-ramp. The traditional Confucian order had been flipped upside down, and a symbolic transfer of power from elders to youth took place.
>
> (Fulford 2003: 92)

Of course, in South Korean politics, the difficult and divisive nature of regionalism originates from a historical and political tension between the two large provinces of Gyeongsang—relatively conservative—and Cholla—relatively liberal, which also played a key role (Hara and Jo 2007), although Roh succeeded in receiving a majority of voters in their twenties and thirties due to the successful online campaign strategy and political use of the internet.

5. Social Media Use and Municipal Elections

Since 2002, South Korean politics, in particular during the elections, both for the presidential and general elections, has greatly relied on digital technologies, not only the internet, but also social media and smartphones. Social networking services (SNSs), including Facebook, Twitter, and Tik Tok, have functioned as a new venue for political engagements and practices over the past fifteen years, sometimes very effectively, and at other times very controversially (Farrell 2012; Baek et al. 2015; McCurry 2020).

Politicians and political parties have continued to utilise SNSs to attract more supports and voters, while many citizens use SNSs as sources for political gathering and protests.

One of the most significant elections supported by social media is the 2011 municipal election, in particular, for the mayorship of Seoul. South Korea's liberal opposition, bolstered by the under-forties and power of social media, could spring a surprise win in this election. The young, more likely to carry smartphones, are mostly liberal and their views are expressed and spread online, often by their smartphones (Kim and Park 2012). Social media has acted as a counterweight to the mainstream media. It prompted young voters who were concerned with issues like growing income inequality and social injustice to swing behind the Democrat United Party (Kim and Park 2012). One of the reasons Twitter works so well is that its 140-character bursts offer a perfect fit for the Korean language, which can pack a lot more into its space than English. 'In English, basically all you can do is to tell someone to check out a YouTube link. In Korean, you can not only describe what the clip is about but how you feel about it' (Kim and Park 2012). As one political consulting company explained, the 2011 municipal election was nothing more than the Twitter election, as Twitter acted as a driver for South Korean youth and young adults to go to the voting places (Kang 2011). The municipal election was the key test of whether the Twitter-using liberals could turn their lock on cyberspace into hard political power, and it was successful (Kim and Park 2012).

The influence of Twitter reached its peak in the by-election for mayor of Seoul in October 2011. Mayor Oh Se-hoon, who had won the election in June 2010, resigned fourteen months later after a referendum that he had called over the provision of free lunches for school children failed (he had opposed the measure, but voters approved). Park Won-sun, the opposition party candidate, had a reputation for being adept at using social media. He had spent his career as a human rights lawyer and founder of leading civil society organisations and philanthropic foundations. He was widely followed on Twitter. Post-election analysis showed that tweets encouraging people to vote skyrocketed during the final two hours of polling time. More importantly, the turnout of voters in their twenties and thirties surged during these two hours, as did the number of votes cast for Park. Votes for Na Kyung-won, the ruling party candidate, 'did not budge during this time. In the end, Park scored an upset victory' (Chang 2014: 31). Twitter became 'political and progressive when it was combined with the offline realities of South Korean society' (Chang 2014: 31).

However, we need to be very careful because Twitter, one of the major social media platforms on politics, could not play a decisive key role in several elections, although it was one of the significant elements for Park Won-sun's victory in this particular municipal election. In South Korea, the number of Twitter users is far fewer than in other countries. As of 2015, only 4.92 million Koreans had Twitter accounts (Statista 2021). Given its advanced networked society, it was quite surprising to learn that Twitter was not that popular. People in the number one country in terms of smartphone penetration rate, ironically, do not use Twitter often. Although the majority of Twitter users lived in either the Seoul or Busan metro areas (the two largest metros in Korea), it was not common for people in Seoul to use Twitter to organise any political activities.

6. Smartphones in South Korean Politics

During the 2017 presidential election, the majority of politicians used both SNSs and smartphones, especially utilising the latter. The smartphone, as the most widely and swiftly diffused technology in South Korea in the 2010s, has replaced the mobile phone (as a feature phone) and changed the form of social mediation. The shift from what South Koreans called feature phones (with physical keys) to those of touch-sensitive smartphones has been evident. Domestically, South Korea had 55.5 million mobile subscriptions as of May 2012, when the presidential election occurred. The number of smartphone users among mobile users spiked to exceed 47.4 million, consisting of 85.4 per cent of total mobile phone users, up from around 1.6 per cent of total mobile phone users in December 2009 (Ministry of Science and ICT (MSIT) 2018).

Based on the rapid growth of smartphone use, presidential candidates and political parties developed new campaign strategies utilising smartphones and social media such as YouTube. In fact, the 2017 presidential election was recorded as the first major election in which new media, including SNSs and smartphones together, played a major role, and therefore, popular media dubbed it as the 'New Media Presidential Election' and/or the 'Smartphone Presidential Election' (Ha 2017). Although the eighteenth presidential election held in 2012 used smartphones and SNSs, candidates did not utilise them much, as the penetration rate of smartphones was about 67 per cent, compared to 85.4 per cent in 2017. Back then, presidential candidates used SNSs to simply convey their messages; however, during the nineteenth presidential election held in 2017, candidates and political parties vehemently utilised SNSs and smartphones (Ha 2017). For example, the Moon Jae-in camp developed a Moon Jae-in app to appeal to smartphone users, which was effective (Cho 2017). The Democratic Party also created the election camp's official Moon Jae-in channel on YouTube and broadcasted the election process (Ha 2017). While there are some differences between presidential candidates, the candidates and their political parties commonly utilised both mobile apps and social media for their campaigns.

As elsewhere, media have continued to play a role as one of the major actors in South Korean politics; however, the situation surrounding media and politics in the South Korean context has fundamentally shifted as digital technologies become major venues, not only to deliver messages, but also to communicate with voters. Digital technologies, from the internet to SNSs and smartphones, have become new actors that South Korean politics must rely on. Although the influence of traditional media in creating agendas has continued, their roles are shrinking due to the emergence of new media. South Korean people have shown their distrust of legacy media due to their misconducts in the past several decades. New media themselves are not exempted from criticism because they also create fake news in major elections.

However, Korean people, in particular youth, are heavily relying on new digital media to get political news, opinions, and information, which greatly influences their voting decisions.

7. Conclusion

This chapter has discussed the ways in which new digital technologies have influenced South Korean politics, in particular in major elections, from presidential to municipal elections. As several digital technologies like high-speed internet, smartphones, and social media have been widely used, South Korean politicians and citizens greatly utilise them in several major political activities. In South Korea, traditional media, both broadcasting and newspapers, have wielded their enormous power in national politics; however, because people distrusted traditional media journalistic standards due to their favouritism to conservative candidates, their dominant roles in South Korean politics have been substituted by digital media. Although digital media alone have not transformed South Korean politics, they certainly now play a key role in South Korean politics. This does not mean that they act as a public sphere, which totally replaces legacy media. As Habermas (1989) pointed out, the logic of the public sphere should be independent of economic and political power. In South Korea, digital technologies have substantively replaced traditional media as the major tool of the public sphere. We cannot deny digital media's opportunities for political participations. However, this does not mean that the principle of the public sphere activated by legacy media was taken over by digital media, although digital technologies have greatly changed the milieu surrounding Korean politics.

The increasing use of digital technologies in politics has been unique in the South Korean context, mainly because it is one of the most networked, if not the most networked, society. With the advent of high-speed internet, South Korea has rapidly advanced wireless wi-fi service, smartphones, and internet portals. South Korea has also advanced instant mobile messengers, such as KakaoTalk and Line, while developing several local-based social media, including Cyworld (now defunct) and Band. These new digital technologies have played a key role in connecting people, and politicians and civic movements leaders cannot lose these great opportunities to organise various political events.

South Korea is not the only place in which people utilise social media and smartphones during national elections. From the United States to small, non-Western countries, politicians use digital technologies as part of their political campaigns. What makes South Korea distinctive is the mentality of the people, which does not trust traditional media, while systematically relying on these digital technologies as major information sources. When South Koreans were sick and tired of legacy media's excessive influences in their daily lives, they started to pay attention to digital technologies as new tools in consuming political news, while appropriating them for political campaigns:

> There are, broadly speaking, two arguments against the idea that social media will make a difference in national politics. The first is that the tools are themselves ineffective, and the second is that they produce as much harm to democratization as good, because repressive governments are becoming better at using these tools to suppress dissent.
>
> (Shirky 2011: 38)

In South Korean politics, the use of digital technologies, including the internet, social media, and smartphones, will continue, and therefore, their influences will be further intensified. As new generations, who have been living with digital technologies since their childhood, come into national politics, their use of, and reliance on, these digital media are not only common, but also crucial.

Bibliography

Ahn, K. S. (2005), 'Newspaper Readership and Subscription Down, Chosun. JoongAng. Dong's Market Share Up', *Media Today*, 19 January, www.mediatoday.co.kr/news/articleView.html?idxno=33896, accessed 23 November 2021.

Baek, Y. M., Jeongb, I., and Rheec, J. W. (2015), 'Political Homophily on Social Network Sites and Users' Poll Skepticism', *Asian Journal of Communication* 25(3), 271–287.

Castells, M., Fernández-Ardèvol, M., Qiu, J. L., and Sey, A. (2009), *Mobile Communication and Society: A Global Perspective* (Cambridge, MA: MIT Press).

Chang, D. J. (2014), 'Leveling the Playing Field: Social Media and Politics in South Korea', *Global Asia* 9(2), 31–35.

Cho, E. H. (2017), 'Increasing Competition in the Presidential Election—Smartphone App War', 2 June, *JoongAng Ilbo*, https://news.joins.com/article/21219426, accessed 23 November 2021.

Farrell, H. (2012), 'The Consequences of the Internet for Politics', *Annual Review of Political Science* 15(1), 35–52.

The Presidential Committee on the 4th Industrial Revolution (2017). 'Plan for the Fourth Industrial Revolution to Promote Innovative Growth'. Seoul: The Presidential Committee on the 4th Industrial Revolution.

Fulford, B. (2003), 'Korea's Weird Wired World', *Forbes*, 21 July 21, https://www.forbes.com/global/2003/0721/058.html#6cea7f56c3da, accessed 23 November 2021.

Ha, J. H. (2017), 'Micro Strategic Map—Make Moon Jae In as President', *Weekly Chosun*, 14 May, https://www.chosun.com/site/data/html_dir/2017/05/12/2017051202314.html, accessed 23 November 2021.

Habermas, J. (1989), *The Structural Transformation of the Public Sphere: Inquire into a Category of Bourgeois Society* (Cambridge: Polity Press).

Hara, N., and Jo, Y. M. (2007), 'Internet Politics: A Comparative Analysis of US and South Korea Presidential Campaigns', *First Monday*, https://firstmonday.org/article/view/2005/1880, accessed 23 November 2021.

Huh, I. H. (2005), 'Role of the Internet in the ROK Presidential Election in 2002', in A. Y. Mansourov, ed., *A Turning Point: Democratic Consolidation in the ROK and Strategic Readjustment in the US–ROK Alliance*, 1–13 (Honolulu, HI: Asia-Pacific Center for Security Studies).

International Telecommunication Unit (2003), 'Top 15 Economies by 2002 Broadband Penetration', https://www.itu.int/ITU-D/ict/statistics/at_glance/top15_broad.html, accessed 23 November 2021.

Jin, D. Y. (2011), 'The Digital Korean Wave: Local Online Gaming Goes Global', *Media International Australia* 141, 128–136.

Jin, D. Y. (2016a), 'How to Understand the Emergence of Digital Korea', in Y.N. Kim (ed.). *Routledge Handbook of Korean Culture and Society*, 179–192 (London: Routledge).

Jin, D. Y. (2016b), *Smartland Korea: Mobile Communication, Culture and Society* (Ann Arbor, MI: University of Michigan Press).

Kang, J. Y. (2009), 'Coming to Terms with "Unreasonable" Global Power: The 2002 South Korean Candlelight Vigils', *Communication and Critical/Cultural Studies* 6(2), 171–192.

Kang, M. H. (2011), 'Park Woon-soon Seoul Mayor—the Victory of PR', The PR News, 3 November, www.the-pr.co.kr/news/articleView.html?idxno=4030, accessed 23 November 2021.

Kim, J., and Park, J.M. (2012), 'South Korea's Twitter Generation May Give Liberals Upset Win', *Reuters*, 9 April, www.reuters.com/article/net-us-korea-politics-socialmedia/south-koreas-twitter-generation-may-give-liberals-upset-win-idUSBRE8380BI20120409, accessed 23 August 2021.

Lee, K. S. (2011), 'Interrogating Digital Korea: Mobile Phone Tracking and the Spatial Expansion of Labour Control', *Media International Australia* 141, 107–117.

Lee, S. H., and Jung, J. I. (1998), 'Telecommunications Markets, Industry, and Infrastructure in Korea', *IEEE Communications Magazine* 36(11), 59–64.

Lim, H. C., and Lee, J. K. (2010), 'Mobile Communication, Political Participation and the Public Sphere: South Korea's Experiences', *Media Asia* 37(4), 244–256.

McCurry, J. (2020), 'How US K-Pop Fans Became a Political Force to Be Reckoned With', *The Guardian*, 24 June.

Ministry of Information and Communication (2002), 'The Status of Korea's Broadband' (press release), 1 November.

Ministry of Science and ICT (MSIT) (2018), 'Mobile Communication Service Statistics of 2017' (Seoul: MSIT).

Oh, M., and Larson, J. (2011), *Digital Development in Korea: Building an Information Society* (London: Routledge).

Organisation for Economic Co-operation and Development (OECD) (2019), 'The Road to 5G Networks: Experience to Date and Future Developments', OECD Digital Economy Papers No. 284 (Paris: OECD).

OECD (2020), *OECD Economics Surveys Korea* (Paris: OECD).

Putnam, R. D. (2000), *Bowling Alone: The Collapse and Revival of American Community* (New York: Simon & Schuster).

Rhee, I. Y. (2003), 'The Korean Election Shows a Shift in Media Power Young Voters Create a "Cyber Acropolis" and Help to Elect the President', *Nieman Reports*, 15 November.

Rheingold, H. (2003), *Smart Mobs: The Next Social Revolution* (Cambridge, MA: Perseus Publishing).

Shin, E. H. (2005), 'Presidential Elections, Internet Politics, and Citizens' Organizations in South Korea', *Development and Society* 34(1), 35–47.

Shirky, C. (2011), 'The Political Power of Social Media: Technology, the Public Sphere, and Political Change', *Foreign Affairs* 90(1), 28–41.

Song, D. H., and Son, C. Y. (2017), 'Comparing the Public Sphere in Social Networking Services during a Period of Political Upheaval: The Three News Channels Facebook Accounts in the 2016 South Korean Presidential Scandal', *International Journal of Digital Television* 8(3), 351–366.

Song, H. G. (2002), 'Primary Contributor to Win the Election', *Weekly DongA*, 26 December, https://weekly.donga.com/List/3/all/11/70183/1, accessed 23 November 2021.

Statista (2021), 'South Korea: Number of Twitter Users 2014–2016', https://www.statista.com/statistics/558435/number-of-twitter-users-in-south-korea/, accessed 23 November 2021.

Ward, A. (2003), 'Love Affair Starts to Grip South Korea's Internet Generation', *Financial Times*, 9 October.

Yoon, J. W. (2016), 'Korean Digital Government Infrastructure Building and Implementation: Capacity Dimensions), in T. G. Karippacheril, S. Kim, R. P. Beschel Jr, and C. Choi, eds, *Bringing Government into the 21st Century The Korean Digital Governance Experience*, 41–59 (Washington, DC: The World Bank).

CHAPTER 25

THE PRESS

KI-SUNG KWAK

1. INTRODUCTION

SINCE democratisation in 1988, the press in South Korea has been legally free to criticise government policy and has adopted a considerably more open political stance than was the case under the previous military regimes. Democratisation has enabled the major South Korean newspapers—the 'big three' of *Chosun Ilbo, Dong-A Ilbo*, and *JoongAng Ilbo*—to take advantage of the political vacuum created by the collapse of the military regimes and transform themselves into a powerful new institution capable of wielding political power. Since that time, they have stayed loyal to the conservative party, and formed strategic alliances with conservative political actors to maintain their position in the ideological power structure. As a result, these newspapers have emerged as a political force that has been able to set agendas and take the lead in protecting conservative interests and ideology.

Since the late 1990s, the press in South Korea has moved away from passive developmental journalism towards a highly selective and partisan journalism where the level of collusive or adversarial reporting has been dependent on which party holds power. This was best illustrated when the major conservative newspapers underwent a sudden shift after the election of a reformist government in 1997. The change of government saw these papers move from close cooperation with the government and a willingness to accept state guidance on preferred media agendas and content to a highly critical stance in relation to government policy and a distinctly adversarial style. The clearest evidence of this was the conservative newspapers' relentless condemnation of President Kim Dae-jung's (1998–2002) 'Sunshine Policy' towards North Korea, in sharp contrast to their former practice of passive journalism. This shift to critical news journalism was not well received by all of South Korea's political parties. Similarly, governments have frequently resorted to various measures designed to implicitly discourage antagonistic reporting. For example, Kim Dae-jung initiated discriminatory tax audits targeted at conservative papers critical of his reformist policy.

While democratisation has meant that the newspapers are freer than they were under the previous governments, the relationship between political parties and the press worsened when Roh Moo-hyun (2003–2007) won the 2002 presidential election. A long-time critic of conservative newspapers, Roh distrusted the media, a distrust that surfaced when he imposed a series of media reforms that widened the gap between government and the press. Like his predecessor, Roh Moo-hyun tried to bring the antagonistic (conservative) press under control through the frequent use of libel and defamation charges. Indeed, the number of complaints and law suits filed against the conservative newspapers by the Roh government exceeded those initiated by any other government.

In 2008, the nation saw the triumphant return of the conservative party after a decade of rule by reformist governments, and the same party continued to hold power after its candidate, Park Geun-hye, won the 2012 presidential election. President Lee Myung-bak (2008–2012) and the ruling party strengthened its relationship with the 'big three' conservative newspapers by granting each of them a comprehensive cable TV licence, which allowed them to produce news and current affairs programmes. Then, after a decade of conservative rule, in 2017 the nation saw the return of the progressive party led by Moon Jae-in following the impeachment of Park Geun-hye (2013–2016). Throughout this period, political shifts, regardless of which party held power, did not alter the partisan outlook of the newspapers.

Against this backdrop, this chapter examines how partisanship and progressive–conservative divisions have influenced the press and the relationship between the press and political parties in South Korea since the 1990s. In order to better understand this dynamic, the chapter begins with an identification of the major features of the South Korean press, which help to explain the complex interplay between the press and political parties in South Korea. This is followed by an examination of the way in which the legacy of authoritarianism has affected political reporting and the press–party relationship, with a special focus on the press club system and the transformation of journalists into politicians.

2. Main Features of the South Korean Press

2.1 Ideological Narrowness

The ideological spectrum of the South Korean press, once determined by the anti-communist ideology of the military regimes, widened with the launch of *Hankyoreh*, a left-leaning daily, in the late 1980s. The progressive *Hankyoreh* was joined by another paper, *Kyunghyang Shinmun*, to provide a stronger counter to conservative views in 1999, when *Kyunghyang*'s editorial stance dramatically shifted to 'progressive' with its ownership being transferred from *Hanhwa*, a business conglomerate, to the newspaper's own employees. There have been attempts made by some newspapers—such as the *Hankook Daily* and *Seoul Daily*—to position themselves more in the centre, taking the middle ground. These newspapers, however, have been less popular and less influential than the big three conservative newspapers and the two progressive papers, and their opinions in practice often lean towards the progressive side. This means that there has been little room among the newspapers to allow middle-ground papers to emerge as a major threat to the conservative or progressive papers, and so perhaps to reduce the intensity of ideological conflicts.

Unlike the newspapers, which have maintained their ideological orientation and political stance regardless of the changes in government, broadcasters in South Korea, terrestrial television in particular, have remained under the control of the government of the day (Kwak 2012). This is because the governments and the ruling parties have imposed and exercised structural constraints upon public service broadcasters (the Korean Broadcasting System [KBS] and Munhwa Broadcasting Corporation [MBC]), which allowed them to have a dominant position in appointing key personnel and programming. Indeed, whenever there was a change of government, a reshuffle of key positions (e.g. president and board members) in the KBS and MBC soon followed (Kwak 2012). Despite strong resistance from the incumbent presidents and the members of the board, who had been appointed by the previous government, they were all eventually forced to resign under enormous pressure and threats from the incoming government. The basic principles of public service broadcasting, such as independence from vested interests and the production of high-quality programmes, have been subordinated to the ideological orientation of the president of the nation and their party. Under the current progressive Moon Jae-in government, current affairs and talk show programmes on terrestrial TV and radio channels have often focused on the flaws and shortcomings of the opposition conservative party and conservative newspapers. Under the previous conservative governments, the focus of these programmes was on criticising progressive ideology.

In common with trends in the rest of the developed world, the readership and subscription rate of newspapers in South Korea have significantly dropped in the past two decades, due to the development of technologies that have allowed the emergence of digital devices and multi-platforms. However, while the readership and subscription rate of print (as opposed to online) newspapers is low (see Table 25.1), the combined media readership (i.e. the ratio of those who have read newspaper articles in the past week through at least one of the media platforms such as print newspapers, fixed-line and mobile internet, smart phones) stood at 79.6 per cent in 2018 (Korea Press. Foundation (KPF) 2019).

Despite the decrease in the readership and subscription rate of the newspapers over the past two decades, the rate of paid circulation (number of printed copies) in the 2010s has been rather static (see Table 25.2).

Conservative newspapers, which have largely remained under family control, are the biggest in terms of readership, subscriptions, and revenue. On the other hand, progressive papers—either publicly owned (*Hankyoreh*) or owned by employees (*Kyunghyang*)—are

Table 25.1: Newspaper readership and subscription rate in South Korea (1996–2018)

	1996	1998	2000	2002	2004	2006	2008	2010	2012	2014	2016	2018
*Newspaper readership	85.2	83.8	81.4	82.1	76.0	68.8	58.5	52.6	40.9	30.7	20.9	17.7
**Daily readership	43.5	35.1	35.1	37.3	34.3	25.1	24.0	13.0	15.7	10.4	6.5	5.7
Subscription rate (%)	69.3	64.5	59.8	52.9	48.3	40.0	36.8	29.0	24.7	20.0	14.3	9.5

Note:
* Newspaper readership: the ratio of those who have read newspaper articles in the past week (unit: %);
** Daily readership: average time spent per day reading print newspapers in the past week (unit: minute).
Source: KPF (2019).

Table 25.2: Daily paid circulation of major South Korean national dailies (in 000s)

	2011	2012	2013	2014	2015	2016	2017	2018	2019
Chosun	1,393	1,353	1,326	1,294	1,295	1,267	1,254	1,239	1,194
Dong-A	983	944	917	811	795	750	720	726	737
JoongAng	867	750	753	707	737	732	729	737	713
Hankyoreh	225	210	210	201	199	201	202	200	200
Kyunghyang	133	135	140	147	149	158	163	167	165
Hankook	200	187	176	169	169	167	165	165	173
Munhwa	145	148	140	141	149	158	164	170	176
Seoul	117	113	110	108	110	113	116	117	118

Source: KPF (2018, 2019).

financially weak in terms of subscription and revenue. Among the main national dailies, with the exception of the economic newspapers (i.e. the *Korea Economic Daily* and *Maeil Business Newspaper*) and newspapers that are owned and operated by religious organisations (i.e. *Kookmin Ilbo* and *Sekye Ilbo*), 'the big three' conservative newspapers (*Chosun*, *Dong-A*, and *JoongAng*) have the largest rate of paid circulations, while the two progressive papers (*Hankyoreh* and *Kyunghyang*) have maintained a relatively steady number of subscribers. This indicates that there have been loyal readers who have continued to support the newspapers that share their ideological leanings.

A more tangible example, which shows the extent to which the conservative–progressive division dominates in the South Korean press (including broadcast journalism), can be found in audience perception of the television news coverage of the Cho Kuk scandal that swept through South Korean politics in the second half of 2019. When Cho Kuk, the former senior secretary to the President for Civil Affairs in the Moon Jae-in government, was appointed as Minister for Justice in August 2019, despite protests from the opposition parties, the local news media were filled with allegations of misconduct by Cho Kuk and members of his family. His wife had been charged with fabricating official documents—such as an internship certificate from the Korea Institute for Science and Technology, and an award certificate from the university where she worked—to facilitate her daughter's admission to a medical school in 2015.

Consistent with their long-established practice of biased news in favour of the government of the day, the nation's public service broadcasters, KBS and MBC, reported the scandal mainly from the perspective of Cho Kuk and his family (Ko 2020). Their coverage was largely devoted to statements by Cho Kuk's supporters, who claimed that the family had been unfairly targeted by prosecutors because Cho had been so determined to reform the Prosecutors Office. On the other hand, TV Chosun and Channel A—cable channels owned by *Chosun* and *Dong-A*, respectively—heavily criticised Cho Kuk's alleged wrongdoings and highlighted the implications of the scandal on South Korean society (Citizens' Coalition for Democratic Media [CCDM] 2019).

Another comprehensive cable TV channel, JoongAng TongYang Broadcasting Company (JTBC), which was launched in 2011 as an affiliate of *JoongAng*, took a more cautious approach with its motto 'factual, fair, objective and balanced news' (JTBC 2020), has consistently been voted the most trusted news organisation by the South Korean people (*PD Journal* 2019). In reporting the Cho Kuk scandal, the channel maintained a neutral stance, with factual and balanced reporting (Jung 2020). Unlike its competitors in the conservative camp, JTBC did not set out to blame or criticise Cho Kuk and his wife's alleged wrongdoings. Equally, it did not support Cho Kuk's position, nor that of the Prosecutor's Office, as the progressive media outlets had done. These one-sided messages provided by conservative broadcasters (TV Chosun and Channel A) and the public service broadcasters (KBS and MBC), gave the audience an easily digestible version of news in the expectation that it would be shared with others. JTBC, however, satisfied neither the pro-Cho Kuk nor anti-Cho Kuk factions. According to a survey of the coverage of the scandal conducted in October 2019, MBC and TV Chosun were ranked the first and second news channels, respectively for the best coverage, while JTBC was ranked third (*Media Today* 2019a). TV coverage of the Cho Kuk scandal showed that the exposure to the partisan media/press strengthens the bonds between citizens and parties and their ideologies (Hallin and Mancini 2004: 28).

2.2 Excessive Focus on Partisan Conflicts and Lack of Diversity in Political Reporting

The narrowness of the ideological spectrum has inevitably limited the diversity of perspectives and views on political issues. The South Korean political system has been dominated by the two major parties, and this has meant that political reporting has been centred on these two parties. The voices of, or news about, minor political parties have been rarely heard or appeared in the political reporting. This partisan nature of the press affects the selection of subject matter and editorial perspective in news coverage.

One of the main reasons for the lack of diversity in political reporting is that news reports normally rely on one-sided sources and information. Journalists working for conservative newspapers obtain their information from sources supportive of conservative ideologies, while those working for progressive newspapers collect information mainly from those who share their progressive ideologies. These partisan differences also exist among newspaper subscribers. Conservatives who subscribe to newspapers are more likely to believe that their newspaper is the most reliable source of news, while the same is true for subscribers of progressive newspapers. A number of studies have produced similar findings on partisan reporting, partisan readership, and the relationship between the two (Min and Lee 2015; Kim 2009). For example, in his research on the relationship between the partisan press and its readers on the issue of Lee Myung-bak's four rivers project, Kim (2009) found that the partisan tone reflected in the conservative newspapers was stronger than the level of partisanship among conservative readers, while the progressive newspapers also showed a stronger degree of partisanship than their progressive readers. Those who have strongly partisan political opinions, whether conservative or progressive, tend to perceive newspaper editorials as more hostile or friendly to themselves than those who hold neutral political opinions (Song 2014).

These examples support the argument that South Korean readers choose news sources slanted towards their own political or ideological views, rather than sources that adopt a neutral stance. In many developed countries, the increased availability of news media outlets allows the audience to selectively seek out the information consistent with their ideological predisposition (Hahn et al. 2015; Allern 2010). In this context, the newspapers are obliged to reflect a one-sided perspective for their loyal readers, confirming their distrust of the opposition. While this can be a typical survival strategy for many newspapers, enabling readers to match their news consumption with their ideological preferences (Iyengar and Han 2009), it poses a serious challenge to the basic ideals of objective journalism.

The South Korean press has suffered from an excessive focus on partisan conflicts and a lack of in-depth analyses of the causes of political conflicts. During the past three decades of democratisation, the ways in which newspapers with different ideological biases have reported political issues have been the subject of many studies. Among these issues, the subject of North Korea (and inter-Korean relations) deserves particular attention, as this has been one of the most pertinent issues the country has faced (Choi 2018), and the source of the major ideological conflicts in South Korea. A number of studies have found that there was a huge gap between ideological perspectives in reports on North Korean issues in the South Korean press (Hong et al. 2011; Kim and Rho 2011; Lee, S.S. 2007; Lee, W.S. 2007b; Hwang et al. 2007; Choi 2010), and that these different ideological outlooks have been maintained regardless of changes of government (Lee, W.S. 2007a; Kim 2015). In framing their stories, South Korean newspapers frequently rely on stereotypes, generalisations, and prejudices. Sources are selected to justify the newspapers' ideological inclinations and stories are framed in such a way as to give news reports a particular ideological cast (Kim and Rho 2011; Park 2011; Choi and Ha 2016; Son and Hong 2019). For example, in reporting North Korea's nuclear threats in the 2010s, conservative newspapers described North Korea as a hostile, aggressive, closed society and represented it as irrational and inconsistent in its response to South Korea (Kim and Rho 2011). The conservative newspapers condemned North Korea's rocket launches as a serious violation of its obligations under several UN resolutions, while the progressive newspapers put the blame more on the conservative South Korean government's hard-line reciprocity policy towards North Korea, claiming that this policy provided the North with an excuse for developing its own long-range missile tests. In framing partisan views on denuclearisation, unconditional vs conditional divide characterised reporting on the inter-Korean and US–North Korea summits held in 2018. When the second US–North Korea summit in Hanoi broke down in February 2019, the conservative newspapers condemned North Korea's gesture towards denuclearisation as 'fake', while the progressive papers maintained the view that dialogue should continue (Song 2019).

The ideological gap was also visible in reports on the parliamentary inspections of government organisations, which took place in 2014 and 2018. The press overwhelmingly reported the inspection as an event, with little in-depth commentary or analysis. Newspapers merely repeated what the lawmakers stated, rather than providing any independent, critical reporting. This is a clear indication that the South Korean press reported the parliamentary inspections from a 'political' perspective, rather than a 'policy' perspective (Lee et al. 2020). Similarly, during plenary sessions of the National Assembly, most of the newspapers carry more report on the activities of the political parties than reports and analyses of legislative activities (Choe and Kim 2002).

2.3 Competition Based on Bickering over Non-Substantive Issues

The South Korean press has also been criticised for a lack of coherent and consistent policy platforms and an excessive focus on personality, rather than an attempt to analyse the background and causes of particular conflicts. In reporting the activities of the political parties, newspapers have often confronted each other with mutual accusations and personal attacks, rather than engaging in political debate (Willnat and Min 2016). This was well demonstrated in the reporting of a series of controversial bills tabled in the National Assembly in late April 2019: a bill to create a new corruption investigation agency for high-ranking public officials; two bills to redistribute investigative powers between the police and the prosecution; and reform of the election law. All these proposals sparked enormous conflicts in South Korean politics. In reporting these 'fast-track' items, the press merely reported the claims of the pro-fast track and anti-fast track camps, without any fact-checking or analysis of each camp's claims (*Journalist* 2019). Similarly, the bill to create a new investigative agency under the direct control of the President met with strong opposition from the main opposition United Future Party (renamed 'People Power' in 2020), which claimed that the agency could ultimately be controlled by the President. Despite these controversies, the South Korean press focused its reports more on the fact that 'they are fighting', rather than helping readers understand 'why they are fighting'. A similar observation can be made in relation to reporting on the proposed revision of the election law, which was difficult for ordinary South Koreans to follow because of the complexity involved. Again, the press was more concerned with highlighting the dispute itself, rather than informing readers about the proposed changes to the new election law and their implications (*Media Today* 2019b).

3. The Authoritarian Legacy of the South Korean Press

3.1 Press Clubs and Designated News Beats

One of the main factors affecting the relationship between the press and political parties is the *Kijadan* or press club system. The South Korean press club is similar to that in other countries, for example, the National Press Club in the United States, the National Press Gallery in Australia, and the Lobby in the United Kingdom, in that it is the key mechanism through which political information is disseminated to the public. However, what distinguishes the press club in South Korea from its counterparts in other countries is its functional characteristics, which bind journalists to the informal rules and customs within each of the press clubs (Feldman 1993; Yoon 1994). The press clubs, the remnants of Japanese colonial influence, were introduced in the 1960s by Park Chung-hee and have existed in most government agencies and ministries and political parties, functioning as a channel through which government or party officials distribute political information to the members of the press clubs. Through these press clubs, selected journalists from the mainstream media are invited to access government/party personnel and activities, while this information is denied to the non-mainstream media. Under the authoritarian regimes, the government used press clubs to 'co-opt' the news media, a system which placed pressure on member journalists to report in favour of the government and its policies. Under this practice, the government, in consultation with press club members when necessary, determined who would and would not have access to government news sources.

The role of the press clubs has long been controversial. While supporters have argued that the press club system ensures that journalists have quick access to government sources and information, symbolising the watchdog status of the media, critics have consistently maintained that the system merely produces an unethical 'cosiness' between journalists and their governmental or political sources. More seriously, the press clubs have been seen as a mechanism for corrupting the press (Youm 1994). Indeed, the cumulative effect of the press clubs under the authoritarian regimes was to blunt the knife of aggressive journalism (Halvorsen 1994: 237). Until the end of the 1990s, South Korean journalists had learned how to develop survival mechanism and anticipate the government's will.

Recognising the major issues surrounding the press clubs, such as their exclusivity to the mainstream media, President Roh Moo-hyun introduced a series of reform measures in 2007. These included: the closure of press clubs in government buildings, the holding of regular news briefings, and an end to restrictions on access to official news sources. Roh's reform attempts to transform the existing press club system into a more open briefing system, however, were short-lived. Journalists collectively claimed that Roh's reform measures were designed to restrict their access to political information and mounted strong opposition to the reforms. It is interesting to note that Roh's attempt to introduce a more open and democratic 'briefing system' was rejected not by the opposition party, but by the journalists themselves, in favour of the existing press club system. Press clubs in the government organisations were resumed when Lee Myung-bak won the 2008 presidential election, and since then this system has continued to operate without any serious challenges.

In his early study of press clubs in Japan, Feldman (1993: 69) observed that press clubs shape the nature of the relationship between the information source and journalists, affect the contents of the information provided to journalists, and even affect the role and orientations of journalists themselves. Similar observations can be made in the case of press clubs in South Korea. Most of the journalists working for mainstream news outlets are assigned to the press clubs in government organisations, agencies, and political parties consistent with their background and interests, or at the request of their employers. One of the well-known critical journalists stated that 'the news media outlets send their journalists to the designated government organisations because they want to share power with political elites. They send journalists to the Blue House to show that they can access information from the most powerful politicians in South Korea' (Lee Sang-ho, cited in a KBS journalism talk show on 19 July 2020). Members of the Blue House press club seek access to the inner circles of government as a way of demonstrating their power status. Journalists rankings tend to be determined by the hierarchic power structure of the government organisations to which their press clubs are attached. This hierarchy not only dictates the value and significance of the information distributed to the press clubs, but limits the boundaries of access to the news sources. As such, it comes as no surprise that the biggest scoops to have influenced South Korean politics (e.g. 'Choi Soon-sil gate' and the Cho Kuk scandal) were covered not through the press clubs, but through the information obtained by field journalists. The press club system constricts the role and orientations of journalists.

3.2 Journalists as Politicians

Another characteristic of the relationship between political parties and the press in South Korea is the transformation of journalists into politicians. In democratic countries, political parties and the press are expected to play different roles with different responsibilities. Political parties promote policy positions and party manifestos, while journalists are supposed to be independent of political power and follow their professional ideology (Nygren and Johansson 2019). More specifically, journalists are meant to be 'independent pontificators, objective observers of governance, and a key part of the accountability process, but are not meant to cross over into party politics with all the vile distortions (spin-doctoring) which accompany contemporary adversarial games' (Dempster 2010). In South Korea, however, the functions of the political parties and the press overlap. The parties and the press both want to control public opinion and pursue power by providing their supporters and audience with one-sided views. 'The relationship between the political elite and journalists is about power—who is able to get attention and influence the public image of politics and political actors. It is about conflicting interests as well as mutual interests when both sides are dependent on one another' (Nygren and Johansson 2019: 10).

Prior to the late 1990s, authoritarian governments and political parties (mainly the ruling conservative party) lured elite media personnel into positions of power as a means of controlling the media (Kang 2000; Park 2014). This mechanism enabled the systematic mobilisation of journalists as a network of power elites. It is worth noting that between the 1960s and the 1980s, between 12 and 18 per cent of elected members of parliament were former journalists, the highest proportion of any occupation represented in the parliament (Kang 2004). This was a clear indication of the conservative governments' attempts to co-opt the media, and as a result, the integrity of the practice of journalism during that time suffered significantly. The political representation of journalists under the authoritarian governments has been seen as a symbolic practice that showed the collusion of political power and the press. Since the late 1990s, however, these journalist-turned-politicians have been seen as agents who act as what Ciaglia (2013) calls, 'partisan actors' in the political game.

In the past, concerns about journalist-turned-politicians mainly involved their ability to control the particular media they had worked for before entering parliament. In more recent years, the problem has been seen as one of professional ethics. As parliamentarians, these former journalists' personal interests and the interests of their party easily come to supplant the standards of objectivity and accountability that governed their former careers. However, these concerns are often overshadowed by the tendency to see these journalists-turned-politicians as the profession's success story.

Between 1945 and 2016, a total of 377 South Korean journalists have made the transition to parliamentarians. Nearly half have been re-elected more than twice, and this has resulted in a total of 760 seats in the National Assembly going to former journalists (Kim 2017). Many of these journalist-turned-politicians have served in high-ranking

Table 25.3: Number of journalist-turned-lawmakers who served in the key political positions (1945–2016)

Positions	Numbers
President, prime minister, deputy prime minister	5
Government minister	45
Presidential secretary, senior aide to president, presidential spokesperson	30
Party leader, party president, senior party member	41

Source: Compiled from Kim (2017).

political positions (Table 25.3). This trend has encouraged enthusiastic journalists to pursue a career in politics.

While journalists can transition to politicians and lawmakers through parliamentary elections, they can also become members of political elites through a patronage system that operates during and after changes of government. Many career-conscious journalists who join the political camps during an election become special aides to the president, presidential secretaries, high-ranking government officials, or spokespersons for political parties.

When a journalist moves into politics, it is not only difficult for the public to trust their previous work as a journalist, but it also reinforces the distrust of the press as a whole. This has particularly been the case when the journalist-turned-politicians have been involved in cases of suspected or proven corruption. For example, Choi Si-joong—a former editor/journalist for *Dong-A* (1965–1993), Commissioner of the Korean Communications Commission (KCC), and presidential aide to Lee Myung-bak—was forced to resign at the end of 2011, when he was arrested on bribery charges in relation to the licensing of a complex logistics centre in Seoul. During Lee Myung-bak's presidency, Shin Jae-min (former journalist for *Chosun*, Deputy Minister for Culture, Sports and Tourism), Kim Doo-woo (former journalist for *Joong-Ang*, Senior Presidential Secretary for Public Relations), and Lee Dong-kwan (former journalist for *Dong-A*, Special Presidential Press Secretary) were regarded as key controversial figures involved in media control (*Media Today* 2012). More recently, in 2018, Kim Eui-kyeom, who worked for more than twenty-five years as a senior journalist for *Hankyoreh*, was handpicked by Moon Jae-in as spokesperson for the Blue House. Kim was one of several journalists involved in the revelation of the 'Choi Soon-sil gate' in 2016, which eventually led to the impeachment of Park Geun-hye. However, he was forced to resign in March 2019, following the controversy surrounding a case of illegal real estate speculation, possibly involving inside information. After Kim took out a 1 billion won loan to purchase property in an area marked for redevelopment in the southern part of Seoul, the value of the property reportedly soared far above the amount of the loan itself (*The Korea Herald* 2019).

Since the 1960s, it has been the practice of political parties and the government to recruit experienced journalists into their own camps. While some journalists see this as an opportunity to put their years of advocating for change into action, others merely use their journalistic profiles as a springboard to a political career. Before the late 1990s, the career paths of the journalists in South Korea were decided by authoritarian governments as part of the strategy to control the media. Since that time, the movement of journalists into politics has been an ongoing issue in South Korea, but the large number of former journalists—elected or re-elected in every parliamentary elections, or transformed into politicians with changes in government—is a clear indication that the link between the press and political power is broadly acknowledged.

4. Conclusion

South Korea has made some headway in liberating the media, and the country's press has enjoyed a great degree of freedom since democratisation in 1988. However, this does not mean that watchdog journalism has been fully nurtured. In a country where ideological conflict has always been at the heart of political life, the South Korean press has failed to slough off the remnants of its ideological attachments of the Cold War period. As a result, the increasing level of press freedom since 1988 hardly broadened the ideological spectrum. On the contrary, it has led to the strengthening of press–party parallelism and has deepened lines of antagonistic bipolarisation, further hampering objective reporting. This has resulted in an increasing level of distrust in the press on the part of the public. Research by Reuters Institute showed that the South Korean people's level of trust in the news was the lowest (22 per cent) among the thirty-eight countries studied, and only 21 per cent of South Korean people believed that the South Korean media were monitoring politicians and the exercise of political power (Newman et al. 2019). The same distrust of the media has been found in journalists' self-assessment. According to KPF's Journalist Survey (2017a), only 17.4 per cent of South Korean journalists believed that the South Korean media could be trusted. The same survey showed that 9.8 per cent and 17 per cent of the journalists surveyed regarded the South Korean media as 'fair' and 'accurate', respectively (KPF 2017b: 70).

This chapter has also revealed that the interplay between the press and the political elites throughout the three decades of democratic transition has continued to be marked by elements of a parallel relationship between the two. Choi (2018: 37–38) identifies the main characteristics of political parties in South Korea as follow: an extremely narrow ideological spectrum among the political parties; a lack of diversity in the representation of voices; a lack of cooperation among political parties and politicians; and, a lack of consensus in approaching the most pertinent issues of conflict, that is, 'class conflict' and 'inter-Korean relations'. The major features of the South Korean press reviewed in this chapter mirror these characteristics. Although 'middle-ground' newspapers do exist, the conservative–progressive ideological spectrum has been too rigid to reflect diverse voices and opinions. The two-party-centred political reporting has hampered the growth of diversity in the range of themes and perspectives represented in the news, as well as in-depth analysis. Apart from an excessive focus on partisan conflicts, political reporting tends to be event-focused, and derived from one-sided sources and information. These features reinforce the trends that have characterised the major political parties since the early days of democratic transition in the 1990s to the more recent top-down democratic regime. Another feature evident in the three decades of democratic transition is that the journalism practice and operational practice of the press have not significantly improved. As shown in this chapter, the legacy of authoritarianism—the press club system and the phenomenon of journalists transforming themselves into politicians—has been a feature of contemporary debates about the press–party parallelism that still exists in South Korea.

Political parties and the press have been seen to play prime roles in democratic societies as guardians of public accountability. Ironically, however, parties and the press have emerged as the major contributors to the current conservative–progressive divisions in South Korea. Indeed, these two institutions, which reflect the opinions of citizens and shape public opinion, have polarised opinions of party supporters and the newspaper readership. Political parties lead citizens' opinions in more biased directions, and the polarised media both reinforce and amplify this situation. In this sense, it is fair to say that the press in South Korea has been continuously subjugated to its own political and ideological commitments—pursuing its own interests within the boundaries of political parallelism (Willnat and Min 2016)—and this has been the main barrier to the growth of more probing journalism.

Bibliography

Allern, S. (2010), 'From Party Agitators to Independent Pundits. The Hanged Historical Roles of Newspaper and Television Journalists in Norwegian Election Campaigns', *Northern Lights. Film and Media Studies Yearbook* 8, 141–66.

Choe, S. Y., and Kim, H. S. (2002), 'A Study of Negativism in Newspaper Reporting of the National Assembly', *Korean Journal of Legislative Studies* 8(1), 158–197.

Choi, H. J. (2010), 'A Study on the Diversity of Korean Newspapers: Analysing the Tendencies of Covering Three Major Issues', *Korean Journalism Research* 54(3), 399–426.

Choi, J. H., and Ha, J. H. (2016), 'News Frames of Korean Unification Issues: Comparing Conservative and Progressive Newspapers', *Korean Journal of Communication Studies* 24(2), 127–151.

Choi, J. J. (2018), 'Korean Democracy in a Hyper-Centralized State'. in Mosler, H. B., Lee, E. J., and Kim, H. J., eds., *The Quality of Democracy in Korea. Three Decades after Democratization*, 27–49 (Cham, Switzerland: Palgrave Macmillan).

Ciaglia, A. (2013), 'Politics in the Media and the Media in Politics: A Comparative Study of the Relationship between the Media and Political Systems in Three European Countries', *European Journal of Communication* 28(5), 541–555.

Citizens' Coalition for Democratic Media (CCDM) (2019), *Television News Coverage of Cho-Kuk Scandal* (Seoul: Citizens' Coalition for Democratic Media).

Dempster, Q. (2010), 'Journalists as Politicians', *The Drum*, 13 October, https://www.abc.net.au/news/2010-10-13/journalists-as-politicians/2296686, accessed 30 November 2021.

Feldman, O. (1993), 'Relations between the Diet and the Japanese Press', *Journalism Quarterly* 64(2), 845–849.

Hahn, K. S., Ryu, S. J., and Park, S. J. (2015), 'Fragmentation in the Twitter Following of News Outlets: The Representation of South Korean Users' Ideological and Generational Cleavage', *Journalism & Mass Communication Quarterly* 92(1), 56–76.

Hallin, D., and Mancini, P. (2004), *Comparing Media Systems* (Cambridge: Cambridge University Press).

Halvorsen, D. E. (1994), 'Confucianism Defies the Computer: The Conflict within the Korean Press', in *Elite Media amidst Mass Culture: A Critical Look at Mass Communication in Korea*, 215–271 (Seoul: Nanam).

Hong, S. K., Ha, T. K., Sohn, K. J., and Lee, J. C. (2011), *News Coverage of North Korea since Kim Dae Jung Government: Focusing on Human Rights in North Korea and Security Issues* (Seoul: Korea Press Foundation).

Hwang, C. S., Lee, K. S., and Kim, C. S. (2007), *North–South Summit and Media Coverage* (Seoul: Korea Press Foundation).

Iyengar, S., and Han, K. (2009), 'Red Media, Blue Media', *Journal of Communication* (59), 19–39.

Joongang Tongyang Broadcasting Company (JTBC) (2020), 'Code of Ethics', http://jtbc.joins.com/company/ethics, accessed 30 November 2021.

Journalist (2019), 'Who Should Be Blamed: National Assembly or the Media?', *Journalist*, 8 May, www.journalist.or.kr/news/article.html?no=46182, accessed 30 November 2021.

Jung, C. W. (2020), 'Declining TV Anchors, Emerging YouTube Anchors', *Newspapers and Broadcasting* 591, 10–14.

Kang, J. M. (2000), *Change of Power: The History of Korean Press* (Seoul: InmulgwaSasang-Sa).

Kang, M. K. (2004), 'Media War and the Crisis of Journalism Practice', *Korean Journal of Journalism & Communications Studies* 48(5), 319–48.

Kim, D. Y. (2015), 'Media Manners and Frames on the North Korea Nuclear Test: Comparing with Conservative, Progressive and Local Newspaper', *Journal of Communication Science* 15(1), 48–87.

Kim, K. H., and Rho, K. Y. (2011), 'A Comparative Study of News Reporting about North Korea on Newspapers in South Korea', *Korean Journalism Research* 55(1), 361–87.

Kim, S. E. (2017), 'From Journalists to Politicians: A Socio-Historical Analysis of Korean 'Polinalists', *Korean Journal of Journalism & Communication Studies* 61(3), 7–54.

Kim, Y. O. (2009), *Partisan Press seen by the Readers*. Seoul: Korea Press Foundation.

Ko, J. S. (2020), 'The Comparison of the White Book and Black Book of Cho-Kuk', *ShindongA* 733, 122–135.

Korea Press Foundation (KPF) (2017a), *Korea Press Yearbook 2017* (Seoul: Korea Press Foundation).

KPF (2017b), *Korean Journalists Survey 2017* (Seoul: Korea Press Foundation).

KPF (2018), *Korea Press Yearbook 2018* (Seoul: Korea Press Foundation).

KPF (2019), *Korea Press Yearbook 2019* (Seoul: Korea Press Foundation).

Kwak, K. S. (2012), *Media and Democratic Transition in South Korea* (Abingdon and New York: Routledge).

Lee, S. S. (2007), 'The News Report of the North–South Summits', *Newspapers and Broadcasting* 442, 72–79.

Lee, W. S. (2007a), 'Ideological Disposition and Assessment of the Government Policies Appeared in Media Reports on the Subject of Inter-Korean Issues', *Korean Journalism Review* 1(2), 88–112.

Lee, W. S. (2007b), 'Media Coverage of North–South Issue during the Rho Mu-Hyun Government', *Northeast Asia Research* 52, 325–366.

Lee, W. S., Yang, Y. Y., and Bae, J. Y. (2020), 'Affiliation between the Media and Political Parties: The Media's Asymmetrical Agenda for Reporting National Audits by Political Parties', *Korea Journal of Legislative Studies* 26(2), 73–111.

Media Today (2019a), 'Democratic Party–MBC, Future Korea Party–TV Chosun: Results of Media Today/Research View Survey', *Media Today*, 1 November, www.mediatoday.co.kr/news/articleView.html?idxno=203370, accessed 30 November 2021.

Media Today (2019b), 'Election Law, Democracy and Conservative Newspapers', *Media Today*, 28 December, www.mediatoday.co.kr/news/articleView.html?idxno=204397, accessed 30 November 2021.

Media Today (2012), 'Yesterday's Journalists Become Today's Politicians', *Media Today*, 11 January, www.mediatoday.co.kr/news/articleView.html?idxno=99711, accessed 30 November 2021.

Min, H., and Lee, W. (2015), 'Voter's Ideological Orientation and Media Use', *Korean Party Studies Review* 14(1), 157–176.

Newman, N., Fletcher, R., Kalogeropoulos, A., and Nielsen, R. (2019), *Reuters Institute Digital News Report 2019*, Reuters Institute (Oxford: Oxford University Press).

Nygren, G., and Johansson, K. M. (2019), 'The Interplay of Media and the Political Executive Introduction and Framework', in Johansson, K. M., and Nygren, G., eds., *Close and Distant. Political Executive–Media Relations in Four Countries*, 9–26 (Göteborg: Nordicom).

Park, K. S. (2011), 'A News Frame Analysis on Socially Controversial Issue: Comparing Three Korean Daily Newspapers Attitude on Lee Myung-Bak Government's Four Major Rivers Restoration Project', *Korean Journalism Research* 55(4), 5–26.

Park, Y. K. (2014), 'Changes in Professional Identity of Journalists during the Park Chung-hee Regime', *Journal of Communication Research* 51(2), 34–76.

PD Journal (2019), 'Survey on Trust in Media', *PD Journal*, 6 September, https://www.pdjournal.com/news/articleView.html?idxno=70435, accessed 30 November 2021.

Son, J. S., and Hong, J. H. (2019), 'Newspaper Frame Analysis on the Nuclear Crisis in Korean Peninsula', *Journal of Political Science & Communication* 22(3), 175–210.

Song, H. J. (2019), 'Fake Denuclearisation vs Dialogue: Partisan Press Framing of USA–North Korea Summit', *Newspaper and Broadcasting* 580, 13–17.

Song, I. D. (2014), 'Biased Media Perception Based on Media Partisanship and Audience's Political Disposition: In Case of Newspaper Editorials', *Communication Theory* 10(3), 222–257.

The Economist (2020), 'Sensitive Seoul; Banyan', *The Economist*, 22 August.

The Korea Herald (2019), 'Blue House Spokesman Offers to Resign Over Real Estate Controversy', *The Korea Herald*, 29 March, www.koreaherald.com/view.php?ud=20190329000413, accessed 30 November 2021.

Willnat, L., and Min, Y. (2016), 'The Emergence of Social Media Politics in South Korea. The Case of the 2012 Presidential Election', in Bruns, A., Enli, G., Skogerbø, E., Larsson, A. O., and Christensen, C., eds., *The Routledge Companion to Social Media and Politics*, 391–405 (London: Routledge).

Yoon, Y. C. (1994), 'Democratisation and Media Control in South Korea', a paper presented at the nineteenth IAMCR conference, 3–8 July, Seoul.

Youm, K. H. (1994), 'South Korea's Experiment with a Free Press', *Gazette* 53, 111–126.

CHAPTER 26

PUBLIC INTELLECTUALS

NAMHEE LEE

1. INTRODUCTION

INTELLECTUALS, whose character and social role have evolved closely following the vicissitudes of history, have remained central in modern Korean political, social, and cultural history. Intellectuals write and speak on the issues of importance to society on behalf of the public and not for their personal, religious, or ideological interests. 'Public intellectual', however, is a new term, first coined in the 1980s in the United States, which began to circulate in South Korea only recently. While the term generally denotes a publicly engaged intellectual, it also has been used to refer to a celebrity intellectual who has achieved name recognition in public, often with a negative connation of a careerist ambition for fame or monetary gain. There is yet no clear consensus on what makes an intellectual a public intellectual or how a public intellectual is different from a political, cultural, or religious leader.

Even if the term itself is relatively new, Korea has in fact had a rich and long tradition of intellectuals playing the role of the public intellectual throughout its history. Key to intellectuals' social criticism was the Confucian concept of knowledge, which was a source for both political power and prestige, as well as a mandate that knowledge be employed not only to enhance one's own status and position in society, but also to maintain the proper and stable order of society; that is, to acquire knowledge was to take up the moral responsibility to speak the truth, which was presumed to be universal, and to rectify what has gone amiss in society. For Confucian scholars, scholarly and moral enterprises were in principle indistinguishable. One's moral authority came from the fact that one practiced what one knew—the principle of *jihaeng ilchi* ('correspondence between knowledge and conduct') (Lee 2007).

The principle of *jihaeng ilchi* has remained one of the core tenets for anyone who takes up the role of public intellectual. Starting from the late nineteenth century, intellectuals' engagement with creating the public sphere became another critical horizon as they sought to interpret and guide the development of the public sphere and public discourse. The group of intellectuals involved in the 'civilisation and enlightenment' movement produced knowledge of modern Korea that also became the basis for the nationalist discourse, which constituted the public sphere of the era (Schmid 2002). During the Japanese colonial period (1910–1945), the recovery of Korea's sovereignty was widely acknowledged as the goal of the nation; as such, those who resisted the colonial rule, directly or indirectly, constituted the era's public intellectuals.

After Korea regained its liberation from Japan in 1945, the future vision and trajectory of the nation and what constituted 'public' became deeply contested. The country's division by two competing superpowers at the time (in 1945) and the subsequent establishment of separate governments (in 1948), the Korean War (1950–1953), and the decades of authoritarian regimes (1948–1987) that gave rise to the vociferous democratisation movement propelled intellectuals to rise as dissident intellectuals. South Korea's democratic transition in the late 1980s, combined with the worldwide transformation of the late 1980s, has attenuated the organic linkage between the public intellectual and the democratisation movement.

This chapter will provide a brief overview of the evolution of the ideas, roles, and characteristics of the public intellectual, with the main focus on the post-democratisation transition period, starting from the 1990s. In what follows, section 2 briefly discusses the core elements of the public intellectuals during the authoritarian regimes and presents some of the representative figures. Section 3 focuses on the post-1987 period and shows how the combined forces of the institutionalisation of liberal democracy, the simultaneous path of neoliberal restructuring, and the advent of the internet that brought about the information revolution as well as the changed status of intellectuals in general in South Korean society, among others, transformed the intellectual landscape in general and the concept of the public intellectual in particular. Section 4 analyses a new type of public intellectual tentatively called 'counter expert', who engages with social issues based on and utilising their professional expertise. A concluding section summarises the key points.

2. Public Intellectuals during the Authoritarian Period

In post-1945 South Korea, the emergence of the public intellectual was intimately connected to the evisceration of civil society and the overdeveloped state, manifested in pervasive political repression; economic inequality; the collusion between the state and corporate conglomerates (*jaebeol*); massive rural-to-urban migration, which led to the rise of the urban poor; and low wages and harsh working conditions for workers, among others. The state ideology of anticommunism, encapsulated in the infamous National Security Law that stood above and beyond the nation's constitution, functioned to silence any alternative visions and critical voices to the existing political order. A small number of intellectuals invoked their duty to 'reveal the falsehood of the ruling system and enlighten the public'. They were distinguished by their willingness to suspend their own personal interests and welfare in the pursuit and defence of what they perceived to be the truth and universal values. Most crucial in their pursuit of truth were various forms of writing—historical accounts of past events and critical analyses of current issues, fiction, poetry, cultural and social commentary, biographies and autobiographies, and manifestos and petitions. Their writings become the vehicle of a public discussion about the nature of society—the current condition, the gap between its promise and its reality, its conflicts, its future vision, and direction. Their activities, more often than not, were considered subversive by the state and led them to dismissal from their jobs, house arrest, detention, torture, imprisonment, and even death in the case of Jang Jun-ha, the founder of the influential journal *Sasanggye* ('World of Thought'), whose cause of death has not been determined to this day.

From the 1970s, as the democratisation movement that became known as the *minjung* ('common people') movement erupted and spread widely, the public intellectual became an integral part of this movement. *Minjung* denoted an alternative interpretive framework, in which ordinary South Koreans—such as farmers, factory workers, and the urban poor—were to be the main subjects of historical development, rather than just victims of oppression (Lee 2007). Together with the *minjung* movement, intellectuals participated in creating and sustaining the 'counterpublic sphere', a sphere in which they challenged the state-established public agenda and redefined the grounds of social and political discourse. This process involved re-evaluating and contesting the most foundational and normative ideological underpinnings of the state: the state ideology of anticommunism and the implied perpetuation of the division of North and South, South Korea's 'unequal' relationship with the United States, the priority of economic growth over distributive justice, and the attendant subordination of labour, among others (Lee 2007).

Ham Seok-heon (1901–1989), philosopher, educator, and writer, as well as social movement activist, was one of the representative public intellectuals in post-1945 South Korea. He played the role of prophet to 'awaken public consciousness', providing a trenchant critique of the Park Chung-hee regime from the time of the military coup, when other intellectuals were largely silent. Ham also founded a monthly journal, *Ssiasui sori* (*Voice of Seed*) in 1970, which articulated the *minjung*-orientated perspective on the pressing issues of the time. Ham's thinking was also influential in the articulation of *minjung* sociology and *minjung* theology during this period (Kang 2017). Ham was arrested and imprisoned numerous times.

Lee Yeong-hui (1929–2010) was another public intellectual active in the 1970s and early 1980s. His 1974 *Jeonhwan sidae eui nolli* (*Logic of the Era of Transition*), published at the height of the Yusin rule (1972–1979), and a piercing critique of the 'fanatical' anticommunism, the 'barbarity' of military dictatorship, and South Korea's involvement in the Vietnam War, among other topics, was a must-read among the intellectuals, university students, and anyone who considered themselves to be socially conscious (it was reprinted thirteen times in just two years and was banned in 1979). Lee wrote: 'My only aim to write starts from and ends with the pursuit of truth. Truth cannot be monopolised by one person and needs to be shared. Writing is an act of rational challenge to the idolatry' (Yoon 2008). Lee was arrested five times, stood trial four times, was imprisoned, dismissed from his earlier journalist position, and later dismissed from his teaching position twice from the same university.

Yet another representative public intellectual of the authoritarian period is Baek Nak-cheong [Paik Nak-chung] (1931–), English literature professor and founder of the quarterly *Changjak kwa bipyeong* (*Creation and Criticism*), a leading journal known for its critical intellectual discourse for more than half a century. A renowned figure of 'national literature' and 'participatory' (as opposed to 'pure') literature in the 1970s and 1980s, Baek devoted himself to the analysis of the relationships between the national division and the two Koreas' ongoing socio-political problems and to the promotion of a deeper understanding and overcoming of the division system. He was also dismissed from the university between 1974 and 1980, and the journal was banned between 1980 and 1988 (Hwang 2016).

In all of these cases, the intellectuals saw themselves as a social critic first, more than an intellectual. If any conflict arose between an intellectual's commitment to the public interest and the interests of academic or professional knowledge, each would have shown clearly that public interest came first. As such, they were also thrust into leadership positions in democratisation movement organisations.

3. The Post-1987 Neoliberal Order and Intellectual Life

Since the late 1980s, the character of intellectual life, especially its relationship to society, has undergone a fundamental shift. South Korea successfully transitioned to a representative democracy in 1987, and since then has undergone a high level of democratisation in all spheres of public life. However, a series of economic downturns and financial crises in 1997 (known as the 'IMF [International Monetary Fund] Crisis') veered the country simultaneously down a path of all-out neoliberal restructuring, giving priority and acquiescing to the demands of the market. As in other parts of the world, by the early 2000s, South Korea was governed by neoliberal rationality, where all features of life were becoming economised.

By the 1990s, the global transformation ushered in by the demise of the 'actually existing socialism', the progress of formal democracy and the growth of civil society, the profusion of consumer culture, the rise of the internet and the consequent advent of the information age, and the high number of the university educated, radically transformed the status and role of intellectuals in society. Intellectuals also 'failed' to predict the coming of the IMF Crisis, which contributed further to their fallen status. The Kim Dae-jung government also initiated a campaign called *sinjisigin* ('New Intellectuals'), calling for citizens to acquire new kinds of knowledge to meet the demands of the digital age and the information–intellectual industry. The campaign was to promote the country's global competitiveness, among other things, and to give due recognition to individuals who had made significant contributions in the fields that had not been previously recognised. The state project was widely criticised as reflecting a societal tendency to value knowledge only for its potential commodity worth (Kang 2015). All of these developments made it difficult to argue for the relevance of the educated scholarly elite or the virtues of disinterested academic research. The traditional role of the intellectual as the prophetic voice and conscience of the nation was fast becoming a relic of the past by the 1990s (Kyunghyang Sinmun teukbyeolchwijaetim 2008). In fact, anyone who harboured such an 'illusion' would be considered to be behind the times, or even obstinate—someone who was unable to adjust to the transformed reality.

3.1 The Rise of the Citizens' Movement and Polifessors

With the democratisation, social movements also went through profound changes. Post-1987, social movements no longer had an overarching goal or centre, ideologically or organisationally; the state was no longer the single locus of power; and no single issue could galvanise society as it had done in the previous decades. A dizzying array of new public issues began to emerge, ranging from issues on tactics and strategies for consolidating democratisation further, to consumer and environmental protection, to LGBTQ rights, which led to the mushrooming of what became known as the *simin undong* ('the citizens' movement'), led by autonomous associations, including diverse activist groups and interest groups (Choi 2000).

Many of the intellectuals and former movement activists were involved in founding such organisations, *Gyeongsillyeon* ('Citizens' Coalition for Economic Justice' [CCEJ]) being one of the most well known. Founded in 1989 to promote economic justice and protection of the environment, many of its campaigns, such as the public concept of land ownership, use of real name in financial transactions, asset declarations of government officials, autonomy of the Korean Bank, transparency of political funds, and revision of election law, were adopted as policy by the government. The 'Minority Shareholders' Campaign' spearheaded by *Chamyeo yeondae* ('People's Solidarity for Participatory Democracy' [PSPD]), organised in 1994, was yet another representative case of the citizens' movement. Kim Dong-choon, co-founder of the PSPD and Professor of Sociology at SungKongHoe University, became a well-respected public intellectual during this period for his continuous engagement with issues of critical importance, both as a scholar and as a public servant, serving as the Commissioner for the Truth and Reconciliation Commission (Kim 2012).

Some of the high-profile members of these organisations went into politics after a few years of activism, having gained a working relationship with government on various policy issues. Some of them moved on to become high-ranking officials of the administration or national assembly members, a phenomenon encapsulated in the widely circulated term 'polifessor', a compound of 'politics' and 'professor' (Kang 2015). It is difficult to discern if and to what degree the disdain with which the term was frequently invoked reflected the sentiment of the public or the mass media that coined the term in 2012. It could very well be that the public at large saw intellectuals' institutional affiliation and professionalism as 'betrayals' of the higher purposes of intellectual life. The changing status and role of intellectuals in society and their relationship to the public have also to do with the changing nature and status of universities in society. Universities have increasingly become embedded in larger political economies, subject to relentless 'specialisation' and 'professionalisation', as well as to markets, and a close working relationship with the neoliberal state (Kang et al. 2017).

3.2 Intellectuals during the Conservative Era (2008–2017) and the Rise of Socialtainers

With the presidencies of Lee Myung-bak (2008–2013) and Park Geun-hye (2013–2017), South Korea saw society moving towards the right and changing relations with intellectuals. Some of the prominent former *minjung* practitioners became members of neoconservative New Right (Lee 2019). One of the iconic public intellectuals during the authoritarian period, poet Kim Ji-ha, known for his biting satire of the Park Chung-hee regime, announced his support of Park, daughter of former dictator Park Chung-hee, under whose watch Kim was sentenced to death (later commuted). Kim also began to indiscriminately accuse some of the former activists of the democratisation movement as mindless followers of North Korean ideology (*jongbuk jwapa*). The label of *jongbuk jwapa* was all the more incriminating since it was used indiscriminately by the state and the conservative mass media to charge anyone whom they perceived to be political opponents of the governments of Lee and Park, and has functioned to discredit groups or individuals associated with the previous governments of Kim Dae-jung (1998–2003) and Roh Moo-hyun (2003–2008) (Doucette and Koo 2013). Kim's public renouncement of the *minjung* paradigm and what it had previously stood for became a bellwether of what was to come.

Even before the conservative governments' wholesale discrediting of the allegedly soft-headed liberalism of the previous governments of Kim Dae-jung and Roh Moo-hyun for their various reform drives and engaging North Korea through economic assistance co-operation, the conservatives had been relentless in their scathing and often debilitating criticism of the liberal governments. The intellectuals behind their reforms, who, more often than not, had been activists in the democratisation movement of the earlier period, also became the target of criticism for the conservatives (Kyunghyang Sinmun teukbyeolchwijaetim 2008). In this context, it seemed as if the role of the public intellectual fell to the conservatives. The trio of ultra-conservative mass media was responsible for promoting the prominent figures of the right, such as science fiction writer Bok Geo-il and the celebrated novelist Yi Mun-yeol, as the public intellectuals of the era. In fact, the media's vigorous promotion of Bok and Yi, providing various platforms for them to comment on the various issues of South Korean society, enhanced the power of their political remarks on the affairs of South Korean society. In the case of Bok, and to a certain degree Yi as well, there was a convergence between their literary output, especially works published from the late 1990s until the 2000s, and their public espousals of neoliberal, free-market convictions and their ferocious anti-communism stance (Lee 2019).

The Lee and Park governments also resorted to measures used by the previous authoritarian regimes to silence critique and opposition, by interfering with and trying to control the press (Park 2011a) and compiling blacklists. Reflecting the transformed nature of South Korean society, where media and popular culture play an increasingly important role in arbitrating social issues, the blacklists included many who were called *gaenyeom insa* or 'socialtainers'—celebrity figures who express their opinions on social issues and advocate social justice. Much like 'polifessors', the term is a compound of 'social' and 'entertainers', and was coined by the mass media around 2008, when a few celebrity figures expressed their critical views of the government decision to import US beef that was suspected of being contaminated with mad cow disease. Socialtainers range from film directors, actors, musicians, and media and TV personalities to novelists, and they are usually active on social networking service (SNS) sites, such as Twitter and Facebook (Park et al. 2014).

The scope of issues that socialtainers tackle has also widened over time. Actor Kim Yeo-jin staged a one-person protest demanding the reduction of college tuition by half; she supported the Hongik University's dismissed janitorial workers; and she led one of the most memorable solidarity movements called 'Hope Bus', a caravan of ordinary citizens coming from all walks of life to support the striking union workers at Hanjin Heavy Industries in Busan in 2011 (Choe 2011). Popular singers Lee Seung-hwan, Lee Hyo-ri, and comedian Kim Je-dong gave their support for the dismissed workers at Ssang Yong Motors. When refugees from Yemen arrived in Jeju Island seeking asylum in the summer of 2018, actor Jeong U-seong was one of the few public figures who spoke out for the granting of asylum, instigating the public debate that lasted for nearly two months (Kang and Lee 2019).

Blacklisted individuals were removed from their leadership positions as directors of a government funded cultural organisation, from their assigned roles on a radio or TV programme, or faced cancellation of their fellowships, grants, or performances or art exhibitions with the vaguest of explanations (Park et al. 2014). They were also subjected to public sanction and criticised for seeking to further their own fame rather than the security of the country, as in the case of Jeong U-seong, or more generally that they should not make their opinion public (Kang and Lee 2019).

By virtue of their ability to capture the attention of the public and their willingness to engage with the public and intervene in current debates, socialtainers play a similar role as the dissident intellectuals of earlier times. In an age of instant communication, their engagement with the public is necessarily time bound, and they are sometimes criticised for oversimplifying the issues at hand or holding contradictory views. But they do challenge the traditional modes of intellectual thinking and writing, as increasingly intellectuals need to operate on various platforms using multiple rhetorical strategies. For intellectuals wishing to engage with the public, writing and thinking have become part of a wide-ranging public performance.

4. New Types of Public Intellectuals: 'Counter-Experts'

Even as the neoliberal order has become relentless and ubiquitous and the phenomenon of socialtainers has blurred the boundary between celebrity activism and the traditional public intellectual, there has also emerged a new group of intellectuals whose mode of engagement with social issues differs from the previous public intellectuals. While they are prompted by the same sense of responsibility and desire to offer alternative scenarios in regard to topics of a political, social, and ethical nature, what distinguishes them from their predecessors is that they engage in issues on the basis of their professional expertise, whether as a physicist, medical doctor, or engineer. They examine issues that are in the domain of their own specialised field but bring in their knowledge and expertise to be used for a greater gain for, and to have a greater impact on, society (Kim 2012). In so doing, they put forth a new public agenda or dispute, or reshape a government policy, or contest truth on a scientific basis. Sociologist Kim Jong-yeong calls these intellectuals *daehang jeonmunga* ('counter-experts') (Kim 2016). This category of intellectual is analogous to Michel Foucault's 'specific intellectual', who, rather than claiming universal truth, as in the case of the previous era, engages in the issues that are congruent with their field of specialisation. The aim of the intervention is not to expand or universalise the influence of their knowledge, or to speak on others' behalf, but to make use of their knowledge and analyses for the issue at hand. By focusing on a specific problem that has larger societal significance, the intellectual feels compelled to speak to an audience broader than that normally prescribed by their specialty (Foucault 1977).

Discussed below are only some of the more well-known cases: medical doctor Gongyu Jeong-ok, who, in the process of working with Samsung workers who became ill with leukaemia, made occupation illness a social agenda item and public health issue; environmental engineer Kim Jeong-wook, who contested the Lee Myung-bak government's Major Rivers Restoration Project; and physicist Seung-Hun Lee and political scientist Jae Jung Suh, who contested the international team report on the cause of the explosion of the navy ship Cheonan.

4.1 Industrial Medicine and Samsung's Semiconductor Industry

Samsung is currently one of the largest semiconductor manufacturers in the world. In March 2007, Hwang Yu-mi, a former worker at a Samsung Electronics factory in Giheung, died of leukaemia. In June, Hwang's bereaved family applied for industrial accident compensation, the first time this had been done for a semiconductor plant employee. The claim was rejected on the grounds that 'the causal relationship between work and disease was not established'. Five months later, nineteen labour unions, labour health civic groups, and human rights organisations formed the Joint Action Committee for Learning the Facts about the Outbreak of Leukemia at Samsung Semiconductors and for Securing the Basic Rights of Labor. At the time when the committee was launched, Hwang's family was still the only family who had applied for industrial accident compensation for a semiconductor worker. But after it became known that there were a number of cases of workers getting sick or dying of leukaemia, lymphoma, and multiple sclerosis, not only at Samsung semiconductor plants but also at plants run by other companies, the action committee changed its name to Supporters for the Health and Rights of People in the Semiconductor Industry (SHARPS, *Banollim* in Korean) and launched its campaign to learn the truth about occupational diseases and industrial accidents in the semiconductor industry and to provide workers with compensation (Gongyu 2010).

Gongyu Jeong-ok, who was trained in industrial medicine and has worked with factory workers as a member of the grass-roots organisation, Hanguk Nodong Anjeon Bogeon Yeunguso (Korea Institute of Labor Safety and Health), was at the front and centre of *Banollim* for more than a decade. The primary aim of *Banollim* was to obtain proper treatment and right to livelihood through recognition of the workers' industrial accident, to demand that the company provide compensation to victims' families and acknowledge the link between their factory work and leukaemia and other diseases, and to prevent such accidents from happening again by improving the working conditions that contribute to accidents.

Samsung's notorious 'no union' policy made it difficult for Gongyu to organise victims of the occupational diseases or to prove the link between the factory work and the cause of the diseases. Not only did workers not have an organisational base, but they also did not even have basic information about their work environment (such as the names of chemicals they were working with), nor were they able to participate in the investigation of their working conditions. Few who were still working at Samsung were willing to testify. Many were afraid that their family members, friends, or close associates might be penalised for providing testimony about the working environment and their illnesses. Some of the victims were 'bought off' by Samsung to testify against their fellow workers or to deny what their fellow victims testified during official investigations (Gongyu 2010).

Despite many difficulties and obstacles, Gongyu persisted in her efforts to gather information about the working environment at Samsung's factory and the nature of diseases, meeting with the victims and their family members, organising protests at various sites, publishing her findings in journals, and presenting at academic conferences. Three years later, in May 2010, fifty Samsung workers who had been affected came forward. In November 2018, Samsung and the family members reached a deal and signed an agreement to accept the mediation ruling of an arbitration committee. Samsung Electronics also issued a statement of apology, acknowledging only partial management responsibility, but not a causal link with the leukaemia cases. It was a hard-won compromise that no one had thought possible before. The acceptance of the mediation plan also marked the end of the demonstrations, which had continued for 1,023 days since beginning on 7 October 2015.

4.2 Environmental Engineering and the Four Major Rivers Restoration Project

Professor Kim Jeong-wook was an environmental engineer by training and taught at the Graduate School of Environmental Studies at Seoul National University from 1976 until he retired in 2011. His public engagement began even before the then president Lee Myung-bak announced his $19.2 billion public works scheme called the Major Rivers Restoration Project (hereafter the Restoration Project) in January 2009. Befitting his image as a former chief executive officer (CEO) of Hyundai and his nickname as the Bulldozer, Lee designated the Restoration Project as a centrepiece of his government's Green New Deal, a strategy of economic growth through ecofriendly projects in an era of climate change and scarcity of resources. The Restoration Project sought to strengthen the three main functions of rivers: ensuring water quantity, water quality, and water environment, as well as facilitating a water-friendly environment where nature and people coexist. Lee promised that the Restoration Project would also generate thousands of jobs, while providing a model for environmentally sound development. It involved deepening the waterbeds of the four major rivers in the nation and building three dams and sixteen giant weirs (barriers that alter river flow) to increase water reserves and slow down water flow. Earlier, Lee had announced as an election pledge a similar grand project linking the Han and Nakdong Rivers to create a 'Grand Waterway Project', which was scrapped due to public opposition.

Opposition to the Restoration Project arose immediately and spread widely, from ordinary citizens, to environmental non-governmental organisations (NGOs), to the opposition parties. The Nationwide Response Committee for the Four Major Rivers Restoration, which was made up of environmental civic groups and various religious groups of Catholics, Protestants, Buddhists, and Won Buddhists, as well as ordinary citizens, carried out nation-wide protests. The Lee administration and construction companies mobilised legal resources and used other strategies to break the demonstrations up, from asking the courts to levy daily fines (up to $8,500) against protestors who occupied the construction sites to cancelling a popular investigative journalism programme, MBC's *PD Note*, which questioned the feasibility of the project, three hours before it was scheduled to air (Im and Ryu 2010).

At the forefront of scholarly effort to provide scientific analyses for the opposition was Professor Kim Jeong-wook. He co-founded and became a senior representative of the National Association of Professors against the Grand Waterway Project, launched on 25 March 2008. Kim began to mobilise experts in various fields, such as economics, civil engineering, the environment, logistics, culture, local development, and real estate, to examine the feasibility and potential impact of the Waterway Project. As the government cancelled the Waterway Project and launched the Restoration Project, scholars of the Association and the opposition maintained that despite some major changes from the earlier plan, the Restoration Project included core elements of the Waterway Project, such as dredging work and weir construction.

More specifically, the scholars argued that the government did not fully comply with official review processes, such as a preliminary feasibility study and an environmental impact assessment. The evaluation, conducted within just three months, did not produce any valid basic data and did not properly estimate the environmental impact of the project (Lah et al. 2015). They also argued that the Restoration Project was against the current trend of the global flood control policy paradigm, which had evolved from embankment works and dam construction to wetland creation and flood plain restoration; that dredging river bottoms would disrupt the ecosystem and that the new dams would create catch basins, worsening pollution and flooding. In terms of both water supply and quality, the Restoration Project did not fulfil its intended goals: the water stored by the project could not reach the arid regions on the upper reaches of small tributaries, where water shortage was most acute. As for improving water quality, the main causes of water pollution in South Korea are insufficiently treated waste water from households and industry and the leaching of nutrients and pesticides from agriculture (Kim 2013). Rather than creating new jobs, scholars estimated that the Restoration Project would cost Korean taxpayers around 800 million US dollars per year in maintenance alone, once the construction of sixteen dams and river dredging, the two main elements of the project, were completed (Park 2011b). Based on their findings, and together with more than 10,000 individuals and civic organisations, scholars and environmental organisations filed a lawsuit against the Restoration Project on November 2009 and again in May 2010 (Park 2011a).

4.3 Physics and the Cheonan Incident

On 26 March 2010, the South Korean naval vessel ROKS Cheonan sank off the country's west coast near the sea border with North Korea, killing 46 of 104 seamen on board. Barely two months later, on 20 May 2010, an official investigation led by South Korea, with a team of international experts called the Joint Civilian–Military Investigation Group (JIG) presented a summary of its findings, concluding that the warship had been sunk by a North Korean torpedo fired by a midget submarine.

There were many inconsistencies in the conclusions of the report, leading several media outlets and the public, including minority party politicians and the two members of the JIG, to express their doubts about the conclusions. In a poll commissioned by Seoul National University's Institute for Peace and Unification Studies, only 32.5 per cent of respondents expressed confidence in the report's conclusions (Certo et al. 2010). The Cheonan incident quickly became one of the most contentious political issues: it was not only South Korea's worst military disaster since the end of the three-year Korean War in 1953, but the government also tried to muzzle any criticism or questions from the public with legal and extra-legal measures, all the while heightening the tension with North

Korea with its retaliatory measures, which included imposing sanctions and a call to halt all inter-Korean exchanges. President Lee Myung-bak publicly called the individuals who raised suspicions about the conclusions advanced by the official investigation 'a pro-North Korean group inside the South who repeat the argument of (North Korea)', a labelling that could land them a prison term for a violation of the National Security Law. The Navy Headquarters filed a media mediation request against eight newspapers for their critical reporting, and the Korea Communications Commission handed down a heavy penalty to KBS for its broadcast of the findings of its own experiment that had failed to discover oxide, a natural by-product of a torpedo explosion, which was cited in the JIG report. The Minister of National Defence also sued for defamation a former officer in the South Korean Navy, who served as a civil expert for the JIG, for his suggestion that the warship sank after running aground, not after being torpedoed. Several conservative groups also brought lawsuits against individuals and groups who questioned the findings, such as the People's Solidarity for Participatory Democracy (PSPD), claiming defamation and violation of the National Security Law (Suh and Nam 2012).

While scientists in South Korea largely remained silent about the findings of JIG for fear that they would be labelled as *jongbuk jwapa* ('followers of North Korea'), two scholars based in the United States felt that it was their responsibility to point out inconsistencies in the report. Jae-Jung Suh, a political scientist at Johns Hopkins University at the time, who also majored in physics as an undergraduate student at the University of Chicago, was active in public discussions in South Korea on matters related to North–South relations. Suh initially found that the X-ray data submitted in the report contained inconsistencies and questioned the integrity of the data. Suh approached Seung-Hun Lee, a physicist at the University of Virginia's neutron and X-ray scattering laboratory and an expert in the X-ray technologies used by the investigative team of JIG, for help to verify his findings (S. H. Lee 2010).

The JIG report concluded that the Cheonan sank after a torpedo exploded in waters near its hull, causing a 'bubble effect' and destroying the ship with its shockwaves. The discovery of a torpedo fragment with 'No. 1' written on it in Korean led the team to implicate North Korea. After replicating the tests carried out by the JIG, Lee and Suh found that their results did not match with the findings of the JIG report and also that there was an anomaly in the JIG test: among others, the blue ink marking on the torpedo reading 'No. 1' would have been burned off in a detonation (Lee and Suh 2013). They also indicated that the 'white compounds' found on both the recovered ship and the torpedo were not substances resulting from an explosion, but were most likely 'rusted' aluminium exposed to moisture or water for a long time (Lee and Suh 2013). Neither suggesting a definite cause of the explosion nor blaming any side, they appealed to the South Korean government to reopen the investigation and that it be carried out by a group of experts independent of the government (Lee and Suh 2013).

Lee and Suh published their findings in various academic and popular journals, appeared as witnesses in courts for defamation cases, as well as on TV programmes and podcasts. The conservative press, which had advanced the torpedo theory even before the official investigation was concluded, saw a 'pro-North Korea follower' in whoever raised questions or concerns about the JIG report. *Daily NK* encapsulated the conservative viewpoint with its headline, 'South Korea, violated by Lee and Suh'. It also questioned the expertise of these scholars, claiming that their findings were an outcome of their reputed leftist convictions, rather than scientifically driven. It even insinuated that North Korea's denial of its reputed responsibility for the explosion was to provide a cover for those North Korean followers in the South (Sin 2011).

Lee and Suh were well aware of the pervasive anti-communist sentiment in South Korea and the danger of being labelled as pro-communist if they were to raise questions about the government's handling of the Cheonan case. But JIG's investigation and its conclusions were announced 'in the name of science', and Lee felt obligated to respond as a scientist (S. H. Lee 2010). Suh was equally motivated by his sense of scholar's responsibility; he, as a scholar, was obligated to seek the truth and to raise questions about what was questionable in the findings of the JIG, regardless of the prevailing public sentiment (J.-T. Lee 2010).

In each of the above cases, the key terms around which the contentious debates were conducted were 'science' and 'expertise'. Gongyu Jeong-ok and *Banollim* fought for over ten years to prove the causal link between the work environment and the leukaemia cases at Samsung Semiconductor, Kim Jeong-wook and his National Association of Professors provided scientific analyses of the problems of the Restoration Project (Yoon 2009), and Lee and Suh raised questions based on their expertise in physics to evaluate the JIG investigation. When many intellectuals aligned themselves with the state or corporate interest based on their credentials as experts, or remained silent due to the fear of reprisals, these 'counter-experts' aligned with ordinary citizens to counter policies or measures that they perceived to be adversarial or counter to the rights and interests of the public. Their involvement in the fields that require specific expertise, such as medicine, science, and technology, also indicates that the ways in which they engage with social issues differ from the public intellectual of the previous era—they rely on and mobilise their own expert knowledge, rather than base their claims on presumed universal truth or general knowledge. They also work alongside and with—not for—their fellow citizens, who, along the way, reconstitute themselves as co-creators and co-producers rather than just consumers of knowledge (Kim 2016).

5. Conclusion

As we have seen in this chapter, the defining characteristics and roles of the public intellectual in South Korea have evolved closely following the socio-political and cultural development of the country. During the authoritarian period, public intellectuals took on the characteristics of 'dissident intellectuals', and they became constitutive of the democratisation movement. From the late 1980s, South Korea's democratic transition and the growth of civil society, the advent of the internet and the information age, the high number of university graduates, and the university's close collaboration with industry and the state, along with the global neoliberal restructuring, have greatly transformed the character of intellectual life and the status and role of the intellectual. An intellectual is no longer seen as—and the society seems no longer to need—a prophetic voice and a seeker of truth. The place and role of the public intellectual have accordingly changed significantly, if not fundamentally.

At the same time, the emergence of 'counter-experts' indicates that some intellectuals still share the same motive and goal as the public intellectuals of the previous era—to employ one's knowledge to close the gap between principle and reality in society—while adopting different modes of engagement by reconstituting the public agenda and disputing or reshaping a policy or a dominant perspective. More recently, however, a new kind of public engagement by bloggers, YouTubers, and influencers also increasingly dominates the public sphere, with various platforms of social media at their disposal. South Korean society has entered the era of 'post-truth'—more and more people think that their beliefs should have equal sway with the established sources of reason and evidence—with all that entails. The defining characteristics and roles of the public intellectual will likely undergo further transformation as the trend continues.

Bibliography

Certo, P., Chaffin, G., and Kim, H.-E. (2010), 'The Cheonan Incident: Skepticism Abounds', *Institute for Policy Studies* 15, https://ips-dc.org/the_cheonan_incident_skepticism_abounds/, accessed 23 November 2021.

Choe, E.-Y. (2011), 'Kim Yeo-jin: Hamkke haengbokhan salmul kkumkkuneun socialtainer' [Kim Yeo-jin: A socialtainer who dreams of a world where everyone is happy together], *Inmul kwa sasang* (September), 74–89.

Choi, J. (2000), 'Democratization, Civil Society, and the Civil Social Movement in Korea: The Significance of the Citizens' Alliance for the 2000 General Election', *Korea Journal* 40(4), 26–55.

Doucette, J., and Koo, S. (2013), 'Distorting Democracy: Politics by Public Security in Contemporary South Korea', *Asia Pacific Journal* 11(48), (Dec. 2).

Foucault, M. (1977), 'The Political Function of the Intellectual', *Radical Philosophy* 17 (Summer), 12–14.

Gongyoo, J.-O. (2010), 'Samsung jeonja jikeopbyeong t'ujaengui jaengjeomgwa gwaje' [(Key Issues and Tasks Facing the Struggles of the Occupation-Related Disease Victims at Samsung Electronics], *Jinbo pyeongnon* 33(June), 120–140.

Hwang, S. (2016), 'Dissident Readings: Paik Nak-Chung and the Politics of Engagement in South Korean Literature', PhD dissertation, University of Michigan.

Im, Y.-J., and Ryu, I.-H. (2010), '"PD Sucheop" MBC sajang jejiro bulbang' ['PD Notes' Not Aired Due to Pressure from MBC President], *Kyeonghyang sinmun* (August), 18, http://news.khan.co.kr/kh_news/khan_art_view.html?artid=201008180025215&code=940705, accessed 23 November 2021.

Kang, J.-G., and Lee, G.-S. (2019), 'Textmining eul tonghae bon Jeju Yemen nanmin Naver news daetguleul jungsim euro' [A Stud on Yemen Refugees in Jeju Island Viewed through

Text-Mining Focusing on Naver News Comments], *Damunhwa kontentsu yeongu* 30(April), 103–135.

Kang, M.-G. (2015), 'Jisikin eui jeongchi chamyeo e kwanhan yeongu: daehak gyosu reul jungsim euro' [A Study on the Political Participation of Intellectuals: Focusing on University Intellectuals], *Hanguk kwa gukje jeongchi* 31(3) (Fall), 1–24.

Kang, N.-H., Lee, J.-K., Lim, J.-Y., Hong, G.-D, and Yoon, J.-K. (2017), 'Chotbul ihu, gyosu jisikin undong eui jeonwhan eul wihayeo' [To Seek a Transition in the Movement of University Professors and Intellectuals in the Aftermath of the Candlelight Protests], *Daehak: Damnon gwa jaengjeom* 2 (August), 119–148.

Kang, S.-T. (2017), 'Ssial kwa jisikin: Ham Seok-heon eui jisikinnon yeongu' [People and Intellectuals: On Ham Seok-heon's Thoughts on Intellectuals], *Sahoe wa iron* (November), 91–131.

Kim, D.-C. (2012), 'Hanguk sahoe ui gongongseong gwa gongcheok jisigin: geu gujojeok teungjing gwa byeonhwa' [Publicness and Public Intellectuals in South Korea: Structural Characteristics and Historical Changes], interview conducted by Pak Yeong-do, *Dongbanghakji* 159 (September), 299–345.

Kim, J. (2013), 'The Environmental Fallout of the Four Major Rivers Project', *Hankyoreh*, 3 August, http://english.hani.co.kr/arti/english_edition/e_national/598190.html, accessed 23 November 2021.

Kim, J.-Y. (2016), 'Jisik jeongchiwa jimin: Gwahak gwa jeongchi eui geyonggye neomgieseo jisik minjoojooeuiro' [The Politics of Knowledge and Citizen-Intellectuals: Towards Intellectual Democracy beyond the Boundary of Science and Politics], *Hanguk gwahak gisulhaehoe haksul daehoe* (December), 13–36.

Kyunghyang Sinmun teukbyeolchwijaetim (2008), *Minjuhwa 20-nyon: Jisikineui jooeum* [20 Years since the Democratization: The Death of Intellectuals] (Seoul: Humanitas).

Lah, T. J., Park, Y., and Cho, Y. J. (2015), 'The Four Major Rivers Restoration Project of South Korea: An Assessment of Its Process, Program, and Political Dimensions', *Journal of Environment & Development* 24(4) (December), 375–394.

Lee, J.-T. (2010), '"Cheonanham pigyeok" euimun jegi Suh Jae-Jung Johns Hopkinsdae gyosu' [Johns Hopkins University's Professor Jae-Jung Suh Raises Issues about the Cheonan Sinking], *Kyunghyang sinmun*, 26 July, http://news.khan.co.kr/kh_news/khan_art_view.html?art_id=201007261759302, accessed 23 November 2021.

Lee, N. (2007), *The Making of Minjung: Democracy and the Politics of Representation in South Korea* (Ithaca, NY: Cornell University Press).

Lee, N. (2019), 'Social Memory of the 1980s and Unpacking the Regime of Discontinuity', in S. Park, *Revisiting Minjung: New Perspectives on the Cultural History of 1980s South Korea*, 17–45 (Ann Arbor, MI: University of Michigan Press).

Lee, S. H. (2010), *Gwahakeui yangsim, Cheonanham eul chujeokhada* [Conscience of Science, the Pursuit of the Cheonan Sinking] (Seoul: Changbi).

Lee, S. H., and Suh, J. J. (2013), 'South Korean Government's Failure to Link the Cheonan's Sinking to North Korea: Incorrect Inference and Fabrication of Scientific Data', *International Journal of Science in Society* 4(1), 15–24.

Park, S.-G., Choe, M.-il, and Jeong, E.-J. (2014), 'Socialtainer hwaldong kwallyon bodowa je3ja hyogwa e gwanhan yeongu' [A Study on the Media Coverage of the Socialtainers' Activities and Their Impact], *Bangsong tongsin yeongu* (January), 135–162.

Park, S. Y. (2011a), 'Restoring or Killing Rivers? The Political Economy of Sapjil and Citizens Movements in Lee Myung-bak's South Korea', *Asia-Pacific Journal* 9(48), 28 November.

Park, Y. (2011b), 'Wangongdwiedo 'donmeokneun 4daegang' … yeon yujibi 2400 eok-1 joweon' [The 'Money-Eating Four Major Rivers Restoration Project' Even after its Completion … Yearly Maintenance Fee between 240 and 800 million US dollars], *Hankyoreh*, 15 June, https://www.hani.co.kr/arti/economy/economy_general/482936.html, accessed 23 November 2021.

Schmid, A. (2002), *Korea Between Empires, 1895–1919* (New York, NY: Columbia University Press).

Sin, J.-H. (2011), 'Lee Seung-hun, Seo Jae-jung du saramege yurindwen Daehanminguk' [South Korea, Violated by Seung-hun Lee and Jae-Jung Suh], *DailyNK*, 21 March, https://www.chogabje.com/board/view.asp?C_IDX=37724&C_CC=AZ, accessed 23 November 2021.

Suh, J. J. (2010), 'Race to Judge, Rush to Act: The Sinking of the Cheonan and the Politics of National Insecurity', *Critical Asian Studies* 42(3), 403–424.

Suh, J. J., and Nam, T. (2012), 'Rethinking the Prospects for Korean Democracy in Light of the Sinking of the Cheonan and North–South Conflict', *Asia Pacific Journal*, 11(10), 11 March.

Yoon, M.-H. (2008), '*Jeonwhan sidae* eui *nolli* wa Lee Yeong-hui' [*Logic in the Era of Transition and Lee Yeong-hui*], *Sindonga*, 6 October, https://shindonga.donga.com/3/all/13/107856/1, accessed 23 November 2021.

Yoon S.-J. (2009), 'Hanbando daeunhawa kwahak kisul' [The Major Rivers Restoration Project, Science, and Technology], *SNU NOW*, 12 January, https://www.snu.ac.kr/snunow/snu_story?md=v&bbsidx=79897, accessed 23 November 2021.

CHAPTER 27

POLITICS AND POPULAR MUSIC

JOHN LIE

1. INTRODUCTION

POPULAR music may be mere entertainment, but it would be difficult to identify a better locus to make sense of South Korean politics and political economy. Consider two vignettes.

Almost exactly one year after the end of the Second World War and the end of Japanese colonial rule, the leading Korean newspaper *Dong-a Ilbo* (1946) exhorted fellow nationals to 'massacre' Japanese music. Among its manifold negative attributes was its 'vulgarity'. The supersession of Japanese popular music—and popular music then was largely Japanese—opened the door to the yet undefined post-Liberation music, popular or traditional, and post-Liberation politics in general. After thirty-five years of colonial rule, the newspaper's declaration is as clear as any expression of the hopes and aspirations of post-Liberation Korea.

On 20 June 2020, nearly three-quarters of a century later, President Donald Trump's rally imploded. Expecting throngs to show up, merely 6,200 arrived at the BOK Center in Tulsa, Oklahoma. Amidst allegations of leftist conspiracy and understandable worries about COVID-19 transmission, an unlikely factor for the low turnout emerged. K-pop fans and especially the Bangtan Boys (BTS) fan group, ARMY, had falsely registered to generate high expectation and thereby foil the Trump campaign. The transnational reach of K-pop in this instance illustrates its primacy and significance, not only for South Korea, but also indeed for the world outside the Korean Peninsula.

Popular music was not central to post-Liberation politics and K-pop fandom did not torpedo the Trump re-election campaign, to be sure. Nevertheless, wherever we cast our gaze, there are small but indelible footprints of popular music which, in turn, illuminate the nature and contours of South Korean politics, culture, and society. Exemplary and symptomatic, the incidents and trends that are discussed in this chapter do not merely reflect and refract underlying reality. From time to time, popular music affects and shapes the course of contemporary politics. The exploration of politics and popular music is worthwhile and illuminates the hitherto unrelated realms of human endeavour.

2. Post-Liberation Efflorescence

The end of Japanese colonial rule ended the preponderant impact of Japanese culture in the Korean Peninsula (Lie 1998). After more than a generation of outright rule, and one that intensified its efforts to render Korea Japanese, the Japanese hegemony ended abruptly and almost completely. We cannot ignore the profound role of Japan in shaping modern Korea, and the thesis is no less true in the realm of politics as in that of popular music.

Two caveats are noteworthy. First, the music that the Japanese brought was deeply influenced by the West, whether the rudiments of classical European music taught in the official school curriculum or the popular songs ('jazz' that encapsulated several distinct genres) aired in movie theatres, cafes, and other venues of post-traditional urban life (Lie 2015). Symptomatic was the oft-mentioned first popular-music sensation in Korea, which was a waltz sung in Western operatic style. The Japanese authorities, in other words, were not enforcing traditional Japanese music, whether classical (*gagaku*) or folk. Rather, the music that disseminated especially in urban Korea was not much different from that in urban Japan. Second, the Korean appropriation of Japanese and Western music generated not only the foundation of post-Liberation musical life (most importantly, musical education and musicians themselves), but also the beginnings of distinct, Korean popular songs, some of which were exported to the Japanese archipelago (Pak 1987). Nevertheless, the Japanese influence, including the continuous import of the latest Japanese pop hits, would cast a long shadow on South Korean musical life (North Korea was much more effective in ending the Japanese influence), and the outsized importance of Japan would not be superseded for another four decades in South Korea.

Given the eruption of nationalist sentiments after Liberation, one might expect the emergence of a nationalist effort to reinvigorate traditional Korean music. Nothing of the sort happened. Korean classical music experienced a steady decline and survives primarily as a government-supported cultural preservation programme in twenty-first-century South Korea (Lie 2015). Folk music, such as the quasi-operatic genre of *pansori*, survived, but its marginalisation in post-Liberation South Korea is graphically expressed in Im Kwon-taek's masterly film *Sopyonje* (1999). The father–daughter duo of *pansori* performers is overwhelmed—indeed, silenced—by a Western brass band (and the listeners abandon the former and follow the latter). What remains is an imaginary museum of the past, the traditional that appeals to an extremely narrow circle of enthusiasts (cf. Lee 2018). Put differently, classical music in South Korea is Western classical music, and almost never Korean classical music. We see in this instantiation a clear sense of how South Korea has superseded the Korean past.

Beyond the Korean War that overwhelmed the peninsula (sounds of guns and bombs rocked both North and South Korea), the new, dominant sound could be heard around US military bases and camp towns. Contemporary US music came to South Korea more or less directly to entertain GI soldiers stationed in South Korea. Later, AFKN—radio and television transmission for the US military forces—would disseminate the latest in US pop music to eager—usually young and urban—South Koreans (Pak 2010). Not surprisingly, copycat acts and groups proliferated in South Korea: the Kim Sisters, after the Andrews Sisters, for instance. Thus a new subgenre was born: rank imitation of US acts.

US dominance of South Korea, to be sure, was skin deep. The penchant for giving oneself American first names did not extend beyond top politicians and others working with American GIs. Similarly, musical preference remained stubbornly conservative for the majority of the population (Lie 2015). Rural, agrarian populations sang folk songs, and most urbanites retained their allegiance to Japanese-style pop songs, though now sung in Korean. There was, then, something of a dual-structure characteristic of many a colonial and post-colonial society: the elite layer of metropolitan influence and the vast foundation of local culture, however, tinged by Japanese and Western impact (cf. Sin et al. 2005).

Thus, US-style popular music's surface, albeit superficial, popularity is emblematic of the US domination of South Korean politics in the 1950s. The nominally democratic polity was far from being a country steeped in democratic culture. The superficial penetration of democratic values can be correlated to the surface spread of US-style popular music in South Korea in the 1950s.

3. THE PARK DECADES

After the 1961 military coup, South Korea entered a long period of increasingly authoritarian rule (Lie 1998). Park Chung-hee came to dominate South Korean politics until his death in 1979 (and provided a mirror image to that of Kim Il-sung in North Korea). Befitting a military strongman, his preferred mode of rule privileged hierarchy and repression. The veneer of political democracy became thinner year after year, leading to the establishment of an outright autocracy in the early 1970s. The same sort of dynamic can be seen in the realm of popular music.

Park's musical preference was decidedly of his time and place, which is to say that he was steeped in slow, Japanese-influenced ballads, usually called *enka* in Japanese and *trot* in Korean. The long shadow of Japanese influence is manifest in *trot*, and Yi Mi-jae, the dominant singer of the 1960s, exemplified the genre. In spite of his personal preference, however, Park actively sought to discourage, and even ban outright, *trot* music for manifesting Japanese 'colours' (Lie 2015). Yi's mega-hit, '*Dongbaek agassi*' ('The Camelia Girl'), was first in a line of songs that would be outlawed for manifesting presumed

Japanese influence. Why would Park and his coterie care about popular music, especially as Park liked the genre (and was rumoured to invite Yi for a personal recital at the Blue House, the South Korean White House)? Park was seeking to combat the common allegation that he was pro-Japanese—most obviously for his espousal of the 1965 Normalisation Treaty between Japan and South Korea that generated a nationwide protest—and his anti-Japanese rhetoric and symbolic gesture, such as discouraging, repressing, and banning Japanese cultural products, would accentuate manifest anti-Japanese cultural policy and popular sentiments well into the twenty-first century (Kim 2014). Far from demonstrating a straight line between colonial-era anti-Japanese politics, South Korea's anti-Japanese politics and culture was encouraged by the military ruler steeped in Japanese popular music. Therein lies some of the underexplored complexities of modern South Korean politics and culture, including the essential ambivalence towards the erstwhile colonial power, Japan (and much the same can be said about Kim Il-sung, though his anti-Japanese credentials were more solid than that of Park). The ambivalence comprised emulation and plagiarism, the sincerest form of flattery, as well as rejection and censorship.

Park's other target for repression and censorship was for music that he seemed to detest outright. Repulsed by the rampant corruption of the Rhee Syngman regime in the 1950s, the ambit of corruption extended to the loose morals and loud music of the West, which seemed to go hand in hand. Being a client state of the United States, he could hardly hope to ban American music in US military bases or AFKN broadcast, but he made every effort to curb the spread of the rock 'n' roll associated with youth culture and, especially, the student anti-government protests (Lie 2015). Especially during the years of the Yusin Constitution (the height of authoritarian rule in the mid 1970s), many pop songs, such as the Beatles' hits—faced outright censorship. Put simply, Western popular music was fine for American GIs, but not for South Koreans, who were discouraged from entertaining sex, drugs, and rock 'n' roll, along with political democracy, of course.

Finally, it would seem in retrospect that Park and his allies rarely liked any popular music save the traditional, Japanese-influenced sort. Western pop and rock-influenced music came under censure, often for association with sex and drugs. In one unlikely instance, Kim Chu-ja, who danced to the tune of rock-influenced music, was arrested for allegedly sending signals to North Korea (Lie 2015). In an era when most singers sung erect, with almost no gestures or movements, the gyrating figure of Kim and her ilk appeared to transgress the normal and the acceptable, though the ne plus ultra of the abnormal and the unacceptable remained North Korea. Park's rule was all business; little space was given to play, and it is not surprising that popular music was almost always an object of suspicion and censure. More directly, the rapidly expanding student movement, as well as allied forces in workers', farmers', Christians', and other anti-authoritarian movements, championed not so much rock but rather modern folk music. Kim Min-gi, who became the banner singer of the student movement, was repeatedly imprisoned. Opposing political cultures could readily be identified by what they listened to and sang.

In short, the Park decades show, in the realm of popular music as well as in larger society, the pervasive authoritarian and repressive streak. To be sure, Park's long rule was far from being uniform or straightforwardly authoritarian, and the regime's changing policies towards popular music is as good an indicator as any in delineating the granular details of the political change, and especially the turn towards autocracy. Top-down surveillance and censorship, outright repression and imprisonment, repressed a wide swathe of popular music. Nevertheless, we can also see countervailing movements, not only in the persistence of Japanese-influenced popular music, whatever the official government position, but also more importantly in the genres that appealed to youths, such as rock and, more significant, folk. Beneath the muffler of authoritarian rule, there were sounds of a different future that could be heard throughout South Korea in the 1970s.

4. The 1980s Interlude

Park's death unleashed massive protests, dubbed the Seoul Spring, but their brutal suppression sustained military rule under Chun Doo-hwan. Lacking Park's ruthlessness and charisma, Chun nevertheless continued to stress Park's favoured legitimation principles: economic growth, national security (anticommunism), and anti-Japanese nationalism. However, it became clear that the regime was reaching limits on deploying outright repression. Hence, there were efforts to shore up tottering rule. New measures to enhance support for military rule included cultural liberalisation (Lie 2015).

The newly enriched and affluent urbanites, especially youths, sought popular entertainment, and popular music was part of the panoply. In the 1980s, television was the king of entertainment and popular music programmes played a preponderant role on the airwaves (Chŏng and Chang 2000). No longer as willing to raise the ire of the public by outlawing popular songs, the government became reticent in deploying censorship and imprisonment. Instead, the authoritarian rulers sought to employ popular music to enhance its legitimacy. Harking back to the Japanese colonial repertoire, it promoted 'healthy music' (*gonjong eumhak*). Bubbly, upbeat songs, usually sung by telegenic younger singers, celebrated South Korea and all things Korean (Lie 2015). If there were any convincing sign of the military losing its grip on power, surely its turn to popular music to enhance popular support was it. Not surprisingly, however, the propaganda effort by another means did not generate much enthusiasm. It remains one of the enduring beliefs of popular musicians, as well as scholars of popular music, that top-down creation of popular songs is doomed to failure.

In spite of efforts to enhance legitimacy, the tragedy of military rule was that it relied on old habits. Kim Wan-seon, dubbed the Madonna of Korea, was arrested for dancing in a suggestive manner on national television in 1986 (Lie 2015). Anti-government folk singers, including rock musicians, faced harassment and arrest. Japanese popular music, though not officially censored, faced informal ban and widespread rejection. The unruly world of popular music was a conspicuous redoubt of authoritarian tendencies and practices.

What dominated South Korea in the 1980s was a congeries of musical genres, ranging from classical Western music to US-dominated rock and pop, but the dominant strands remained slow ballads (tracing their roots to the colonial period in some ways) (Pak 2009; Lie 2015). *Trot*, then known as *kayo*, was probably the most popular genre of music in urban South Korea, though Western pop music was making serious inroads. Western classical music was the favoured genre for elites and upwardly mobile urbanites. As with other eastern Asian countries, piano lessons marked the rite of passage for many a middle-class (and other 'aspiring classes') child. Folk music was the prescribed musical genre of anti-government activists. We also see in this period the very beginnings of idol pop music that catered to urban youths. Discoes and night clubs blared dance music into the small hours. Put differently, it is in the 1980s that we can identify the proliferation of subcultures and subgenres that continue to this day (Furuya 2005). The range of musical expression far exceeded that of the post-Liberation period, and is a testament to the growing affluence and the transnational reach of the South Korean listening public.

In short, the 1980s presaged the limit of authoritarian rule. The affluent public began to demonstrate a multiplicity of tastes. Even as something akin to a unified national popular culture emerged, it was being torn asunder by multifarious currents and genres. By listening to the variegated expressions of popular music in the air, we can hear the rumbles of an era's end.

5. The Post-Democratisation Era

The end of military authoritarianism, coeval with the 1988 Seoul Olympics, recapitulated the cultural efflorescence of the post-Liberation era. As with Liberation, the transition from authoritarian rule to political democracy is shrouded in chiaroscuro, but there is no question that the late 1980s marked the eruption of new cultural expressions. In retrospect, it is well nigh impossible to identify the transition from the dark decades of military rule to the bright dawn of democracy and the realm of popular music was certainly no exception. As repression and censorship receded, new genres and influences gushed forth, often from diasporic and transnational sources.

One trend is noteworthy. Although ballads, or *trot* music, continued to be the favoured genre of popular music, there was a decisive shift away from Japanese influences and the wholehearted embrace of the US trends (Lie 2015). To be sure, as noted, US influences have been something of a constant in post-Liberation South Korea, but the ambit of avid listeners remained circumscribed. What distinguished the late 1980s was the almost instantaneous import of the latest trends and songs from the United States, and their widespread appeal, especially for young urbanites.

The eclipse of Japanese influence and the rise of US impact became unquestionable in the course of the 1980s (Lie 1998, 2015). There is, of course, the waning proportion of South Koreans, with schooling and memory of Japanese language and culture. To the generational shift was grafted the nationalist turn in curriculum and culture. The centuries-long reliance on Chinese characters, for instance, gave way to the newfound stress on learning English and relying solely on native Korean script (*hangeul*). In the 1970s, any educated South Korean would be able to make sense of a Japanese-language book given the widespread usage of Chinese characters in both countries. By the late 1990s, fewer South Koreans would have the requisite literacy in Chinese characters. Another inescapable trend was the decisive shift in South Koreans' orientation from Japan to the United States. What was true at the level of top politicians would be true for the population at large by the 1980s. One element of this shift was the growing impact of the Korean diaspora, not to mention the massive wave of South Koreans studying abroad, in the United States. From economic activities to cultural knowledge, South Korean immigrants in the United States would emit influence and information about the latest trends in the United States.

The most spectacular example of this phenomenon in the realm of popular music was Seo Tae-ji and Boys, who introduced rap and hip hop to mainstream TV audiences in 1992 (Kang 1995). Although adults in the room were horrified by the noise and break dancing, the band would become a sensation and etched the beginning of a new era in South Korean popular music. Obsolescent at once was the previously staid appearance and demeanour of performers, as well as the normative character of gesticulation and body movements. Needless to say, it is not difficult to see the impact of MTV and its marquee stars, such as Michael Jackson and Madonna, but it also speaks to the vibrant presence of diasporic and transnational Koreans: emigrants to the United States (and elsewhere) and their children who came back to South Korea, or students and others who spent a spell abroad and returned with the latest from the United States and elsewhere. We should not forget, too, the sheer force of cultural globalisation, abetted as it was by new technologies. Lee Soo-man, the founder of the representative K-pop agency SM Entertainment, is a not-untypical example (Lie and Oh 2014). Steeped in anti-government movement and its anthems, primarily folk songs, he studied in southern California in the early 1980s and absorbed the impact of MTV and the latest trends in African-American-dominated popular music, including rap and hip hop. He would go on to become a central figure in the genesis and development of K-pop.

Seo Tae-ji and Boys are important for a non-musical reason as well. When one of their songs was censored, they sued and won a decisive victory in the courts (Lie 2015). Although censorship and repression never disappeared completely (they were to make something of a comeback during the reign of Park Chung-hee's daughter, Park Geun-hye in the 2010s), active political control of popular music ceased to be a major force from the mid-1990s. Much the same can be said about all manner of political and cultural expression in South Korea. In popular music, then, we see a proof, if one were needed, of the rapidly expanding and hegemonic notion of political and cultural democracy in the 1990s.

It would be misleading to characterise the 1990s as an era of innovation and disruption, however. Just as mainstream listeners continued to favour crooner love songs, imports dominated the latest and the best in the world of South Korean pop music aficionados. Enrichment and technological advance facilitated the instantaneous influx of the latest hits from the United States, often in the form of music videos. Furthermore, South Koreans continued to rely disproportionately on mimicking, and at times plagiarising, foreign sources, especially from Japan. Put differently, no one in the mid 1990s expected the imminent emergence of K-pop as a global sensation. In this state of affairs, however, popular music was no different from any other major industrial sectors. No one would accuse Hyundai or Samsung in the 1990s of being a disruptive and innovative force in the world of manufacturing or design.

In short, the 1990s exhibited the sprouting of political and cultural democracy. The trend was especially evident in the realm of popular music, which at once ended the reign of authoritarian politics and augured a new era of political-economic and cultural differentiation as well as the potential for innovation.

6. K-Pop

K-pop's origin can be traced to the mid-1990s (see Lie 2015, Choi 2017, and Kim 2018). As Kim Dae-jung's economic policy sought to limit the monopolistic power of South Korean conglomerates, the progressive regime unwittingly laid the seedbed of a new music genre. All three major K-pop agencies—SM, YG, and JYP—were formed in the mid-1990s. Combining the latest artistry of African-American-influenced popular music (everything from back beats to break dancing), they created a musical genre that was *au courant* to the prevailing trends in the United States.

Several features of K-pop articulated well with the regnant South Korean political economy. First, it was designed to be exported. The widespread consensus of South Korean businesspeople is the limited nature of the domestic market and the consequent imperative to export. It is tantamount to a religion in contemporary South Korean business—and a striking contrast to contemporary Japan—and the belief that K-pop entertainment entrepreneurs followed (Lie 2015; cf. Sakamoto and Epstein 2020). Not only was this a break from the past of domestic popular music, it was also an idea that was unusual, if not unique. US popular music is exported all around the world, but the intention of the artists and the producers is usually focused on the domestic market. Important in this regard is that the leading K-pop producers were in line with the prevailing export-orientated mindset of South Korean businesses. Just as important was that they had deep exposure to the United States and exemplified the diasporic and other networks that tightly bound South Korea and the United States.

Second, the leading K-pop entertainment agencies embraced the digital revolution. This was part and parcel of the Kim Dae-jung regime's stress on the new digital technologies, but also spoke to their embrace of the recent US innovations, such as music videos and, later, YouTube and its ilk. Put simply, they forged a new business model for popular music that depended less on CD sales and downloads and relied more on the new digital media to disseminate their products and to generate revenues in other ways, such as holding events and selling goods to fans. In this regard, the K-pop agencies sought to cultivate enthusiastic fandom, who would do everything from promoting their favourite act to purchasing its paraphernalia (Kim 2019).

Finally, the K-pop agencies relied less on the bottom-up generation of pop music stars—the proverbial garage band to superstardom as the royal road in popular music—and more on the top-down creation of stars and idols (Lie 2015; Kim 2019). K-pop idols usually undergo between five and ten years of intensive training before they debut, and they are taught everything from voice and dancing lessons to foreign languages (the export market) and fan interaction skills. In this regard, the agencies instituted a global division of labour, outsourcing everything from composition and choreography to fashion and advertising. The three leading K-pop agencies converged on the new business model and K-pop as a global phenomenon solidified towards the end of the first decade of the twenty-first century. In short, K-pop was cultivated in hit factories that trained and managed talent.

Initially, the export target was the neighbouring Japan. SM Entertainment, for example, cultivated a young female singer, BOA, to become fluent in Japanese and debut as a Japanese pop star in the early 1990s. Although the extent of passing became attenuated over time, K-pop was initially J-pop done by South Koreans. Yet as the agencies promoted idol music, they realised that they had found a triumphant formula that would work not only in Japan, but also in China and elsewhere. K-pop emerged out of this insight, and from the late 1990s K-pop and idol music became synonymous (Lie and Oh 2014; Lie 2015). In so doing, the export orientation shifted from just Japan to the rest of the world. It is not surprising that the People's Republic of China, which in the 1990s was less than a decade away from the 1989 Tiananmen Incident and still a developing country, would struggle to produce high-quality popular music. C-pop remains inchoate as of 2020, and this is not surprising for a country that long devalued, and even banned, popular music. Yet what of Japan? In point of fact, J-pop was popular throughout eastern Asia in the 1990s. As has been noted, we cannot make sense of South Korean popular music in the first three decades after Liberation without appreciating the influence of Japanese popular music. But what stunted the possibility of global J-pop is the cultural involution that gripped Japan after the property-speculation bubble burst in the early 1990s (Lie 2021). Redolent with pop music stars and songs in the 1990s, J-pop music agencies exhibited little or no interest in exporting them or expanding the ambit of J-pop. At the same time, J-pop, once an innovative and vibrant genre, became calcified and conservative, and decidedly outside the mainstream of US-led popular music that would have limited appeal beyond Japan (Lie 2019).

K-pop's success abroad made it probably the single best-known thing about South Korea, superseding the tragic past, such as the Korean War, or its marquee industrial might, such as Samsung smartphones, by the 2010s. The global sensation called BTS—itself a permutation from the original K-pop formula in stressing the idols' individuality and originality—ensured that no one in South Korea, or indeed around the world, would gainsay the centrality of K-pop to contemporary South Korean identity. Each successive president, at least since Lee Myung-bak, took note, actively seeking to promote K-pop. Put polemically, in spite of the fact that K-pop did not emerge from government plan or encouragement, conservative and progressive governments alike seized on K-pop as the embodiment and exemplar of New South Korea: cool and innovative. Over time, K-pop became a poster child for the general societal enthusiasm for entrepreneurship and innovation (Lie 2015).

It is therefore not an accident that the South Korean government—as well as corporations and other organisations—routinely deploy K-pop to promote the notion of cool Korea. When President Trump visited South Korea in 2018, President Moon Jae-in had the K-pop boy band Exo in tow. Put differently, K-pop is the public and global face of South Korea. One shudders to think what Park Chung-hee would have made of K-pop, however. We have travelled galaxies and millennia from the post-Liberation decades when popular music was routinely a phenomenon of opprobrium and repression.

In summary, South Korea's export-orientated economy, seeking in the 2010s to be innovative and disruptive, found its ideal expression in K-pop. Far from reflecting the regnant political–economic system, popular music is at once the public face and the leading edge of the sort of South Korea the political and business establishments want the country to become.

7. Thematic Coda

What are some lessons we might draw from pondering the changing relationship between politics and popular music?

First, the preponderant role of exogenous forces. It is a truism that the Korean peninsula has been buffeted by waves from abroad, whether the omnipresent imperial might of China or successive streams of invaders, including Mongolians, Japanese, and Americans, to name a few. The half-baked insight holds true in the realm of popular music. The decisive impact of Japan during the colonial period and its long shadow cannot be underestimated. Even after nearly a decade of Park's anti-Japanese rhetoric, probably the pop song that was most widely aired in South Korea in the early 1970s was the Japanese singer Ishida Ayumi's 'Blue Light Yokohoma', and it was almost impossible to escape the repetitive playing of the fellow Japanese Itsuwa Mayumi's '*Koibito yo*' ('Lover') in Seoul cafes in the 1980s. Unofficial proscription and intermittent boycott of Japanese popular music hardly dented domestic and demotic enthusiasm—even as others decried the latest manifestation of pro-Japanese sentiments—and emulation, at times sliding into the zone of plagiarism, underscored the profound influence of Japan in post-Liberation Korea. The decline of Japan was simultaneous with the rise of the United States as the predominant political-economic and cultural influence. With direct nexuses provided by diasporic Koreans and Koreans studying or living abroad, all the latest trends in the United States would be reproduced in Seoul by the late 1980s. The ascent of K-pop, a permutation of African-American-influenced popular music, cannot be told apart from the convergence of taste culture across the Pacific, forged in part by the diasporic networks. As I stressed, the export-orientation of South Korea is a crucial component of K-pop's global ascent.

Wherever we look, then, we cannot avoid the essential place of the external in South Korea. It is a defiant counterpoint to the nationalist, and often hyper-nationalist, historiography and social science of South Korea that stresses the traditional and the endogenous. Diasporic, transnational, and global relations and forces are ubiquitous and they are critical to any adequate understanding and explanation of contemporary South Korea. In this regard, K-pop has become the representative face of South Korea to the world, embodying at once South Korea's deep commitment to export-orientation and globalisation and the newfound zeal to forge an innovative and disruptive industrial leader.

Second, the expunction of the traditional. In a society that insists on its nationalist character and its long, uninterrupted past—from the putative founder of Korea *Dangun* to the multi-ethnic present, often described hyperbolically as 5,000 years of Korean history—what emerges from our overview are serial chasms that separate the past from the present (Lie 2015). To be sure, past influences do not evaporate overnight, but the profound presence of Japan has been effaced in the past quarter-century, and with it a crucial component of the Korean past. The rise of K-pop has entailed squelching every aspect of traditional Korean music, including Confucian mores and even Korean physique and appearance. To take a small example, until four decades ago, plastic surgery was frowned upon precisely because it altered the gift that parents had bestowed upon their children. In the twenty-first century, plastic surgery is normative. To be sure, each stage is said to be 'Korean' to the nationalist mindset, but we shouldn't overlook the simple reality that past normative practices—the use of the pentatonic scale or the traditional Korean rhythm, the Confucian norm of demure female attire and demeanour, and so on—have disappeared, and there is a pervasive cultural amnesia about norms and practices from even the very recent past. The forward-looking mindset, itself something of a US import, makes possible disruptive innovation, such as K-pop, but it also speaks to the hollowing out of the traditional. Good for economic innovation, not so good for cultural preservation: K-pop exemplifies the modal mindset of South Korea in 2020, and speaks loudly about the Korean present and future.

Third, the transformation of South Korean politics. The ambient sound of an era accompanies the ruling regime's ethos and provides a clear window into its legitimating ideas. The landlord-dominated elite that was the Rhee regime had politicians who went by American first names and, fittingly, the popular songs of the time were predominantly American or US-influenced. Park Chung-hee's increasingly repressive regime banned a widening circle of songs and genres for being pro-Japanese, anti-government, and other undesirable traits, so much so that very little was left of popular music that was not suspicious. The tottering regime of Chun Doo-hwan sought to mix repression with legitimation, producing 'healthy music' that would promote popular enthusiasm. The failure of the 'healthy music' campaign is symptomatic of the manifold failures of the Chun regime. The democratic era opened up all genres of popular music, but the post-Asian currency crisis South Korean political economy doubled down on export orientation and, not surprisingly, produced export-orientated music. The surprising global success of K-pop rendered it as the leading edge of the idealised South Korean self-conception as a progressive, innovative, and cool country. Conservative and progressive governments alike in turn would latch onto K-pop to promote not only their own regime, but also all things Korean. The road from repression to promotion, marginalisation to mainstream, speaks volumes about the changing place of popular music in South Korea, but also just as decisively about the transformation of South Korean politics. Tell us what you are listening to, and that will tell a great deal about what sort of politics reigns in that time and place. As unlikely as this insight may seem, politics and popular music are intimately intertwined, and it would behove analysts to consider the unlikely locus of popular music for clues on politics and political economy.

8. Conclusion

By reviewing the transformation of South Korean popular music, this chapter has sought to illuminate the changing character of South Korean politics. Needless to say, political economy, geopolitics, and culture have a profound impact on the character of popular music, a robust generalisation for modern, post-industrial societies, but the causal arrow does not always point in one direction. Popular music not only becomes an unlikely site of political and cultural struggles, but it also becomes a focal point of interest and aspiration for the body politic. K-pop is, as I have emphasised, the leading edge and the favoured representation of South Korean political and business elites. At the very least, as irrelevant or marginal as popular music may be to power politics or political economy, it is very good to think with and about these weighty topics.

Bibliography

Choi, J. (2017), *K-pop* (Abingdon: Routledge).
Chŏng S.-il, and Chang, H.-S. (2000), *Han'guk TV 40-nyŏn ŭi paljachwi* (Seoul: Hanul).
Dong-a, I. (1946), 13 August.
Furuya, M. (2005), *K Generation* (Tokyo: DHCo).
Kang, M.-S. (1995), *Sŏ T'ae-ji rŭl ilgŭmyŏn munhwa ka poinda?!* (Seoul: Hansol Midiŏ).
Kim, S.-M. (2014), *Sengo Kankoku to Nihon bunka* (Tokyo: Iwanami Shoten).
Kim, S.-Y. (2018), *K-pop Live* (Stanford, CA: Stanford University Press).
Kim, G. (2019), *From Factory Girls to K-pop Idol Girls* (Lanham, MD: Lexington Books).
Lee, K. I.-Y. (2018), *Dynamic Korea and Rhythmic Form* (Middletown, CT: Wesleyan University Press).
Lee, H. J. (2019), *K-pop Idols* (Lanham, MD: Lexington Books).
Lie, J. (1998), *Han Unbound* (Stanford, CA: Stanford University Press).

Lie, J. (2015), *K-pop* (Oakland, CA: University of California Press).
Lie, J. (2019), 'Popular Music and Political Economy', *Culture and Empathy* 2(1), 3–17.
Lie, J. (2021), *Japan, the Sustainable Society* (Oakland, CA: University of California Press).
Lie, J., and Oh, I. (2014), 'SM Entertainment and Soo Man Lee', in T. F.-L. Yu and H. D. Yan, eds, *Handbook of East Asian Entrepreneurship* (Abingdon: Routledge).
Pak, C.-H. (1987), *Kankoku kayōshi* (Tokyo: Shōbunsha).
Pak, C.-H. (2009), *Han'guk kayosa*, vol. 2 (Seoul: Miji Puksŭ).
Pak, S.-S. (2010), *Han'guk Chŏnjaeng kwa taejung kayo, kirok kwa chŭngŏn* (Seoul: Ch'aek i innŭn P'unggyŏng).
Sakamoto, R., and Epstein, S., eds (2020), *Popular Culture and the Transformation of Japan-Korea Relations* (Abingdon: Routledge).
Sin, H.-J., Yi, Y.-U., and Ch'oe, C.-S. (2005), *Han'guk p'ap ŭi kogohak 1960* (Seoul: Han'gil'at'ŭ).

PART 7

PUBLIC POLICY AND POLICY-MAKING

CHAPTER 28

POLITICAL CONTROL AND BUREAUCRATIC AUTONOMY

HUCK-JU KWON

1. INTRODUCTION

SOUTH Korea has achieved a great transformation from a war-torn, poor country to an affluent industrial society over the past six decades. The country has been successful not only in economic development but also in democratisation, with a number of peaceful government changeovers occurring in the past thirty years (Ringen et al. 2011). During the recent COVID-19 pandemic, South Korean society has been relatively unscathed by the outbreak and spread of the virus. The South Korean government was able to keep the spread of infection to a minimum, while other Organisation for Economic Co-operation and Development (OECD) countries like the United Kingdom, the United States, and Italy were unable to effectively deal with the epidemic. This signifies that another developmental achievement, the welfare state in South Korea, works well even in a time of crisis.

At the same time, however, there has been growing concerns about the sustainability of South Korean democracy in general and the competence of the bureaucracy in particular. The last three former South Korean presidents had tragic experiences after their tenures in office: one committed suicide and two others were sentenced to prison. While two presidents were charged with corruption, the other president, President Park Geun-hye, was removed from office by impeachment, and she was sentenced to more than twenty years in prison. Many bureaucrats were also caught in the middle of these political struggles. Many career bureaucrats were dismissed because they served in important positions for the previous governments. The South Korean bureaucracy has been criticised for not exercising professionalism or utilising its expertise due to political control and mobilisation as new administrations act on the basis of different political convictions (Han 2018). According to one senior official while giving a presentation to the Presidential Transition Committee in 2008, 'the South Korean bureaucracy has lost its soul'. Further, the South Korean bureaucracy has been criticised as being complacent and slow to react to policy challenges, relying on past achievements. With such observations and interpretations, two important questions emerge: what is the relationship between democratically elected governors (in particular, the presidents and political appointees) and bureaucracy in the post-developmental and democratisation era and what should these relationships be like in the future in order to serve the people effectively in a democracy?

This chapter examines such relationships from the viewpoint of accountability. It defines accountability as the balance between political control and bureaucratic autonomy and professionalism. In a democratic polity, bureaucracy must be controlled by elected officials such as the president and political appointees. At the same time, bureaucracy should have autonomy to a certain degree in order to design public policies in a scientific and rational manner and implement them effectively. It should also consist of professional experts as this is a necessary condition for their autonomy in the policy process (Fukuyama 2015).

In order to analyse the accountability of bureaucracy in a democratic polity, this study examines government policies including institutional arrangements and political measures which were intended to enhance political control and accountability. It pays special attention to institutional arrangements that hold the bureaucracy accountable. In particular, the chapter examines the performance management system as one instrument to hold bureaucrats accountable. Drawing on such an analysis, it attempts to draw out the implications of the relationship between elected governors and the bureaucracy with an eye towards providing lessons needed in order to sustain a vibrant democracy in South Korea.

2. Political Control and Bureaucratic Autonomy: Accountability

This study examines the relationship between elected governors and bureaucracy through the perspective of accountability. In a democratic polity, sovereignty rests with the citizenry, and citizens delegate political power to their representatives through elections. Holding elections and giving public offices to elected politicians, however, is only one side of the democratic political process. The other side of the political process is to ensure that those trusted with a political mandate to implement public policies have done their job properly. Checks and balances between the three branches of the government provide an institutional rationale for such an idea (Persson et al. 1997). Within the constitutional structure in South Korea, the National Assembly, the legislature, holds the executive branch headed by the president accountable. The president, who in turn delegates their power to the bureaucracy to work on public administration, holds it accountable. The accountability of bureaucrats is a building block of the democratic political process.

Meanwhile, bureaucrats either in policymaking or in policy implementation have to make decisions according to the situation in which they carry out their tasks. Those decisions are not always made based on instructions from laws and elected governors, and they need to exercise discretion. Bureaucratic discretion arises due to the delegation of responsibility for public policy. According to Brandsma and Schillemans (2013: 953), accountability is to ensure that bureaucratic discretion in implementing public policies is checked. Accountability in its simplest form is to explain one's actions or behaviour (Romzek and Dubnick 1987). It is, however, necessary to further elaborate the notion of accountability in order to examine the institutional process in a democratic polity. According to Bovens (2010), the actual account giving consists of three components. First, it is essential that public officials are obliged to inform their trustors about their conduct by providing various types of information about the processes, outputs, and outcomes of carrying out their tasks. Second, it is necessary for trustors to interrogate public officials and question the adequacy of data as well as the effectiveness and efficiency of their work. Third, trustors may pass judgement on the conduct of officials, and there must be a possibility of sanctions so that accountability carries responsibility (Bovens 2010: 952). In short, accountability takes place in three stages: informing, questioning, and judgement.

It is important to note that there are necessary preconditions for accountability: the delegation of a mandate and autonomy of work. We do not hold private individual persons accountable for their conduct. People engaged in their own private business may choose not to give information about their conduct even though it may be requested. Public officials, however, need to be held accountable because they are entrusted to carry out public duties. In order to fulfil their duties, public officials need to have professional expertise in their work. They are also allowed to have a certain degree of autonomy in implementing their duties. If they just do what they are ordered to do, it would not be necessary to hold them accountable. Public officials are given a certain degree of autonomy when necessary in the process of implementing their duties (Goodin 1988; Lipsky 1980). Maintaining professional expertise and autonomy that public officials need can be summarised as bureaucratic autonomy and professionalism. In this context, this study views accountability as a relationship between political control and bureaucratic autonomy and professionalism and uses this concept of accountability as an analytical framework for the study of the South Korean government in the post-developmental and democratisation era.

If accountability is utilised as an analytical framework, where should the focus be regarding the scope of the research? Bovens (2010) provides a very useful framework for analysing accountability. According to his literature review, a group of accountability studies tends to use accountability as a normative concept or as 'a set of standards for the evaluation of behaviour' of public officials (Bovens 2010: 947). Another group of accountability scholars sees accountability as 'a social mechanism' or as an institutional arrangement through which public officials are held accountable. From the perspective of seeing accountability as a norm, the locus of research should be given to behavioural standards of actors and the focus would be on making evaluative and prescriptive findings. In the logic of accountability as social mechanism, the analytical attention needs to be on the institutional process of accountability. Research findings will be about the dynamics of institutional process of accountability (Bovens 2010).

This study uses both perspectives of accountability in its analysis of the South Korean bureaucracy. In particular, it first adopts the concept of accountability as a norm in order to examine the relationship between elected governors and bureaucrats in the post-developmental and democratisation era. It offers a historical overview with the tone of an evaluative description. This historical analysis provides the overall context for the accountability of bureaucracy to the elected governors.

Second, the study adopts the concept of accountability as an institutional mechanism in order to examine the institutional arrangement for accountability. In particular, the study analyses the performance management and evaluation systems developed in the South Korean government since the 2000s. Performance management and evaluation systems are government efforts to manage government administrative activities by measuring the performance of government organisations (Peters 2018). Performance management systems can be an important mechanism for presidents and their ministers to hold bureaucrats accountable. The current framework of the performance management system in the South Korean government was established in 2006 (Oh 2018). The system requires government agencies to provide information about their activities and policy outcomes, as well as policy objectives, and the system is used to evaluate those outcomes of performance. In other words, the performance management system has the basic components of the accountability process. This study examines the performance management and evaluation system as an institutional mechanism of accountability and discusses whether it has functioned effectively. The 'Concluding Remarks' section summarises the analysis of the study and discusses the implications of this research for future policies.

3. The Legacy of the Developmental State and Political Control of the South Korean Bureaucracy

Before we start to examine the accountability of the South Korean bureaucracy in the era of democratic politics, it is necessary to review political control of bureaucracy and autonomy under the developmental state since it would give us an idea about the political context in which the South Korean governments introduced policies and institutional arrangements to enhance political control of the bureaucracy in the later period.

It will also give us a normative dimension for evaluating changes in the accountability of the South Korean bureaucracy in the post-developmental era.

According to a large body of literature on economic development in South Korea, her successful transformation from a poor to an affluent industrial society was largely due to the developmental state (Adelman 1997; Evans 1995; White 1988; Woo 1991). The developmental state is defined as a kind of institutional arrangement in which top policymakers and elite bureaucrats make economic development a top priority and mobilise financial and institutional resources to achieve it (Gough 2004; Johnson 1999). The government headed by President Park Chung-hee, who presided over economic development in the 1960s and 1970s, is a typical example of such institutional arrangements. Subsequent governments in the 1980s, those of Presidents Chun and Rho, could also be regarded as types of a developmental state.

Within the institutional arrangement of the developmental state, the bureaucracy played a very important part in steering public policy for economic development and consequently enjoyed a considerable degree of policy autonomy from society in general and the National Assembly in particular. Among the government ministries, the Economic Planning Board (EPB) and the Ministry of Finance were central in planning and coordinating public policies (Choi 2014). Here, it is necessary to note that state-led development policy was implemented not only in South Korea but also in many other development countries in the 1960s. It was recommended by United Nations (UN) agencies, and in the case of South Korea, the UN Report authored by the Nathan Commission gave the South Korean government similar policy programmes (UN Nathan Report 1954). Such state-led development strategies were based on Keynesian theories of economic development, but they did not lead to successful outcomes in most newly independent developing countries, where social and economic infrastructure necessary for Keynesian economic policies to be effective was not in place.

Why, then, were the state-led development policies successful in South Korea? One of the main reasons was that an effective bureaucracy was in place in South Korea when the South Korean government embarked on the state-led development policies in the 1960s under the leadership of President Park. It is true that there has been a long tradition of bureaucracy in South Korea since the Koryo dynasty in tenth century. More recently, however, in the late 1960s, the South Korean government was able to recruit highly competitive and motivated young graduates to the bureaucracy with a number of incentives. Young graduates were attracted to stable employment and pensions while they were highly motivated to participate in state-led development efforts (Yoon and Park 2016). These young graduates were products of the massive expansion of the public education system in the 1950s. Studies of economic history in this period show that the land reform policies implemented after South Korea became independent from Japan in 1945 enabled families in rural areas to send their children to school (Cho 2003). The government bureaucracy was a well-organised and highly qualified social organisation, which in turn enjoyed a high degree of autonomy from society. The bureaucracy, then, was able to drive economic development while pursuing policies of building economic infrastructure such as motorways and ports for newly emerging industries.

While effective in terms of economic development, the developmental state was authoritarian in terms of politics. Taking a critical perspective, some scholars see it as a bureaucratic authoritarian regime (Im 1987; O'Donnell 1973). It is true that the South Korean bureaucracy was largely unaccountable to the National Assembly and the public under political insulation by authoritarian presidents. At the same time, public officials working in the bureaucracy were subject to political control of the authoritarian regime headed by the president. In the Blue House, the presidential office, there was a large presidential staff which closely oversaw the workings of the ministries. Furthermore, the state intelligence agency, at first called the Korean Central Intelligence Agency and then later the Korean National Security Planning Agency, watched carefully over public officials and their ministries to make sure that they did not step outside their technical and professional boundaries.

In this context, the notion of bureaucratic authoritarian regimes put forward by O'Donnell describes accurately the relationship between the authoritarian president and bureaucracy in South Korea (O'Donnell 1973). Within the policy paradigm of 'economic growth first', the South Korean bureaucracy spearheaded by the EPB and the Ministry of Finance could make technocratic and professional decisions without necessarily considering other social pressures. For instance, their goals were set in terms of economic growth rates, fiscal stability, and balance of payments (Choi 2014). Trade union rights were severely restricted and people living in urban shanty towns were forcefully removed to the outskirts of cities without due legal process. While the South Korean bureaucracy was tightly controlled by the authoritarian president, it enjoyed bureaucratic autonomy towards society at large. The National Assembly controlled by the governing party was not able to hold the South Korean bureaucracy accountable. This political situation continued in the 1980s after President Chun Doo-hwan took power in 1980, although some liberalisation measures were introduced.

Throughout the 1980s, South Korean society witnessed rising social movements, including student movements and trade union strikes, that demanded democratisation. As political confrontation intensified during the democratisation process in the late 1980s, the developmental state became subject to strong criticism for various reasons. First, the overgrown bureaucracy became too powerful without democratic political control (Ahn and Cheong 2007). Democratisation was not only about democratic elections but also about accountability of the bureaucracy. Second, state intervention in the economy, which the South Korean bureaucracy led during the developmental era, was no longer conducive to economic growth. Government intervention was seen as ineffective as well as arbitrary. There were rising calls for liberalisation of the market. These two critical points towards the bureaucracy became the major agenda for reforms of the South Korean government in the democratic era.

4. Does Democratic Control Make the Bureaucracy More Accountable?

4.1 Liberalisation and Small Government Reforms

The developmental state became a kind of *ancien régime* subject to fundamental reform once democracy became the constitutional norm in the South Korean polity in the 1990s. The Roh Moo-hyn government, the first elected under the democratic Constitution of 1987, did not carry through significant reforms. In contrast, the Kim Young-sam government (in office 1993–1998) was able to undertake reforms in the area of economic policy and government bureaucracy, especially by disempowering economic ministries. While President Rho Tae-woo, a former military general, was only able to preside over a transition from authoritarian to democratic government, President Kim Young-sam, with a long political career in the democratic opposition, could initiate crucial reforms. His reforms were intended to remove authoritarian legacy in the government and to establish a market economy with minimal government intervention (Kim 2007).

The reforms had a three-pronged approach to addressing the legacies of the developmental state. First, the military was targeted. The government disbanded secret political societies within the military so that the military elite would not interfere with civilian political affairs in the future. The infamous Hana Society, whose members included young army lieutenants such as Chun Doo-hwan and Rho Tae-woo, the two spearheads of the military coup d'état in 1979, was made illegal. Military personnel would no longer be allowed to organise informal societies. Second, the government implemented an anti-corruption drive against the triangle of collusion among politicians, the bureaucracy, and business (Ahn 1995). A number of senior politicians and bureaucrats were prosecuted for corruption and tax evasion in the early period of the Kim Young-sam government. Third, the twice implemented administrative reforms by the Kim government changed the structure of the government ministries. Administrative reforms aimed at reducing the power of the EPB and other economic ministries. The EPB was merged into the Ministry of Finance and Economy, which was intended to signal that the government would not steer the economy as it used to under the developmental state. The Ministry of Commerce and the Ministry of Energy and Resources were merged into the newly created Ministry of Trade and Industry, while the Ministry of Transportation and Construction absorbed two ministries concerned with transportation and construction. More than 1,000 positions in the central government bureaucracy were eliminated. Park Jae-yoon, Senior Adviser to the President at the Blue House, explained the policy direction of administrative reforms in a succinct manner during at an interview with a national newspaper.

> Under the authoritarian regime in the past, government planning and control were the driving force of the economic development. In the democratic system,

only voluntary participation and creativity of citizens can make the economy prosper.... In order to establish the New Economy, it is necessary to restructure administrative organization and to implement full scales reform of administration, public finance and financial market.

(*Kookmin Ilbo*, 22 December 1992)

One of the most significant and enduring reforms undertaken by the Kim Young-sam government was the introduction of real-name financial transactions in the financial market. The new law required all financial transactions to be made under the real names of account holders in contrast to the past practices in the financial market, which allowed customers to conduct financial transactions without verifying their real names. This greatly enhanced transparency in the financial markets and prevented activities such as money laundering through banking transactions. The government could now impose taxes on financial gains in an equitable manner as well as cut channels for black money to enter the financial market. This financial reform was regarded as a significant achievement of the Kim Young-sam government as it improved the institutional basis for the financial market so that South Korea could compete in the global financial market. Furthermore, the financial market reform established an institutional infrastructure for public transparency and accountability since illegal financial transactions, including those related to political corruption, could be tracked.

In a nutshell, the Kim Young-sam government tried to dismantle the policy regime of the developmental state and to bring the overgrown bureaucracy under the control of democratically elected governors such as the president. Nevertheless, the old practices of the developmental state died hard and new ideas of liberalisation were not always immediately adopted by the elected governors and bureaucrats. For instance, the Kim government launched the 'One-Hundred-Day Plan for the New Economy' to boost the economic situation and introduced new industrial policies for small and medium enterprises and regulations on prices of basic necessities for low-income families. According to Kang (2000: 314), these measures contradicted the government policy rationale of a liberalising market economy and reducing the role of the bureaucracy. Such inconsistency between policy ideas and practices brought about many policy failures to the Kim government, one of which was the financial crisis in 1997–1998, the most catastrophic event in the recent history of the South Korean economy. Mismanagement of the liberalisation of the financial market and opening to the global market were the immediate cause of the financial crisis, but there was underlying policy inconsistency between the ideas of liberalisation and the old practices of the developmental state that could explain such failures.

4.2 The New Public Management Reform and Political Control of the Bureaucracy

In the midst of the financial crisis in 1997, the long-time opposition leader Kim Dae-jung (in office 1998–2003) was elected president. His government carried out public sector reform as one of the major reform programmes together with reforms of financial sectors, the labour market, and corporate governance after the economic crisis (Weiss 2000). Those reforms were conditions of the emergency loan from the International Monetary Fund (IMF). Regarding financial market reform, state-owned banks were privatised, while some large private banks were allowed to be sold to international capital. Together with privatisation, the financial supervisory commission was established to monitor the financial market. This was also intended to reduce the power of the Ministry of Finance and Economy.

Regarding public sector reform, the Kim Dae-jung government introduced reforms that established new agencies modelled on the Next Step agencies in the UK following the rationale of new public management. This reform was intended to make public agencies deliver better public services to citizens. Although this idea came from new public management, it reflected a significant shift in the standing of the bureaucracy from a dominating institution to an agency for public service delivery. It is important to note that President Kim Dae-jung considered social policy to be a high-priority government policy, embarking on an initiative of productive welfare (Kwon 2001; Ringen et al. 2011). While social policies were regarded as only secondary policy instruments for economic consideration under the policy regime of the developmental state, the Kim Dae-jung government gave high priority to social policies. The Employment Insurance Programme which was introduced on a small scale in 1995 was extended rapidly in order to respond to high unemployment caused by the economic crisis. A new public assistance programme was introduced to support low-income households in 2000. The National Health Insurance Programme was established, integrating the fragmented existing public health insurance funds.

These social initiatives were carried out following the social consensus that was forged in the tripartite committee which included trade unions, business organisations, and the government (Kwon 2001). The tripartite committee was established to negotiate labour market reform, which inevitably required significant concessions from the trade unions. Given the rapid increase in labour costs above the level of productivity increases before the East Asian economic crisis, labour market reform which would bring about flexibility in employment contracts was considered an essential part of the reform programmes in the wake of the financial crisis. At the tripartite committee, a deal was made in which flexible labour market reform would be implemented by the trade unions while the government would strengthen the welfare state in order to provide social protection to unemployed people and low-income families. Significant public decisions were made through political deals among various social groups. This was another salient break from the policy regime of the developmental state in which top policymakers and elite bureaucrats played a predominant role in decision-making.

Nevertheless, it was not clear whether the Kim Dae-jung government really made a clear departure from the developmental state in terms of the rationale of governance. The government bureaucracy still played a crucial role in the efforts to navigate the economic crisis and to upgrade the South Korean economy to another level by spearheading high-technology industries such as IT, mobile telephones, car manufacturing, and shipbuilding. As in the past, the government could control financial institutions such as commercial banks in the restructuring process (Lee 2002).

While the basic characteristics of the developmental state in terms of policymaking remained, despite certain modifications and changes, President Kim Dae-jung tried to take a firm grip of political control of the bureaucracy. As the first government taking power through a transition between the governing and opposition parties, the Kim Dae-jung government felt that it was very important to command loyalty from the bureaucracy. In particular, since the political and bureaucratic elite from the southwest Jeolla region had been outside the governing coalition for many years, it was an imperative for the Kim government to control the bureaucracy which had been a core of the governing coalition of the developmental state and included political and bureaucratic elites from the southeast Yeongnam region. To accomplish this, the Kim government appointed senior politicians from the party to ministerial positions (Kwon and Lee 2001). In some government positions which required expertise in the policy areas concerned, academics and professional managers who came from the Jeolla region were appointed. As the bureaucracy was essentially a hierarchical organisation, senior officials could control government ministries and agencies.

4.3 Performance Evaluation and Accountability

The Kim Dae-jung government did not only rely on political control but also introduced institutional mechanisms that could hold the bureaucracy accountable. Reflecting on government failure to prevent the economic crisis in 1997, the Kim Dae-jung government identified the inadequacy in monitoring and evaluating the performance of various government ministries and agencies as one of the underlying causes. In 2001, the Kim Dae-jung government introduced a performance management system for government ministries as part of a new public management reform (Yang 2003). The performance management system was intended to manage government ministries based on their performance outcomes. Although there were evaluating mechanisms in the government before 2001, they were mainly to evaluate public policies and programmes, analysing outcomes and outputs of public policies (Kim 2003; Oh 2018). The new system was designed to manage and evaluate government ministries, public organisations, and bureaucrats working for those institutions in a systematic manner.

In 2006, the Roh Moo-hyun government (in office 2003–2008) strengthened the performance management system by introducing the Basic Law on Government Performance and Evaluation (Law No. 7928). President Roh Moo-hyun emphasised making innovations in public management rather than pursuing small government. It was a clear contrast to the previous governments, which tried to weaken the strong bureaucracy in order to overcome the legacies of the developmental state. He demanded that government ministries implement public policies in innovative ways so that the government could meet new challenges. President Roh did not shy away from new public management reforms, although he came from a centre-left political background.

The new performance systems integrated various categories of evaluations into one comprehensive system: major policy goals, public finance, and management. It also set up the processes of performance management. Under the overall responsibility and coordination of the prime minister's office, the ministries of central government and local governments prepared annual performance plans for the financial year, implemented tasks according to plans during the year, and prepared self-evaluation reports for the end of the year. Each government ministry or public organisation needed to define its missions and responsibilities and set up mid-term organisational goals and short-term objectives. It then needed to devise a strategy to achieve those goals and objectives and set evaluative criteria of performance to ascertain to what extent it achieved these objectives and goals. Based on the results of the performance evaluation, policy choices, budgets, and sizes of organisations could be adjusted for government ministries (Kim 2019: 50).

From a perspective of accountability, which comprises three components of information, interrogation, and judgement, the performance management system provides a very useful institutional basis to hold the bureaucracy accountable. Through planning performance evaluations and preparing self-evaluation reports, government institutions gather the necessary information in a systematic manner according to goals, objectives, and outcomes. The evaluation committees, including outside experts, interrogate officials regarding the self-evaluation reports. The prime minister's office is in charge of the evaluations together with the presidential office, making final judgements on the performance of government ministries and institutions at the end.

Using this performance management system, the president can hold the government bureaucracy and public organisations accountable for their policy objectives and performance outcomes. Holding the bureaucracy accountable through the performance management system is in sharp contrast to the political control over senior bureaucrats through political loyalty. Such methods include appointment of the president's political lieutenants to senior government positions and promotion of bureaucrats to senior positions according to political loyalty. By using a performance management system, the president can give a certain degree of autonomy to bureaucracy, which allows public officials to exercise their professional expertise to produce intended outcomes. It was a basic rationale of the reinforcement of the public performance management system under the Roh Moo-hyun government (Kim 2003). Together with the performance management system, the Roh Moo-hyun government introduced a performance-related global budget system so that the government ministries could have a certain degree of autonomy in allocating the budget within their own organisation. In real-world democracies, the president needs to use both methods to control the bureaucracy and maintain accountability and political control. In the end, the president decides how to balance between these two methods of controlling the bureaucracy.

Since the introduction of the performance management system in 2006, government ministries and public institutions have carried out evaluations according to the evaluation criteria. However, the following governments of President Lee Myung-bak (in office 2008–2013) and Park Geun-hye (in office 2013–2017) resorted more to the method of political control than the performance management system. This was partly because there were weaknesses within the performance management system at the institutional level, which have been identified over the past decade-and-a-half of implementation (Kim 2019: 54–60). First, there are overlaps among different evaluations within the performance evaluation system. Each ministry needs to undertake different evaluations of outcomes for different oversight offices: their main policies (the prime minister's Office), public expenditure (the Ministry of Finance and Strategy), and organisation and personnel (Ministries of Public Administration and Personnel Management). These evaluations are often concerned with the same policy programmes and some evaluations are consequently undertaken to assess what has been evaluated. Such problems undermine the efficiency of performance evaluation activities. Second, public officials who are responsible for preparing evaluation plans and final reports in each ministry do not work closely with people in implementing departments of the same ministry. Planning evaluations and preparing reports do not thoroughly reflect what government ministries do. Such weakness led to a question about the relevance of performance evaluations. Third, the evaluation committees, who are responsible for first-order evaluations, are not given enough time for evaluation. The evaluation processes of review and interrogation are often carried out in a formal manner rather than a comprehensive way. In addition to these institutional weaknesses, there are more fundamental problems of the performance management system. Foremost, the president does not give evaluation outcomes serious consideration in his personnel management of senior officials of the government. The president does not award the ministers with good evaluation results, for instance, with promotions to higher positions, nor sanction those with poor performance. The other important limitation of the performance management system is the fact that the president and political allies do not give autonomy to the government ministries.

Instead of holding the bureaucracy accountable through the performance management system, the presidents, including the former Presidents Lee and Park, as well as the incumbent President Moon Jae-in, resorted to political control in managing the bureaucracy. At the beginning of new governments, many senior officials were dismissed because they had served the previous governments without due consideration of their professional capabilities and past performances. Those political advisers to the ministers, who were appointed from political parties and presidential campaigns, exercised increasing influence in managing administration of the ministries. To those ambitious bureaucrats, political loyalty became a necessary condition for promotion before professional expertise. Such opportunistic attitudes became problematic since public officials would not take the necessary decisions based on their expertise when policy challenges arose. Instead, they were waiting for political decisions on how to deal with those issues. The remark 'The South Korean bureaucracy has lost its soul' reflects this situation. Given the fact that the president's tenure is one five-year term, the bureaucracy will be further politicised and their competency will be continually undermined.

5. Concluding Remarks

This chapter has examined the relationship between elected presidents and the bureaucracy in the post-developmental and democratisation era from the perspective of accountability. Under the developmental state, the authoritarian president exercised strong political control over the bureaucracy, while it was unaccountable to the National Assembly and the public in general. In the post-developmental and democratic era, placing the overgrown bureaucracy under democratic control was identified as a major governance challenge facing elected presidents. The ruling political power spearheaded by the president could resort to their prerogative of appointment of senior personnel in order to command political loyalty. They could also hold the bureaucracy accountable for their work using institutional mechanisms. Adopting the concept of accountability, this chapter has examined the relationship between the elected president and the bureaucracy, focusing on the performance management system which was reinforced in 2006 under the Roh Moo-hyun government and was established as an accountability mechanism.

This chapter has shown that Korean presidents after democratisation undertook reforms to dismantle the policy regime of the developmental state and to reduce the size and influence of the bureaucracy. In particular, the presidents tried to control the bureaucracy by both the methods of political control and the institutional mechanisms of accountability, especially the performance management system. It was designed to evaluate government ministries and public institutions in a systematic way while giving them a certain degree of autonomy. Under the overall coordination of the prime minister's office, the government ministries and public institutions needed to prepare performance evaluation reports which included comprehensive information about institutional objectives, policy implementation, and outcomes.

This chapter has argued that holding the Korean bureaucracy accountable through the performance management system has not been effective. First, successive governments did not place strong importance on managing the bureaucracy, although the performance management system is still in place. Presidents came back to rely on the conventional method of political control. Political loyalty became the prevailing currency in the relationship between political power and the bureaucracy. Second, opportunistic behaviour among senior public officials between outgoing and incoming governments are to blame. Political neutrality and professionalism have been weakened. Third, the required autonomy for accountability in general and performance management in particular was never given to the bureaucracy. This is mainly because political competition among politicians and parties has been so intense that elected governors could not trust the bureaucrats unless they are certain about their political loyalty. Such tendencies have undermined the competence of the South Korean bureaucracy. It is a kind of paradox of democracy: while the bureaucracy became subject to political control, its accountability has been seriously weakened.

In order to balance between political control and bureaucratic autonomy, the bureaucracy should be controlled through the mechanism of accountability. On the bureaucratic side, it will be necessary to further develop the institutional arrangement of accountability including the performance management system. The bureaucracy needs to work more effectively and transparently to earn the trust it might be given. Elected politicians, most importantly the president, need to trust the bureaucracy with professional expertise and hold it accountable with fair systems of accountability. It is important to realise that accountability as a concept of government ethics applies not only to the bureaucracy but also to elected politicians.

Acknowledgement

This study is supported by the Oversea Training Expenses of Humanities & Social Science (2021–2022) through Seoul National University.

Bibliography

Adelman, I. (1997), 'Social Development in Korea, 1953–1993', in D. Cha, K. Kim, and D. Perkins (eds), *The Korean Economy 1945–1995* (Seoul: Korea Development Institute), 509–540.

Ahn, B., and Cheong, M. (2007), 'Minjujuui, Peongdeung, Geurigo Hyaengjeong (Democracy, Equality and Public Administration)', *Korea Review of Public Administration* 41(3), 1–40 (in Korean).

Ahn, M. (1995), 'Munminjeongbuui Haengjeonggyaeghyeok (Public Reform in the 'Civilian' Government)', *Korea Public Administration Review* 4(1), 30–57 (in Korean).

Bovens, M. (2010), 'Two Concepts of Accountability: Accountability as a Virtue and as a Mechanism', *West European Politics* 33(5), 946–967.

Brandsma, G. J., and Schillemans, T. (2013), 'The Accountability Cube: Measuring Accountability', *Journal of Public Administration Research and Theory* 23(4), 953–975.

Cho, S. (2003), 'Hangukui Tojigyaeghyeokkwa Jabonjuui' (Land Reform and Capitalism in Korea)', in C. Yoo (ed.), *The History of the Korean Development Model and its Crisis* (Seoul: Cobook), 285–314 (in Korean).

Choi, B.-S. (2014), 'Managing Economic Policy and Coordination: A Saga of the Economic Planning Board', in H. J. Kwon and Min Gyo Koo (eds), *The Korean Government and Public Policies in a Development Nexus*, 1 (New York: Springer), 31–54.

Evans, P. B. (1995), *Embedded Autonomy: States and Industrial Transformation* (Princeton, NJ: Princeton University Press).

Fukuyama, F. (2015), *Political Order and Political Decay: From the Industrial Revolution to the Globalization of Democracy*, ed. F. Fukuyama, 1st paperback edn (New York: Farrar, Straus and Giroux).

Goodin, R. E. (1988), *Reasons for Welfare: The Political Theory of the Welfare State* (Princeton, NJ: Princeton University Press).

Gough, I. (2004), 'East Asia: The Limits of Productivist Regimes', in I. Gough and G. Wood (eds), *Insecurity and Welfare Regimes in Asia, Africa and Latin America: Social Policy in Development Context* (Cambridge: Cambridge University Press), 169–201.

Han, S. (2018), 'Jeonggwongyochewa Gwanryojeui Jeongchijeok Jungrip (Government Change and Political Neutrality of Bureaucracy)', in H Kwon (ed.), *Governance for Effective Government: Democratic and Republican Perspective* (Seoul: Bakyeong SA), 55–86 (in Korean).

Im, H. (1987), 'The Rise of Bureaucratic Authoritarianism in South Korea', *World Politics* 39(2), 231–257.

Johnson, C. (1999), 'The Developmental State: Odyssey of a Concept', in M. Woo-Cumings (ed.), *The Developmental State* (Ithaca, NY: Cornell University Press), 32–60.

Kang, K. (2000), 'Singyeongje Pyaekil Gyehoik (New Economy 100 Days Plan)', *Economic Papers* 39(3), 311–323 (in Korean).

Kim, H. G. (2003), 'Hangukui Gigwanpyeongga Ironjeok Nongo (A Theoretical Review of Korean Agency Evaluation)', *Korean Public Administration Review* 37(4), 57–79 (in Korean).

Kim, H. J. (2007), 'Kim Young-sam Daetongryongui Rideosipgwa Munminjeongbuui Kaehyeok Pyonggwa (President Kim Yongsam's Leadership and Evaluation of Governance of the "Civilian" Government)', in Korean Association of Political Studies (ed.), *Presidential Leadership in Korea and National Development* (Seoul: Inkansarang), 199–244 (in Korean).

Kim, J. (2019), 'Jungang Jeongbuui Jachepyeonggae Deahan Yeongu (A Study on the Self-Evaluation of the Central Government Agencies)', in Research Center for State-Owned Entities (ed.), *2019 Public Agencies and Public Policies* (Sejong: Korea Institute of Public Finance), 37–70.

Kookmin Ilbo (1992), 'New Economy is Autonmy', 22 December, 1922.

Kwon, H. J. (2001), 'Globalization, Unemployment and Policy Responses in Korea: Repositioning the State?', *Global Social Policy* 1(2), 213–234.

Kwon, K. D., and Lee, H. C. (2001), 'Jeongchi Gwonryeokui Gyochewa Haengjeong Eliteui Chungwon (The Change of Political Power and the Administrative Elite in Korea)', *Korean Policy Studies Review* 10(1), 117–140 (in Korean).

Lee, Y. (2002), 'Debate on the Emergence of the Regulatory State in Financial Sector Reform in Korea', *Korea Sociology* 36(4), 59–88.

Lipsky, M. (1980), *Street-Level Bureaucracy: Dilemmas of the Individual in Public Services* (New York: Russell Sage Foundation).

O'Donnell, G. A. (1973), *Modernization and Bureaucratic-Authoritarianism; Studies in South American Politics*, Politics of modernization series (Berkeley, CA: Institute of International Studies).

Oh, C. (2018), 'Performance Management and Evaluation', in K. Namgung, K.-H. Cho, and S.-M. Kim (eds), *Public Administration and Policy in Korea: Its Evolution and Challenges* (London: Routledge), 157–176.

Persson, T., Roland, G., and Tabellini, G. (1997), 'Separation of Powers and Political Accountability', *The Quarterly Journal of Economics* 112(4), 1163–1202.

Peters, B. G. (2018), *The Politics of Bureaucracy: An Introduction to Comparative Public Administration*, 1, 7th edn (Florence: Routledge).

Ringen, S., Kwon, H., Yi, I., Kim, T., and Lee, J. (2011), *The Korean State and Social Policy: How South Korea Lifted Itself from Poverty and Dictatorship to Affluence and Democracy* (New York: Oxford University Press).

Romzek, B. S., and Dubnick, M. J. (1987), 'Accountability in the Public Sector: Lessons from the Challenger Tragedy', *Public Administration Review* 47(3), 227–238.

UN Nathan Report (1954), 'An Economic Program for Korean Reconstruction' (New York: United Nations Korean Reconstruction Agency).

Weiss, L. (2000), 'Developmental State in Transition: Adapting, Dismantling, Innovating, Not "Normalizing"', *The Pacific Review* 13(1), 21–55.

White, Gordon (ed.) (1988), *Developmental States in East Asia* (New York: St Martin's).

Woo, J. (1991), *Race to the Swift: State and Finance in Korean Industrialization* (New York: Columbia University Press).

Yang, J. (2003), 'Jeonggwongyochewa Gwanryocheui Jeongchijeok Tongchee Gwanhan Yeongu (An Analysis of Political Control over the Bureaucracy and Change of Political Power)' *Korea Public Administration Review* 37(2), 263–287.

Yoon, G., and Park, J. (2016), 'Gaebalyeondaeui Gukgagwanryocheui Jeongchaekjiphaenge Gwanhan Yeongu (An Analysis of Policy Implementation of the State Bureaucracy in the Developmental Era)', *Korea Public Administration Review* 50(4), 211–242 (in Korean).

CHAPTER 29

THE DEVELOPMENT OF WELFARE PROGRAMMES

JOOHA LEE

1. INTRODUCTION

This chapter begins by identifying the unique aspects of the East Asian welfare model as compared with Western welfare capitalism. Next, it examines the key principles and features underlying the welfare programmes of South Korea, which can be captured by the notion of 'developmental welfarism' or 'welfare developmentalism'. Since the 1997 Asian Financial Crisis, there has been a series of welfare reforms under the two centre-left governments (1998–2007) and the two conservative governments (2008–2017). To what extent did these welfare reforms represent a major departure from policy legacies of developmental welfarism?

Welfare politics can be largely assessed through three political prisms: bureaucratic politics, partisan politics, and social politics. The most influential theoretical stream in explaining the welfare development in East Asia, including South Korea, is the state-centred approach that highlights bureaucratic politics (Goodman et al. 1998; Lee 2008; Tang 2000; Takegawa 2005). However, a surge of new research has focused on the burgeoning role played by partisan politics in the welfare reforms of South Korea (Fleckenstein and Lee 2020; Kim 2012; Yang 2017). In addition, a new wave of research analysing South Korean welfare reforms has focused on social politics (e.g. Lee and Kim 2019). The increasing attention attracted by those two arenas does not deny the salience of bureaucratic politics, nor does it mean that the state-centred model is of secondary importance. Finally, the concluding section will briefly address the challenges facing the South Korean welfare state today.

2. Developmental Welfarism and Its Legacies

The best-known and most influential typology in the study of welfare states is the one constructed by Esping-Andersen (1990). He clustered welfare regimes into liberal (Anglo-Saxon), conservative/corporatist (Continental European), and social democratic (Nordic) models to examine the extent to which social policy 'decommodifies' labour. In terms of his typology, the welfare state in East Asia, including South Korea, has often been viewed as belonging to either the conservative model, the liberal model, or a hybrid regime of liberalism and conservatism (see, for instance, Kim 2002). Esping-Andersen (1997) himself asserted that Japan should be considered not as a unique fourth type of regime, but as a hybrid of key elements of the conservative regime (e.g. occupational segmentation and familialism) with a liberal, US-style dominance of private welfare systems. Although East Asian welfare states have accepted many aspects of Western welfare models, they depart from Western experiences in practice.

2.1 The East Asian Welfare Regime

In contrast to the classification of Western welfare states, there have been a number of efforts to provide an Indigenous typology for East Asia, such as the 'Confucian welfare state' (Jones 1993), the 'East Asian welfare model' (Goodman and Peng 1996; Goodman et al. 1998), the 'productivist welfare regime' (Gough 2004; Holliday 2000), and the 'developmental welfare state/regime' (Chung 2006; Kwon 2005; Ringen et al. 2011). These studies share a common finding that social welfare in East Asia is strictly subordinate to the overriding policy objective of economic efficiency and growth. As stated by Holliday and Wilding (2003): 'when the chips are down, Western states have always given the economy priority over social policy, but that priority has generally been less explicit and more reluctant. It has been a stance in need of justification, rather than a policy given' (2003: 14).

Social and economic goals are often compatible and closely linked, insofar as social welfare does not hinder economic development. The developmental strategies of the East Asian newly industrialised countries (NICs), which are concerned with export-oriented and labour-intensive industrialisation, have depended on the effective utilisation of human resources, while maintaining a disciplined and low-cost labour force. Under these circumstances, economic development was energised by welfare programmes that strengthened labour productivity and training. Given the cultural heritage in these countries, which assigns great value to education and a high status to educated people, the policies also promoted investments in human resources through education (Lee 2014b).

The overwhelming priority in the economic development of East Asia was to impose a minimum financial burden to the state by maintaining a low level of public spending on social welfare. Compared with their Western counterparts, East Asian governments are low social spenders that are less involved in providing and financing social welfare. At the same time, they are 'regulators' that enforce welfare programmes without providing sufficient direct finance (Goodman et al. 1998, 13). Instead, private actors such as family and community members, as well as voluntary and commercial sectors, have been expected to play a prominent welfare role, buttressed by Confucian cultural ideology. Conservative gender roles and the gendered division of paid and unpaid work went hand in hand with the developmental welfare strategy of the East Asian states (Fleckenstein and Lee 2020; S. C. Lee 2018). In addition, the East Asian developmental states claimed that the social needs of their populations would be best met by increasing the real income in the labour market, driven by high and stable economic growth, together with low unemployment. These states might be seen as ardent believers in the trickle-down theory, which held that increasing the national income by prioritising economic growth would have a trickle-down effect throughout the population—even to the poorest people (Shin 2003; Tang 2000).

Finally, it is worth highlighting three key interrelated notions that illuminate and identify the specific characteristics underlying East Asian welfare states by broadening the conventional concept and analysis of welfare programmes through the inclusion of 'functional equivalents' (Estevez-Abe 2008), 'surrogate social policy' (Kim 2010), and 'multifunctional institutions' (Kwon and Yi 2009). Estevez-Abe (2008) extends the traditional approach that focuses on a narrow range of social spending schemes by introducing the concept of functional equivalent programmes (e.g. public works, subsidies to rural families, market restricting regulations, and employment protections) as various types of state intervention that are not typically considered social policy instruments. In an attempt to recalibrate the relationship between economic and social policies to capture the hidden aspects of state intervention in social welfare, Kim (2010) adopts the term 'surrogate social policy' (Chang 2004), which includes various subsidies and regulations in favour of rural farmers and small- and medium-sized businesses. Another focus should be on how the government mobilises and coordinates public institutions, such as rice-purchasing schemes, education institutes, and public health facilities, to perform a variety of functions to achieve its goals of economic development and poverty reduction (Kwon and Yi 2009).

2.2 Features and Legacies of Welfare Programmes in South Korea

As the East Asian developmental welfare state prioritised economic growth and industrialisation, the fact that the state provided minimum financial commitment to welfare within the lens of fiscal conservatism enormously influenced the subsequent

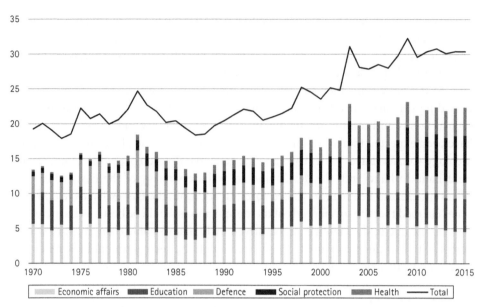

FIGURE 29.1: General government spending in Korea, 1970–2015 (% of GDP)

Source: OECD (2021a).

development of social policy in South Korea (Chung 2006; Kwon 2005; Lee 2008). As shown in Figure 29.1, a large share of general government spending was devoted to the productive sectors of the economy (i.e. economic affairs and education, on the one hand, and defence, on the other). In the course of the export-led and labour-intensive industrialisation, the South Korean developmental welfare state focused on improving human capital, which was expected to strengthen not just the productive potential of individuals, but also their self-reliance. Hence, there was a high proportion of general government spending on education, despite the small proportion of spending on social protection expenditure (see also Jacobs 2000). The allocation of the social spending, which was already limited by the developmental strategy, was further restricted by the extraordinary requirements of national defence expenditure in the South-North division of Korea—particularly during the authoritarian military regimes before the political democratisation of 1987. Consequently, the high amounts of public spending on national defence and economic development left little for social expenditure on social protection and health.

As noted previously, in East Asia, including South Korea, the state is not just a low social spender but also plays a substantial welfare role as a regulator. Prior to the 1987 democratisation, the authoritarian developmental welfare state used its regulatory power to shift the responsibility for welfare onto companies and families. It thus developed a welfare system that relied heavily on the occupational welfare sector in terms of the close relationship between social policy and labour control policy (Yi 2007). Family welfare, which is encouraged by Confucian cultural ideology (e.g. filial piety, individual self-help, and family interdependence), mitigated much of the need for state welfare. This caused the responsibility for providing social care and service to rest with families (Lee et al. 2016). Furthermore, to maximise the state's investment in economic development, it was critical for women to generally serve as unpaid caregivers (Lee 2018).

Given the state's role as a low social spender, the major welfare programmes depended on the social insurance principle which maintains that a person should first contribute before claiming any benefit (Kwon 1999; Lee 1999). This can be referred to as the 'mandatory but privately-financed' social insurance principle in which the state's role as a provider is minimal. The Industrial Accident Insurance Programme (1964), the National Health Insurance Programme (1977), the National Pension Programme (1988), the Employment Insurance Programme (1995), and the Long-Term Care Insurance (2008) were all financed from contributions paid by the insured and their employers, with little financial contribution from the state beyond administrative costs. The initial choice of policy design, which relied on the mandatory but privately financed insurance programme, was determined and reinforced by the minimum financial commitment of the state to welfare. The social insurance programmes were fragmented along occupational lines because the authoritarian developmental welfare state used them to appease certain sectors of the public, starting with civil servants, the military, private school teachers, and industrial workers in large companies. In addition to the prevalent role of enterprise welfare, the social insurance programmes were linked to work at their inception. In short, there was a link between work and welfare because of the work-based, contributory insurance programmes, as well as strong company welfare.

Furthermore, without socially guaranteed minimum standards of welfare provision, there was a strong emphasis on self-reliance. This was well illustrated in the old social assistance programme enacted in 1961, the Livelihood Protection System (LPS). The LPS did not grant a guaranteed income benefit as a social right, as it emphasised the spirit of self-reliance and work incentives. The number of social assistance recipients under the LPS tended to be restricted because the allocated budget was generally considered short of what was needed to protect the entire poor population at that time (Organisation for Economic Co-operation and Development (OECD) 2000). The Basic Law of Social Security, which was enacted in 1963 and replaced by the 1995 Social Security Act, also specified 'self-help, work incentives, and a minimal level of government involvement in social welfare, all of which were symbolic manifestations of developmentalism in the Korean welfare system' (Chung 2006: 156).

The 'economy-first' developmental strategy and its marginalisation of social policy were initiated and advocated for by the conservative ruling coalition among authoritarian political leaders, economic officials, and big businesses (Chung 2006; Kwon 1999; Shin 2003). The crucial interventionist role of the developmental state was amplified through 'organisational and institutional links between politically insulated state developmental agencies and major private-sector firms' (Deyo 1987: 19). Accordingly, the developmental welfare state before the 1987 democratisation relied on a combination of coalescence between the authoritarian regimes and Chaebol, as well as the political subordination of civil society and labour.

The welfare programmes espoused by the South Korean developmental state not only served an economic function advancing the developmental strategy, but also had political purposes, such as establishing political legitimacy, social control, and nation building. Even the authoritarian regimes still had to maintain popular support by providing social welfare; 'Life is somewhat easier for non-democratic states—but only slightly, as they too must enjoy public support if they are to remain in office for long and rule effectively' (Ramesh 2004: 8). According to Kwon (1999), welfare programmes were initiated in an attempt to enhance the legitimacy of the authoritarian regimes at critical junctures, such as the military coup of 1961, the constitutional reform of 1972, and the political turmoil of 1980. Given the social and political instability in these times, the conservative ruling elites 'made some anticipatory concessions to industrial workers in order to block the transformation of labour from a potential to a real threat to the regimes' (Joo 1999: 406).

In sum, the characteristics of the welfare programmes offered by the South Korean developmental welfare state ('developmental welfarism' or 'welfare developmentalism') can be encapsulated in the following interrelated components: (a) the state's role as a regulator and a low social spender (in combination with the prominent welfare role demanded of the private sector); (b) the mandatory but privately financed social insurance principle; (c) the link between work and welfare through an enterprise-centred and employment-centred system; and (d) a strong emphasis on human capital investment and self-reliance without a commitment to socially guaranteed minimum standards of provision. The historical legacies of the developmental welfare state remained embedded until the economic crisis of 1997, specifically in terms of 'interaction effects between institutional arrangements and other elements of a particular political configuration' (Pierson 2001: 9). In a sense, these can serve as a yardstick for measuring the lines of continuity, as well as the major departures in the welfare development of South Korea.

3. Welfare Reforms since the 1997 Economic Crisis

The welfare reform following the Asian Financial Crisis of 1997 was a turning point in the history of South Korean welfare development (e.g. Kim 2002; Ringen et al. 2011). The origins of the 1997 economic crisis remain a matter of controversy, but whatever the causes, it had devastating economic and social repercussions, such as declining macroeconomic conditions, increasing unemployment, and greater income disparities. In a sense, the economic crisis might be seen as what Wilsford (1994) calls 'conjunctural forces' or what Sabatier and Jenkins-Smith (1999) identify as 'significant perturbations external to the subsystem', which are a critical prerequisite to major policy change. Although the economic crisis prompted welfare reform, including the expansion of state welfare in South Korea, other countries in the region, such as Hong Kong and Singapore, weathered the crisis without undertaking welfare reform (Tang 2000). Therefore, the substance of welfare reform was more profoundly affected by an interaction between institutional arrangements and strategic manoeuvring by political actors, which constitutes welfare politics.

3.1 Welfare Reforms under Centre-Left (1998–2007) and Conservative (2008–2017) Regimes

Although the economic crisis itself did not automatically translate into welfare reform, it did lead to the conditions that strengthened the possibility of changes to the policy legacies of the developmental welfare state. Given the minimal role of state welfare and the strong emphasis on self-reliance, South Korea had insufficient public provisions for the unemployed, as the state had maintained near-full employment before the 1997 economic crisis. In addition, family and company welfare, which obviated much of the need for state welfare, could not fulfil its welfare role in the context of the economic crisis. According to Kwon (2005), the post-crisis welfare reform was viewed as a transformation within welfare developmentalism, namely, from 'selective welfare developmentalism' (based on productivism, selective social investment, and authoritarianism) to 'inclusive welfare developmentalism' (productivism, universal social investment, and democratic governance). In a selective form of the developmental welfare state before the 1997 crisis, welfare programmes were used as an instrument of economic policy (productivist), structured in such a way that risk-pooling was narrow within particular social categories (selective), and motivated mainly by political justification of the authoritarian regime (authoritarian). The post-crisis welfare reform was carried out in order to change the South Korean welfare state in the latter two dimensions, while maintaining a productivist orientation (Kwon 2005).

In the wake of the economic crisis, Kim Dae-jung, as the erstwhile political opponent of military authoritarianism, won the presidential election, which marked the first democratic transition of power from the long-entrenched, conservative ruling party to an opposition party. President Kim Dae-jung (1998–2002) advocated for productive welfare as the new South Korean welfare paradigm (Presidential Committee for Quality of Life 1999). President Kim was more committed to social welfare than his predecessors, who were in favour of developmental ideas prioritising the economy above all. The Kim government's flagship productive welfare initiative included the introduction of the new social assistance, National Basic Livelihood Security Act (NBLSA), the expansion of the National Pension and Employment Insurance Programmes, and the adoption of an integrated system in the National Health Insurance (see Chung 2006; Lee 2014a; Ringen et al. 2011).

Kim Dae-jung's successor, President Roh Moo-hyun (2003–2007), announced the Vision 2030 plan as a comprehensive long-term strategy aiming to strike a balance between economic growth and social welfare. The centrepieces of the Roh government's welfare reform were childcare services, the tax-based Basic Pension Programme, the Long-Term Care Insurance for the elderly, and the Earned Income Tax Credit (see Lee et al. 2016; Lee 2018; Peng 2014; Yang 2017). However, despite these efforts, welfare reform under the Roh government 'was increasingly neutralised by benefit cuts for financial sustainability and a rising gap within the working class in terms of income, job security, corporate welfare, and entitlements to social insurance benefits' (Yang 2017: 154). Moreover, pro-welfare reforms during the two centre-left presidencies of Kim Dae-jung and Roh Moo-hyun were bounded by dilemmas ensuing from the Kim and Roh administrations' neoliberal economic policies, such as financial liberalisation and labour market flexibilisation.

The centre-left governments (1998–2007) were followed by the return of right-wing governments under the leadership of Lee Myung-bak (2008–2012) and Park Geun-hye (2013–2017), who inherited the political base of the previous authoritarian regime. The key concern of these conservative governments was based on market-conforming priorities in an overall policy paradigm designed to promote small government and neoliberal principles. However, the Lee and Park administrations were also sympathetic to pro-welfare reform in attempts to gather popular support and mobilise votes. The conservative embrace of a welfare agenda is also closely associated with the emergence of so-called new social risks in a post-industrial society. New social risks include precarious employment, labour market segmentation, working poverty, single parenthood, work–life imbalance, and long-term care for an ageing population; by contrast, old social risks refer to unemployment, illness, disability, and poverty in the post-war Keynesian welfare state era. As a new welfare paradigm, the social investment approach is committed to coping with new social risks in terms of public investments in early childhood care, education, training, reconciliation policies, lifelong learning, and active ageing (e.g. Bonoli 2007; Morel et al. 2012).

Given that South Korea currently has the lowest fertility rate and the most rapidly ageing population among the OECD countries, family policy expansion is inevitable, even for conservative actors which strongly uphold minimal state welfare and fiscal austerity. As argued by Fleckenstein and Lee (2017, 2020), the conscious efforts made by the Lee and Park administrations to surpass the advancements made by their centre-left predecessors represented a remarkable policy U-turn from the conservative party, which was originally in favour of traditional family and gender role values; the two conservative governments continued to support 'a social investment turn in family policy', such as improving free universal childcare and parental leave benefits. However, it should also be noted that the Lee government did not compromise its stance on tax cuts, and President Park took the contradictory position of 'more welfare with no tax increase' (see Yang 2017). In other words, the conservative governments were more than willing to agree with conservative (economic) officials and other entrenched coalitions of the right on economy-first developmental welfare and fiscal conservatism, while also asserting that work is the greatest form of welfare.

3.2 Two Rationales for the Inclusive Type of Developmental Welfarism

To what extent has the series of welfare reforms after the 1997 crisis departed from the policy legacies of developmental welfarism, specifically, selective welfare developmentalism? To answer this question, there are two interrelated criteria that should be considered for the successful implementation of inclusive welfare developmentalism. The first criterion is that the government should strengthen social rights, social inclusion, and redistribution, at least by guaranteeing a minimum living standard to all those in need. To achieve this, and to differentiate itself from the historical legacies of the developmental welfare state, which were in support of minimal income support combined with low social spending, new welfare reform needs to improve income maintenance benefits. This also implies a meaningful shift in the previous role of the state as a low spender and a regulator, specifically by increasing the state commitment to social welfare as a provider.

The second criterion is enhancing employability and social investment throughout the whole lifetime of a person. It should be noted that the main priority of the developmental welfare state was employability and investment in human resources, mainly aiming towards self-reliance and economic productivity. However, this did not mean that the South Korean government's spending effort prior to the 1997 economic crisis was devoted to active labour market measures. For example, in 1996, the public spending on active labour market programmes was only 0.1 per cent of gross domestic product (GDP) (Martin 1998). During the economic buoyancy of the past few decades, the developmental welfare state was content to rely exclusively on economic growth to meet employment needs, while additionally facilitating company training (Lee 2014b).

The social investment strategy can be traced back to the Swedish 'active manpower policy', which includes benefits as part of the 'productivist' approach. However, the current approaches, such as a US-style 'workfare' and the UK 'welfare-to-work', emphasise the activation of benefit payments, thereby promoting training and work experience at the expense of passive forms of income support for the unemployed and labour market outsiders (see Clasen 1999: 161–162). At this point, the inclusive developmental welfarism in South Korea, which has relatively few 'passive' benefits to be activated, should not be simply equated with Western social investment strategies. In addition, the main problem of the South Korean welfare system has been neither an excessive welfare budget nor welfare dependency, as has been claimed for Western welfare states. Instead, social provision in South Korea used to be accused of having low levels of welfare budget and income maintenance benefits due to the state's minimal commitment to welfare.

To what extent did the welfare reforms represent a breakaway from the policy legacies of developmental welfarism in light of the aforementioned two criteria? The answer is mixed. On some level, the welfare reforms since the 1997 crisis did mark a significant change because the South Korean governments have strengthened income maintenance benefits, such as social assistance and unemployment benefits, by extending their coverage and raising the benefit level (Kwon 2005; Ringen et al. 2011). This means that the reforms departed from some policy legacies, such as the commitment to minimal income support and a strong emphasis on self-reliance without socially guaranteed minimum standards of provision.

However, the beneficiaries of the new social assistance of NBLSA, which was the Kim government's key reform initiative, represented too small a portion of the poor due to its strict eligibility rules, particularly the family support criterion. To be eligible for social assistance benefits in South Korea, claimants must prove an absence of private support from extended-family members, called 'supporters'. As of 2018, social assistance benefits are provided to 1.74 million people, which is approximately 3.4 per cent of the population (Korean Statistical Information Service (KOSIS) 2020a); this is well below the 16.7 per cent of the population in relative poverty, which is one of the highest portions among OECD member countries (OECD 2021b).[1] Altogether, this indicates that the family support criteria should be rapidly abolished. Since the 1997 economic crisis, the governments in power have taken increasing responsibility in financing social welfare. However, as Figure 29.2 clearly demonstrates, South Korea's social expenditure was 12.2 per cent of its GDP, which is far short of the OECD average of 20 per cent. Consequently, the South Korean state can still be regarded as a low social spender and a regulator. This is closely related to the fact that the total tax as a percentage of GDP was 27.4 per cent for South Korea, thus ranking thirty-first among thirty-seven OECD countries, as shown in Figure 29.2.

As discussed in section 3.1 'Welfare Reforms under Centre-Left (1998–2007) and Conservative (2008–2017) Regimes', some welfare reforms since the 1997 Asian Financial Crisis exhibited a social investment turn in family policy that departed from the Confucian path of family policy (see Fleckenstein and Lee 2020). According to Peng (2014), social investment in South Korea has become more inclusive, specifically by expanding its focus from the productive sector alone to embrace vulnerable populations such as children, women, and the elderly; at the same time, new investment in social care has been used as a main tool to develop the social service industry and mobilise the underutilised human capital of women. Regarding the social investment turn in labour market policy, the South Korean governments have implemented a strong activation framework, specifically consisting of workfare-oriented activation policies. Due to the neoliberal economic reforms after the 1997 crisis, the labour-market duality between regular and non-regular employment deepened. Given that South Korea's labour market is characterised by a high degree of duality, a very low job tenure, and a high level of informality, a recent OECD report (2018) concludes that significant additional action is necessary to make income and employment supports more effective and inclusive. Social investment strategies can be pursued in either a more protective way or a more productive way (Lee 2014b), and the South Korean developmental welfare state needs more of the former than the latter.

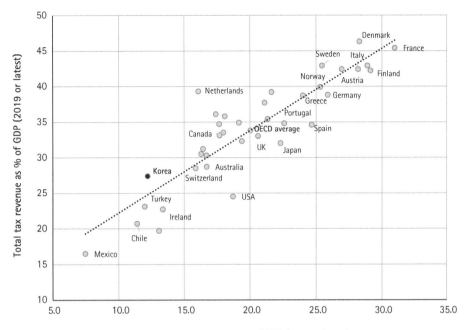

FIGURE 29.2: Public social expenditure and total tax revenue in OECD countries

Source: OECD (2020a, 2020b).

4. THREE ARENAS OF WELFARE POLITICS

Any analysis of welfare politics should aim to accomplish two goals: to identify the salience of institutional arrangements and effects; and to embrace the important roles of political agency, conflict, and choice, thus mirroring the essential debates that have taken place in social science research on the relationship between agency and structure/institution.[2] A proper explanation of welfare politics should also focus on the complex interweaving of state and society, while avoiding a dichotomy between the society-centred power resources model and the neo-Weberian, state-centred analyses. On this basis, welfare politics can be examined in terms of three approaches: bureaucratic politics, partisan politics, and social politics.

4.1 The Bureaucratic Politics of Welfare Reform

Competent and autonomous state bureaucracy plays a significant role in (social) policymaking; this is postulated not only by the state-centred framework in comparative studies (Evans et al. 1985; Skocpol 1992), but also by key studies examining East Asian welfare states (Goodman et al. 1998; Ringen et al. 2011; Takegawa 2005; Tang 2000). As argued by Skocpol (1992: 42), state officials have their own ideas and organisational interests, and they pursue policies that will further those ideas and interests, or at least not harm them. Key bureaucrats with professional knowledge and expertise play a decisive role in an era of welfare-state retrenchment, as well as in times of welfare-state expansion (Dahlström 2009; Marier 2005).

The developmental strategy in East Asian countries such as South Korea was initiated and advocated by conservative state elites, including economic bureaucrats. Specifically, it was based upon the institutional arrangement that necessitated the involvement of powerful state elites. The decision-making framework used in South Korea can be characterised by the centralisation of power in the president and the exceptional authority of the economic bureaucracy. The pivotal role of the president as a chief policymaker is derived from the office's constitutional authority, as established in Chapter IV of the Constitution. Then, owing to the political power and status of the presidency, the presidents' ideas were magnified in the structure of welfare provision and infused into welfare institutions 'through formal legislation, financial supports, stimulation through government campaign and regulation through monitoring and supervision' (Yi 2007: 308).

The economy-minded developmental strategy established a strong economic bureaucracy, which had a higher status in the government structure than other ministries. Economy-related ministries determined the overall budget and expenditure items of each ministry. Along with controlling the budgetary process, senior economic officials were regularly promoted into leadership positions in other ministries, including the Ministry of Health and Welfare (MOHW) and powerful presidential secretariats in the Office of the President. This means that economic officials were a type of 'veto player', that is, an 'individual or collective decision-maker whose agreement is required for the change of the status quo' (Tsebelis 2000: 442). Whereas economy-related ministries were the dominant forces at the level of national state administration, the MOHW was peripheral to decision-making; the marginalisation of social welfare was further fuelled by the MOHW's marginal status, and hence passive administrative culture.

Although state actors have had dwindling power and control over societal actors since the 1987 democratisation, the strong presidential system and powerful economic bureaucracy still retain executive authority and therefore remain crucial in decision-making. Following the onset of democratisation, South Korean state elites, particularly economic officials, have still commanded strong institutional resources afforded by the historical legacies of the developmental state. As pointed out by Evans and his colleagues (1985), officials in the treasury and finance departments tend to have strongly conservative policy orientations. As a result, economic bureaucrats are in support of cost containment, competitive austerity, a strong work ethic, and minimal state welfare, which have represented the main obstacles for the MOHW and pro-welfare groups. Finally, the disproportionate power and organisational capacity between economy-related ministries and other ministries have deeply affected the whole policy process, including not only central decision-making, but also local-level implementation (see Lee 2009, 2014a).

4.2 The Partisan Politics of Welfare Reform

The development of the three worlds of welfare capitalism is 'largely the product of different patterns of partisan government experienced by the end of first three postwar decades' (Iversen and Stephens 2008: 28). In other words, when attempting to understand and identify the development of different welfare regimes in Western advanced democracy, it is useful to consider partisan politics; such politics, which have been somewhat overlooked by the neo-institutionalist explanations, can still have a substantial impact in the restructuring process of the Western welfare state (Huber and Stephens 2001; Iversen and Stephens 2008; Ross 2000). According to Häusermann, Picot, and Geering (2013), the 'new school' of partisan politics highlights the changing electoral constituencies in the post-industrial age, the role played by the party systems, and the competition existing between parties, while simultaneously questioning the assertions of the traditional partisan politics: that there is a linear and direct relationship between the type of party in power (e.g. social democratic, liberal, or conservative) and the policy output.

The evolution of welfare systems in East Asia reflects neither the Western experience of right–left party politics nor the partisan composition of the government in power at the time (Estevez-Abe 2008; Goodman et al. 1998; Tang 2000). Given the conservative dominance of partisan politics in East Asia, Western explanations, which are often couched in terms of the power wielded by left parties, appear to be less relevant to East Asian cases. For example, Japanese politics is often depicted as a 'one-party dominant regime' (Pempel 1990), wherein the conservative Liberal Democratic Party has enjoyed a majority in Japan's bicameral legislature for most of the post-war period. Meanwhile, in Korea, the South–North division resulted in an exclusive inclination towards a conservative political culture, and because of this there were no left-leaning or labour parties in South Korea's unicameral legislature before the 2004 parliamentary elections. However, considering partisan politics—such as the key features of the rules of electoral competition and the structures of party systems—can help to draw a more accurate picture of welfare politics in East Asia, including South Korea.[3]

Partisan politics in South Korea became regionally based following the democratisation of 1987. This regionalism has been reinforced by the South Korean electoral system, which is based on a first-past-the-post and single-member district system. This has benefitted the major existing parties, whose supporters are geographically concentrated in certain areas, and it has made it difficult for a new progressive party to make inroads into parliament (Lee 2008; Ringen et al. 2011). Given the historical weakness of the political left in South Korea, the electoral competition between the centre-left party and the conservative party must be considered in any explanation of welfare reforms. In recent pension reform, the two political parties took a crucial role in shaping both policies and public opinion, and the vibrant strategic interactions among the parties determined the details of the revised legislation (Kim 2012). During the ten years that centre-left governments were in power (1998–2007), the work/family reconciliation policy gained political salience, while family policy continued to expand under the two conservative governments (2008–2017) to attract young voters and young women voters (see Fleckenstein and Lee 2020). Therefore, the new school of partisan politics seems better suited than the traditional partisan theory for understanding the development of welfare states in South Korea.

4.3 The Social Politics of Welfare Reform

The discourse surrounding social politics can begin with the power resources model, which views welfare state development in terms of the organisational and political power held by the working class and the social democratic parties (Esping-Andersen 1990; Korpi 1983). The original power resources model mainly argues that the strength of class mobilisation and class coalitions has historically had a substantial effect on the trajectory of welfare state development. In Western welfare states, both partisan politics and social politics have the same political underpinnings—namely, the influence of working-class forces and social democratic or labour parties. The weakness of the organised working class and leftist parties may account for the fact that the East Asian welfare systems have lagged behind those of states in which organised labour has regularly wielded political power. However, this does not explain how specific social policies could be introduced (Kwon 1999), as in Skocpol's argument regarding the US case (Skocpol 1992).

The locus of power in the union organisations of South Korea is at the enterprise level, although there are industry-wide federations. Enterprise unionism has contributed to the fragmented structure of trade unions and the decentralised nature of collective bargaining practices. Company-based unions tend to limit their demands and activities to firm-level issues such as wage increases, labour conditions, and occupational welfare (Yi 2007). Not only are these unions poorly centralised within enterprise unionism, but they also lack sufficient strength in terms of union density. Following the Great Labour Struggle of 1987, union density in South Korea peaked at almost 20 per cent in 1989, then gradually declining to a low 10.3 per cent in 2005, and it currently remains at about 11 per cent (KOSIS 2020b). This is because both workers in small- and medium-sized firms and non-regular (i.e. temporary and daily) workers found it difficult to maintain their union memberships. In 2018, only 0.1 per cent of workers in firms with fewer than 30 employees were unionised, whereas large companies with more than 300 workers reached unionisation of 50.6 per cent (KOSIS 2020b). Due to enterprise unionism, low union density, and labour-market duality, trade unions have a restricted influence on East Asian welfare politics, so more attention should be paid to the crucial roles played by other non-parliamentary social forces as a basis for power mobilisation and new political constellations.

The notion of solidarity or coalition-building within civil society can better elucidate how social politics affect welfare development in non-Western democracies that have neither strong (industry-level) unions nor a significant social democratic influence. Particular attention should be paid to the alliance between the class-oriented, old social movement (i.e. trade unions) and the citizenship-oriented, new social movement (i.e. civic advocacy groups). Along with solidarity within civil society, pro-welfare reform can be more readily driven by a strategic coalition between civil society and other political spheres, such as the government and political parties. Within this context, the structure of social politics consists of the interplay among civic advocacy groups, labour unions, and political leadership (for more details, see Lee and Kim 2019).

In South Korea, where civic advocacy groups are well developed at the national level, the pro-welfare alliance within civil society can play a pivotal role in welfare politics. Since the 1987 democratisation, civic advocacy groups have steadily developed a cohesive agenda-setting capacity, strengthened their financial independence, and increased their power as policy initiators. As a result, South Korean civic advocacy groups have often been able to successfully pursue an 'insider' strategy (i.e. speaking directly with political elites in private meetings or cultivating long-term relationships with them), as well as a classic 'outsider' strategy (i.e. calling for demonstrations or getting people into the street to protest) (for more details on insider and outsider advocacy strategies, see Pekkanen et al. 2014). To this end, the pro-welfare solidarity cultivated by civic advocacy groups is the primary locus of social politics in South Korea's welfare reform.

5. Conclusion

The series of welfare reforms following the 1997 economic crisis exhibited a notable deviation from some of the policy legacies of developmental welfarism, but these did not translate into a wholesale shift in the welfare regime. A robust pro-welfare alliance within civil society can facilitate pro-welfare reform and, when combined with support from political leadership that wields strong institutional resources, enables the further expansion of welfare in the South Korean developmental welfare state (Lee and Kim 2019). Finally, it is worth noting the pending agenda and challenges ahead.

First, the coverage of social insurance as the main pillar of the South Korean welfare state should be strengthened. Compared with other OECD countries, South Korea has a relatively high share of non-standard workers, such as non-regular (i.e. temporary and daily) and self-employed workers, who have been hit hard by the COVID-19 pandemic. Whereas regular workers in South Korea are both labour market insiders and social security insiders, non-regular workers and marginal workers in small companies have a substantially lower chance of being protected by social insurance programmes. For example, only about one-half of workers are enrolled in the Employment Insurance Programme (EIP). In addition to the low EIP coverage among non-regular workers, self-employed workers in South Korea make up about 25 per cent of total employment, which is higher than the OECD average of 15 per cent, and most of these self-employed workers are not covered by the EIP (OECD 2018; People's Solidarity for Participatory Democracy (PSPD) 2020). Before the COVID-19 outbreak, South Korea was 'facing the challenge of reducing dualities between regular and non-regular workers, the latter of which account for around 30 per cent of all employees, and the pandemic is aggravating that duality' (International Labour Organisation (ILO) 2020: 7). Therefore, there is an urgent need for the introduction of a full-scale expansion of the EIP to cover all workers, including non-standard workers, by setting new eligibility criteria based on an individual's total income, regardless of employment type (PSPD 2020).[4]

Another key policy agenda is the provision and governance of social care in the midst of the current unprecedented demographic transition, namely, the most rapidly ageing society with the lowest fertility rate of all OECD countries. In particular, care service providers are mostly private and operate on a fee-for-service basis, and South Korea has a fragmented delivery system with weak local autonomy. The South Korean welfare state therefore needs to enhance its steering capacity in governing a welfare mix and monitoring the service quality of care providers (Lee et al. 2016). Finally, the South Korean government is still a low social spender, operating within fiscal conservatism. Increasing attention should be paid to a 'catching up' process or effort that can be undertaken by South Korea to reach the average level of OECD countries.

Notes

1. Despite the increasing number of those receiving the Livelihood Benefit as the main income support of the NBLSA, the total number of social assistance recipients did not change much compared with the old system, with 1.41 million recipients in 1997 and 1.42 million in 2001. After the 2008 global economic crisis, the total recipients peaked at 1.57 million in 2009, then gradually declined to 1.33 million in 2014 (KOSIS 2020a; Ministry of Health and Welfare [MOHW] 2015). Therefore, it is apparent that the NBLSA left certain segments of the poor unprotected.
2. This section draws on the author's previous research, Lee and Kim (2019), 'Social Politics of Welfare Reform in Korea and Japan: A New Way of Mobilising Power Resources', *Voluntas* 20: 393–407.
3. Prior to the 1996 elections, the Japanese electoral system used a single non-transferable vote in a multi-member district, which facilitated 'clientalist politics' in which candidates delivered electoral bribes to their supportive constituencies without needing to appeal to whole constituencies (Anderson 1993; Neary 2002). The new mixed system of regional block proportional representation and single-member districts no longer favours particularistic constituent groups, yet makes the ruling party vulnerable to potential electoral backlashes against unpopular policies (Estevez-Abe 2008).
4. In response to the COVID-19 crisis, the Moon Jae-in government (2017–2022) has introduced a range of measures, such as emergency relief payments to all households,

emergency employment security subsidies for vulnerable workers, and increased subsidies for job retention schemes (OECD 2020c; see also ILO 2020). The idea of a universal basic income, which has received renewed interest due to the fourth industrial revolution and 'platform capitalism', has risen to the surface with this implementation of one-time, universal emergency relief payments.

Bibliography

Anderson, S. J. (1993), *Welfare Policy and Politics in Japan* (New York, NY: Paragon House).

Bonoli, G. (2007), 'Time Matters: Postindustrialization, New Social Risks, and Welfare State Adaptation in Advanced Industrial Democracies', *Comparative Political Studies* 40(5), 495–520.

Chang, H.-J. (2004), 'The Role of Social Policy in Economic Development: Some Theoretical Reflections and Lessons from East Asia', in T. Mkandawire, ed., *Social Policy in a Development Context*, 4246–261 (Basingstoke: Palgrave).

Chung, M. K. (2006), 'The Korean Developmental Welfare Regime: In Search of a New Regime Type in East Asia', *Shakai Seisaku Gakkai Shi (Journal of Social Policy and Labour Studies, Japan)* 16, 149–71.

Clasen, J. (1999), 'Unemployment Compensation and Other Labour-Market Policies', in J. Clasen, ed., *Comparative Social Policy: Concepts, Theories and Methods*, 159–177 (Oxford: Blackwell).

Dahlström, C. (2009), 'The Bureaucratic Politics of Welfare–State Crisis', *Governance* 22(2), 217–238.

Deyo, F. C., ed. (1987), *The Political Economy of the New Asian Industrialism* (Ithaca, NY: Cornell University Press).

Esping-Andersen, G. (1990), *The Three Worlds of Welfare Capitalism* (Cambridge: Polity).

Esping-Andersen, G. (1997), 'Hybrid or Unique? The Japanese Welfare State between Europe and America', *Journal of European Social Policy* 7(3), 179–189.

Estevez-Abe, M. (2008), *Welfare and Capitalism in Postwar Japan* (Cambridge: Cambridge University Press).

Evans, P., Rueschemeyer, D., and Skocpol, T., eds (1985), *Bringing the State Back In* (Cambridge: Cambridge University Press).

Fleckenstein, T., and Lee, S. C. (2017), 'The Politics of Investing in Families: Comparing Family Policy Expansion in Japan and South Korea', *Social Politics*, 24(1): 1–28.

Fleckenstein, T., and Lee, S. C. (2020), 'Roads and Barriers towards Social Investments: Comparing Labour Market and Family Policy Reforms in Europe and East Asia', *Policy and Society* 39(2), 266–283.

Goodman, R., and Peng, I. (1996), 'The East Asian Welfare States: Peripatetic Learning, adaptive Change, and Nation-Building', in G. Esping-Anderson, ed., *Welfare States in Transition: National Adaptations in Global Economies*, 192–224 (London: Sage).

Goodman, R., White, G., and Kwon, H. J., eds (1998), *The East Asian Welfare Model: Welfare Orientalism and the State* (London: Routledge).

Gough, I. (2004), 'East Asia: The Limits of Productivist Regimes', in I. Gough, G. Wood, A. Barrientos, P. Bevan, P. Davis and G. Room, eds, *Insecurity and Welfare Regimes in Asia, Africa and Latin America: Social Policy in Development Contexts*, 169–201 (Cambridge: Cambridge University Press).

Häusermann, S., Picot, G., and Geering, D. (2013), 'Review Article: Rethinking Party Politics and the Welfare State—Recent Advances in the Literature', *British Journal of Political Science* 43(1), 221–240.

Holliday, I. (2000), 'Productivist Welfare Capitalism', *Political Studies* 48, 706–723.

Holliday, I., and Wilding, P. eds (2003), *Welfare Capitalism in East Asia* (Basingstoke: Palgrave).

Huber, E., and Stephens, J. D. (2001), *Development and Crisis of the Welfare State* (Chicago, IL: University of Chicago Press).

International Labour Organisation (ILO) (2020), *Republic of Korea: A Rapid Assessment of the Employment Impacts of COVID-19. ILO Policy Brief* (Geneva: ILO).

Iversen, T., and Stephens, J. D. (2008), 'Partisan Politics, the Welfare State, and Three Worlds of Human Capital Formation', *Comparative Political Studies* 41, 600–637.

Jacobs, D. (2000), 'Low Public Expenditures on Social Welfare: Do East Asian Countries Have a Secret?', *International Journal of Social Welfare* 9, 2–16.

Jones, C. (1993), 'The Pacific Challenge: Confucian Welfare States', in C. Jones. ed., *New Perspectives on the Welfare State in Europe*, 184–202 (London: Routledge).

Joo, J. H. (1999), 'Explaining Social Policy Adoption in South Korea: The Cases of the Medical Insurance Law and the Minimum Wage Law', *Journal of Social Policy* 28(3), 387–412.

Kim, Y. M., ed. (2002), *Hanguk bokjikukga seonggyeok nonjaeng* (*Debate on the Characteristics of the Korean Welfare State*) (Seoul: Human and Welfare Publishing).

Kim, P. (2010), 'The East Asian Welfare State Debate and Surrogate Social Policy', *Socio-Economic Review* 8(3), 411–435.

Kim, Y. S. (2012), 'Are Korean Welfare Politics Changing? The Politics of the First and Second Pension Reforms in Korea', *Korean Social Sciences Review* 2(2), 93–129.

Korpi, W. (1983), *The Democratic Class Struggle* (London: Routledge).

Korean Statistical Information Service (KOSIS) (2020a), 'Livelihood Protection Recipients Statistics', https://kosis.kr/eng/, accessed 25 November 2021.

KOSIS (2020b), 'National Union Organisation Status', https://kosis.kr/index/index.do, accessed 25 November 2021.

Kwon, H.-J. (1999), *The Welfare State in Korea* (London: Macmillan).

Kwon, H.-J., ed. (2005), *Transforming the Developmental Welfare State in East Asia* (Basingstoke: Palgrave).

Kwon, H.-J., and Yi, I. (2009), 'Economic Development and Poverty Reduction in Korea', *Developmental and Change* 40(4),: 769–792.

Lee, H. K. (1999), 'Globalization and the Emerging Welfare State—the Experience of South Korea', *International Journal of Social Welfare* 8(1), 23–37.

Lee, J. (2008), 'Politics of Social Policy-Making in South Korea and Japan', *The Korean Journal of Policy Studies* 22(2), 109–133.

Lee, J. (2009), 'Another Dimension of Welfare Reform: The Implementation of the Employment Insurance Programme in Korea', *International Journal of Social Welfare* 18(3), 281–90.

Lee, J. (2014a), 'What Happens after the Passage of Reform Initiatives? Two Dimensions of Social Policy Reform in Korea), *International Review of Administrative Sciences* 80(1), 193–212.

Lee, J. (2014b), 'Institutional Linkages between Social Protection Measures and Industrialization in South Korea', in I. Yi and T. Mkandawire, eds, *Learning from the South Korean Developmental Success*, 91–107 (London: Palgrave Macmillan).

Lee, S. C. (2018), 'Democratization, Political Parties and Korean Welfare Politics: Korean Family Policy Reforms in Comparative Perspective', *Government and Opposition* 53(3), 518–41.

Lee, J., and Kim, T. (2019), 'Social Politics of Welfare Reform in Korea and Japan: A New Way of Mobilising Power Resources', *VOLUNTAS: International Journal of Voluntary and Nonprofit Organization* 30(2), 393–407.

Lee, J., Chae, J.-H., and Lim, S. H. (2016), 'Governing a Welfare Mix: Operation of Long-Term Care Policies in England and South Korea', *Korea Observer* 47(1), 167–197.

Marier, P. (2005), 'Where Did the Bureaucrats Go?', *Governance*, 18(4), 521–44.

Martin, J. P. (1998), *What Works among Active Labour Market Policies: Evidence from OECD Countries' Experiences*, Labour Market and Social Policy–Occasional Papers No. 35 (Paris: OECD Publishing).

Ministry of Health and Welfare (MOHW) (2015), *2015 Bogeonbokji tonggyeyeonbo* (*2015 Yearbook of Health and Welfare Statistics*) (Seoul: MOHW).

Morel, N., Palier, B., and Palme, J. (2012), *Towards a Social Investment Welfare State? Ideas, Policies and Challenges* (Bristol: Policy Press).

Neary, I. (2002), *The State and Politics in Japan* (Cambridge: Polity).

Organisation for Economic Co-operation and Development (OECD) (2000), *Pushing Ahead with Reform in Korea* (Paris: OECD Publishing).

OECD (2018), *Connecting People with Jobs: Towards Better Social and Employment Security in Korea* (Paris: OECD Publishing).

OECD (2020a), 'OECD Social Expenditure Database', www.oecd.org/social/expenditure.htm, accessed 25 November 2021.

OECD (2020b), *Revenue Statistics 2020* (Paris: OECD Publishing).

OECD (2020c), *OECD Employment Outlook 2020: Worker Security and the COVID-19 Crisis* (Paris: OECD Publishing).

OECD (2021a), 'General Government Spending (Indicator)', https://doi.org/10.1787/cc966 9ed-en, accessed 25 November 2021.

OECD (2021b), 'Poverty Rate (Indicator)', https://doi.org/10.1787/0fe1315d-en, accessed 25 November 2021.

Pekkanen, R. J., Smith, S. R., and Tsujinaka, Y. (2014), *Nonprofits and Advocacy: Engaging Community and Government in an Era of Retrenchment* (Baltimore, MD: Johns Hopkins University Press).

Pempel, T. J. (1990), *Uncommon Democracies: The One-Party Dominant Regime* (Ithaca, NY: Cornell University Press).

Peng, I. (2014), 'The Social Protection Floor and the "New" Social Investment Policies in Japan and South Korea', *Global Social Policy* 14(3), 389–405.

People's Solidarity for Participatory Democracy (PSPD) (2020), 'Modeun ilhaneun salamdeului goyong·sodeug anjeonmang ileohge mandeulja! chamyeoyeondaega jeanhaneun jeongugmingoyongboheom doib bangan' (Let's Make the Employment and Income Safety Net for All Working People! PSPD's Plan to Introduce a Universal Employment Insurance System), www.peoplepower21.org/Welfare/1735634, accessed 25 November 2021.

Pierson, P. (2001), 'Coping with Permanent Austerity: Welfare State Restructuring in Affluent Democracies', in P. Pierson. ed., *The New Politics of the Welfare State*, 410–456 (Oxford: Oxford University Press).

Presidential Committee for Quality of Life (1999), *DJ Welfarism: A New Paradigm for Productive Welfare in Korea* (Seoul: Office of the President).

Ramesh, M. (2004), *Social Policy in East and Southeast Asia: Education, Health, Housing, and Income Maintenance* (London: RoutledgeCurzon).

Ringen, S., Kwon, H.-J., Yi, I., Kim, T., and Lee, J. (2011), *The Korean State and Social Policy: How South Korea Lifted Itself from Poverty and Dictatorship to Affluence and Democracy* (New York: Oxford University Press).

Ross, F. (2000), 'Beyond Left and Right': The New Partisan Politics of Welfare', *Governance* 13(2), 155–183.

Sabatier, P. A., and Jenkins-Smith, H. C. (1999), 'The Advocacy Coalition Framework: An Assessment', in P. A. Sabatier, ed., *Theories of the Policy Process*, 117–166 (Boulder, CO: Westview Press).

Shin, D. M. (2003), *Social and Economic Policies in Korea: Idea, Networks and Linkages* (London: RoutledgeCurzon).

Skocpol, T. (1992), *Protecting Soldiers and Mothers* (Cambridge, MA: The Belknap Press of Harvard University Press).

Takegawa, S. (2005), 'Japan's Welfare-State Regime', *Development and Society* 34(2), 169–190.

Tang, K.-L. (2000), *Social Welfare Development in East Asia* (New York: Palgrave).

Tsebelis, G. (2000), 'Veto Players and Institutional Analysis', *Governance* 13(4), 441–474.

Wilsford, D. (1994), 'Path Dependency, or Why History Makes It Difficult But Not Impossible to Reform Health Care Systems in a Big Way', *Journal of Public Policy* 14(3), 251–283.

Yang, J.-J. (2017), *The Political Economy of the Small Welfare State in South Korea* (New York: Cambridge University Press).

Yi, I. (2007), *The Politics of Occupational Welfare in Korea* (Fukuoka: Hana-Syoin Press).

CHAPTER 30

DECENTRALISATION AND LOCAL GOVERNMENT

YOOIL BAE

1. INTRODUCTION

A long tradition of centralism has dominated the development and democratisation of South Korea. Since the Japanese colonial period, South Korea has been known as a strong state, where the central political world tightly controlled localities and civil society in the name of the country's modernisation, maintaining social order, and preparing for reunification with the northern part of the Korean Peninsula. As argued by the developmental state theorists, the mobilisation of national resources for rapid industrialisation and the active intervention of central bureaucrats were indeed inevitable (Amsden 1989; Evans 1995). Even politicians from the opposition parties claimed the introduction of local elections as a part of national democratisation against the authoritarian regime. This means that decentralisation and local democracy were not the priorities of the democratic movement. National politicians were embroiled with revising the non-democratic constitution, introducing direct presidential elections, and building democratic institutions at the central level. As such, since the first Constitution of the Republic in 1948, discussions on the introduction of local autonomy and democracy have been, at best, secondary issues for national politicians (Yoo 1994).

It was not until the early 1990s that some central politicians began to proactively push for the decentralisation and reintroduction of local elections that had existed for a short period in the 1950s. After the Roh Tae-woo administration (1988–1993) attempted to postpone implementing fully fledged local autonomy (1992), a few prominent politicians, including former President Kim Dae-jung, who was one of the key opposition leaders at the time, strongly demanded immediate implementation of local democracy. Since the initial enactment of the Local Autonomy Act in 1988, there have been several revisions to expand the scope of local government functions and the local political arena. In the end, a fully fledged local election ranging from *si, gun, gu* (community level) to gubernatorial level, followed by local democratic institutions and mechanisms, was introduced in the mid-1990s. This trend towards decentralisation is also consistent with the World Bank's projection that about 95 per cent of countries across the globe pursue some form of decentralisation reform today (World Bank 2000).

The practice of local democracy, despite a few drawbacks, has brought about some positive changes in the landscape of post-1987 South Korean politics. In addition to the popular election of local representatives (legislators and executives) at all levels, there has been a transfer of administrative and fiscal resources to lower levels of government. In turn, many local governments have been able to deal with local affairs with more discretion and have been motivated to meet the demands of the residents in a local-friendly manner. A few local governments often develop solutions for local development that reflect the localities' history and identity (Kim 2015). Moreover, this reinstated local democracy, or 'School for democratic citizenship', as the earlier thinkers often labelled it, has produced a few highly regarded politicians in both the local and national political arenas. Therefore, contrary to the initial attitude towards local democracy, over 80 per cent of South Koreans have come to recognise that local autonomy is an essential part of democratic politics (Ministry of the Interior and Safety (MOIS)–Korea Research Institute for Local Administration (KRILA) 2015).

In the following sections, this chapter first highlights the flashpoints of decentralisation reform during the post-1987 period, followed by an evaluation of the current state of local democracy and decentralisation from a comparative perspective. Second, the chapter also identifies several challenges and vexing problems for South Korean local democracy, including growing inequality and an ageing population, that pose additional threats to the current state of South Korean local democracy. This job is critical, as local leaders and academic communities continue to claim that the current state of decentralisation is far from the desired level, regardless of several reform measures. Also, deepening local democracy is often hampered by the widening gap between the centre and the periphery (Yoo 2018).

2. Post-1987 Decentralisation and Local Democratisation

Decentralisation has continuously garnered academic and practical interests because it was expected to facilitate changes in politics, economy, and society by migrating power and resources from the centre to lower levels of government. In literature, the term *decentralisation* is often defined as a multidimensional process, including political, fiscal, and administrative decentralisation (Falleti 2010: 8). *Political decentralisation* is an enactment of a new constitutional or legal design for subnational political actors and usually includes the popular election of local representatives (local executives and legislators). On the other hand, *fiscal decentralisation* is designed to increase the fiscal capacity and autonomy of subnational governments by transferring taxation authority and fiscal resources. Finally, *administrative decentralisation* means the general transfer of public service and administrative functions, such as social services, education, development, and welfare, to subnational government. Other scholarly works also include devolution, de-concentration, or privatisation under certain circumstances as different types of decentralisation that possibly disperse the concentration of power and resources (Turner 1999).

Over the past two decades, perspectives on decentralisation and the central–local relationship in South Korea have gradually shifted from political to economic, reflecting the aspects of decentralisation as mentioned in the previous paragraph (Bae 2016: 71). The initial call for decentralisation during the earlier democratisation period predominantly focused on the promotion of democracy by weakening the strong state institutions that possessed enormous policymaking authority and capacity to shape the politics and the economy without much consideration for localities and civil society (Lee 1996; Yoo 1994). However, there has been a back-and-forth in central–local relationships over neoliberalism since the 1997 Asian Financial Crisis. The structural economic problems and inefficient centralisation certainly posed political–economic threats to the centralised state and, to some extent, brought about the precipitous decline of the 'developmental state' (Minns 2001; Pirie 2007). Simultaneously, the widening gap between the Seoul Metropolitan Area (SMA) and non-SMA and the increase in the number of shrinking cities (stemming from the ageing population and domestic migration) requires more systematic collaboration for balanced development between the centre and the localities. This means that the traditional dichotomous view of local governments and decentralisation may not adequately capture the whole picture of subnational democracy.

2.1 Democratisation and Decentralisation: Towards Local Democracy

After the fall of the authoritarian regime (1961–1987) which suspended the implementation of local democracy under the guise of national reunification, administrative efficiency for economic growth, national security, and financial scarcity of local governments, a nationwide democratic movement for democratisation eventually produced the new democratic Constitution of 1987 containing the foundations of several democratic mechanisms and institutions. This included the introduction of the popular election of the president (Article 67), basic human rights (Articles 10-37), a constitutional court (Article 111), and local governments (Articles 117-8). The candidates running for president in the 1987 election (i.e. Roh Tae-woo, Kim Young-sam, and Kim Dae-jung) pledged to amend the Local Autonomy Act to structure local government systems through direct elections and open an era of local autonomy (Lee 1996). However, although decentralisation during the earlier period of democratisation made a significant step towards local democracy, the strong centralism of the past created a path dependency, making it difficult for the pro-decentralists to push for fully fledged local democracy. The older generation of politicians and central bureaucrats were disinclined to share authority with localities. Whereas democratic movements at the national level flourished in this period, the mobilisation of local forces and civil society to influence the process of decentralisation was, at best, minimal (Bae and Kim 2013; Kim 2006).

It was not until the mid-1990s that there was somewhat substantial progress towards decentralised governance by allowing direct election of local councilmen and executive heads of local government through the newly revised Local Autonomy Act (1994). Since then, local governments have enacted their own bylaws and ordinances regarding local affairs within the scope of legal and constitutional boundaries (Articles 22–23). The various administrative and financial, as well as functional, capacities of local governments have also been gradually strengthened to deal with growing demands from residents.

The economic crisis in 1997 was a significant turning point in that South Korea pursued further decentralisation from an economic perspective. The civilian government officials put forth structural reform and government reorganisation to address economic inefficiency and 'globalisation' of economic issues. Although his reform package was only partially successful, former President Kim Young-sam's *segyehwa* ('globalisation') strategy pushed central bureaucrats to reorganise inefficient central ministries (Kihl 2005: 152–154). Under the Kim Dae-jung administration (1998–2003), the government reorganisation programmes were popularised, and several reform committees were created to carry out the downsizing of the central ministries (Kim 1999). In the government reorganisation context, the Kim Dae-jung administration also passed the Law for the Promotion of Transfer of Central Authorities. It established the Presidential Committee on Devolution Promotion in 1999 to accelerate the transfer of central functions to subnational governments and government innovation.

The various decentralisation reforms from the mid-1990s up to the Kim Dae-jung administration were implemented and favourably assessed in general. Nevertheless, at the same time, they also left many unfinished tasks. Scholars such as Choi and Wright (2004) noted that decentralisation in this period at minimum created room for local politics and citizen participation in local affairs. Local governments, with limited decisional and fiscal authority, also began to make efforts to meet their residents' various demands. However, although President Kim Dae-jung was often called 'Mr Local Autonomy' and received much support during the recovery process from the International Monetary Fund (IMF) crisis, the decentralisation reform under his administration was, overall, half-hearted. The government transferred administrative affairs without proper fiscal resources and often faced strong bureaucratic resistance internally from the central ministries. Instead, his reform drive based on neoliberalism required a faster top-down decision from the central ministries to effectively recover the national economy (Bae 2018: 208).

2.2 Consolidation of Local Democracy in the 2000s: Change and Continuity

The scale of decentralisation reform under the Kim Dae-jung administration was not as great as expected by the people, but the Roh Moo-hyun administration was inaugurated with better conditions. Whereas the previous administrations considered decentralisation as part of broader reform agendas, the Roh administration brought it to the fore as a top national priority (Bae 2016; Koo and Kim 2018). President Roh was elected as the sixteenth president of South Korea in December 2002 and showed strong intent to carry out decentralisation, de-concentration, and balanced development policies during his term in office. His administration claimed that the ailing South Korean politics and economy originated from inefficient distribution of resources between the centre and the periphery and suggested five directions for major reform (so-called roadmaps), such as administrative reform, public personnel reform, e-government, financial and tax reform, and decentralisation (Park 2008).

The Roh administration undertook decentralisation reform with clear goals highlighted in 'the decentralisation roadmap', which was designed to realign the structure of central–local relations within a given period. For example, based on trust to local governments and citizens, the central ministries were required to transfer their affairs to the subnational governments first and then to fix unexpected problems (*first delegate then fix later*). This principle was suggested because one of the causes of the delay in decentralisation was that the central government lacked confidence in local governments' capacity. The decentralisation idea was based on the belief that various government affairs must belong to subnational governments where residents live (*subsidiary guideline*), as the central government had possessed too many functions dealing with purely local affairs, such as local government organisations, urban planning function, and resident welfare. Finally, the central government was required to delegate both functions and authorities (*comprehensive guideline*), as the problem of the past decentralisation reform was that the government delegated functions without allocating appropriate financial and human resources (Lee 2005: 356).

Whereas the previous decentralisation reforms faced severe resistance from the 'pro-centre' political figures, including central bureaucrats and national politicians, decentralisation programmes in this period (2003–2007) were carried out under the leadership of strong 'pro-local' president and reformists in the government. When President Roh took office in February 2003, he brought forward many of his staffs' policy recommendations in national agendas concerning the resolution of decades-long disparities between the centre and periphery. In particular, *jibangbungwon* ('decentralisation') and *gyunhyeongbaljeon* ('balanced development') became two of the most important priorities to be completed in his government. There was undoubtedly organised resistance against this policy direction in different phases of decentralisation, but President Roh appointed his key policy advisors as leaders of reform institutions, including the Ministry of Government and Home Affairs, Chief Policy

Advisor to the President, and the Presidential Committee on Government Innovation and Decentralisation (PCGID); to some extent he succeeded in reducing resistance and cultivating support from the bureaucrats (Bae 2016).

As a result, the Roh administration could pass the Special Act on Decentralisation (2004), which contains rational allocation of authority between the central and the local governments, transferring fiscal resources to the lower levels of government, strengthening local capacities and responsibilities, vitalising civil society, and more. The PCGID and other related central ministries carried out reform agendas listed in the roadmap and designed new institutions to meet the roadmap's requirements. These reform efforts were followed by the introduction of resident petitioning (2004), group litigation (2006), Jeju Special Self-Governing Province (2006), and the resident recall system (2007), among many other initiatives (Bae, 2016: 67). In 2006, the local allocation tax rate increased from 15 to 19.24 per cent to strengthen subnational governments' fiscal capacity. Although the promotion of decentralisation reform lost strength after the failed attempt to impeach President Roh in 2004 and faced bureaucratic resistance, decentralisation measures under the Roh administration were notable achievements.

The successive Lee Myung-bak (2008–2013), Park Geun-hye (2013–2017), and Moon Jae-in (2017–2022) governments have continued to advance the Roh administration's unfinished decentralisation tasks. Similar to the Roh administration's actions, these three administrations have enacted similar special laws and representative reform committees to continue transferring central authority and resources to subnational governments and strengthen local and civic capacities, as Table 30.1 indicates. The Lee

Table 30.1: Decentralisation reform agencies and special laws, 1999–2018

Administrations	Special laws	Reform agencies
Kim Dae-jung	Law for the Promotion of Transfer of Central Authorities (1999)	Presidential Committee for Promotion of Local Empowerment
Roh Moo-hyun	Special Act on Local Decentralization (2004)	Presidential Committee on Government Innovation and Decentralization
Lee Myung-bak	Special Act on Decentralization Promotion (2008) Special Act on Restructuring of Local Administrative Systems (2010)	Presidential Committee for Decentralization Presidential Committee for Promotion of Reform of Local Administrative System
Park Geun-hye	Special Act on Local Decentralization and Restructuring of Local Administrative Systems (2013)	Presidential Committee for the Development of Local Autonomy
Moon Jae-in	Special Act on Local Autonomy and Decentralization, and Restructuring of Local Administrative Systems (2018)	Presidential Committee on Autonomy and Decentralization

Source: Presidential Committee on Autonomy and Decentralization, www.pcad.go.kr/eng/, accessed 29 November 2021.

administration established the Decentralisation Promotion Committee and pursued twenty major tasks in seven areas, including authority migration, new local income tax (5 per cent of VAT) and local capacity-building. However, more emphasis was placed on restructuring the local administrative system, such as merging smaller cities (e.g. merging Masan, Changwon, and Jinhae in 2010) for economic efficiency. Likewise, the Park Geun-hye administration launched a separate organisation for decentralisation and implemented reform programmes to complete decentralisation, but failed to meet expectations as a whole. The Moon administration has promoted measures to improve resident participation and revitalise local democracy with the goal of building a 'decentralised state' comparable to that of the federal system. The Moon administration inaugurated its term with a pledge to create a decentralised state by establishing a Presidential Committee on Autonomy and Decentralisation and passing a Special Law on Local Autonomy and Decentralisation and Restructuring of Local Administrative Systems in 2018, similar to the previous governments. The Moon administration revised the Local Autonomy Act in December 2020, which strengthens residential participation and balanced national development.[1]

Taken together, efforts to materialise the idea of local democracy and decentralisation reform have continued over the past two decades and brought about some notable achievements. First, needless to say, the reinstatement of local elections of different scales was the most crucial change. The introduction of elements of direct democracy, such as resident petition, referendum, resident recall, group litigation, and resident auditing to encourage citizens' communication with local officials and politicians, have been a significant accomplishment.

Second, in addition to building democratic institutions at the local level, strengthening the administrative, fiscal, and functional capacities of local government has served the local citizens' needs in various ways and deepened local democratic politics further. With more discretion and power, 'entrepreneurial politicians' have emerged in the local political arena to lead various local development projects. In terms of functional diversity, the local government portion of total functions increased from 19 per cent in 1999 to 32 per cent in 2014 (Yoo 2018). Fiscal resources were transferred from the central government to subnational governments by adjusting local allocation tax and introducing new tax items (local consumption tax). Local governments with improved functional and administrative capacities often instituted 'bottom-up' policy initiatives, such as the Information Discloser Ordinance in 1992 (Chung-ju) and participatory budgeting in 2003 (Gwang-ju), which spread across the country later.

Third, empowered local democracy has strongly motivated local politicians—particularly local executives—to address local problems and issues in a proactive manner. Along with newly introduced local democracy, competition among localities pushed local leaders to introduce local government service charters and improve their administration quality (Kim, 2010). Interestingly, a recent disaster relief fund during the COVID-19 pandemic (2020) was the outcome of policy initiatives by local government leaders.

Fourth, the introduction of local democracy has nurtured democratic citizenship at local levels and promoted participation in local political affairs via various channels, including elections, petitioning, and participatory budgeting (Kim, 2015). The empowered local citizenship is also linked to the rise of local politicians in the national political arena. Since the introduction of local elections, many prominent political appointees in important government positions such as prime minister, ministers, and party leadership have run for metropolitan city mayors or provincial governors. At the same time, politicians who made their debut in localities are increasingly playing a significant role in national politics today. For example, in the eighteenth and nineteenth presidential elections, more than half of the candidates who passed the primaries in the major political parties were former or incumbent local government heads.

Of course, the success of local democracy has not progressed without challenges and problems over the past two decades. Some scholars, mass media, and even leaders of the lowest levels of government (community level) take extreme positions and often complain that the current form of decentralisation and distribution of authority and fiscal resources is not sufficient to practice local democracy. To name a few: regardless of a series of decentralisation reforms, the distribution of public servants (60 per cent vs 40 per cent) and administrative affairs (70 per cent vs 30 per cent) between the central and the local governments are still disproportionate. Considering the increasing role of local governments in public policy implementation, such as local welfare service provision, uneven distribution of central–local finance (80 per cent vs 20 per cent) has added more difficulties in providing public services locally (Kim 2015). Local tax income accounts for around 20 per cent of total tax revenue at best, and local governments have limited discretion in expanding local tax bases (Koo and Kim 2018: 298). As Figure 30.1 shows, unlike the common expectations of decentralisation, local financial independence has steadily declined since the early 2000s, whereas local tax income is still heavily dependent upon national taxation policy and the changing macroeconomic situation. From a political perspective, many countries, such as the United States, legally limit the role of national parties in local elections (Sellers et al. 2020). Nevertheless, there are many criticisms in South Korea that local political autonomy has been seriously restricted by the exercise of nomination rights in local elections by the national political parties.

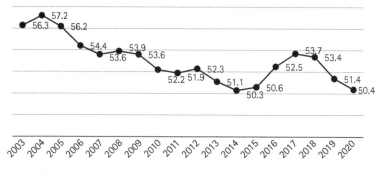

FIGURE 30.1: Changes in local financial independence ratio (%)

Source: e-National Index, www.index.go.kr, accessed 29 November 2021.

To summarise, it is true that local democracy in South Korea has made unprecedented progress, along with national-level democratisation, but it still needs further development. In this regard, the Moon Jae-in administration inaugurated in 2017 declared the introduction of 'the decentralised constitution' which sought the coexistence of the centre and the localities and has continued to empower local government, as well as encourage citizen participation. However, as Goldsmith and Page (1987) once mentioned, only countries conducting many affairs at the local level tend to 'constitutionalise' local autonomy. The efforts to build local constitutional democracy in South Korea must be relentless. This change and continuity in central–local relations call for a more systematic global comparison to more precisely diagnose the state of local democracy in South Korea.

3. The State of Local Democracy: An International Comparison

A systematic international comparison makes a more accurate assessment of local democracy in South Korea possible, although there have been surprisingly few comparative studies of localities (Sellers 2019). Most of them focused heavily on 'formal' institutions at the national level, as it is difficult to capture variance within nations. Even existing comparative studies of local democracy made only smaller-scale analysis within a specific region such as Western Europe, without much consideration of informal institutions at different scales (Goldsmith and Page 1987; Hesse and Sharp 1991).

However, recent developments in comparative local democracy literature show that local autonomy and capacity are not merely decided by local factors, such as level of decisional authority, discretion, administrative, and financial resources. A recent study of the Regional Authority Index (RAI) by Hooghe et al. (2010), for instance, divided local autonomy and authority into 'self-rule' components and 'shared-rule' components to assess the power of localities in eighty-one countries. Here, *self-rule components* refer to the local governments' authority to govern their territories, which indicates the degree of autonomy from higher levels of government. In contrast, *shared-rule components* refer to local governments' capacity to influence and shape national policymaking, such as constitutional revision, new taxation policies, and normal legislation through a bottom-up process (Hooghe et al., 2010). According to the RAI report, this shared rule is often ignored in literature, but is as important as self-rule because the modern public policy process requires a closer collaboration between central and local governments.
Comparatively speaking, the RAI data indicate the relative position of local and regional power in South Korea. As seen in Figure 30.2, South Korea has made some progress in the transfer of the central authority and policy implementation power to the subnational governments. Still, local governments' institutional authority (e.g. personnel, organisation) depends on the central approval and local borrowing and taxation authorities

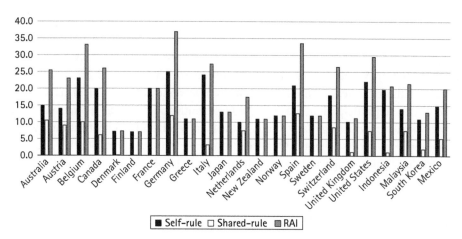

FIGURE 30.2: Regional authority index scores

Source: Hooghe et al. (2010).

attached to national policies. Due to this limited nature of decentralisation, the self-rule component of local governments in South Korea (in blue) scored relatively low, equivalent to that of Japan (Hooghe et al. 2010). In addition, local governments in South Korea do not have effective policy communication channels with the central government and are not effectively represented in the policymaking process at the national level, as the 'shared-rule' score (in orange) indicates. The Local Autonomy Act guarantees the formation of local government associations to represent local governments' interests, but they have limited negotiation power over local borrowing or other financial burdens in national projects (Bae 2018). The Moon administration provides local governments with a chance to have 'prior' conversations, which occur before the national government delegates some administrative burden. However, these local voices are often ignored or systemically marginalised in national policymaking. Therefore, regardless of improvement in the building of 'democratic institutions' at the subnational level, localities in South Korea are less integrated with the central government, with relatively higher supralocal supervision, weak fiscal capacity, and an inefficient communication channel to the centre, which often hamper further consolidation of local democracy and effective policy collaboration for citizens.

However, the formal institutions of local democracy that appeared in the RAI have a clear limitation in assessing the overall effectiveness of local democracy, which requires a closer investigation of social forces. Sellers et al. (2020), inspired by the concept of 'infrastructural power' proposed by Michael Mann (1984), which emphasises the state's effectiveness *through society*, assured the significance of the democratic institutional arrangement and civil society within cities and communities. They argued that both state–society and central–local relations at different levels of government in modern states account for a degree of democracy and policy effectiveness; that is, the extent to which localities and civil society engage in, or are integrated with, national policymaking is critical in understanding the genuine progress of local democracy.

According to this research, 'inclusive' democratic infrastructure at the local level that mediates linkages between communities and the hierarchies of the state has been crucial for effective local governance and democratic incorporation (Sellers et al. 2020). For example, in Scandinavian welfare states, the national government and political party decide welfare programmes. Still, without the influence and participation of localities and civil society through various participation channels (which were ignored in the formal institution-focused RAI index), fair and effective implementation of welfare programmes would be impossible.

Interestingly, a few empirical studies exploring local politics in newly established local democratic settings in South Korea have commonly perceived that a mayor-centred electoral coalition and local elites—including local developers, businesses, and media—dominate local politics without proper participation or consideration of civil society (Park 2000). Local politicians are devoted to building a clientelist connection to the national-level party organisations because nomination for the next election depends on the central party leaders. Political parties are supposed to mediate the political world and the citizens, but the linkage role is limited in the South Korean context, as local citizens are more often occupied with national than local issues. Civic associations at the local level, led by local elites, played notable roles in some policy areas, but overall, the slow growth of local citizen participation has been a recurring issue since the inception of local democracy (Bae and Kim 2013).

In summary, although South Korea has successfully built democratic institutions at both national and local levels, it lacks wider participation from the citizens—a requirement for effective state and local democracy, as well as policy implementation, to rely on more than formal state apparatus and institution. In the past two decades, voter turnout for local elections has been much lower than that for the National Assembly and presidential elections. A few participatory measures, such as local referendum and resident recall, have rarely been used or could not meet legal requirements (Bae 2018: 267). This 'dual' nature of South Korean local democracy (i.e. institutions without substantive participation) has deterred further decentralisation and more responsible democratic politics. More involvement of localities and civil society in national decision-making through extensive political and policy integration is critical for consolidating local democracy. As will be discussed in the next section, because transboundary environmental problems, an ageing population, shrinking cities, pandemics, and other risks pose additional threats to local democracy, more systemic collaboration beyond simple decentralisation is needed.

4. Local Democracy as a Wicked Problem: Emerging Challenges

South Korea's local democracy, as seen in the comparative analysis, has many remaining tasks, but a few new challenges and a rapidly changing environment for localities greatly threaten further decentralisation and the consolidation of local democracy. Some extremists currently demand a more comprehensive decentralisation package with a catchphrase, '20 percent local autonomy', symbolising uneven distribution of authority and finance to the localities and highlighting the limited nature of the decentralisation drive of the previous administrations (Yoo 2018). Contrary to their arguments, however, it is also questionable whether more transfer of power and decentralisation would effectively resolve the challenges that local governments face today. This is because issues such as population cliffs, shrinking cities, and unbalanced development of localities are extremely complex, ambiguous, and difficult to resolve with current decentralisation strategies. These are called 'wicked problems', which are by nature challenging to resolve or too complicated (Head and Alford 2015).

First, the excessive concentration of politics, economy, and population in the SMA is not a new problem, but the government has failed to resolve this issue over the past fifty years, regardless of the implementation of various policy measures (Chung and Kirby 2002). The problem of population concentration began in the 1960s, and eventually, as of 2020, more than 50 per cent of the total population lived in the narrow space of the SMA, occupying only 11 per cent of the nation's land (Figure 30.3). Although the government has attempted to address this overconcentration in the SMA since the 1970s, the non-SMA population has continued to decline for the past decades, for example, the migration of population and industrial facilities (businesses and manufacturers) to newly developed areas and the restriction of development in the designated area ('green belt') embarked on in the 1970s (OECD 2001). Even the Roh Moo-hyun administration recognised the growing seriousness of the regional disparities and tried to combine decentralisation and de-concentration ('national balanced development') policies by migrating government agencies and public enterprises to a new administrative capital (Sejong) and other local cities.

Nevertheless, for over twenty years, there have been no substantial changes. The concentration of business headquarters, public organisations, and prestigious universities in the SMA has created a greater economic gap between the SMA and the non-SMA.

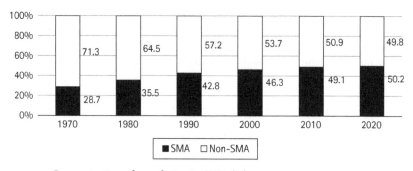

FIGURE 30.3: Concentration of population in SMA (%)

Note: SMA: Seoul metropolitan area.

Source: Korean Statistical Information Service, https://kosis.kr/index, accessed 29 November 2021.

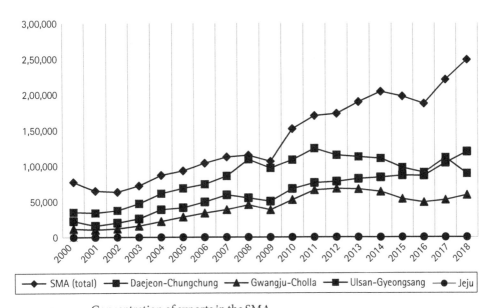

FIGURE 30.4: Concentration of exports in the SMA

Note: SMA, Seoul metropolitan area (unit: regional export total, Million USD).

Source: Korean Statistical Information Service, https://kosis.kr/index, accessed 29 November 2021.

The regional growth pole cities or industrial centres such as Ulsan and Gumi have experienced sharp economic decline lately, whereas the SMA (Seoul, Gyeonggi, and Incheon) and areas near the SMA (e.g. Chungnam Province) have rapidly expanded their share in the national economy (Figure 30.4). The Moon administration is trying to address this issue by establishing the National Committee for Balanced Development. However, balanced development is not compatible with decentralisation either, given that it is beyond a locality's capacity. This affects the quality of local public service and infrastructure development by failing to meet the citizens' needs in localities.

Second and relatedly, shrinking cities—disappearing cities—in local areas have become a serious concern for local and central policymakers. According to a Korea Research Institute for Human Settlement report (2017), more than twenty cities face a trend of declining population and empty homes due to the ageing population, low fertility, and outmigration of the young. Furthermore, other reports expected that at least 100 municipalities (small towns and villages) were on the verge of disappearing, with most experiencing a fast-growing ageing population (*Chosun-Ilbo* 2020). This shrinking-city phenomenon directly hit most local governments' development-orientated policies because declining local population substantially reduces disposable local income and increases financial ineffectiveness. Despite the shrinking population, local politicians considering the next local elections continue to spend the local budget for infrastructure development and housing, which eventually creates serious fiscal deficits and pushes local governments to depend more on central grants. The declining population is also a very complex issue, negatively affecting local commercial activities and local universities. More importantly, the collapse of local communities due to shrinking cities poses a serious threat to local democracy. In this context, it is certain that resolving the problem of shrinking cities by employing one-off policy measures or simply strengthening decentralisation reform would not be effective.

Last but not least, widening economic disparity among the localities also has negative implications for deepening local democracy. Indeed, the implementation of local democracy has produced many local entrepreneurs. It is also true that the mayor of Seoul and the Gyeonggi Province governor, with a larger population size and relatively affluent financial resources, for example, are very influential political figures, even in national politics. Nevertheless, at the same time, many small-sized local governments are struggling not only to improve the quality of public service in their territory but also to pay for local officials on time, due to weak financial and administrative capacities. Should the central government possess approval authority for local borrowing and establishing new local tax items, it is evident that these small-scale localities would experience the double trouble of outflow of population and local financial difficulties.

These ongoing and upcoming challenges make the meaning of Tocquevillian local democracy itself a wicked problem because it is clear that the classical idea of local democracy cannot accommodate all these challenges and problems. Local democracy and decentralisation are good ideas that should be implemented and cannot be ignored. However, to deal with these complex problems, careful consideration of the 'effectiveness' of local democracy and creative solutions beyond simple decentralisation is necessary (Koo and Kim 2018: 300). In this regard, the newly revised Local Autonomy Act (2020) attempted to create a clear policy tie between the central and the local governments by introducing central–local collaborative meetings (Article 164 and Article 186) to discuss policy issues that might affect balanced national development (MOIS 2020). The government also provided a legal basis for municipal merging or special financial support for mega-sized cities for effective decision-making and rational resource allocation.

5. Conclusion

Considering that there are several stages of political and economic, as well as social, development, it is true that South Korea's local democracy and decentralisation is late. South Korea's rapid industrialisation and national-level democratisation created vested interests in central politics and somehow forced regions and localities to sacrifice themselves for more effective and coherent execution of public policies at the national level. Even compared with other developing countries, such as Indonesia, which carried out decentralisation in the late 1990s, South Korea's full-scale decentralisation beyond simple local elections did not begin until the early 2000s. The polarised or unequal development strategy for rapid modernisation also hindered a smooth transition towards local democracy because the long tradition of central dominance help create vested interests—for example, central politicians and bureaucrats—and impeded more effective, faster transfer of authority to local governments.

Under this circumstance, reforms for local democracy and decentralisation required a favourable political–economic environment and strong supports from political reformist leaders and politicians in the government to overcome the organised resistance. The Asian Financial Crisis in 1997 brought about a crack in the centralised system, and the rise of pro-local politicians, including Kim Dae-jung and Roh Moo-hyun, as well as other reformists armed with the idea of decentralisation, facilitated the process over the past two decades. This eventually resulted in some notable accomplishments (Bae 2016): Restoring local elections and building local democratic institutions created the local political arena and pushed more political participation from local residents, to name just a few effects.

Nevertheless, rapid local democratisation and decentralisation did not come without problems and challenges. First, South Korea's local democracy suffers from *duality*, which means the institutionalisation of local democracy without an actual increase in citizen participation. There are readily available local institutions and participatory mechanisms for local citizens—such as petitioning and resident recall—that are rarely used. Second, piecemeal adjustment of local finance and transfer of authority without proper fiscal decentralisation puts local governments in financial trouble. The widening economic gap among local governments has further burdened the weak regions and cities.

To conclude, the central–local relationship in South Korea is not a zero-sum game anymore. The wicked problems discussed herein are serious challenges and create greater ambiguity and uncertainty for local democracy in South Korea. These problems are not likely to be resolved through the exercise of local autonomy. Instead, to effectively address these challenges and issues, local governments' accountability to their citizens and much broader democratic constituencies through the bottom-up process is critical. In addition to the continuous transfer of central authority and resources, for the national government, closer integration with localities and civil society in national policymaking would increase the effectiveness of local democracy and help escape the duality of South Korean local democracy. As Sellers et al. (2000) note, a multilevel democracy beyond the simple top-down-style decentralisation is critical for enduring and substantive democracy.

Note

1. In 2020, the Moon administration passed the fully revised Local Autonomy Act containing several reform elements such as strengthening of local councils (Article 41 and Article 123), creating special cities (Article 198), providing a foundation for merging cities and counties, and so forth. For details, see the Ministry of Interior and Safety (2020), https://www.mois.go.kr/frt/bbs/type010/commonSelectBoardArticle.do?bbsId=BBSMSTR_000000000008&nttId=81594, accessed 30 November 2021.

Bibliography

Amsden, A. (1989) *Asia's Next Giant: South Korea and Late Industrialization* (Oxford: Oxford University Press).

Bae, Y. (2016), 'Ideas, Interests, and Practical Authority in Reform Politics: Decentralization Reform in South Korea in the 2000s', *Asian Journal of Political Science* 24(1), 63–86.

Bae, Y. (2018), *Hangugui ijungjeong jibang minjujuui: aidieowa jedo, geurigo dayanghan jibangbungwon* (*South Korea's Dual Local Democracy: Ideas and Institutions, and Varieties of Decentralization*) (Goyang: Moonwoo-Sa).

Bae, Y., and Kim, S. (2013), 'Civil Society and Local Activism in South Korea's Local Democratization', *Democratization* 20(2), 260–286.

Choi, Y., and Wright, D. S. (2004), 'Intergovernmental Relations (IGR) in Korea and Japan: Phases, Patterns, and Progress toward Decentralization (Local Autonomy) in a Trans-Pacific Context', *International Review of Public Administration* 9(1), 1–22.

Chosun-Ilbo (2020), 'Pocheon·Yeojusido 30nyeon dwi somyeor wigi' (Pocheon·Yeoju Cities are also on the Verge of Extinction in Thirty Years), 17 November, https://www.chosun.com/national/national_general/2020/11/17/WDTOPDR3GNFOBDE4XR33ATPA6U/, accessed 10 December 2020.

Chung, J.-Y., and Kirby, R. (2002), *The Political Economy of Development and Environment in Korea* (Routledge: London).

Evans, P. (1995), *Embedded Autonomy: States and Industrial Transformation* (Princeton, NJ: Princeton University Press).

Falleti, T. G. (2010), *Decentralization and Subnational Politics in Latin America* (Cambridge: Cambridge University Press).

Goldsmith, M., and Page, E. (1987), *Central and Local Government Relations: A Comparative Analysis of West European Unitary States* (London: Sage).

Head, B., and Alford, J. (2015), 'Wicked Problems: Implication for Public Policy and Management', *Administration and Society* 47(6), 711–739.

Hesse, J., and Sharp, L. J. (1991), 'Local Government in International Perspective: Some Comparative Observations', in J. Hesse and L. J. Sharp, eds, *Local Government and Urban Affairs in International Perspective: Analyses of Twenty Western Industrialized Countries*, 603–621 (Nomos: Baden-Baden).

Hooghe, L., Marks, G., and Schakel, A. H. (2010), *The Rise of Regional Authority: A Comparative Study of 42 Democracies* (New York: Routledge).

Kihl, Y.-W. (2005), *Transforming Korean Politics: Democracy, Reform and Culture* (New York: M. E. Sharpe).

Kim, D. (2010), 'Jibangjachi 20neyon Mueoseul Eotgo Mueoseul Ireonneunga' (20 Years of Local Autonomy, What We Earned and What We Lost), *Jachi Hangjeong* (*Autonomy Administration*) 265, 47–50.

Kim, P.-S. (1999), 'Administrative Reform in the Korean Central Government: A Case Study of the Dae Jung Kim Administration', *Public Performance and Management Review* 24(2), 145–160.

Kim, S. (2006), 'Civil Society and Local Democracy', *Korea Journal* 46(4), 62–86.

Kim, S. E. (2015), 'Jibangjachi 20neyonui Pyeongga' (The Evaluation of 20 Years of Local Autonomy), *Ipbeopgwa Jeongchaek* (*Legislation and Policy*) 7(1), 57–82.

Koo, J., and Kim, B.-J. (2018), 'Two Faces of Decentralization in South Korea', *Asian Education and Development Studies* 7(3), 291–302.

Korea Institute for Human Settlement (2017), *Jeoseongjang Sidaeui Chuksodo-si Siltaewa Jeongchaek Yeon-gu* (*Urban Shrinkage in Korea: Current Status and Policy Implications*) (Seoul: Korea Institute for Human Settlement).

Ladner, A., Keuffer, N., and Baldersheim, H. (2016), 'Measuring Local Autonomy in 39 Countries', *Regional and Federal Studies* 26(3), 321–357.

Lee, J.-S. (1996), 'The Politics of Decentralization in Korea', *Local Government Studies* 22(3), 60–71.

Lee, S.-J. (2005), 'Nomuhyeon Jeongbuui Jibangbungwonjeongchang Pyeongga' (An Evaluation of the Decentralization Policy of the President Roh's Government), *Hangjeong Nonchong* (*Korea Journal of Public Administration*) 43(2), 351–379.

Mann, M. (1984), 'The Autonomous Power of the State: Its Origins, Mechanisms and Results', *European Journal of Sociology* 25(2), 185–213.

Ministry of the Interior and Safety (MOIS) (2020), 'Jibangjachibeom 32nyeon Mane Jeonbugaejeong, Jachibungwon Hwakdae Giteul Maryeon' (Local Autonomy Act Completely Revised in 32 Years, a Framework for Expanding Decentralization of Autonomy Laid), 9 December, https://www.mois.go.kr/frt/bbs/type010/commonSelectBoardArticle.do?bbsId=BBSMSTR_000000000008&nttId=81594, accessed 30 November 2021.

Ministry of the Interior and Safety–Korea Research Institute for Local Administration (MOIS–KRILA) (2015), *Jibangjachi 20nyeon Pyeongga* (*The Evaluation of 20 Years of Local Autonomy*) (Seoul: Ministry of the Interior and Safety).

Minns, J. (2001), 'Of Miracles and Models: The Rise and Decline of the Developmental State in South Korea', *Third World Quarterly* 22(6), 1025–1043.

Organisation for Economic Co-operation and Development (OECD) (2001), *OECD Territorial Reviews: Korea* (Paris: OECD).

Park, B.-G. (2008), 'Uneven Development, Inter-Scalar Tensions, and the Politics of Decentralization in South Korea', *International Journal of Urban and Regional Research* 32(1), 40–59.

Park, C.-M. (2000), 'Local Politics and Urban Power Structure in South Korea', *Korean Social Science Journal* 27(2), 41–67.

Pirie, I. (2007), *The Korean Developmental State: From Dirigisme to Neo-Liberalism* (London: Routledge).

Sellers, J. (2019), 'From within to between Nations: Subnational Comparison across Borders', *Perspectives on Politics* 17(1), 85–105.

Sellers, J. M., Lidström, A., and Bae, Y. (2020), *Multilevel Democracy: How Local Institutions and Civil Society Shape the Modern State* (New York: Cambridge University Press).

Turner, M. (1999), 'Central–Local Relations: Themes and Issues', in M. Turner, ed., *Central–Local Relations in Asia-Pacific: Convergence of Divergence?*, 1–19 (New York: St. Martin's Press).

World Bank (2000), *The World Development Report, 1999–2000* (Washington, DC: World Bank).

Yoo, J. (1994), 'Jibangjachiui Jeongchi: Jeongdangui Yeokareul Jungsimeuro' (The Politics of Local Autonomy: The Role of Political Parties), *Hangukaengjeonghakbo* (*Korean Public Administration Review*) 28(2), 499–523.

Yoo, J. (2018), 'Assessing Central–Local Government Relations in Contemporary South Korea: An Application of Page & Goldsmith's Comparative Framework', *Lex Localis— Journal of Local Self-Government* 16(3), 505–528.

CHAPTER 31

CORRUPTION

KYOUNG-SUN MIN

1. INTRODUCTION

IN the late 1980 and 1990s, social scientists started to pay significant amounts of attention to corruption because corruption scandals were rampant worldwide (Lopez-Claros 2014). One motivation for studying corruption is its corrosive effect. It is widely believed that corruption harms income inequality (Gupta et al. 2002), social stability (Theobald 1990), trust (Seligson 2002), and government legitimacy (Clarke and Xu 2004). Most of all, many experts insist that corruption hurts economic development (Mauro 1995; Mo 2001; Pellegrini and Gerlagh 2004; Shleifer and Vishny 1993).

However, some scholars believe that corruption can positively affect economic growth under certain conditions (Barreto 2001; Huntington 2002; Leff 1964). South Korea was perceived as an example of the positive relationship between corruption and economic achievement. Many scholars point out that despite South Korea's extraordinary economic development, the level of corruption has not decreased (Choi 2018; Bhargava and Bolongaita 2004; Jun et al. 2019; Ko and Cho 2015; You 2005). For example, Lee Myung-bak and Park Geun-hye, two former presidents, went to prison due to corruption scandals.

Although scholars assert that a level of corruption is high in South Korea, this perception is not valid due to the decoupling of petty corruption from grand corruption. Corruption can be divided into two types: petty and grand corruption. Empirical evidence shows that petty corruption has decreased. For example, in the 1970s and the 1980s, it was natural for ordinary citizens to bribe police officers to avoid getting a traffic ticket, but today this is unimaginable. Underdeveloped countries and developing countries are trying to learn the anti-corruption policies of South Korea. Many scholars believe that the level of grand corruption is positively correlated to the level of petty corruption (You 2005; Andvig et al. 2001). However, South Korea shows the decoupling of petty corruption from grand corruption.

Current literature focuses mainly on the causes of grand corruption in South Korea (e.g. Kang 2002; You 2005). These studies do not explain the causes of corruption in South Korea by differentiating petty corruption from grand corruption. However, this chapter investigates the level of petty and grand corruption in South Korea with various measures. The results show that petty corruption has decreased. What leads to successful control of petty corruption? What causes grand corruption to still run rampant? To answer these questions, this chapter explains the difference between petty and grand corruption and measures the level of petty and grand corruption with various indices. The chapter also analyses the decoupling of petty and grand corruption by using historical institutionalism. A critical juncture explains a low level of petty corruption, and path dependence helps us to understand a high level of grand corruption in South Korea. A critical juncture was created by the Asian Financial Crisis of 1997, democratisation, and internet technology. Path dependence was fortified by crony capitalism and prosecutorial power. It is widely believed that political will is essential for fighting grand corruption. This chapter evaluates a level of political will by examining anti-corruption policies of South Korea.

2. Definitions: Corruption, Petty Corruption, and Grand Corruption

While the definition of corruption has generated long-running debates, there is still no single definition that satisfies everyone. One of the reasons is that discussions on corruption are related to the context (Johnston 2005). Corruption is understood differently depending on the state's context, in which the discussion of corruption takes places (Costantini 2017). While some countries construe a particular action as corruption, other countries may find the same behaviour acceptable (Klitgaard 1988). For this reason, it might be challenging to measure the level of corruption among different countries with one standard. However, this blurred line does not mean we cannot differentiate a bribe from a gift. Despite the definition of *bribery* varying amongst many countries, people can tell an illegal bribe from a legal gift (Klitgaard and Baser 1998).

Considering the goal of the study, this chapter defines *corruption* as the intentional misuse or abuse of public power by public officials to increase private interests while doing damage to people through their actions. Corruption can be classified as either petty or grand. Some scholars have sought to clarify the difference. Heidenheimer (2002: 150) claims, 'Petty corruption refers to bending of official rules in favour of friends, as manifested in the somewhat untruthful reporting of details, the ignoring of cut-off dates, the 'fixing' of parking tickets, and so on.' Holmes (2015) argues that petty corruption occurs in ordinary people's daily lives, while grand corruption happens only at the elite level. Others define grand corruption as more sophisticated than petty corruption (Lambsdorff 2005; Poeschl and Ribeiro 2012).

Some anti-corruption experts prefer to use the term '*venal corruption*' instead of '*grand corruption*' (Rotberg 2017: 32; Wallis 2006: 25). Some scholars suggest sophisticated classifications to deeply analyse the impact of corruption. For example, Ang (2020) classifies corruption as petty theft, speed money, grand theft, and access money. Although it might be better to investigate corruption with sophisticated classifications, this chapter uses the simple corruption classification. It is not perfect, but it is widely used and easy to understand.

It should be mentioned that petty corruption is not petty: it is a serious problem. It can be more harmful than grand corruption (Elliott 1997; Johnston 2005). Two main reasons can be suggested here. First, although the dollar value of petty corruption in a single case is small, the effect of the summation of petty corruption in total cases is not small. Second, the contagious effect of petty corruption can be stronger than that of grand corruption. Petty corruption can generate a negative externality effect (Abbink et al. 2002). While grand corruption is relatively hard to observe, petty corruption is relatively well observed because it relates to people's everyday lives. Thus, 'petty corruption is obviously not petty' (Riley 1999: 191).

3. THE LEVEL OF CORRUPTION IN SOUTH KOREA

To evaluate the state of corruption in South Korea, this section examines various corruption indices. The Corruption Perceptions Index (CPI) is the most popular index and is widely used. The CPI is a composition index created by Transparency International, which measured the perceptions of corruption in 180 countries using 13 different datasets (Transparency International 2020). The maximum score is 100, which indicates the lowest level of corruption. The minimum score is zero, which means the highest level of corruption.

Figure 31.1 shows the results of the CPI. The upper line is the average score of 37 Organisations for Economic Co-operation and Development (OECD) countries, and the lower line is South Korea's score. That score is lower than the average score of the OECD countries, but it has been improving since 2016. In 2019, South Korea's score was 59, and the average score of the OECD countries 66.9.

The perception of corruption does not precisely estimate corruption experience (Donchev and Ujhelyi 2014). This chapter explores survey datasets created by the Anti-Corruption and Civil Rights Commission (ACRC) to measure the level of corruption by experience. Since 2006, the ACRC has conducted surveys to gather crucial data related to corruption. In 2019, the respondents included 1,400 citizens, 700 business executives,

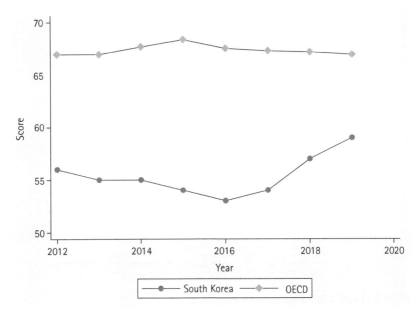

FIGURE 31.1: Comparison of corruption perceptions index between South Korea and the OECD (score)

Source: Transparency International (2020).

400 foreigners, 630 experts, and 1,400 public employees (ACRC 2019). Figure 31.2 shows the results of a survey question: 'Have you ever offered public officials a bribe during the past year?' (ACRC 2018: 3). From 2006 to 2019, the experience of giving bribes has generally decreased. In 2006, the citizens' experience was 3.9 per cent; the business persons' experience, 17.2 per cent; and the foreigners' experience, 11.8 per cent. In 2019, the citizens' experience was 0.6 per cent; the business persons' experience, 1.4 per cent; and the foreigners' experience, 2.3 per cent.

These results show several trends that capture the level of corruption in South Korea. First, the level of perception of corruption in South Korea has improved. Second, this level is still higher when we compare South Korea's score with the average of the OECD countries. Finally, the gap between perception and experience is considerable. While corruption perception is still high, corruption experience is low.

These trends help us to understand the level of corruption in South Korea. First, although perception has slowly decreased, corruption experience was already low. While experiences could have quickly changed, perception changed slowly because people stick to their previous perception (Rose-Ackerman and Palifka 2016). Second, whereas petty corruption has decreased, grand corruption has not significantly diminished in South Korea. Although ordinary people have little experience with petty corruption, they do not believe that their country is free from corruption because of recent grand corruption cases (Rose-Ackerman and Palifka 2016). For example, in 2016, Park

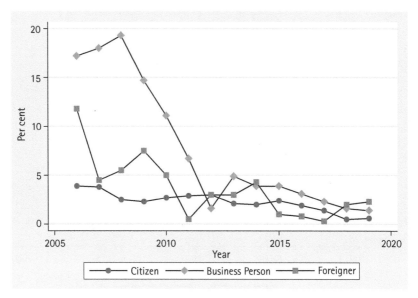

FIGURE 31.2: Experience of giving bribes (%)

Source: The Anti-Corruption and Civil Rights Commission (2019).

Geun-hye, the former president of Korea, was impeached due to corruption scandals (Choi 2018).

4. Explaining Corruption with Historical Institutionalism

4.1 Critical Juncture and Petty Corruption: IMF Global Standard, Democratisation, and E-Government

This chapter adopts the concept of historical institutionalism to explain the changes in the levels of corruption in South Korea. What leads to successful control of petty corruption? The idea of a critical juncture can answer this question. The popular definition of a *critical juncture* is 'a period of significant change, which typically occurs in distinct ways in different countries (or other units of analysis) and which is hypothesised to produce distinct legacies' (Collier and Collier 2002: 29). In South Korea, petty corruption visibly decreased after the occurrence of a critical juncture. Three main factors created the critical juncture that affected the path dependence of petty corruption in South Korea: International Monetary Fund (IMF) global standard, democratisation, and e-government.

4.1.1 *IMF Global Standard*

In 1997, the Asian Financial Crisis forced South Korea to ask the IMF to help. The Asian Financial Crisis changed South Korea's perceptions of corruption: from being a relatively incorruptible bureaucracy to a country controlled by crony capitalism (You 2005). Before the Asian Financial Crisis, the collaboration between the government and the conglomerates was seen as a positive factor for increasing South Korea's economic growth (Evans 1999; Wedeman 1997). However, after the crisis, pointing to the corrosive effect of corruption, many experts asserted that South Korea should abandon crony capitalism (Kang 2002; Kim and Im 2001; Göbel 2008; Moon and McLean 2003).

Political leaders in South Korea accepted this criticism and pushed the public and private sectors to adopt global standards. For example, since the Kim Dae-jung government believed that a low level of transparency in private companies affected the economic crisis, the government made firms implement global standards of auditing and accounting (Ko and Cho 2015). To fight corruption in the public sector, the government also established the Presidential Committee of Corruption Prevention in 2002. These changes came from the impact of the Asian Financial Crisis.

4.1.2 *Democratisation*

Democracy does not always reduce corruption (You 2005). The impact of democracy on corruption is controversial (Schopf 2018), but it is widely accepted that advanced democracy reduces corruption (Sung 2004; Caiden and Kim 1993). In a consolidated democracy, civil society is active and influential. Democracy with a robust civil society has generally a positive effect on curbing corruption (Ko and Cho 2015).

In South Korea, it is evident that democracy and civil society positively affect curbing corruption (You 2005; Schopf 2018; Setiyono et al. 2017). Since Kim Young-sam, the first civilian president after authoritarian regimes, was elected in 1992, political coups have not occurred. Today, South Korea successfully consolidates democracy and increases political stability with economic development (Ko and Cho 2015). With a consolidated democracy, non-profit organisations (NGOs) fervently work to fight corruption. For example, in 1998, an NGO, People's Solidarity for Participatory Democracy, proposed the Anti-Corruption Act; it was finally enacted in 2001 (Ko and Cho 2015). NGOs conducted a negative campaign to defeat corrupt candidates in the National Assembly election of April 2000, and 70 per cent of them finally lost the election (You 2005). The Citizens' Coalition for Economic Justice and the People's Solidarity for Participatory Democracy, established in 1989 and 1994, respectively, fought corruption by asking to build an anti-corruption agency (Bhargava and Bolongaita 2004). Partly due to their efforts, the Presidential Committee of Corruption Prevention was established in 2002. Thus, social pressure from civil society can curb corruption (Collier 2002).

4.1.3 *E-Government*

Since the end of the 1990s, the South Korean government has adopted and implemented information technology (IT) in government agencies. Now, South Korea is one of the

Table 31.1: Number and rate of disclosure of information

Category	2015	2016	2017	2018	2019
Number of organisations	484	603	609	613	614
Number of disclosures	6.95 million	5.80 million	5.20 million	4.59 million	6.38 million

Source: ACRC (2020b).

top e-government countries (United Nations 2020: 10). It is widely accepted that e-government with IT has a positive effect on controlling corruption (Andersen 2009; Mistry and Jalal 2012; Shim and Eom 2008). When countries adopted IT in their governments, the primary purpose of building an e-government was to increase efficiency (Von Haldenwang 2004). What are the channels from building e-government to controlling corruption?

First, e-government increases transparency (Shim and Eom 2008). With a high level of transparency, citizens can monitor public administration with low monitoring costs. For example, The Seoul Metropolitan Government launched the Online Procedures Enhancement for civil applications (OPEN) in 1999 (Schopf 2018). This internet service system dealt with various civil affairs related to transportation, housing, and so on. With this system, citizens could submit public complaints and requests as well as monitor procedures, and civil servants could not abuse their administrative power. According to a survey conducted by the Gallup Poll in 2000, 49 per cent of the citizens felt that corruption decreased with this new system (Cho and Choi 2004). Today, this system is implemented in various public agencies, including central governments, local governments, and state-owned enterprises (ACRC 2020b). Table 31.1 shows the number and rate of disclosure of information from 2015 to 2019.

Second, e-government helps citizens to report corruption with ease. For instance, since 2000, many police stations have created websites, including bulletin boards. Citizens can quickly access the boards and report corrupt police officers who asked them to give bribes. Over the years, the chiefs of police stations monitored the bulletin boards and ordered audit departments to investigate the cases. Today, it is difficult to find a case in which a police official asks for a bribe on the street.

4.2 Path Dependence and Grand Corruption: Crony Capitalism and Prosecutorial Power

While petty corruption decreased after the critical junctures occurred, grand corruption in South Korea has not dramatically decreased. What causes grand corruption to still run rampant? The concept of path dependence can help us answer this question. *Path dependence* can be defined as 'what has happened at an earlier point in time will affect the possible outcomes of a sequence of events occurring at a later point in time' (Sewell 1996: 262–263). In South Korea, path dependence has been fortified by crony capitalism and prosecutorial power.

Political leaders were not free from the connection between politics and business (Jun et al. 2019; Tsai 2009). For example, Lee Myung-bak, a former president, was charged in 2018 and sentenced to seventeen years in prison in 2020 with sixteen criminal allegations, including embezzling from DAS, an auto parts company, and receiving bribes from Samsung, a South Korean conglomerate (Woo 2020). Furthermore, Park Geun-hye, Lee Myung-bak's successor, was sentenced to twenty years in prison in 2020, with criminal allegations including receiving bribes from Lee Jae-yong, the chairman of Samsung (Jang 2020). These cases show that crony capitalism is not over in South Korea.

Prosecutorial power without checks and balances has been closely related to fortifying path dependence for failing to control grand corruption. According to Article 16 of the Constitution of the Republic of Korea, 'In case of search or seizure in residence, a warrant issued by a judge upon request of a prosecutor shall be presented.' This means that prosecutors have monopolistic power to request warrants. Since other investigative agencies have no power to request warrants, they should ask prosecutors to request warrants. According to Article 247 of the Criminal Procedure Act, 'A prosecutor may not institute a public prosecution, considering the matters under Article 51 of the Criminal Act.' This means that prosecutors have discretionary power to make decisions for indictment. These Articles give the prosecution office monopolistic power in the Korean criminal justice system (Pyo 2007).

Furthermore, the Prosecutor's Office does not want to share this monopolistic power with other investigative organisations (Ko and Cho 2015). Even if other investigative agencies assert that the suspects should be indicted, prosecutors can refuse to indict the suspects. For this reason, the objection to the prosecutor's decision is usually ignored. For example, in 2019, the ACRC received about 1,400 complaints related to the prosecution office, but most of the complaints were referred to the prosecution office because the ACRC has no power to investigate these cases (Foglesong et al. 2020). Political and business elites want to make connections with prosecutors to avoid the possibility of indictments. Thus, the connection between the elites and prosecutors hurts the curbing of grand corruption.

5. Anti-Corruption Policies in South Korea

5.1 The Political Will to Fight Grand Corruption

If grand corruption is persistent, what should we do? Many experts argue that political will, accompanied by demonstrated commitment, is essential to implement anti-corruption strategies for fighting corruption (Altamirano 2007; Brinkerhoff 2010; Rotberg 2017; Zhang 2015). *Political will* can be defined as 'the demonstrated credible intent of political actors to take meaningful action toward reform' (Quigley 2009: 16). Thus, without the strong political will to fight grand corruption, it will not decrease.

In South Korea, political will has not been enough to fight grand corruption. A lack of punishment is an obstacle to fighting grand corruption, and punishment is weak in South Korea (Bhargava and Bolongaita 2004). While various institutional reforms have been implemented, political elites have not been interested in fortifying punishment. According to the survey conducted by the ACRC in 2019, all respondents except public officials believe that fortifying punishment is an urgent issue. Table 31.2 shows the results of a survey question: 'What is the foremost issue to fight corruption?' (ACRC 2018: 4). More than 30 per cent of citizens answered that increasing the probability and severity of punishment should be the most important strategy to fight corruption. Without fortifying punishment related to grand corruption, path dependence that exacerbates grand corruption cannot be broken.

Table 31.2: Survey results: policy preference

	citizens	Business executives	experts	Foreigners	Public employees
N	1,400	700	630	400	1,400
Increasing the probability and severity of punishment	30.4%	34.7%	22.9%	26.4%	16.9%
Monitoring the corrupt behaviour of leaders and high-ranking officials	20.3	24.6	20.6	16.5	29.1
Improving laws and institutions related to corruption	15.1	16.0	20.3	18.8	12.4
Changing culture related to corruption	11.9	11.0	20.6	20.2	28.7
Building strong anti-corruption investigative agencies	9.1	3.9	5.2	4.8	4.0
Forfeiting the profit of corruption	8.6	3.6	4.8	2.5	3.3
Increasing transparency in business activities	2.5	4.3	1.6	8.3	2.7
Others	2.1	2.0	4.0	2.5	2.9

Source: ACRC (2019).

5.2 A Brief History of Anti-Corruption Policies

To evaluate political will to fight grand corruption, this section introduces a brief history of anti-corruption policies in South Korea. Overall, some political leaders of South Korea were not interested in implementing anti-corruption policies. Authoritarian leaders focused only on disciplining street-level bureaucrats. Although some democratic political leaders introduced anti-corruption reforms, their reforms did not fortify punishment related to grand corruption.

Before democratisation, authoritarian leaders construed the goal of anti-corruption policies as fortifying discipline in public services. For example, in 1981, the Chun Doo-hwan government disciplined more than 35,000 public employees involved in corruption (Ko and Cho 2015). However, various anti-corruption policies, including institutional reforms, had not been implemented. After democratic transition, democratic leaders adopted and implemented anti-corruption policies to differentiate themselves from the former dictators.

Kim Young-sam, president from 1993 to 1997, began to implement anti-corruption policies by enacting new laws, such as the Act on Real Name Financial Transactions in 1993 (Göbel 2008). Before enacting this law, politicians and the rich could open bank accounts anonymously. Due to this law, irregular political funds and bribery have been exposed (Bhargava and Bolongaita 2004). The Election of Public Officials and Prevention of Election Malpractices Act was also established in 1994. This Act prevented candidates from receiving bribes and buying votes (Ko and Cho 2015). Kim Young-sam also empowered the Bureau of Audit and Inspection and the Prosecutor's Office to investigate public officials' corruption (Ko and Cho 2015). Because anti-corruption policies were not wholly invented and developed, the Kim Young-sam government's reform focused mainly on regulation.

Kim Dae-jung, the president from 1998 to 2002, was interested in anti-corruption policies. The Anti-Corruption Act was established in 2001. It was the first comprehensive law that dealt with anti-corruption policies. By the law, the Korea Independent Commission against Corruption, the first holistic anti-corruption agency, was also established in 2002 (Göbel 2008). The Kim Dae-jung government vigorously adopted and implemented systematic anti-corruption policies, but the anti-corruption agency was too small to deal with corruption cases and had no investigative power (Ko and Cho 2015).

Roh Moo-hyun, the president from 2003 to 2007, adopted a holistic and comprehensive strategy to fight corruption, including punishment and systematic reforms (Ko and Cho 2015). The Consultative Council of Anti-Corruption Affiliated Agencies was launched in 2004, and council meetings were regularly held under the president's chairmanship (ACRC 2020b). The council made decisions for implementing various anti-corruption policies, and the Korea Independent Commission against Corruption played a leading role in the council. Moreover, the Public Official Election and Anti-Corruption Act in 2004 forced the government to fully refund all election costs if a candidate got more than 15 per cent of the vote.

Lee Myung-bak, president from 2008 to 2012, did not seem to be too interested in anti-corruption policies. The Consultative Council of Anti-Corruption Affiliated Agencies was disbanded when the Lee Myung-bak government was inaugurated. The ACRC was established in 2008. Other anti-corruption measures were also implemented by the ACRC. For example, the Protection Law of Public Interest Whistle-Blowers was enacted in 2011, and the Anti-Corruption Training Institute was established in 2012. Although the chairperson of the ACRC has the security of tenure, the ACRC faced massive criticism from civil society due to a lack of independence (People's Solidarity for Participatory Democracy 2018). One of the reasons for this criticism is that whereas the former anti-corruption agency was subject to the president, the ACRC is subject to the prime minister.

Park Geun-hye, president from 2013 to 2017, also did not seem to hold much interest in anti-corruption policies. However, ironically, the Improper Solicitation and Graft Act, known as the Kim Young-ran Act, was enacted in 2015 during her term. Kim Young-ran, the former chairperson of the ACRC from 2011 to 2012, sponsored the Act's draft in 2012. It was not easy to enact because this Act evoked strong opposition among the privileged class, including lawmakers. However, the impeachment of Park Geun-hye forced the politicians to pass this Act in 2015.

Moon Jae-in, president from 2017 to 2022, took some anti-corruption actions. The Anti-Corruption Policy Consultative Council, the Consultative Council of Anti-Corruption Affiliated Agencies' successor, was established in 2017 (ACRC 2020b). At the second Anti-Corruption Policy Consultative Council in 2018, the Five-Year Comprehensive Anti-Corruption Plan was announced (ACRC 2020a). This plan can be construed as a long-term anti-corruption strategy that includes various anti-corruption policies implemented by government agencies, NGOs, and other actors.

The Act for Building the Corruption Investigation Office for High-Ranking Officials (CIO) was also enacted in December 2020, and the CIO's head was appointed in January 2021. The CIO can be a tool to fight grand corruption by increasing the probability and severity of punishment. However, the future of the CIO is not clear. While some politicians and experts assert that political leaders will use the CIO as a tool to retaliate against their rivals, others argue that the agency will fight corruption seriously. A survey conducted in October 2019 shows that while 51 per cent of respondents supported building the agency, 41 per cent of them opposed the Act (Realmeter 2019). The opponents believe that the CIO's primary purpose is to control the Prosecutor's Office and not fight corruption. Political leaders should show their commitment that the CIO is for fighting grand corruption and not for retaliating their enemies.

5.3 Today's Anti-Corruption Policies

To understand present anti-corruption policies in South Korea, this section examines some anti-corruption policies that the ACRC adopted. The ACRC is making efforts to curb corruption. The ACRC was launched in 2008 by integrating the Ombudsman of Korea, the Korea Independent Commission against Corruption, and the Administrative Appeals Commission (ACRC 2020a). The effectiveness of the ACRC is controversial, but the ACRC executes its mission and tasks without serious problems. In fighting corruption, the ACRC has the responsibility to coordinate various anti-corruption policies (ACRC 2020a). This section explains two unique anti-corruption measures: integrity assessment and the Improper Solicitation and Graft Act.

5.3.1 *Integrity Assessment*

Since 2002, the ACRC has conducted an integrity assessment of public organisations to measure the level of integrity among public organisations (ACRC 2017). The Integrity Assessment survey mainly captures experiences and perceptions of corruption among citizens, public employees, and experts. More than 500 organisations were evaluated in 2017 (ACRC 2017). The ACRC (2017: 16) defines a public organisation's *level of integrity* as 'the degree to which a public official carries out his/her duties transparently and fairly without committing an act of corruption'. According to Article 2 of the Act on the Prevention of Corruption and the Establishment and Management of the Anti-Corruption and Civil Rights Commission, the act of corruption is 'the act of any public official's abusing his/her position or authority or violating statutes in connection with his/her duties to seek gains for himself/herself or any third party'.

Table 31.3 shows the composition of comprehensive integrity. The Integrity Assessment has three indices: internal integrity, external integrity, and policy customer evaluation. The ACRC conducted annual surveys of hundreds of thousands of respondents (ACRC 2017). Public employees participated in the internal integrity survey, citizens answered the external integrity survey, and experts gave their opinion to the policy customer evaluation survey.

The use of the Integrity Assessment of South Korea is one of the more well-known and useful anti-corruption policies. The Integrity Assessment won first place in the 2012 UN Public Service Awards. Today, the ACRC helps developing countries, such as Indonesia, Thailand, Malaysia, Vietnam, and Mongolia, to adopt and implement the Integrity Assessment (ACRC 2017). Since the Integrity Assessment can measure the level of corruption in organisations, it can help us to investigate the relationship between corruption and other variables. For example, using the Integrity Assessment and other datasets, Min (2019) showed the effectiveness of anti-corruption policies among public agencies in South Korea.

5.3.2 *The Improper Solicitation and Graft Act*

The Improper Solicitation and Graft Act passed in 2015, but was enforced in 2016 to have a grace period. According to Article 1, this Act aims to prohibit improper solicitations and prevent public officials from receiving bribes and other advantages. Thus, this Act has two parts: the prohibition of improper solicitations and accepting financial or other benefits. According to Article 5 of the Act, no one shall make improper solicitations to public officials. According to Article 8, no public officials can accept money and goods 'exceeding one million won at a time or three million won in a fiscal year from the same person'. According to Article 2, this Act applies to all types of public organisations, including constitutional institutions, local governments, and state-owned enterprises, as well as specific organisations, such as educational foundations and press companies.

Table 31.3: Composition of comprehensive integrity (2017)

Section	Index	Indicators
External integrity (0.601)	Corruption index (0.638)	Direct and indirect experience and perception of corruption, including the offering of money, gifts, entertainment or convenience, and improper pursuit of private interest (thirteen survey questions)
	Corruption risk index (0.362)	Transparency and accountability in the performance of duties (four survey questions)
Internal integrity (0.250)	Integrity culture index (0.433)	Prevalence of corrupt practices and effectiveness of anti-corruption systems (nine survey questions)
	Work integrity index (0.567)	Transparency and fairness in personnel management, budget execution, and order by superiors (twenty-four survey questions)
Policy customer evaluation (0.149)	Perception of corruption (0.427)	Perception of favour for former public officials, waste of budget, transparency/fairness in decision-making and overall work process, etc. (nine survey questions)
	Control of corruption (0.294)	Perception of strict punishment, efforts to prevent corruption, etc. (three survey items)
	Experience of corruption (0.279)	Experience and perception of offering of money, gifts, and entertainment, etc. (one survey items)

Note: The numbers in parenthesis are weights.
Source: ACRC (2017).

Table 31.4: Approval rating for the Improper Solicitation and Graft Act (%)

	2017	2018	2019	2020
Citizen	87.3	87.5	87.7	88.1
Public employee	93.4	95.0	96.6	97.2
Journalist	71.1	81.0	79.2	82.1
School teacher	91.6	91.9	92.8	94.4

Source: ACRC (2020b).

Thus, not only politicians and public employees but also teachers and journalists are presumed to be public officials.

This Act has been working effectively. According to surveys conducted by the ACRC, the majority of about 2,000 respondents believes that the Act affects the reduction of corruption. Table 31.4 shows the approval rating for the Act. The trends demonstrate that the approval rating has increased among all types of respondents.

6. Conclusion

This chapter has explored petty and grand corruption in South Korea, utilising various studies and indices. The theory of institutionalism helps us understand the decoupling of petty corruption from grand corruption. The Asian Financial Crisis, democratisation, and IT created a critical juncture that controlled petty corruption in South Korea. Crony capitalism and prosecutorial power have fortified path dependence that obstructs a decrease in grand corruption. Political will to fight grand corruption is critical to fighting against grand corruption, but it has not been enough in South Korea. Although some democratic political leaders have adopted anti-corruption policies, their reforms did not aim to fortify punishment related to grand corruption.

Various indices and cases indicate that petty corruption has decreased. It is also evident that grand corruption persists. This situation is not unique. Developed countries also suffer from grand corruption, although petty corruption is hardly observed. For example, Atkinson (2011) argues that although Canada gets good scores in corruption indices, political corruption scandals continue to occur. This means that fighting against grand corruption is not just South Korea's problem.

This chapter shows that we need different strategies to fight different types of corruption. An anti-corruption policy that works for curbing corruption might fail to control grand corruption. If we want to curb grand corruption, what types of anti-corruption policies should we adopt? The CIO can be an answer, but we do not know its effectiveness. The effectiveness of the CIO might depend on political will. How can we increase political will? That is our next question to be answered.

Bibliography

Abbink, K., Irlenbusch, B., and Renner, E. (2002), 'An Experimental Bribery Game', *Journal of Law, Economics, and Organization* 18(2), 428–454.

Anti-Corruption and Civil Rights Commission (ACRC) (2017), 'A Practical Guide to Integrity Assessment', http://www.acrc.go.kr/en/file/file.do?command=downFile&encodedKey=Mjk2MzRfNg%3D%3D, accessed 25 November 2021.

ACRC (2018), 'Bupae insigdo josa seolmunji' ('Corruption Perception Survey Questionnaire'), https://www.acrc.go.kr/acrc/board.do?command=searchDetail&menuId=05020703&method=searchDetailViewInc&boardNum=71534&currPageNo=1&confId=36&conConfId=36&conTabId=0&conSearchCol=BOARD_TITLE&conSearchSort=A.BOARD_REG_DATE+DESC%2C+BOARD_NUM+DESC, accessed 25 November 2021.

ACRC (2019), '2019 Bupae insigdo josa' ('Corruption Perception Report 2019'), https://www.acrc.go.kr/acrc/board.do?command=searchDetail&menuId=05020703&method=searchDetailViewInc&boardNum=82910, accessed 25 November 2021.

ACRC (2020a), 'ACRC Korea Annual Report 2019' (Sejong, South Korea: ACRC), 7 July, https://www.acrc.go.kr/en/board.do?command=searchDetail&method=searchDetailViewInc&menuId=020504&boardNum=83623, accessed 25 November 2021.

ACRC (2020b), 'Republic of Korea Anti-Corruption Report', 23 November, https://www.acrc.go.kr/en/board.do?command=searchDetail&method=searchDetailViewInc&menuId=020504&boardNum=84853, accessed 25 November 2021.

Altamirano, G. D. (2007), 'The Impact of the Inter-American Convention against Corruption', *University of Miami Inter-American Law Review* 38(3), 487–547.

Andersen, T. B. (2009), 'E-Government as an Anti-Corruption Strategy', *Information Economics and Policy* 21(3), 201–210.

Andvig, J. C., Fjeldstad, O.-H., Weltzien, Å., Amundsen, I., Sissener, T. K., and Søreide, T. (2001), *Corruption: A Review of Contemporary Research*, CMI Report (Bergen: Chr. Michelsen Institute).

Ang, Y. Y. (2020), 'Unbundling Corruption: Revisiting Six Questions on Corruption', *Global Perspectives* 1(1), 1–19.

Atkinson, M. M. (2011), 'Discrepancies in Perceptions of Corruption, or Why Is Canada So Corrupt?', *Political Science Quarterly* 126(3), 445–464.

Barreto, R. A. (2001), *Endogenous Corruption, Inequality and Growth: Econometric Evidence*, School of Economics Working Papers (Adelaide: University of Adelaide).

Bhargava, V. K., and Bolongaita, E. (2004), *Challenging Corruption in Asia: Case Studies and a Framework for Action* (Washington, DC: World Bank).

Brinkerhoff, D. W. (2010), *Unpacking the Concept of Political Will to Confront Corruption*, U4 Brief (Bergen: Chr. Michelsen Institute).

Caiden, G. E., and Kim, J. H. (1993), 'A New Anti-Corruption Strategy for Korea', *Asian Journal of Political Science* 1(1), 133–151.

Cho, Y. H., and Choi, B. D. (2004). 'E-Government to Combat Corruption: The Case of Seoul Metropolitan Government', *International Journal of Public Administration* 27(10), 719–735.

Choi, J. W. (2018), 'Corruption Control and Prevention in the Korean Government: Achievements and Challenges from an Institutional Perspective', *Asian Education Development Studies* 7(3), 303–314.

Clarke, G. R., and Xu, L. C. (2004), 'Privatization, Competition, and Corruption: How Characteristics of Bribe Takers and Payers Affect Bribes to Utilities', *Journal of Public Economics* 88(9–10), 2067–2097.

Collier, M. W. (2002), 'Explaining Corruption: An Institutional Choice Approach', *Crime, Law and Social Change* 38(1), 1–32.

Collier, R. B., and Collier, D. (2002), *Shaping the Political Arena: Critical Junctures, the Labor Movement, and Regime Dynamics in Latin America* (Notre Dame, IN: University of Notre Dame Press).

Costantini, I. (2017), 'The Politics of Corruption and Anti-Corruption Measures in Conflict-Affected Countries: An Exploration through the Lens of Hybridity', in B. Bellak, J. Devdariani, B. Harzl, and L. Spieker, eds, *Governance in Conflict: Selected Cases in Europe and Beyond*, 171–192 (Vienna: LIT Verlag).

Donchev, D., and Ujhelyi, G. (2014), 'What Do Corruption Indices Measure?', *Economics and Politics* 26(2), 309–331.

Elliott, K. A. (1997), 'Corruption as an International Policy Problem: Overview and Recommendations', in K. A. Elliott, ed., *Corruption and the Global Economy*, 175–236 (Washington, DC: Institute for International Economics).

Evans, B. R. (1999), *The Cost of Corruption*, Tearfund discussion paper, http://auxbeacon.org/wp-content/uploads/2016/03/corruption23.pdf, accessed 25 November 2021.

Foglesong, T., Pasca, T., Zhao, S., and Kim, S. (2020), *The Role of Complaints in Public Prosecution* (Toronto: Munk School Report).

Göbel, C. (2008), 'Warriors in Chains: Institutional Legacies and Anti-Corruption Programmes in Taiwan and South Korea', in L. de Sousa, B. Hindess, and P. Larmour, eds, *Governments, NGOs and Anti-Corruption: The New Integrity Warriors*, 102–119 (London: Routledge).

Gupta, S., Davoodi, H., and Alonso-Terme, R. (2002), 'Does Corruption Affect Income Inequality and Poverty?', *Economics of Governance* 3(1), 23–45.

Heidenheimer, A. J. (2002), 'Perspectives on the Perception of Corruption', in A. J. Heidenheimer and M. Johnston, eds, *Political Corruption: Concepts & Contexts*, 141–154 (New Brunswick, NJ: Transaction Publishers).

Holmes, L. (2015), *Corruption: A Very Short Introduction* (Hampshire, Great Britain: Oxford University Press).

Huntington, S. P. (2002), 'Modernization and Corruption', in A. J. Heidenheimer and M. Johnston, eds, *Political Corruption: Concepts & Contexts*, 253–264 (New Brunswick, NJ: Transaction Publishers).

Jang, Y. (2020), 'Park Geun-hye Receives Reduced Sentence of 20 Years', *Hankyoreh*, 13 July, http://english.hani.co.kr/arti/english_edition/e_national/953463.html, accessed 25 November 2021.

Johnston, M. (2005), *Syndromes of Corruption: Wealth, Power, and Democracy* (Cambridge: Cambridge University Press).

Jun, I.-W., Kim, K.-I., and Rowley, C. (2019), 'Organizational Culture and the Tolerance of Corruption: The Case of South Korea', *Asia Pacific Business Review* 25(4), 534–553.

Kang, D. C. (2002), *Crony Capitalism: Corruption and Development in South Korea and the Philippines* (New York: Cambridge University Press).

Kim, B. K., and Im, H. B. (2001), 'Crony Capitalism in South Korea, Thailand and Taiwan: Myth and Reality', *Journal of East Asian Studies* 1(1), 5–52.

Kim, S. (2008), 'The Assessment of Bureaucratic Corruption Control in South Korea: The Importance of Political Will in Government's Anti-Corruption Efforts', PhD thesis, University of Sheffield.

Klitgaard, R. (1988), *Controlling Corruption* (Berkeley, CA: University of California Press).

Klitgaard, R., and Baser, H. (1998), *Working Together to Fight Corruption: State, Society and the Private Sector in Partnership* (Santa Monica, CA: RAND Corporation).

Ko, K., and Cho, S. Y. (2015), 'Evolution of Anti-Corruption Strategies in South Korea', in Y. Zhang and C. Lavena, eds, *Government Anti-Corruption Strategies: A Cross-Cultural Perspective*, 103–122 (Boca Raton, FL: Taylor & Francis).

Lambsdorff, J. G. (2005), 'Between Two Evils—Investors Prefer Grand Corruption', Working paper, University of Passau.

Leff, N. H. (1964), 'Economic Development through Bureaucratic Corruption', *American Behavioral Scientist* 8(3), 8–14.

Lopez-Claros, A. (2014), 'Why Is Corruption Today Less of a Taboo Than a Quarter Century Ago?', http://blogs.worldbank.org/futuredevelopment/why-corruption-today-less-taboo-quarter-century-ago, accessed 25 November 2021.

Mauro, P. (1995), 'Corruption and Growth', *Quarterly Journal of Economics* 110(3), 681–712.

Min, K. (2019), 'The Effectiveness of Anti-Corruption Policies: Measuring the Impact of Anti-Corruption Policies on Integrity in the Public Organizations of South Korea', *Crime, Law and Social Change* 71(2), 217–239.

Mistry, J. J., and Jalal, A. (2012), 'An Empirical Analysis of the Relationship between E-Government and Corruption', *International Journal of Digital Accounting Research* 12, 145–176.

Mo, P. H. (2001), 'Corruption and Economic Growth', *Journal of Comparative Economics* 29(1), 66–79.

Moon, Y. L., and McLean, G. N. (2003), 'The Nature of Corruption Hidden in Culture: The Case of Korea', in F.-J. Richter and J. Kidd, eds, *Fighting Corruption in Asia: Causes, Effects and Remedies*, 297–315 (Singapore: World Scientific).

Pellegrini, L., and Gerlagh, R. (2004), 'Corruption's Effect on Growth and Its Transmission Channels', *Kyklos* 57(3), 429–456.

People's Solidarity for Participatory Democracy (2018), *Petition for Building Anti-Corruption Agency*, http://www.peoplepower21.org/Petition/1581134, accessed 25 November 2021.

Poeschl, G., and Ribeiro, R. (2012), 'Everyday Opinions on Grand and Petty Corruption: A Portuguese Study', Observatório de Economia e Gestão de Fraude (OBEGEF) Working paper.

Pyo, C. (2007), 'Prosecutor, Police and Criminal Investigation in Korea: A Critical Review', *Journal of Korean Law* 6(2), 191–200.

Quigley, F. (2009), 'Growing Political Will from the Grassroots: How Social Movement Principles Can Reverse the Dismal Legacy of Rule of Law Interventions', *Columbia Human Rights Law Review* 41, 13–66.

Realmeter (2019), 'Gonsucheo chanseong 51% bandae 41%' (Poll for Building the Corruption Investigation Office for High-Ranking Officials: Pros 51% and Cons 41%), 21 October, http://www.realmeter.net/%ea%b3%b5%ec%88%98%ec%b2%98-%ec%84%a4%ec%b9%98-%ec%b0%ac%ec%84%b1-51-vs-%eb%b0%98%eb%8c%80-41/, accessed 25 November 2021.

Riley, S. P. (1999), 'Petty Corruption and Development', *Development in Practice* 9(1–2), 189–193.

Rose-Ackerman, S., and Palifka, B. J. (2016), *Corruption and Government: Causes, Consequences, and Reform* (Cambridge: Cambridge University Press).

Rotberg, R. I. (2017), *The Corruption Cure: How Citizens and Leaders Can Combat Graft* (Princeton, NJ: Princeton University Press).

Schopf, J. C. (2018), 'Cutting Corruption without Institutionalized Parties: The Story of Civic Groups, Elected Local Government, and Administrative Reform in Korea', *Korea Observer* 49(4), 573–604.

Seligson, M. A. (2002), 'The Impact of Corruption on Regime Legitimacy: A Comparative Study of Four Latin American Countries', *Journal of Politics* 64(2), 408–433.

Setiyono, B., Adnan, M., and Astrika, L. (2017), 'Combating Corruption during Democratic Transition: The Role of CSOs in South Korea and Indonesia', *Sociology and Anthropology* 5(11), 968–976.

Sewell, W. H. (1996), 'Three Temporalities: Toward an Eventful Sociology', in T. J. McDonald, ed., *The Historic Turn in the Human Sciences*, 245–280 (Ann Arbor, MI: University of Michigan Press).

Shim, D. C., and Eom, T. H. (2008), 'E-Government and Anti-Corruption: Empirical Analysis of International Data', *International Journal of Public Administration* 31(3), 298–316.

Shleifer, A., and Vishny, R. W. (1993), 'Corruption', *Quarterly Journal of Economics* 108(3), 599–617.

Sung, H. E. (2004), 'Democracy and Political Corruption: A Cross-National Comparison', *Crime, Law and Social Change* 41(2), 179–193.

Theobald, R. (1990) *Corruption, Development, and Underdevelopment* (Hampshire, London: Macmillan Press).

Transparency International (2020), 'Corruption Perceptions Index 2020: Short Methodology Note', https://www.transparency.org/en/cpi/2020/index, accessed 25 November 2021.

Tsai, J. (2009), 'Political Structure, Legislative Process, and Corruption: Comparing Taiwan and South Korea', *Crime, Law and Social Change* 52(4), 365–383.

United Nations (2020), 'United Nations E-Government Survey 2020', https://publicadministration.un.org/egovkb/en-us/Reports/UN-E-Government-Survey-2020, accessed 25 November 2021.

Von Haldenwang, C. (2004), 'Electronic Government (E-Government) and Development', *European Journal of Development Research* 16(2), 417–432.

Wallis, J. J. (2006), 'The Concept of Systematic Corruption in American History', in E. L. Glaeser, ed., *Corruption and Reform: Lessons from America's Economic History*, 23–62 (Chicago, IL: University of Chicago Press).

Wedeman, A. (1997), 'Looters, Rent-Scrapers, and Dividend-Collectors: Corruption and Growth in Zaire, South Korea, and the Philippines', *Journal of Developing Areas* 31(4), 457–478.

Woo, J. (2020), 'Supreme Court Confirms 17-Year Prison Term for Ex-President Lee Myung-bak in Corruption Case', *Yonhap News*, 29 October, https://en.yna.co.kr/view/AEN20201029003451315, accessed 25 November 2021.

You, J. S. (2005), *Embedded Autonomy or Crony Capitalism? Explaining Corruption in South Korea, Relative to Taiwan and the Philippines, Focusing on the Role of Land Reform and Industrial Policy* (Washington, DC: Citeseer).

Zhang, Y. (2015), 'What Can We Learn from Worldwide Anti-Corruption Practices?', in Y. Zhang and C. Lavena, eds, *Government Anti-Corruption Strategies: A Cross-Cultural Perspective*, 247–261 (Boca Raton, FL: CRC Press).

PART 8

THE INTERNATIONAL ARENA

CHAPTER 32

FOREIGN POLICY

RAMON PACHECO PARDO

1. Introduction

THE foreign policy of South Korea since the Sixth Republic was established in 1987 has remained remarkably stable. In terms of structures, goals, and tools, there has been little change across administrations. This stems from a high degree of elite consensus regarding South Korean foreign policy objectives and the policies that the country can realistically use to achieve them. Continuity also comes from structural constraints on South Korean foreign policy, especially a long-standing alliance with the United States, its geographical position in Northeast Asia surrounded by great powers, and the division between the two Koreas. Logically, South Korea's foreign policy has been influenced by developments such as the end of the Cold War, China's rise, the Asian and Global financial crises, or growing Sino–American competition. And there have been differences regarding how to approach relations with North Korea once it became a nuclear power. But for the most part, South Korean foreign policy has remained stable during this period—allowing the country to achieve many of its goals.

The structures underpinning South Korea's foreign policymaking process reflect the country's strong presidentialism, dating back to 1987 (Im 2020). Thus, the president and its office (*Cheong Wa Dae* or Blue House until 2022) dominate foreign policy decision-making. A relatively small number of ministries, the intelligence services, the National Assembly, other organisations, and civil society influence decision-making and implementation. But the president has a lot of leeway in taking decisions and directing how to implement them.

In terms of goals, South Korean foreign policy has remained stable. In common with all other countries, strengthening national security remains the ultimate goal. Autonomy has been another crucial objective. This relates to (South) Korea's centuries-old concern of being a 'shrimp among whales', with little scope to pursue its chosen foreign policy path. Korean reunification—or at least reconciliation—is another main goal, which underscores that Korea remains divided after centuries as a single nation. Other important foreign policy objectives include balancing relations with the great powers (particularly the United States and China), promoting economic openness at the global level, and influencing international affairs.

When it comes to foreign policy tools, South Korea prioritises its alliance with the United States, strong military capabilities, multilateralism and cooperation, soft power and public diplomacy, and trade multilateralism and bilateralism. The Republic of Korea–US (ROK–US) alliance is seen both as a security guarantee and as an enabler of South Korean foreign policy because it significantly boosts South Korean strength, even though sometimes it can also constrain foreign policy autonomy. The development of strong military capabilities is crucial for South Korean autonomy and security. Multilateralism and cooperation through institutions such as the United Nations (UN) or the G20 levels the playing field between South Korea and greater powers, which benefits Seoul. Soft power and public diplomacy enhance South Korean reputation, and allow Seoul to benefit from the success of *Hallyu* or the Korean Wave to advance its foreign policy interests. As for multilateral and bilateral trade agreements, they underpin South Korea's quest for economic openness—a vital goal for a trade-dependent economy, which cannot rely on its domestic market for growth.

Ultimately, South Korea is a middle power (Kim 2015). Middle powers are hard to define. In simple terms, middle powers are countries that clearly do not have great power status, while having enough power to influence global affairs and not simply be defined by them. East Asian neighbours such as Japan, European countries such as Spain or the United Kingdom, and G20 members, including Australia and Canada, belong to this category. Dating back to the Roh Tae-woo administration that inaugurated the Sixth Republic, South Korea has self-consciously identified as a middle power. As opposed to the weak power dependent on the United States and threatened by North Korea that South Korea was throughout much of the Cold War, middle power South Korea has sought to use its strengths to proactively pursue its preferred foreign policy goals.

This chapter is organised as follows. The next section outlines in detail South Korea's foreign policymaking structures since its transition to democracy in 1987. Section 3 focuses on Seoul's foreign policy during the first post-transition administrations, when South Korea started to open up to the rest of the world: Roh Tae-woo and Kim Young-sam (1988–1998). The following section then analyses foreign policy during the first decade of liberal rule in South Korean history, with a renewed focus on North Korea and East Asia under Kim Dae-jung and Roh Moo-hyun (1998–2008). Section 5 then examines the conservative decade under Lee Myung-bak and Park Geun-hye (2008–2017), when South Korea focused on a more global policy. The section after analyses foreign policy under the liberal Moon Jae-in (2017–2022), with its emphasis on a balanced approach, and the conclusion section then summarises the key findings from this chapter.

2. South Korea's Foreign Policy-Making Structures

South Korea's foreign policy structures encompass institutions formally tasked with its making and implementation, together with institutions that explicitly or implicitly seek to influence policy debates. With regards to the institutions with a formal role in foreign policy decision-making and implementation, in theory their tasks are clearly defined, even if in practice task compartmentalisation is not clear cut. The president and its office sit at the top, and ministries, intelligence services, the National Assembly, and other governmental institutions are tasked with implementation. These other institutions also provide input to inform foreign policy, together with civil society organisations.

As befits a presidential system, the president is formally tasked with taking foreign policy decisions. Legally, the president is the head of state, head of government, and commander in chief of the armed forces.[1] It is the president's prerogative to decide how much input other institutions may have, and to what extent they will be involved in the decision-making process. The Presidential Office, colloquially known as *Cheong Wa Dae* until 2022, is the key institution supporting the president. It is staffed by secretaries and special advisors appointed by the president and with different areas of expertise (*Cheong Wa Dae* 2020b). Traditionally, there have been secretaries for foreign affairs, security, defence, peace and reunification, and trade/economic affairs. They assist the president in their areas of expertise. In addition, there is a National Security Council (NSC) or Office for National Security (ONS) (*Cheong Wa Dae* 2020b). It deals with these issues, as well as intelligence. The NSC/ONS has an advisory role. Both *Cheong Wa Dae* and the NSC/ONS have become more powerful foreign policy actors since South Korean presidents have centralised more aspects of foreign policymaking.

There are four ministries that strongly influence South Korea's foreign policy. They are the Ministry of Foreign Affairs (MOFA),[2] the Ministry of National Defense (MND),[3] the Ministry of Unification (MOU),[4] and the Ministry of Trade, Industry and Energy (MOTIE);[5] from 1998 to 2013, MOFA was also tasked with trade (MOFAT), with separate ministers for foreign affairs and trade. This underscores the centrality of trade to South Korean foreign policy. These ministries focus, respectively, on foreign policy, security and defence, North Korea, and trade. It should be noted, however, that their areas of work inevitably overlap—especially between MOFA, MND, and MOU. These ministries are tasked with policy implementation, information gathering, and policy evaluation. Together with the heads of *Cheong Wa Dae* and NSC/ONS, ministers attend the regular State Council meetings chaired by the president or the prime minister; the latter plays a role akin to a vice president.

These ministries operate several institutions and resources to support foreign policy implementation. In the case of MOFA, at the start of 2020 it had 120 embassies and permanent missions and 2,405 diplomatic staff, plus 332 resident officers from other ministries (MOFA 2020). MOFA also operates the Korea International Cooperation Agency (KOICA), set up in 1991 to manage and distribute South Korean aid. As of 2020, KOICA had forty-four offices across Africa, Asia, Latin America, Middle East, and international organisations (KOICA 2020). In addition, the Korea Foundation (KF), established in 1992 as a public diplomacy organisation, is affiliated with MOFA. As of 2020, KF operated eight offices overseas (Korea Foundation 2020). As for MND, the South Korean military comprised 599,000 active personnel and 3,100,000 reserve personnel at the start of 2020 (International Institute for Strategic Studies 2020). In addition, by law, and since 1957, all able-bodied male citizens between the ages of eighteen and forty have to complete a military service of almost two years. In the case of MOTIE, it has been operating the Korea Trade Promotion Agency (KOTRA) since 1962. KOTRA was renamed as the Korea Investment Trade Promotion Agency in 1995. Its main goals are to promote South Korean exports and inward foreign direct investment. KOTRA operated 10 offices and 129 business centres across the world as of 2020 (KOTRA 2020). Meanwhile, South Korea has been setting up Korean Cultural Centers (KCC) overseas since 1979. Managed by the Ministry of Culture, Sports and Tourism, as of 2020 there were thirty-two centres across Africa, the Americas, Asia-Pacific, Europe, and the Middle East (KOCIS 2020). The KCC support South Korea's soft power through the promotion of Korean traditional culture and South Korean contemporary culture.

Two organisations collect intelligence and conduct counter-intelligence operations to support South Korea's foreign policymaking, among other things, especially in the area of national security. The National Intelligence Service (NIS) was established in 1961 under the name of the Korean Central Intelligence Service. It then changed its name to the Agency for National Security Planning in 1981, before switching to its current name of NIS in 1999 (NIS 2015). The NIS responds directly to the president. In addition, the MND has been operating the Defense Security Support Command (DSSC) since 2018. The DSSC replaced the Defense Security Command (DSC), formed in 1977 (DSCC 2020).

South Korea's unicameral National Assembly also plays a formal role in the country's foreign policy. It scrutinises, checks, and monitors foreign policy decisions. Committees are in charge of these tasks. There are permanent committees on foreign affairs, national defence, trade, and intelligence (The National Assembly of the Republic of Korea 2020a). There are also inter-parliamentary councils and parliamentary friendship groups conducting inter-parliamentary diplomacy, to strengthen links with other parliaments (The National Assembly of the Republic of Korea 2020b). In the specific area of trade, the National Assembly also has to formally approve free trade agreements (FTAs) signed by MOTIE.

With regards to civil society, it is involved in foreign policy through a wide range of institutions that participate in decision-making informally. The most relevant institutions include think tanks. These can be divided into government-funded, but independently run, think tanks, such as the Institute of Foreign Affairs and National Security (IFANS),[6] the Korea Institute for Defense Analyses (KIDA),[7] or the Korea Institute for National Unification (KINU),[8] and private think tanks, such as The Asan

Institute for Policy Studies[9] or Sejong Institute.[10] In addition, university graduate schools for international studies and think tanks also influence policy. They include Korea University,[11] Seoul National University,[12] and Yonsei University.[13] These think tanks and universities issue policy papers, organise conferences, and provide expertise, and there is a 'revolving door' between them and government. In addition, South Korean media also actively informs about and robustly debates foreign policy, particularly North Korea policy, the ROK–US alliance, and Northeast Asian relations (Kwak 2012). Finally, business groups and trade unions seek to influence trade policy (see chapter 34 by Soohyun Zoe Lee on Foreign Economic Policy).

3. SOUTH KOREAN FOREIGN POLICY UNDER ROH TAE-WOO AND KIM YOUNG-SAM: OPENING UP TO THE REST OF THE WORLD

South Korea was under authoritarian rule for almost the whole period since its founding in 1948 to the democratic elections of 1987. Throughout these decades, South Korea's foreign policy priorities were clear: to protect itself from a possible North Korean attack and to maintain the ROK–US alliance as the anchor of South Korean security and prosperity (Heo and Roehrig 2014). Shaken by the Korean War and in dire need of economic development, these were the key tenets of the foreign policy approach of Rhee Syngman, Park Chung-hee, and Chun Doo-hwan, the three presidents who dominated South Korean politics until 1987. They resulted in South Korea's steadfast support for US foreign policy, including participation in the Vietnam War (Heo and Roehrig 2014: 58). Certainly, Korean reunification was another key foreign policy priority, but both forceful absorption and a diplomatic approach were unrealistic (Heo and Roehrig 2014: 31–32). In July 1972, however, there was a potential breakthrough in inter-Korean relations as the two Koreas issued a joint communiqué establishing the three principles for reunification: independence, peace, and national unity.[14] The communiqué came in the context of Sino–American rapprochement. However, there was in fact no breakthrough and inter-Korean relations continued to be marked by antagonism and competition. Besides these issues, South Korean foreign policy, for the most part, maintained a low profile.

South Korea's foreign policy took a qualitative and quantitative change with the advent of democracy. Seoul hosted the Summer Olympic Games in 1988, less than a year after its first ever truly free elections. The Games were symbolic of South Korea's economic development and diplomatic 'victory' over North Korea, which asked fellow communist countries to boycott the Games, only to see the Soviet Union and China lead the communist bloc in attending (Han 1989: 34–35). Imbued by a sense of pride, the newly elected Roh Tae-woo announced *Nordpolitik* in July 1988—two months before the Games. *Nordpolitik* established that Seoul would promote trade and people-to-people exchanges between the two Koreas, establish diplomatic relations with the

Soviet Union, China, and other communist countries, and support North Korea's normalisation with the United States and Japan (Han 1989: 34–35). It was a marked shift in paradigm: moving towards autonomy from Washington (which actually supported *Nordpolitik*), taking a new approach towards Korean reunification, improving relations with China and the communist bloc at large, and opening new markets for South Korean exporters. In the case of inter-Korean relations, *Nordpolitik* has implicitly or explicitly underpinned South Korea's approach ever since.

The Roh government therefore inaugurated the era of South Korea as a middle power, seeking to raise its profile at the global level. Seoul normalised relations with several communist countries in quick succession from 1989, including the Soviet Union in 1990 and China in 1992. In 1991, both Koreas joined the United Nations (UN) at the same time (Heo and Roehrig 2014: 173). This was a de facto recognition of the division of Korea into two. But it was also part of South Korea's wish to use multilateralism to show its autonomy, balance relations with the great powers, and start to influence international affairs. Furthermore, joint UN membership supported inter-Korean relations. In December 1991, the two Koreas signed the Agreement on Reconciliation, Non-Aggression and Exchanges and Cooperation, or the Basic Agreement, whereby they recognised each other's systems, peace, and cooperation as the basis for reconciliation.[15] One month later, in January 1992, the two Koreas signed the Joint Declaration of the Denuclearisation of the Korean Peninsula.[16] One month before this agreement, the United States had removed its tactical nuclear weapons from South Korea. This was another step in reducing Seoul's dependence on Washington, but also symbolised that South Korea did not feel threatened by North Korea to the same extent as before anymore.

Upon his inauguration in 1993, Kim Young-sam launched his *Segyehwa* or Globalisation policy. Firmly anchored in a conception of South Korea as a middle power, *Segyehwa* sought to strengthen South Korea's diplomatic and economic links outside of their usual regions of focus (Snyder 2018: 78)—namely, the Korean Peninsula, Northeast Asia, and the ROK–US alliance. Kim wanted South Korea to become a more open economy, more influential in global affairs, and to look beyond Korean reunification as its only focus. At the global level, therefore, South Korea became more active in the UN. In 1994, South Korea sent its first-ever peacekeepers to support UN missions in Western Sahara, Georgia, and the Indo–Pakistani border. From then onwards, South Korea would contribute soldiers, medical staff, observers, and other personal to most UN missions (Ko 2015: 72). In addition, in 1996–1997, South Korea joined the UN Security Council as a non-permanent member for the first time ever. Even though both Koreas had joined the UN at the same time, there was no doubt which of the two was becoming a more active and recognised member of the international community.

Its quest for international recognition as a symbol of autonomy and an influential actor in global affairs also led Seoul to prioritise Organisation for Economic Co-operation and Development (OECD) membership. South Korea joined this organisation in 1996, only the second Asian country to do (OECD 2020a). The Kim government and South Koreans more broadly celebrated membership, seen as proof that the country had left poverty behind. Shortly after, in 1997, the Bank of Korea joined the Bank for International Settlements (BIS) (Bank of Korea 2020). Less celebrated in public, BIS membership was another clear sign that the Kim government was pursuing a policy of economic openness and liberalisation to strengthen the South Korean economy. Instead, however, South Korea's financial openness and deepening integration in global capital flows were a direct reason why the country was one of the most heavily affected by the Asian Financial Crisis (AFC). Seoul was forced to go cap in hand to the International Monetary Fund (IMF), which approved and led a US$58 billion bailout (IMF 2000)—the largest in its history until then. South Koreans saw this as an act of national humiliation. Inevitably, the AFC had an impact in South Korean foreign policy.

4. South Korean Foreign Policy under Kim Dae-jung and Roh Moo-hyun: A Liberal Decade with a Focus on East Asia

The onset of the AFC coincided with the election of Kim Dae-jung. In 1998, Kim would take office as South Korea's first liberal president since the early 1960s. Upon his election, he had to contend with the effects of the AFC. To this end, Kim turned his attention to East Asian regional cooperation. Ultimately, it had not been North Korea, but a financial crisis that had impacted the (economic) security of the South Korean population. Furthermore, China had applied for World Trade Organisation (WTO) membership. This threatened South Korea's export-led economic model. The Kim government saw regional cooperation as a means to boost South Korean economic security. Seoul was therefore fully behind the formalisation of ASEAN + 3 cooperation also involving ASEAN, China, and Japan. And in 2000, Seoul also supported the launch of the Chiang Mai Initiative (CMI) (Nabers 2003). This was a network of bilateral currency swap arrangements among ASEAN + 3 countries, essentially to try to prevent reliance on the IMF. At the same time, the Kim government launched bilateral FTA negotiations to strengthen economic security and to withstand competition from China—and also since the United States and the European Union (EU) were moving in the direction of regionalism and bilateral deals. In 1999, South Korea launched FTA negotiations with Chile (Asia Regional Integration Center 2020c).

South Korea's foreign policy under Kim, in any case, was best known for the launch of the 'Sunshine Policy' (Kim 2019: 493). Kim believed in inter-Korean economic cooperation and people-to-people exchanges to build trust, moving towards inter-Korean reconciliation by reducing tensions in the Korean Peninsula, and laying the groundwork for future reunification. In June 2000, Kim travelled to Pyongyang and met with North Korean leader Kim Jong-il; this was the first ever inter-Korean summit (Kim 2019: 630). From Seoul's perspective, the summit was also a symbol of (South) Korean autonomy.

Certainly, the United States supported the summit, as US President Bill Clinton pursued its own engagement policy under the Agreed Framework signed by Washington and Pyongyang in 1994.[17] But the inter-Korean summit seemed to show that South Korea could press ahead with one of its key foreign policy goals regardless of US policy. The election of US President George W. Bush, however, put an end to this belief. The Bush government took a radically different approach towards North Korea, even including the country in an 'Axis of Evil' threatening global security (Pacheco Pardo 2019: 43). Kim, as a result, could not press ahead with inter-Korean reconciliation.

The Kim administration was also the first to actively make use of soft power to advance South Korea's interests. At the same time as the AFC was hitting the country, South Korean cultural products were becoming popular across East Asia. In the late 1990s, Chinese media started to talk about *Hallyu* or the Korean Wave (Kim 2013: 1). This referred to the success of South Korean dramas, pop, and cinema in the country, later replicated in Japan and Southeast Asia. The Kim government supported *Hallyu* as a way to increase cultural exports, which would reduce South Korea's reliance on the export of goods. It was also a means to enhance South Korean influence overseas (Kim 2013). Indeed, South Korean soft power increased thanks to *Hallyu*. Soft power was also enhanced by the successful co-hosting of the 2002 football World Cup, together with Japan, which for many South Koreans was a source of pride (Lee 2003: 71). For many South Koreans, the national team's success by reaching the semi-finals of the tournament came to symbolise that the country had recovered from the crisis.

Roh Moo-hyun replaced Kim in 2003. Similarly to his predecessor, he pursued a policy of engagement with North Korea. But the situation had changed. In 2002, North Korea had admitted possession of a highly enriched uranium programme, in breach of the Agreed Framework. As a result, the Six-Party Talks to address North Korean's nuclear programme were launched in 2003. South Korea was part of them, along with North Korea, the United States, China, Japan, and Russia (Pacheco Pardo 2019: 56). Thus, inter-Korean engagement was now part of a broader framework to deal with North Korea. This created tensions between Seoul and Washington. Furthermore, Roh implemented a strategy to make South Korea a 'balancer' in Northeast Asia (Sheen 2008). This meant that South Korea would seek to facilitate relations among the region's major powers, especially the United States and China. However, the policy raised tensions with Washington, which interpreted it as a sign that Seoul might lean towards Beijing. These tensions were exacerbated by even more tensions following the killing of two schoolgirls by a US armoured vehicle in 2002, which led to months of protests and heightened tensions that still lingered the year after (Lee 2003: 74). In addition, Roh officially raised the transfer of wartime operational control (OPCON) of the ROK–US forces in 2005. From the perspective of many South Koreans, their country will not be fully autonomous until wartime OPCON transfer takes place (Yoon 2015: 92).

Since the Roh government already had differences with the United States regarding North Korea and its 'balancer' policy was met with suspicion in Washington, its official raising of the OPCON transfer issue raised tensions between the two allies further. In the end, Seoul and Washington signed an OPCON transfer agreement in 2007. The agreement indicated that OPCON transfer should take place by 2012 (Yoon 2015: 93). That same year, Roh held South Korea's second ever inter-Korean summit with Kim Jong-il (Pacheco Pardo 2019: 85), as US–North Korea tensions had decreased thanks to a Six-Party Talks Joint Statement in 2005 and two more agreements in 2007. In the end, the US–ROK alliance remained on a solid footing, despite years of tensions.

Roh also prioritised economic openness through bilateral trade agreements to strengthen South Korea's economic security. The FTA negotiations with Chile were an eye-opener for South Korean negotiators. The agreement was only signed in 2003, with South Korean farmers protesting against what they saw as too much opening of the domestic market to Chilean agricultural products (Park and Koo 2007: 268). Shortly after the negotiations finished, the Roh government adopted an 'FTA Roadmap' in September 2003 (Institute for International Trade 2014). The roadmap indicated that South Korea risked its prosperity as bilateral and regional FTAs proliferated elsewhere and the Doha Round of WTO trade negotiations stalled. The roadmap called for South Korea to sign as many FTAs as possible in the shortest time feasible, to pursue multiple negotiations in parallel, and, crucially, to prioritise FTAs with big economies. Thus, South Korea launched FTA negotiations with the United States in 2006. Both countries would sign an agreement one year later dubbed KORUS (Park and Koo 2007: 260). This was another sign that the alliance was not as weakened as some thought. In 2007, South Korea started FTA negotiations with the EU (Park and Koo 2007: 260). The roadmap would continue to inform South Korea's FTA policy in future administrations.

5. South Korean Foreign Policy under Lee Myung-bak and Park Geun-hye: A Conservative Decade with a Global Focus

The Lee Myung-bak government took office in 2008, starting a decade of conservative rule. Upon his inauguration, Lee launched a 'Global Korea' policy (MOFAT 2008: 5). He wanted to promote a global role for South Korea, and also saw supporting the globalisation of South Korean businesses as one of the goals of the country's foreign policy. These priorities had strong links with Kim Young-sam's *Segyehwa*. The Global Financial Crisis (GFC) ravaging the global economy throughout 2007–2008 provided Seoul with an opportunity to strengthen its global role. In 2008, the G20 was upgraded to a head of government-level institution to address the GFC. South Korea—a member of the institution since its launch in 1999—was one of five Asian countries taking part (G20 2020). It was also one of only three developed countries not to suffer a recession during the GFC (OECD 2020b). The Lee government pushed for South Korea to become the first non-Western country to host a summit of the upgraded G20, which it achieved in 2010.

Meanwhile, the Lee government also pushed a green growth agenda at the domestic and international levels. In terms of foreign policy, the UN decided to open its Office for Sustainable Development (UNOSD) in Incheon in 2011 (UNOSD 2020) and the treaty-based Global Green Growth Initiative (GGGI)—originally launched as a think tank in 2010—in Seoul in 2012 (GGGI 2020). In other words, in the period 2010-2012, South Korea was at the forefront of initiatives to address key global governance issues. This supported the goals of global influence and autonomy.

Concurrently, the Lee government believed that the two previous governments had weakened the ROK–US alliance. Therefore, he set out to 'reset' South Korea–US relations by drawing Seoul closer to Washington. Lee pushed back OPCON transfer until 2015 (Yoon 2015: 93). Seoul also hosted the second edition of the Nuclear Security Summit in 2012 (Sohn and Kang 2013: 204). This was an initiative launched by the US President Barack Obama to address nuclear terrorism. Hosting its second edition showed that the ROK–US alliance could enable Seoul's global role. The Lee government also agreed to renegotiate KORUS, after several US congresspeople refused to ratify it because they believed that South Korea should made more concessions in the automobile and beef sectors (Koo and Jho 2013). In an instance of domestic politics directly influencing foreign policy, however, huge anti-US beef protests throughout 2008 forced Lee to reverse the lifting of a ban on US beef imports. This was reflected in the renegotiated KORUS, where public health safety-related restrictions were considered. An updated version of KORUS was signed in 2010 and launched in 2012 (Snyder 2018). This was one year later than the FTA with the EU, also signed in 2010 but launched in 2011 (Koo and Jho 2013).

In terms of inter-Korean relations, Lee moved away from his predecessors' 'Sunshine Policy'. Lee had to contend with a nuclear North Korea, which had carried out its first ever nuclear test in 2006 (Pacheco Pardo 2019: 72). He vowed to continue engagement and his goal remained inter-Korean reconciliation, but only if North Korea took steps towards denuclearisation. This approach was similar to that of the Obama administration. Coupled with the ill health of Kim Jong-il, who would pass away in December 2011, the result was that inter-Korean relations deteriorated dramatically. Most notably, in 2010 Pyongyang sank the ROKS *Cheonan*—killing forty-six crew members—and shelled Yeonpyeong, a South Korea island close the inter-Korean maritime border—killing four people (Pacheco Pardo 2019). The Lee government thus decided to actively join the global sanctions campaign against Pyongyang.

Park Geun-hye succeeded Lee in 2013. Despite also being from the conservative party, however, her foreign policy had several differences from that of her predecessor. Park pushed for a middle power diplomacy that continued from Lee's engagement in global governance. But Park's approach also prioritised new formats. At the global level, Seoul held a seat at the UN Security Council for the second time in 2013–2014 (Heo and Roehrig 2014: 2). It prioritised issues such as climate change and strengthening peacekeeping that can only be addressed multilaterally. South Korea was also instrumental in setting up MIKTA in 2013—a group comprising Mexico, Indonesia, South Korea itself, Turkey, and Australia (MOFA 2014: 4). MIKTA's goal was to boost the influence of these five countries, but it soon became clear that the differences among them in terms of thematic and geographical priorities prevented full cooperation. Arguably more closely aligned with South Korea's core interests were the Park government's Northeast Asia Peace and Cooperation Initiative (NAPCI) and Eurasia Initiative. NAPCI was a long-term process to build confidence and boost regional cooperation. Meanwhile, the Eurasian Initiative aimed at connecting South Korea with Central Asia, Southeast Asia, and Europe (MOFA 2014: 29–30). The initiative had echoes of *Nordpolitik*, in that it sought to diversify Seoul's foreign relations, including economic links. Indeed, one of its most tangible outcomes was an FTA with Vietnam, which, by 2019, had become one of South Korea's five largest trading partners (World Integrated Trade Solution 2020). It also sought to benefit from *Hallyu*, which had grown very popular in Southeast Asia (Kim 2010). Overall, the Park government was seeking to diversity South Korea's foreign policy links.

The Park government also made a strong push to balance relations between the United States and China. The Lee government had launched bilateral FTA negotiations with Beijing in 2012. Park made conclusion of the FTA with Beijing—by then Seoul's largest trading partner—a priority. An agreement was signed in 2015 (Asia Regional Integration Center 2020b). That same year, South Korea joined China's Asian Infrastructure Investment Bank (AIIB) in spite of the Obama administration's pressure on allies not to do (Chan 2017). But for the Park government, the United States continued to be South Korea's key partner. Therefore, Park continued to delay OPCON transfer into the mid-2020s (Yoon 2015: 93). And more importantly, Seoul agreed to host Washington's Terminal High Altitude Area Defense (THAAD) anti-missile system. The announcement was made in 2016. Ostensibly, THAAD was to protect South Korea against North Korean missiles. However, China strenuously denounced its deployment and imposed economic sanctions on South Korea, including banning tourists groups from travelling to the country and banning *Hallyu* stars from Chinese media (Park et al. 2019). The Obama administration did not help Seoul to withstand Beijing's pressure. Thus, South Korea once again felt like a 'shrimp among whales', with its autonomy curtailed.

On North Korea, the Park government launched a *Trustpolitik* policy aimed at reversing the hostilities of the Lee years and opening a window to reconciliation. However, Park continued to emphasise that Pyongyang had to take steps towards denuclearisation to engage with South Korea (Pacheco Pardo 2019: 133). In contrast, North Korea had accelerated its nuclear and missile programmes under its new leader Kim Jong-un. The Park government therefore hardened Seoul's stance towards Pyongyang. In 2016, the government effectively closed down the Kaesong industrial complex— a joint industrial zone in North Korean territory that symbolised inter-Korean cooperation—and the National Assembly passed the North Korean Human Rights Act to impose sanctions on Pyongyang due to its human rights abuses (Pacheco Pardo 2019: 141). In other words, South Korea continued to join the Obama government and the international community in pressurising North Korea.

6. South Korean Foreign Policy under Moon Jae-in: Balancing across the World

Moon Jae-in became South Korea's third liberal president in 2017, following Park's impeachment. The thrust of his foreign policy was the concept of 'Balanced Diplomacy' (*Cheong Wa Dae* 2020a). This referred to the balancing of relations between the United States and China, as well as the balancing of relations across regions. To this end, the Moon government launched the Northeast Asia Plus Community of Responsibility (NAPCR) (MOFA 2017)—which had echoes of NAPCI. Its two key pillars were the New Northern Policy and the New Southern Policy. The New Northern Policy aimed at building stronger economic links with the rest of Eurasia (The Presidential Committee on Northern Economic Cooperation 2020). This necessitated better inter-Korean relations. And indeed, Moon took a leaf from his liberal predecessors and put inter-Korean reconciliation at the top of his agenda. Taking advantage of the 2018 PyeongChang Winter Olympic Games, he held high-level talks with a visiting North Korean delegation. The initial results were three inter-Korean summits in 2018 (only two had ever been held before), opening the door for Pyongyang and Washington to host their historic, first ever summit in June 2018.[18] Relations between both Koreas improved significantly from the lows of the Lee and Park years. But the New Northern Policy would need proper inter-Korean reconciliation to be implemented.

As for the New Southern Policy, it was reminiscent of the Eurasian Initiative. But Moon was much more proactive in pursuing his vision. He was the first South Korean president to visit all ASEAN countries plus India, which was also included in the policy (Presidential Committee on New Southern Policy 2020). Furthermore, Indonesia agreed to sign an FTA with South Korea in 2019 (Asia Regional Integration Center 2020a). Indonesia was the largest ASEAN economy, and it was notoriously reluctant to sign trade agreements compared to other Southeast Asian countries. In addition, the Moon government decisively supported Regional Comprehensive Economic Partnership (RCEP) (Kang 2020). This was an FTA encompassing ASEAN + 3 along with Australia, India, and New Zealand. India eventually dropped out of the agreement though.

With respect to the ROK–US alliance, Moon wanted to increase autonomy, but his government believed that this relationship remained a cornerstone of South Korean foreign policy. To this end, he revised the idea of OPCON transfer with a view to completing it by the end of his five-year term in office (Heo and Roehrig 2018: 216). Meanwhile, US voters had elected President Donald Trump, who had a negative view of US allies, which he saw as 'free-riders'. Thus, he pressed Seoul to renegotiate KORUS. Renegotiations were completed in 2017, with limited changes to the agreement (Pacheco Pardo 2019: 147). He also pressed South Korea to substantially increase its payments towards the costs of maintaining US troops in the country. After a one-year agreement in 2018, negotiations then dragged on throughout 2019–2020 without the prospect of a deal (Jeong 2020). In a sense, the Moon government was standing up to US demands. At the same time, the Moon government followed a 'peace-through-strength' policy, leading to substantial increases in military spending. The goal was to strengthen South Korea's autonomous military capabilities to show that the country was ready to take control of OPCON, act as a deterrent against potential North Korean provocations to support inter-Korean reconciliation, and, ultimately, to boost South Korean autonomy.

7. Conclusion

South Korea's foreign policy has remained stable since the Sixth Republic was launched. In spite of the presidentialism inherent to South Korea's political system and the fact that presidents can only be in office for five years, goals and policies have not changed significantly throughout the decades. Arguably, the biggest difference has been with regard to the policies to pursue inter-Korean reconciliation. But ever since Roh Tae-woo launched *Nordpolitik*, inter-Korean reconciliation—and eventual reunification—has been the goal. Some presidents have emphasised engagement over sanctions to achieve this goal, but even those who have pressed for a sanctions-first approach had dialogue within their toolkit. Ultimately, South Korean governments agree that both talks and pressure are necessary to deal with North Korea.

With regards to other goals that successive South Korean governments have pursued, autonomy tops the list. Both conservative and liberal governments have tried to make South Korea a more independent foreign policy actor. Indeed, other goals—such as balancing relations between the United States and China, pushing for economic openness especially through trade agreements, and influencing global affairs through multilateralism, soft power, and other means—are goals in and by themselves, but also strengthen South Korean autonomy. From Seoul's perspective, autonomy boosts national security in a post-Cold War environment in which China's rise means that the United States is not the only superpower and cannot be South Korea's only guarantor.

Throughout the decades, South Korean foreign policy objectives and policies have resulted in a more globalised foreign policy. Seoul is not satisfied with focusing on North Korea and the ROK–US alliance. Starting with Kim Young-sam's *Segyehwa* and all the way to Moon Jae-in's New Northern and New Southern policies, South Korea has been looking beyond the small confines of the Korean Peninsula and Northeast Asia—and into Eurasia, elsewhere in Asia, and the rest of the world. Multilateralism and cooperation have underpinned this shift in South Korean foreign policy. But Seoul has tried to move away from being rule-taker to rule-shaper and, sometimes, to rule-maker.

We can expect South Korean foreign policy to continue along the same path for the foreseeable future. South Korean policymakers see their country as a middle power, with a strong alliance with the United States, but also needing to balance US influence, while benefiting from multilateralism. This consensus has not been challenged since South Korea regained its democracy in 1987, and there is no reason why it should for years to come. Ultimately, South Korean autonomy has, and will, involve making use of all existing capabilities for Seoul to act in the way that serves its interests best.

Notes

1. *The Constitution of the Republic of Korea*, 29 October 1987.
2. Ministry of Foreign Affairs, Republic of Korea (MOFA) (2020), www.mofa.go.kr/eng/index.do, accessed 25 November 2021.
3. Ministry of National Defense, Republic of Korea (MND) (2020), https://www.mnd.go.kr/mbshome/mbs/mndEN/, accessed 25 November 2021.
4. Ministry of Unification, Republic of Korea (MOU) (2020), https://www.unikorea.go.kr/eng_unikorea/, accessed 25 November 2021.
5. Ministry of Trade, Industry and Energy, Republic of Korea (MOTIE) (2020), http://english.motie.go.kr/www/main.do, accessed 25 November 2021.
6. Institute of Foreign Affairs and National Security (IFANS) (2020), www.ifans.go.kr/knda/ifans/eng/main/IfansEngMain.do, accessed 25 November 2021.
7. Korea Institute for Defense Analyses (KIDA) (2020), https://kida.re.kr/index.do?lang=en, accessed 25 November 2021.
8. Korean Institute for National Unification (KINU) (2020), https://www.kinu.or.kr/main/eng, accessed 25 November 2021.
9. The Asan Institute for Policy Studies (2020), http://en.asaninst.org/, accessed 25 November 2021.
10. Sejong Institute (2020), www.sejong.org/eng/main/, accessed 25 November 2021.
11. Korea University (2020), Division of International Studies. Graduate School of International Studies, https://int.korea.edu/kuis/index.do, accessed 25 November 2021.
12. Seoul National University (2020), Graduate School of International Studies, https://gsis.snu.ac.kr, accessed 25 November 2021.
13. Yonsei University (2020), Graduate School of International Studies, https://gsis.yonsei.ac.kr/main/default.asp, accessed 25 November 2021.
14. The July 4 South–North Joint Communique, 4 July 1972.
15. Agreement on Reconciliation, Non-Aggression and Exchanges and Cooperation between the South and the North, 13 December 1991.
16. Joint Declaration of the Denuclearization of the Korean Peninsula, 20 January 1992.
17. Agreed Framework of 21 October 1994 between the United States of America and the Democratic People's Republic of Kore, 21 October 1994.
18. Joint Statement of President Donald J. Trump of the United States of America and Chairman Kim Jong Un of the Democratic People's Republic of Korea at the Singapore Summit, 12 June 2018.

Bibliography

Asia Regional Integration Center (2020a), 'Indonesia-Republic of Korea Free Trade Agreement', 18 December, https://aric.adb.org/fta/korea-indonesia-free-trade-agreement, accessed 25 November 2021.

Asia Regional Integration Center (2020b), 'People's Republic of China–Republic of Korea Free Trade Agreement', https://aric.adb.org/fta/peoples-republic-of-china-korea-free-trade-agreement, accessed 25 November 2021.

Asia Regional Integration Center (2020c), 'Republic of Korea–Chile Free Trade Agreement', https://aric.adb.org/fta/korea-chile-free-trade-agreement, accessed 25 November 2021.

Bank of Korea (2020), 'Overview', https://www.bok.or.kr/eng/main/contents.do?menuNo=400198, accessed 25 November 2021.

Chan, L.H. (2017), 'Soft Balancing Against the US 'Pivot to Asia': China's Geostrategic Rationale for Establishing the Asian Infrastructure Investment Bank', *Australian Journal of International Affairs* 71(6), 568–590.

Cheong Wa Dae (2020a), 'Moon Jae-in. President of the Republic of Korea', http://www.korea.net/FILE/pdfdata/2018/06/MoonJae-in_PRESIDENTOFTHEREPUBLICOFKOREA_en.pdf, accessed 25 November 2021.

Cheong Wa Dae (2020b), 'The Moon Jae-in Administration. Organization', http://english1.president.go.kr/President/Administration, accessed 25 November 2021.

Defense Security Support Command (DSSC) (2020), '군사안보지원사령부' (Defense Security Support Command), https://www.dssc.mil.kr/main.do?cmd=main, accessed 25 November 2021.

G20 (2020), 'What Is the G20?', https://g20.org/en/about/Pages/whatis.aspx, accessed 25 September 2021.

Global Green Growth Institute (GGGI) (2020), 'About GGGI', https://gggi.org/about/, accessed 25 November 2021.

Han, S.-J. (1989), 'South Korea in 1988: A Revolution in the Making', *Asian Survey* 29(1), 29–38.

Heo, U., and Roehrig, T. (2014), *South Korea's Rise: Economic Development, Power and Foreign Relations* (Cambridge: Cambridge University Press).

Heo, U., and Roehrig, T. (2018), *The Evolution of the US–South Korea Alliance* (Cambridge: Cambridge University Press).

Im, H. B. (2020), *Democratization and Democracy in South Korea, 1960–Present* (London: Palgrave Macmillan).

International Institute for Strategic Studies (2020), *The Military Balance* (London: Routledge).

International Monetary Fund (IMF) (2000), 'Republic of Korea: Economic and Policy Developments', IMF Staff Country Report No. 00/11, February.

Institute for International Trade (2014), '한국 FTA 추진 10년의 발자취' (Ten Years of South Korea's FTA Promotion), *Trade Focus* 13(18), 1–25.

Jeong, A. (2020), 'To Make Korea Pay More for Security, Trump Has to Show His Shopping List', *Wall Street Journal*, 7 January.

Kang, Y.-S. (2020), 'S. Korea Joins Efforts to Conclude RCEP Negotiations This Year', *Yonhap News Agency*, 2 February.

Kim, D.-J. (2019), *Conscience in Action. The Autobiography of Kim Dae-jung* (London: Palgrave Macmillan).

Kim, E. (2015), 'Korea's Middle Power Diplomacy in the 21st Century', *Pacific Focus* 30(1), 1–9.
Kim, J. K. (2010), 'The Korean Wave: Korea's Soft Power in Southeast Asia', in Steinberg, D. I., *Korea's Changing Roles in Southeast Asia: Expanding Influence and Relations*, 283–303 (Singapore: ISEAS Publishing).
Kim, Y. (2013), 'Introduction: Korean Media in a Digital Cosmopolitan World', in *The Korean Wave: Korean Media Go Global*, 1–27 (London: Routledge).
Ko, S. (2015), 'The Foreign Policy Goal of South Korea's UN Peacekeeping Operations', *International Peacekeeping* 22(1), 65–80.
Koo, M. G., and W. Jho (2013), 'Linking Domestic Decision-Making and International Bargaining Results: Beef and Automobile Negotiations between South Korea and the United States', *International Relations of the Asia-Pacific* 13(1), 65–93.
Korea Foundation (2020), 'Global Offices', https://en.kf.or.kr/?menuno=3779, accessed 25 November 2021.
Korea International Cooperation Agency (KOICA) (2020), '해외사무소' (Overseas Offices), www.koica.go.kr/koica_kr/863/subview.do, accessed 25 November 2021.
Korean Cultural and Information Service (KOCIS) (2020), 'Korean Cultural Centers, www.kocis.go.kr/eng/openInformation.do, accessed 25 November 2021.
Korean Investment Trade Promotion Agency (KOTRA) (2020), 'Global Networks' https://www.kotra.or.kr/foreign/main/KHEMUI010M.html, accessed 25 November 2021.
Kwak, K.-S. (2012), *Media and Democratic Transition in South Korea* (London: Routledge).
Lee, H. Y. (2003), 'South Korea in 2002: Multiple Political Dramas', *Asian Survey* 43(1), 64–77.
Ministry of Foreign Affairs (MOFA) (2014), '2014 Diplomatic White Paper', Seoul.
MOFA (2017), *Northeast Asia Platform for Peace and Cooperation* (Seoul: MOFA).
MOFA (2020), 년도 외교부 예산개요 (국회확정) (*Budget Summary of the Ministry of Foreign Affairs for the Year (Confirmed by the National Assembly)*) (Seoul: MOFA).
Ministry of Foreign Affairs and Trade (MOFAT) 2008. '2008 Diplomatic White Paper', Seoul.
Nabers, D. (2003), 'The Social Construction of International Institutions: The Case of ASEAN+3', *International Relations of the Asia-Pacific* 3(1), 113–136.
National Intelligence Service (NIS) (2015), 'Establishment of the National Intelligence Service', https://eng.nis.go.kr/EID/1_5_1.do, accessed 25 November 2021.
Organisation for Economic Co-operation and Development (OECD) (2020a), 'Where: Global Reach', https://www.oecd.org/about/members-and-partners/, accessed 25 November 2021.
OECD (2020b), 'Quarterly National Accounts: Quarterly Growth Rates of Real GDP, Change over Previous Quarter', https://stats.oecd.org/index.aspx?queryid=350, accessed 25 November 2021.
Pacheco Pardo, R. (2019), *North Korea–US Relations from Kim Jong Il to Kim Jong Un* (London: Routledge).
Park, J. H., Lee, Y. S., and Seo, H. (2019), 'The Rise and Fall of Korean Drama Export to China: The History of State Regulation of Korean Dramas in China', *International Communication Gazette* 81(2), 139–157.
Park, S., and Koo, M. G. (2007), 'Forming a Cross-Regional Partnership: The South Korea–Chile FTA and Its Implications', *Pacific Affairs* 80(2), 259–278.
Presidential Committee on New Southern Policy (2020), 'New Southern Policy', 8 July, www.nsp.go.kr/eng/main.do, accessed 15 November 2021.
Sheen, S.-H. (2008), 'Strategic Thought Toward Asia in the Roh Moo-hyun Era', in Rozman, G., I.-T. Hyun and S.w. Lee (eds.), *South Korean Strategic Thought Toward Asia*, 101–126 (London: Palgrave Macmillan).

Snyder, S. (2018), *South Korea at the Crossroads: Autonomy and Alliance in an Era of Rival Powers* (New York: Columbia University Press).

Sohn, Y., and Kang, W.-T. (2013), 'South Korea in 2012: An Election Year under Rebalancing Challenges', *Asian Survey* 53(1), 198–205.

The National Assembly of the Republic of Korea (2020a), 'Committees', https://korea.assembly.go.kr:447/int/org_06.jsp, accessed 25 November 2021.

The National Assembly of the Republic of Korea (2020b), 'On Parliamentary Diplomacy', https://korea.assembly.go.kr:447/int/act_04_01_01.jsp, accessed 25 November 2021.

The Presidential Committee on Northern Economic Cooperation (2020), 'The Presidential Committee on Northern Economic Cooperation', https://www.bukbang.go.kr/bukbang_en/, accessed 25 November 2021.

United Nations Office for Sustainable Development (UNOSD) (2020), 'About UNOSD', https://unosd.un.org/content/about, accessed 25 November 2021.

World Integrated Trade Solution (2020), 'Korea, Rep. Trade', https://wits.worldbank.org/countrysnapshot/en/KOR, accessed 25 November 2021.

Yoon, S. (2015), 'South Korea's Wartime Operation Control Transfer Debate: From an Organizational Perspective', *Journal of International and Area Studies* 22(2), 89–108.

CHAPTER 33

SECURITY AND DEFENCE POLICY

SUNG-HAN KIM AND ALEX SOOHOON LEE

1. INTRODUCTION

IN a highly complex system of international politics, a nation's security policy is often a language that implicitly or explicitly presents its intent. While the foreign policy of a nation mainly engages in diplomatic approaches through peaceful means for resolving issues with other nations, security policy primarily comes from military strategy. Foreign policy concerns a nation's economic and political relations, whether good or bad, with other nations, whereas security policy predominantly deals with a nation's defence and survival. In this light, the overlap between the two policies usually occurs within the area of 'alliance politics and coercive diplomacy' (Jordan et al. 1993: 6) since alliance-based coercive diplomacy tends to be implemented with the threat to use force.

In this respect, security policy is made to prevent threats that may endanger 'the survival of regimes, citizenry, or the society's way of life' (Mandel 1994: 21–22). However, since the end of the Cold War, the scale and scope of national security has expanded. Traditionally, the determinants of national security have only included coercive measures, usually military means. However, the concept of national security has enlarged in scope with the inclusion of new issues such as climate change, terrorism, and pandemics (Chandra and Bhonsle 2015: 341). They are now being called non-traditional security threats. Although this chapter mainly focuses on explaining South Korea's traditional security policy, it also touches upon the non-traditional security pillar when expounding on the ROK-US alliance.

There are certain factors the South Korean government considers when determining its national security policy. First, there is a geopolitical factor showing that South Korea is surrounded by the United States, China, Japan, and Russia, whose geopolitical interests diverge, rather than converge, on the Korean Peninsula. Located in the eastern tip of the Eurasian continent, South Korea's security policy has been affected by great power politics, especially the US–China strategic competition. Second, historical factors influence South Korea's security policymaking as well. For instance, China's long-time historical ties with the Korean Peninsula, and their contemporary ramifications coming from the rise of China, tend to be considered in South Korea's security and defence policymaking, particularly on North Korea. Japanese colonial legacies influence South Korea's policy as well when security is not detached from the problem of the past.

Finally, the division of the Korean Peninsula raises various challenges and dilemmas for South Korea, which is tasked with resolving the division and achieving reunification of the peninsula. In particular, the nuclear problem involving North Korea remains a three-decade-long conundrum that puts a lot of stress on South Korea's defence and military policymaking vis-à-vis the surrounding countries. In this light, this chapter is devoted to explaining the security and defence policy of South Korea.

To that end, the following section assesses the security environment of the Korean Peninsula. It defines and verifies the threats posed to South Korea. The third section reviews the actual policies regarding the North Korean nuclear threat, the ROK–US alliance, and US–China strategic competition, over the past three decades. The fourth section analyses the lingering internal challenges that South Korea faces, and the concluding section discusses a prospective role that South Korea could play in the arena of international security.

2. THE SECURITY ENVIRONMENT OF THE KOREAN PENINSULA

2.1 Geopolitical Destiny

South Korea is destined to confront both continental and maritime forces. Since H. J. Mackinder, a British geographer, categorised Korea as a bridging nation along with France, Italy, Egypt, and India, that act as 'bridgeheads' when outside navies challenge the pivot (Mackinder 1904: 436), South Korea's geopolitics have been destined to confront various challenges posed by surrounding nations. Facing such geopolitical risks, the division of the Korean Peninsula has exacerbated the situation. Although South Korea has achieved miraculous economic development and successfully accomplished democratisation, such innate hardships rooted in geopolitics have not subsided.

Barricaded by North Korea and surrounded by the most powerful nations in the world, South Korea's security environment has confronted dynamic challenges and opportunities. Prior to the foundation of ROK, the territorial ambitions of surrounding nations were the biggest security challenge for the peninsula. The Japanese occupation of Korea (1910–1945) and the Korean War (1950–1953) crippled the development of the nation. Moreover, due to its geographical location, South Korea was caught in the middle of international power politics, which has reduced its security policy options. Such a phenomenon has continued in the modern era as well. South Korea has often been pressurised to take sides between the United States and China since China began to flex its muscles over the Korean Peninsula after the US-led Global Financial Crisis in 2008.

Seven decades ago, the scope of the Korean War pushed the peninsula to the edge. The world's most powerful nations, the United States, the Soviet Union, and China, were involved in the war. During the early years of the ideological confrontation between the United States and the Soviet Union, the Korean War was referred to as a proxy war, which resulted in the division of the peninsula. After the war, the ROK–US alliance became the cornerstone of South Korea's security and the engine for the 'Miracle on the Han River'. The United States, a superpower located on the other end of the Pacific, did not reveal territorial ambition, which made itself the closest ally of South Korea.

2.2 The North Korean Military Threat

North Korea has remained the most imminent threat to South Korea since the outbreak of the Korean War. As North Korean soldiers crossed the thirty-eighth parallel on 25 June 1950, the war broke out and soon escalated into an international conflict when the United Nations and China intervened. Apart from the Armistice Agreement signed on 27 July 1953, a peace agreement that would officially end the war is yet to be signed, thus leaving the two Koreas technically at war up to this moment (Kim 2020c). Even after the war, North Korea has consistently carried out provocations towards South Korea in an attempt to communise the peninsula.

North Korea, with a population little over 25 million, utilises roughly 20 per cent of its population for the military. The number of North Korean active military personnel is about 1,280,000, consisting of 1,100,000 army, 60,000 navy, and 110,000 air force troops. It is about twice the size of the South Korean military (International Institute for Strategic Studies (IISS) 2020). The North Korean navy is equipped with 73 submarines, outnumbering 22 South Korean submarines, and its artillery, at 21,600, is twice as big as South Korea's, which is about 11,067 (IISS 2020: 288). North Korea's conventional forces remain 'reliant on increasingly obsolete equipment supplemented by a number of indigenous designs and upgrades' (IISS 2020: 285). While North Korea's conventional weapons capability is not as threatening as its nuclear warheads and ballistic missiles, its destructive power is multiplied when these two capabilities operate in tandem (Park 2018: 230).

While South Korea was concentrating on economic development after establishing the Mutual Defence Treaty with the United States in October 1953, North Korea initiated a nuclear development programme. In November 1968, the late North Korean leader Kim Il-sung visited the Hamhung branch of the State Academy of Sciences and encouraged scientists to develop nuclear weapons and long-range missiles capable of directly attacking the continental United States. After procuring the Soviet Union reactor, IRT-2000, and Scud missiles from Egypt in 1967 and 1976, respectively, North Korea's nuclear and missile development has accelerated (2020c).

Over the past two decades, North Korea has conducted six nuclear weapons tests. After threatening to withdraw from the Non-Proliferation Treaty (NPT) in 1993, North

Korea revealed its nuclear ambition. In 2005, North Korea announced its possession of nuclear weapons and in 2006 tested its first atomic bomb. Since then, North Korea has conducted five more tests up until 2017. Each test presented the progress made in yield, magnitude, and even type of the bomb. North Korea's nuclear weapon tests, or provocations, were conducted strategically and in a timely manner. Such provocations were undertaken to illustrate its growing influence over the international society, particularly the United States (Lee, H. 2020: 16).

Over the past six tests, North Korea's nuclear yield has consistently increased. The first nuclear test yield was around 0.5–2 kilotons (kt) of TNT. The yield had increased to 2–4 kt in 2009, 6–9 kt in 2013, 7–10 kt in January 2016, 10 kt in September 2016, and 140 + kt in 2017 (Center for Strategic and International Studies (CSIS) 2020). To compare, the yield of the atomic bomb, or so-called Little Boy, that had been dropped on Hiroshima in 1945 and killed tens of thousands, was equivalent to detonating 12–18.5 kt of TNT (Kennedy et al. 1984: 8). The explosive yield of North Korea's latest test in 2017 was 'reported to be at least five times larger' than the previous one and it was known as the type of hydrogen bomb that can be fitted onto the warheads of Inter-continental ballistic missiles (ICBMs) (CSIS 2017).

Since 1984, ninety-four incidents of North Korean missile launches have been monitored by the international society (CSIS 2020). The launches include ICBMs, inter-regional ballistic missiles (IRBMs), short-range ballistic missiles (SRBMs), and cruise missiles. For North Korea, 'missile' denotes the transportation vehicle that delivers a nuclear bomb to the target. Therefore, obtaining ICBM capability is the key to countering the United States across the Pacific. North Korean leader Kim Jong-un believes that once a North Korean ICBM was capable of reaching the continental United States, North Korea would secure more bargaining power vis-à-vis the United States. In this regard, the direction of North Korea's nuclear development is crystal-clear: to polish the ICBM capability and miniaturise the nuclear warhead. If North Korea, under brinkmanship, decides to use nuclear weapons on South Korea, there would be two options left to decide for Seoul: either fight to the death or surrender. For this reason, North Korea's nuclear capability is the most serious threat that both South Korea and the United States must deter.

2.3 US–China Rivalry

The security environment of the Korean Peninsula is largely influenced by the US–China rivalry. China, with its dramatic economic growth, threatens the United States, which has long enjoyed a world operating under the unipolar system after the end of the Cold War. The two gigantic nations are now in a fierce competition. Although Kenneth Waltz (1964) claimed the world operating in a bipolarity, as seen in the Cold War structure, is safer than the one functioning under a unipolarity or multipolarity, the US–China rivalry is not making the Korean Peninsula safe.

China's World Trade Organisation (WTO) accession in 2001 was a chance for the United States to gradually incorporate China into a liberal world order and contain its rise. However, the outbreak of the Global Financial Crisis in 2007 soon crippled the US economy and left little power for the United States to overwhelm China. Ever since then, the US–China rivalry has become the major consideration when South Korea makes its security policy. From Korea's national security perspective, the US–China rivalry has often acted as a stumbling block, rather than a building block. The US deployment of the Terminal High Altitude Area Defence (THAAD) missile battery in South Korea in 2016 belonged to the former. Although deploying THAAD was an 'alliance decision' to 'protect alliance forces from North Korea's weapons of mass destruction and ballistic missile threats' (US Department of Defense 2016), it certainly triggered Chinese resentment and eventually became a major problem between South Korea and China (Swaine 2017), which led to a coercive Chinese economic policy against South Korea.

The US security policy in Asia mainly concerns China, which, in turn, affects South Korea's security policy. After withdrawing from the Intermediate-range Nuclear Forces (INF) Treaty in 2019, the United States planned to build a missile base in one of its allies' territories. China publicly 'opposed the US plan to deploy land-based medium-range missiles in the Asia Pacific' (Reif and Bugos 2020). China's opposing stance on the deployment of THAAD and the INF missile base has also been applied to any kind of security cooperative framework initiated by the United States, including the Indo-Pacific strategy and the Quadrilateral Security Dialogue (Quad). In this regard, South Korea's security policy options are very limited.

US policy on China is shifting from 'containment' to 'transformation'. The Biden administration, employing liberal internationalist values of multilateral cooperation, free trade, and democracy, is different from the previous administration. While the Trump administration's policy on China embraced a containment strategy that mainly deterred China's military expansion, Biden's focus appears to be concentrated on the strategy of transformation, which aims to change the behaviour of China. In doing so, the United States utilises its allies and partners for military deterrence against China (Kim 2020b). In this light, the US strategy on China consists of strengthening military deterrence based on an alliance network; technology alliances with key allies in the area of artificial intelligence, next-generation semi-conductors, and quantum computing; and multilateralism, including global governance. Having the United States as the closest security ally and China as the biggest trade partner, South Korea's policy options have been limited.

3. South Korea's Security and Defence Policy

3.1 Denuclearising North Korea

The major threat that North Korea poses is nuclear. Without its nuclear capability, North Korea would not be as threatening as it is today. Knowing this, North Korea has tested its nuclear capability numerous times over the past two decades. North Korea's nuclear capability has been presented in twofold: nuclear weapons and missile tests. Through these developments, North Korea's Kim dynasty has sustained and survived. In 1985, North Korea joined the NPT and, together with South Korea, signed the South–North Declaration on the Denuclearisation of the Korean Peninsula in 1992. But after a series of disputes over the inspections by the International Atomic Energy Agency (IAEA), North Korea announced its intention to withdraw from the NPT in 1993 (Lee, H. 2020: 13).

This event, called the North Korean first nuclear crisis, was settled between the United States and North Korea after they had signed on the Agreed Framework in Geneva in 1994. Prior to this, former US President Jimmy Carter had visited North Korea and laid the groundwork for high-level bilateral talks with the United States. Back then, South Korea's President Kim Young-sam imposed a hard-line policy on North Korea and, as a result, US–North Korea bilateral negotiations took place instead of inter-Korean negotiation. Embracing the Geneva Agreed Framework, North Korea agreed to freeze, and eventually dismantle, nuclear facilities and, in response, it received two light water reactors provided by the Korean Peninsula Energy Development Organisation (KEDO), an organisation jointly founded by South Korea, the United States, and Japan (Pollack 2010: 114), where South Korea contributed 70 per cent of the fund (Kim 2000: 104).

The second nuclear crisis approached a decade later when the United States, immediately after the September 11 attacks, found a secret nuclear programme developed by North Korea in 2002. It was a clear violation of the Geneva Agreed Framework and led to North Korea's withdrawal from the NPT in the following year. Unlike the first bilateral attempt to overcome the first nuclear crisis, a multilateral framework of Six-Party Talks was formed by South Korea, North Korea, the United States, China, Russia, and Japan. However, five rounds of negotiations conducted by the six nations did not accomplish North Korea's denuclearisation (Kim 2008: 137). Furthermore, regardless of the international society's concerted efforts, North Korea has continued its nuclear and missile programmes.

Meanwhile, coping with the North Korean nuclear missile threat, South Korea has developed its own defence system on top of joint preparations with the United States. Building a solid and effective missile defence system is the simplest way to deter the North Korean nuclear threat. South Korea's missile development is fundamentally aimed at defensive use and is not for offensive capabilities. South Korea did not develop a missile that reaches beyond the Korean Peninsula; rather, it focused on developing a space launch rocket (Hong 2015). It was only after the revision of the ROK–US missile guidelines in 2020 that South Korea was authorised to use solid fuel, which 'allows greater efficiency and mobility in launching rockets or missiles with the significantly reduced preparation time' (Lee, S. H. 2020). The four-decade-old missile guidelines had been terminated in the 2021 South Korea-US Summit.

South Korea's missile defence system is known as the Korea Air and Missile Defence (KAMD), which is yet to be completed. Before North Korea launches a missile, South Korea detects and pre-emptively strikes North Korea's 'nuclear, missile, and long-range artillery facilities', a strategy known as Kill Chain. If Kill Chain fails to cease North Korea's missile launch, Korea Massive Punishment and Retaliation (KMPR) is next in line, directly targeting the North's capital and the regime (CSIS 2021). KAMD operates under the Patriot Advanced Capability-2 (PAC-2) and PAC-3 systems and THAAD, a US missile defence system, supplements Korean missile defence.

A slightly new approach in dealing with the North Korean nuclear issue was presented by President Trump. President Trump believed that denuclearisation of North Korea could be realised in the bilateral summit setting. In this top-down approach, President Trump directly negotiated denuclearisation terms with North Korean leader Kim Jong-un in a series of summits. From Singapore to Hanoi, three US–North Korea denuclearisation talks were held (Sigal 2020). President Trump, with an entrepreneurial background, seemed confident in handling the negotiation. President Moon Jae-in supported this setting in various ways, including the proactive role of mediator between the United States and North Korea. Nonetheless, North Korea has not given up its nuclear programme, and neither has President Trump been re-elected.

The South Korean government, for the past three decades, has embraced both engagement and containment policies on North Korea. Although economically much larger than the North, South Korea will always be vulnerable as long as the North possesses nuclear weapons. In this regard, South Korea is required to work towards the complete denuclearisation of North Korea, which will be in a form of 'aggressive peace' rather than 'submissive peace' (Kim 2020c).

3.2 Strengthening the ROK–US Alliance

The ROK–US alliance has altered forms over the past seven decades. It started as a blood alliance when the two allies shed blood together in the Korean War. During the Cold War, as South Korea adopted liberal democracy and a market economy, the relationship developed into a form of value-based alliance. In this setting, South Korea had economically and politically thrived under US leadership. In the post-Cold War era, rather than redefining and upgrading their relationship, the two countries focused on ending their asymmetrical relationship, which led to a transitional alliance exploring a new relationship. After the September 11 attacks in the United States, President Lee Myung-bak and President George W. Bush agreed to expand the scope of the alliance beyond the Korean Peninsula to a regional and global level, on which a strategic alliance would be working in non-military ways. To bring the ROK–US alliance to more strategic level, the Lee administration believed that South Korea must actively engage in regional and global roles such as 'peacekeeping, counter-terrorism, piracy' (Kim 2010: 276–277). However, the strategic alliance has been somewhat downgraded, referred to as transactional alliance (Patrick 2017), mainly due to Trump's 'America First' credo.

Both the conservative and progressive governments of South Korea acknowledged the significance of the ROK–US alliance in dealing with North Korean nuclear issues. However, progressive governments have devoted more efforts to seek inter-Korean cooperation, despite North Korea's continued nuclear threat (Kim 2017). In this regard, whether a progressive or conservative government is formed in South Korea is a critical issue, which the United States considers when dealing with North Korea, or the Korean Peninsula as a whole. In addition, for the sustainability of the alliance, the division of responsibility and cost in defence have become important. Thus, defence cost-sharing and transition of wartime operational control (OPCON) turned out to be the main agenda between the allies.

South Korea's '2018 Defence White Paper' reads, "for the last 65 years, the ROK–US Alliance has not only defended South Korea from external threats but also contributed to the country's political and economic development" (Republic of Korea Ministry of National Defense 2020b). There are four security agenda that link the two allies: defence cost-sharing, United States Forces in Korea (USFK), joint military exercise, and wartime OPCON transfer. These are the core pillars that can make the alliance sustainable.

First, defence cost-sharing requires South Korea and the United States to share the cost for maintaining USFK. Negotiations of the Special Measures Agreement (SMA) had been smooth before the Trump administration came in as a pillar of the shared commitment to the defence of South Korea by combined US–ROK forces. The SMA, a type of burden-sharing agreement, is the mechanism by which South Korea shares the costs of USFK to defend South Korea. The SMA, financial backbone of the ROK–US combined defence, is essential for South Korea's security, where the allies signed ten SMAs since its first agreement in 1991 (Lee 2021). Trump's 'America First' policy, however, undermined the negotiation and demanded an unreasonably high contribution from South Korea (Ban 2020: 14). South Korea, which spends more than 2.5 per cent of its gross domestic product (GDP) on its defence budget, the highest among US allies, found no reason to acquiesce to the unreasonable demands (IISS 2020). Seoul and Washington were able to conclude the 11th SMA, which had been stalled for almost two years, after the inauguration of President Joe Biden.

Second, USFK is the backbone of South Korea's defence capability. Deterring North Korean conventional and nuclear threats requires the USFK and its strategic weapons. USFK presence had begun even before the Korean War and it is the third largest US overseas presence after Germany and Japan. As a part of United States Indo-Pacific Command, the USFK consists of 28,500 personnel. The army, with 19,200 soldiers, is the biggest group in the USFK, followed by 8,800 air force and 250 navy personnel (IISS 2020). Although there have been local social groups that demand withdrawal of the USFK from South Korea, even the progressive governments have recognised the value of US military presence.

Third, the ROK–US joint military exercise has been the core of South Korea's defence strategy. Composed of three main exercises; Key Resolve, Foal-Eagle and Ulchi-Freedom Guardian, the ROK–US joint military exercises are aimed at maintaining the readiness to defend against a North Korean conventional and nuclear attack (Jeon 2010: 409). The Trump administration, however, requested to cease or delay them to promote US–DPRK denuclearisation talks. According to Trump, minimising exercises would protect soldiers from COVID-19 and allow denuclearisation talks to gain momentum. As long as the North Korean threat continues and the Commander of the US–ROK Combined Forces Command claims the necessity of the exercise to maintain readiness, the exercise is expected to gradually revert to routine.

Finally, OPCON transfer has been the most strained issue between the allies for over a decade. Transferring wartime operational control to the South Korean command, the current plan is to establish Future Combined Forces Command (F-CFC) and appoint a South Korean four-star general to be the commander and a US four-star general as the deputy (Nishizuka 2018: 466). If the transition is completed, there comes a new security paradigm for the South Korean military. However, the timing and the method remain disputed. For South Korea to take command, its military capability must be reviewed by the United States, in a process called Full Operational Control (FOC) and Full Mission Control (FMC). Although OPCON transfer has been overly politicised, it is still the most important agenda that the ROK–US alliance must manage.

South Korea and the United States, beyond the scope of joint security, have also emphasised the importance of cooperation in the non-traditional security areas. The 2009 Declaration of Joint Vision for ROK–US Alliance states that the alliance will work together in dealing with non-traditional security threats such as energy security, human rights, humanitarian assistance, development assistance cooperation, and counter-terrorism (Choi 2013: 554–555). In light of the starkly increased importance of non-traditional security threats after the outbreak of COVID-19, the ROK–US alliance is at a critical juncture, where they should explore the ways to contribute to the improvement of human security at regional and global levels.

3.3 Making Security Policy under US–China Strategic Competition

As addressed in this chapter, South Korea's security policy is largely affected by the US–China strategic rivalry. The US–China competition is clearly portrayed in their defence budget. The United States spent 738,000 million dollars on defence in 2020, and that amount is larger than the total sum of the remaining top ten nations' budget. The amount that the United States spent on its defence in 2010 was nearly nine times what China spent in the same year, but the difference was reduced to only four times by 2020. The gap between China and the United States has been narrowed in a period of ten years, where China has been catching up with the United States in terms of defence budget at a dramatic pace (IISS 2020).

South Korea, spending 42.2 billion dollars on defence in 2020 (Republic of Korea Ministry of National Defense 2020a), had been ranked tenth in the world's defence spending (IISS 2020) and has been pursuing a policy of strategic ambiguity in the dilemma laid out by US–China competition. South Korea depends on the ROK–US alliance for security, while maintaining larger economic relations with China than with the United States. 'Straddling' has been the most optimal option, with a higher return than the other two options to choose and to vacillate. Nevertheless, South Korea could soon have to choose, rather than straddle. Meanwhile, US–China strategic competition is likely to intensify and, as such a phenomenon continues, South Korea's strategic ambiguity may become difficult.

The future of US–China competition will be accelerated in the high-tech sector, which is highly relevant to the military dimension. China's effort to export fifth-generation wireless (5G) infrastructure in Latin America, Africa, and Europe could be understood as such. The future warfare between the United States and China would be extended to every sector of ICT, including next-generation semiconductors, artificial intelligence, and quantum computing. Straddling between the United States and China, while obtaining both technology and experience, South Korea will continue to be locked into a dilemma defined by US–China competition (Kim 2020d).

4. Challenges for South Korean Security and Defence

4.1 Growing Challenges for the ROK–US Alliance

Despite South Korea's effort in establishing security policies to overcome the challenges stated in this chapter, there remain steadily rising challenges both in and out of the nation. The issues concerning the challenges for the ROK–US alliance and three sets of competing beliefs on the South Korean domestic front are defined as new challenges. First, the challenges for the ROK–US alliance concerns South Korea's stance in accordance with the competition and the combined defence structure of the alliance in dealing with the North Korean nuclear threat. As previously explained, the Biden administration's plan for creating a united front of allies to deal with China would be a serious challenge for South Korea. As the ROK–US alliance has traditionally been working on the peninsula, any extra burden or increased accountability for other countries or issues may jeopardise South Korea's strategic posture in the alliance.

Moreover, the fundamental question revealing the inconvenient truth of how to share the strategic burden of dealing with other threats than North Korea may arise. In this case, the *raison d'etre* of the ROK–US alliance would be put to the test. For instance, the United States asking Korea to join the Indo-Pacific strategy or Quad could put Seoul into a difficult situation. South Korea would have to think deeply about whether to choose or to continue to straddle.

Another issue between the United States and South Korea is the reliability of the US nuclear umbrella in dealing with the North Korean nuclear threat. While the US deterrence capability for punishment is high in North Korea, its resolve is not sufficient. The US deterrence capability for denial is not very high either when we see the insufficient THAAD deployment in South Korea and the uncertain defence system against North Korea's ICBMs on the US continent. In this regard, from South Korea's security perspective, the possible options are (a) the deployment of tactical nuclear weapons; (b) nuclear sharing with the United States; (c) joint operational planning of extended deterrence; and (d) deterring with conventional weapons (Kim 2020a).

As a way of properly dealing with the North Korea nuclear threat, South Korea could set up a ROK–US joint operational plan for extended deterrence. Moreover, in a longer measure, two allies could consider a redeployment of tactical nuclear weapons and even discuss nuclear sharing in contingencies where North Korea conducts strategic provocations, such as nuclear and ICBM tests (Kim 2020a).

4.2 Competing Beliefs on the Domestic Front

Examining three sets of competing beliefs concerning South Korean security requires understanding the diverse perspectives embedded in South Korean society. First, there are 'inter-Korean' versus 'alliance' schools in dealing with North Korean issues. The alliance school argues that North Korea developing nuclear weapons has nothing to do with the survival of the nation. The only reason for the development is to reinforce its totalitarian regime security and dominate the inter-Korean rivalry. The inter-Korean school believes, on the other hand, that North Korea is developing nuclear weapons solely for its self-defence, and inter-Korean relations should thus be delinked from US–North Korean confrontation so that inter-Korean cooperation can be cultivated (Kim 2017: 246).

In other words, the inter-Korean school places Korean peace before the denuclearisation of North Korea, while the alliance school puts denuclearisation before inter-Korean cooperation. In addition, the alliance school believes that the ROK–US alliance and the US military presence in South Korea constitute the backbone of sustainable peace on the peninsula. On the other hand, the inter-Korean school believes that South Korea should make an effort to promote inter-Korean peace, while reducing its dependence on the United States for its security (Kim 2017: 246–247).

Although the Korean Peninsula has been divided for the past seventy years, the North Korean people are also considered in principle as 'the Korean people'. This is the notion that motivates a group of South Koreans to seek inter-Korean cooperation regardless of security circumstances. On the other hand, there is a group that places the ROK–US alliance before inter-Korean cooperation (Ryu 2017: 192). This group, although embracing the 'Korean people' notion, takes a more realistic approach by considering security as the top priority of the nation. In their view, the North Korea regime is the most serious threat to South Korea. The two groups embracing competing beliefs support different approaches in policies on North Korea and the United States.

The second set of competing beliefs regards South Korea–Japanese relations. The South Korea–Japan relationship, being an independent variable, affects South Korea–US–Japanese trilateral relations and possibly the ROK–US alliance (Kim 2015: 83). Due to the colonial experience, Korea's relationship with Japan has never taken an easy path.

Since the international society also understands the historical background of the bilateral relationship, making peace between the two has rarely been an important agenda until the US–China competition intensified. The United States, in competing with China, has started to recognise South Korea–US–Japan security cooperation as the key to deterring China and to maintaining peace and prosperity in the region.

In this light, the South Korean government seems to be taking the US stance on this trilateral relationship seriously. In this new setting, the South Korean government has to strike a balance between strengthening South Korea–US–Japan security cooperation and holding a firm position on South Korea–Japan historical disputes. South Korea and Japan have been working out ways to settle the issues over comfort women and forced labour during the colonial period, which is still an ongoing diplomatic headache. Furthermore, whether to renew the South Korea–Japan general security of military information agreement (GSOMIA) has also been an issue that must be resolved before moving forward (Park 2019).

The third set of competing beliefs concerns the 'South–South conflict'. The term, 'South–South Conflict' first appeared when the Kim Dae-jung government referred to the conflict between the political conservatives and progressives in the Korean society. Back then, based on the one's alignment with the 'Sunshine Policy', one's political orientation could be defined (Min 2016). The progressives supported the 'Sunshine Policy' and the conservatives opposed it. Ever since, the 'South–South Conflict' has been the major obstacle hindering the government's effective policymaking on North Korea.

The South–South conflict has also appeared in conservative governments. President Lee Myung-bak, a conservative, mainly focused on resolving the North Korean nuclear issue with carrots and sticks. But President Lee's denuclearisation-focused policy was condemned by the progressives and the international humanitarian groups for not assisting North Korean citizens. President Park Geun-hye's efforts in initiating the 'trust-building process on the Korean Peninsula', was undermined by North Korea's continued tests of its nuclear weapons and missiles (Min 2016: 207–208).

Those two conservative governments also put emphasis on the human rights situation in North Korea with a view to changing the behaviour of the North Korean regime in the areas of the nuclear problem, let alone the gross human rights violation (Min 2016: 207–209). In this regard, the 'South–South conflict' regarding policymaking in North Korea divides South Korea into two groups holding completely opposite beliefs. This conflict has often prevented the South Korean government from making a consistent policy on North Korea.

The abovementioned challenges, or competing beliefs, have caused South Korean security policymaking to deteriorate seriously. They are fundamentally different from the threats explained in the beginning of the chapter. While the threats explained earlier are innate to South Korea's geopolitical location and history, the challenges presented here have been created by people with different political orientations, especially concerning North Korea and the United States. In this light, these challenges are more difficult to overcome than coping with external threats.

5. Conclusion

South Korea's security is largely affected by the two entities, North Korea and the United States. In this chapter, the security environment of the Korean Peninsula, South Korea's security and defence policies, and the internal challenges for South Korean security have been discussed. However, the scope of South Korea's security is more complex than it appears at face value. Based on a dramatic economic growth, South Korea's GDP ranks twelfth (World Bank 2020) and sixth in military strength (Global Fire Power 2020). With its economic size and military strength, South Korea is expected to play a more active role in international security, both in traditional and non-traditional sectors.

Reflecting this trend, South Korea's military outreach has been active and constructive over the past decade. The size of South Korea's overseas deployment is 1,039 as of February 2021, where half of the soldiers are dispatched to United Nations peacekeeping operations (PKOs) and the other half are in active duty, either in multinational forces or defence cooperation. South Korea has deployed its soldiers to Lebanon and South Sudan under the UN PKO mission, and Somalia, for a peace operation conducted by a multinational force (Republic of Korea Joint Chiefs of Staff 2020). Korea also participated in the US-led war on terror, serving in Iraq and Afghan missions. South Korea is proud to join peacekeeping operations that have contributed to the world's peace and prosperity.

South Korea's efforts to respond to international non-traditional security threats has become essential as well. The United Nations Development Programme (UNDP) published the Human Development Report in 1994, and the concept of human security has gradually permeated through the non-traditional security sector ever since. As a calling to expand the scope of security to cover non-military sectors, human security has become a major security discourse in international security (Lee and Jeong 2019) and South Korea has been securitising non-traditional sectors such as climate change, food, and health (Yu 2011: 228). South Korea's response to the recent COVID-19 pandemic 'has become a global point of reference for epidemic prevention' (Klingebiel and Tørres 2020).

South Korea still faces the security challenges posed by great power politics and inter-Korean relations. It has, however, successfully set an example by accumulating both economic and military power with a view to striking an ideal balance between geopolitical and geo-economic challenges. Therefore, the future of South Korean security and defence depends on what those efforts will produce in the years to come.

Bibliography

Ban, K. J. (2020), 'The Two-For-One Entity and a "For Whom" Puzzle: UNC as Both a Peace Driver and the US Hegemony Keeper in Asia', *Asian Journal of Political Science*, https://doi.org/10.1080/02185377.2020.1814364.

Center for Strategic and International Studies (CSIS) (2017), 'Ramifications of North Korea's Sixth Nuclear Test', 5 September 2017, https://www.csis.org/analysis/ramifications-north-koreas-sixth-nuclear-test, accessed 26 November 2021.

CSIS (2020), 'Missiles of North Korea (Missile Threat: CSIS Missile Defense Project)', 14 June 2018, last modified 30 November, https://missilethreat.csis.org/country/dprk/, accessed 26 November 2021.

CSIS (2021), 'Missiles of South Korea (Missile Threat: CSIS Missile Defense Project)', https://missilethreat.csis.org/country_tax/south-korea/, accessed 26 November 2021.

Chandra, S., and Bhonsle, R. (2015), 'National Security: Concept, Measurement and Management', *Strategic Analysis* 39(4), 337.

Choi, K. (2013), 'Retrospect and Prospects for the ROK–U.S. Alliance at 60 and Beyond', *Korean Journal of Defense Analysis* 25(4), 549–559.

Global Fire Power (2020), 'Military Strength Ranking', https://www.globalfirepower.com/countries-listing.asp, accessed 26 November 2021.

Hong, K. D. (2015), 'Building a Better Strategy for Missile Defense: Lessons from the THAAD Controversies', *New Asia* 22(4), 110–134.

International Institute for Strategic Studies (IISS) (2020), 'The Military Balance 2020', https://milbalplus.iiss.org/member/DataAnalysisEconomics.aspx, accessed 26 November 2021.

Jeon, J. G. (2010), 'Driven by Peace Operations: A Balanced Development of the ROK–U.S. Alliance', *Korean Journal of Defense Analysis* 22(4), 407–420.

Jordan, A. A., Taylor, W. J. Jr, and Korb, L. J. (1993), *American National Security: Policy and Process*, 4th edn (Baltimore, MD: The Johns Hopkins University Press, 1993).

Kennedy, L. W, Roth, L. A., and Needham, Charles E. (1984), 'Calculations to Assist in a New Hiroshima Yield Estimate', 15 June, https://digital.library.unt.edu/ark:/67531/metadc1192979/, accessed 26 November 2021.

Kim, H. S. (2017), 'The Possibility of Policy Integration on North Korea between Conservative Government and Progressive Government', *Korean Journal of Unification Affairs* 29(2), 241–269.

Kim, S. H. (2008), 'Searching for a Northeast Asian Peace and Security Mechanism', *Asian Perspective* 32(4), 127–156.

Kim, S. H. (2010), 'From Blood Alliance to Strategic Alliance: Korea's Evolving Strategic Thought Toward the United States', *Korean Journal of Defense Analyses* 22(3), 265–281.

Kim, S. H. (2015), 'Three Trilateral Dynamics in Northeast Asia: Korea–China–Japan, Korea–US–Japan, and Korea–US–China Relations', *Journal of International Politics* 20(1), 71–95.

Kim, S. H. (2020a), 'Assessment of U.S. Extended Deterrence on the Korean Peninsula', 국제관계연구: 일민국제관계연구원 (*Journal of International Politics*) 25(2), 33–59.

Kim, S. H. (2020b), 'Growing Challenges Ahead for ROK–US Relations', Center for East Asian Peace and Cooperation Studies, Ritsumeikan University, 16 November, http://en.ritsumei.ac.jp/research/ceapc/insight/detail/?id=34, accessed 26 November 2021.

Kim, S. H. (2020c), 'No Denuclearization, No Peace', *Korea JoongAng Daily*, 18 August, https://koreajoongangdaily.joins.com/2020/08/16/opinion/columns/195053-Korean-War/20200816193600298.html, accessed 26 November 2021.

Kim, S. H. (2020d), 'US Policy to China: From Containment to Transformation; Growing Challenge for ROK–US Alliance; From Top-Down to Bottom-Up for North Korean Denuclearization', talking points presented at Chey–CSIS workshop, 8 December.

Kim, Y. H. (2000), 'Multilateral Approaches to the Korean Problems: A Comparative Analysis of the KEDO and Four Party Talks', *Korean Journal of Policy Studies* 15(1), 101–110.

Klingebiel, S., and Tørres, L. (2020), 'Republic of Korea and COVID-19: Gleaning Governance Lessons from a Unique Approach', Pathfinders, UNDP, September, www.undp.org, accessed 26 November 2021.

Lee, H. (2020), 'Motives for North Korea's Nuclear Weapons Development and Denuclearization', *Korean Journal of Military Art and Science* 76(1), 1–32.

Lee, S. H. (2020), 'Korea Faces New Missile Guidelines', *The Korea Times*, 9 September, www.koreatimes.co.kr/www/opinon/2020/09/197_295711.html, accessed 26 November 2021.

Lee, S. H. (2021), 'SMA in the Biden Administration', *Korea JoongAng Daily*, 20 January, https://koreajoongangdaily.joins.com/2021/01/20/opinion/columns/SMA-in-the-Biden-administration/20210120104100620.html, accessed 26 November 2021.

Lee, S. W., and Jeong, H. W. (2019), 'Korean People's "New Security Perception": Change and Continuity', *21st Century Political Science Journal* 29(2), 73–98.

Mackinder, H. J. (1904), 'The Geographical Pivot of History', *Geographical Journal* 23(4), 421–437.

Mandel, R. (1994), *The Changing Face of National Security: A Conceptual Analysis* (Michigan, Westport, Conn.: Greenwood Press).

Min, T. E. (2016), 'South–South Conflict: Humanitarian Aid to North Korea', *Korea Journal of Legislative Studies* 49, 201–230.

Nishizuka, C. R. (2018), 'Demystifying the U.S.–ROK Command and Control Structure: How "OPCON Transfer" Can Advance the Unity of Effort on the Korean Peninsula', *Korean Journal of Defense Analysis* 30(4), 455–473.

Park, C. H. (2019), 'Deepening South Korea–Japan Conflict and the Future of Security Cooperation between the Two', *KRINS-Quarterly* 4(2), 117–144.

Park, H. R. (2018), 'An Influence of North Korean Nuclear Weapons on Military Balance between South Korea and North Korea: A Pilot Analysis', *Journal of Parliamentary Research* 13(2), 225–248.

Patrick, S. M. (2017), 'Trump and World Order: The Return of Self-Help', *Foreign Affairs* 96(2), 52–57.

Pollack, J. D. (2010), 'Chapter Four: From Kim Il-sung to Kim Jong-il', *Adelphi Series* 50, 99–130.

Reif, K., and Bugos, S. (2020), 'US Aims to Add INF-Range Missiles', Arms Control Association, October, https://www.armscontrol.org/act/2020-10/news/us-aims-add-inf-range-missiles, accessed 26 November 2021.

Republic of Korea Joint Chiefs of Staff (2020), '해외파병현황' (Overseas Deployment of Armed Forces), https://new.mnd.go.kr/mbshome/mbs/jcs2/subview.jsp?id=jcs2_030102010000, accessed 26 November 2021.

Republic of Korea Ministry of National Defense (2020a), 'Defense Budget', https://www.mnd.go.kr/mbshome/mbs/mndEN/subview.jsp?id=mndEN_030900000000, accessed 26 November 2021.

Republic of Korea Ministry of National Defense (2020b), '2018 Defense White Paper', https://www.mnd.go.kr/user/mndEN/upload/pblictn/PBLICTNEBOOK_201908070153390840.pdf, accessed 26 November 2021.

Ryu, H. K. (2017), 'Successive Governments (Progressive/Conservative) of North Korea Policy, Comparative Research', *Military Forum* 91(0), 172.

Sigal, L. V. (2020), 'Paved with Good Intentions: Trump's Nuclear Diplomacy with North Korea', *Journal for Peace and Nuclear Disarmament* 3(1), 163.

Swaine, M. D. (2017), 'Chinese Views on South Korea's Deployment of THAAD', *China Leadership Monitor*, 14 February, https://www.hoover.org/research/chinese-views-south-koreas-deployment-thaad, accessed 26 November 2021.

US Department of Defense (DOD) (2016), 'US to Deploy THAAD Missile Battery to South Korea', *DOD News*, 16 September, https://www.defense.gov/Explore/News/Article/Article/831630/us-to-deploy-thaad-missile-battery-to-south-korea/, accessed 26 November 2021.

Waltz, K. (1964), 'The Stability of a Bipolar World', *Daedalus* 93(3), 881.

World Bank (2020), 'GDP Ranking (Data Catalog)', updated 29 October 2021, https://datacatalog.worldbank.org/dataset/gdp-ranking, accessed 26 November 2021.

Yu, H. S. (2011), 'The Military and Human Security: Theory, Cases and Policy Implications for Korea', *Korean Political Science Review* 45(5), 221.

CHAPTER 34

FOREIGN ECONOMIC POLICY

SOHYUN ZOE LEE

1. INTRODUCTION

SINCE 1987, South Korea's foreign economic policies (FEPs) have undergone remarkable transformation, attributable not only to the dynamics of domestic politics since the country's democratisation but also to globalisation, which began with the end of the Cold War. South Korea has become much more reliant on foreign investment and trade in the past three decades. Now more than ever, global financial crises have quicker and more significant impacts on the local economy. South Korea's FEP strategies have adapted and adjusted in response to these changes. The country's timely response to changes in the international economic environment has become critical for maintaining its highly trade-dependent economy and ensuring a stable financial market.

Most visibly, as a middle-power country, highly vulnerable to changes in its external trade relations, South Korea has developed multilayered economic ties. It joined the Asia-Pacific Economic Cooperation (APEC) in 1989 and the Asia–Europe Meeting (ASEM) in 1996 as a founding member. In the same year, it became a member of the Organisation for Economic Co-operation and Development (OECD) and became regarded as an advanced industrialised state. The Asian Financial Crisis (AFC) during 1997–1998 further accelerated the changes to South Korea's FEPs. To promote regional economic stability, South Korea took part in regional economic initiatives, such as the Chiang Mai Initiative (CMI) and the Asian Bond Market Initiative (ABMI). Policies based on state-led, export-oriented growth and inward foreign direct investment were redirected towards achieving market-oriented liberalisation through deregulation and promotion of transparent market transactions (Dent 2000). Further, South Korea began actively engaging in free trade agreements (FTAs) at bilateral, regional, and cross-regional levels. Since the late 2010s, as the US–China rivalry has intensified, South Korea has sought to diversify its diplomatic ties further through the New Northern Policy (NNP) and the New Southern Policy (NSP).

Nevertheless, traditional actors, including the government and, to a lesser degree, the Chaebols, continue to play pivotal roles in the country's contemporary FEP decision-making process. FEP goals and decision-making structures have been largely dependent on the government and are susceptible to changes in political leadership. In other words, South Korea's institutions and FEP directions have been sensitive to the different motivations and objectives of each administration. Simultaneously, however, South Korea's institutions have evolved since its democratisation to accommodate an increased level of influence by interest groups and the civil society. This gradual change has been driven by both external economic shocks and the country's domestic agenda to increase the transparency of its decision-making process.

To examine these developments further, this chapter explores the interaction between the dynamics of South Korea's domestic and international economies that shape its contemporary FEPs. Hence, the second section introduces the institutional structure of South Korea's FEPs. The following sections investigate the developments of South Korea's FEPs by analysing the country's FEPs prior to the AFC, the post-AFC developments, and the recent progress after the Global Financial Crisis and the rise of China. This analysis has focused on how domestic politics have responded to the externalities, as FEPs are products of domestic decision-making processes that reflect the changes in the international economic environment. The final section concludes with a discussion of South Korea's FEPs.

2. THE FEP DECISION-MAKING STRUCTURE

The executive branch of the government is central to South Korea's FEP decision-making process and is characterised by strong presidential powers and bureaucratic elites. This concentration of power shapes South Korea's current FEP agendas; however, institutions have evolved to reflect South Korea's transition from an authoritarian to a democratic state. First, as Im (2017: 18) noted, 'the resources of bureaucracy, which during the developmental period were solely in the service of the authoritarian leadership, were exercised toward democratisation'. Since the late 1980s, FEP decision-making has developed to accommodate increased participation from non-governmental actors, transforming it into a multilayered process (Bae 2020). This is not only attributable to the increased demand for democratic decision-making but also to the nature of FEPs, which has a direct distributional impact on domestic industries. Furthermore, the state–Chaebol connections have significantly weakened, particularly since the AFC, which has reduced the Chaebols' role in the FEP decision-making process.

Under the current South Korean semi-presidential system, the president, as head of state and chief diplomat, enjoys substantial autonomy in determining South Korea's foreign policy and is not restricted to the economic sphere. The prime minister's power is limited because the prime minister is appointed by, and is subject to the order of, the president. However, since the sixth revision of the Constitution in 1987, the president's term of office has been restricted to a five-year, single-term presidency to prevent the potential development of an authoritarian rule. Due to the substantial presidential authority exercised within a limited time framework, South Korea's FEPs have been revised with each administration change. For instance, the Kim Dae-jung administration's FEP focus was on East Asia. Under the Roh Moo-hyun administration, the focus was redirected towards a multitrack FTA strategy, which in the long run aimed at concluding FTAs with large and powerful economies such as the United States and the European Union (EU). Currently, under the Moon Jae-in administration, South Korea has been aiming at diversifying and expanding its economic relations beyond its traditional focus on major powers such as the United States, China, Japan, and Russia.

Similarly, FEP-related bureaus have undergone numerous structural changes and subsequent relabelling with each change in administration. The trade function, for example, was originally under the Ministry of Trade and Industry, but has undergone several transformations since. In 1993, for instance, the Kim Young-sam administration incorporated the Ministry of Energy and Resources into the Ministry of Trade and Industry, creating a Ministry of Trade, Industry and Energy (MOTIE). In 1998, under the Kim Dae-jung administration, trade bureaus were merged to the Ministry of Foreign Affairs (MOFA) to centralise trade policymaking structures, resulting in a redesignation of the agency as the Ministry of Foreign Affairs and Trade (MOFAT). When the Park Geun-hye administration began in 2013, however, the trade bureau was rehoused to MOTIE to emphasise the linkages between trade and domestic industries. This structural change consequently had a fragmenting effect on FTA decision-making authority (Choi and Oh 2017).

At present, multiple bureaus are involved in the FEP decision-making process. These include the Ministry of Economy and Finance (MOEF); MOTIE; MOFA; the Ministry of Agriculture, Food and Rural Affairs; the Ministry of Environment; the Ministry of Land, Infrastructure and Transport; the Ministry of Science and Information and Communication Technology; the Ministry of Small and Medium-Sized Enterprises and Start-Ups; and the Office for Government Policy Coordination/Prime Minister's Secretariat. These bureaus work closely with national policy research institutes, such as the Korea Institute for International Economic Policy and the Korea Development Institute, to analyse and evaluate the impacts of FEPs. Depending on specific FEPs, some bureaus are more involved than others and apply more specific protocols to their decision-making processes; for instance, trade-related policies are led by MOTIE, while MOFA and MOEF are primarily responsible for overseas development assistance (ODA)-related policies. Because FEPs involve various bureaucracies, inter-bureaucracy conflicts have at times slowed down decision-making processes, most notably until the 1990s (Choi and Oh 2011).

To promote inter-bureaucracy coordination, the Ministerial Meeting on International Economic Affairs (MMIEA) has been held since 2001 under the direct order of the president (Solis 2013). To conduct this meeting, ministers in FEP-related ministries gather twice a month, in principle, or more frequently if required. Some of the core tasks of the MMIEA include reviewing international economic trends and setting policy directions; promoting bilateral, regional, and multilateral economic cooperation; and discussing the economic issues to be included in the Summit meetings. Further, the MMIEA evaluates the impact of domestic economic policies on South Korea's foreign economic relations and determines the medium-to-long-term distribution of South Korea's financial expenditure in relation to its FEPs (Presidential Decree 2017). The results from these discussions are passed on to Cabinet meetings. Eventually, the president decides the final FEP based on these discussions.

Since the late 1990s, FTAs have become major FEP tools in South Korea, which have shaped its bilateral and regional economic relations. Since FTAs are treaties, an additional procedure—ratification by the National Assembly—is required once negotiations have been concluded. The key role of the National Assembly is to monitor and give consent for what has been negotiated and concluded; in this respect, it is not directly involved in shaping South Korea's FTA strategies. Nevertheless, the FTA ratification processes have at times caused substantial delays for agreements to take effect, due to the politicisation of South Korea's sensitive agricultural sector and the actions of legislators from agricultural districts (Park and Koo 2007; Koo and Jho 2013); the South Korea–Chile FTA and the South Korea–US FTA (KORUS FTA) most representatively demonstrate these delays. To avoid such potential conflicts, FEP-related bureaucrats regularly communicate and share policy directives with legislators (Cheong and Cho 2009; Lee 2017).

While South Korea's concentration of power has permitted the president to pursue streamlined FEPs with efficiency, influence from non-governmental actors has been relatively weak in comparison with other democracies that imbue more power to the legislative branch of the government. Interest groups exert their influence via political parties; however, because South Korea's party system is weakly linked to voters, such influence occurs only to a limited extent (Park and Moon 2006). Nonetheless, institutions have been evolving to accommodate more influence from non-governmental actors, such as academics, the private sector, and civil society. This change has been driven not only by major structural reforms conducted after the AFC but also by the public's growing demand for transparency in the government's decision-making process.

The Chaebols continue to influence South Korea's FEPs; however, their influence notably weakened after the AFC, as major reforms took place under the Kim Daejung administration to dismantle the state–Chaebol nexus (Dent 2000). Their influence has waned further since President Park Geun-hye's corruption scandal, which led to investigations into the Chaebols and the restructuring of the Federation of Korean Industries (FKI).

3. FEPs Prior to the AFC (1987–1998)

By the early 1980s, South Korea's FEPs had begun shifting away from the policies of the 1960s–1970s, which had focused on promoting economic growth through a government-led, export-orientated strategy. Internationally, the second oil crisis and high inflation had worsened South Korea's terms of trade (Lee 2005). The country was also facing growing pressure from the United States, its largest trade partner at the time, as it continued to record high trade surpluses based on protectionist policies (Kwon 2004). Domestically, General Chun Doo-hwan established a new government through a military coup in 1980 after the assassination of President Park Chung-hee. Against this unfavourable economic backdrop, General Chun appointed US-educated neo-classical economists to compensate for his own lack of expertise. The newly appointed economists led South Korea's FEPs, based on the Washington Consensus, effectively sustaining South Korea's economic growth throughout the 1980s (Lee 2005).

These liberalising policies continued to shape South Korea's FEP directions from the late 1980s to the mid-1990s. The FEPs also diversified, both internationally and domestically. At the international level, South Korea's regional and global networks expanded through participation in various regional and international economic organisations, including APEC in 1989 and ASEM and the OECD in 1996. After joining the General Agreement on Tariffs and Trade (GATT) as a developing country in 1967, a rapidly growing South Korea faced intense international pressure to increase its contribution to the Uruguay Round negotiations and the subsequent World Trade Organisation (WTO) negotiations. As Dent (2000: 294–285) assessed, 'the combination of partial economic liberalisation, diversified bilateral economic relations, and increased participation in international economic regimes led to greater emphasis on promotive, rather than defensive, economic diplomacy by the mid-1990s'.

At the domestic level, South Korea faced greater challenges after democratisation, while incorporating different voices in its FEP decision-making process. The Chaebols' influence began to increase, as their reliance on government support declined (Kim 1997; Lee 2005). Their development increasingly depended on market-orientated policies, which enabled them to mobilise their economic capacity into political power (Cha 1993; Graham 2003). Reduced state intervention also indicated greater participation of interest groups, academics, the media, consumer organisations, and the public (Lee 2005). Inter-ministry coordination problems and domestic protests added further complications to South Korea's FEP decision-making processes, particularly in trade; farmers and the Ministry of agriculture aggressively opposed the Uruguay Round and the WTO negotiations. During this period, trade-involved ministries and relevant sectoral interests had strong direct links that resulted in frequent disagreements among different ministries (Choi and Oh 2011).

Furthermore, the end of the Cold War precipitated a considerable change in South Korea's existing trade relations and a significant growth in trade volume. Between 1990 and 1997, South Korea's total exports more than doubled, from US$ 65 billion to US$ 136.2 billion. South Korea's trade with China and the Association of Southeast Asian Nations (ASEAN) began rapidly catching up to the level of trade between South Korea and its traditional major trade partners—the United States, Japan, and the EU (Kang 2014). In 1990, South Korea's exports to the United States were US$ 20.6 billion, accounting for 31.6 per cent of its total exports, followed by exports to Japan (US$ 13.5 billion) and the EU (US$ 10.4 billion), or 20.6 per cent and 15.8 per cent of South Korea's total exports, respectively. Exports to China and the ASEAN were merely US$ 584 million and US$ 5.2 billion, or 0.8 per cent and 8 per cent of the total exports, respectively. In 1997, the United States continued as South Korea's largest export destination, accounting for a total of US$ 21.6 billion. By this time, however, ASEAN had become South Korea's second largest export destination with US$ 20.4 billion, overtaking the EU, which accounted for exports of US$ 19.2 billion. Furthermore, exports to China closely followed those to Japan, which totalled US$ 13.6 billion and US$ 14.8 billion, respectively (see Table 34.1).

However, the liberalisation trends and trade growth do not allow us to conclude that FEPs, which had been promoted since the late 1980s, were consistent across different administrations. Rather, they were highly responsive to the changing global and domestic environment, and both protectionist and liberal policies co-existed in broader trends. The Roh Tae-woo administration (1988–1993) promoted FEPs to stabilise South Korea's high surplus in international trade, against the backdrop of growing pressure from the United States on East Asian economies that it thought were responsible for its high trade deficit. To reduce trade tensions with the United States, the Roh administration sought to ease import restrictions, cut back on export support schemes, reduce tariffs, and liberalise financial and foreign exchange markets (Park 2009; Jameson 1991).[1]

President Roh's *Nordpolitik* (Northern Policy), which was announced in 1988 and aimed at building new relations with the communist bloc, gained an impetus with the end of the Cold War. After the two Koreas simultaneously joined the United Nations in 1991, the administration particularly focused on improving relations with North Korea. As a part of this strategy, trade with North Korea was officially authorised for the first time since Korea was divided in 1945. This policy directly resulted in a significant growth in trade with North Korea, which surged from US$ 1 million in value in 1988 to US$ 200 million in 1992 (Presidential Archives 1992). The Roh administration further sought to facilitate economic relations with Russia and China after the normalisation of the respective diplomatic relations in 1991 and 1992 (Park 2009).

The succeeding president, Kim Young-sam (1993–1998), carried on with market-based reforms, although in a much different domestic and global context. To accommodate the rapidly changing global dynamics, President Kim made *Segyehwa* (globalisation) his administration's new comprehensive policy in 1994. This change was aimed at increasing productivity and market flexibility, while diversifying economic diplomacy, which had been heavily focused on South Korea–US relations (Saxer 2013). South Korea also actively engaged in the Uruguay Round negotiations, as well as the WTO negotiations and worked towards promoting economic deregulations that had

Table 34.1: South Korea's major export destinations, 1990–2020 (in thousand US$)

	1990	1995	1997	2000	2005	2015	2020
United States	20,638,993	24,131,474	21,625,432	37,610,630	41,342,584	69,832,103	74,159,016
Japan	13,456,797	17,048,871	14,771,155	20,466,016	24,027,438	25,576,507	25,092,517
EU* (2007, 27; 2013, 28 countries)	10,381,809	17,850,230	19,226,547	24,890,795	43,658,877	48,079,270	52,143,733
China	584,854	9,143,588	13,572,463	18,454,540	61,914,983	137,123,934	132,555,008
ASEAN	5,216,736	17,978,998	20,365,332	20,133,786	27,432,172	74,824,364	89,050,647
Total exports	65,015,731	125,057,988	136,164,204	172,267,510	284,418,743	526,756,503	512,788,730

Source: K-Stat (stat.kita.net).

traditionally targeted the manufacturing industry towards services and investment (Kwon 2004; Park 2009). These developments became precursors for South Korea to act as a mediator between industrialised and developing states in multilateral fora (Kwon 2004).

President Kim structurally reshuffled the ministries and established new committees. In the economics dimension, the Ministry of Finance and Economy was established, which brought the Economic Planning Board and the Ministry of Finance together to reduce the role of the once powerful Economic Planning Board, as well as the overall role of government in the market (Graham 2003). To minimise inefficiencies caused by overlapping functions, the Ministry of Trade and Industry and the Ministry of Energy and Resources were merged to form the Ministry of Trade, Industry and Energy (MOTIE).[2] The Economic Deregulation Committee and Industrial Deregulation Committee were formed to promote further economic liberalisation (Choi 2001). To bid for OECD membership, President Kim's administration pursued policies that liberalised foreign exchange and capital transactions, despite fierce opposition from the civil society and labour unions (Kim 2012; Saxer 2013); the president's authority over FEPs successfully resulted in South Korea's entry into the OECD in 1996.

The FEPs based on *Segyehwa*, however, were severely hit by the AFC, which loomed over East Asia in 1997; this consequently limited President Kim's capacity to pursue his policy agenda effectively (Park 2009).

4. Post-AFC FEPs (1998–2008)

After the AFC, the evolution of South Korean FEPs entered a new phase marked by post-crisis market-oriented reforms, the decline in the Chaebols' influence, the rise of the civil society, and the emergence of FTAs. The Kim Dae-jung administration (1998–2003) carried out substantive reforms as part of the International Monetary Fund's (IMF) bailout plan, including tightening monetary and fiscal policies, establishing the foreign exchange market, increasing foreign competition, conducting structural reforms in financial sector and labour markets, improving corporate governance, and liberalising trade. To attract foreign investors, the administration promoted bilateral investment treaties (BITs) with the United States and Japan. The BIT negotiation with the United States failed due to opposition from domestic film industries, which strongly resisted the reduction of 'screen quotas',[3] while the BIT with Japan came into force in 2001. President Kim further agreed to the CMI in 2000, which consisted of multiple bilateral swap agreements among the ASEAN + 3 countries; the initiative was expected to stabilise South Korea's foreign exchange market, while reducing its reliance on the IMF.

The government further introduced new regulations on the practice of cross-guarantees among Chaebol members' entry into new business sectors, and on high debt–equity ratios, demanding the improvement of transparency in their financial statements (Kwon 1998; Dent 2000). The crisis and these subsequent measures significantly reduced the Chaebols' political and economic power and their ability to shape South Korea's FEPs. Contrarily, the civil society's influence and their ability to mobilise joint actions increased. Its presence was extended in the making of foreign policy process; the Yangju highway incident, an accident in which a US Army vehicle killed two South Korean schoolgirls, sparked a series of anti-US movements on issues that followed later, such as deployment of Korean non-combat troops to Iraq and Afghanistan, and the KORUS FTA negotiations (Saxer 2013).

Another significant change in South Korea's FEPs after the AFC was its shift of emphasis from WTO-based multilateralism to regionalism and bilateralism. Prior to the crisis, despite a global rise of bilateral and regional trade agreements, policymakers had refrained from pursuing FTAs; they considered South Korea to be one of the largest beneficiaries of multilateralism as a developing country (Park and Koo 2007; Lee 2021). Against the background of the growing inefficiency of multilateral negotiations and the competitive rise of FTAs, policymakers began to reposition their perception towards FTAs (Lee 2021). In a reflection of this change, President Kim, in 1998, housed the function of trade under MOFAT and established the Office of the Minister for Trade. In the same year, Chile was selected as South Korea's first FTA partner. The MMIEA was created in 2001 to unite the ministries involved in South Korea's FEPs under a single set of meetings. Since then, this centralisation of the trade policymaking structure, combined with strong presidential power, significantly reduced the conflict among the different ministries (Choi and Oh 2011). The Kim administration further explored the potential for FTAs with Singapore, Thailand, and Japan.

South Korea's FTA strategy significantly progressed when President Roh Moo-hyun (2003–2008) announced the FTA Roadmap, which aimed at negotiating FTAs with 'big and advanced economies'. The Roadmap, led by President Roh and Trade Minister Hyun-chong Kim, shifted South Korea's conventional focus on East Asia to cross-regional and multitrack FTAs (Lee 2021). Considering the fierce domestic opposition and South Korea's lack of experience in negotiating in-depth and highly liberalising trade agreements with major economies, the change had been perceived as radical and risky (Sohn 2019; Lee 2021). Therefore, in the short run, the Roh administration strategically promoted FTAs with partners such as Singapore, ASEAN, and the European Free Trade Association (EFTA), which took less than a year to negotiate; the South Korea–Singapore FTA negotiations were concluded in 2004, and the South Korea–ASEAN trade in goods agreement, as well as the EFTA negotiations, were concluded by the end of 2005. Along with other FTA negotiations (such as those with Canada, India, and Mexico) that soon followed, these early agreements acted as a gateway to the Roadmap's long-term goal of reaching towards FTAs with the United States and the EU (Lee 2017; Lee 2021). These agreements with the United States and the EU were concluded by 2007 and 2009, respectively, enhancing South Korea's diplomatic position as a trade hub and a middle-power country.

Most FTAs promoted during this period were efficiently negotiated within a time frame of one or two years and were backed by a streamlined presidential leadership and centralised trade decision-making authority. However, little room was left for other domestic actors, often leaving them unsatisfied. This dissatisfaction resulted in aggressive protests and subsequent delays in the ratification process, particularly for FTAs that had substantial political or economic implications for the country. Most representatively, South Korea's FTA with Chile faced strong opposition from the agricultural sector, causing severe delays in the ratification process. Yet, the role of the National Assembly was limited regarding reflecting the protesters' positions. While the members of the National Assembly, representing rural districts, liaised with farmers, their actions took place individually, rather than at the party or the National Assembly level, and that too only after all negotiations had been concluded (Lee 2010). To complement these limitations, the FTA Procedure Regulation was introduced in June 2004 to specify the procedures that should be adopted before, during, and after FTA negotiations.[4]

The government was again confronted with opposition from interest groups and the public when the KORUS FTA negotiations began in February 2006. In response to these reactions, the National Assembly formed a Special Committee that met for the first time in July 2006 to check and balance the executive's promotion of the KORUS FTA negotiations and South Korea's overall FTA strategies (Lee and Kim 2010). During this period, however, the institutions were still evolving to incorporate these changing domestic and international environments. The KORUS FTA further faced protests and delays during the ratification process, demonstrating the limitations of the FEP decision-making process.

5. CONTEMPORARY FEPs (2008–2021)

In recent years, South Korea has once again experienced substantial growth in the role of civil society groups, while the Chaebols' influence on the FEP decision-making process has further declined. Similarly, South Korea's FEPs have become much more inconsistent than those of the past, due to a prolonged global economic downturn since the Global Financial Crisis of 2008, and the rise of China, along with South Korea's increasing economic dependence on the Chinese market. The average economic growth rate of 5.15 per cent from 2004 to 2007 had reduced to 3 per cent in 2008 and remained at an approximate range of 2–3 per cent throughout the 2010s (Korean Statistical Information Service (KOSIS) 2020).[5] South Korea's exports to China had already surpassed its exports to the United States by the mid-2000s, and the figures continued to rise rapidly. By 2015, South Korea's exports to China totalled US$ 137.1 billion, compared to US$ 69.8 billion worth of exports to the United States (see Table 34.1). South Korea, as a longstanding ally of the United States, struggled to strike a balance in its FEPs as the US–China hegemonic rivalry began to intensify, beginning in the late 2000s.

South Korean economic growth waned under the Roh administration, which led to the electoral success of the competing Grand National Party's presidential candidate, Lee Myung-bak, whose business and economic expertise appealed to the public. As soon as he assumed office in February 2008, President Lee's administration (2008–2013) began working towards ratifying the KORUS FTA, which had been stalled by both the South Korean National Assembly and the US Congress. In the hope of facilitating the ratification of the KORUS FTA by the US Congress, President Lee, in his first visit to the United States in April 2008, promised to lift the ban on the import of US beef as part of the KORUS FTA; this revised agreement would allow the United States to export all its beef and other cattle products irrespective of age (Jurenas and Manyin 2008). In reaction to this unexpected announcement, civil society groups and the public immediately mobilised themselves against the renegotiation of the FTA through a series of candlelight protests. The reason behind these protests was two-fold: first, the removal of the ban that had been in place since 2003, due to the outbreak of Mad Cow disease, might pose a risk to public health; and second, objection to the president's unilateral decision-making and lack of transparency in South Korea's FEP policymaking process (Lee 2010).

These protests acted as negotiating leverage on the South Korean side, pushing President Lee to revoke his promise to the United States and limit US beef import to cattle less than thirty months old for an unspecified period (Jurenas and Manyin 2008). Nevertheless, the FKI, largely backed by the Chaebols, continued to support the KORUS FTA, arguing that South Korea would benefit from increased exports to the US market. The President's power had also been sufficiently strong to pressure the ruling party, which led to the ratification of the agreement by November 2011 (Saxer 2013). At an international level, the ratification of the KORUS FTA provoked Beijing to accelerate its own FTA with South Korea to counterbalance the growing influence of the United States in shaping regional trade rules (Sohn 2019). Therefore, the South Korea–China FTA (KCFTA) negotiations began in May 2012 and progressed under newly elected President Park Geun-hye (2013–2017).

Alongside the KCFTA negotiations, President Park announced her new plans for South Korea's FEPs, which significantly diverged from the previous two administrations' approaches. In President Park's view, the previous FEPs, which had focused on the export-oriented and multitrack FTA policy, were no longer suitable to revive the sluggish economy (Oh 2013). The New FTA Roadmap in June 2013 aimed to strengthen linkages between domestic industries and trade policies. This contrasted with Roh's and Lee's administrations that aimed to expand South Korea's economic territory and focused on the international economy. The New Roadmap's goal was for South Korea to become a 'linchpin' in regional mega-FTA initiatives, such as the Trans-Pacific Partnership (TPP), the Regional Comprehensive Economic Partnership (RCEP), and the China–Japan–South Korea (CJK) FTA (Kim 2015). As part of this New Roadmap, the previous administrations' focus on significant and advanced economies, such as the United States and the EU, was redirected towards emerging economies. Furthermore, President Park announced the increase of ODA as well as the promotion of cooperation with other middle powers. To reflect these changes, trade bureaus under MOFAT were rehoused to MOTIE and physically moved from Seoul to the new administrative capital, Sejong.

Despite its initial ambitions, however, the Park administration's achievements in FEPs were limited. This was in part due to the relocation of the trade bureau, which had fragmented the FTA decision-making authority, while strengthening the influence of protectionist sectoral interests (Choi and Oh 2017). In addition, diplomatic resources were diverted to the KCFTA negotiations, rather than to mega-regional FTAs, which consequently took almost three years to conclude (from 2012 to 2015). More crucially, the corruption scandal around President Park in late 2016 that eventually led to her impeachment was critical enough to put a pause on South Korea's FEPs. Due to the FKI's involvement in this scandal, four of South Korea's major Chaebols left the federation and its budget source was cut by more than half, which incapacitated the FKI (*Nikkei Asian Review* 2017). In contrast, the civil society's influence further grew and matured, as civil society groups were successfully able to check President Park through candlelight protests, while putting a halt to corrupt practices between the state and the Chaebol. As a result of this mass movement, on 9 December 2016, the National Assembly voted, with more than two-thirds majority, to temporarily suspend the presidential executive powers and to impeach the president. The Constitutional Court unanimously upheld this ruling on 10 March 2017.

Since President Moon Jae-in (2017–2022) came into power, South Korea's FEPs have once again been subject to transformation. In response to the changing global economic environment and the deepening of the US–China rivalry, the Moon administration has sought to diversify South Korea's diplomatic relations by strengthening ties with Eurasia, Southeast Asia, and India through the NNP and the NSP. These policies were developed in response to external pressure from both the United States and China; South Korea became one of the earliest targets of President Donald Trump's 'America First' policy, when President Trump announced the renegotiation of the KORUS FTA. The KORUS FTA was hence renegotiated and signed by the two parties in September 2018, with relatively minor changes in the agreement, in contrast to President Trump's initial proclamations.[6] Contrarily, China's unofficial economic sanctions on South Korea, triggered by South Korea's acceptance of the US proposal for the deployment of the Terminal High Altitude Area Defense (THAAD) system, increased pressure on the economy. This series of events highlighted the need to reduce South Korea's heavy reliance on the United States and China by expanding its diplomatic relations through the NNP and the NSP.

After the withdrawal of the United States from the TPP, South Korea has focused on promoting 'simultaneous and individual/bilateral FTAs', as outlined by the 190th Economic Ministers' Meeting in January 2017 (Park 2017) and concluding the RCEP. To institutionally support emerging issues in FEPs, MOTIE's trade negotiation bureaus were internally reorganised in March 2018. The KORUS FTA Division, Trade Legal Affairs and Planning Division, and the Digital Trade Policy Division were newly created. In addition, existing divisions were rebranded into the Northern Trade and Coordination Division and the New Southern Trade Policy Division (MOTIE 2018). Backed by these institutional adjustments, South Korea has been negotiating an FTA with Malaysia since 2019, while concluding its FTAs with Indonesia, Cambodia, and the Philippines in November 2019, February 2021, and October 2021, respectively.

The continuation of the US–China trade war since 2018 has further strengthened the Moon administration's commitment to accelerate the diversification strategy. Since the onset of the COVID-19 pandemic, the administration has sought to further utilise the NNP and the NSP as key drivers of its diplomatic power. For instance, at the 213th Economic Ministerial Meeting held on 27 April 2020, Namki Hong, the Vice Minister and Minister of MOEF, announced that, as part of the NNP and the NSP, South Korea would increase its ODA by US$ 7 billion—twice its existing ODA for the past three years. Further, the NSP Plus Strategy was announced in November 2020, to expand South Korea's regional and global role amid the economic downturn caused by the COVID-19 pandemic and to address the growing demand for cross-border digital economic activities (Do 2020). Nevertheless, the NSP has been drawing increasing attention from the United States and China, even though South Korea set out the strategy as a means of diversification. The two powers have been competitively situating the NSP under their respective regional initiatives: the United States' Indo-Pacific strategy and China's Belt and Road Initiative.

At the multilateral level, South Korea has officially withdrawn from receiving special and differential treatment for developing countries in the WTO since October 2019. The decision was a direct response to the United States' criticism that advanced economies should not be receiving special treatment as developing countries (Lee and Nicolas 2021). As Lee and Nicolas (2021: 67) note, however, 'the South Korean government made it explicit that its intention is not to "forego" its developing country status, but rather, "not seek" preferential treatment' to avoid backlash from the agricultural sector.

Given these recent developments, it will remain a challenge for South Korea to execute a consistent strategy as a middle power among the global power dynamics, while balancing the domestic interests with the national interests.

6. Conclusion

Since South Korea's democratisation in the late 1980s, its FEPs have been constantly evolving to move in consonance with the changing global environment, while embracing the principles of democratic capitalism. Deregulation and liberalisation trends have shaped the overall direction of South Korea's FEPs throughout the 1990s and 2000s. In contemporary South Korea, the country's conventional links with the United States and the WTO have had a paramount influence that shapes its FEP strategies. Simultaneously, however, South Korea has also expanded its bilateral, regional, and cross-regional economic ties by diversifying and strengthening its economic links across the globe to extend its market access and ensure a stable economy. At the domestic level, South Korea's FEP institutions have developed to include diverse domestic actors in their decision-making process. In contrast, with the introduction of reform measures after the AFC and the shrunken role of the FKI since the late 2010s, the influence of the Chaebols has significantly declined. The influence of non-governmental actors has increased; however, their activities are largely limited to protests and mass mobilisation because there are few formal communication channels with the government.

Despite South Korea's remarkable transformation of its FEPs at both international and domestic levels, several agendas remain unaddressed. The FEP decision-making process continues to be dominated by the executive branch of the government because South Korea's institutional structure accords strong decision-making authority to the president. The structure has allowed the country's FEPs to progress with high efficiency; however, this structure has also left room for enhancing transparency and incorporating more participation from domestic actors through official channels. Additionally, the fast-paced revamp of FEP agendas with every change in administration poses major challenges to producing consistent policy outcomes. These challenges have become prominent since the late 2000s, as the global economic environment entered a new phase of the financial crisis, followed by the increasing US–China rivalry and the COVID-19 pandemic. Therefore, the future of South Korean FEPs will hinge on how the power dynamics among the domestic actors evolve, and how they effectively manage South Korea's diplomatic relations as a middle-power country.

Notes

1. While these policies successfully induced trade deficits, their side effects had to be counterbalanced by the policies of September 1991, which included goals such as reducing the trade deficit with Japan, reducing foreign currency loans, minimising crude oil stocks, and encouraging people to save more, while localising production of parts and components for manufacturing goods (Park 2009).
2. MOTIE (2016), http://english.motie.go.kv/en/am/introduction/indtoruction.jsp, accessed 26 November 2021.
3. Screen quotas, enforced in 1967, allocate a minimum number of screening days to domestic films to protect the domestic film industry from foreign competition.
4. See Lee (2010: 296) for the details of the Free Trade Agreement Procedure Regulation.
5. KOSIS (2020), www.kosis.kr, accessed 26 November 2021.
6. See Lester, Manak, and Kim (2019) for the details of the renegotiated KORUS FTA.

Bibliography

Bae, J. (2020), 'Korean Foreign and National Security Policy: Actors, Structures, and Process', in C. Moon and M. Moon (eds), *Routledge Handbook of Korean Politics and Public Administration*, 1st edn (Abingdon, UK and New York: Routledge), 144–159.

Cha, V. (1993), 'Politics and Democracy under the Kim Young Sam Government: Something Old, Something New', *Asian Survey* 33(9), 849–863.

Cheong, I., and Cho, J. (2009), 'The Impact of Free Trade Agreements (FTAs) on Business in the Republic of Korea', ADB Working Paper no. 156, https://www.adb.org/sites/default/files/publication/156011/adbi-wp156.pdf, accessed 26 November 2021.

Choi, B., and Oh, J. S. (2011), 'Asymmetry in Japan and Korea's Agricultural Liberalization in FTA: Domestic Trade Governance Perspective', *The Pacific Review* 24(5), 505–527.

Choi, B., and Oh, J. S. (2017), 'Reversed Asymmetry in Japan's and Korea's FTAs: TPP and Beyond', *Pacific Focus* 32(2), 232–258.

Choi, D. (2001), 'A Radical Approach to Regulatory Reform in Korea', paper presented at the Annual 2001 Conference of the American Society for Public Administration at Rutgers University, New Jersey, March.

Dent, C. (2000), 'What Difference a Crisis? Continuity and Change in South Korea's Foreign Economic Policy', *Journal of the Asia Pacific Economy* 5(3), 275–302.

Do, J. (2020), 'Moon Announces "New Southern Policy Plus Strategy"', *The Korea Times*, 12 November, https://www.koreatimes.co.kr/www/nation/2020/11/113_299218.html, accessed 26 November 2021.

Graham, E. (2003), 'Reforming Korea's Industrial Conglomerates', Peterson Institute for International Economics, January, https://www.piie.com/bookstore/reforming-koreas-industrial-conglomerates, accessed 26 November 2021.

Im, T. (2017), *The Experience of Democracy and Bureaucracy in South Korea (Public Policy and Governance)* (Bingley: Emerald Publishing).

Jameson, S. (1991), 'Roh Tae Woo: South Korea's President Wants a Polity to Match Its Economy', *Los Angeles Times*, 23 June, https://www.latimes.com/archives/la-xpm-1991-06-23-op-1801-story.html, accessed 26 November 2021.

Jurenas, R., and Manyin, M. (2008), 'U.S.–South Korea Beef Dispute: Negotiation and Status', *CRS Report for Congress*, 24 July, https://www.everycrsreport.com/reports/RL34528.html, accessed 26 November 2021.

K-Stat (n.d.) 'K-stat', stat.kita.net, accessed 13 December 2021.

Kang, M. (2014), 'South Korea's Foreign Economic Relations and Government Policies', in S. Pekkanen, J. Ravenhill, and R. Foot, eds, *The Oxford Handbook of the International Relations of Asia*, 199–217 (New York: Oxford University Press).

Kim, C. (2015), '21세기 산업- 通商시대의 新통상정책 방향]' ('21segi saneop-tongsangsidaeui sintongsangjeongchaeng banghyang), *Nara Economy*, Korea Development Institute, pp. 48–49.

Kim, E. (1997), *Big Business, Strong State* (New York: State University of New York Press).

Kim, Y. (2012), '김영삼 정권, 세계화의 덫에 스스로 걸려들다' ('Kim Young-sam jeonggwon, segyehwaui deoche seuseuro geollyeodeulda), Pressian News, 26 https://m.pressian.com/m/pages/articles/106708#0DKW, accessed 26 November 2021.

Koo, M., and Jho, W. (2013), 'Linking Domestic Decision-Making and International Bargaining Results: Beef and Automobile Negotiations between South Korea and the United States', *International Relations of the Asia-Pacific* 13(1), 65–93.

KOSIS, 2020, *Korean Statistical Information Service*, viewed 04 December, 2020, <www.kosis.kr>.

Kwon, Y. (1998), 'The Korean Financial Crisis: Diagnosis, Remedies and Prospects', *Journal of the Asia Pacific Economy* 3(3), 331–357.

Kwon, Y. (2004), 한국의 개방정책 진단 (*Hangugui gaebangjeongchaeng jindan*) (Seoul: KERI).

Lee, C. (2005), 'The Political Economy of Institutional Reform in Korea', *Journal of the Asia Pacific Economy* 10(3), 257–277.

Lee, H. (2010), 'Ratification of a Free Trade Agreement: The Korean Legislature's Response to Globalisation', *Journal of Contemporary Asia* 40(20), 291–308.

Lee, S. (2017), 'A Step Towards East Asian Regionalism? Comparing the Negotiation Approaches of South Korea and Japan in Their Preferential Trade Agreements with ASEAN', PhD thesis, London School of Economics and Political Science, London, http://etheses.lse.ac.uk/3717/, accessed 26 November 2021.

Lee, S. (2021), 'Ideas and Policy Transformation: Why Preferences for Regionalism and Cross-Regionalism Diverged in Japan and South Korea', *The Pacific Review*, 34(2), 290–320.

Lee, Y., and Kim, W. (2010), 'South Korea's Meandering Path to Globalisation in the Late Twentieth Century', *Asian Studies Review* 34(3), 309–327. https://www.tandfonline.com/doi/abs/10.1080/10357823.2010.507864

Lee, S., and Nicolas, F. (2021), 'Trade', in Ramon Pacheco Pardo, ed. *South Korea-EU Cooperation in Global Governance*, KF-VUB Korea Chair Report, https://brussels-school.be/publications/other-publications/south-korea-eu-cooperation-global-governance

Lester, S., Manak, I., and Kim, K. (2019), 'Trump's First Trade Deal: The Slightly Revised Korea–US Free Trade Agreement', *Free Trade Bulletin* 73, 13 June, https://www.cato.org/publications/free-trade-bulletin/trumps-first-trade-deal-slightly-revised-korea-us-free-trade, accessed 26 November 2021.

Ministry of Trade, Industry and Energy (MOTIE) (2018), '통상역량 강화를 위해 '신통상질서전략실' 신설한다' (To Create 'Office of International Trade and Legal Affairs' to Strengthen Trade Capacity), www.motie.go.kr/, accessed 26 November 2021.

MOTIE 2016, *Ministry of Trade, Industry and Energy (MOTIE)*, viewed 1 October 2020, <http://english.motie.go.kr/en/am/introduction/introduction.jsp>.

Nikkei Asian Review (2017), 'Park Scandal Leaves Korean Business Lobby in Shrunken Role' *Nikkei Asian Review*, 29 April, https://asia.nikkei.com/Business/Park-scandal-leaves-Korean-business-lobby-in-shrunken-role, accessed 26 November 2021.

Oh, C. (2013), '박근혜 정부, 대외경제정책도 MB와 선 긋기' (Park Geun-hye jeongbu, daeoegyeongjejeongchaekdo MBwa seon geutgi), *The Kyunghyang Shinmun*, 5 April, http://news.khan.co.kr/kh_news/khan_art_view.html?art_id=201304052155195#csidxad2b2232c23531196094ab83ce64f4d, accessed 26 November 2021.

Park, J. (2009), 한국 역대정권의 주요 경제정책 (*Hanguk yeokdaejeonggwonui juyo gyeongjejeongchaek*) (Seoul: KERI).

Park, J. (2017), '메가FTA시대 저물고 양자협정 시대로 … 정부, 동시다발적 개별FTA추진 배경' (Mega FTA Sidae jeomulgo yangjahyeopjeongui sidaero … jeongbu, dongsidabaljeok gaebyeo FTA chujin baegyeong', *JoongAng Ilbo*. 26 January, https://news.joins.com/article/21181468, accessed 26 November 2021.

Park, S., and Koo, M. (2007), 'Forming a Cross-Regional Partnership: The South Korea–Chile FTA and Its Implications', *Pacific Affairs* 80(2), 259–278.

Park, Y., and Moon, B. (2006), 'Korea's FTA Policy Structure', https://faculty.washington.edu/karyiu/confer/seoul06/papers/park-moon.pdf, accessed 26 November 2021.

Presidential Archives (1992), '북방경제정책의 성과와 추진방향' (Bukbanggyeongjejeongchaegui seonggwawa chujinbanghyang), https://www.pa.go.kr/research/contents/policy/index.jsp?scate=PS1_08&tcate=PS1_08_03, accessed 26 November 2021.

Presidential Decree (2017), No. 28211, National Law Information Center, https://www.law.go.kr/법령/대외경제장관회의규정, accessed 26 November 2021.

Saxer, C. (2013), 'Democratization, Globalization and the Linkage of Domestic and Foreign Policy in South Korea', *The Pacific Review* 26(2), 177–198.

Sohn, Y. (2019), 'South Korea under the United States–China Rivalry: Dynamics of the Economic–Security Nexus in Trade Policymaking', *The Pacific Review* 32(6), 1019–1040.

Solis, M. (2013), 'South Korea's Fateful Decision on the Trans-Pacific Partnership', Brookings Institute Policy Paper, no. 31, September https://www.brookings.edu/wp-content/uploads/2016/06/0918-south-korea-trans-pacific-partnership-solis.pdf, accessed 26 November 2021.

CHAPTER 35

THE SOUTH KOREAN DEVELOPMENT MODEL

EUN MEE KIM AND NANCY Y. KIM

1. INTRODUCTION

SOUTH Korea's spectacular rise from rags to riches in just a few short decades is certainly an appealing and inspirational development story. In the 1950s, following the Korean War, South Korea was one of the poorest countries in the world. It has a dramatic and tumultuous history of rapid and compressed economic development starting from extreme poverty during the 1950s. It was marred with a politically brutal and economically exploitative colonial period (1910–1945), and nearly 80 per cent of its economic capacity was destroyed during the Korean War (1950–1953), which has still not officially ended nearly seventy years after the armistice was signed in 1953. The country suffers from having relatively few natural resources. It has experienced a military-based authoritarian regime that lasted from 1961 to 1987. During the Asian Financial Crisis (1997–1998), its economy appeared to slow down once again. However, in spite of these tumultuous events, the country has achieved rapid industrialisation and a reduction of poverty in one generation and achieved democratisation through civil uprising. In 1996, it joined the Organisation for Economic Co-operation and Development (OECD) group of advanced economies, and by 2019, it was the tenth largest economy in the world. Between 1945 and 1999, South Korea received $12.7 billion in aid (KOICA History available at http://www.koica.go.kr/koica_en/3392/subview.do). When it joined the OECD Development Assistance Committee in 2010, it was the first major recipient to do so. It now disburses approximately $2 billion in aid annually to developing countries, including many that were wealthier than South Korea in the 1950s and 1960s (OECD Statistics, Creditor Reporting System, 2019; The World Bank, 2019). But is the South Korean development experience a model that can be replicated by other countries? Or was it a product of a unique set of factors and circumstances which cannot be emulated?

And if it is indeed a model, what are the critical features of the model? In this chapter, we argue that South Korea's development was not an accident of history or nature; it developed by pursuing a deliberate, planned approach which enabled it to transcend the factors and circumstances with which it was initially endowed. We highlight in particular three core features of this approach: (a) state-led economic development; (b) social development and capability enhancement; and (c) strategic use of aid for development.

We also address the issue of the applicability of the South Korean development model—in the context of the changing nature and purported decline of the developmental state, as well as South Korea's growing aid programme, via which it actively, but not always consistently, promotes its development model. This brings South Korea's development story full circle, as large inflows of foreign aid and South Korea's strategic use of such aid were critical to its development. This makes South Korea a particularly politic poster child for the aid and development cooperation community, which struggles to find examples of aid effectiveness. That South Korea is eager to share and promote its path to development through its own growing aid programme enhances the appeal of the South Korean development model. However, we caution against the notion of a one-size-fits-all model. Indeed, the evolution of the South Korean developmental state—from its earlier authoritarian, neo-mercantilist iteration to its current democratic and globalised model—is a testament to the fact that development is a contextual, adaptive process.

This chapter is structured as follows. Section 2 lays out the key features of South Korea's development model. Section 3 then explores inconsistencies and ambiguities of the South Korean development story, which some see as invalidating it as a model. Section 4 reconsiders these ambiguities and argues that they can be reinterpreted as evidence of South Korea's constructive, balanced, and bridging role in development and development cooperation. We recommend that South Korea pursue its middle power and development cooperation ambitions via this 'middle way'. A concluding section summarises the key points.

2. Features of the South Korean Development Model

Like other emerging donors (e.g. China, Brazil, Russia), South Korea is eager to supply 'new narratives of development and globalisation' (Fourie 2017; Mawdsley 2012). More so than many other countries, it has a credible development story to tell, having been the first major recipient country to 'graduate' to the OECD Development Assistance Committee in 2010. South Korea actively promotes its development experience through its official development assistance (ODA) programme, which has steadily increased in volume from US$23.5 million in 1987 to US$1.8 billion in 2013—growth of nearly seventy-five times in twenty-six years, which is one of the fastest ODA growth rates among emerging donors (Stallings and Kim 2017). Below we describe the key and widely acknowledged features of South Korea's development model, including its economic and social development mandates and strategic use of aid for development.

2.1 State-Led Economic Development

Perhaps the best-known feature of South Korea's development model is its state-led economic development. This is widely considered to have emerged in the 1960s under the Park Chung-hee regime (1961–1979) as the primary ambition and strategy of his developmental state. However, the years following independence from Japan and preceding the Park regime (1945–1961) are instructive as a foil against which to illustrate the economic development orientation of the developmental state. The Rhee Syngman (1945–1960) and Chang Myon (1960–1961) regimes were also statist in that the state directed and intervened in the economy. But that direction was personalistic rather than nationalist. Government and business elites (Chaebols) colluded to line their own pockets (including with diverted foreign aid), rather than collaborating to achieve national economic development (Woo 1991). The developmental state is all the more compelling as a model because it was so clearly and deliberately launched in 1961 as a repudiation of the classically corrupt, rent-seeking, underdeveloped state that preceded it.

Park Chung-hee came to power through a military coup in 1961, and from the outset linked the legitimacy of his regime to achieving national 'economic self-sufficiency and prosperity' (Park 1966). Park's first order of business was to refashion the corrupt, collusive, and co-dependent state–Chaebol relations that pervaded by disciplining Chaebols by charging them with illicit accumulation of wealth; asserting the state as the lead partner in the relationship; and then co-opting the most promising Chaebol to work towards the national economic development project (Amsden 1989; Glassman and Choi 2014; Kim 1997). Through a newly established bureaucracy, including the Economic Planning Board (EPB), the Ministry of Finance, and the Ministry of Commerce and Industry, the developmental state took firm control of both long-term planning (via Five Year Economic Development Plans) and implementation (via allocation of domestic and foreign capital and facilitation of access to technology and markets) (Kim 1997).

A prime example of state-planned and led economic development was the South Korean government's pursuit of heavy and chemical industries (HCI) development in the 1970s eschewing mainstream economic theory and advice that this would run counter to South Korea's comparative advantage. HCI, of course, ultimately formed the backbone of the modern South Korean economy—steel, shipbuilding, cars, etc. (Amsden 1989; Stallings and Kim 2017; Stern et al. 1995). The role of the state is perhaps more obvious in the authoritarian developmental state years. But the end of the strongman state was not the end of the developmental state. Developmental state-led development has continued since South Korea's democratic transition in 1987. Even the

International Monetary Fund (IMF)-advised economic liberalisation undertaken by the Kim Dae-jung regime in the aftermath of the Asian Financial Crisis (AFC) has been shown to be 'shaped by an active state' (Kalinowski 2008). Thus, it is not surprising to find that, despite the newfound independence of the Bank of Korea, the state continues to influence the financial sector through the Financial Supervisory Commission (Lim and Lee 2009) and by tolerating preferential access to finance for Chaebols (Witt 2015). Nor is it surprising that the Ministry of Strategy and Finance has taken on the influential finance and budget planning functions of the former Ministry of Finance and Economy and the Ministry of Planning and Budget; or that industrial policy planning continues via sectoral agencies in lieu of the dismantled EPB (Witt 2015; Wong 2004).

Proponents of South Korea's developmental state model highlight the benefits of a strong (capable, meritocratic) state that plays a prominent role in the economy, including economic planning in the long-term national interest that transcends short-term interests; coordination of political and economic actors around the plan/strategy; and country ownership and channelling of finance, including foreign aid (Amsden 1989; Kim 1997; Stallings and Kim 2017). They view state interventions as producing 'higher and more equal growth than otherwise would have occurred' (World Bank 1993 cited in Chang 2009).

South Korea's record-breaking economic success is seen as a validation of its state-led economic development approach. Per capita gross national income increased 500-fold from $76 in 1953 to over $33,000 in 2018 (Bank of Korea, cited in Park 2019). From one of the poorest countries in the world in the 1950s, it has become the tenth largest economy in the world (World Bank 2019). When South Korea joined the Development Assistance Committee (DAC) of the OECD in 2010, it was the first country to transition from major aid recipient to DAC member since its establishment in 1961.

Together with the state-led economic development successes of China and Japan, South Korea's development narrative is recounted by critics of the Washington Consensus to disrupt its 'neoliberal prescriptions for development' (Doucette 2020). South Korea is seen as having achieved the economic successes described above as a result of throwing off the neoliberal-prescribed 'golden straightjacket' (Chang 2010). While South Korea itself is more 'veiled' in its critique of the hitherto mainstream neoliberal orthodoxy, it also seems to conceive of and present its economic development model as an 'alternative'—an alternative that is to 'theory-oriented policy recommendations from advanced countries' (Korean Development Institute 201, cited in Doucette 2020).

Interest in South Korea's economic development model has grown since the early 2000s as the Washington Consensus loses currency as a one-size-fits-all development model. The developmental state model—and particularly its economic and industrial policies—have been emulated by developing countries in Asia, Africa, and Latin America (Childs and Hearn 2017; De Waal 2013; Edigheji 2010; Mkandawire 2001; OECD–DAC 2012). In 2018, the President of the African Development Bank cited South Korea as 'a perfect model' for Africa's economic development. (African Development Bank 2018, cited in Kim 2019).

2.2 Social Development and Capability Enhancement

While the economic development ambitions of South Korea's developmental state are widely studied and acknowledged as its top priority, the social development narrative is still evolving. Much of the developmental state literature focuses on the suppression of labour rights and wages in support of export-led industrialisation and economic growth (Kim 1997; Vogel and Lindauer 1997). Statistics such as the number of hours worked per week (longest of any nation in the 1970s and 1980s) (ILO 1970; ILO 1980), wage level (minimal increases, and even real wage decreases, in the 1960s, despite increasing labour productivity) (Choi 1989; Kim 1997), and public social spending (3.4 per cent of gross domestic product (GDP), well below the OECD average of 17.4 per cent, in 1997) (OECD 2020a) provide support for this narrative.

On the other hand, the developmental state envisioned from the outset that national economic development should benefit the entire society, albeit via a trickle-down, business-first and growth-first process. This was evident in Park Chung-hee's personal commitment to eradicating poverty (Kim 1997); and his successor Chun Doo-hwan's statements that 'economic stability is the very core of welfare' and that 'a system of welfare that is ... suited to our realities ... should be based on stable economic growth and equal job opportunities for all people' (Chun 1984). These were not just empty promises by the developmental state. It delivered handily on poverty alleviation, reducing the poverty rate from 60 to 70 per cent in the mid-1960s to under 4 per cent in the mid-1990s (Henderson et al. 2002).

Taking a broader and more structural human development perspective, we can see that South Korea's development model included 'renowned levels of investment in human capital' (Evans 2014). Indeed, even as early as 1945–1948, the US military government-advised regime which preceded the developmental state adopted a 'Koreanisation' policy which included education of manpower at all levels (Kim and Kim 2014). In addition to targeting poverty alleviation and meeting basic consumptions needs, development prior to the 1960s paid early and intensive attention to education and laid the groundwork for the South Korean developmental state to successfully pursue long-term economic development via industrialisation from the 1960s. It achieved universal primary and secondary education by 1960 and 1980, respectively (Ministry of Education, Republic of Korea 2015); increased health care coverage from 0.06 per cent in 1970 to 92 per cent in 1989 (Economic Planning Board 1990); and extended life expectancy from sixteen years below the OECD average in 1960 to two years above the average today (OECD 2020b). Moreover, and counter to global trend, South Korea's spectacular economic growth has been accompanied by relatively equal income distribution compared to other countries that have experienced rapid development, such as those in Latin America (Kim et al. 2011; Siddiqi and Hertzman 2001). Indeed, it is lauded as one of a few exceptional success stories in achieving 'growth with equity' (World Bank 1993, cited in Lee 1996).

The limited attention to South Korea's social development mandate—as compared to its economic development mandate—may stem in part from lack of consensus regarding its welfare regime. The jury is still out regarding whether South Korea is an underdeveloped version of one of three ideal-typical welfare regimes: liberal, conservative/corporatist, social democratic (Esping-Andersen 1990) or an altogether different model, such as developmental-productivist (Holliday 2011; Kim et al. 2014; Rudra 2007) or Confucian-familial (Finer 1993; Gould 1993). Lee (2014) posits that the South Korean welfare regime may indeed depart from the traditional 'Eurocentric' welfare regime types—that low public social spending does not tell the full story. Rather than direct provision of social benefits, the South Korean state ensured welfare through regulation, which shifted some of the welfare burden onto the private sector (Kim et al. 2014; Lee 2014). That the South Korean developmental state supported (via subsidies, tax relief, and other measures) selected businesses and industries to grow is widely agreed. In turn, however, business was expected—and even regulated—to share some of its gains with society through employment (e.g. full employment, lifelong employment) and financing of occupational (employment-based) social insurance (e.g. sickness, unemployment) programmes (Kim et al. 2014; Lee 2014). In addition, the South Korean state also co-opted the voluntary (non-governmental organisation) sector to shoulder some of the administrative burden of implementing welfare programmes (Kim et al. 2014). Kim et al. (2014) compellingly depict the South Korean state's early efforts at social policy—in fact, initiated by the First Republic and consolidated by the developmental state, whereby businesses were the state's instruments of financing social services and voluntary agencies were the state's instruments of delivering (relatively cheaply) social services.

Increasingly, the government has taken on more direct responsibility for welfare provision. From 1985 to 1995, there was significant expansion (over 25 per cent) of social spending in South Korea alongside democratisation and civil society mobilisation (Evans 2014). Social protection continued to expand in subsequent decades, concurrent with economic growth and expanding government fiscal space. While the delivery channels and spending figures have evolved over time, the key take-away is that South Korea's development model did indeed '[reflect] the desire to extend benefits to all of society ... [including] minimum living standards for all ... [and] human-resource development' (World Bank 2004). Through a variety of state-led, business-financed and civil society-implemented arrangements, the South Korean developmental state has prioritised and achieved key human development outcomes.

While less prominent, and sometimes considered constitutive of its economic development model, at least certain elements of South Korea's social development model are globally recognised. In particular, South Korea's human resource development strategies are widely promoted and studied. Education is the second largest sector to which South Korea allocates its ODA (OECD 2021); and South Korea is among the top ten bilateral education aid donors (*Education at a Glance* 2021). The government of South Korea promotes education as 'the driving force for the development of Korea' and seeks to share its 'virtuous cycle of educational development and national development' with the international community (Ministry of Education, Republic of Korea 2015).

2.3 Strategic Use of Aid and Other Flows

A final and compelling component of South Korea's development model is that large inflows of foreign aid and South Korea's strategic use of such aid were critical to its development. This makes South Korea a particularly politic poster child for the foreign aid community, which struggles to find examples of aid effectiveness. In particular, proponents of South Korea's development model highlight the importance of country ownership and strategic use of diverse aid and other flows.

South Korea is seen as a pioneer in pursuing country ownership of aid—decades before it became a part of development cooperation best practice via the 2005 Paris Declaration on Aid Effectiveness (Kim et al. 2013). Policies were localised or translated, rather than unilaterally transferred and aid was assimilated, coordinated, and deployed to support host country (rather than donor country) priorities and objectives (Stallings and Kim 2017; Kim 2014). Indeed, as early as the Rhee regime, the country pushed back on the United States, its primary donor at the time, most notably refusing to integrate South Korea into a regional Co-Prosperity Sphere with Japan (Woo 1991). The Park regime was even more assertive in efforts to lessen dependence on and increase ownership of foreign aid. Park's developmental state was a 'tough negotiator' (Kim and Kim 2014) with donors, and consequently was able to use aid for its own economic development priorities rather than just accepting (often short-term, consumption-boosting) activities pushed by donors (Stallings and Kim 2017). For example, the Park regime pursued heavy and chemical industries (HCI) development in the 1970s, in spite of major donors' refusal to support the initiative because of South Korea's lack of comparative advantage. When the United States declined to finance the Pohang Iron and Steel Mill project, a lynchpin of South Korea's HCI drive, it sought and secured funding from Japan instead as part of the reparation fund for the Japanese Colonial Period (Kim and Kim 2014). Other examples of South Korean aid ownership include its selectivity in engaging foreign technical advisors to help develop the Korea Institute of Science and Technology (Stallings and Kim 2017); its development of the Korean Cable Company (Kim et al. 2013); and its construction of the Seoul–Busan Expressway Project (Kim et al. 2013).

Another way in which South Korea strategically leveraged aid for development was its effective and differential stewardship of grants, concessional loans, and other official flows. From 1945 to 1999, South Korea received 55 and 45 per cent of its total aid via grants and concessional loans, respectively (Chun et al. 2010). This is a much larger share of concessional loans than the current global norm (more than 80 per cent of bilateral ODA-delivered via grants) (OECD–DAC 2008). South Korea also made strategic use of other financial flows, such as foreign investment. With its strict state control of finance, it was able to allocate foreign and domestic capital to support its industrial policies (Kim et al. 2013). From 1945 to 1960, South Korea was primarily focused on escaping poverty and it was able to do so utilising grant aid (Lee 2014). Later, during the developmental state era (from 1961), concessional loans overtook grant aid and South Korea productively used these, other official flows, foreign direct investment (FDI), and trade to achieve record-breaking economic growth (Lee 2014). Now, as a donor, South Korea delivers a relatively large portion of ODA via concessional loans; and links its ODA to FDI and trade, the so-called trinity approach to economic development cooperation (Stallings and Kim 2017).

Country ownership and diversification of development finance are currently relevant and still evolving issues in the development sector. South Korea is one of the most credible advocates of these approaches, having recently and successfully applied them as an aid recipient; and now as a donor, at least in principle, offering aid to developing-country partners on these terms. South Korea has also played a key role in facilitating constructive dialogue on these issues amongst development actors with divergent positions, most notably while advocating for a shift in paradigm from aid effectiveness to development effectiveness at the Fourth High Level Forum on Aid Effectiveness (Kim et al. 2013; Kim and Lee 2013). However, while many developing countries naturally welcome the greater autonomy and expanded options inherent in the principles of aid ownership and diversification, as we discuss in the next section, South Korea's actions as a donor are not always consistent with its experiences as a recipient.

3. AMBIGUITY AND INCONSISTENCY OF SOUTH KOREA'S DEVELOPMENT MODEL

Notwithstanding the economic and human development successes of South Korea, the applicability, desirability, and even existence of its development model have been challenged. In this section, we describe the challenges in delineating a South Korean development model via the exploration of several conceptual inconsistencies. Some of the inconsistencies relate to South Korea's 'double transition' since the 1990s towards economic liberalism and democracy (Kim and Kim 2014), which some see as a repudiation of South Korea's authoritarian, mercantilist developmental state. Another inconsistency is not exclusive to South Korea. As with most donors, there is some ambiguity regarding South Korea's motives for giving aid—whether recipient needs or donor interests come first. As we describe in further detail below, it is not always easy to discern a clear South Korean development model because the country does not always put forward a consistent narrative.

3.1 The 'Double Transition' Dilemma

One particular contention is that economic reforms adopted by South Korea in the aftermath of the AFC signal the end of South Korea's developmental state; and that its very demise challenges its viability as a development model (Pirie 2007, 2016). The dismantling of the EPB, the state's looser grip on finance, and a more welcoming stance on FDI are all seen as examples of the developmental state ceding power to the market (Kim 1997). The neoliberal camp actively promotes this view, for example, the IMF's endorsement of South Korea as a successful case of trade liberalisation (Doucette 2020).

Even some who accept that South Korea's economic development was state-led hesitate to promote it as a model. They believe that the pathways pursued by South Korea are no longer open to others—that South Korea's unorthodox neo-mercantilist policies were tolerated by global powers like the United States due to Cold War dynamics (i.e. U.S. desire to keep allies in their camp); and because it was an *early* late industrialiser (i.e. it was one of just a few rising competitors and thus not a significant threat to the developed world) (Kim and Kim 2014). This variant of the neoliberal challenge to South Korea's developmental state model posits that the hegemony of economic liberalism—as upheld by the (holy or unholy, depending on one's view of neoliberalism) trinity of international organisations, the World Trade Organisation, the IMF, and the World Bank—makes it difficult to pursue statist, protectionist economic strategies (Kim and Kim 2014).

South Korea's other transition—towards democracy—is the basis for another major challenge to South Korea's developmental state model. The democratic camp questions the desirability and continuity of South Korea's original authoritarian developmental state. Certainly, the first few decades of South Korean development were marked by low wages, poor working conditions, and limited labour rights (Kim 1997). Some describe South Korea's economic development as having been built on the backs of suppressed and exploited workers (Kim and Park 2011; Kwon 2020). Anti-authoritarian challengers to the developmental state argue that authoritarianism is 'an utterly immoral system of government'. Hence, neither authoritarianism nor the developmental state, with its authoritarian antecedents, should be tolerated as a viable form of political, social, or economic governance (Kim and Kim 2014).

The democratic camp celebrates South Korea's democratic transition and consolidation. The inclusion of labour unions in the Tripartite Commission in 1998, the recognition of an independent umbrella labour union (the Korean Confederation of Trade Unions) in 1999, and the founding of the Democratic Labor Party in 2000 are cited assigns of increased labour power (Kalinowski 2009: 292). More broadly, civil society organisations (CSOs) have become more active in serving as watchdogs and whistle-blowers to hold government accountable and check the power of Chaebols (Lee 2005: 297–298). Similar to neoliberal interpretations of South Korea's economic liberalisation, these and other political reforms in South Korea are viewed as a repudiation of the developmental state model (Kim and Kim 2014).

South Korea tends to gloss over these inconsistencies. The South Korean development model is set forth as an 'alternative to traditional development models ... but the prescriptive content of what that alternative is remains obscure' (Doucette 2020). This may be from a reluctance to critique prevailing market-based approaches to development and/or due to a real ambivalence in understanding how and in what ways South Korea's development has been driven by state intervention versus market-led approaches (Doucette 2020). This leads to incongruities such as South Korea's Knowledge Sharing

Programme (a flagship initiative launched in 2004, through which South Korea exports its development experience) introducing the successes of South Korea's EPB to developing economies, while informing them of the 'adverse effects of planning' and encouraging them to follow market-led growth (Doucette 2020).

South Korea also employs this 'non-approach' of ignoring away an issue in dealing with the developmental state's authoritarian history. Cultural explanations—for example, Asian or Confucian values such as self-sacrifice and diligence—are sometimes used to explain the human toll of national development while glossing over the coercive, human rights-abusing elements of the developmental state (Doucette 2020). Modularising and presenting the South Korean development model in technical, 'politically odourless' terms is another way in which South Korea masks the role that authoritarianism and oppression played in its development (Kim 2019). The sterilisation of the controversial, politically motivated and politically manipulated (i.e. to rally rural support for the authoritarian Park regime) Saemaul Movement and its subsequent export as a grassroots community/rural development programme is one example of 'camouflaging' by 'rendering technical' (Kim 2019; Doucette and Muller 2016).

3.2 Disentangling Aid Motivations

As with many other donors, South Korea is charged with being inconsistent in its aid motives. Within the wide body of literature, there is evidence that South Korea's aid is motivated by geopolitical/middle power ambitions (Hwang 2014; Kim and Gray 2016), national economic interests (Kalinowski and Park 2016; Park and Lee 2015), humanitarian needs (Kim and Oh 2012), and even the personal and political agendas of presidents (Kim and Oh 2012; Mawdsley et al. 2017). This 'kitchen sink' approach to aid giving is not uncommon among donors, but poses a particular problem for South Korea because it brands its aid as empathetic and 'reflect[ing] the needs of the recipient country rather than those of the donor' (Kim and Garland 2019; Mawdsley 2012).

On the other hand, and in common with fellow Asian donors China and Japan, South Korea advocates the principle of mutual benefit through development cooperation (Mawdsley 2012). While this is couched in terms of solidarity (i.e. shared experiences as developing countries) and rejecting the hierarchical relations imposed by traditional donors (Mawdsley 2012), in reality this is often an excuse for the unabashed pursuit of donor interests. For example, South Korea prioritises aid to relatively high-income countries with which it trades and in which it invests, rather than to countries with the most development need (Kim and Oh 2012; Lee 2012). Given this commercial motivation, a large portion of South Korean aid is tied, allocated to economic infrastructure, and delivered via concessional loans. ODA is thus synergised with trade and FDI to expand business opportunities for South Korean companies.

Taking a more critical stance, Kim and Garland (2019) view South Korean attempts to market its goods and services to developing countries via aid as 'neo-colonial' (i.e. the giver has a certain amount of control over the resources or economy of the receiver and uses such control to achieve goals that are not in the best interest of the receiver, and the benefits to the giver outweigh those to the receiver). In a similar vein, Kim (2019) portrays South Korea's promotion of its development model—including by appealing to common legacies of colonialism and poverty—as 'embedded in its global aim of expanding its realm of influence'. While these perspectives are perhaps overly harsh and judge South Korea by more stringent standards than other donors, they serve to caution South Korea against veering from experience-sharing to narcissism (Kim and Garland 2019), or from mutual benefit to extraction.

4. Middle Power, Middle Way Forward

Having 'graduated' from major aid recipient to major donor, South Korea is justifiably proud of, and actively promotes, its development experience through its development cooperation programme. However, as we discuss in section 3, there are inconsistencies in South Korea's development and development cooperation narratives. We argue in this section that these inconsistencies are a natural outgrowth of a dynamic, adaptive development process; and that ambiguity (in the sense of being open to several possibilities) may be a better development norm than ideology.

Some consider South Korea's development model to be ambiguous because it employed a wide and diverse range of development theories, strategies, and modalities. We posit that the evolution of South Korea's development model—and the conceptual inconsistencies which stem from dynamic, adaptive development—is a key strength, rather than a sign of weakness. South Korea has successfully developed by evolving and adapting to domestic and external circumstances. This is why it is so difficult to pin down the South Korean development model. There is no fixed model; there have been different iterations that have used different strategies under different circumstances at different times.

Similarly, there is no fixed ideology. South Korea has been opportunistic about harnessing ideologies and strategies to achieve national development. With national development as the goal, the developmental state is open to a wide array of ideologies and approaches. Neomercantilism, neoliberalism, productive welfare, protective welfare— to the South Korean developmental state, these are all potential means to an end (national development). Thus, post-AFC, the South Korean developmental state used neoliberal reforms to 'discipline the Korean *chaebol* to become viable global businesses' (i.e. able to participate in and profit from the international market system without relying on state subsidies and protection) (Kim 1997); while also extending protective welfare to cover the larger number of people made vulnerable by the AFC and South Korea's neoliberal response. The Green New Deal that has recently emerged to spur the recovery of the economy after the COVID-19 pandemic looks to be a shift back to infant industry protection, this time of digital and green technology industries (Kalinowski 2021). In this era of digital and green growth, however, the South Korean developmental state will focus more on providing access to 'inputs' that enable innovation and development of high-technology industries (e.g., research and development, ecosystem/networking), rather than directing capital for large-scale manufacturing facilities as in the past (Kim 2012; Wong 2004).

Perhaps rather than trying to distil a South Korean development model and establish the primacy of one approach over another (e.g. loans over grants, economic over social infrastructure), the South Korean experience is more useful as a reminder that development is highly contextual and that different development approaches may work for different countries at different stages of development. In this vein, Kim, Kim, and Kim (2013) propose that South Korea should develop and share various development alternatives or options, rather than a one-size-fits-all model; and Kim and Lee (2013) view South Korea as playing an important 'bridging' role between developed and developing countries; and traditional (DAC) and emerging (South–South Development Cooperation) donors. South Korea is uniquely suited to such a role, as it has itself been open to, and employed, a wide range of approaches in its development and development cooperation efforts. It has not constrained itself by taking unnecessarily polarized or ideological positions on grants versus loans (it received and gives ODA fairly evenly, split between the two modalities); social versus economic (in 2018, it allocated 34 per cent of ODA to social infrastructure and services and humanitarian aid and 54 per cent to economic infrastructure and production) (OECD 2021); recipient needs versus donor interests (it advocates mutual benefit); etc. In fact, with the shift in paradigm from aid effectiveness to development effectiveness that is currently underway, more development partners are moving towards the balanced, pragmatic position that South Korea has occupied for some time. Such a role of promoting an open, balanced approach to development—a 'middle' way—also befits the middle-power status of South Korea.

5. Conclusion

This chapter has summarised the critical features of South Korea's development model. We posit that South Korea's transformation from one of the poorest countries in the world in the 1950s to the tenth largest economy in the world in 2019 was shepherded by the developmental state—in particular, the developmental state's attention to both economic and social facets of nation building, as well as its ability to continually adapt development approaches to evolving development needs and priorities. The phenomenal success of South Korea's 'miracle on the Han River', as well as its strategic use of foreign aid to achieve that success, make it a storied development model. The depressingly limited number of development (and particularly aid) success stories contributes to the allure of the South Korean model. As an increasingly generous and confident donor, and with the commendable intention of giving back what it received in the past, South Korea now actively promotes its development model. Some see it as one of several Asian donors that is leading a 'silent aid revolution' (Woods 2008) which provides alternatives to the Washington Consensus' overly prescriptive 'golden straightjacket' (Friedman 1999) approach to development.

The South Korean development model is not without its detractors. Various inconsistencies and ambiguities—particularly related to South Korea's double transition of economic liberalisation and democratisation—are seen as invalidating the existence of a development model. Its own inconsistent and avoidant (i.e. glossing over hard-to-incorporate issues such as the developmental state's authoritarian history) recounting of its development story also makes it difficult to discern a clear development model. With this in mind, we urge caution in promoting a one-size-fits-all South Korean development model. As the South Korean experience aptly demonstrates, development is a highly context-specific and evolving process. Crucial to successful, sustainable development—of the kind achieved by South Korea —is the willingness and ability to consider and draw on a diverse range of ideologies, strategies, and approaches. Through this lens, we can make sense of the South Korean development model's various and seemingly incongruent iterations. Neo-mercantilist, neoliberal, neo-developmental, export-led growth, green growth—these are all testament to the ideological freedom and flexibility of South Korea's developmental state-led development model. The primary ideology and raison d'etre of a developmental state, after all, is development.

The pathways to development are many and varied. South Korea's development model is most helpful when viewed in stages—various iterations of the developmental state employed a range of policies and measures at different stages of development. However, all of this was done—under democratic and undemocratic regimes alike—with the ultimate aim of nation building, which encompasses the notion of enhancing the capabilities of all those that make up the nation (i.e. human development) (Evans 2014; Igbafen 2014). This reminder to the development community to keep its eye on the prize (development) rather than the game (development ideologies) comes at an opportune time, as the decades-long primacy of the Washington Consensus loses currency and the conception of development moves beyond economic development to multi-dimensional human development. Having achieved both economic and social development in record time, and if it can continue to expand and deliver multidimensional well-being without ideological stagnation, South Korea does indeed offer a credible development model worthy of study and contextualised application.

Bibliography

Acharya, A., Fuzzo de Lima, A. T., and Moore, M. (2006), 'Proliferation and Fragmentation: Transaction Costs and the Value of Aid', *Journal of Development Studies* 42(1), 1–21.

African Development Bank (2018), 'Korea Is a Model for Africa's Industrialization, Says President Adesina', 22 May, https://am.afdb.org/en/press-releases/korea-model-africas-industrialization-sayspresident-adesina, accessed 27 November 2021.

Amsden, A. H. (1989), *Asia's Next Giant: South Korea and Late Industrialization* (New York: Oxford University Press).

Chang, D. (2009), *Capitalist Development in South Korea: Labour, Capital and the Myth of the Developmental State* (London: Routledge).
Chang, H. J. (2010), *Bad Samaritans: The Myth of Free Trade and the Secret History of Capitalism* (New York: Bloomsbury Press).
Childs, J., and Hearn, J. (2017), ' "New" Nations: Resource-Based Development Imaginaries in Ghana and Ecuador', *Third World Quarterly* 38(4), 844–861.
Choi, C. J. (1989), *Labor and the Authoritarian State: Labor Unions in South Korean Manufacturing Industries, 1961–1980* (Seoul: Korea University Press).
Chun, D. H. (1984), *Towards Peace and Prosperity: The President's Annual Summer Press Conference* (Seoul: Korea Overseas Information Service).
Chun, H.-M., Munyi, E. N., and Lee, H. (2010), 'South Korea as an Emerging Donor: Challenges and Changes on Its Entering OECD/DAC', *Journal of International Development* 22(6), 788–802.
De Waal, A. (2013), 'The Theory and Practice of Meles Zenawi', *African Affairs* 112(446), 148–155.
Doucette, J. (2020), 'Anxieties of an Emerging Donor: The Korean Development Experience and the Politics of International Development Cooperation', *EPC: Politics and Space* 38(4), 656–673.
Doucette, J., and Muller, A. R. (2016), 'Exporting the *Saemaul* Spirit: South Korea's Knowledge Sharing Program and the "Rendering Technical" of Korean Development', *Geoforum* 75, 29–39.
Economic Planning Board (1990), *Major Statistics of the Korean Economy* (Seoul: Economic Planning Board).
Edigheji, O. (ed.) (2010), *Constructing a Democratic Developmental State in South Africa: Potentials and Challenges* (Cape Town: HSRC Press).
Education At a Glance (2021), 'Donor Tracker', 19 February 2021, https://donortracker.org/sector/education, accessed 27 November 2021.
Esping-Anderson, G. (1990), *The Three Worlds of Welfare Capitalism* (Princeton, NJ: Princeton University Press).
Evans, P.B. (2014), 'The Capability Enhancing Developmental State: Concepts and National Trajectories', in E. M. Kim and P. H. Kim, eds, *The South Korean Development Experience: Beyond Aid*, 83–110 (London: Palgrave Macmillan).
Finer, C. J. (1999), 'Trends and Developments in Welfare States', in J. Clasen, ed., *Comparative Social Policy: Concepts, Theories and Methods*, 15–33 (Oxford: Blackwell).
Fourie, E. (2017), 'The Intersection of East Asian and African Modernities: Towards a New Research Agenda', *Social Imaginaries* 3(1), 119–146.
Friedman, T. (1999), *The Lexus and the Olive Tree* (New York: Farrar, Straus, Giroux).
Glassman, J., and Young-Jin Choi. (2014), 'The Chaebol and the US Military—Industrial Complex: Cold War Geopolitical Economy and South Korean Iindustrialization.' *Environment and Planning A* 46(5), 1160–1180.
Gould, A. (1993), *Capitalist Welfare Systems: A Comparison of Japan, Britain and Sweden* (London: Longman).
Henderson, J., Hulme, D., Phillips, R., and Kim, E. M. (2002), *Economic Governance and Poverty Reduction in South Korea*. Manchester Business School, University of Manchester Business School Working Papers. No. 439.
Hwang, K. D. (2014), 'Korea's Soft Power as an Alternative Approach to Africa in Development Cooperation: Beyond Economic Interest-Led Perspectives of Korea–Africa Relations?', *African and Asian Studies* 13(3), 249–271.

Igbafen, M. L. (2014), 'South Korea's Development Experience as an Aid Recipient: Lessons for Sub-Saharan Africa', in *The South Korean Development Experience*, pp. 111–135 (Palgrave Macmillan, London).

International Labour Office (ILO) (1970, 1980, 1990, 1991), *Yearbook of Labour Statistics* (Geneva: International Labour Office).

Jeong, U. J. (2010), 'Successful Asian Recipient Countries: Case Studies of Korea and Vietnam', International Development Cooperation, KOICA (March).

Kalinowski, T. (2008), 'Korea's Recovery since the 1997/98 Financial Crisis: The Last Stage of the Developmental State', *New Political Economy* 13(4), 447–462.

Kalinowski, T. (2009), 'The Politics of Market Reforms: Korea's Path from Chaebol Republic to Market Democracy and Back', *Contemporary Politics* 15(3), 287–304.

Kalinowski, T. (2021), 'The Politics of Climate Change in a Neo-Developmental State: The Case of South Korea', *International Political Science Review* 42(1), 48–63.

Kalinowski, T., and Park, M. (2016), 'South Korean Development Cooperation in Africa: The Legacy of a Developmental State', *Africa Spectrum* 51(3), 61–75.

Kim, E. M. (1997), *Big Business, Strong State: Collusion and Conflict in South Korean Development, 1960–1990* (Albany, NY: State University of New York Press).

Kim, S. Y. (2012), 'Transitioning from Fast-Follower to Innovator: The Institutional Foundations of the Korean Telecommunications Sector', *Review of International Political Economy* 19(1), 140–168.

Kim, T. K. (2014), 'Learning through Localizing International Transfers: South Korea's Development Experiences', in I. C. Yi and T. Mkandawire, eds, *Learning from the South Korean Developmental Success*, 1st edn, 216–234 (Geneva: United Nations Research Institute for Social Development).

Kim, S. W. (2019), 'The Misadventure of Korea Aid: Developmental Soft Power and the Troubling Motives of an Emerging Donor', *Third World Quarterly* 40(11), 2052–2070.

Kim, W. K., and Kim, I.C. (2008), 'Hangook sanupjungchekui gwaguwa hyunje geurigo mire (Korea's Industrial Policy – Past, Present, Future)', *E-KIET Sanupkyungjejungbo*, 379, 1–6.

Kim, E. M., and Park, G. S. (2011), 'The Chaebol', in B. K. Kim and E. F. Vogel, eds, *The Park Chung Hee Era: The Transformation of South Korea*, 265–294 (Cambridge, MA: Harvard University Press).

Kim, E. M., and Oh, J. (2012), 'Determinants of Foreign Aid: The Case of South Korea', *Journal of East Asian Studies* 12(2), 251–274.

Kim, E. M., and Lee, J. E. (2013), 'Busan and Beyond: South Korea and the Transition from Aid Effectiveness to Development Effectiveness', *Journal of International Development* 24, 787–801.

Kim, E. M., and Kim, P. H. (2014), *The South Korean Development Experience: Beyond Aid* (London: Palgrave Macmillan).

Kim, S. Y., and Gray, K. (2016), 'Overseas Development Aid as Spatial Fix? Examining South Korea's Africa Policy', *Third World Quarterly* 37(4), 649–664.

Kim, J. H., and Garland, J. (2019), 'Development Cooperation and Postcolonial Critique: An Investigation into the South Korean Model', *Third World Quarterly* 40(7), 1246–1264.

Kim, T. K., Kwon, H. J., Lee, J. H., and Yi, I. C. (2011), 'Poverty, Inequality, and Democracy: "Mixed Governance" and Welfare in South Korea', *Journal of Democracy* 22(3), 120–134.

Kim, E. M., Kim, P. H., and Kim, J. K. (2013), 'From Development to Development Cooperation: Foreign Aid, Country Ownership, and the Developmental State in South Korea', *Pacific Review* 26(3), 313–336.

Kwon, P. B. (2020), 'Building Bombs, Building a Nation: The State, Chaebŏl, and the Militarized Industrialization of South Korea, 1973–1979', *Journal of Asian Studies* 79(1), 51–75.

Lee, J. W. (1996), 'Economic Growth and Human Development in the Republic of Korea, 1945–1992', Background paper for the UNDP Human Development Report 1996, UNDP Occasional Paper 24.

Lee, K. W. (2012), 'Do Emerging Donors Allocate Aid as DAC Members Do? The Case of Korea in the Millennium Era', *Journal of International Development* 24, 977–988.

Lee, J. H. (2014), 'Institutional Linkages between Social Protection Measures and Industrialization in South Korea', in I. C. Yi and T. Mkandawire, eds, *Learning from the South Korean Developmental Success*, 1st edn, 91–107 (Geneva: United Nations Research Institute for Social Development).

Lim, H. R., and Lee, H. N. (2009), 'Political Economy of Financial Supervisory Reform in Korea', *Journal of Korean Politics* 18(1), 119–146.

Mawdsley, E. (2012), *From Recipients to Donors: Emerging Powers and the Changing Development Landscape* (London: Zed Books).

Mawdsley, E., Kim, S. M., and Marcondes, D. (2017), 'Political Leadership and "Non-Traditional" Development Cooperation', *Third World Quarterly* 38(10), 2171–2186.

Ministry of Education, Republic of Korea (2015), *Education, the Driving Force for Development of Korea* (Seoul: Ministry of Education).

Mkandawire T. (2001), 'Thinking about Developmental States in Africa', *Cambridge Journal of Economics* 25(3), 289–314.

Organisation for Economic Co-operation and Development (OECD–DAC) (2008), *OECD DAC Peer Review on Korea* (Paris: OECD Publishing).

OECD–DAC (2012), *OECD DAC Peer Review on Korea* (Paris: OECD Publishing).

OECD–DAC (2018), *OECD DAC Peer Review on Korea* (Paris: OECD Publishing).

OECD (2020a), 'Social Spending (Indicator)', https://doi.org/10.1787/7497563b-en.

OECD (2020b), 'Life Expectancy at Birth (Indicator)', https://doi.org/10.1787/27e0fc9d-en.

OECD (2021), 'Korea', in *Development Co-operation Profiles* (Paris: OECD Publishing), https://doi.org/10.1787/2dcf1367-en.

OECD–Development Assistance Committee (DAC). 'Aid at a glance', https://www.oecd.org/dac/financing-sustainable-development/development-finance-data/aid-at-a-glance.htm.

Park, C. H. (1966), *The Road toward Economic Self-Sufficiency and Prosperity* (Seoul: Ministry of Public Information).

Park, E. J. (2019), 'GNI Per Capita Is Up 500 Fold since End of the War', Korea JoongAng Daily.

Park, B. Y., and Lee, H. S. (2015), 'Motivations for Bilateral Aid Allocation in Korea: Humanitarian, Commercial, or Diplomatic?', *Asian Economic Papers* 14(1), 180–197.

Pirie, I. (2007), *The Korean Developmental State: From Dirigisme to Neo-Liberalism* (London: Routledge).

Pirie, I. (2016), 'South Korea after the Developmental State', in Y. Chu, ed., *The Asian Developmental State* (New York: Palgrave Macmillan).

Rudra, Nita (2007), 'Welfare States in Developing Countries: Unique or Universal?', *Journal of Politics* 69(2), 378–396.

Siddiqi, A., and Hertzman, C. (2001), 'Economic Growth, Income Equality, and Population Health Among the Asian Tigers', *International Journal of Health Services* 31(2), 323–333.

Stallings, B., and Kim, E. M. (2017), *Promoting Development: The Political Economy of East Asian Foreign Aid* (Singapore: Palgrave Macmillan).

Stern, J. J., Kim, J. H., Perkins, D. H., and Yoo, J. H. (1995), *Industrialization and the State: The Korean Heavy and Chemical Industry Drive* (Cambridge, MA: Harvard University Press).

Vogel, E. F., and Lindauer, D. L. (1997), 'Toward a Social Compact for South Korean Labour', in *The Strains of Economic Growth: Labour Unrest and Social Discrimination in Korea*, 93–121 (New Haven, CT: Harvard University Press).

Witt, M. A. (2015), 'South Korea: Plutocratic State-Led Capitalism Reconfiguring', in M. A. Witt and C. Redding, eds, *The Oxford Handbook of Asian Business Systems*, 216–237 (Oxford: Oxford University Press).

Wong, J. (2004), 'The Adaptive Developmental State in East Asia', *Journal of East Asian Studies* 4, 345–362.

Woo, J. E. (1991), *Race to the Swift: State and Finance in Korean Industrialization* (New York: Columbia University Press).

Woods, N. (2008), 'Whose Aid? Whose Influence? China, Emerging Donors and the Silent Revolution in Development Assistance', *International Affairs* 84(6), 1205–1221.

World Bank (1993), *The East Asian Miracle* (New York: Oxford University Press).

World Bank (2004), 'Republic of Korea: Four Decades of Equitable Growth', case study from Reducing Poverty, Sustaining Growth What Works, What Doesn't, and Why A Global Exchange for Scaling Up Success.

World Bank (2019), World Development Indicators. GDP (current US$).

CHAPTER 36

KOREAN REUNIFICATION

YOUNG-KWAN YOON

1. Introduction

The Cold War international order ended when the Soviet Union collapsed in 1991. The Korean Peninsula, however, still remains as a hotspot of the outdated Cold War, with the highest military tension in the world. Inter-Korean relationship is generally confrontational, even though there have been some political efforts now and then to turn it into a peaceful coexistence. The confrontational inter-Korean relationship is structurally woven into international competitions among neighbouring powers, for example, between the United States and the Soviet Union during the Cold War and between the United States and China post-Cold War.

In this sterile political environment, even for maintaining peace, discussing the issue of reunification of the Korean Peninsula may look impractical. But it would be worthwhile from a long-term perspective to analyse power dynamics related to reunification, identify some of the challenges lying ahead of the Korean people, and think over how to overcome those challenges.

Examples of peaceful reunifications are rare and the 1990 German reunification is one of those. A review of German reunification shows that a peaceful reunification can be explained as the result of an interaction between the centrifugal forces in international dimension in favour of the status quo and the centripetal forces in internal dimension towards reunification. Reunification occurred especially when international forces against German reunification were minimised while internal (i.e. inter-German) forces for reunification were maximised.

Adopting this framework, the first question this chapter raises is how the centrifugal forces have been working internationally against Korea's reunification. It will look at positions and intentions of four neighbouring states—the United States, China, Japan, and Russia—on the issue of Korean reunification. The second question is how the Koreans have tried to foster centripetal forces for mutual cooperation and integration. In this regard, the chapter will mainly focus on South Korean government's efforts and its North Korea policies pursued in the past. Then, it will explain a few important factors affecting operations of centrifugal and centripetal forces and how Koreans might influence these factors in order to achieve reunification.

2. THE GERMAN REUNIFICATION EXPERIENCE

Germany was lucky in the sense that *Glasnost* and *Perestroika*, pursued by President Gorbachev in the Soviet Union since 1985, provided the critical opportunity for weakening the centrifugal forces against German reunification. From a geopolitical competition perspective, the Soviet Union could be regarded as the state which would oppose a West Germany-led reunification most strongly. But its international position was much weakened due to political and economic difficulties during President Gorbachev's domestic reforms. Chancellor Kohl succeeded in persuading President Gorbachev to agree to the idea of a reunited Germany remaining as a member of the North Atlantic Treaty Organisation (NATO) in return for providing a significant amount of economic assistance to the Soviet Union (Zelikow and Rice 1996: 335–338).

Germany was lucky also in the sense that the relative influence and power of the United States, most likely a strong supporter of German reunification were at the peak at the time of German reunification. Chancellor Kohl successfully mobilised strong support of President George H. W. Bush for reunification, which turned out to be important in calming down anxieties of the other states, such as the United Kingdom and France.

Witnessing the fall of the Berlin Wall on 4 November 1989, UK Prime Minister Margaret Thatcher and French President François Mitterrand were nervous about the possibility of German reunification. They met several times to discuss the issue of German reunification after Chancellor Kohl announced a ten-point plan for reunification on 28 November 1989. In their meeting at the Elysée Palace in Paris on 20 January 1990, President Mitterrand worried about how German reunification would lead to re-emergence of the 'bad' Germans who had once dominated Europe (Powell 1990). The assurances of Chancellor Kohl and Foreign Minister Genscher that German reunification would not lead to the 'Germanisation of Europe', but rather the 'Europeanisation of Germany' also helped mitigating European neighbours' concerns (Zelikow and Rice 1996: 234).

In this way, Chancellor Kohl successfully minimised the centrifugal forces that were working against German reunification in international politics. However, this was only half of the story. West German political leaders could gradually strengthen inter-German centripetal forces in favour of mutual cooperation and integration for two decades before reunification.

Chancellor Willy Brandt from the Social Democratic Party initiated *Ostpolitik*, a new diplomatic strategy pursuing reconciliation and mutual cooperation with East

Germany and Eastern European socialist states in the early 1970s. It was politically bold and an imaginative approach at the high time of the Cold War confrontation. The initial response of the US government to *Ostpolitik* was cold. National Security Advisor Henry Kissinger criticised Chancellor Brandt as pursuing a nationalistic, unrealistic, and risky policy (Del Pero 2009: 95–95).

It was extraordinary to see that Chancellor Kohl from the conservative Christian Democratic Union inherited *Ostpolitik* from his rival party, Social Democratic Party, after he gained power in 1982. As a result of the continued pursuit of *Ostpolitk* for two decades, the momentum for inter-German political, economic, and social integration continued to strengthen. In other words, centripetal forces were created and strengthened, uninterrupted for two decades, and laid the foundation for successful reunification in 1990 and integration thereafter.

3. The International Politics of Korean Reunification (Centrifugal Forces)

Unlike Germany at the time of reunification, centrifugal forces working against Korean reunification remain strong even after the end of the Cold War in 1991. The public positions of all four neighbouring states—the United States, China, Japan, and Russia—are that they support a peaceful reunification of Korea. However, official government positions are one thing and their short-term policy preferences are another. The current state of international power dynamics and each state's policy preferences are in favour of the status quo, continued division of the Korean Peninsula, rather than reunification.

At the time of Korea's liberation from Japanese colonial rule in August 1945, the United States and the Soviet Union made a political compromise to divide the Korean Peninsula temporarily through the thirty-eighth parallel. A balance of power between two big powers could be maintained through division of Korea. In the following years of the Cold War period, a fault line was drawn between the three liberal democratic states—South Korea, the United States, and Japan—and the three communist states—North Korea, the Soviet Union, and China.

After the end of the Cold War in 1991, the fault line remained basically the same, except that China replaced Russia as the dominant power among the three Northern communist states. The only difference is that the ideological aspect of confrontation dimmed, while the *realpolitik* aspect became distinctive. This international dynamic has been strengthening the centrifugal forces simply because both camps pulled each of the Koreas further into their own camps, leaving inter-Korean hostility high. Now, let's look at each individual state's concern and strategic intention on Korea's reunification.

3.1 The United States

Historically, the US policy towards Korea swung back and forth between neglect and intervention. The US recognition of Japan's colonisation of Korea in 1905 and the US Secretary of State Dean Acheson's deletion of Korea from the defence line in January 1950 are examples of neglect. However, when North Korea invaded South Korea in June 1950, President Harry S. Truman quickly decided to intervene. The conclusion of the US–Republic of Korea (ROK) alliance in 1953 institutionalised US commitment to South Korea, which provided South Korea with the secure environment for democratic and economic development over the past seven decades. And the US–ROK alliance has become 'the linchpin of peace and prosperity in Northeast Asia, as well as the Korean Peninsula' (US Department of Defense 2019).

Among the four neighbouring states of Korea, the United States would probably be the most enthusiastic supporter of reunification, led by its ally, South Korea. It would mean the expansion of democracy to the Northern part of Korea and the elimination of North Korea's security threats, such as nuclear programme and human rights problems.

However, US policymakers would be concerned about the strategic uncertainty that would follow after Korea's reunification. For example, once reunification occurs, it will not be easy for the United States to rationalise for continuation of the US–Korea alliance unless the Korean people want it. The United States may want to continue its alliance with the unified Korea and the stationing of US troops in order to strategically engage in Northeast Asia. In addition, if US troops were to leave Korea, the rationale for the stationing of US troops in Japan might also be weakened (Brzezinski 1997: 190–191; Kissinger 2001: 132–134) or should be reformulated. This kind of uncertainty may make US policymakers hesitate to break the status quo on the Korean Peninsula. At present, US policymakers are giving much higher priority to the issue of denuclearising North Korea, which is regarded as the most urgent threat to US national security.

3.2 China

Despite the Chinese government's official rhetoric, most China experts in the West think that the geopolitical strategy of China is becoming Asia's regional hegemon. One way of pursuing that goal would be to push US influence out of Asia, including Korea. For instance, at the time of President Lee Myung-bak's visit to Beijing in 2008, the spokesperson of the Chinese Foreign Ministry made a statement that the US–ROK alliance was a historical relic of the Cold War (*The Korea Times* 2008). This statement is just one example of China's strategic intention on the Korean Peninsula.

Considering this strategic goal, China is likely to oppose Korean reunification if a unified Korea continues to be allied with the United States. From the Chinese perspective, that kind of reunification would mean the expansion of US influence up to the Yalu and Tumen Rivers. Actually, the same concern about losing North Korea as a buffer zone was why Mao Zedong decided to intervene in the Korean War in the winter of 1950 (Kissinger 2011: 144–145). There are also secondary reasons for China's fear, such as the massive inflow of North Korean refugees into China, possible negative political impacts on the Korean–Chinese community in the Northeastern provinces, and a possible territorial dispute. This is why China has supported the North Korean regime by providing food and energy for a long time.

China also has been reluctant to apply tough sanctions on North Korea, always setting a higher priority on the stability of the North Korean regime than denuclearisation. President Xi Jinping has faithfully followed this traditional geopolitical strategy of China (Grossman 2018; Kissinger 2011: 496–497). In this way, China has been contributing to strengthening centrifugal forces against Korea's reunification.

3.3 Japan

The rising power of China and its assertive diplomacy since the 2008 Global Financial Crisis have been Japan's most important strategic concern (Abe 2012). Japan has been wishing South Korea to join Japan and the United States to confront China as a coalition. The problem has been that Japanese political leaders didn't understand South Korea's dilemma that South Korea needs China's cooperation in resolving the North Korea problem and building peace on the Peninsula. Another problem for South Korea has been some Japanese political leaders' adoption of historical revisionism regarding the Japanese colonial rule of Korea (Kingston 2015). These two factors strained South Korea–Japan relations in recent years.

Regarding the issue of Korean reunification, Japan shares a similar concern to its ally, the United States, on what would happen after Korean reunification. It worries about the possibility of the unified Korea getting closer to China and becoming confrontational towards Japan (Brzezinski and Scowcroft 2008: 128). This has for long been a geopolitical concern of Japan. In the 1880s, the head of a German training mission to the Japanese army, Major Jacob Meckel, said that Korea was 'a dagger aimed at the heart of Japan' (Duus 1998: 49). Thus, the preference of Japan may not be reunification, but rather to maintain the status quo. Even in the case of a Korean reunification, Japanese leaders will wish for the unified Korea to remain as a non-nuclear ally of the United States. Japan would probably wish the continued presence of US troops in the unified Korea as a shield against the rising China.

3.4 Russia

Russia shares a border with North Korea. Similar to China, Russia wants stability and peace on the Korean Peninsula, which will provide Russia with the security of its border and territories. Russia's official position is that it supports peaceful reunification of Korea, free from foreign influences (Vorontsov 2013). However, like other major states,

Russia tends to view Korean issues from the perspective of its own strategic games with other big powers. Russia is maintaining close strategic cooperation with China in confronting the United States. For instance, on North Korea's denuclearisation, Russia has taken a position similar to that of China (Lukin 2019). In other words, Russian leaders' judgement on what position Russia would take on Korea's reunification will be significantly influenced by its relationship with the United States and China at the time of reunification (Jackson 2015). If Russia is hostile to the United States while remaining close to China, Russia would be less cooperative with South Korea and the United States.

Compared to China, however, Russia may be less reserved on the Korean reunification. Russia has long wished to develop the Siberian Far East and advance towards the Asia-Pacific. Thus, Russia is the only country which has pursued trilateral projects of economic cooperation with both Koreas such as connecting railroads, gas pipelines, and power lines since the early 1990s (Timonin 2011). In addition, Russia has been enthusiastic on establishing a multilateral mechanism of security cooperation regarding the Korean Peninsula. For example, Russia took the chairmanship of the working group on multilateral security cooperation under the September 19th Agreement by the Six-Party Talks in 2005.

3.5 Factors Affecting Centrifugal Forces

There may be many factors that affect strengthening or weakening of the centrifugal forces regarding Korea's reunification. However, the following three factors seem to be the most relevant and fundamental factors from the perspective of Northeast Asian power politics.

3.5.1 *Multilateralisation of North Korean Issues*

Unlike in Europe, there was no multilateral institution for security cooperation in Northeast Asia, which strengthened the centrifugal forces against Korean reunification even more. Due to the lack of a multilateral institution, there were no collective principles, norms, rules, and decision-making procedures to regulate state behaviour effectively in Northeast Asia. This made each state more suspicious of the others' intentions regarding the Korean Peninsula and made it more difficult for Korea's four neighbouring states to arrive at a certain agreement on reunifying both Koreas. Thus, multilateral negotiations on the North Korean issues would be a meaningful method of reducing mutual suspicion and competition and increasing cooperation among Korea's neighbouring states.

The first major multilateral talks on the Korean Peninsula issues in the post-Cold War period were the Four-Party Talks which began in December 1997 and lasted over twenty-one months. South Korean President Kim Young-sam and US President Bill Clinton first proposed Four-Party Talks (ROK, United States, Democratic People's Republic of Korea [DPRK], China) in their summit meeting in Jeju Island on 16 April 1996. Both leaders intended to reduce tensions and build a more permanent peace mechanism, which would replace the armistice agreement in Korea. Despite arduous negotiation process, the Four-Party Talks could not produce meaningful results. It was mainly because the North consistently demanded what the United States and South Korea could not accept. The North argued for withdrawal of the US troops from South Korea and the conclusion of a peace treaty between North Korea and the United States, excluding South Korea. The South wanted to begin with the easy things first focusing on confidence-building and tension reduction (Kwak 2003: 13–17).

The second major multilateral talks on the Korean Peninsula issues were the Six-Party Talks (ROK, US, The Democratic People's Republic of Korea (DPRK), China, Japan, and Russia) to denuclearise North Korea. The Six-Party Talks lasted from 27 August 2003 to 14 April 2009, when the North Korean authority declared that they would no longer participate. After North Korea's reluctant admission of the existence of the uranium enrichment programme in October 2002, the George W. Bush administration, which did not like to deal with North Korea bilaterally, initiated the Six-Party Talks. The six parties produced a major agreement on 19 September 2005, which can be regarded as the most comprehensive multilateral agreement on the denuclearisation of North Korea. However, this agreement could not be implemented. The influential key policymakers in the Bush administration were reluctant to accept the diplomatic solution of the September 2005 agreement (Oberdorfer and Carlin 2014: 406–411). During the later period of 2007–2009, North Korea did not cooperate on the issue of verification and, even worse, had a missile launch and the second nuclear test early in Obama's presidency in 2009 (Oberdorfer and Carlin 2014: 431–435).

In this way, multilateralisation of the North Korean issues were not successful in the past. However, this does not necessarily mean that multilateral efforts in the future would also fail. Domestic and international situations of the major state actors in the region now are very different from those of two or three decades ago. In addition, the burden of providing a security guarantee and economic assistance to North Korea in return for denuclearisation would have to be shared by neighbouring states and South Korea. A multilateral format would also help, to some extent, to prevent the increasing US–China competition over a wide range of international issues from spilling over into the Korean Peninsula issues.

3.5.2 *Political Relations between the United States and North Korea*

One fundamental source of the North Korea problem has been the continued international isolation of North Korea. This has worsened North Korea's paranoid security concern. In the critically unstable post-Cold War period in the 1990s, North Korea pushed for nuclear development as a survival strategy.

Actually, North Korea has continuously wanted to improve political relations with the United States. For instance, Kim Il-sung delivered that message in early 1992 through the first high-level official meeting in New York (Oberdorfer and Carlin 2014: 207). Making progress on North Korea's strategic goal of improving relations with the United States was a major reason for striking a deal, the Geneva Agreed Framework in October 1994 (Oberdorfer and Carlin 2014: 276). The 2000 joint communiqué between the

United States and North Korea decided to end hostile relations (US Department of State Archive 2000). Even the first clause of the Singapore Agreement of 2018 is on improving US–North Korea relations. However, each time, the United States declined the North Korean offer or rescinded from previous agreements on improving the US–North Korea relationship.

Basically, the US position was that the United States would provide the reward of an improved relationship only after North Korea denuclearised itself. North Korea violated numerous international laws and norms such as the Nuclear Nonproliferation Treaty and United Nations Security Council Resolutions, and defected from various agreements with the United States and other countries. Thus, applying maximum pressure would be the only remaining option. Some people even argued for regime change (*Newsweek* 2018). However, in retrospect, this moralistic coercive approach underestimated North Korea's survival instincts and willingness to do whatever was necessary to achieve the goal of regime survival. So the vicious circle has continued for the past three decades.

There were a few South Korean diplomatic efforts in the past to break this vicious circle by helping to improve relations between the United States and North Korea. But those efforts did not bear fruit. For example, President Kim Dae-jung tried hard but failed to persuade the newly elected US President George W. Bush in his summit meeting in March 2001 to continue Clinton's engagement policy towards North Korea. President Roh Moo-hyun mentioned in early 2003 to the author of this chapter, the Minister of Foreign Affairs and Trade, that he would not mind the United States having trilateral talks on denuclearisation, even without South Korea's participation, if the United States could only begin to talk to North Korea. President Moon Jae-in also tried hard to prepare a favourable political atmosphere for the US–DPRK summit in early 2018. Despite all these efforts, the conviction of US policymakers on the utility of the conventional approach turned out to be quite strong.

3.5.3 *China's Concern on Korea's Reunification*

Despite some different interpretations of China's intention (Mastro 2018), the conventional view is that China has been worried about the disappearance of a buffer zone through reunification led by South Korea, an ally of the United States. Especially, China has been much concerned about the possibility of US forces moving up to the North in the case of reunification (Freeman 2018). Since the beginning of the Trump administration, US–China relations have undergone a fundamental change in a more confrontational direction. As the result, China may become even more sensitive to this issue. In a trilateral second-track conference among US, Chinese, and South Korean researchers some fifteen years ago, the author of this chapter could confirm Chinese participants' strong concern on the possible move of the US forces to the North in the case of North Korean contingencies.

One way of mitigating Chinese concerns on Korea's reunification and preventing any military conflicts due to misunderstandings at the time of the North Korean contingency would be to have candid dialogues in advance among authorities from China,

South Korea, and the United States. However, Chinese government officials have been very reluctant to discuss this sensitive issue, for fear of sending a negative signal to North Korea. Yet, there seem to have been a few occasions where the high-level US officials could talk on the subject with their Chinese counterparts. For example, former US Secretary of State Tillerson once mentioned that he exchanged his view on this matter with his Chinese counterpart (*New York Times* 2017).

South Korean political leaders also wished to build a close relationship with China with the hope of gaining China's cooperation on Korea's reunification. For example, both governments agreed to upgrade the bilateral relationship to the level of 'strategic cooperative partnership' in May 2008. However, it ended up being empty political rhetoric. Both countries could not share any concrete vision for strategic cooperation regarding the future of the Korean Peninsula. Yet, South Korea may need to continue to assure China that the united Korea will cooperate with China closely on issues such as US troop deployment, North Korean refugees, territory, and the rights of the Chinese businesses in the North.

4. INTER-KOREAN POLITICS (CENTRIPETAL FORCES)

4.1 Cold War Period

The history of Cold War inter-Korean relations is full of hostile confrontations. Above all, North Korea's invasion of the South in June 1950 set the hostile tone of the inter-Korean relations afterwards. The Korean War was ended on 27 July 1953 by the Armistice Agreement, signed between the United Nations Command on the one hand and the Korean People's Army and the Chinese People's Volunteers on the other (UN Peacemaker 1953). Thus, legally speaking, the Korean War has not ended because combatant states have not yet concluded a peace treaty. This means that domestic and inter-Korean political environments became too rigid for political leaders to pursue any kind of inter-Korean reconciliation.

However, there were a few intermittent attempts for dialogue between the two Koreas. The most important case was the South Korean Central Intelligence Agency (CIA) Director Lee Hu-rak's secret visit to Pyongyang in May 1972 (Wilson Center Digital Archive 1972a). After witnessing sudden rapprochement between their patrons, the United States and China, in 1971 and 1972, the top leaders of both Koreas thought that it would be meaningful to open dialogues with the other side. Both sides agreed on a 4 July joint communiqué which declared three principles of pursuing independent and peaceful unification and a great national unity as one people (Wilson Center Digital Archive 1972b). However, there were only a few rounds of high-level official meetings thereafter and the friendly atmosphere between the two Koreas quickly disappeared.

In this way, there was little room for the Koreans to find a way towards mutual cooperation and integration. In a nutshell, both Koreas simply played the role of front-line bases of the Cold War confrontation. Furthermore, under the military dictatorship in South Korea, idealists who dared to dream of reconciliation with the North could be easily punished as communists. As such, centrifugal forces for division were maximised, while centripetal forces for inter-Korean cooperation were minimised during the Cold War.

4.2 Post-Cold War

The end of the Cold War order opened up space for both Koreas to search for an alternative mode of inter-Korean relationship. South Korean political leaders began to take initiatives for reconciliation and peaceful coexistence with the North. For instance, on 11 September 1989, President Roh Tae-woo proposed to form a 'Korean National Commonwealth' as an interim stage in which both Koreas recognised the coexistence of two different systems. This would be preceded by the stage of reconciliation and cooperation and succeeded by the stage of a unified Korea of one nation and one state (Yang 2016). This approach was based on three principles—independence, peace, and democracy—and was adopted as the baseline of the South Korean government's approach to reunification by Roh's successors.

President Roh Tae-woo pursued the Northern Policy (*Nordpolitik*) aiming to normalise South Korea's relations with former enemies like the Soviet Union in 1990 and China in 1992. He said that the goal of the Northern Policy was not to isolate North Korea but to induce it to open up (Roh 2011: 140). However, the US and South Korean governments declined Kim Il-sung's offer in 1991–1992 to normalise diplomatic relations with the United States (Roh 2011: 280; Oberdorfer and Carlin 2014: 208). Kim tried to find an exit from his country's dire situation through a diplomatic opening with the United States, but in vain.

On 27 September 1991, US President George H. W. Bush declared that the United States would unilaterally withdraw tactical nuclear warheads all over the world, including in South Korea (National Security Archive 2016). This decision changed inter-Korean relations quite positively. For the first time, a comprehensive agreement between the South and the North was produced on 13 December 1991. It was the Agreement on Reconciliation, Non-Aggression, Exchanges and Cooperation, in which both Koreas agreed on a wide range of measures for peaceful and cooperative inter-Korean relations (UN Peacemaker 1991). Furthermore, both Koreas produced the Joint Declaration of the Denuclearisation of the Korean Peninsula on 31 December 1991 (UN Peacemaker 1992).

However, the inter-Korean détente brought by the fundamental change of the international political atmosphere quickly disappeared due to the increasing tension over North Korea's nuclear programme. The US and South Korean military authorities decided in early October 1992 to resume the next year's Team Spirit joint military exercise to pressurise North Korea towards cooperating on the nuclear issue. North Koreans strongly protested against the decision and cut all inter-Korean contacts immediately (Oberdorfer and Carlin 2014: 213). This incident was an early precedent of what would happen repeatedly in later periods. Any efforts to improve inter-Korean relations by the liberal governments such as those of Kim Dae-jung, Roh Moo-hyun, and Moon Jae-in hit the same stumbling block of North Korea's nuclear programme.

The first fully fledged political efforts for inter-Korean reconciliation were exerted by President Kim Dae-jung after his inauguration in 1998. His Sunshine Policy was based on three basic principles: no armed provocations by the North, no attempt by the South to absorb the North, and the South seeking cooperation and promoting reconciliation towards the North (Kim Dae-jung 2010: 72). As a result, there was a rapid increase in economic, human, and cultural exchanges between the South and the North (Ministry of National Unification 2004: 173, 193). Two signature projects were the Mount Kumgang Tourism Project and the Kaesong Industrial Complex Project.

In June 2000, the first inter-Korean summit between President Kim Dae-jung and Chairman Kim Jong-il occurred, agreeing on the 15 June South–North Joint Declaration. Both leaders agreed on five points: to resolve the question of reunification independently, to promote reunification with recognition of a common element between the South's concept of confederation and the North's formula for a loose form of federation, to resolve humanitarian issues such as reunion of separated families, to promote balanced development of the national economy through economic cooperation and exchanges in various fields, and to hold a dialogue between relevant authorities to implement the above agreements (UN Peacemaker 2000).

One important point to note is the fact that both sides could agree on recognising the existence of a common element between the South Korean approach and the North Korean approach to reunification. The South Korean approach from President Roh Tae-woo to President Moon Jae-in has been based on a functionalist approach. It argued for beginning cooperation from the functional, easy-to-do, non-political and non-sensitive areas, such as exchanging goods, sports teams, mails, people, and reunion of separated families, etc. Habits of cooperation in these areas would be supposed to spill over to the more sensitive military and security areas thereafter. Gradual convergence between the two different systems would appear during the process and thus lead to the final stage of reunification.

However, the North Korean approach was a kind of federalist approach. It argued for starting from cooperation in the political and security fields. For example, Kim Il-sung's 1993 Ten-Point Programme of the Great Unity of the Whole Nation for the Reunification of the Country proposed to build a pan-national unified state, while leaving the existing systems and governments intact. It would be a federal state which would be independent from any other great powers. He argued for building the Democratic Federal Republic of Koryo (DPRK Government 1994). The agreement of both leaders to recognise the existence of a common element between these two different approaches revealed a small but meaningful possibility of accomplishing the goal of a 'Korean National Commonwealth' in political reality.

President Kim Dae-jung's relatively successful implementation of inter-Korean reconciliation and cooperation was assisted by the strong support of US President Bill Clinton. President Clinton trusted and helped President Kim Dae-jung by engaging North Korea himself (Kim 2010: 84). He promoted exchanges of high-level officials with North Korea. President Clinton also adopted a US–North Korea joint communiqué agreeing to end the hostile relationship when Vice Marshal Jo Myong Rok, a top military leader of North Korea, visited Washington in October 2000 (US Department of State Archive 2000).

The three-year period from 1998 to 2000, when Presidents Kim Dae-jung and Clinton worked together, was the peak of South Korea's engagement policy. This three-year experience showed that a fundamental change of inter-Korean relations into a cooperative one would be difficult without the improvement of US–North Korea relations. It marked the first historical example of showing the possibility of weakening centrifugal forces and strengthening centripetal forces on reunification of the Korean Peninsula.

The situation quickly became aggravated when George W. Bush was elected as the new US president in 2000. His policy towards North Korea was exactly the opposite of President Clinton's. Despite President George W. Bush's hard-line approach and designation of North Korea as an 'Axis of Evil', President Roh Moo-hyun inherited Kim Dae-jung's engagement policy. But full implementation of an engagement policy was not easy because of the mismatch between the South Korean and US approaches to North Korea. President Roh Moo-hyun held the second inter-Korean summit on 4 October 2007 with Chairman Kim Jong-il and signed a peace declaration. The declaration included clauses on promoting and expanding joint economic, military, and family reunion projects and replacing the armistice agreement with a permanent peace treaty (United Nations Peacemaker 2007).

The centripetal forces working for inter-Korean cooperation which began to blossom during the Kim Dae-jung and Roh Moo-hyun period were doomed when a new conservative president, Lee Myung-bak, took office in February 2008. President Lee was reluctant to accept North Korea's wish to continue the existing inter-Korean relationship on the basis of what the two previous South Korean administrations accomplished with the North. However, as the presidential candidate of the Grand National Party in February 2007, he announced his North Korea policy to help North Korea's per capita income to grow up to $3,000 USD if North Korea gave up its nuclear programme and opened its economy (Lee, M. 2015: 303–307). However, the North declined this offer of 'Denuclearisation, Opening, 3000'. The North even attacked the South Korean corvette *Cheonan* on 26 March 2010, killing forty-six soldiers and bombarded Yeonpyeong Island on 23 November 2010, killing four South Koreans.

The next president Park Geun-hye adopted the policy of trust-building, *Trustpolitik* (Park 2011). However, her government did not clarify concrete operational means of implementing it. Later, President Park promoted the 'Unification Bonanza' theory, but again did not explain how to approach unification. During her presidency, inter-Korean relations remained hostile. President Park closed the last remaining symbol of inter-Korean cooperation, Kaesong Industrial Complex, in February 2016 in response to North Korea's fourth nuclear test in January and its launching of a long-range rocket on 7 February (*The Guardian* 2016).

President Moon Jae-in inherited the engagement policy from his liberal predecessors, Kim Dae-jung and Roh Moo-hyun. Until early 2018, he faced a serious security crisis due to the confrontation between the United States and North Korea on North Korea's nuclear programme. US President Donald Trump applied maximum pressure against North Korea, mobilising harsh international economic sanctions and military threats. As a result, military tension on the Korean Peninsula was very high in 2017. President Moon was able to turn the crisis into the beginnings of active diplomacy by utilising the 2018 Winter Olympic Games in PyeongChang (South Korea) (*New York Times* 2018). As a result, there were three inter-Korean summits and two summits and a brief meeting between President Trump and Chairman Kim Jong-un during 2018–2019.

This does not mean that President Moon's initiative for settling a peace process on the Korean Peninsula was successful. The US–North Korea and inter-Korean summits did not make substantial progress in denuclearising North Korea. This situation put the Moon government in a difficult situation. Even though he wanted to pursue a fully fledged engagement policy, by resuming the Kaesong Industrial Complex and Mount Kumgang Tourism projects, he could not do so, simply because the political cost of defecting from the international coalition of sanctioning North Korea would be too high. Inter-Korean relations turned sour after the failure of the second Trump–Kim summit in Hanoi in January 2019.

4.3 Factors Affecting Centripetal Forces

There may be various factors that affect strengthening or weakening of the centripetal forces regarding Korea's reunification. However, the following two factors seem to be the most fundamental and structural factors from the perspective of each of two Koreas' internal political economy.

4.3.1 *The South Korean Factor: Reaching a Bipartisan Consensus*

The most important reason for South Korea's failure to strengthen centripetal forces was probably the lack of bipartisan consensus between the liberal and the conservative political camps on North Korea policy. For example, when the power was transferred from the liberal Roh Moo-hyun government to the conservative Lee Myung-bak government in 2008, there was reversal of North Korea policy and the nature of inter-Korean relations.

North Korea's attack of the corvette *Cheonan* on 26 March 2010 and President Lee Myung-bak's response left a serious long-term impact on inter-Korean dynamics. Probably due to the difficulties of immediate retaliation in kind, President Lee chose to punish North Korea by economic means and ceased almost all economic and human interactions except the Kaesong Industrial Complex Project on 24 May. Though the rationale for taking the punitive measures against North Korea was quite understandable, centripetal forces were significantly weakened as the result of the 'May 24th Measures'. For example, the South–North trade decreased from USD 1.912 billion in 2010 to USD 1.136 billion in 2013. Furthermore, the May 24th Measures led to the strengthening of the centrifugal forces by making North Korea much more dependent on China than before. In 2004, China took 48.5 per cent of North Korea's trade, but by 2012, China's share had increased to 88 per cent (Gray 2016: 43).

One of the fundamental differences between the supporters of engagement policy and their criticisers is how to perceive North Korea (Lee, S. 2015). While the former view North Korea as the partner for coexistence and cooperation, the latter tend to view North Korea as the target which should, or will soon, collapse. According to the criticisers, engagement policies of the liberal governments prolonged the life of the rogue state, North Korea, by providing economic aid which might have been diverted to build the nuclear stockpile. Supporters of engagement, however, argue that the confrontational approach of the conservative camp based on a collapse scenario will make North Korea even more desperate and non-cooperative towards South Korea, leading to higher tension and possibility of disastrous arms conflicts.

South Korea's winner-takes-all type of politics is the main factor which contributes to the divisiveness of North Korea policy. Power is heavily concentrated in the hands of the president. Once a political party loses power, it doesn't have any room to influence the formation of North Korea policy unless the president and the ruling party open the door for discussion with the opposition parties, which has been rare. So there were radical switches of North Korea policy when the power shifted to the other parties. Korean politicians have long been talking about reforming this kind of political system through revision of the constitution. However, each time, their myopic personal calculation of political interests have made it impossible to agree on how and when to reform the constitution.

4.3.2 *The North Korean Factor: Marketisation, Economic Opening, and Denuclearisation*

Another important factor which worked against strengthening of the centripetal forces through increased inter-Korean interaction was North Korean leaders' reluctance to open the country to the outside world. Top leaders of North Korea feared the possible infiltration of negative political ideas and influences from the outside world, which would endanger their regime control. However, Chairman Kim Jong-il broke this pattern to some extent for the first time and responded positively to President Kim Dae-jung's engagement policy.

Despite ups and downs in the cycle of inter-Korean relations during the past three decades, it has become clear that the momentum for economic openness in North Korea has been growing gradually. When the public distribution system collapsed in the mid-1990s, the North Korean top leader couldn't but acquiesce to the market transactions among people. And as marketisation proceeded, the scope of economic transactions with the outside world also expanded. Now, the North Korean economy is a quasi-market and open economy. Actually, North Korean economy has become so open that it cannot survive without trade (Kim 2017: 64–70). Foreign trade has become the main source of the government budget and income for powerful state organisations. This is why Kim Jong-un's announcement of return to self-reliance in January 2020 (*Rodong Sinmun* 2020) contradicts the reality of the North Korean political economy.

As of 2020–2021, the North Korean economy is suffering seriously because of international sanctions and self-imposed isolation due to the COVID-19 pandemic. One key issue which will decide the future dynamics of the North Korean political economy is whether and how far Chairman Kim Jong-un would cooperate with the United States in terms of denuclearisation. If Kim makes a strategic decision to denuclearise in return for economic assistance (including the lifting of sanctions) and security guarantee, then the opportunity for inter-Korean economic cooperation will be significantly improved. This would mean strengthening of the centripetal forces.

If the North Korean leader continues to decline to make compromises on denuclearisation, then international sanctions and diplomatic isolation will continue. This will make North Korea's economic situation even worse if China keeps sanctioning North Korea. Then, the critical issue would be how much longer the North Koreans would continue to support Kim. The likelihood of regime instability is present in North Korea, which, in the worst case, may lead to the opening of a Pandora's box for the future of the Korean Peninsula.

5. Conclusion

Focusing on two diametric forces, centrifugal and centripetal, this chapter intended to explain some factors which would weaken or strengthen the momentum for reunification. For example, if the North Korean issues such as denuclearisation could be effectively multilateralised, if US–North Korea relations can be improved and North Korea could get out of diplomatic isolation, and if China's concern on possible negative impacts of Korean reunification for its strategic interest could be mitigated, then the centrifugal forces would be weakened and the likelihood of reunification would increase. And if South Korean politicians could achieve bipartisan consensus on North Korea policy through political reforms and cooperation, and if the North Korean leader decides to cooperate with the United States on denuclearisation and get economic sanctions removed, then the centripetal forces will be strengthened and the likelihood of reunification will increase.

The result of this review reveals that the prospect for Korean reunification is not bright at present. The centrifugal forces working at international level are strong, mainly due to mutual suspicions among the four powers and their fear of uncertainties of a united Korea's future diplomacy. The centripetal forces at inter-Korean level are weak due to some structural obstacles at the level of internal political and economic dynamics inside each of the two Koreas. Only time will tell whether the Korean people will be able to overcome those challenges.

From the analytical point of view, the relevance of each of the five factors that the author chose to focus on may be subject to further scrutiny and debate. Yet, the discussion in this chapter may be regarded as meaningful if it could provide a useful framework for analysing such a dubious but important subject as Korean reunification.

Bibliography

Abe, S. (2012), 'Asia's Democratic Security Diamond', 27 December, Project Syndicate.

Brzezinksi, Z. (1997), *The Grand Chessboard* (New York: Basic Books).

Brzezinski, Z., and Scowcroft, B. (2008), *America and the World* (New York: Basic Books).

Del Pero, M. (2009), *The Eccentric Realist: Kissinger and the Shaping of American Foreign Policy* (Ithaca, NY: Cornell University Press).

Democratic People's Republic of Korea (DPRK) Government (1994), 'DPRK Government's Memorandum on Issues Connected with the Plan for Founding the Federal State of the Democratic Federal Republic of Koryo', 11 August.

Duus, P. (1998), *The Abacus and the Sword: The Japanese Penetration of Korea* (Oakland, CA: University of California Press).

Freeman, C. P. (2018), 'Testimony before the U.S.–China Economic and Security Review Commission', Developments in China's North Korea Policy and Contingency Planning, 12 April, https://www.uscc.gov/sites/default/files/transcripts/Hearing%20Transcript%20-%20April%2012,%202018.pdf, accessed 28 November 2021.

Gray, K. (2016), 'Between Politics and Economics in Seoul's North Korea Policy', *North Korean Review* 12(1) (Spring), 35–50.

Grossman, D. (2018), 'China's Reluctance on Sanctions Enforcement in North Korea', 4 January, https://www.rand.org/blog/2018/01/chinas-reluctance-on-sanctions-enforcement-in-north.html, accessed 28 November 2021.

Jackson, V. (2015), 'Putin and the Hermit Kingdom: Why Sanctions Bring Moscow and Pyongyang Closer Together', *Foreign Affairs*, 22 February.

Kim, B. (2017), *Unveiling the North Korean Economy: Collapse and Transition* (Cambridge: Cambridge University Press).

Kim, D.-J. (2010), *Kim Dae-jung:* Memoir, Vol. 2 (in Korean) (Seoul: Sam-in).

Kingston, J. (2015), 'Abe's Revisionism and Japan's Divided War Memories', *The Japan Times*, 22 August.

Kissinger, H. (2001), *Does America Need a Foreign Policy?: Toward a Diplomacy for the 21st Century* (New York: Simon & Schuster).

Kissinger, H. (2011), *On China* (New York: The Penguin Press).

Kwak, T. (2003), 'The Korean Peninsula Peace Regime Building through the Four-Party Peace Talks: Re-Evaluation and Policy Recommendations', *Journal of East Asian Affairs* 17(1) (Spring/Summer), 1–32.

Lee, M.-B. (2015), *Hour of the President: 2008–2013* (in Korean) (Seoul: RHK).

Lee, S. (2015), 'A Geo-Economic Object or an Object of Geo-Political Absorption? Competing Visions of North Korea in South Korean Politics', *Journal of Contemporary Asia* 45(4), 693–714.

Lukin, A. (2019), 'Russia's Policy Toward North Korea: Following China's Lead', *38 North*, 23 December.

Mastro, O. S. (2018), 'Why China Won't Rescue North Korea: What to Expect If Things Fall Apart', *Foreign Affairs* (January/February), 58–66.
Ministry of National Unification (2004), 'White Paper on National Unification' (in Korean), Seoul.
National Security Archive (2016), 'Unilateral U.S. Nuclear Pullback in 1991 Matched by Rapid Soviet Cuts', 30 September, https://nsarchive.gwu.edu/briefing-book/nuclear-vault-russia-programs/2016-09-30/unilateral-us-nuclear-pullback-1991-matched, accessed 28 November 2021.
New York Times (2017), 'A Tillerson Slip Offers a Peek into Secret Planning on North Korea', 17 December.
New York Times (2018), 'Can South Korea's Leader Turn an Olympic Truce into a Lasting Peace?', 25 February.
Newsweek (2018), 'John Bolton Blasts Trump's New North Korea Sanctions as Worthless', *Newsweek*, 23 February.
Oberdorfer, D., and Carlin, R. (2014), *The Two Koreas: A Contemporary History* (New York: Basic Books).
Park, G. (2011), 'A New Kind of Korea: Building Trust between Seoul and Pyongyang', *Foreign Affairs* (September/October), 13–18.
Powell, C. D. (1990), 'Letter from Mr. Powell (No.10) to Mr. Wall', 20 January, <WRL 020/1> Secret and Personal, 10 Downing Street, U.K. Archive (Cabinet Office), German Unification: No.10 Memorandum of Conversation (MT & President Mitterrand) 'Prospect of Unification Had Turned Them into "the 'Bad' Germans They Used to Be"' (declassified 2010), https://www.margaretthatcher.org/document/113883, accessed 28 November 2021.
Rodong Sinmun (2020), 'Let Us Break Through Head-On Present Difficulties in Offensive Spirit of Mt Paektu', *Rodong Sinmun*, 22 January.
Roh, T. (2011), *Roh Tae-woo: Memoir, Vol. 2* (in Korean) (Seoul: Chosunnews Press).
The Guardian (2016), 'Seoul Shuts Down Joint North–South Korea Industrial Complex', 10 February.
The Korea Times (2008), 'Chinese Official Calls Korea–US Alliance Historical Relic', 28 May.
Timonin, A. (2011), 'Kommersant Correspondent Alexander Gabuev's Interview with Ambassador Alexander Timonin', 30 November, https://www.kommersant.ru/doc/1827381, accessed 28 November 2021.
United Nations Peacemaker (1991), 'Agreement on Reconciliation, Non-Aggression and Exchanges and Cooperation between the South and the North', 13 December, https://peacemaker.un.org/korea-reconciliation-nonaggression91, accessed 28 November 2021.
United Nations Peacemaker (1953), 'Armistice Agreement Volume I Text of Agreement', 27 July, https://peacemaker.un.org/sites/peacemaker.un.org/files/KP%2BKR_530727_Agreement ConcerningMilitaryArmistice.pdf, accessed 29 December 2021.
United Nations Peacemaker (1992), 'Joint Declaration of the Denuclearization of the Korean Peninsula', 20 January, https://peacemaker.un.org/sites/peacemaker.un.org/files/KR%20KP_920120_JointDeclarationDenuclearizationKoreanPeninsula.pdf, accessed 28 November 2021.
United Nations Peacemaker (2000), 'South-North Joint Declaration', 15 June, https://peacemaker.un.org/sites/peacemaker.un.org/files/KP%20KR_000615_SouthNorth%20Joint%20 Declaration.pdf, accessed 28 November 2021.
United Nations Peacemaker (2007), 'Declaration on the Advancement of South–North Korean Relations, Peace and Prosperity', 4 October, https://peacemaker.un.org/sites/peacemaker.

un.org/files/KP%20KR_071004_Declaration%20on%20Advancement%20of%20South-North%20Korean%20Relations.pdf, accessed 28 November 2021.

US Department of Defense (2019), 'Indo-Pacific Strategy Report: Preparedness, Partnerships, and Preparing a Networked Region', 24 June, https://media.defense.gov/2019/Jul/01/2002152311/-1/-1/1/DEPARTMENT-OF-DEFENSE-INDO-PACIFIC-STRATEGY-REPORT-2019.PDF, accessed 28 November 2021.

US Department of State Archive (2000), 'U.S.–D.P.R.K. Joint Communique', 12 October, https://1997-2001.state.gov/regions/eap/001012_usdprk_jointcom.html, accessed 28 November 2021.

Vorontsov, A. (2013), 'The Russian Perspective on Korean Unification', *Tong-il gwa Pyonghwa (Unification and Peace)*5(1).

Wilson Center Digital Archive (1972a), 'Conversation between Kim Il Sung and Lee Hu-Rak', 4 May, https://digitalarchive.wilsoncenter.org/document/110780, accessed 28 November 2021.

Wilson Center Digital Archive (1972b), 'On the Three Principles of National Reunification, Conversations with the South Korean Delegation to the High-Level Political Talks between North and South Korea', 3 May, https://digitalarchive.wilsoncenter.org/document/110851, accessed 28 November 2021.

Yang, C. (2016), 'Review of Previous ROK Government Policies for Reunification and Future Policy Options in View of German Reunification', December (SAIS: US–Korea Institute).

Zelikow, P., and Rice, C. (1996), *Germany Unified and Europe Transformed* (Cambridge, MA: Harvard University Press).

CHAPTER 37

THE ROK–US ALLIANCE

Drivers of Resilience

VICTOR D. CHA AND KATRIN KATZ

1. Introduction

The South Korea–US alliance was formed with the signing of the Mutual Defense Treaty on 1 October 1953. The treaty, designed to protect South Korea from a second North Korean invasion and deter communist expansion during the Cold War, commits both sides to come to each other's aid in the event of an external attack and grants the United States permission to station military forces on South Korea's territory (The Avalon Project 2008).[1] Over the decades, the alliance has expanded beyond its original mandate into a much broader partnership involving economic, political, and security cooperation at the peninsular, regional, and global levels.

Several dramatic changes have taken place since the alliance was established— including South Korea's remarkable economic growth and transition to democracy, the end of the Cold War, and the rise of China to become the world's second largest economy. In the midst of these transitions, the alliance has weathered a number of difficult phases—including the 'Nixon and Carter shocks' involving unilateral plans to remove US troops from the peninsula during the Cold War, the wave of anti-US sentiment and tensions over North Korea policy in the early 2000s, and the more recent years of 'America-First' policies under the Trump administration that involved haggling over narrow alliance issues such as military cost-sharing, while coordination on pressing security challenges related to North Korea and China was sparse.

Each of these periods of transition and strain within the alliance has also brought new voices in South Korea and the United States calling for the partnership to be adjusted or abandoned altogether. Although public support for the alliance remains strong in both countries (Green et al. 2020; Friedhoff 2020),[2] the arguments of those who see alternative security arrangements as preferable to the alliance have gained new traction in recent years. For instance, in 2018, Moon Chung-in, senior adviser to South Korean President

Moon Jae-in, suggested that alliances are a 'very unnatural state of international relations' and that, eventually, 'the best thing is to really get rid of alliance' (Friedman 2018). In the United States, commentaries arguing that the alliance has become outdated, too expensive, and even dangerous have become more prominent (Bandow 2017, 2020).

1.1 What Explains the Alliance's Resilience in the Midst of Significant Countervailing Forces over the Past Nearly Seventy Years?

This chapter addresses this question through a review of alliance patterns since the early 1950s. It highlights the degree to which the alliance has consistently been affected by a combination of centrifugal forces (pulling the allies apart) and centripetal forces (pushing the allies together), often simultaneously. Two dynamics, in particular, have had centrifugal effects during different phases of the alliance. First, during the mid-Cold War years and some phases thereafter, US policy shifts spurred South Korean fears of abandonment, which, in turn, prompted Seoul to prepare alternative security arrangements. Second, South Korea's development and growing nationalism has led to a drive for greater autonomy in its foreign policy decision-making, which has fostered resentment and, at times, misinterpretations of Seoul's motives in Washington.

The chapter argues that three centripetal forces account for the alliance's persistence and growth over time, even as centrifugal forces created tensions in the alliance. These include: (a) the continuity of common security interests in the midst of broader geopolitical transitions; (b) Washington's willingness to provide security assurances in response to Seoul's fears of abandonment; and (c) South Korea's increased capacity and willingness to forge new areas of alliance cooperation in parallel with its economic and political development.

The chapter begins with an overview of centrifugal and centripetal forces in the alliance over three phases, including the early 1950s, the mid-Cold War, and the post-Cold War period. The second section explains the alliance's resilience in each phase on the basis of the centripetal dynamics listed above. The third section considers the implications of this analysis in assessing the Trump–Moon years.

2. The Alliance over Time: Forces of Convergence and Divergence

2.1 Alliance Formation: The Origins and Institutionalisation of Mutual Security Interests

In the years immediately following the Second World War, Korea did not figure prominently in Washington's strategic plans for the region (Cha 2016: ch. 3; Green

2017: 272–278). Budget pressures and a focus on the adoption of a maritime, rather than a continental, strategy in Asia put Japan and the Philippines above Korea on Washington's list of priorities (Rapp-Hooper 2020: 52). The United States accepted the surrender of Japanese forces south of the parallel as a result of a hasty arrangement with Moscow in 1945, but it was eager to redirect military resources in Korea to defence commitments elsewhere in the world (Green 2017: 265–286). The United States withdrew combat troops from South Korea in June 1949. Six months later, Secretary of State Dean Acheson's January 1950 speech on the US defence perimeter left out the Korean Peninsula (Cha 2016: 43–44).

These US moves are believed to have factored into North Korean leader Kim Il-sung's decision to invade South Korea, assessing that he could unify the peninsula before Washington became involved (Heo and Roehrig 2014: 52). On 25 June 1950, North Korean troops in Soviet-built tanks crossed the thirty-eighth parallel, marking the start of the Korean War as well as a shift in US assessments regarding the strategic importance of South Korea. Two days later, President Truman ordered US air and naval forces to join South Korea under the auspices of the United Nations in fighting North Korean, and later Chinese, forces, who intervened on the North Korean side in October 1950.

When hostilities ended in July 1953, an armistice agreement set a new border close to the thirty-eighth parallel and established a 2.5 mile-wide demilitarised zone (DMZ) to serve as a buffer between the North and South. The three-year conflict resulted in a significant human toll,[3] as well as a US strategy that now tied South Korea to broader US Cold War objectives (Cha 2016: 56–57).

The United States pursued a formal defence relationship with South Korea to achieve three goals. First, it aimed to establish a continental foothold in South Korea to fend off communist threats in the Cold War and protect the centre of US Pacific operations in Japan (Rapp-Hooper 2020: 52). Second, the United States wanted to avoid another costly conflict with North Korea, particularly at a time when Washington still aimed to focus the bulk of its time and energy on defence plans in Europe (Cha 2016: 63; Green 2017: 278). Third, and closely related to the second objective, Washington saw the need to restrain the mercurial and unpredictable South Korean leader, Rhee Syngman, who attempted to block ceasefire negotiations and was eager to 'march north' to reunify the peninsula on South Korea's terms (Cha 2016: 105–107).

For Seoul, the alliance provided security guarantees from a remote power with none of its own territorial ambitions, as well as opportunities to receive much-needed economic and military aid. Overall, the deal transformed US entrapment fears into a centripetal force that pulled the two sides into a mutually beneficial arrangement.

The treaty also formed the basis for further cooperation and agreements, including the formalisation of US operational control over South Korean forces by the United Nations Command in November 1954 (Cha 2016: 118).[4] From 1954 until 1971, approximately 63,000 US troops were stationed across 100 bases in South Korea. Many of the soldiers were situated close to the DMZ to function as a 'trip wire', signalling that the United States would automatically become involved if North Korea were to launch a second attack (Heo and Roehrig 2014: 54).[5] The United States later deployed tactical nuclear weapons on the peninsula from 1958 to 1991 to strengthen extended deterrence

(Roehrig 2017: 125). Bilateral economic cooperation in the early years of the alliance also fortified the relationship (Cha 2016: 114).

2.2 The Mid-Cold War: South Korean Abandonment Fears Followed by US Security Assurances

In the early years of the Cold War, South Korea became a key hub in the US strategy to maintain a favourable balance of power vis-à-vis the Soviet Union, while managing threats to US security far from its shores (Rapp-Hooper 2020: 61).

For South Korea, the alliance remained essential for different reasons. South Korean President Park Chung-hee, who seised power in a coup in 1961 and oversaw the country's rapid industrialisation in the two decades that followed, was driven by a desire to free South Korea from reliance on outside powers, including the United States. But Park was also aware of the harsh realities South Korea faced at that time. The country still had a long road ahead in recovering from the devastation of the Korean War, and North Korea was faring better than the South in its post-war economic recuperation. Increased North Korean provocations along the DMZ in the early 1960s heightened Park's sense of vulnerability. As a result of these circumstances, South Korea's strategic options were severely constrained. Park chose to remain closely aligned with the United States to address the threat from North Korea, while seeking maximal security and economic assistance from Washington as a foundation for South Korea's own development (Snyder 2018: 30–31).

The Vietnam War stoked concerns in Seoul that the United States would divert its troops from the Korean Peninsula to Vietnam, thereby providing North Korea with an opportunity to invade. This fear of US abandonment drove President Park to offer to send Korean troops to Vietnam in 1961 (Lee 2011: 409). In total, South Korea committed approximately 48,000 troops to Vietnam, the largest contingent of foreign combat troops aside from the United States (Heo and Roehrig 2014: 58). In return, Park received increased military and economic aid, a pledge to maintain troops in South Korea at the same level, and political acceptance of his authoritarian rule (Snyder 2018: 31–33; Lee 2011: 415–20).

The alliance was seriously tested when Washington ultimately did develop plans for troop withdrawals in the late 1960s, and again during the 1970s. In July 1969, President Nixon announced the Guam doctrine, calling for US allies in Asia to bear a larger share of the responsibility for their self-defence. As the Vietnam War dragged on, Nixon aimed to draw down forces in the theatre, but, to avoid the appearance of defeat, he needed to apply the Guam doctrine elsewhere. South Korea became the natural choice (Cha 1999: ch. 3). In order to reassure allies, President Nixon declared that the United States would provide a 'shield if a nuclear power threatens the freedom of a nation allied with us or of a nation whose survival we consider vital to our security' (Richard Nixon Presidential Library 2017). Nixon's reference to the US 'nuclear umbrella' was intended to demonstrate that US security guarantees would not be diminished by his troop withdrawal plans.

For South Korea, the Guam doctrine precipitated intense abandonment fears (Cha 1999: ch. 3). The stakes of the situation were made more severe by the increasing frequency of North Korean provocations around the same time, including a failed assassination attempt on President Park and the capture of the *USS Pueblo* in 1968 (Snyder 2018: 43–44; Cha 1999: ch. 3). By 1972, US troop levels had been lowered from approximately 64,000 to 40,000 with the removal of the Seventh Infantry Division. To offset the troop drawdowns, the United States provided significant military assistance, including a contribution of $1.5 billion to support South Korea's Five-Year Military Modernisation Plan from 1971 to 1975 (Lee 2011: 422–423).

Military assistance aside, Park remained concerned that US security commitments were waning. Announcements about Washington's secret efforts to engage China around the same time did not help. Park's abandonment fears ultimately prompted his decision to clandestinely pursue a nuclear weapons programme (Cha 1999: 113; Snyder 2018: 43). By the mid-1970s, Washington was aware of Park's nuclear initiative and pressurised him to abandon the programme (Oberdorfer 1997: 72). Park eventually succumbed partially to US demands, shutting down sizable portions of the programme, while keeping some elements open on a smaller scale (Snyder 2018: 46).

This episode sparked concerns in the United States about the potential for its influence to wane in the region as it disengaged militarily. In order to reassure Seoul that it did not need nuclear weapons of its own, the Ford administration in 1975 formally acknowledged the presence of US nuclear weapons on the Peninsula and reaffirmed the U.S. commitment to South Korea's security (Roehrig 2017: 126; Hong 2011: 508).

Jimmy Carter again ignited South Korean abandonment fears in 1975 when he pledged, during his presidential campaign, to withdraw all US ground troops from South Korea, linking his plan to President Park's poor human rights record. Once he became president, Carter announced his intent to complete the troop withdrawals within four or five years (Kim 2011: 467).

President Park was again deeply concerned about the loss of US defensive capabilities and requested security concessions, including cutting-edge military equipment and the establishment of a Combined Forces Command (CFC) (Cha 1999: ch. 5) Washington further agreed to offer $1.9 billion in compensatory military assistance and to participate in annual joint military exercises (Kim 2011: 470). Park accepted these offers, but remained wary. He restarted South Korea's nuclear weapons programme, which, by that time, was easier to conceal as a civilian programme (Hong 2011: 508–509).

However, centripetal forces again pulled the allies together. President Carter's key security advisors expressed serious reservations about the troop pull-out plan, arguing that the security of South Korea was too critical to US Cold War strategy in Asia and pointing to revised US intelligence estimates about the North Korean threat (Kim 2011: 478–479; Green 2017: 379). A scandal that came to be known as 'Koreagate'—involving allegations of US congressmen being bribed by Korean Central Intelligence Agency (KCIA)-affiliated South Korean lobbyists—made it politically infeasible for Congress to approve Carter's compensatory military aid package for Seoul (Boettcher 1980). The USSR's invasion of Afghanistan in 1979 was the final straw, spurring President

Carter to rethink his own strategy and commit to a global focus on containment, rather than human rights concerns. Carter dropped the troop pull-out plan in 1979.[6]

When Ronald Reagan defeated Carter in the presidential election of 1980, he immediately took steps to restore trust in the US–South Korea alliance, issuing assurances that further US troop reductions would not occur (Lee, C. 2020: 31). Reagan accepted considerable political risk in these moves, as they required legitimising the rule of then South Korean President Chun Doo-hwan, another hardline military leader who came to power by force in 1980 after Park Chung-hee was assassinated in 1979. In the months prior to Reagan's election, the United States had been harshly criticised for its toleration of Chun's use of the South Korean military to crush a political uprising in Kwangju in May 1980 (Gleysteen 2000; Oberdorfer 1997: 128–130; Clark 1996).

Reagan struck a deal with Chun, offering a White House meeting in exchange for the commutation of political dissident Kim Dae-jung's death sentence. Reagan helped to restore South Korea–US relations following the turbulent Carter years, but he also sent the signal that human rights concerns were not at the top of Washington's agenda (Lee, C. 2020: 15–58; Oberdorfer 1997: 136–137). Nonetheless, the Reagan administration's efforts to assure Seoul of Washington's security commitments made an impact, as indicated by Chun's decision to abandon President Park's nuclear programme (Snyder 2018: 47).

2.3 The Post-Cold War: South Korea's Autonomy Push Tempered by New Areas of Cooperation

US consideration of troop reductions re-emerged due to the end of the Cold War, as well as the transformation of South Korea into an economic powerhouse with the capacity to take on more defence responsibilities. A 1990 US Defense Department report noted that the US forward presence would remain a critical element of its strategy in Asia, but also laid out plans for a three-phase drawdown of troops in South Korea over a ten-year period (United States Department of Defense 1990: 11–13). However, these force reduction plans were later suspended, first by the George H. W. Bush administration and later by the Clinton administration, as concerns increased regarding North Korea's pursuit of nuclear weapons. As a result, US troop levels on the peninsula remained fixed at 37,500 throughout the 1990s (Heo and Roehrig 2014: 55).

The Bush administration announced that it was removing tactical nuclear weapons from South Korea in 1991, mostly to encourage reciprocal steps elsewhere in the world by the Soviet Union, but also to facilitate negotiations on the nuclear issue with North Korea. Potential South Korean abandonment fears from this move were mollified by Washington's efforts to consult Seoul more closely on this decision than it had prior to previous troop withdrawal announcements. It also provided direct assurances at high levels that the US nuclear umbrella would remain intact (Oberdorfer 1997: 260). South Korea's own engagement efforts with North Korea at that time, resulting in two landmark agreements on political and nuclear issues with Pyongyang in 1991–1992, also helped to dampen the impact of President Bush's decision.

Centrifugal forces in the alliance in the early post-Cold War years stemmed less from South Korean fears of abandonment than from Seoul's desire to pursue a more autonomous foreign policy.[7] Whereas patron–client dynamics had predominated in the early decades of the alliance, by the 1990s, South Korea was asserting its own preferences in the relationship. South Korean leaders following the democratic transition also became more attuned to shifts in public opinion, which did not always align with Washington's preferences.

Tensions in the alliance in the 1990s and early 2000s emerged as Seoul and Washington disagreed over the most effective approach to thwart North Korea's pursuit of nuclear weapons.

The first North Korean nuclear crisis erupted when International Atomic Energy Agency (IAEA) inspectors detected discrepancies between North Korea's reporting and IAEA sampling, with suspicions of non-compliance later verified by US imagery. This process ultimately culminated in North Korea's announcement of its withdrawal from the Non-Proliferation Treaty (NPT) in March, which spurred the opening of US–North Korea negotiations. This direct bilateral channel created anxiety for the newly elected South Korean leader Kim Young-sam, who worried about the optics of Seoul being sidelined on an issue that was central to its security (Oberdorfer 1997: 288; Snyder 2018: 74). Kim also believed that the United States was naïve in its offers of economic and political incentives to North Korea to spur denuclearisation.[8]

In a demonstration of South Korea's new willingness to question US policies, President Kim criticised the US negotiation strategy in interviews with major news outlets, including the *New York Times* and the BBC (Snyder 2018: 75). He also confronted President Clinton during his first official visit to Washington in November 1993, demanding that North and South Korea exchange envoys prior to the next round of US–North Korea talks and that Seoul be granted the decision to determine whether US–Korea joint military exercises would be cancelled (Oberdorfer 1997: 297).

Tensions within the alliance over North Korea policy became even more pronounced under the progressive leadership of South Korean presidents Kim Dae-jung and Roh Moo-hyun, both of whom pursued engagement-focused policies in dealings with Pyongyang. President Kim's 'Sunshine Policy', which culminated in the historic North–South summit meeting in June 2000, clashed with President George W. Bush's preference for a hard-line approach to Pyongyang, particularly following the 2002 discovery of a clandestine uranium enrichment programme in North Korea (Sanger 2002). President Bush was also highly critical of the North Korean leadership, referring to North Korea, along with Iran and Iraq, as a member of the 'axis of evil' in his 2002 State of the Union address (*Reuters* 2007).

The Bush administration's hard-line approach to Pyongyang created resentment among the South Korean public, whose perceptions of North Korea had softened following exposure to televised family reunions and other events after the 2000 summit. South Koreans also increasingly saw themselves as capable of managing a greater share of their own defence responsibilities and were offended by US moves that seemed to disregard Seoul's policy preferences. Within this context, a tragic accident involving a US military vehicle running over and killing two South Korean school girls sparked a massive wave of protests, known as the Candlelight protests, in South Korea. This movement played a major role in Roh Moo-hyun's success in the presidential elections of 2002, as he had advocated in his campaign for a more 'equal' relationship with the United States, which resonated with the public at that time (Struck 2002).

President Roh's approach to North Korea built on the foundations of Kim Dae-jung's Sunshine Policy, focusing on tension reduction and 'co-prosperity' to address the nuclear issue. This clashed with the Bush administration's efforts in the Six-Party Talks to withhold economic concessions until Pyongyang took concrete steps towards denuclearisation (Cha 2012: ch. 7).

President Roh also developed a regional policy that envisioned a 'balancer' role for South Korea among the powers of Northeast Asia. This approach sparked concerns in Washington that Seoul was seeking alternative, multilateral security arrangements to eventually replace the alliance. South Korea's growing economic ties with China—with Beijing becoming Seoul's largest trading partner in 2004—also led some in the United States to believe that Seoul might eventually choose Beijing over Washington as its main regional partner.

In spite of the South Korea–US rift during the Bush–Roh years, cooperation in the alliance remained solid, and even grew in some areas. The United States and South Korea launched a joint plan for US base realignment on the peninsula and concluded negotiations on a free trade agreement (FTA) in 2007. South Korea also despatched the third-largest ground contingent to support US operations in Iraq and sent medics, engineers, aid workers, and eventually a full provincial reconstruction team (PRT) to Afghanistan (Cha 2007; Heo and Roehrig 2014: 59–61). Notably, the Pentagon also withdrew approximately 9,000 troops from South Korea to support US operations in Iraq and Afghanistan during this period, bringing the overall level to 28,500, where it remains today. This decision generated concern in Seoul, but South Korea's military capabilities by that time had grown strong enough to take over some of the US role without detracting from the country's defence posture. Overall, the US–South Korea partnership endured, and even managed to become stronger and broader in some areas during the Bush–Roh years, even as political tensions dominated the headlines.

3. Analysis: Past Drivers of Alliance Resilience

The preceding section illustrates the degree to which the endurance and expansion of the US–South Korea alliance over the past several decades has been far from inevitable. Since its founding, the alliance has faced challenges due to changing geopolitical dynamics, South Korean fears of abandonment, and Seoul's desire for greater autonomy. Collectively, and perhaps even individually, these forces could have led to the collapse of the alliance. Conditions that increase the likelihood of alliance collapse include changing perceptions of threat, a decrease in credibility of security commitments, and shifting domestic politics, among other things (Walt 1997: 159–179). As the above review of alliance patterns indicates, all of these conditions have been present to varying degrees since the alliance was founded in 1953. Importantly, however, these centrifugal forces have been met with countervailing centripetal forces that, thus far, have prevailed in keeping the alliance steady and strong.

Three centripetal dynamics, in particular, have buttressed the resilience of the alliance over the past sixty-nine years. *First, since the alliance was formed, both sides have viewed it as an effective tool to advance important national security interests.* In the founding days of the alliance, both Seoul and Washington identified the alliance as the best means of prevention of a second Korean War and fending off communist threats.

The Vietnam War decreased US capabilities—and therefore its ability to continue to devote the same level of resources to alliance commitments. But Nixon's Vietnamisation initiative did not undermine the ongoing centrality of alliances in the US Cold War strategy for Asia. Even President Carter, who attempted a strategic redesign that prioritised human rights over security concerns, ultimately reverted to traditional Cold War containment policies that relied heavily on alliances.

The end of the Cold War eliminated one of the original rationales for the US–South Korea alliance, but the alliance's primary rationale remained intact: deterring and, if necessary, defeating, a second North Korean invasion. The end of the Cold War actually fortified the latter rationale when Pyongyang invigorated its pursuit of nuclear weapons in the 1990s. In other words, as one threat (the USSR) dissolved at the end of the Cold War, the other (North Korea) increased. The United States remained concerned about the instability that a second Korean War would unleash and was increasingly worried about the proliferation risk emanating from North Korea's nuclear programme.

Common security interests also remained intact in the context of testy relations between presidents Bush and Roh in the early 2000s. South Korea sought a more autonomous foreign policy, but it also recognised that its alliance with the United States still provided the best means available for South Korea to defend itself against external threats.[9]

Notably, the importance of the US–South Korea alliance for pursuing mutual interests was again affirmed in the early days of the Obama administration, when China's resistance to cooperating with the United States, Japan's move towards a more 'independent' foreign policy under the leadership of the Democratic Party of Japan, and North Korean provocations spurred President Obama to identify the alliance as 'the linchpin of not only security for the Republic of Korea and the United States but also for the Pacific as a whole'.[10]

In summary, despite the many rocky patches Seoul and Washington have experienced since the alliance was formed, both sides have continued to view the alliance as: (a) a mutually beneficial arrangement; (b) a power asset, not liability, that furthers individual interests; and (c) an institution that provides security and non-security benefits.

The *second* factor that has buttressed alliance resilience over the decades has involved *US security assurances in response to South Korean fears of abandonment, which have helped to prevent Seoul from pursuing alternative security arrangements.* These efforts, most pronounced in the mid-Cold War years, have included enhanced military aid, agreements to hold joint military exercises, public affirmations of the nuclear umbrella, and pledges to freeze troop reductions, among other things.

These security assurances did not succeed in completely eliminating Seoul's concerns regarding the continuity of US security commitments during the Nixon and Carter administrations. This was evident in Park's decision to pursue a clandestine nuclear programme even after the United States offered $1.5 billion to support Seoul's military modernisation efforts. However, the impact of the Nixon and Carter shocks would likely have been more severe and long-lasting had the United States neglected to make any efforts to reassure South Korea. Furthermore, by the time President Reagan entered office, US actions to restore the alliance and security assurances had more credibility, ultimately precipitating President Chun's decision to abandon South Korea's nuclear programme.

Third, *South Korea's willingness to deepen and expand alliance cooperation in new areas over the lifetime of the alliance has softened the impact of its periodic pushes for greater autonomy.* These efforts were evident during the early 2000s, when President Roh pursued South Korea–US FTA negotiations and agreed to contribute to US military operations in Iraq and Afghanistan, even as he pushed back on the Bush administration's approach to North Korea and envisioned a balancing role for South Korea in the region. During the Obama and Biden administrations, South Korea also pursued a host of issues in cooperation with the United States that provided public goods to the international system, including on climate change, nuclear safety and security, supply chains, and development assistance. As a result, the alliance has managed to survive, and even expand, through one of its most turbulent periods to date.

The second and third centripetal dynamics listed above are related insofar as they constitute deliberate alliance management strategies employed by Washington and Seoul to keep the alliance on track in the midst of challenges. Common security interests have constituted a necessary condition in upholding the resilience of the US–South Korea alliance; they have provided its raison d'etre. But they have not been sufficient. Further misunderstandings or political missteps, combined with the absence of specific policies to buffer tensions, could have resulted in considerably more serious and permanent alliance rifts in the 1970s and early 2000s. For this reason, agency in the alliance has been essential in ensuring that periods of tension have not metastasised to precipitate the collapse of the alliance.

4. Assessing the Trump–Moon Years

Alliance dynamics under the Trump and Moon administrations were uniquely challenging for three reasons. First, the Trump–Moon years involved compounded centrifugal dynamics—stemming both from US policy shifts, which spurred South Korean fears of abandonment, and from Seoul's desire for greater autonomy, particularly related to its policy towards North Korea, but also tied to differing approaches to China's rise.

Regarding US policy shifts, President Trump endorsed an 'America-First' agenda that devalued alliances globally. This manifested in a transactional approach that treated alliance equities like bargaining chips and structured interactions between the allies in zero-sum terms. President Trump said he was open to withdrawing US troops from South Korea as well as Japan if Seoul and Tokyo did not pay more to cover the costs of stationing troops there (Cha and Lim 2019). Trump also expressed comfort with the notion of South Korea and Japan developing their own nuclear weapons. Military cost-sharing negotiations became deadlocked in 2019 because Trump demanded a five-fold increase in South Korea's contributions to $5 billion per year. In the economic area, President Trump imposed import restrictions on several products from South Korea and said he would withdraw from the South Korea–US Free Trade Agreement (KORUS FTA) if Seoul did not agree to a renegotiation process.

These moves diminished goodwill in the alliance, while creating fresh concerns in Seoul regarding the credibility of Washington's security commitments. This, in turn, appears to be linked to a surge in support among South Korean politicians from centrist and conservative parties for the procurement of nuclear weapons, either through restationing US tactical nuclear weapons on the peninsula or through restarting South Korea's own programme (Dalton and Han 2020). The Moon administration also stepped up its military spending and pressed to accelerate the transfer of wartime operational control (OPCON) to Seoul from Washington, in part to increase South Korea's security independence and prepare for the possibility of a future without the alliance.

South Korea's pursuit of autonomy was most apparent in President Moon's prioritisation of engagement with North Korea, even as Pyongyang improved its capabilities to reach the continental United States with a nuclear weapon. The Moon administration sought to relax sanctions and establish a peace regime on the peninsula, alongside, and even in the absence of, progress on denuclearisation (Kim 2021). This clashed with the Trump administration's desire to only lift sanctions in exchange for concrete progress towards denuclearisation. In many respects, this rift echoed the divides on North Korea policy between Washington and Seoul during the Bush, Kim, and Roh administrations.

The second factor that made the Trump–Moon years uniquely challenging was the degree to which neither administration took steps to mitigate the effects of these centrifugal forces through US policies of assurance or South Korea's pursuit of new forms of cooperation, as Seoul and Washington did in the past. Specifically, President Trump did not seek to soften the blow of suggested unilateral troop withdrawals through public, high-level affirmations of extended deterrence or reinstating joint military exercises. Instead, Trump left the question of Washington's security commitment open ended and even took steps like downplaying the significance of Pyongyang's short-range ballistic missile tests, which created suspicion that the United States would consider decoupling its security from South Korea's.

South Korea also did not compensate for its independent positions on North Korea through seeking allied cooperation in new areas, as it had done during the Bush–Roh years. For instance, Seoul might have made an attempt to counterbalance its inter-Korean engagement push by joining the United States in its regional initiatives, such as criticising China's increasingly aggressive behaviour in the South China Sea or supporting the US position on 5G technology. Seoul did neither. Overall, rather than balancing policy independence with cooperation across different dimensions of the alliance, South Korea during the Trump-Moon years pursued an intensified autonomy push that drove both its North Korea as well as regional positions (Pacheco Pardo 2018).

Third, and perhaps most importantly, the Trump–Moon years coincided with broad geopolitical shifts in the region tied to China's rise that called into question the degree to which Washington and Seoul's security interests remained aligned. Specifically, as tensions between the United States and China hardened into a multidimensional strategic competition, Seoul maintained neutrality and ambiguity in its dealings with Beijing (Kim 2021). Statements from senior officials in the Moon administration supporting greater autonomy for Seoul in regional affairs heightened suspicions of a strategic disconnect (Lee, H. 2020).

In assessing the significance of these types of statements, it is important to keep in mind that regional policy preferences have differed between Washington and Seoul in the past, even as common security interests remained intact. South Korea has demonstrated a clear preference to not take sides in fights between China and the United States, but it has not gone so far as to indicate that it is ready to abandon the alliance in order to pursue alternative security strategies. South Korea got a taste of what it might be like to rely on China as a security partner in 2017, when Beijing used economic coercion to retaliate against Seoul's decision to deploy the US-made Terminal High Altitude Area Defense (THAAD) system. The result of these dynamics was a unique period in which the ally, South Korea, experienced both abandonment and entrapment fears simultaneously—anxiety about US disengagement, as well as concerns about being pulled into a US–China conflict.

The combination of compounded centrifugal forces and withered centripetal forces made the Trump–Moon years exceptionally difficult. However, the first year of the Biden administration indicated an eagerness in both Seoul and Washington to restore the alliance. On the day of Joe Biden's inauguration, President Moon sent a congratulatory message emphasising Seoul's commitment to close coordination with Washington and later tweeted 'America is back'. Shortly thereafter, on 4 February, President Biden noted in his first foreign policy address, 'we will repair our alliances and engage with the world once again', repeating a pledge he made in his inaugural address. A few weeks later, on 8 March, South Korea and the United States took a further step towards getting relations back on track by concluding Special Measures Agreement (SMA) negotiations, which had been deadlocked for over a year. The reconvening of 2 + 2 talks between the foreign and defence ministers of the United States and South Korea on 18 March, while thin on substantive outcomes, was another indication of the enthusiasm on both sides for reopening channels of communication. These types of 'reset' actions are consistent with previous patterns of alliance restoration following challenging periods. They have been further amplified since the May 2022 inauguration of President Yoon Suk-yeol, who has pursued North Korea and regional policies that align more closely with Washington than those of the Moon administration.

5. Conclusion

This chapter has argued that a combination of common security interests and deliberate alliance management strategies explains the longevity and growth of the US–South Korea alliance over time. Common security interests have evolved but not diminished, as the alliance has weathered several geopolitical transitions since its foundational years in the early 1950s. During the mid-Cold War years and some periods thereafter, US efforts to reassure South Korea of its security commitments played an important role in mitigating South Korea's fears of abandonment. And South Korea's willingness to pursue new areas of alliance cooperation, even as it sought greater autonomy in its foreign policy, helped to mitigate post-Cold War tensions over North Korea and broader regional policy. This combination of centripetal forces has carried the alliance through dramatic geopolitical and domestic transitions and many tense phases in recent decades. More recently, following the difficult Trump–Moon years, the first year of the Biden administration and early months of the Yoon administration have involved a number of security, economic, and political steps by Seoul and Washington, once again, to restore the relationship. These steps include closer alignment on North Korea and regional policies as well as a focus on emerging technologies, global health, and green growth that not only expand the alliance's scope, but also engage new constituencies in the alliance thereby laying a strong foundation for the future.

Acknowledgements

The authors wish to thank Dana Kim, Jaehyun Han, Maika Jones, Seung Ho Jung, and Jaejoon Lee for research assistance.

Notes

1. Specifically, the Mutual Defense Treaty contains a pledge by each party to 'act to meet the common danger in accordance with its constitutional processes' in the event of an armed attack, as well as permission from South Korea 'to dispose United States land, air and sea forces in and about the territory of the Republic of Korea as determined by mutual agreement' (The Avalon Project 2008).
2. An August 2020 survey of the US public and thought leaders conducted by CSIS indicated that support for the defence of South Korea against external threats (China in particular)

was high. When asked, 'On a scale of "1" to "10," how important is it to defend South Korea in the Asia-Pacific if they come under threat from China?', the mean responses among the general public and thought leaders were 6.92 and 8.6, respectively. (Green et al. 2020) An August 2020 report by the Chicago Council on Global Affairs based on a June 2020 poll conducted in Korea indicated that 90 per cent of the South Korean respondents said that they strongly support (32 per cent) or somewhat support (58 per cent) the US–South Korea alliance (Friedhoff 2020).
3. While fatality and casualty figures vary widely, one estimate puts the total fatalities at between 3 and 4 million people, 70 per cent of which may have been civilians (Stack 2018).
4. Operational control (OPCON) of South Korean forces during peacetime was transferred to South Korea in 1994. In 2006, Seoul and Washington agreed to work towards the transfer of wartime OPCON to South Korea and set an initial target date of 2012, but the actual transition was postponed a number of times and has yet to take place due to evolving security conditions on the peninsula.
5. Specifically, the Second and Seventh US infantry divisions were deployed near the border.
6. The Carter administration committed to a review of the policy in 1981, at which point the balance between South and North Korean military forces would be reassessed. (Carter was out of office by that time) (Oberdorfer 1997: 107–108).
7. Since the early 1960s, South Korea has gone from being one of the poorest countries in the world to one of the top twenty economies, and became a member of the Organisation for Economic Co-operation and Development in 1996. South Korea's successful democracy movement resulted in its first democratic election in 1987, followed one decade later by the first peaceful transition of power to an opposition party, with the election of Kim Dae-jung in 1997.
8. Kim thought Pyongyang would likely pocket the US concessions to relieve its political and economic problems, while not taking any concrete steps to give up its programme. He also worried that the United States would make a deal with the North that would undercut South Korea's security (Snyder 2018: 74).
9. Snyder (2018) provides an in-depth analysis of this argument.
10. Remarks by President Obama and President Lee Myung-bak of the Republic of Korea after the Bilateral Meeting, Toronto, on 26 June 2010, at the White House, as cited in Cha and Katz (2011: 55).

Bibliography

Bandow, D. (2017), 'It's Time for America to Cut South Korea Loose', *Foreign Policy*, 13 April.
Bandow, D. (2020), 'Not Even South Korea Deserves Unlimited Defense from America', CATO Institute, 13 March.
Boettcher, R. (1980), *Gifts of Deceit* (New York: Holt, Rinehardt and Winston).
Cha, V. D. (1999), *Alignment Despite Antagonism: The U.S.–Korea–Japan Triangle* (Stanford, CA: Stanford University Press).
Cha, V. D. (2007), 'Winning Asia', *Foreign Affairs* 86(6), 98–113, November/December.
Cha, V. D. (2012), *The Impossible State: North Korea, Past and Future* (New York: Ecco).
Cha, V. D. (2016), *Powerplay* (Princeton, NJ: Princeton University Press).
Cha, V. D., and Katz, K. (2011), 'South Korea in 2010: Navigating New Heights in the Alliance', *Asian Survey* 53(1), 55.

Cha, V. D., and Lim, A. (2019), 'Database: Donald Trump's Skepticism of U.S. Troops in Korea Since 1990', *Beyond Parallel*, 25 February, https://beyondparallel.csis.org/database-donald-trumps-skepticism-u-s-troops-korea-since-1990/, accessed 29 November 2021.

Clark, D. N. (1996), 'U.S. Role in Kwangju and Beyond', *Los Angeles Times*, 29 August.

Dalton, T., and Han, A. (2020), 'Elections, Nukes, and the Future of the South Korea–U.S. Alliance', The Carnegie Endowment for International Peace, 26 October.

Friedhoff, K. (2020), 'Troop Withdrawal Likely to Undermine South Korean Public Support for Alliance with United States', *The Chicago Council on Global Affairs*. https://www.thechicagocouncil.org/sites/default/files/2020-12/2020_sma_korea_brief_0.pdf.

Friedman, U. (2018), 'A Top Adviser to the South Korean President Questions the U.S. Alliance', *The Atlantic*, 17 May.

Gleysteen, W. (2000), *Massive Entanglement, Marginal Influence: Carter and Korea in Crisis* (Washington, DC: Brookings Institution Press).

Green, M. J. (2017), *By More Than Providence: Grand Strategy and American Power in the Asia Pacific since 1783* (Columbia University Press).

Green, M. J., Blanchette, J., Glaser, B., Fodale, H., Funaiole, M., Kennedy, S., Lauter, L., and Szechenyi, N. (2020), 'Mapping the Future of U.S. China Policy', Center for Strategic and International Studies, https://chinasurvey.csis.org/, accessed 29 November 2021.

Heo, U., and Roehrig, T. (2014), *South Korea's Rise: Economic Development, Power and Foreign Relations* (Cambridge: Cambridge University Press).

Hong, S. G. (2011), 'The Search for Deterrence: Park's Nuclear Option', in Kim, B.-K. and E. Vogel, eds, *The Park Chung Hee Era: The Transformation of South Korea* (Cambridge, MA: Harvard University Press), 483–510.

Kim, D. (2021), 'Washington and Seoul Must Heal Their Alliance', *Foreign Affairs*, 26 January.

Kim, Y.-J. (2011), 'The Security, Political, and Human Rights Conundrum, 1974–1979', in B.-K. Kim and E. Vogel, eds, *The Park Chung Hee Era: The Transformation of South Korea* (Cambridge, MA: Harvard University Press), 457–482.

Lee, C.-J. (2020), *Reagan Faces Korea: Alliance Politics and Quiet Diplomacy* (Cham, Switzerland: Palgrave MacMillan imprint with Springer Nature).

Lee, H.-A. (2020), 'S. Korea Can Now "Choose" between U.S., China', *Yonhap News Agency*, 4 June.

Lee, M. Y. (2011), 'The Vietnam War: South Korea's Search for National Security', in B.-K. Kim and E. Vogel, eds, *The Park Chung Hee Era: The Transformation of South Korea* (Cambridge, MA: Harvard University Press), 403–429.

Oberdorfer, D. (1997, 2001), *The Two Koreas: A Contemporary History, Revised and Updated* (New York, NY: Basic Books).

Pacheco Pardo, R. (2018), 'Will America Lose Seoul? Redefining a Critical Alliance', *War on the Rocks*, 5 September.

Rapp-Hooper, M. (2020), *Shields of the Republic: The Triumph and Peril of America's Alliances* (Cambridge, MA: Harvard University Press).

Reuters (2007), 'Factbox: Previous U.S. Comments about Kim Jong-Il', *Reuters*, 6 December.

Richard Nixon Presidential Library (2017), 'President Richard Nixon Address to the Nation on the War in Vietnam, November 3, 1969' (White House Oval Office, Washington, DC).

Roehrig, T. (2017), *Japan, South Korea, and the United States Nuclear Umbrella: Deterrence after the Cold War* (New York: Columbia University Press).

Sanger, D. E. (2002), 'North Korea Says It Has a Program on Nuclear Arms', *New York Times*, 17 October.

Snyder, S. (2018), *South Korea at the Crossroads: Autonomy and Alliance in an Era of Rival Powers* (New York: Columbia University Press).

Stack, L. (2018), 'Korean War, a "Forgotten" Conflict That Shaped the Modern World', *The New York Times*, 1 January.

Struck, D. (2002), 'Anti-U.S. Mood Lifts South Korean', *The Washington Post*, 20 December.

The Avalon Project (2008), 'Mutual Defense Treaty between the United States and the Republic of Korea; 1 October 1953(1)', https://avalon.law.yale.edu/20th_century/kor001.asp, accessed 29 November 2021.

United States Department of Defense (1990), *A Strategic Framework for the Asian Pacific Rim: Looking Toward the 21st Century* (Washington, DC: Department of Defense).

Walt, S. (1997), 'Why Alliances Endure or Collapse', *Survival* 39(1), 159–179.

Chapter 38

Evolving Relations with China

Heung-Kyu Kim

I. Introduction

Korea is a neighbouring country of China, sharing a border of 1,416 km in length that today is between North Korea and China. Korea is the sixth biggest among China's fourteen adjacent countries. Frequent contacts between the two date back to the Prehistoric period, as the resemblances between relics excavated in both countries' coastal areas well illustrate. According to their ancient myth, Koreans have taken the '檀君 (Dangun)' dynasty established in 2333 BC as the origin of the Korean nation. In the case of China, the myth of the '黃帝 (Huangdi)' dates back its foundation to 2698 BC. Since then, people in both areas have been in close contact throughout history (Liu 2011; Wang 2014).

According to South Korean scholar Rhu Pong-young, Korea has been invaded by outside forces a total of 931 times—438 of them through the northern border (Rhu 1970). Most major invasions came from the north because most southern invasions comprised pirates from Japan. Although the total does not necessarily meet any academic standard, we can still determine the frequency of the number of invasions. South Koreans often utilise this source when describing the unique DNA of Koreans as opposed to Chinese.

Therefore, how to best deal with China has been an unresolved question for Koreans throughout history. Indeed, there have been many wars between Korean and Chinese dynasties. And it is noteworthy that many Chinese dynasties have disappeared as a consequence of military defeats and interventions in Korea. The best-known cases include the fall of the 隋 (Sui), 明 (Ming), and 清 (Qing) dynasties of China right after military interventions in Korea. And the Korean War intervention (1950–1953) by the People's Republic of China (PRC, hereafter China) severely damaged the then newly established country. The intervention blocked hopes for unification with Taiwan and led to a prolonged confrontation with the United States. Meanwhile, the ancient Korean dynasties of Goguryeo and Baekje collapsed due to attacks by China's 唐 (Tang) dynasty in the seventh century. Korea has been the object of military invasions whenever power transitions have occurred in Northeast Asia, and new dynasties rose in China. The history of military clashes between Korea and China begs the question of how Korean dynasties in the past could survive without being annexed by their big neighbour. According to David Kang (2009), Korea and other countries adjacent to China accepted economic dependence and political constraints to join a peaceful China-centred system for the most of their history. However, China was never able to annex the whole of Korea and its ambition to be a gravitational centre failed on the Korean Peninsula (Kaplan 2012; Kim 2020).

In the meantime, Korea has embraced a vast cultural and ideational legacy from China, particularly Confucian. The Chinese regard Korea as the closest country in terms of the affinity of Confucian culture (Liu 2011). Due to the rule of the Qing dynasty, non-汉 (Han) ethnicities, and the detrimental impacts of the Cultural Revolution in mainland China, Confucian traditions were severely damaged in the very place where Confucian culture was born. The traditions have survived in Korea more so than in China. Koreans are proud of themselves as the sole inheritors of Confucian traditions, particularly after the fall of the Ming dynasty in China. For Koreans, these complex love–hate experiences with China have become a defining factor in the perception of, and relationship with, their neighbour.

Korea has long faced one of the worst geopolitical environments, similar to Poland in Eastern Europe. It has been a bridge between continental and maritime powers, subjecting it to military invasions. From a geopolitical perspective, as Robert Kaplan succinctly pointed out, 'Korea is in a shatter zone' (Denmark 2012). John Mearsheimer has also argued that 'Korea, Poland, and Ukraine are in the worst geopolitical locations' (Mearsheimer 2018). Koreans share the pride of not losing their statehood, despite the magnitude of an existential threat from China. Both Koreas seem to share the DNA of how to survive the Chinese.

2. The Road to Normalisation and the Honeymoon Period

2.1 The Cold War Period

South Korea and China had been adversaries since the latter entered the Korean War (1950–1953). During the Cold War period, South Korea regarded China as an enemy, accepting Taiwan as the only legitimate government in mainland China. China also recognised North Korea as the sole legitimate state on the Korean Peninsula.

From China's perspective, South Korea was a subordinate, weak, and dependent ally of the United States. However, during the Cold War period, the relationship between North Korea and China was not necessarily without problems (Lee 2000; Eouyang 2008;

Choi 2009; Kim 2010; Shunji 2013). North Korea trusted neither China nor the Soviet Union, although it was an ally of both of them. North Korea resisted intervention from the Soviet Union and China and balanced the Soviet Union against China to pursue its strategic interests. The rapprochement between the United States and China, starting with US President Richard Nixon's visit to Beijing in 1972, reinforced North Korea's distrust of its socialist ally. It fortified its independent posture under the slogan of *Juche*.

The launch of China's reform and opening-up policy in 1978 provided a new window of opportunity to turn around hostile South Korea–China relations. China had gradually expanded its contacts with South Korea via Hong Kong and Singapore in the 1980s. Their trade volume jumped from almost zero in 1978 to US$6.4 billion in 1992, when the two normalised relations. During the 1980s, South Korea had gradually developed a two-China policy in practice, although it maintained the one China policy recognising Taiwan as the only legitimate China in principle. China also maintained its one Korea policy, but gradually recognised South Korea as a political entity (Kim 2013).

In the first half of the 1980s, two critical incidents occurred that facilitated bilateral relations: the Chinese civil airplane asylum incident of 1983 and the Chinese torpedo incident of 1985. In May 1983, some Chinese defectors kidnapped a civil aeroplane flying from Shenyang to Shanghai. They requested asylum after arriving at Chuncheon airport in South Korea. Chinese authorities dispatched a delegation to negotiate the return of the aeroplane and its passengers. It was the first official contact between South Korean and Chinese authorities and implied official recognition of each other. After the negotiation, South Korea allowed the defectors to go to Taiwan, but returned the aeroplane and other Chinese civilians to China. According to South Korean Ambassador Kim Ha-joong, afterwards China adjusted its policy orientation to South Korea away from no contact and towards gradual improvement (Kim 2013).

In March 1985, two crew members of a Chinese torpedo gunboat revolted and murdered the other six members, later fleeing into South Korean territory. Upon a Chinese request following negotiations, South Korea rendered all the members and the ship back to China. In return, China decided to participate in the Asian Games held in Seoul in 1986 and in the Seoul Olympic Games of 1988. Despite internal debates in China regarding whether to improve the relationship with South Korea due to Beijing's traditional alliance with North Korea, the government decided to develop better relations with South Korea under Deng Xiaoping's leadership in the 1980s (Kim 2013).

2.2 Towards a Honeymoon Period

China officially adopted a two-Korea policy when it supported both Koreas becoming United Nations (UN) members in 1991, even though psychologically and ideologically China still favoured North Korea. Nonetheless, and despite strong opposition from North Korea, South Korea and China normalised their diplomatic relations in 1992. The driving forces behind the normalisation were Beijing's desire for economic development and to escape international isolation following the Tiananmen incident of 1989, the collapse of most socialist regimes in the early 1990s, and Seoul's pursuit of *Nordpolitik* projects under the Roh Tae-woo government to encircle North Korea. Normalisation meant that South Korea accepted China as the only legitimate government representing the whole of China in both principle and practice. However, China's two-Korea policy remained intact (Cui 2000; Chen and Wang 2002; We 2008).

As shown in Table 38.1, after the normalisation, the trade volume has grown significantly from US$6.37 billion in 1992 to a peak of US$313.4 billion in 2018, according to Chinese statistics (Ministry of Foreign Affairs of the Republic of Korea 2021). China has been the largest trading partner and the largest destination for South Korean foreign direct investment and tourism since 2004 (Snyder 2009). The exchange of top-level visits has been brisk too. Beginning with Roh Tae-woo in 1992, successive South Korean presidents have made official visits to China. This included Kim Young-sam in 1994, and later Kim Dae-jung in 1998. In return, Jiang Zemin, then Chinese leader, also paid an official visit to South Korea in 1995, which was the first time in history that the top Chinese leader had visited the country (Chung 2011a). This contrasted with the souring relationship between China and North Korea in the mid-to-late 1990s. North Korea was shocked by the normalisation, and also suffered several natural disasters and a famine during the period.

Table 38.1: Evolution of South Korea–China formal relations

Leaders	Official description of bilateral relations (year)	Trade, billion US $ (year)	People-to-people exchanges, million (year)
Roh Tae-woo–Jiang Zemin	Friendship and cooperation relations (1992)	6.37 (1992)	0.13 (1992)
Kim Dae-jung–Jiang Zemin	Cooperative partnership (1998)	41.15 (2002)	2.26 (2002)
Roh Moo-hyun–Hu Jintao	Comprehensive cooperative partnership (2003)	145.0 (2007)	5.85 (2007)
Lee Myung-bak–Hu Jintao	Strategic cooperative partnership (2008)	215.1 (2012)	6.90 (2012)
Park Geun-hye–Xi Jinping	Materialization of strategic cooperative partnership (2014)	240.0 (2017)*	8.03 (2017)
Moon Jae-in–Xi Jinping	Substantial strategic cooperative partnership (2017)	268.6 (2018) 243.4 (2019)	10.37 (2019)

Note: * South Korea and China agreed to reach the target of US$300 billion by 2015. The target was fulfilled in 2018, with US$313.4 billion, according to Chinese statistics (US$268.6 billion according to South Korean statistics).

Sources: Ministry of Foreign Affairs of the Republic of Korea, each year.

During the South Korea–China honeymoon period, the most symbolic event took place in 1997 when then North Korean highest-ranked defector, Hwang Jang-yop— primarily responsible for crafting *Juche*, the official state ideology of North Korea— entered the South Korean embassy in Beijing. China allowed Hwang to depart to South Korea, despite North Korea's strong opposition (Chung 2011b). China's decision signalled that it had already left behind the Cold War orientation of its foreign policy on the Korean Peninsula.

However, there has always been a trust deficit in political and security relations between South Korea and China. Beijing's two-Korea policy and China's quasi-alliance with North Korea were the main obstacles. The unresolved triangular relationship remains a defining factor in the South Korea–China relations at the time of writing. In the case of South Korea–China relations, therefore, trade had to drive bilateral relations ahead of politics and security. South Korea hoped that increasing economic interdependence could shift China's prioritisation of, and security relations with, North Korea. During the honeymoon period, both countries had different dreams while lying on the same bed.

From a Chinese perspective, the Asian Financial Crisis of 1997–1998 tore apart the myth of a South Korean economic miracle. China witnessed the vulnerability of the South Korean economy. The bilateral relationship gradually transformed into a normal relationship, in which both countries saw differences in terms of interests in various areas. Despite a growing trade volume, China did not establish a strategic relationship with South Korea until 2008. From a South Korean perspective, one objective of relations with China related to North Korea, and Beijing did not want to discuss North Korea political issues with South Korea in public until 2008—only economic ones (Chung 2011a).

Even during the honeymoon period, there were disputes. A trade dispute, the so-called garlic battle, took place in 1999–2000 (Chung 2011a). When South Korea adopted provisional safeguards and raised tax rates on China-imported garlic to protect its agricultural sector, China retaliated by raising taxes on South Korea-exported electronic goods. The magnitude and subsequent shock waves of the trade dispute were so intense that many China watchers in South Korea felt that it would be the end of the honeymoon period.

2.3 The Early Twenty-First Century: Making Efforts to Maintain the Honeymoon

China's entry to the World Trade Organisation (WTO) in 2001 changed its ideas about South Korea and the rest of the world. Due to the Asian Financial Crisis, South Korea was no longer the ideal model for China's economic development. However, China recognised South Korea's value to develop its economy and as a source of investment. Since the beginning of the twenty-first century, steadfast institutionalisation and substantial upgrades to the relationship between the two countries have rendered an unprecedented number of contacts at the summit level, formal diplomatic exchanges, people-to-people contacts, and governmental dialogues on the economy, diplomacy, and even security.

However, a history dispute about Goguryeo—an ancient Korean dynasty from the Three Kingdoms period—broke out in 2004 (Chung 2011a). China's controversial Northeast Project claimed Goguryeo and other Korean kingdoms as Chinese tributary states. This new attempt to interpret ancient Korean history ignited the nationalism of both countries.[1] It is widely known that the name of Goguryeo was the origin of the current name of Korea. Thus, both countries made considerable efforts not to damage the rapidly developing economic relationship. Nevertheless, the scars remained (Chung 2011b). Furthermore, Chinese illegal fishing boat issues have erupted regularly in South Korea's West Sea area.

Both countries could manage a series of disputes in the early 2000s due to rapidly growing economic cooperation. Since that period, South Korea–China relations have improved remarkably. Kim Dae-jung, then South Korea's president, launched a new rapprochement policy towards North Korea—the so-called Sunshine Policy—and China welcomed it (Gong 2018). Chinese foreign policy also became more flexible towards other countries with the launch of the 'new security concept' at the end of the twentieth century. This concept regarded international relations as non-zero-sum rather than zero-sum. Improvements in US–China relations after the 9/11 incident provided a new security environment to further facilitate the relationship between South Korea and China.

South Korean President Roh Moo-hyun paid visits to China in 2003 and 2006. The conservative President Lee Myung-bak had ten summit meetings with Chinese President Hu Jintao during his tenure. Including the meetings with Chinese Premier Wen Jiabao, both countries held almost four summit meetings every year. President Hu Jintao also visited Seoul in 2005 and 2012, and Premier Wen Jiabao did so in 2007 (Chung 2011b).

Under Hu Jintao's leadership from 2002, his foreign policy strategists made a critical decision to transform the China–North Korea relationship into a normal state-to-state relationship (Lim 2008). North Korea's nuclear ambitions touched a nerve in China. When Beijing desperately needed stable relations with the United States and a stable security environment right after the WTO accession, the second North Korean nuclear crisis began in 2002. Hu Jintao left aside the previous position of 'hesitant interventionist policy' regarding the North Korean issue. Instead, China took a more active role as a mediator and sought a better international image as a' 'responsible great power' by successfully launching the Six-Party Talks in 2003. The second North Korean nuclear crisis brought the Korean Peninsula to Chinese foreign policy and strategic attention. Under China's new policy, North Korea was not necessarily a strategic asset, but more likely a burden. The overall trend of the relationship between South Korea and China indeed strengthened and changed in favour of South Korea over North Korea.

Seoul and Beijing elevated their formal relationship from a comprehensive cooperative partnership to a strategic cooperative partnership in 2008. This is one of the highest levels for Chinese foreign policy. Both countries started to hold strategic dialogues at the vice-minister level in the areas of foreign affairs and security. Both also increased the number of dialogues at various levels (Ministry of Foreign Affairs of the Republic of Korea 2020).

Concurrently, there was a process of power shift between China and Japan. China became the second biggest economy in the world. Economic competition between the United States and China at the global level intensified. Accordingly, South Korea became of more strategic value to China. South Korea was seen as a 'swing state' in the eyes of China. If South Korea sided with Japan and the United States, China would have been affected and forced to live in a Cold War-like environment. Instead, South Korea became a key supplier of products in manufacturing industries, technologies, and semiconductors to China. South Korea's role in maintaining stability on the Korean Peninsula and Seoul's strategic value in Northeast Asian geopolitics could not be neglected.

China welcomed progressive President Roh Moo-hyun's more balanced diplomacy between the United States and itself. There were frequent consultations between Seoul and Beijing concerning the North Korean nuclear issues and the security situation on the Korean Peninsula. During Roh's tenure, both countries started track-1.5 strategic dialogues, even to deal with North Korea issues. China closely communicated with South Korea during the Six-Party Talks to recognise that Seoul's Peace and Prosperity Policy towards North Korea matched its strategic interests of peace and stability on the Korean Peninsula. During these years, the two governments established a hotline, a rare action in their bilateral security and military relationship regarding North Korea.

Despite this development, considerable distrust between South Korea and China remained. China still regarded South Korea as a weak diplomatic state because it was a US 'puppet' ally. Furthermore, the inauguration of conservative president Lee Myung-bak in 2008 ended the short honeymoon with China. Although the formal relationship was upgraded to a strategic cooperative partnership under Lee Myung-bak's government in 2008, China believed that the newly established South Korean conservative government's foreign policies returned to a typical weak state diplomacy, strengthening the alliance with the United States and seeking North Korea's collapse. This perception strained bilateral relations, in spite of frequent contacts.

Furthermore, growing frictions and disputes between China and the United States after the United States declared its 'pivot to Asia' increased the strategic value of North Korea to China. These frictions increased tensions in the relationship between Lee's South Korea and Hu's China. Incongruous attitudes towards the two Koreas as part of Chinese foreign policy complicated Beijing's strategic and short-term objectives. China still favoured South Korea for economic cooperation. However, North Korea remained valuable as a geopolitical buffer zone and a potential strategic card against the United States and South Korea. Although China strongly opposed North Korea's nuclear development, stability and the status quo on the Korean Peninsula were more critical and imminent Chinese foreign policy objectives.

3. Building a Strategic Cooperative Partnership

3.1 Diverse Ideas about the Korean Peninsula in China

China's foreign policy during the Jiang Zemin era (1989–2002) is best described through the 韜光養晦 (*taoguangyanghui*) 'hide-your-capacities-and-bide-your-time' principle introduced by Deng Xiaoping, the core idea of the 'developing country diplomacy school' among China's thinkers. However, reflecting China's growing capabilities, the strategic policy during the Hu Jintao era (2002–2012) gradually changed into 有所作爲 (*yousuozuowei*) 'being able to accomplish something'. This was the main idea of the 'newly rising to great power school'. Under Hu Jintao, China gradually took a more active foreign policy to achieve the international status of a great power, as illustrated in Table 38.2. During the second term of the Hu era, China searched for a new foreign policy towards the Korean Peninsula. Furthermore, China's growing confidence after the Global Financial Crisis of 2008–2009 allowed Chinese foreign policy to cross the Rubicon. The principle of *taoguangyanghui* would no longer be a guiding Chinese foreign policy. Instead, different strategic thoughts appeared in Chinese foreign policy discourses, including the 傳統地政學派 ('traditional geopolitics school'), the 開發途上國派 ('developing country school'), and the 新興大國派 ('rising great power school') (Kim 2020). Chinese diverse discourses were reflected in China's two-Korea policy, which became the most controversial Chinese foreign policy issue in the second term of the Hu Jintao period (2007–2012).

By the end of Hu's second term, the 'newly rising great power school' became mainstream in China's strategic thinking. It regarded China as a rising great power, reflecting growing Chinese nationalism and self-confidence. This group's ideas were gradually becoming more popular among the Chinese general population and elites by the time of the seventeenth Party Congress, so even before the Global Financial Crisis (Kim and Guo 2015).

This school favoured playing a more active role in foreign policy, as befitted a great power. Although this group was very cautious of, and reluctant to challenge, the United States, it became more audacious in protecting China's self-declared core national interests. The school even gradually expanded the scope of Beijing's core national interests, including in the South China Sea. School members were not shy of placing pressure on North Korea if its behaviour would damage China's national interests. This group of people became mainstream in future leader Xi Jinping's inner foreign policy circle.

China's evolving strategic thinking certainly influenced its Korean policies, providing South Korea space to play its more independent middle power diplomacy, and was also more favourable to South Korea in the face of North Korea provocations. However,

Table 38.2: The main trends in China's foreign policy orientations

	Traditional geopolitics school	Developing country school	Newly rising great power school	Great power school
China's international status	(Traditional) big power	Developing country	Newly rising great power	Great/global power
Period of dominance	Jiang to Hu's first term, 1993–2007	Hu's first–second term, 2003–2012	Late Hu's second term–Xi's first term 2010–2017	Xi's second term, 2018–
Key term	Geopolitics/buffer zone	Hide capacities and bide time	Taking necessary measures	China's dream, belt and road, China production 2025
Relationship with the United States	Competitive	Cooperative	Hedging	Competition and rivalry
Policy direction	Challenging	Bandwagoning to hedging	Mixture of hedging and soft balancing	Expansion and hard balancing
Policy towards the Korean Peninsula	Recovery of influence	Status quo	Status quo with potential for change	Balancing and expansion of influence
Policy towards South Korea	Not friendly	Subject for diplomatic inclusiveness and management	Opportunistic, but leaning towards South Korea	Pressure and inclusion
Perception of North Korea	Buffer zone	Troublemaker	Troublemaker/strategic card	Troublemaker and strategic asset
Policy means towards North Korea	Political support and economic aid	Economic aid and diplomatic persuasion	Complex means, including coercion	Limited economic and military aid/pressure

Sources: Kim 2010, 2017.

on the Korean Peninsula security issue, China maintained its traditional position, opposing any unilateral intervention in North Korea either by the United States or by South Korea. China maintained its equidistant policy towards the two Koreas under Xi Jinping's leadership. However, North Korea conducted its third nuclear test in 2013 against China's will, and Xi was outraged. Thus, the South Korea–China relationship quickly improved up to the level of there being discussions about the resurrection of the Seoul–Beijing honeymoon. Some Chinese scholars in the great power school, such as Wang Yiwei and Yan Xuetong, even audaciously suggested to South Korea the idea of a South Korea–China alliance.

3.2 South Korea–China Relations at Their Peak

Presidents Park Geun-hye and Xi Jinping had many similarities, from their wretched childhood to difficulties in rising to power. They certainly shared an emotional attachment. In the early period of Park in office, the relationship between South Korea and China drastically improved. South Korea adopted an active engagement policy towards China, embracing the strategic idea of 聯美和中 ('allying with the US and seeking harmonious relations with China') (Kim 2012).

This strategy reflected Beijing's growing international status in light of power shifts between the United States and China. South Korea sought to promote shared interests with China and to bridge differences (救同縮異), and thus deepen its bilateral relationship with Beijing. This strategy aimed to maximise South Korea's economic and security interests by utilising China's 'peaceful rise and harmonious world' strategy. South Korea hoped to induce more positive collaboration from China on North Korea's nuclear issue, considering the changing tide in China's strategic thinking (Kim 2012).

The two countries exchanged special envoys right after Park won the South Korean presidential election in 2012. They then strengthened cooperation following from the third North Korean nuclear test, agreed on UN Resolution 2094 without considerable frictions, and appeared to have entered a new honeymoon period. At the summit meeting on 27 July 2013, the two leaders announced that they would materialise the pre-existing strategic cooperative partnership. For the first time, they agreed on the North Korea denuclearisation principle in public and announced further cooperation (Kim 2012).

Political trust between the previous governments of Lee and Hu had remained relatively low. However, Park and Xi sought to elevate the political relationship drastically. South Korea's strategic value to China had increased under Xi's bold foreign policy adjustments. To deal with deepening the US–China competition, Xi emphasised neighbour diplomacy. South Korea and India were the primary targets of China's new neighbour diplomacy as a critical note states during Xi's first term as leader. China's goal was to pull South Korea into an orbit of friendly neighbours. China hoped South Korea to be China's ally in its territorial disputes against Japan, thanks to the two countries' similar experiences under Japanese imperialism a century before. Park also stood on

Tiananmen Square along with Xi and Russian President Vladimir Putin to celebrate the seventieth anniversary of China's victory in the Second World War despite tremendous pressure from Western countries. It symbolised the culmination of the honeymoon in the Park–Xi period.

During the honeymoon period, South Korea and China were able to finalise a bilateral free trade agreement (FTA) on 20 December 2015. After the United States and South Korea signed their FTA on 30 June 2007, China immediately began to seek an FTA agreement with South Korea as well (Chung 2011b). The country had been South Korea's largest trading partner since 2004. South Korea bestowed China a 'market-oriented economy' status. The international division of labour in the global economy deepened cooperation between the two.

A South Korean decision to take the side of China would have been a tremendous loss for the United States, psychologically, symbolically, and militarily. South Korea had been the symbol of a successful US engagement policy and the strongest inter-operational military alliance in the post-Second World War period. The loss of South Korea to China would likely be a turning point in US hegemony. Under this scenario, it would be almost impossible for the United States to maintain its hub-and-spoke system in Southeast Asia and Australia in the future. Therefore, the political pressure from the U.S. and domestically came to Park government not to lean on China heavily.

As a result, South Korea's diplomacy under Park took a somewhat balanced approach and remained cautious of full cooperation with China, even though they were already at the zenith in the history of their bilateral relationship. During summit meeting negotiations in 2013 and 2014, China prioritised making a coalition with South Korea against Japan. However, South Korea refused to follow the Chinese suggestion in return for Beijing's more active cooperation on the North Korean nuclear issue. South Korea also rejected China's suggestion to upgrade the strategic cooperative partnership to a comprehensive strategic cooperative partnership. This would have led to bilateral military cooperation, but the Park government still prioritised the Republic of Korea (ROK)–US alliance.[2] South Korea hoped to maintain a balance between Washington and Beijing, while still respecting its alliance with the United States. South Korea was the only country to object to anti-(US) alliance statements among participants in the fourth Conference on Interaction and Confidence Building Measures in Asia, held in Shanghai in 2014, and played a critical role in preventing such statements. During the conference, Xi promoted the 'new Asian Security Concept' based upon his new idea of a 'community of common destiny'. South Korea was cautious enough not to include 'the anti-US alliance' statements in its final reports (Kim 2021).

During the presidential campaign, Park had suggested 'a policy of *Trustpolitik*' to build ties between South and North Korea (Office of National Security 2014). During her tenure, South Korea sought to promote a trilateral strategic dialogue between South Korea, the United States, and China. It received China's support, but Washington was reluctant to endorse such an idea in the face of Japanese opposition. However, Park's emphasis gradually moved towards the denuclearisation issue and placing pressure on

North Korea to abandon its nuclear ambitions upon her election. Meanwhile, China was reluctant to fully cooperate with South Korea, due to its apprehension about the fate of North Korea. Pyongyang has been keen to create and exploit policy differences between South Korea and China, developing a new Cold War-like security environment in Northeast Asia under which North Korea could reap the most benefits. In this regard, the bilateral relationship between South Korea and China was vulnerable to strategic manoeuvring by North Korea, despite their honeymoon.

3.3 The Broken Honeymoon between Seoul and Beijing

Seoul and Beijing thus enjoyed a short period of renewed honeymoon, until the Terminal High Altitude Area Defense (THAAD) issue broke out in 2015. In the face of strong opposition by China and the international society, North Korea's fourth nuclear test on 6 January 2016 created a security dilemma for South Korea. The Blue House thus made a strategic decision to deploy the THAAD in July 2016, even though Xi expressed his strong opposition. This was a US anti-missile system that in theory would allow South Korea to intercept North Korean missiles. The first launchers would become operational in May 2017. By then, the THAAD issue has dramatically deteriorated the Seoul–Beijing relationship throughout 2016. Nonetheless, the trade volume between the two countries had reached its peak in 2014 at US$240 billion, targeting US$300 billion by 2015. Also, the number of people-to-people exchanges was increasing and reached ten million in 2019, as seen in Table 38.1.

The conservative Park government promoted a friendly relationship with China, hoping that Beijing would exert its influence to manage North Korea's provocations and nuclear weapons development. However, this hope vanished. The other agenda item in relations with China was related to South Korea's strategic concerns not to alienate Japan, despite its disputes over history and war-time crime issues. Even during the progressive government of Moon Jae-in, South Korea set up its policy goal in its relationship with China as the 'realisation of the Strategic Cooperative Partnership' instead of upgrading to a comprehensive one (Kim 2021).

3.3.1 *A Return to Normal Relations after the THAAD Issue*

South Korea–China relations significantly deteriorated after Seoul announced its intention to deploy THAAD, which China strongly opposed. Beijing imposed unofficial economic sanctions on South Korea to stop its move to deploy the missile system. South Korea and China, for the first time since their diplomatic normalisation, faced a clash of strategic interests. To secure its alliance with the United States and protect its territory from the North Korean nuclear threat, the South Korean government was decisive. However, the Chinese government vehemently opposed the deployment of THAAD on South Korean soil because of its security concerns. The relationship between South Korea and China experienced a severe setback and there were scars in the hearts of people in both countries, due to rising nationalistic feelings.

The trauma related to the introduction of THAAD guided South Korea's foreign policy afterwards. Right after the United States deployed the THAAD on South Korean soil in 2017, China retaliated against South Korea by banning South Korean products and Chinese tourism to South Korea. China thus imposed various economic and cultural sanctions on South Korea. However, even the newly elected progressive Moon Jae-in government allowed the United States to deploy its THAAD missile defence system (Snyder 2020).

However, South Korea was also bitter towards the United States, due to its position on the THAAD issue. The United States never helped South Korea effectively beyond some verbal support amid China's sanctions against South Korea. China's THAAD-related bullying encouraged South Korea to seek out and diversify its economic and strategic options. To this end, in late 2017 the Moon government launched its New Southern Policy (NSP) to boost ties with Association of Southeast Asian Nations (ASEAN) member countries and India (Office of National Security 2018). Its main objective was to diversify away from its strong trade dependence on China.

From South Korea's perspective, the relationship with China thus turned into a thorny issue marked by ambivalence. On the one hand, South Korea desperately needed help from China to resolve the North Korean nuclear issue, maintain stability on the Korean Peninsula, and boost the economic relationship. South Korea fell into a trap: the more North Korea posed a threat, the more South Korea increased its expectations towards China. On the other hand, China's rapid rise and strategic competition between the United States and China imposed a tremendous burden on South Korea's foreign policy and the ROK–US alliance. China became the main threat to the United States. However, the main threat for South Korea came from North Korea instead of China. Thus, there was a widening strategic interest gap in the ROK–US alliance, and Washington put pressure on South Korea to turn against China. South Korea thus faced pressure to transform the goal of the alliance from deterring North Korea to dealing with China.

The historical experience shows that China's main concern on the Korean Peninsula has been consistent: maintaining the status quo of two Koreas, preserving stability, and deterring US influence over the whole of the Korean Peninsula. The denuclearisation of North Korea and unification under a South Korea-style system have not been priorities for Chinese foreign policymakers, which is a big difference from South Korean expectations. South Korea has gradually recognised such differences, eliminating any illusions towards China. However, Seoul respects China's contribution and role in stabilising the Korean Peninsula and its economy. Thus, China has sought and enjoyed deep relations with both Koreas under Xi Jinping's leadership. At the same time, China is striving to avoid running the risk of a bigger crisis and facing an uncertain political and security scenario due to any sudden change on the Korean Peninsula (Zhu 2016).

3.3.2 *Impact of the Strategic Competition between the United States and China*

The United States and China are locked in a strategic battle over the future of the Indo-Pacific region. Not only the Indo-Pacific, but also the whole world are heading into a period of turbulence due to the US–China strategic competition. The triangular relationship between South Korea, the United States, and China resembles the triangular relationship between Korea (then, *Koryo*), Liao, and Song from the tenth to thirteenth centuries. Korea struggled for its own survival in the strategic competition between Liao and Song, waging war with Liao three times (Ledyard 1983; Northeast Asian History Foundation 2018).

The Donald Trump administration unveiled its free and open Indo-Pacific (FOIP) strategy in 2017, following from the Obama administration's rebalancing strategy towards Asia. After Trump became president, he took unprecedented, bold, and aggressive policies against China. The US National Security Strategy report published in December 2017 defined China as a 'strategic competitor' and 'revisionist' towards the current international order (White House 2017). The strategic competition between the United States and China is likely to be a defining factor in the South Korea–China relationship. There might be catastrophic consequences for their relationship in the future if South Korea mishandles these relations.

Indeed, South Korea finds itself caught between the two competing great powers. South Korea has been a staunch ally of the United States and a strategic cooperative partner of China. It heavily depends on the United States for its security because it faces an existential threat from North Korea's growing nuclear weapon capabilities. Meanwhile, its economy depends on China for about 34 per cent of its trade as of 2020 (Ministry of Foreign Affairs of the Republic of Korea 2021). Neither the United States nor China can replace the role of the other for South Korea.

Moon Jae-in's foreign policy orientation is based on a close alliance with the United States, while developing a substantial 'strategic cooperative partnership' with China, as documented in the president's 100 Policy Tasks Five-Year plan. The Moon administration understands FOIP as a strategy driven by geopolitical competition between the United States and China. Beyond circumstantial or domestic political reasons, the dominant factors driving Seoul's policy stance towards FOIP lie on the experience of the THAAD dispute and the Moon government's desire for policy autonomy.

Historically, Korea has been the victim of surrounding great power competition without exception, whether a regional power transition or strategic competition among great powers took place. In the twenty-first century, South Korea sees itself increasingly entrapped in the strategic competition between the United States and China. At the heart of this dilemma is South Korea, pursuing greater foreign policy autonomy from this great power competition (Snyder 2020).

Meanwhile, South Korea is also afraid that adopting FOIP would dramatically deteriorate its relationship with Beijing, South Korea's largest trading partner and a significant stakeholder in establishing a Korean peace regime. Seoul has trodden cautiously with FOIP to avoid overly antagonising Beijing.

3.3.3 *China's South Korea Policy*

From a Chinese perspective, South Korea is a lynchpin in East Asia, a critical objective of its neighbouring foreign policy. Wang Yi once replied to a question about the

Indo-Pacific (Wang 2020, 2021). He said: first, focus on East Asia and Asia. Chinese foreign policy would like to maintain a balanced approach between the two Koreas to extend its influence over the Korean Peninsula. If strategic rivalry deepens, Beijing will pay more attention to China–North Korea relations.

From a Chinese perspective, the most urgent issue with regards to South Korea is not denuclearisation: it is acquiring a stable and sufficient supply of memory chips from Samsung and SK Hynix amid the US–China strategic competition. Probably an even more important security issue is preventing the deployment of US mid-range ballistic missiles in South Korea. If this happened, it could cause a second, Chinese version of the Cuban missile crisis.

Embracing Seoul is the key to the success of China's two circular strategies. Beijing also needs to include Japan and Taiwan in its regional value chain. Therefore, China will pay close attention to establishing a better relationship with South Korea and Japan for the foreseeable future, unless both countries openly take a position against China. For example, Beijing hopes to establish a South Korea–China–Japan FTA. In contrast, the Taiwan issue is more subtle. China generally is more cautious on this issue, despite its firm attitude towards unification.

4. Conclusion

Korea and China share several thousand years of contact and communication. Therefore, the Chinese often describe such relations as a relationship connected by waters and mountains (山水相连). For Korea, however, this history and experiences do not necessarily convey pleasant memories, as is the case for most countries adjacent to great powers. Koreans are proud of themselves for keeping their independence from China, which has never conquered the entirety of Korea.

Without exception, Korea has been a victim of great power competition whenever regional power transitions or strategic competition among great powers has taken place. The centrifugal forces of great powers have affected Korea's domestic politics and created turmoil in Korean society.

In the past, continental forces influenced the fate of Korean and Korean dynasties more strongly. However, after the Second World War, Korea was divided into two adversaries. North Korea became part of the continental forces; South Korea part of the maritime forces for the first time in history.

Chinese reform and opening-up policies adopted from 1978 provided an opportunity for South Korea to normalise its relationship with China in 1992. South Korea and China formally established a strategic cooperative partnership in 2008. Since normalisation, both countries have enjoyed honeymoon periods, despite different ideologies and political systems—until the THAAD issue broke out and US–China strategic competition took hold. Currently, China is South Korea's top trading partner, with over 30 per cent of the trade total. However, China's rise gradually changed relations between South Korea and China. Rivalry replaced mutual complementarity.

As the strategic competition between the United States and China deepens, South Korea sees itself increasingly entrapped by them. South Korea's national policies, dependent on the United States for its security and on China for its economy, are incompatible with the strategic competition. Neither of the two replaces the other's role in relation to the economy and security of South Korea. Thus, Seoul's scope for autonomy is narrowing. Also, the hope of North Korean denuclearisation has almost disappeared. South Korea thus needs to find a new space and thinking in foreign policy beyond the strategic competition.

The year 2022 is the thirtieth anniversary of South Korea–China normalisation. However, both countries are yet to find an exit from the malign influences of the strategic competition. Rocky relations appear to be waiting for them in the future.

Notes

1. Interview, http://news.naver.com/main/read.nhn?mode=LSD&mid=sec&sid1=101&oid=037&aid=0000006961, accessed 29 November 2021.
2. Interview with a then-policy advisor to the Presidential Foreign Affairs Office.

Bibliography

Chen, F. (陈峰君), and Wang, C. (王传剑) (2002), 亚太大国与朝鲜半岛 (*Asian-Pacific Major Powers and the Korean Peninsula*) (Beijing: Beijing University Press).
Choi, M.-H. (2009), 중국·북한동맹관계 (*China's Alliance with North Korea*) (Seoul: Oreum Press).
Chung, J. (2011a) 중국의 부상과 한반도의 미래 (*China's Rise and the Future of the Korean Peninsula*) (Seoul: Seoul National University Press).
Chung, J., ed. (2011b) 한·중관계의 딜레마와 해법 (Dilemma and Solution of South Korea–China Relations) (Seoul: SERI).
Cui, Z. (崔志鹰) (2000), 大国与朝鲜半岛 (*Great Powers and the Korean Peninsula*) (Wanchai: Joyo Publishing Agency Ltd).
Denmark, A. (2012), 'The Revenge of Geography and the Asia-Pacific', interview with Robert Kaplan, National Bureau of Asian Research, 12 September, https://www.nbr.org/publication/the-revenge-of-geography-and-the-asian-pacific/, accessed 29 November 2021.
Eouyang, S. (2008), 중국의 대북조선 기밀파일 (*China's Secret File on North Korea*) (Seoul: Hanwool).
Gong, K. (龚克瑜) (2018), 朝鲜半岛局势与中国 (*Situations on the Korean Peninsula and China*) (Seoul: Shinsung Press).
Kang, D. C. (2009), 'Between Balancing and Bandwagoning: South Korea's Response to China', *Journal of East Asian Studies* 9 (2009), 1–28.
Kaplan, R. (2012), *The Revenge of Geography* (New York: Random House).
Kim, H.-J. (2013), 중국 이야기 (*The Story of China*) (Seoul: Vision and Leadership).
Kim, H.-K. (2010), 'From a Buffer Zone to a Strategic Burden: Evolving Sino–North Korea Relations during the Hu Jintao Era', *Korean Journal of Defense Analysis* 22(1), 57–74.

Kim, H.-K. (2012), 'Enemy, Homager or Equal Partner? Evolving South Korea–China Relations', *Journal of International and Area Studies* 19(2), 47–62.

Kim, H.-K. (2017), 'U.S.–China–South Korea Coordination on North Korea', *CFR Online Journal*, November, www.cfr.org, accessed 29 November 2021.

Kim, H.-K. (2020), 'China's Evolving North Korea Policy', *Focus Asia* (Stockholm: Institute for Security & Development Policy): https://isdp.eu/publication/chinas-evolving-north-korea-policy/, accessed 15 November 2021.

Kim, H.-K. (2021), Inside Interviews as a then-policy advisor to the Presidential Foreign Affairs Office.

Kim, H.-K., and Guo, S. (2015), '시진핑시기 중국의 대한반도 전략사고의 변화와 함의' (Changes of Strategic Thinking on the Korean Peninsula during Xi's Era and Its Implication), 신아세아(*New Asia*) 22(4)호. 36–59.

Kim, S.-K. (2020), 송대 동아시아의 국제관계와 외교의례 (*International Relations in East Asia and Diplomatic Rituals in the Era of Song Dynasty*) (Seoul: Sing-A Press).

Ledyard, G. (1983), 'Yin and Yang in the China–Manchuria–Korea Triangle', in Morris Rossabi, ed., *China among Equals* (Berkeley, CA: University of California Press), 313–353.

Lee, J.-S. (2000), 북한-중국관계: 1945–2000 (*North Korea–China Relations: 1945–2000*) (Seoul: Joongshim Press).

Lim, D.-W. (2008), 피스메이커 (*Peacemaker*) (Seoul: Joongang Books).

Liu, S. (刘顺利), ed. (2011), 中国与朝韩五千年交流年历 (*A Chronology of Five Thousand Years of Contacts between China and Korea*) (Beijing: Xuefan).

Mearsheimer, J. (2018), 'Presentation at the Chey Institute', https://www.chey.org/Eng/issues/IssuesContentsView.aspx?seq=563, accessed 29 November 2021.

Ministry of Foreign Affairs of the Republic of Korea (2021), 중국 개황 2020 (*China Factbook*) (Seoul: Ministry of Foreign Affairs).

Northeast Asian History Foundation(2018), 한국 대외관계와 외교사: 고려 (*South Korea's Foreign Relations and the History of Diplomacy: Koryo* (Seoul: Northeast Asian History Foundation).

Office of National Security (2014), 국가안보전략(*National Security Strategy*) (Seoul: Office of National Security).

Office of National Security (2018), 국가안보전략(*National Security Strategy*) (Seoul: Office of National Security).

Rhu, P.-Y. (劉鳳榮) (1970), 'Foreign Invasions and the Ten Places of Security Listed in Chung-Kam-Rok' 白山學報 (*Baek-san-hak-bo*), 223.

Shunji, H. (2013), 북한중국관계 60 년 (*60 Years of North Korea China Relations*) (Seoul: Sun-In Press).

Snyder, Scott. A. (2020), *South Korea at the Crossroads: Autonomy and Alliance in an Era of Rival Powers* (New York: Columbia University Press).

Snyder, Scott. (2009), *China's Rise and the Two Koreas* (Boulder, CA: Lynne Rienner Publishers).

Wang, Xiaopu. (王小甫) (2014), 中韩关系史 (*A History of Sino–Korean Relations*), Vols I, II, and III (Beijing: Social Science Academic Press).

Wang, Yi. (2020), '王毅就当前中美关系接受新华社专访 (Interview with Wang Yi on China-US Relations by Xinwha News Agency)', 新華網, 5 August, www.china.com.cn/opinion/think/2020-08/06/content_76351781.htm, accessed 29 November 2021.

Wang, Yi. (2021), '王毅就2020年国际形势和外交工作接受新华社和中央广播电视总台联合采访(Interview with Wang Yi on 2020 International Relations and China's Foreign

Policies by Xinwha News Agency)', 新華網 2 January, www.xinhuanet.com/mrdx/2021-01/02/c_139636018.htm, accessed 29 November 2021.

Wei, Z. (魏志江) (2008), 冷战后中韩关系研究 (*Study on China–ROK Relations after the Cold War Period*) (Guangzhou: Zhongshan University Press).

White House (2017), 'National Security Strategy', Washington DC, https://trumpwhitehouse.archives.gov/wp-content/uploads/2017/12/NSS-Final-12-18-2017-0905.pdf, accessed 29 November 2021.

Zhu, Zhiqun. (2016), 'Comrades on Broken Arms: Shifting Chinese Policies Toward North Korea', *Asian Politics & Policy* 8(4), 14.

Index

Tables are indicated by *t* following the page number

A

administrative law *see* civil service; corruption; decentralisation; executive accountability; local government; public policy
ageing society, social welfare and 486
armed forces
   coups *see* history
   global ranking of strength 558
   overseas deployments 558
   policies *see* defence policy
   strategy *see* national security
   Terminal High Altitude Area Defence (THAAD) missile system 640–641
arts and culture
   handbook's contributors' approaches to 11–12
   international impact of Korean culture 3, 4
   see also cinema; popular music; public intellectuals; television
Asian Financial Crisis (1997)
   corruption, and 513
   foreign economic policy, and 562, 569
   social welfare reform 473–476, 485
   trade (labour) unions, and 349–353, 354
'associational' interest groups 328, 332
associative interest groups *see* interest groups
attitudes *see* public opinion
authoritarian presidentialism *see* presidentialism

B

big business *see* Chaebol
business and industrial organisations 329–331

C

campaigns, election *see* elections
Candlelight Uprising (2016-17) 3, 315–316
Chaebol (big business)
   competition policy, and 128–131
   conceptualisation of 121–123
   controversy as to 120
   definition of 120
   developmental state, and 116–117, 118
   economic policy, and 123–128, 129, 133
   foreign economic policy, and 563, 565, 566, 569–572
   global competitiveness of 132–133
   growth of 123–128, 133
   handbook's contributors' approaches to 120–121
   industrial policy, and 123, 124, 125, 127
   innovativeness of 132
   political economy of reform of 128–132
'Cheonan' (Korean Navy ship) explosion controversy 433–435
China
   Cold War relations with 630–631
   Comprehensive cooperative partnership (2003) 632, 634, 639, 640
   Cooperative partnership (1998) 632
   deterioration and recovery during THAAD issue 640–641
   foreign policy as to Korean Peninsula 636–638
   free trade agreement 639
   geopolitical impact 630
   historical link with 629, 643
   honeymoon period (1991-2001) 631–633
   Korea economic relations 567, 571–575

China (cont.)
  Korean reunification, and 598–599, 602–603
  North Korea, and 629–644
  one Korea policy 631
  present-day South Korea policy 642–643
  relationship building since 2000 633–635
  relationship ebbs and flows 643–644
  strategic cooperative partnership (2008) 632, 634–643
  Substantial strategic cooperative partnership (2017) 632, 642
  Terminal High Altitude Area Defence (THAAD) missile system issue, and 640–641
  trade with 631–633, 640, 641, 642, 643
  two-Korea policy 631–633, 636
  US rivalry 549–550, 554–555, 629, 635, 636–639, 642–644
  wars with 629
  zenith of relations with 638–640
cinema
  censorship of 380–383
  democratisation, and 378
  handbook's contributors' approaches to 380
  importance and influence of 377
  introduction in Korea 377–378
  during Japanese occupation 377
  political and social commentary function of 378–379, 385–387
  post-democratisation relationship with politics 389
  progressive political storytelling 380–383
  pursuit of popularity to preserve political independence 390
  storytelling function of 377–380
  television contrasted 377
  vehicle for young people's political participation, as 389
  see also television
civil service, historical development of 183–184
civil society see public participation
Cold War see China; Korea (reunification); Korean War; Korea–United States alliance
collapse mode of democratisation 89
colonialism see Japan

communication, political see elections
competition, global competitiveness of Chaebol (big business) 132–133
competition policy, Chaebol (big business) and 128–131
Confucianism 423, 630
Constitution
  authoritarian presidentialism (1952-80), and 155–160
  demand for further reform of 165
  democratic reform (1987) 160–164
  longevity and success of 1987 Constitution 165
  making of 1948 Constitution 153–155
  resource distribution, power of 183
  separation of powers 51, 183, 186, 199, 200, 203, 207, 370, 372, 456–457
  see also executive power; judiciary; National Assembly
Constitutional Court
  creation of (1987) 199
  judicial review, power of 210
  opposition to 199
  political role of 199
  Supreme Court, and 210
conversion mode of democratisation 89
cooperative ('pacted transition') mode of democratisation 89, 90
corporations see Chaebol
corruption
  anti-corruption policies, current policies 518–520
  anti-corruption policies, historical overview of 517–518
  anti-corruption policies, political will for 515–516, 521
  Asian Financial Crisis (1997), and 513
  critical juncture approach to 512
  crony capitalism 513, 514–515, 521
  democracy and reduction of 513
  e-government and reduction of 513–514
  grand corruption, anti-corruption policies against 515–520
  grand corruption, definition and distinction 508–510, 521
  grand corruption, no decrease in 509, 511, 514, 521

grand corruption, path dependence
　　and 514–515
grand corruption, political will to curb 515–
　　516, 521
grand corruption, studies of 509
historical institutionalism approach to 512–
　　515, 521
IMF Global Standard, adoption of 513
Improper Solicitation and Graft Act
　　(2015) 519–520
integrity assessment 519
level of 508, 510–512
no decrease in 508
path dependence approach to 514–515
petty corruption, critical juncture approach
　　to 512–514
petty corruption, decrease in 508–509, 511,
　　515, 521
petty corruption, definition and
　　distinction 508–510, 521
petty corruption, impact of 510
positive effect on economic growth 508
social scientific studies of 508
'venal corruption' 510
'counter-experts' 430–435, 436
courts *see* judiciary
COVID-19 pandemic, success of response
　　to 455
critical juncture approach to corruption 512
crony capitalism 513, 514–515, 521

D

decentralisation
　　centralism, tradition of 491
　　global trend towards 492
　　handbook's contributors' approaches to 492
　　historical development of reform
　　　　process 493–494
　　lateness of development of 504–505
　　post-1987 democratic regime, and 492–493
　　renewed demands for 491
defectors from North Korea, attitudes
　　towards 298–299
defence policy
　　geopolitical factor 547–548
　　handbook's contributors' approaches to 14,
　　　　547

historical factors 547
North Korea, and 547
North Korean military threat 548–549
North Korean nuclear weapons 550–552
public opinion, and 556–557
Terminal High Altitude Area Defence
　　(THAAD) missile system
　　deployment 640–641
US alliance 552–554, 555–556
US-China rivalry, and 549–550
see also armed forces; foreign policy;
　　national security
democracy
　　Candlelight protests and revival of 358
　　centralism, tradition of 491
　　collapse mode of democratisation 89
　　conceptualisation of democratic
　　　　support 362–363
　　conservative democratisation 88–89,
　　　　96–99
　　conservative democratisation
　　　　process 89–90
　　consolidation of 358–362
　　Constitution of 1987 92–94
　　conversion mode of democratisation 89
　　cooperative ('pacted transition') mode of
　　　　democratisation 89, 90
　　corruption reduction, and 513
　　critique of current literature on 89–91
　　cultural perspective on deconsolidation
　　　　of 372–373
　　decline in public support for 358–359
　　deconsolidation of 358–362, 372–373
　　democratic backsliding 358
　　foreign intervention mode of
　　　　democratisation 89
　　foundational presidential election
　　　　(1987) 91–92
　　global support for, perspectives on 358, 372
　　handbook's contributors' approaches
　　　　to 15–16
　　history *see* history
　　incomplete democracy, problems
　　　　of 372–373
　　majoritarian electoral system 92–94, 99
　　nationalism, and 145–146
　　Philippines transition contrasted 89–90

democracy (*cont.*)
  popular preference for 88
  pre-democratisation process 91
  presidentialism, and 88, 99
  public participation's role in
      democratisation 90, 91, 99
  regionalism, and 88, 94–96
  relevance of democratic support 362–363
  revival strategy for 373
  shift in balance of support for democracy or
      authoritarianism (1996-2018) 363–372
  success of 3, 87–88, 98–99
  sustainability of, concerns about 455–456
  Taiwan transition contrasted 90
  transition to 3–4
  29 June Declaration (1987) 44, 90–92, 95, 161–162
  see also Constitution; decentralisation;
      elections; executive accountability;
      interest groups; local elections; local
      government; minorities (political);
      National Assembly; political parties;
      politics; presidentialism; public
      intellectuals; public participation;
      social movements; trade (labour)
      unions
Democratization Uprising (1987) 44–45
developmental state
  adaptability of 579, 590
  centralism, tradition of 491
  Chaebol (big business), and 116–117, 118
  conceptualisation of 104–105
  conflicting interests arising from increase in
      social diversification 327, 338
  'double transition' dilemma 585–587
  executive accountability, and 458–460, 467
  finance 114–116, 118
  foreign aid inflows 584
  industrial policies 111–115, 117–118
  international politics of 107–111, 117–118
  middle power ranking 588
  North Korea, and 110, 114
  origins of 105–107
  post-1945 division of Korea, and 107
  social development, and 582–583
  social welfare, and 472–476, 479–481
  state-led economic development 580–581

  success of 589
  US support 107–110, 118
digital technologies
  emergence of digital media 397–399
  handbook's contributors' approaches
      to 394–395
  new media in digital networked
      society 395–396, 404–405
  smartphones, politics and 403–404, 404–405
  transformation of politics by 394, 404–405
  see also internet; social media
diplomacy *see* foreign policy
'double transition' dilemma *see* economic
      development

E

economic development
  aid motives, inconsistency of 587–588
  corruption, and 508
  critique of 585–588
  'double transition' dilemma 585–587
  executive control of 186–189
  features of 579–585
  foreign aid inflows 584–585
  global ranking of economic strength 558, 578
  handbook's contributors' approaches
      to 578–579
  middle power ranking 588–589
  model 578–590
  replicability of 578–579
  social development, and 582–583
  state-led economic development 580–581
  success of 3, 578
  transition to modern economy 3
  see also developmental state
Economic Planning Board
      (*Gyeongjegihoikwon*) (EPB)
  abolition of (1994) 192, 461, 581, 586
  creation of (1961) 38, 186
  economic policy initiatives 189–190
  economic policymaking 195, 460
  influence of 192
  leadership of 42, 187*t*, 188, 188–190, 196n3
  power of 183–184, 186, 195, 459, 461, 580
  reform of 188, 190

status of 186
success of 188, 586
weakness of 184, 186
economic policy
    Chaebol (big business), and 123–128, 129, 133
    foreign policy, and *see* foreign economic policy
    liberalisation 183–184
    new political issues as to 286–289
    redistribution issues 286–287
    welfare issues 286–287
e-government and reduction of corruption 513–514
elections
    candidates' use of social media 273–275, 280
    communication technology, use of 270
    handbook's contributors' approaches to 270
    historical overview of campaign communication 271–273, 280
    municipal elections, social media use in 401–402
    political communication, role of 270
    social media and political participation 270, 276–280
    social media and vote choice 270, 279–280
electoral system
    campaign strategies 252
    generational voting 252–253
    inter-Korean issues, dominance of 266–267
    majoritarian 92–94, 99
    multiparty system, obstacles to emergence of 252, 266
    party systems, and 253–257
    redistributive issues 252, 266–267
    regional voting 253, 263–266
    two-party system 252
    voters' political attitudes 252–253, 257–262
    see also elections
employment relations *see* trade (labour) unions
EPB *see* Economic Planning Board
executive accountability
    concerns about executive competence 455–456
    democratic control, effectiveness of 461–468
    democratic government reforms, and 461–462, 467
    developmental state political control, and 458–460, 467
    handbook's contributors' approaches to 456
    New Public Management reforms 462–464
    performance management, and 464–466, 467–468
    political control and bureaucratic autonomy in relation 456–458, 468
executive power
    administrative reform (1980-2002), and 189–192
    bureaucratic autonomy political and control in relation 468
    bureaucratic politics of welfare reform 471, 481–483
    democratisation era (2003-present) 193–195
    economic development, and 186–189
    economic liberalisation, and 183–184
    historical development of 183–186, 195
    resource distribution 183

F

female representation *see* women
FEP *see* foreign economic policy
Fifth Republic (1979-79) 100n11, 160, 170, 171, 177
finance, developmental state and 114–116, 118
Financial Crisis (1997) *see* Asian Financial Crisis (1997)
First Republic (1948-60) 35–37
foreign aid *see* economic development
foreign economic policy (FEP)
    after Asian Financial Crisis (1998-2008) 569–571
    Asian Financial Crisis (1997), and 562, 569
    China, and 567, 571–575
    contemporary FEPs (2008-21) 571–574
    COVID-19 pandemic, and 575
    decision-making structure 563–565
    free trade agreements 562–563, 564, 565, 569–573, 639
    handbook's contributors' approaches to 563
    international/regional economic agreements 562–563, 565, 566, 567–574

foreign economic policy (FEP) (*cont.*)
   Japan, and 569
   middle power ranking 562
   New Northern Policy (NNP) 563, 567
   New Southern Policy (NSP) 563
   North Korea, and 567
   political and private sector actors 563–566, 569–572
   post-democratisation (1987-98) 566–569
   post-democratisation transformation of 562
   United States, and 564, 565, 567, 569, 571–575, 639
foreign intervention mode of democratisation 89
foreign policy
   alliances *see* national security
   consensus and continuity 529, 541–542
   conservative era (2008-17) 537–539, 541
   decision factors 529
   economic policy, and *see* foreign economic policy
   function of 546
   globalisation, and 541
   handbook's contributors' approaches to 14, 530
   institutional structure 529, 531–533
   Korean reunification *see* Korea (reunification)
   liberal era (1998-2008) 535–537, 541
   liberal era (2017-) 540–541
   middle power ranking 530, 541–542
   national autonomy, protection of 529, 541–542
   overlap with security policy 546
   peaceful settlement of disputes 546
   post-democratisation (1987-98) 533–535
   presidentialism, and 529, 541
   success of 529
   tools of 530
   US alliance *see* Korea-United States alliance
   US-China rivalry, and 530
   see also China; defence policy; Korea (reunification); Korea-United States alliance; national security
Four Major Rivers Restoration Project controversy 432–433

Fourth Republic (1972-79) 170, 383
free trade agreements (FTAs) *see* foreign economic policy
freedom of the press 408–409, 419
FTAs (free trade agreements) *see* foreign economic policy
full cleavage theory of regionalism 77–79

G

gender
   conflicts 291–295
   gender gap 289–291
   new political issues as to 289–295
   see also women
generational political representation 234, 247, 248
generational voting 252–253
German and Korean reunification compared 595–597
globalisation
   Chaebol (big business), and 132–133
   decentralisation, and 492
   foreign policy, and 541
   nationalism, and 146–147
   popular music, and 448–449
government administration
   centralism, tradition of 491
   e-government 513–514
   see also civil service; corruption; decentralisation; local government
grand corruption *see* corruption
Gwangju Uprising (1980) 43–44
Gyeongjegihoikwon see Economic Planning Board

H

health *see* public health
historical institutionalism approach to corruption 512–515, 521
history
   China-Korea link 629
   Democratization Uprising (1987) 44–45
   First Republic (1948-60) 35–37
   Gwangju Uprising (1980) 43–44
   introduction to 34
   key concepts 5–7
   military coup (1961) (Park Coup or May Coup) 38

military coup (1980) (Chun Coup) 43–44
Park Government (1961-79) 38–43
pre-1945 *see* Korea (pre-1945 history)
Second Republic (1948-61) 38
Yushin Constitution (1972-79) 41–43
human security, national security and 558

I

IMF Global Standard on corruption, adoption of 513
immigration *see* migrants
Improper Solicitation and Graft Act (2015) 519–520
industrial development *see* developmental state; economic development
industrial policy
    Chaebol (big business), and 123, 124, 125, 127
    developmental state, and 111–115, 117–118
integrity assessment 519
intellectuals *see* public intellectuals
interest groups
    'associational' interest groups 328, 332
    attitudes towards 327
    business and industrial organisations 329–331
    conflict coordination system, need for 339
    conflicts arising from increase in social diversification 327, 338
    conflictual pluralism from 2010s 337–338
    democracy undermined by 327
    democratic society, in 326, 328
    emergence of 328
    handbook's contributors' approaches to 327, 343
    importance and influence of 326
    industrialisation, and 328, 338
    intrinsic part of democracy and social development 327
    legal prohibition of political participation by 338–339
    negative perspectives on 327, 338
    own special interests, pursuit of 327
    political mobilisation groups during authoritarian regimes 328, 339
    political parties contrasted 326–327
    positive perspectives on 327, 338
    post-democratisation changes in 333–338
    post-democratisation competitive pluralism 335–337
    pre-democratisation dependence on state power 333–335
    professional organisations 331–332
    public interest groups 332–333
    purpose of 326
    social stability reduced by 327
    trade (labour) unions 328–329
    types of 328
    see also public participation; social movements; trade (labour) unions
international economic agreements *see* foreign economic policy
international relations
    cultural aspects of *see* arts and culture
    diplomacy *see* foreign policy
    handbook's contributors' approaches to 14–15
    see also China; defence policy; foreign policy; Korea, Democratic People's Republic of (North Korea); national security; United States
internet
    e-government and reduction of corruption 513–514
    new digital technologies, and 394–395
    politics, and 399–401, 404–405
    see also social media

J

Japan
    cinema 377–378, 381, 387, 388
    cinema during Korea occupation 377
    colonial rule over Korea 6, 17, 22–26, 30–31, 123–124, 137–139, 144, 146, 153, 185, 186, 377–378, 381, 415, 424, 491, 547, 584
    developmental state, and 26–28, 104–112, 114–118, 124
    economic development 6–7, 581, 584, 587
    global democracy ranking 87
    Korea–China relations, and 635, 638, 639, 640, 643
    Korean nationalism, and 7, 136–141, 137–139, 146–147, 153
    Korean republicanism, and 28–30

Japan (*cont.*)
　　Korean reunification, and　597–601
　　Korea–United States alliance, and　621, 623
　　liberation from　5, 34, 54, 168, 183, 377, 424, 439, 459, 580, 615
　　music　439–449
　　Normalization Treaty (1965)　36, 39–40
　　press clubs　416
　　Protectorate of Korea (1905-10)　18–21
　　public participation　320–321
　　security policy　556–557
　　trade (labour) unions　342, 350
　　trade with　567–572
　　welfare　472, 483
　　zaibatsu (corporations)　130–131
jihaeng ilchi ('correspondence between knowledge and conduct'), principle of　423
journalism *see* press
judicial independence *see* judiciary
judiciary
　　institutional structure of courts　202–205, 210
　　judicial independence　199, 211
　　judicialisation of politics　210–211
　　political role of　198–199, 205–206, 210–211
　　political understanding of judicial power　200–202
　　politicisation of　210–211
　　recent cases on political role of courts　207–209
　　see also Constitutional Court

K

Kim Dae-jung　219, 220, 221–225, 227, 229
Kim Jong-pil　221–225, 227, 229
Kim Young-sam　219, 221–225, 227, 229
Korea (pre-1945 history)
　　critique of current literature on　17, 30–31
　　divisions within independence movement　23–26
　　economic development　26
　　handbook's contributors' approaches to　18
　　Japanese Protectorate (1905-10)　18–21
　　legacy of　17, 30–31
　　modern nationalism　21–23

monarchy, end of　29–30
rise of republicanism　26
Korea (reunification)
　　China, and　598–599, 602–603
　　Cold War legacy　595
　　Cold War North Korea relations　603–604
　　defence policy, and　547
　　domestic political consensus on　607–608
　　foreign policy goal of　529–530, 533–535, 541
　　German reunification compared　595–597
　　handbook's contributors' approaches to　595–596
　　inter-Korean politics　603–609
　　international politics of　597–603
　　Japan, and　597–601
　　multilateralisation of North Korean issues　600–601
　　North Korean openness　608–609
　　post-Cold War North Korea relations　604–607
　　prospects for　609–610
　　Russian Federation, and　599–600
　　United States, and　598
　　US/North Korea relations　601–602
Korea, Democratic People's Republic of (North Korea)
　　China and　629–644
　　Cold War relations with　603–604
　　defectors from, attitudes towards　298–299
　　developmental state and　110, 114
　　Korean reunification, and *see* Korea (reunification)
　　military threat from　548–549
　　nuclear weapons　547, 550–552, 634–635, 639–644
　　openness　608–609
　　political consensus on　607–608
　　post-Cold War relations with　604–607
Korea, Republic of (South Korea)
　　global ranking of strength　558
　　middle power ranking　530, 541–542, 562, 588–589
　　transition and modernisation　3–5
Korean War, nationalism during　141–142
Korea–United States alliance
　　abandonment fears and US assurances　616–618

balancing of autonomy and cooperation 618–620
beginning of 613, 614–616
changes in 613
critique of 620–622
early Cold War period 614–616
foreign policy 529, 530, 533, 534, 536–538, 540–542
Korean dependency 630, 644
mid-Cold War period 616–618
Mutual Defence Treaty (1953) 613, 615–616
post-Cold War period 618–620
public support for 613–614
resilience of 614, 625
security policy 552–556
Terminal High Altitude Area Defence (THAAD) missile system deployment 640–641
Trump-Moon era 622–625
K-pop *see* popular music

L

labour movements *see* social movements
labour unions *see* trade (labour) unions
legislation
 consultations as to 170–171
 legislative process 171–178
legislative branch *see* National Assembly
liberalism
 economic policy 183–184
 see also neoliberalism
local elections
 introduction of 491–492
 renewed demands for 491
local government
 centralism, tradition of 491
 consolidation during 2000's 495–499
 expansion of 491
 future reform, challenges for 501–505
 handbook's contributors' approaches to 492, 492–493
 historical development of reform process 493–494
 international comparison 499–501
 lateness of development of 504–505
 positive political impacts of 492
 Regional Authority Index (RAI) 499–501

M

May Coup (1961) 38
media *see* arts and culture; cinema; digital technologies; elections; internet; press; social media; television
middle power ranking 530, 541–542, 562, 588–589
migrants
 immigrants, attitudes towards 296–297
 immigration issues 295–299
 North Korean defectors, attitudes towards 298–299
 political representation 234, 247, 248
military coups *see* history
military forces *see* armed forces; national security
military strategy *see* national security
minorities (political)
 democratisation, and 233
 generational representation 234, 247, 248
 handbook's contributors' approaches to 234, 253
 interest in 233–234, 247–248
 level of representation of 234
 migrants 234, 247, 248
 National Assembly, in 243–247
 party nomination for 237–240
 political divisions, and 234–236
 political systems reform 235–236, 247–248
 regionalism, and 234
 representative democracy, in 233
 women's representation 234, 247–248
mobile phones, use in political campaigns 403–404
moral element of intellectualism 423–424
multiparty system *see* electoral system
music *see* popular music
Mutual Defence Treaty (1953) *see* Korea-United States alliance

N

National Assembly
 Cabinet formation, and 58–60
 constitutional status of 167
 executive-introduced legislation, and 60–63
 historical overview of 168–170

National Assembly (*cont.*)
   increase of powers of 167, 179
   inter-party consensus 178–179
   legislative consultation system 170–171, 178–179
   legislative process 171–178
   minority representation in 243–247
   parliamentary parties, dominant role of 175–178
   partisan conflict within 179
   presidentialism, and 57, 167
   public opinion of 167–168
   resource distribution, power of 183
   standing committees 172–175
   see also legislation; political parties
national security
   'alliance politics and coercive diplomacy' 546
   decision factors 546
   function of 546
   geopolitical factor 546–548
   handbook's contributors' approaches to 547
   historical factors 547
   human security, and 558
   military strategy, and 546
   new issues for 546
   non-traditional threats, responses to 558
   North Korea, and 547, 548–549
   North Korean nuclear weapons 550–552
   overlap with foreign policy 546
   policy as expression of intent 546
   priority given to 529–530
   public opinion, and 556–557
   scale and scope of 546, 558
   US alliance *see* Korea-United States alliance
   US-China rivalry, and 549–550, 554–555
   see also armed forces; defence policy
nationalism
   conceptualisation of 147
   democracy, and 145–146
   distinctive characteristics 136–137
   globalisation, and 146–147
   handbook's contributors' approaches to 137
   importance of 136, 147
   Japanese colonialism, and 137–139, 147
   Korean War, and 141–142
   nation state, and 142–144

   post-1945 division of Korea, and 139–142
   progressive politics, and 144–145
neoliberalism
   New Public Management reforms, executive accountability and 462–464
   public intellectuals and 426–427
networked social movements 315–316
new digital technologies and media *see* digital technologies; elections; internet; social media
New Northern Policy (NNP) *see* foreign economic policy
new political issues *see* politics
New Public Management reforms, executive accountability and 462–464
New Southern Policy (NSP) *see* foreign economic policy
news *see* press
NNP (New Northern Policy NNP) *see* foreign economic policy
North Korea *see* Korea, Democratic People's Republic of
NSP (New Southern Policy) *see* foreign economic policy
nuclear weapons *see* national security

P

parliament *see* National Assembly
path dependence approach to corruption 514–515
performance management, executive accountability and 464–466, 467–468
petty corruption *see* corruption
polifessors 427–428
political communication *see* elections
political mobilisation groups during authoritarian regimes 328, 339
political parties
   changes to parties and party system 225–228
   characteristics of parties and party system 218–220, 229
   conflicts between 179
   consensus amongst 178–179
   decline of 229
   democratic institutionalisation of 217–218
   difficulties of 229

handbook's contributors' approaches to 218
historical legacies as to development
    of 220–221, 229
interest groups contrasted 326–327
party leaders' dominance of 222–223
party system institutionalisation (PSI), need
    for 217–220, 223, 227–229
'partyless' democracy, concept of 222
peaceful power transfer, success of 218, 220
political institutions, and 224
regionalism, and 223
role in democratic governance 217, 229
'three Kims' politics, and 219, 220, 221–225,
    227, 229
two-party system, causes of 220–224
working-class parties 342
see also elections; electoral system;
    minorities (political)
politics
  anti-corruption policies, and *see* corruption
  centralism, tradition of 491
  control over executive *see* executive
    accountability
  critique of current literature on 4–5
  definition of 183
  democratic transition 3–4
  developmental state, of 107–111, 117–118
  digital technologies, and *see* digital
    technologies; internet; social media
  dynamic perspective on 4
  economic issues 286–289
  gender issues 289–295
  handbook's contribution to literature 4–5
  immigration issues 295–299
  judiciary, and *see* judiciary
  Korean reunification *see* Korea
    (reunification)
  nationalism and progressive
    politics 144–145
  new issues, influence of 285, 299–300
  political mobilisation groups during
    authoritarian regimes 328, 339
  political process 7–9
  political theory *see* social theory
  popular music, and *see* popular music
  redistribution issues 286–287
  static perspective on 4

welfare *see* social welfare
see also Constitution; democracy; interest
    groups; minorities (political); political
    parties; public participation; social
    movements; trade (labour) unions
popular music
  during authoritarian regimes 441–443
  global influences on 448–449
  Japanese music, rejection of 439, 440
  K-pop, rise of 446–448, 450
  K-pop and Donald Trump rally
    sabotage 439, 448
  1980's 443–444
  political change, and 449–450
  political impact of, examples of 439–440
  post-democratisation era (1987-) 444–446
  post-liberation (1945-61) 440–441
  rejection of tradition 449
  US influence on 440–441
prejudice theory of regionalism 74–75, 79
president *see* presidentialism
presidentialism
  conceptualisation of 51–54, 63
  Constitution and 155–160
  critique of current literature on 49–50
  democracy, and 88, 99
  foreign policy, and 529, 541
  handbook's contributors' approaches to 50–
    51, 63–64
  historical development of 54–57, 183
  hyper-presidentialism ('imperial
    presidency') 49–50, 60, 61, 63
  parliamentary elements of 57–63
  press, and 415–419, 420
  separation of powers 51, 155–160, 183, 186,
    199, 200, 203, 207, 370, 372, 456–457
  shift in balance of support for democracy or
    authoritarianism (1996-2018) 363–372
  social movements during authoritarian
    regimes 307–308
  trade (labour) unions, and 343–345, 354
press
  authoritarian legacy features of 415–419,
    420
  democratisation of, success of 408–409,
    419–420
  designated news beats 415

press (*cont.*)
   diversity in political reporting 412–414, 420
   focus on non-substantive issues 414–415
   freedom 408–409, 419
   handbook's contributors' approaches to 409, 424
   ideological spectrum of 409–412, 419
   journalists as politicians 417–419
   partisan journalism 408–409, 412–414, 419
   press clubs (*Kijadan*) 415–416
   public trust in 419
   relationship with political parties 409, 419–420
pressure groups *see* interest groups
professional organisations 331–332
professionals as public intellectuals 430–435
protests *see* social movements
PSI (party system institutionalisation) *see* political parties
public administration *see* civil service
public health, COVID-19 pandemic response 455
public intellectuals
   during authoritarian regimes 424–426
   'Cheonan' (Korean Navy ship) explosion controversy 433–435
   citizens' movement (*simin undong*), and 427–428
   Confucian scholarship, and 423
   Conservative Era (2008–17), during 428–429
   contesting (as 'counter-experts') on specific issues, examples of 430–435
   'counter-experts' 430–435, 436
   democratisation movement, and 425–426
   Four Major Rivers Restoration Project controversy 432–433
   historical tradition of 423
   importance and influence of 423
   jihaeng ilchi ('correspondence between knowledge and conduct'), principle of 423
   moral element 423–424
   neoliberalism, and 426–427
   new types of ('counter-experts') 430–435
   origin and meaning of 'public intellectual' 423
   polifessors 427–428
   post-1987 democratic regime, and 426–427
   professionals as ('counter-experts') 430–435
   role of intellectuals, changes in 423–424, 435–436
   Samsung semiconductor workers leukaemia controversy 430–432
   socialtainers 428–429
public interest groups 332–333
public opinion
   authoritarianism, for 363–372
   democracy, for *see* democracy
   immigrants, on 296–297
   interest groups, on 327
   Korea-United States alliance 613–614
   National Assembly, of 167–168
   North Korean defectors, on 298–299
   voters' political attitudes 252–253, 257–262
public participation
   democratic transition, in 3
   democratisation, and 90, 91, 99
   handbook's contributors' approaches to 10–11
   success of 3
public policy
   handbook's contributors' approaches to 12–14
   see also corruption; decentralisation; executive accountability; local elections; local government

R

RAI *see* Regional Authority Index
redistribution, new political issues as to 286–287
Regional Authority Index (RAI) 499–501
regional economic agreements *see* foreign economic policy
regionalism
   conceptualisation of 72–73
   democracy, and 88, 94–96
   distinctive characteristics 68–69
   electoral system, and 253, 263–266
   full cleavage theory of 77–79
   origins of 70–72
   political parties, and 223
   prejudice theory of 74–75, 79
   social identity theory of 75–76, 79–80

Russian Federation, Korean reunification and 599–600

S

Samsung semiconductor workers leukaemia controversy 430–432
Second Republic (1948-61) 38
security policy *see* national security
separation of powers 51, 183, 186, 199, 200, 203, 207, 370, 372, 456–457
  see also executive power; judiciary; National Assembly
Sixth Republic (1987-present) 167–168, 170, 171–172, 529, 530, 541
smartphones, use in political campaigns 403–404
social development, economic development and 582–583
social identity theory of regionalism 75–76, 79–80
social media
  municipal elections, use in 401–402, 404–405
  new digital technologies, and 394–395
  see also internet
social media in election campaigns *see* elections
social movements
  during authoritarian regimes 307–308
  Candlelight protests 315–316
  conceptualisation of 306–307
  current state of progress 305
  decentralisation of 315
  democratisation, and 305, 321–322
  diversification of 312–313
  handbook's contributors' approaches to 305–306
  ideological division of 315
  importance and influence of 305
  international comparison of 319–321
  left-right division of 316–317
  networked movements 315–316
  new movements since 2010s 317–319
  post-democratisation growth 308–311
  'social movement society,' growth of 322
  structural complexity of, increase in 322
  uneven development of 313–315

  see also interest groups; trade (labour) unions
social politics of welfare reform 471, 484–485
social scientific studies of corruption 508
social stability, reduction by interest groups 327
social structure, transition to modern society 3–4
social theory, key concepts 5–7
social welfare
  ageing society, and 486
  bureaucratic politics of reform 471, 481–483
  centre-left reforms (1998-2007) 477–478
  conservative reforms (2008-17) 478
  developmental state, and 472–476
  East Asian model of 472–473
  features and legacies of welfare programmes 473–476
  future reform, challenges for 485–486
  handbook's contributors' approaches to 471
  inclusive developmental welfarism, rationales for 479–481
  new issue politics 286–287
  partisan politics of reform 471, 483–484
  politics of, conceptualisations of 471, 481
  post-Asian Financial Crisis 1997 reforms 473–476, 485
  social insurance, need for further reform 485–486
  social politics of reform 471, 484–485
  spending increase, need for 486
  typology of welfare states 472
socialtainers 428–429
South Korea *see* Korea, Republic of
standing committees 172–175
state-led economic development *see* developmental state; economic development
Supreme Court
  Constitutional Court, and 210
  judicial review, power of 210

T

television
  cinema contrasted 377
  democratisation, and 378

television (cont.)
   handbook's contributors' approaches to 380
   importance and influence of 377
   introduction in Korea 377–378
   political and social commentary function of 378–379
   political criticism of TV drama 387–390
   politicised regulation of 383–385
   post-democratisation relationship with politics 389
   pursuit of popularity to preserve political independence 390
   storytelling function of 377–380
   vehicle for young people's political participation, as 389
   see also cinema
Terminal High Altitude Area Defence (THAAD) missile system 640–641
Third Republic (1963-72) 100n9, 158, 162–164, 169, 174, 186
trade (labour) unions
   during authoritarian regimes 343–345, 354
   'democracy without labour,' in 343
   enterprise unionism, dominance of 355
   geopolitical reasons for continuance of institutional anti-unionism 355
   Great Workers' Struggle of 1987 345–349
   ideological division, implications of 354–355
   institutional inertia of 355
   interest groups, as 328–329
   labour market outsiders, exclusion of 354–355
   leadership problems 343, 354
   militancy 345–349, 354
   obstacles to growth of labour movement, statist perspective on 342–343, 354
   political marginalisation after 1997 Financial Crisis 349–353, 354
   success of 354
   working-class political movement, and 342

29 June Declaration (1987) 44, 90–92, 95, 161–162
two-party system see electoral system

U

United States
   China rapprochement 631
   China rivalry 549–550, 554–555, 629, 635, 636–639, 642–644
   developmental state, support for 107–110, 118
   free trade agreement 639
   interest groups 327
   judicial independence 211
   Korea economic relations 564, 565, 567, 569, 571–575
   Korean reunification, and 598, 601–602
   North Korea relations 601–602
   post-liberation (1945-61) influence on popular music 440–441
   public intellectuals 423
   Terminal High Altitude Area Defence (THAAD) missile system deployment 640–641
   see also Korea–United States alliance

V

'venal corruption' 510
voting see electoral system

W

welfare, new political issues as to 286–287
welfare state see social welfare
women
   gender conflicts, and 291–295
   gender gap, and 289–291
   political representation 234, 247–248
worker representation see trade (labour) unions

Y

young people see generational political representation
Yushin Constitution (1972–1979) 41–43